ALSO BY MAX HASTINGS

REPORTAGE

America 1968: The Fire This Time
Ulster 1969: The Struggle for Civil Rights in Northern Ireland
The Battle for the Falklands (with Simon Jenkins)

BIOGRAPHY

Montrose: The King's Champion
Yoni: Hero of Entebbe

AUTOBIOGRAPHY

Going to the Wars
Editor

MILITARY HISTORY

Bomber Command
The Battle of Britain (with Len Deighton)
Das Reich
Overlord
Victory in Europe
The Korean War
Armageddon: The Battle for Germany, 1944–1945
Warriors: Extraordinary Tales from the Battlefield

COUNTRYSIDE WRITING

Outside Days
Scattered Shots
Country Fair

ANTHOLOGY (EDITED)

The Oxford Book of Military Anecdotes

RETRIBUTION

RETRIBUTION

THE BATTLE FOR JAPAN, 1944–45

Max Hastings

Alfred A. Knopf · New York · 2008

THIS IS A BORZOI BOOK
PUBLISHED BY ALFRED A. KNOPF

Portions of this work appeared in *World War II* magazine.
Originally published in Great Britain as *Nemesis: The Battle for Japan, 1944–45*,
by HarperPress, an imprint of HarperCollins*Publishers*, London, in 2007.

ISBN 978-0-307-26351-3

Manufactured in the United States of America
Book Club Edition

In memory of my son

CHARLES HASTINGS

1973–2000

CONTENTS

ILLUSTRATIONS

A task group led by U.S. carriers at sea in late 1944. *(© Bettman/CORBIS)*
A pilot in the "ready room." *(Naval Historical Foundation, Washington)*
Launching a Hellcat. *(Naval Historical Foundation, Washington)*
Commander David McCampbell. *(Naval Historical Foundation, Washington)*
U.S. soldiers taking cover on Leyte in November 1944. *(© Associated Press/PA Photos)*
U.S. soldiers fighting through the wreckage of Manila in February 1945. *(© Associated Press/PA Photos)*
The Marines land on Iwo Jima. *(U.S. National Archives/CORBIS)*
Japanese surrendering on Iwo Jima. *(Naval Historical Foundation, Washington)*
Gen. Douglas MacArthur. *(© U.S. National Archives/CORBIS)*
Lt. Bill Bradlee.
Lt. Philip True. *(Courtesy of Philip True)*
Emory Jernigan. *(Courtesy of Vandamere Press)*
Rear Admiral Clifton Sprague. *(© U.S. National Archives/CORBIS)*
British survivor at Nakhon Pathom, Siam, in 1945. *(Imperial War Museum, London: HU 4569)*
Four Australians drag themselves to the U.S. submarine *Pampanito*, which had sunk the transport taking them to Japan. *(Australian War Memorial: PO3651.009)*

INSERT TWO

A Japanese pilot prepares for his final mission. *(© Hulton Archive/Getty Images)*
A suicide plane narrowly misses the U.S. carrier *Sangamon* off Okinawa. *(© U.S. National Archives/CORBIS)*
USS *Franklin* afire. *(© Associated Press/PA Photos)*
Marines in one of the innumerable bloody assaults on Okinawa. *(© W. Eugene Smith/Time & Life Pictures/Getty Images)*
Civilians on Okinawa await their fate. *(© Bettmann/CORBIS)*
A Marine helps a woman and her baby to safety. *(© Bettmann/CORBIS)*
Yoshihiro Minamoto.
Haruki Iki.
Toshio Hijikata.
Renichi Sugano.
Harunori Ohkoshi.
Toshihara Konada.
Kisai Ebisawa.
Yoshiko Hashimoto with her family, who paid a terrible price for the 9 March 1945 USAAF firebombing of Tokyo.

MAPS

War is human, it is as something that is lived like a love or a hatred . . . It might better be described as a pathological condition because it admits of accidents which not even a skilled physician could have foreseen.

—Marcel Proust

"Oh, surely they'll stop now. They'll be horrified at what they've done!," he thought, aimlessly following on behind crowds of stretchers moving away from the battlefield.

—Tolstoy's Pierre Bezukhov at Borodino, 1812

In 1944, there seemed absolutely no reason to suppose that the war might end in 1945.

—Captain Luo Dingwen, Chinese Nationalist Army

INTRODUCTION

Sir Arthur Tedder, Eisenhower's deputy supreme commander in Europe in 1944–45, suggested that warriors educating themselves for future conflicts should study the early phases of past ones: "There are no big battalions or blank cheques then," he wrote ruefully. In the first campaigns, nations which are victims rather than initiators of aggression enjoy scanty choices. They strive for survival with inadequate resources, often unsuitable commanders, all the handicaps of fighting on an enemy's terms. Later, if they are granted time fully to mobilise, they may achieve the luxury of options, of might equal or superior to that of the enemy, of the certainty of final victory tempered only by debate about how to secure this most swiftly and cheaply. Tedder and his Allied comrades experienced all these sensations.

For students of history, however, the manner in which the Second World War ended is even more fascinating than that in which it began. Giants of their respective nations, or rather mortal men cast into giants' roles, resolved the greatest issues of the twentieth century on battlefields in three dimensions, and in the war rooms of their capitals. Some of the most populous societies on earth teemed in flux. Technology displayed a terrifying maturity. Churchill entitled the closing volume of his war memoirs *Triumph and Tragedy*. For millions, 1944–45 brought liberation, the banishment of privation, fear and oppression; but air attack during those years killed larger numbers of people than in the rest of the conflict put together. Posterity knows that the war ended in August 1945. However, it would have provided scant comfort to the men who risked their lives in the Pacific island battles, as well as in the other bloody campaigns of that spring and summer, to be assured that the tumult would soon be stilled. Soldiers may accept a need to be the first to die in a war, but there is often an unseemly scramble to avoid becoming the last.

I have written *Retribution* as a counterpart to my earlier book *Armageddon*, which describes the 1944–45 struggle for Germany. It is hard to exaggerate the differences between the endgames of the Asian and European wars. In the west, American strategy was dominated by a determination to confront the German army in Europe at the first possible moment—which proved much later than the U.S. joint chiefs of staff desired. It was taken for granted that Allied armies must defeat the main forces of the enemy. Uncertainty focused upon how this should be achieved, and where Soviet and Anglo-American armies might meet. The possibility of offering terms to the Nazis was never entertained.

In the Far East, by contrast, there was much less appetite for a ground showdown. Some in the Allied camp argued that the commitment to impose unconditional surrender upon the Japanese should be moderated, if this would avert the necessity for a bloodbath in the home islands. Only in the Philippines and Burma did U.S. and British ground forces encounter, and finally destroy, major Japanese armies—though none was as large as the enemy host deployed in China. The U.S. Navy and Army Air Forces (USAAF) sought to demonstrate that blockade and bombardment could render unnecessary a bloody land campaign in the Japanese home islands. Their hopes were fulfilled in the most momentous and terrible fashion.

The phrase "heavy casualties" recurs in studies of the eastern conflict. It is often used to categorise American losses on Guadalcanal, Iwo Jima, Okinawa and in smaller island battles. It deserves more sceptical scrutiny than it usually receives, however, being justified only in relation to the relatively small forces engaged, and to the expectation of the American people that a nation as rich and technologically powerful as their own should be able to gain victory without great loss of blood. The lives of some 103,000 Americans were sacrificed to defeat Japan, along with those of more than 30,000 British, Indian, Australian and other Commonwealth servicemen, in addition to those who perished in captivity. The U.S. pro rata casualty rate in the Pacific was three and a half times that in Europe. America's total loss, however, represented only a small fraction of the toll which war extracted from the Soviets, the Germans and Japanese, and only 1 percent of the total deaths in Japan's Asian war. Americans came to expect in the Pacific a favourable exchange rate of one U.S. casualty for every six or seven Japanese. They were dismayed when, on Iwo Jima and Okinawa, the enemy fared better, losing only in the ratio of 1.25:1 and 1.3:1, respectively, though almost all the Japanese losses were fatal, compared with less than one-third of the American. Pervading U.S. strategy was a cultural conceit about the necessary cost of victory. This proved justified, but should not have been taken for granted in a conflict between major industrial nations.

I agree wholeheartedly with American scholars Richard Frank and Robert Newman that underpinning most post-war analysis of the eastern war is a delusion that the nuclear climax represented the bloodiest possible outcome. On the contrary, alternative scenarios suggest that if the conflict had continued for even a few weeks longer, more people of all nations—and especially Japan—would have lost their lives than perished at Hiroshima and Nagasaki. The myth that the Japanese were ready to surrender anyway has been so comprehensively discredited by modern research that it is astonishing some writers continue to give it credence. Japanese intransigence does not of itself validate the use of atomic bombs, but it should frame the context of debate.

"Retributive justice" is among the dictionary definitions of *nemesis.* Readers must judge for themselves whether the fate which befell Japan in 1945 merits that description, as I believe it does. The war in the Far East extended across an even wider canvas than the struggle for Europe: China, Burma, India, the Philippines, together with a vast expanse of the Pacific Ocean. Its courses were directed by one of the most extraordinary galaxies of leaders, military and political, the world has ever seen: Japan's emperor, generals and admirals; Chiang Kai-shek and Mao Zedong; Churchill, Roosevelt, Truman, Stalin; MacArthur and Nimitz; LeMay, Slim, Mountbatten, Stilwell—and the men who built the bomb. My purpose, as in *Armageddon,* is to portray a massive and terrible human experience, set within a chronological framework, rather than to revisit the detailed narrative of campaigns that have been described by many authors, and which anyway could not be contained within a single volume. This book focuses upon how and why things were done, what it was like to do them, and what manner of men and women did them.

Many of us gained our first, wonderfully romantic notion of the war against Japan by watching the movie of Rodgers and Hammerstein's *South Pacific.* Memories of its scenes pervaded my consciousness as I wrote *Retribution.* For all that the film is Hollywood entertainment, it catches a few simple truths about what the struggle was like for Americans. A host of innocent young men and a scattering of young women found themselves transplanted into a wildly exotic setting. The Pacific's natural beauties provided inadequate compensation, alas, for the discomforts and emotional stresses which they endured amid coral atolls and palm trees. For every fighting soldier, sailor and Marine who suffered the terrors of battle, many more men experienced merely heat and boredom at some godforsaken island base. The phrase "the greatest generation" is sometimes used in the U.S. to describe those who lived through those times. This seems inapt. The people of World War II may have adopted different fashions and danced to different music from us, but human behaviour, aspirations and fears do not alter much. It is more appropriate to call them, without jealousy, "the generation to which the greatest things happened."

I chose my terms of reference partly in order to depict examples from a wide range of land, sea and air battles. Though there were some great men upon the stage, the history of World War II is, for the most part, a story of statesmen and commanders flawed as all of us are, striving to grapple with issues and dilemmas larger than their talents. How many people are fitted to grapple with decisions of the magnitude imposed by global war? How many commanders in history's great conflicts can be deemed competent, far less brilliant?

While most writers address one eastern campaign or another—Burma, strategic bombing, the war at sea, the island assaults—I have attempted to set all these in context, component parts of the struggle to defeat Japan. I have omitted only the experience of indigenous anti-colonial resistance movements, an important subject so large that it would have overwhelmed my pages. Where possible without impairing coherence, I have omitted familiar anecdotes and dialogue. I have explored some aspects of the struggle that have been neglected by Western authors, notably the Chinese experience and the Russian assault on Manchuria. Nehru once said scornfully: "The average European concept of Asia is an appendage to Europe and America—a great mass of people fallen low, who are to be lifted by the good works of the West." Twenty years ago, that princely historian Ronald Spector puzzled over the fact that Westerners have always been less interested in the war with Japan than in the struggle against Germany. Remoteness, both geographical and cultural, is the obvious explanation, together with our often morbid fascination with the Nazis. Today, however, readers as well as writers seem ready to bridge the chasm with Asia. Its affairs loom huge in our world. An understanding of its recent past is essential to a grasp of its present, especially when Chinese grievances about the 1931–45 era remain a key issue in relations between Beijing and Tokyo.

Some set pieces—Leyte Gulf, Iwo Jima, Okinawa—are bound to be familiar. I have attempted no primary research on the dropping of the atomic bombs, because the archives have been exhaustively explored and the published literature is vast. Other episodes and experiences may come fresh to readers. I have addressed the issue of why Australia seemed almost to vanish from the war after 1943. Australian soldiers played a notable, sometimes dazzling, part in the North African and New Guinea campaigns. Yet the country's internal dissentions, together with American dominance of the Pacific theatre, caused the Australian Army to be relegated to a frankly humiliating role in 1944–45.

All authors of history books owe debts to earlier chroniclers, and it is important to acknowledge these. I am following a path trodden with special distinction by Ronald Spector in *Eagle Against the Sun*, Richard Frank in *Downfall*, and Christopher Thorne in *Allies of a Kind.* John Dower's books offer indispensable insights into the Japanese experience. John Toland's *The Rising Sun* is not a scholarly work, but it contains significant Japanese anecdotal material. These are only the most notable general studies of a period for which the specialised literature is vast. I should add George MacDonald Fraser's *Quartered Safe Out Here*, perhaps the most vivid private soldier's memoir of the Second World War, describing his 1945 experience with Slim's Fourteenth Army.

In Britain and the U.S. I have interviewed some veterans, but focused my research chiefly upon the huge manuscript and documentary collections which are available. My splendid Russian researcher, Dr. Luba Vinogradovna, conducted interviews with Red Army veterans, and also translated a mass of documents and written narratives. In China and Japan I have sought out eyewitnesses. Most published Chinese and Japanese memoirs reveal more about what people claim to have done than about what they thought. I will not suggest that face-to-face interviews with a Westerner necessarily persuaded Chinese and Japanese witnesses to open their hearts, but I hope that the tales which emerge make some characters seem flesh and blood, rather than mere strangled Asian names speaking tortured English.

In most Western accounts of the war, the Japanese remain stubbornly opaque. It is striking how seldom Japanese historians are quoted in U.S. and British scholarly discussions. This is not, I think, a reflection of American or British nationalistic conceit, but rather of the lack of intellectual rigour which characterises even most modern Japanese accounts. There is a small contributory point, that literal translations from the Japanese language cause statements and dialogue to sound stilted. Where possible here, I have taken the liberty of adjusting quoted Japanese speech and writing into English vernacular. Scholars might suggest that this gives a misleading idea of the Japanese use of language. It may help, however, to make Asian characters more accessible. With the same intention, although the Japanese place surnames before given names, I have reversed this in accordance with Western practice.

I have adopted some other styles for convenience. The Japanese called their Manchurian puppet state "Manchukuo." Modern Chinese never speak of "Manchuria," but of "the north-eastern provinces." Nonetheless, I have here retained the name "Manchuria," save when the Japanese political creation is discussed. Modern Indonesia is referred to as the Dutch East Indies, Malaysia as Malaya, Taiwan as Formosa and so on. After much vacillation, however, I have adopted modern pinyin spellings for Chinese names and places, because these are more familiar to a modern readership. I have, however, accepted the loss of consistency involved in retaining the familiar usages "Kuomintang" and "Manchukuo." Naval and military operations are timed by the twenty-four-hour clock, while the twelve-hour clock is used in describing the doings of civilians.

China is the country which today provides a historical researcher with the greatest revelations. I first visited it in 1971 as a TV film-maker, and again in 1985 when writing a book on the Korean War. On neither assignment was it was possible to break through the ironclad culture of propaganda. In 2005, by contrast, I found ordinary Chinese welcoming, relaxed and remarkably open in conversation. Many, for instance, do not hesitate to assert a respect for Chiang Kai-shek, and reservations about Mao Zedong, which were unavowable thirty years ago.

Some Chinese observed bitterly to me that they found the Maoist Cultural Revolution a worse personal experience than the Second World War. Almost all those with Nationalist associations suffered the confiscation and destruction of their personal papers and photographs. Several served long terms of imprisonment—one because wartime service as a Soviet-sponsored guerrilla caused him to be denounced twenty years later as a Russian agent. I conducted almost all my own interviews in China and Japan, with the help of interpreters, but four former Chinese "comfort women" of the Japanese army declined to tell their stories to a man and a Westerner, and instead talked to my splendid researcher Gu Renquan.

In modern China, as in Russia and to some degree Japan, there is no tradition of objective historical research. Absurd claims are thus made even by academics, unsupported by evidence. This is especially true about the China-Japan war, which remains a focus of national passions, fomented by the Chinese government for political purposes. An appropriately sceptical Western researcher, however, can still achieve much more than was possible a decade or two ago. I found it exhilarating to stand on the snowclad border with Russia, where Soviet armies swept across the Ussuri River in August 1945; to clamber through the tunnels of the massive old Japanese fortress at Hutou, some of which have today been reopened as part of the local "Fortress Relics Museum of Japanese Aggression Against China"; to meet peasants who witnessed the battles. In a café in Hutou, at nine in the morning local people were clustered around the big TV, watching one of the melodramas about the Japanese war which Chinese film-makers produce in industrial quantities. These celluloid epics, echoing with the diabolical laughter of Japanese occupiers as they slaughter heroic Chinese peasants, make such Hollywood war movies as *The Sands of Iwo Jima* seem models of understatement.

When I asked Jiang Fushun, in 1945 a teenage peasant in Hutou, if there were any happy moments in his childhood, he responded bitterly: "How can you ask such a question? Our lives were unspeakable. There was only work, work, work, knowing that if we crossed the Japanese in any way, we would go the way of others who were thrown into the river with their hands tied to a rock." In his flat in Harbin, eighty-four-year-old Li Fenggui vividly reenacted for me the motions of a bayonet fight in which he engaged with a Japanese soldier in 1944.

Likewise, in Japan, at the tiny doll's house in a Toyko suburb where he lives, Lt. Cmdr. Haruki Iki cherishes a plastic model of the torpedo bomber which he once flew, alongside a garish painting of the British battle cruiser *Repulse*, which he sank in 1941. To meet him is to encounter a legend. At eighty-seven, former navy pilot Kunio Iwashita retains the energy and quick movements of a man thirty years younger. Today he is known in Japan as "Mr. Zero." I met him when he had just returned from the premiere of a lurid new Japanese movie epic, *Men of the Yamato*. Iwashita overflew the vast battleship on the morning she was sunk in April 1945, and has never forgotten the spectacle. He said with a wry smile: "I sobbed all the way through the film."

I asked another navy fighter pilot, Toshio Hijikata, how he and his comrades spent their hours on Kyushu in the early months of 1945, as they prepared to scramble to meet American B-29 formations in the same fashion as RAF pilots waited for the Luftwaffe five years earlier, during the Battle of Britain. "We played a lot of bridge," said Hijikata. "It was part of the whole ethos of the Imperial Japanese Navy, which tried so hard to emulate the Royal Navy." The notion of Japanese fliers calling "three spades, four clubs" to each other between sorties seemed irresistibly unexpected and droll.

My daughter once observed in a domestic context: "Life is what you are used to, Daddy." This seems an important truth in understanding human responses to circumstances. To a remarkable degree the young, especially, adapt to predicaments which might seem unendurable, if these are all that they have known. Across the globe, the generation which grew to maturity amid the Second World War learned to accept war's terrors and privations as a norm. This applies to many people whose stories I seek to record in this book.

Some general observations can be made about evidence, of which the most obvious is that scepticism is in order, even when reading formal contemporary minutes of meetings, unit war diaries or ships' logs. Few official narratives in any language explicitly acknowledge disaster, panic or failure, or admit that people ran away. Likewise, many splendid lines attributed by historians to participants are probably apocryphal. People find it infinitely easier to imagine afterwards what should have been said in crises, rather than what actually was. Witticisms which survive through the generations retain a certain validity, however, if they seem to catch a spirit of the moment, like "Nuts!," the alleged American response to a German demand for surrender at Bastogne.

Oral evidence collected in the early twenty-first century by interviewing men and women who witnessed events more than sixty years earlier is immensely valuable in illustrating moods and attitudes. But old people have forgotten many things, or can claim to remember too much. Those who survive today were very young in the war years. They held junior ranks and offices, if indeed any at all. They knew nothing worth rehearsing about events beyond their own eyesight and earshot. The reflections of their age group cannot be considered representative of a nation's mind-set and behaviour in 1944–45. It is essential to reinforce their tales with written testimony from those who were at the time more mature and exalted.

It is notable how swiftly historical perceptions change. For instance, in post-war Japan General Douglas MacArthur was a hero, an icon, almost a god, in recognition of his perceived generosity to the Japanese people in defeat. But a modern historian, Kazutoshi Hando, says: "In Japan today, MacArthur is almost unknown." Similarly, a Chinese historian told me that few of his young compatriots have heard of Stalin. I feel obliged to restate a caveat which I entered in the foreword of *Armageddon*: statistics given here are the best available, but all large numbers related to the Second World War must be treated warily. Figures detailing American and British activities—though emphatically not their contemporary estimates of losses inflicted on the enemy—are credible, but those of other nations are disputed, or represent guesstimates. For instance, although the rape of Nanjing falls outside the compass of my narrative, I am persuaded that Iris Chang's well-known book claims a death toll for the city in excess of its actual, rather than previously recorded, 1937 population. This does not invalidate the portrait of horror which she depicts, but it does illustrate the difficulty of establishing credible, never mind conclusive, numbers.

The longer I write books about the Second World War, the more conscious I become that a fundamental humility is necessary when offering judgements upon those who conducted it. Harold Macmillan, British minister in the Mediterranean 1943–45 and later prime minister, once told me a story of his last encounter with Field Marshal Earl Alexander, wartime Allied commander-in-chief in Italy: "We were going into the theatre together, and I turned to him and said one of those old man's things: 'Alex, wouldn't it be lovely to have it all to do over again.' Alexander shook his head decisively. 'Oh, no,' he said. 'We might not do nearly so well.' " Those of us who have never been obliged to participate in a great war seem wise to count our blessings and incline a bow to all those, mighty and humble, who did so.

—MAX HASTINGS
Hungerford, England, and Kamogi, Kenya
April 2007

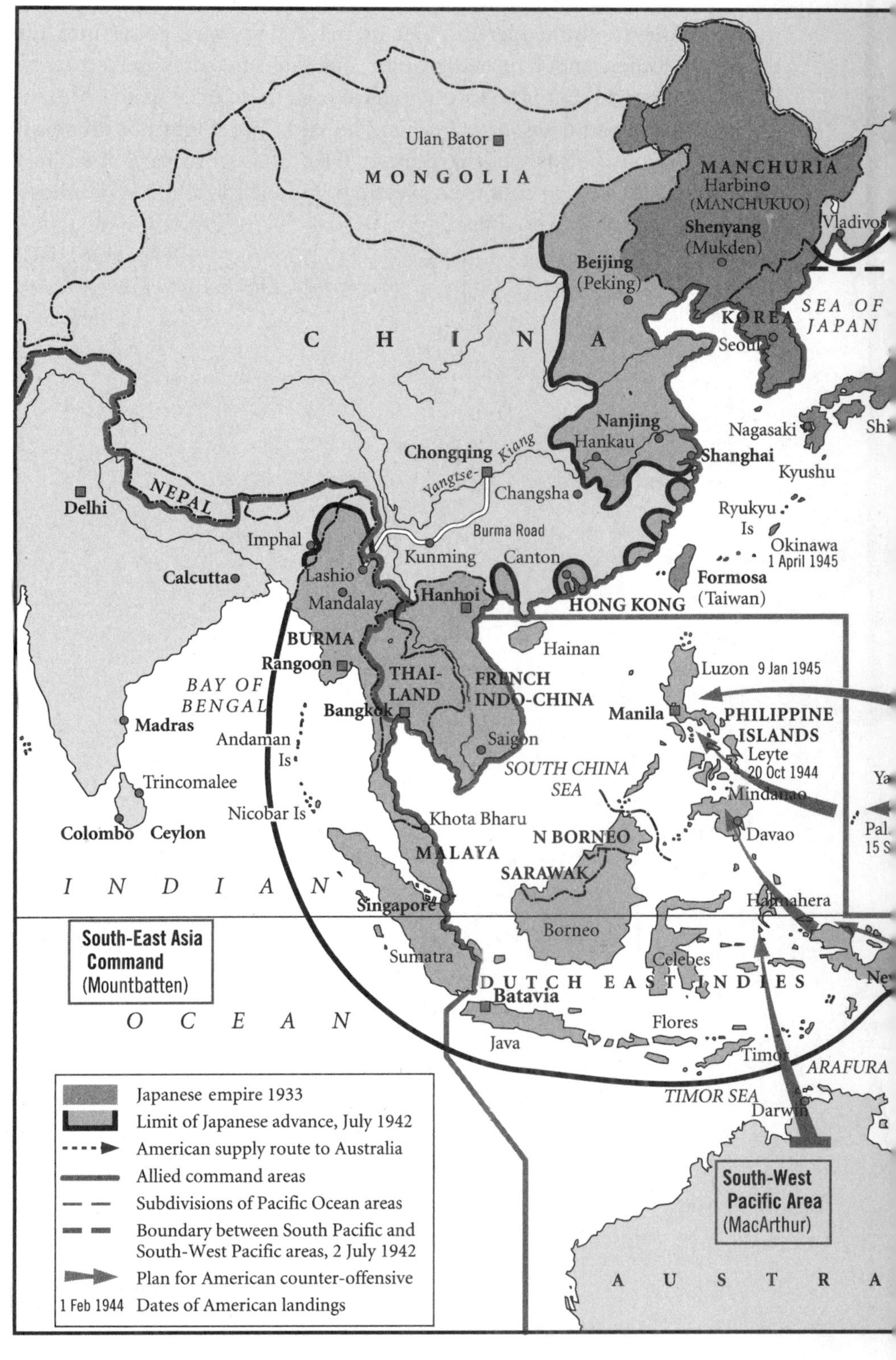
Ulan Bator
MONGOLIA
MANCHURIA
Harbin
(MANCHUKUO)
Shenyang
(Mukden)
Vladivos
Beijing
(Peking)
KOREA
SEA OF
JAPAN
Seoul
C H I N A
Nanjing
Hankau
Nagasaki
Shanghai
Kyushu
Chongqing
Yangtse-Kiang
Changsha
Ryukyu
Is
Okinawa
1 April 1945
NEPAL
Delhi
Imphal
Burma Road
Kunming
Canton
Calcutta
Lashio
Mandalay
Hanhoi
Formosa
(Taiwan)
HONG KONG
BURMA
Hainan
Rangoon
THAI-
LAND
FRENCH
INDO-CHINA
Luzon 9 Jan 1945
BAY OF
BENGAL
Bangkok
Manila
PHILIPPINE
ISLANDS
Madras
Andaman
Is
Saigon
Leyte
20 Oct 1944
SOUTH CHINA
SEA
Mindanao
Trincomalee
Nicobar Is
Khota Bharu
Davao
Colombo
Ceylon
N BORNEO
MALAYA
SARAWAK
I N D I A N
Singapore
Halmahera
Borneo
South-East Asia
Command
(Mountbatten)
Sumatra
Celebes
DUTCH EAST INDIES
Batavia
O C E A N
Flores
Java
Timor
ARAFURA
TIMOR SEA
Darwin
Japanese empire 1933
Limit of Japanese advance, July 1942
American supply route to Australia
Allied command areas
Subdivisions of Pacific Ocean areas
Boundary between South Pacific and South-West Pacific areas, 2 July 1942
Plan for American counter-offensive
1 Feb 1944 Dates of American landings
South-West
Pacific Area
(MacArthur)
A U S T R A

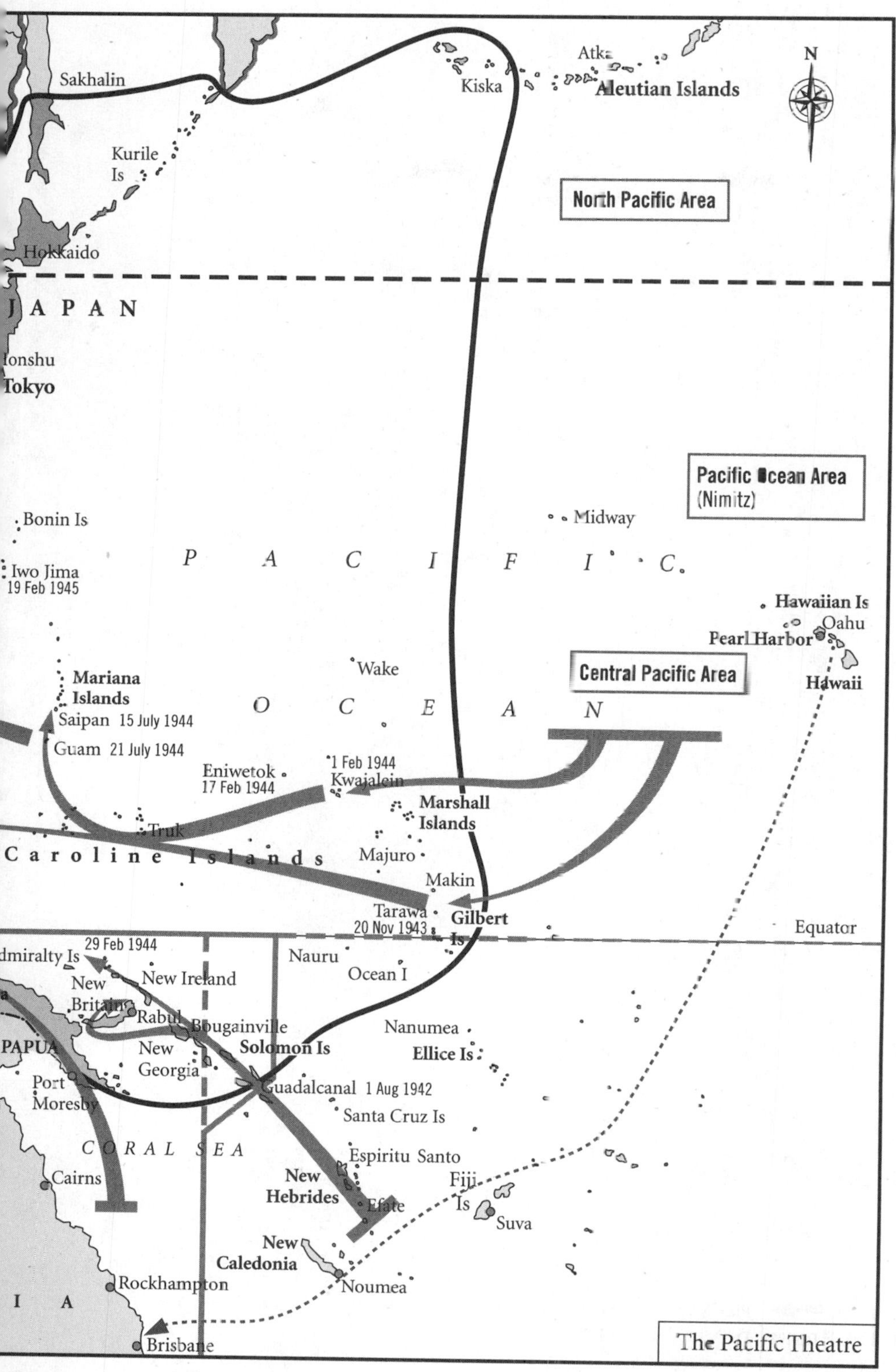
Sakhalin
Kurile Is
Hokkaido
JAPAN
Honshu
Tokyo
Kiska
Atka
Aleutian Islands
N
North Pacific Area
Pacific Ocean Area (Nimitz)
Midway
Bonin Is
Iwo Jima 19 Feb 1945
PACIFIC OCEAN
Hawaiian Is
Oahu
Pearl Harbor
Hawaii
Central Pacific Area
Wake
Mariana Islands
Saipan 15 July 1944
Guam 21 July 1944
Eniwetok 17 Feb 1944
1 Feb 1944 Kwajalein
Marshall Islands
Truk
Caroline Islands
Majuro
Makin
Tarawa 20 Nov 1943
Gilbert Is
Equator
Admiralty Is
29 Feb 1944
Nauru
Ocean I
New Ireland
New Britain
Rabul
Bougainville
PAPUA
New Georgia
Solomon Is
Nanumea
Ellice Is
Port Moresby
Guadalcanal 1 Aug 1942
Santa Cruz Is
CORAL SEA
Espiritu Santo
Cairns
New Hebrides
Efate
Fiji Is
Suva
New Caledonia
Noumea
Rockhampton
Brisbane
The Pacific Theatre

Retribution

CHAPTER ONE

Dilemmas and Decisions

1. War in the East

OUR UNDERSTANDING of the events of 1939–45 might be improved by adding a plural and calling them the Second World Wars. The only common strand in the struggles which Germany and Japan unleashed was that they chose most of the same adversaries. The only important people who sought to conduct the eastern and western conflicts as a unified enterprise were Franklin Roosevelt, Winston Churchill and their respective chiefs of staff. After the 7 December 1941 Japanese attack on Pearl Harbor caused the United States to become a belligerent, Allied warlords addressed the vexed issue of allocating resources to rival theatres. Germany was by far the Allies' more dangerous enemy, while Japan was the focus of greater American animus. In 1942, at the battles of the Coral Sea in May and Midway a month later, the U.S. Navy won victories which halted the Japanese advance across the Pacific, and removed the danger that Australia might be invaded.

Through the two years which followed, America's navy grew in strength, while her Marines and soldiers slowly and painfully expelled the Japanese from the island strongholds which they had seized. But President Roosevelt and General George Marshall, Chief of Staff of the Army, resisted the demands of Admiral Ernest King, the U.S. Navy's C-in-C, and of General Douglas MacArthur, supreme commander in the south-west Pacific, for the eastern theatre to become the principal focus of America's war effort. In 1943 and 1944, America's vast industrial mobilisation made it possible to send large forces of warships and planes east as well as west. Most U.S. ground troops, however, were dispatched across the Atlantic, to fight the Germans. Once Japan's onslaught was checked, the Allies' eastern commanders were given enough forces progressively to push back the enemy, but insufficient to pursue a swift victory. The second-class status of the Japanese war was a source of resentment to those who had to fight it, but represented strategic wisdom.

The U.S. and Britain dispatched separate companies to Europe and Asia, to perform in different plays. Stalin, meanwhile, was interested in the conflict with Japan only insofar as it might offer opportunities to amass booty. "The Russians may be expected to move against the Japanese when it suits their pleasure," suggested an American diplomat in an October 1943 memorandum to the State Department, "which may not be until the final phases of the war—and then only in order to be able to participate in dictating terms to the Japanese and to establish new strategic frontiers." Until 8 August 1945, Soviet neutrality in the east was so scrupulously preserved that American B-29s which forced-landed on Russian territory had to stay there, not least to enable their hosts to copy the design.

To soldiers, sailors and airmen, any battlefield beyond their own compass seemed remote. "What was happening in Europe really didn't matter to us," said Lt. John Cameron-Hayes of 23rd Indian Mountain Artillery, fighting in Burma. More surprising was the failure of Germany and Japan to coordinate their war efforts, even to the limited extent that geographical separation might have permitted. These two nominal allies, whose fortunes became conjoined in December 1941, conducted operations in almost absolute isolation from each other. Hitler had no wish for Asians to meddle in his Aryan war. Indeed, despite Himmler's best efforts to prove that Japanese possessed some Aryan blood, Hitler remained embarrassed by the association of the Nazi cause with *Untermenschen*. He received the Japanese ambassador in Berlin twice after Pearl Harbor, then not for a year. When Tokyo in 1942 proposed an assault on Madagascar, the German navy opposed any infringement of the two allies' agreed spheres of operations, divided at 70 degrees of longitude.

A Japanese assault on the Soviet Union in 1941–42, taking the Russians in the rear as they struggled to stem Hitler's invasion, might have yielded important rewards for the Axis. Stalin was terrified of such an eventuality. The July 1941 oil embargo and asset freeze imposed by the U.S. on Japan—Roosevelt's clumsiest diplomatic act in the months before Pearl Harbor—was partly designed to deter Tokyo from joining Hitler's Operation Barbarossa. Japan's bellicose foreign minister, Yosuke Matsuoka, resigned in the same month because his government rejected his urgings to attack.

Only in January 1943, towards the end of the disaster of Stalingrad, did Hitler make a belated and unsuccessful attempt to persuade Japan to join his Russian war. By then, the moment had passed at which such an intervention might have altered history. Germany's Asian ally was far too heavily committed in the Pacific, South-East Asia and China to gratuitously engage a new adversary. So perfunctory was Berlin's relationship with Tokyo that when Hitler gifted to his ally two state-of-the-art

U-boats for reproduction, German manufacturers complained about breaches of their patent rights. One of Japan's most serious deficiencies in 1944–45 was lack of a portable anti-tank weapon, but no attempt was made to copy the cheap and excellent German *Panzerfaust*.

Japan and Germany were alike fascistic states. Michael Howard has written: "Both [nations'] programmes were fuelled by a militarist ideology that rejected the bourgeois liberalism of the capitalist West and glorified war as the inevitable and necessary destiny of mankind." The common German and Japanese commitment to making war for its own sake provides the best reason for rejecting pleas in mitigation of either nation's conduct. The two Axis partners, however, pursued unrelated ambitions. The only obvious manifestation of shared interest was that Japanese planning was rooted in an assumption of German victory. Like Italy in June 1940, Japan in December 1941 decided that the old colonial powers' difficulties in Europe exposed their remoter properties to rapine. Japan sought to seize access to vital oil and raw materials, together with space for mass migration from the home islands.

A U.S. historian has written of Japan's *Daitoa Senso*, Greater East Asian War: "Japan did not invade independent countries in southern Asia. It invaded colonial outposts which the Westerners had dominated for generations, taking absolutely for granted their racial and cultural superiority over their Asian subjects." This is true as far as it goes. Yet Japan's seizures of British, Dutch, French and American possessions must surely be seen in the context of its earlier aggression in China, where for a decade its armies had flaunted their ruthlessness towards fellow Asians. After seizing Manchuria in 1931, the Japanese in 1937 began their piecemeal pillage of China, which continued until 1945.

Inaugurating its "Greater East Asia Co-Prosperity Sphere," Japan perceived itself merely as a latecomer to the contest for empire in which other great nations had engaged for centuries. It saw only hypocrisy and racism in the objections of Western imperial powers to its bid to match their own generous interpretations of what constituted legitimate overseas interests. Such a view was not completely baseless. Japan's pre-war economic difficulties and pretensions to a policy of "Asia for Asians" inspired some sympathy among subject peoples of the European empires. This vanished, however, in the face of the occupiers' behaviour in China and elsewhere. Japanese pogroms of Chinese in South-East Asia were designed partly to win favour with indigenous peoples, but these in turn soon found themselves suffering appallingly. The new rulers were inhibited from treating their conquests humanely, even had they wished to do so, by the fact that the purpose of seizure was to strip them of food and raw materials for the benefit of Japan's people. Western audiences have been told much since

1945 about Japanese wartime inhumanity to British, Americans and Australians who fell into their hands. This pales into absolute insignificance beside the scale of their mistreatment of Asians.

It is a fascinating speculation, how events might have evolved if the U.S. and its Philippines dependency had been excluded from Japanese war plans in December 1941; had Tokyo confined itself to occupying British Malaya and Burma, along with the Dutch East Indies. Roosevelt would certainly have wished to confront Japanese aggression and enter the war—the oil embargo imposed by the U.S. following Japan's advance into Indochina was the tipping factor in deciding Tokyo to fight the Western powers. It remains a moot point, however, whether Congress and public sentiment would have allowed the president to declare war in the absence of a direct assault on American national interests or the subsequent German declaration of war on the United States.

There was once a popular delusion that Japan's attack smashed the American Pacific Fleet. In truth, however, the six old battleships disabled at Pearl Harbor—all but two were subsequently restored for war service by brilliantly ingenious repair techniques—mattered much less to the balance of forces than the four American aircraft carriers, oil stocks and dockyard facilities which escaped. Japan paid a wholly disproportionate moral price for a modest, if spectacular, tactical success. The "Day of Infamy" roused the American people as no lesser provocation could have done. The operation must thus be judged a failure, rendering hollow the exultation of the Imperial Navy's fliers as they landed back on their carriers on 7 December 1941. Thereafter, Americans were united in their determination to avenge themselves on the treacherous Asians who had assaulted a peace-loving people.

The only important strategic judgement which the Japanese got right was that their fate hinged upon that of Hitler. German victory was the sole eventuality which might have saved Japan from the consequences of assaulting powers vastly superior to itself in military and industrial potential. Col. Masanobu Tsuji, architect of the Japanese army's capture of Singapore and a fanatical advocate of national expansion, said: "We honestly believed that America, a nation of storekeepers, would not persist with a loss-making war, whereas Japan could sustain a protracted campaign against the Anglo-Saxons." Tokyo's greatest misjudgement of all was to perceive its assault as an act of policy which might be reviewed in the light of events. In December 1941 Japan gambled on a short war, swift victory, and acceptance of terms by the vanquished. Even in August 1945, many Japanese leaders refused to acknowledge that the terms of reference for the struggle ceased to be theirs to determine on the day of Pearl Harbor. It was wildly fanciful to suppose that the consequences of military failure might be mitigated through diplomatic parley By choosing to participate in a total war, the nation exposed itself to total defeat.

Although the loss of Hong Kong, Malaya and Burma in 1941–42 inflicted on Britain humiliations to match those suffered at Japanese hands by the U.S., its people cared relatively little about the Far Eastern war, a source of dismay to British soldiers obliged to fight in it. Winston Churchill was tormented by a desire to redeem the defeat in February 1942 of some 70,000 combat troops under British command by a force of 35,000 Japanese. "The shame of our disaster at Singapore could . . . only be wiped out by our recapture of that fortress," he told the British chiefs of staff as late as 6 July 1944, in one of his many—fortunately frustrated—attempts to allow this objective to determine eastern strategy.

To the British public, however, the Asian war seemed remote. The Japanese character in the BBC's legendary *ITMA* radio comedy show was Hari Kari, a gabbling clown. In June 1943 the Secretary of State for India, Leo Amery, proposed forming a committee to rouse the British public against its Asian enemies. The minister of information, Brendan Bracken, strongly dissented:

> It is all very well to say "We must educate the British public to regard the Japanese as if they were Germans, and war in the Pacific as if it were war in Europe." But, while the Japanese remain many thousands of miles away, the Germans have for three years been only twenty miles distant from our shore and, too often, vertically overhead. Interest and feeling follow where friends and loved ones are fighting . . . Europe is very much a home concern, whereas knowledge of or interest in the Far East is sparsely distributed in this country . . . I do not think that any committee could do much to alter "the state of morale" . . . The people have been left under no misapprehension by the PM that it is their duty to turn and tackle Japan when the time comes . . .

Those Britons who did think about the Japanese shared American revulsion towards them. When reports were broadcast in early 1944 of the maltreatment of prisoners, an editorial in the *Daily Mail* proclaimed: "The Japanese have proved a sub-human race . . . Let us resolve to outlaw them. When they are beaten back to their own savage land, let them live there in complete isolation from the rest of the world, as in a leper compound, unclean." The American historian John Dower explains Western attitudes in racist terms. U.S. admiral William Halsey set the tone after Pearl Harbor, asserting that when the war was over, 'Japanese will be spoken only in hell." A U.S. War Department film promoting bond sales employed the slogan: "Every War Bond Kills a Jap." An American sub-machine gun manufacturer advertised its products as "blasting big red holes in little yellow men." There was no counterpart on the European fronts to the commonplace Pacific practices of drying and preserving Japanese skulls as souvenirs, and sending home to loved ones polished bones of enemy dead. A British brigade commander in Burma once declined to accept a report from the 4/1st Gurkhas about the proximity of "Nips." Their colonel, Derek Horsford, dispatched a patrol to gather evidence. Next day, Horsford left three Japanese heads, hung for convenience on a string, beside his commander's desk. The brigadier said: "Never do that again. Next time, I'll take your word for it."

But those who argue that the alien appearance and culture of the Japanese generated unique hatred and savagery seem to give insufficient weight to the fact that the Japanese initiated and institutionalised barbarism towards both civilians and prisoners. True, the Allies later responded in kind. But in an imperfect world, it seems unrealistic to expect that any combatant in a war will grant adversaries conspicuously better treatment than his own people receive at their hands. Years ahead of Pearl Harbor Japanese massacres of Chinese civilians were receiving worldwide publicity. Tokyo's forces committed systemic brutalities against Allied prisoners and civilians in the Philippines, East Indies, Hong Kong and Malaya—for instance, the slaughter of Chinese outside Singapore in February 1942—long before the first Allied atrocity against any Japanese is recorded.

The consequence of so-called Japanese fanaticism on the battlefield, of which much more later, was that Allied commanders favoured the use of extreme methods to defeat them. As an example, the Japanese rejected the convention customary in Western wars, whereby if a military position became untenable, its defenders gave up. In August 1944, when German prisoners were arriving in the United States at the rate of 50,000 a month, after three years of the war only 1,990 Japanese prisoners reposed in American hands. Why, demanded Allied commanders, should their men be obliged to risk their own lives in order to indulge the enemy's inhuman doctrine of mutual immolation?

The Anglo-American Lethbridge Mission, which toured theatres of war assessing tactics, urged in a March 1944 report that mustard and phosgene gases should be employed against Japanese underground defensive positions. The report's conclusion was endorsed by Marshall, U.S. air chief Gen. Henry A. "Hap" Arnold and MacArthur, even though the latter abhorred the area bombing of Japanese cities. "We are of the opinion," wrote the Lethbridge team, "that the Japanese forces in the field will not be able to survive chemical warfare attack . . . upon a vast scale . . . [This] is the quickest method of bringing the war to a successful conclusion."

Despite the weight of opinion which favoured gas, it was vetoed by President Roosevelt.

The Allies certainly perceived victory over Japan as the reversal of a painful cultural humiliation, the defeats of 1941–42. But it seems mistaken to argue that they behaved ruthlessly towards the Japanese, once the tide of war turned, because they were Asians. The U.S. pursued a historic love affair with other Asians, the people of China a nation which it sought to make a great power. A leading British statesman told an audience in February 1933: "I hope we shall try in England to understand a little the position of Japan, an ancient state with the highest sense of national honour and patriotism and with a teeming population of remarkable energy. On the one side they see the dark menace of Soviet Russia; on the other, the chaos of China, four or five provinces of which are actually now being tortured, under Communist rule." Remarkable as it may seem to posterity, the speaker was Winston Churchill, addressing the Anti-Socialist and Anti-Communist Union. Allied hatred of, contempt for, and finally savagery towards their Pacific foes were surely inspired less by racial alienation than by their wartime conduct.

It may be true that Japanese physiognomy lent itself to Anglo-Saxon caricature. But it seems mistaken to argue that—for instance—Americans felt free to incinerate Japanese, and finally to drop atomic bombs upon them, only because they were Asians. Rather, these were Asians who forged a reputation for uncivilised behaviour not merely towards their Western enemies, but on a vastly greater scale towards their fellow Asian subject peoples. If the Allies treated the Japanese barbarously in the last months of the war, it seems quite mistaken thus to perceive a moral equivalence between the two sides.

At its zenith in 1942, the Japanese empire extended over twenty million square miles. Most were water, but even Tokyo's land conquests were a third greater than Berlin's. Japanese forces were deployed from the north-eastern extremities of India to the northern border of China, from the myriad islands of the Dutch East Indies to the jungle wildernesses of New Guinea. Few Allied servicemen were aware that, throughout the war, more than a million enemy soldiers—approximately half Tokyo's fighting formations—were deployed to garrison Manchuria and sustain the occupation of eastern China. By the summer of 1944, while some Japanese formations still held out on New Guinea and Bougainville, American forces had driven westwards across the Pacific, dispossessing the enemy island by island of air and naval bases. Some nineteen divisions, about a quarter of the Imperial Army's strength, were deployed against the British and Chinese in Burma, and garrisoned Malaya. A further twenty-three divisions, some reduced to fragments and amounting in all to a further quarter of

Japanese combat capability, confronted U.S. soldiers and Marines on their oceanic line of advance.

"Americans ought to like the Pacific," asserted a jocular passage of the 1944 official *U.S. Forces' Guide* to their theatre of war. "They like things big, and the Pacific is big enough to satisfy the most demanding . . . Quonset huts and tents are the most profuse growth on the main islands we occupy. In arguments with trees, bulldozers always win. Americans who eat out a lot in the Carolines will have trouble with girth control. The basic food the natives eat is starchy vegetables—breadfruit, taro, yams, sweet potatoes and arrowroot. Gonorrhea is found in at least one-third of the natives, and there is some syphilis."

Almost 400,000 British servicemen served in the Far East, together with more than two million soldiers of Britain's Indian Army. In other words, though the U.S. absolutely dominated the conduct of the war against Japan, the British mobilised far more people to do their modest share. One and a quarter million Americans served in the Pacific and Asia, a zone of operations embracing a third of the globe. Of these, 40 percent of officers and 33 percent of men spent some time in combat, by the most generous interpretation of that word. Over 40 percent saw no action at all, working in the vast support organisations necessary to maintain armies, fleets and air forces thousands of miles from home.

There was a chronic shortage of manpower to shift supplies in the wake of the advancing spearheads. All strategy is powerfully influenced by logistics, but the Pacific war was especially so. Marshall and MacArthur once discussed a proposal to ship 50,000 coolies a month from China to boost the labour force in their rear areas, dismissing it only because the practicalities were too complex. Waste was a constant issue. Americans fighting for their lives were understandably negligent about the care of food, weapons, equipment, vehicles. The cumulative cost was enormous, when every ration pack and truck tyre had to be shipped halfway across the world to the battlefield. Up to 19 percent of some categories of food were spoilt in transit by climate, poor packing or careless handling.

Many of those who did the fighting of 1944–45 had been mere children in September 1939, or indeed December 1941. Philip True was a sixteen-year-old Michigan high school student at the time of Pearl Harbor—"I didn't think I'd be in World War II." By 1945, however, he was navigating a B-29. The merest chance dictated whether a man called to his country's service finished up in a foxhole in Okinawa, in the cockpit of a Spitfire, or pushing paper at a headquarters in Delhi. For millions of people of every nationality, the wartime experience was defined by the need to make journeys far from home, sometimes of an epic nature, across oceans and continents, at risk of their lives.

Many British and American teenagers, without previous knowledge of life outside their own communities, found uniformed service a unifying and educating force. They learned that the only redemptive feature of war is the brotherhood which it forges. "The people are what I really remember," said USAAF pilot Jack Lee DeTour, who bombed South-East Asia from India. If men got home on leave, many felt alienated from civilians who had not shared their perils and sacrifices. "Only shipmates were important to me," wrote U.S. naval rating Emory Jernigan. Eugene Hardy, a bosun's mate, came from a farm family so dirt-poor that he had never set foot in a restaurant until he joined the navy in 1940. Men learned to live with others from utterly different backgrounds, often possessing quite different outlooks. For instance, a million messroom or foxhole arguments between American northerners and southerners featured the line: "You want a nigger to marry your sister?" Somehow, out of it all, most men learned a lot about viewpoints other than their own, and about mutual tolerance.

A British soldier expressed in his journal reflections about wartime conscript experience which have almost universal validity: "Men live conscious all the time that their hearts, roots, origins lie elsewhere in some other life . . . They measure the hardships, privations, weariness here against the memory of a past that they hope to continue in the future . . . Since their hearts reside elsewhere, they face the present with an armoured countenance." The author meant that most warriors seek to preserve their sanity by shielding some corner of themselves from proximate reality, so often unpleasant. U.S. naval officers protested at the assertively unseamanlike outlook of cryptanalysts working at the Pacific Fleet's superb "Magic" code-breaking centre in Honolulu, which played such a critical part in Allied victory. Their commander dismissed their complaints: "Relax, we have always won our wars with a bunch of damned civilians in uniform anxious to get back to their own affairs, and we will win this one the same way."

Winston Churchill often asserted his conviction that the proper conduct of war demanded that "the enemy should be made to bleed and burn every day." The Pacific and Burma campaigns, by contrast, were characterised by periods of intense fighting interspersed with long intervals of inaction and preparation. Whereas on the Russian front opposing forces were in permanent contact, and likewise in north-west Europe from June 1944, in the east Japanese and Allied troops were often separated by hundreds, even thousands, of miles of sea or jungle. Few Westerners who served in the war against Japan enjoyed the experience. It was widely agreed by veterans that the North African desert was the most congenial, or rather least terrible, theatre. Thereafter in ascending intensity of grief came north-west Europe, Italy, and finally the Far East. Few soldiers, sailors or airmen felt entirely healthy during Asian or Pacific service. The stifling heat belowdecks in a warship made daily routine enervating, even before the enemy took a hand. The only interruptions to months at sea were provided by brief spasms in an overcrowded rest camp on some featureless atoll. For those fighting the land campaigns, disease and privation were constants, vying as threats to a man's welfare with a boundlessly ingenious and merciless enemy. "All the officers at home want to go to other theatres because there is more publicity there," wrote one of MacArthur's corps commanders, Lt.-Gen. Robert Eichelberger, in a gloomy letter to his wife.

Eichelberger was a career soldier, one of those whom war provided with dramatic scope for fulfilment and advancement. Civilians in uniform, however, were vulnerable to the misery identified by British novelist Anthony Powell, "that terrible, recurrent army dejection, the sensation that no one cares a halfpenny whether you live or die." "Hello, suckers," "Tokyo Rose" taunted millions of Allied servicemen from Radio Japan. "I got mine last night, your wives and sweethearts probably got theirs—did you get yours?" Corporal Ray Haskel of the U.S. Army wrote from the South Pacific to a Hollywood starlet named Myrtle Ristenhart, whose picture he had glimpsed in *Life* magazine. Rodgers and Hammerstein would have appreciated his sentiments: "My dear Myrtle, guess you are wondering who this strange person could be writing to you. We are here in the Pacific and got kind of lonesome and so thought we would drop you a few lines . . . There isn't any girls here at all but a few natives and a few nurses and we can't get within ten miles of them . . . When you can find time please answer this letter and if you have a small picture we would appreciate it, Sincerely your RAY. PS I am an Indian, full-blooded and very handsome."

"Here it is a Burma moon with not a girl in sight and a few dead Japs trying to stink you out," Sgt. Harry Hunt of the British Fourteenth Army wrote miserably to a relative in England. ". . . It must be lovely to soldier back home, just to get away from this heat and sweat, from these natives, to get together with white men . . . There it comes, the rain again, rain rain that's all we get, then the damp, it slowly eats into your bones, you wake up like nothing on earth, you always feel sleepy. I don't know whether I'm coming or going, better close now before I use bad words, remember me to dad, mum and all."

One of Hunt's senior officers, Maj.-Gen. Douglas Gracey, took as bleak a view from a loftier perspective: "Nearly every Jap fights to the last or runs away to fight another day. Until morale cracks, it must be accepted that the capture of a Japanese position is not ended until the last Jap in it (generally several feet underground) is killed. Even in the most desperate circumstances, 99 percent of the Japs prefer death or suicide to capture. The fight is more *total* than in Europe. The Jap can be compared to the most fanatical Nazi Youth, and must be dealt with accordingly."

"Dear Mother and Dad," Lt. Richard Kennard wrote from one of the Pacific island battles in which he was serving as an artillery forward observer with the U.S. 1st Marine Division. "War is just terrible, just awful, awful, awful. You have no idea how it hurts to see American boys all shot up, wounded, suffering from pain and exhaustion and those that fall down never to move again. After this war is all over I shall cherish and respect more than anything else all that is sweet, tender and gentle. Our platoon leaders and company commanders are more afraid of what their men will think of them if they don't face the enemy fire and danger along with them than of getting shot by the Jap. I have my fingers crossed every minute I am up there in the front lines and pray each night that I won't get hit."

China's people paid a vastly more terrible price than any other belligerent nation, at least fifteen million dead, for its part in the struggle against the Japanese. The country had been at war since 1937. Few Chinese dared to anticipate any end to their miseries, least of all victory. "In 1944," said Captain Luo Dingwen of Chiang Kai-shek's Nationalist army, "there seemed absolutely no reason to suppose that the war might end in 1945. We had no idea how long we might have to keep fighting." One of Luo's comrades, Captain Ying Yunping, described a characteristic 1944 battle which, after two hours' fighting, swung dramatically against the Chinese:

> We got the order to retreat. A mass of men, horses, carts, was streaming back. It was a shambles. I suddenly saw Huang Qixiang, our general, hurrying past us on a horse, wearing pyjamas and only one boot. It seemed so shockingly undignified. If generals were running away, why should ordinary soldiers stay and fight? The Japanese were sending in tanks, and we had nothing to fight tanks with. But I felt we couldn't just let the Japanese walk all over us. I called to my 8th Section, whose commander was the bravest man in the regiment, and told him to take up a blocking position. He held out for hours—the Japanese were completely thrown by meeting resistance just when everything was going their way. We lost the battle—but it seemed something to win even one small part of it. I met our general a little while later. I said that it was quite safe for him to ride back and fetch his uniform.

A vast host of Chinese civilians served merely as victims. Chen Jinyu was a sixteen-year-old peasant girl, planting rice for the Japanese occupiers of Jiamao, her village. One day, she was informed by the Japanese that she was being transferred to a "battlefront rear-service group." She said: "Because I was young, I had no idea what this meant, but I thought any duty must be easier than working in the field." A week later, she discovered the nature of her new role when she was gang-raped by Japanese soldiers. She ran away home, but an interpreter arrived to say that her family would suffer grievously if she did not return to her duties. She remained a "comfort woman" for the local Japanese garrison until June 1945 when, weary of beatings, she fled to the mountains and hid there until she heard that the war was over.

Tan Yadong, a nineteen-year-old Chinese who served the Japanese in the same capacity, was accused by a Japanese officer of failing to be an "obedient person." After two five-day spells of solitary confinement, "I became an obedient person." She was vividly reminded of the consequences of displeasing the Japanese when one of her comrades failed to take contraceptive medicine, and became pregnant. "They didn't want this baby to be born so they hung this poor girl from a tree. They killed her by cutting her open with a knife in front of all the people of our village. I was quite close, only six or seven metres away. I could see the baby moving."

At least a million Vietnamese died in their country's great famine of 1944–45, which was directly attributable to Japanese insistence that rice paddies should be replanted with fibre crops for the occupiers' use. Much Vietnamese grain was shipped to Japan, and rice commandeered to make fuel alcohol. The people of the Philippines and Dutch East Indies also suffered appallingly. In all, some five million South-East Asians died as a result of Japanese invasion and occupation, including 75,000 slave labourers on the Burma railway. If the British could take little pride in their wartime stewardship of the Indian subcontinent, where white guests of Calcutta's clubs could order unlimited eggs and bacon while Bengalis starved in the streets, never did they match the systemic barbarism of Japanese hegemony.

U.S. forces fought their way across the Pacific supported by an awesome array of wealth and technology. American observers on the Asian mainland were appalled by the contrasting destitution which they everywhere perceived, and impressed by the political forces stirring. "There are over a billion people who are tired of the world as it is; they live literally in such terrible bondage that they have nothing to lose but their chains," wrote Theodore White and Annalee Jacoby in 1944. They noted the twenty-seven-year life expectancy in India, jewel in Britain's imperial crown; a China where half the population died before attaining thirty. They described the lifeless bodies of child workers collected each morning outside factory gates in Shanghai; the beatings, whippings, torture, disease and starvation that were commonplace across the continent.

During China's famines, vastly worsened by the Japanese war, people hunted ants, devoured tree roots, ate mud. The *North China Herald* deplored the prevalence of kidnapping and extortion: "In some districts, it has been customary to roast the victims in big kettles, without water, until the flesh falls from the bone." White and Jacoby wrote: "Everywhere in Asia life is infused with a few terrible certainties—hunger, indignity, and violence." This was the world Americans perceived themselves advancing to save, not merely from the Japanese, but from imperialists of every hue—including their closest allies, the British. Churchill nursed the ill-founded delusion that victory over Japan would enable Britain to sustain its rule in India, and reassert command of Burma and Malaya. The U.S. cherished a parallel fantasy, equally massive and misguided, about what it could make of China. Frank Capra's China film in the famous U.S. War Department *Why We Fight* documentary series portrayed the country as a liberal society, and made no mention of Communists.

The Japanese, meanwhile, cherished their own illusions. As late as the summer of 1944, much of their empire still seemed secure, at least in the eyes of humbler members of its ruling race. Midshipman Toshiharu Konada loved his "runs ashore" on Java from the heavy cruiser *Ashigara*. "Everything was so new and exotic to us young men," he said. Once a chorus of local children serenaded a leave party from the fleet with Japanese songs. Konada and a cluster of other men from his ship dined at a local Italian restaurant, ogling the proprietor's daughter, one of the first European girls they had ever seen. "I thought: I am seeing the bright future of Asia here. The whole area seemed so peaceful. Many of the Chinese in Singapore were friendly to us."

Twenty-year-old Konada was the son of a naval officer commanding a Pacific base. He himself had wanted to be a doctor, but relinquished that ambition when he was drafted in 1943. "I knew Japan must be defended, and I wanted to 'do my bit.' " The following year, when *Ashigara* and its consorts were redeployed to northern Japan to guard against an American threat from the Aleutians, "we started to feel a mounting sense of peril." In the gunroom with his fellow midshipmen, "we never talked about what might happen after the war, because it seemed so remote." He knew nothing of his father's fate, because there was no mail from the Pacific islands. The midshipmen simply concentrated on their immediate tasks—studying hard for promotion exams and maintaining journals which were rigorously examined by their divisional officers.

Diversions were few in the long wait for a fleet action: every night,

Konada or some other junior officer commanded a picket boat which patrolled the waters round the ship. Their biggest excitements were spotting the head of an apparent frogman in the darkness, which proved to be a giant turtle, and detecting torpedo tracks which translated into a shoal of tuna. They recognised the power of the American and British navies. However, when they gazed around their anchorage at the serried ranks of battleships, cruisers, destroyers which Japan still possessed, there seemed no grounds for despair. "We understood that this would be a long, hard war. But it seemed worth it, to achieve peace and security for Asia."

Lt. Cmdr. Haruki Iki had been flying in combat since 1938, when he bombed retreating Chinese on the banks of the Yangtse. Iki, now thirty-two, was a famous man in the Japanese navy, the pilot who sank *Repulse* off Malaya. By the summer of 1944 he commanded a squadron flying long-range reconnaissance from Truk. They were bombed almost daily by high-altitude U.S. Liberators. Most of the bombs fell into the sea, but raids caused the Japanese airmen to spend many hours in the caves which served as shelters. In the air, the planes under Iki's command suffered relentless attrition. Replacement crews arrived scarcely trained. He found himself teaching signals procedures to radio operators who knew the principles of Morse code, but had never touched a transmitter. By high summer, the strength of his force had fallen from thirty-six aircraft to twelve. He was recalled to Japan to command a unit of Ginga bombers.

Masashiko Ando, twenty-three, was the son of a Japanese governor of Korea. None of this grandee's three boys had wanted to pursue military careers, but all were obliged to do so. The eldest died fighting on Saipan, the second perished as an army doctor in New Guinea. By July 1944 this left Masashiko the only survivor, just graduating from the Navy Academy's flight school. He had chosen to serve at sea, because an admired uncle was a naval officer. He was lucky enough to be in one of the last classes of cadets to receive thorough training, before fuel and aircraft became scarce. When postings were apportioned, he was the only cadet to apply for seaplane duty. Within a month, he was flying anti-submarine patrols in a single-engined, three-seater Judy dive-bomber.

He and his crew's routine missions lasted two or three hours, covering convoys pursuing their sluggish courses towards Japan from Malaya or the Dutch Indies. Their aircraft were primitive by Allied standards. Lacking radar, they carried only a magnetic ship-detection device, together with a single 120-pound depth charge, for the unlikely eventuality that they found an American submarine. Conducting box searches twice a day, month after month, might seem a dreary task, but it was not so to Ando, who loved to fly. His conscientious crewmen, Kato and Kikuchi, were younger than himself in years, but not in naval experience. They scanned the sea intently, searching for a telltale periscope wake.

After a while, they drank coffee from thermoses and ate their flight rations. These had improved somewhat since a disgusted pilot complained to their messing officer: "Every day might be our last! Is this muck the best you can do for our final meals?" If they needed to urinate while they were in the air, a complex procedure was invoked. Each crew carried a folded oiled paper container which, once filled and sealed with a knot, was handed over the pilot's shoulder to the magnetic search operator in the rear seat, to be thrown out of a window. Carelessness would cause the container to burst open in their faces. Even in the last year of the war, at Japanese bases in Indochina and the Dutch islands, there was enough to eat and plenty of fuel. Only aircrew replacements were in short supply. "We realised that Japan was in a tough spot," Ando said, "but not that we were in danger of losing the war. We young men believed that, whatever was happening, we could turn the tide."

Staff officer Maj. Shigeru Funaki felt almost embarrassed that his life at China Army headquarters in Nanjing was so safe and comfortable—good food and no enemy bombing. "In Japan, one felt very conscious of what a mess we were in. But in China, our lives seemed so normal that we lulled ourselves into thinking that somehow, our country would come through OK. I was always proud of the fact that, whatever happened in other theatres, in China we remained victorious. For that reason, it seemed a good place to serve."

Many young Japanese, however, discovered by experience the growing vulnerability of their nation's empire. In October 1944 Lt. Masaichi Kikuchi was posted to the Celebes, south of the Philippines. Having taken off by air from Japan, he and his draft were forced to land on Formosa by engine failure. They remained marooned there for the next two months, among several hundred others in similar plight, enduring a rain of American bombs. When they finally escaped, it was not to the Celebes, now cut off by the Americans, but to Saigon. A sea voyage which normally took a day lasted a week, as their convoy of empty oil tankers lay close inshore by day, then progressed southwards in a series of nocturnal dashes. The military passengers were kept on almost permanent anti-submarine watch, and the convoy was bombed four times.

Huddled wounded in a cave on a Pacific island, Sgt. Hiroshi Funasaka looked down on an American camp, brightly lit in the darkness: "I imagined the Americans sound asleep in their tents. They might well be easing their weariness by losing themselves in a novel. In the morning they would rise at leisure, shave, eat a hearty breakfast, then come after us as usual. That sea of glowing electric lights was a powerful mute testimonial to their 'assault by abundance' . . . I had a vision of the island divided into adjoining heaven and hell, only a few hundred metres apart."

None yearned more desperately for Allied victory than prisoners of war in Japanese hands, of whom many thousands had already died. Those who survived were stricken by disease, malnutrition and the experience of slave labour. British soldier Fred Thompson wrote on Java: "We have just started a new ten-hour shift. How long the chaps will be able to cope remains to be seen. All of us have given up guessing when we will be out—we have had so many disappointments. We are all louse-ridden, but it is one diversion anyway—big-game hunting. Keep smiling through."

In the summer of 1944, only a few hundred thousand Japanese confronting the Allies in New Guinea, the Pacific islands or Burma, at sea or in the air, had seen for themselves the overwhelming firepower now deployed against their country. Every Japanese was conscious of the privations imposed by the American blockade, but the home islands had suffered only desultory bombing. The prospect of abject defeat, which air attack and massive casualties on the Eastern Front obliged Germans to confront long before the end, was still remote from Japan. By late 1944 Hitler's people had suffered over half their total wartime losses, more than three million dead.

By contrast, a year before capitulation Hirohito's nation had suffered only a small fraction of its eventual combat and civilian casualties. Japan's human catastrophes were crowded into the last months of war, when its fate was sealed, during the futile struggle to avert the inevitable. Japan's commanders and political leaders were privy to the desperate nature of their nation's predicament, but most remained implacably unwilling to acknowledge its logic. In the last phase, around two million Japanese people paid the price for their rulers' blindness, a sacrifice which availed their country nothing. After years in which Japan's armies had roamed Asia at will, killing on a Homeric scale, retribution was at hand.

2. Summit on Oahu

Japan's advance across the Pacific and South-East Asia attained its zenith in the spring of 1942, when Australia seemed threatened with invasion, and the British Army was forced back through Burma into India. Long ground campaigns proved necessary to recover from the Japanese Guadalcanal, Papua New Guinea and other Pacific bases which they had seized. Desultory British attempts to return to Burma were frustrated. The U.S. build-up was slow, in conformity with Washington's commitment to "Germany First"—priority for the western war. America's Pacific Fleet wrested mastery of the seas from the Japanese only after a long succession of clashes, great and small, which cost many ships, planes and lives. The Allied counter-offensive was hampered by the contest for mastery between the U.S. Army and Navy. The two services conducted separate and rival campaigns against the Japanese, spuriously dignified as "the twin-track strategy."

Despite all these difficulties, by the summer of 1944 the material strength of the U.S. was becoming overwhelming, the Japanese comet was plunging steeply. The trauma inflicted on the Americans and their allies by Pearl Harbor, the loss of Hong Kong, Malaya, Singapore, Burma, the Dutch East Indies, and scores of Pacific islands had faded. The challenge confronting the leaders of the Grand Alliance was no longer that of frustrating Japan's advance, but instead that of encompassing its destruction. Strategic choice had become the privilege of the Allies. In the eastern war, this meant that the political, military and naval leadership of the U.S. determined courses, then informed the British.

Early in the afternoon of 26 July 1944, the cruiser *Baltimore* passed Hawaii's Diamond Head inbound for Pearl Harbor. Insecure gossip had prompted a crowd of soldiers and sailors to gather at the navy yard. Off Fort Kamehaha, as the big warship lost way a tug nosed alongside, carrying Admiral Chester Nimitz, commander-in-chief of the Pacific Fleet. Then *Baltimore* moored at Pier 22B, enabling more flag officers and generals to ascend the gangway and form up to salute the cruiser's exalted passenger, the president of the United States. Franklin Roosevelt in the last nine months of his life and in the midst of his fourth presidential election campaign, looked about for Douglas MacArthur, the man he had come to meet. He was told that the general's plane had just landed. MacArthur was on his way from Fort Shafter, and would arrive shortly. Sure enough, cheers and whistles along the Honolulu road heralded America's most famous soldier since Ulysses S. Grant. MacArthur's car swept up to the dockside. The great man emerged in khaki trousers, a brown leather air force jacket, chief of the army's cap and insignia. As bosuns' pipes screeched, he mounted the gangway, saluted the quarterdeck and went below to meet Roosevelt.

This was an encounter MacArthur had not sought, did in fact scorn. George Marshall and Dwight Eisenhower, together with every other American, British, Soviet, German and Japanese commander of the Second World War, acknowledged subordination to their respective national leaderships. MacArthur, by contrast, seemed to reject accountability to any earthly power. His formal title was Allied Supreme Commander, South-West Pacific Area—SWPA. He seldom commanded more than ten divisions committed to combat operations, a fraction of Eisenhower's army in north-west Europe. Indeed, in 1944 he controlled fewer than half the number of ground troops deployed in Italy, itself a secondary commitment. It was a source of bitter chagrin that he was denied overall theatre authority, and obliged to acknowledge Admiral Chester Nimitz, commanding U.S. forces in the central Pacific, as his equal and rival. MacArthur had always opposed the "twin-track strategy," whereby his elements approached Japan from the south-west, while the navy and Marines conducted their own thrusts further north. He believed that he alone was the appropriate arbiter of America's eastern war, and fumed at the waste of resources caused by fighting two parallel campaigns, while never deigning to address the possibility that his own was the obvious candidate for redundancy.

Throughout his tenure of high command, MacArthur, sixty-four in July 1944, bore controversy in his wake. From the day he graduated first of his West Point class, his intellect and inspirational leadership were recognised. As U.S. Army chief of staff, however, he earned notoriety for his ruthless suppression of the 1932 World War I veterans' "bonus march" on Washington. His policy reflected perfervidly right-wing political convictions. Following his retirement in 1935 he returned to the Philippines, the American dependency where he had served in his youth, accepting the appointment of military adviser to its government and commander of its armed forces. As the Japanese threat grew, in July 1941 Roosevelt named MacArthur commander-in-chief of the American garrison as well as of the Filipino troops in the islands. In this capacity the general directed the defence of the islands from their invasion by the Japanese in December 1941 until March 1942. He was then ordered by the White House to escape by PT-boat before the surrender of his starving soldiers, trapped on the Bataan Peninsula.

Army insiders held MacArthur personally culpable for the Philippines débâcle, by failures both of commission and omission. This was unjust. Though his generalship was poor, no commander could have defeated the Japanese onslaught with the weak forces at his disposal. More than a few American senior officers, however, would have been happy to see this elderly autocrat play no further role in the war. Eisenhower, who had served under MacArthur, expressed in his diary during the Bataan siege a belief that it would be a mistake to evacuate him: "If brought out, public opinion will force him into a position where his love of the limelight may ruin him." MacArthur displayed a taste for fantasy quite unsuited to a field commander, together with ambition close to megalomania and consistently poor judgement as a picker of subordinates. Fortunately for his public image, only Roosevelt and a handful of others were aware of the general's acceptance in March 1942 of $500,000 from the Philippines Treasury, as a personal gift from President Manuel Quezon. This was an extraordinarily improper transaction on the part of both donor and recipient.

The British always acknowledged that their own forces and commanders performed poorly in the 1941–42 Burma and Malaya campaigns. Operations in the Philippines were equally mismanaged, but in those dark days Americans yearned for heroes. President and people colluded to make one of MacArthur, to forge a heroic myth around the defender of Bataan. Americans found it unthinkable that the U.S. army which slowly assembled in Australia through 1942 and 1943 should be led into battle by anyone else.

MacArthur presided over campaigns to regain dominance of New Guinea and the islands of the south-west Pacific which proved protracted and bitter, and at first yielded little glory. Yet so formidable was the general's publicity machine, so impressive his personality, that he held his job until the victories began to come. There were demands from the U.S. political right that he should be made the nation's global supreme commander, or accept nomination as a presidential candidate, neither of which notions he seemed eager to dismiss. Foremost among proponents of the "man of destiny" view of history, he was bent upon becoming the lone star of America's Pacific war. Everything within his compass was subordinated to that purpose. A blizzard of personal publicity accompanied his every movement, readily supported by U.S. newspaper moguls—Hearst, McCormick, Patterson—who loved the general. Twelve full-length biographies were published in the course of the war, their flavour conveyed by a sample title, *MacArthur the Magnificent*, which did nothing to check his egomania.

The senior Allied commander who afterwards spoke most warmly of MacArthur was Gen. Sir Alan Brooke, the dour, clever Northern Irishman who was Britain's principal wartime chief of staff. Brooke's assessment was astonishingly effusive: "From everything I saw of him, he was the greatest general of the last war. He certainly showed a far greater strategic grasp than Marshall." Such a testimonial should not be altogether ignored, but Brooke knew little of either MacArthur or the Japanese war. Top Americans obliged to work with the "hero of Bataan" adopted a much more sceptical view. His fitness for high command was disputed by many senior officers, foremost among them the chief of naval operations, Admiral Ernest King, another Olympian autocrat. King's daughter described her father as an entirely even-tempered man: "He was always angry." Such was the admiral's personal animus against the general that, at a joint chiefs of staff meeting, Marshall—himself no admirer of MacArthur—felt obliged to thump the table and silence a tirade from King: "I will not have any meeting carried on with this hatred."

MacArthur's critics believed that an advance across the south-west Pacific was irrelevant to America's strategic requirements, and was promoted only by the general's ambition to liberate the Philippines. He shamelessly manipulated communiqués about his forces' achievements, personally selected photographs of himself for press release, deprived subordinates of credit for successes, shrugged off his own responsibility for failures. He was a man of fierce passions, whom "joy or sorrow would set . . . off on lusty zooms or steep dives," in the words of a subordinate. "At the risk of being naïve and just plain dumb," wrote Maj.-Gen. St. Clair Streett, later commander of the Thirteenth Air Force, assessing Pacific command in October 1942, "the major obstacle for a sane military solution of the problem [is] General MacArthur . . . even the President himself might find his hands tied in dealing with the general." The sooner MacArthur was out of the Pacific, thought Streett, the sooner would it be possible to establish a rational command structure for the theatre.

A senior British airman, no stranger to tensions in his own nation's high command, was nonetheless awed by those between America's armed forces: "The violence of inter-service rivalry . . . in those days had to be seen to be believed, and was an appreciable handicap to their war effort." Even where armed services dislike each other institutionally, successful cooperation can be achieved if individual commanders forge working relationships. MacArthur, however, was interested in achieving harmony only in pursuit of his own objectives. Admiral King likewise placed the long-term interests of the U.S. Navy far above any tactical conveniences related to fighting the Japanese. No overall Pacific supreme commander was ever appointed, because neither army nor navy could stomach the explicit triumph of the other service. And even if the resultant division of authority impeded the defeat of Japan, so prodigious were U.S. resources that the nation felt able to indulge it.

MacArthur was never ill. When there was nowhere more distant to go, he paced his office to assuage his chronic restlessness. He made no jokes and possessed no small talk, though he would occasionally talk baseball to enlisted men, in attempts to deceive them that he was human. Marshall observed that MacArthur had a court, not a staff. Intimates of the "Bataan gang," the handful of officers to whom he granted passage alongside his own family on the PT-boats escaping from the Philippines, remained privileged acolytes to the war's end. SWPA chief of staff Lt.-Gen. Richard

Sutherland felt able to commission his Australian mistress in the American Women's Army Corps, shipping her in his entourage until the scandal was exposed.

MacArthur's belief that his critics were not merely wrong, but evil, verged on derangement. He claimed to perceive a "crooked streak" in both Marshall and Eisenhower, two of the most honourable men in American public service. When the Office of War Information wished to alter for national consumption his legendary remark on quitting the Philippines from "I shall return" to "We shall return," MacArthur demurred. Early in 1944, the general wrote to Henry Stimson: "These frontal attacks by the Navy . . . are tragic and unnecessary massacres of American lives . . . The Navy fails to understand the strategy . . . Give me central direction of the war in the Pacific, and I will be in the Philippines in ten months . . . don't let the Navy's pride of position and ignorance continue this great tragedy to our country." MacArthur's personal behaviour was no worse than that of Patton and Montgomery, but he exercised command under far less restraint than either.

Perhaps most distasteful of all his wartime actions was a flirtation with a 1944 presidential election run against Roosevelt, whose liberalism affronted his own rabidly conservative convictions. MacArthur's staff corresponded with potential campaign backers in the U.S., which they could not have done without his knowledge. Lt.-Gen. Robert Eichelberger asserted: "If it were not for his hatred, or rather the extent to which he despises FDR, he would not want [the presidency]." The influential *New York Times* columnist Arthur Krock wrote in April 1944: "It is generally believed . . . that General MacArthur is dissatisfied with the military strategy of the war as approved by the President and Prime Minister Churchill." This was indeed so. Only when it became apparent that MacArthur could not defeat Thomas Dewey to secure the Republican presidential nomination did he finally exclude himself from candidacy.

He also possessed virtues, however. His air chief, George Kenney, observed shrewdly that "as a salesman, MacArthur has no superiors and few equals." The USAAF responded to the general's enthusiasm for air power by offering its passionate support to his causes. Though MacArthur's hostility towards Britain was well-known, British brigadier Jack Profumo, attached to his staff, praised his private courtesy and warmth. The supreme commander's senior British liaison officer described him to Churchill as "ruthless, vain, unscrupulous and self-conscious . . . but . . . a man of real calibre with a vivid imagination, a capacity to learn rapidly from the past, a leader of men . . . [with] a considerable understanding of personalities and political development." MacArthur's serene assurance, natural authority and charisma lent some substance to his claims to rank. If he was not among history's outstanding commanders, he acted the part of one with unshakeable conviction.

In late summer 1944, MacArthur's credit as a strategist stood higher than it ever had before, or would again. In two months he had conducted a dramatic advance 1,200 miles up Papua New Guinea, bypassing rather than lingering to destroy Japanese garrisons, staging a series of surprise amphibious assaults, of which the most recent and successful took place at Hollandia, where his headquarters was now being transferred. These achievements, however, won headlines without removing fundamental doubts about the usefulness of the army's operations in the south-west Pacific, now that the threat to Australia was lifted. Geographical imperatives made the U.S. Navy the lead service in the Japanese war, to which the army was obliged to defer. Soldiers could nowhere engage the Japanese without being transported to objectives in ships, and supported in action by fleets. MacArthur could bend strategy and sustain his own status as the most famous American participating in the struggle. But try as he might, he could not contrive absolute personal mastery.

This, then, was the background against which the supreme commander of SWPA arrived on Oahu, Hawaii, in July 1944, to meet Roosevelt and Nimitz. MacArthur's tardy arrival reflected his distaste for the encounter. If he chafed at the need to parley by signal with the joint chiefs of staff in Washington, he found it intolerable to be obliged to fly several thousand miles to confer with a civilian politician, albeit the greatest in the land. MacArthur believed that Roosevelt had summoned the Hawaii meeting for political purposes, to further his re-election campaign by showcasing himself before the American people as their commander-in-chief. "The humiliation of forcing me to leave my command to fly to Honolulu for a picture-taking junket!" the general exclaimed furiously during the twenty-six-hour flight from Australia. For once, his paranoia was probably justified. His scepticism about the Hawaii meeting was shared by Admiral King. Roosevelt was always party to the big decisions, and on several important occasions—for instance, when he insisted upon the November 1942 North African landings despite the deep reluctance of his chiefs of staff—he dictated them. Nonetheless, U.S. strategy in the Second World War was dominated by compromises between rival service chiefs. This explains the curled lips of King and MacArthur when, in July 1944, Roosevelt sought to be seen to play the part of supreme warlord as he offered himself to the American people for an unprecedented fourth term.

The struggle with Japan had moved many thousands of miles since the Hawaiian Islands fell victim to the 7 December 1941 air assault, but they remained America's principal rear base and staging area for the Pacific campaign. "Pearl was mostly brass and hookers," in the laconic words of cruiser bosun's mate Eugene Hardy. Combat officers who visited the islands' headquarters complexes were irked by the sybaritic comfort in which staffs did their business. Regular Saturday-night dances were held at Schofield Barracks. "There were dinner parties, beach parties and cocktail parties," wrote a Marine general, O. P. Smith. "At some of the parties the women guests wore evening gowns. You had the feeling that you were half in the war and half out of it." Personnel based on Hawaii shrugged that it would give no help to the men at the sharp end to impose a spurious austerity. After protests by visitors from the combat zone, however, officers' clubs abandoned the practice of serving steak twice a day.

Roosevelt's most important meetings on Hawaii took place at the Kalaukau Avenue mansion of a prominent Waikiki citizen, Chris Holmes. Naval aviators had been billeted there for some time, and for a week before the grandees' arrival, working parties from the submarine base laboured overtime to repair the fliers' depredations. The house then became the setting for performances by two remarkable thespians, the president and the General of the Army, together with a supreme professional, the Pacific Fleet's C-in-C. The only issue which interested MacArthur was resolution of the Pacific route by which the U.S. should continue its advance upon Japan. Even as Roosevelt, Nimitz and MacArthur conferred, the U.S. Navy and Marines were completing the capture of the Mariana island group. On 19 and 20 June 1944, in the "Great Marianas Turkey Shoot," carrier planes of Admiral Raymond Spruance's Fifth Fleet had inflicted devastating defeat, indeed near annihilation, upon Japan's naval air force. Around 475 enemy aircraft were destroyed, by comparison with the 60 Luftwaffe planes shot down by the RAF on 15 September 1940, the biggest day of the Battle of Britain. The island chain, a mere 1,400 miles south-east of Japan, represented a vital link in the American advance. Its capture made possible the construction of air bases from which B-29 bombers could reach Tokyo. Its loss was by far the most important Japanese defeat of 1944, a decisive moment of the war.

Because no minutes were taken of Roosevelt's meetings with his commanders, uncertainty has persisted about exactly what was said. The historical narrative relies on fragmentary and highly partial accounts by the participants. "Douglas, where do we go from here?" Roosevelt asked. This form of address must have irked MacArthur, who signed even letters to his wife, Jean, with his surname. "Leyte, Mr. President, and then Luzon!" was the recorded response, naming two of the foremost Philippine islands. These exact words are implausible, for at that stage U.S. plans called for an initial landing further south, on Mindanao. The thrust of MacArthur's argument is not in doubt, however. He asserted, as he had done since 1942, that strategic wisdom and national honour alike demanded the liberation of the Filipino people, whose territory would then become the principal stepping-stone for the invasion of Japan.

In October 1943, the joint chiefs had allocated the U.S. Navy its own route across the central Pacific via the Marshall, Caroline and Mariana islands, assaulted principally by Marine divisions, while MacArthur's soldiers advanced by way of the Solomons, the Bismarck Archipelago, and the hills and jungles of Papua New Guinea. All these objectives were now achieved. The names of their torrid conquests had become written in blood into American history: Guadalcanal and Kwajalein, Tarawa, Saipan and Guam. Each had been the scene of a contest for a few square miles of rock or coral on which to create airstrips and anchorages to support the greatest fleets the world had ever seen. The Pacific war was fought almost entirely within gunshot of the sea. Amid the vast, empty expanses of the world's largest ocean, men flung themselves upon outcrops of land, painted livid green by vegetation, with a passion mocked by their coarse beauty. In the first eighteen months of the conflict, though Japan's supply lines were grossly over-extended, her armed forces engaged the Americans on not unequal terms. Until late 1943, for instance, the U.S. Pacific Fleet never possessed more than four aircraft carriers. Thereafter, however, American strength soared, while that of Japan shrank.

A host of ships, planes, men and guns flooded west from the U.S. to the battlefields. At peak production in March 1944, an aircraft rolled out of an American factory every 295 seconds. By the end of that year, almost one hundred U.S. aircraft carriers were at sea. American planes and submarines were strangling Japanese supply routes. It had become unnecessary systematically to destroy Japan's Pacific air bases, because the enemy possessed pitifully few planes to use them. Between 26 December 1943 and 24 October 1944, Japanese aircraft failed to sink a single significant American ship. Similarly, surviving Japanese army garrisons presented no threat, for Tokyo no longer had means to move or supply them. But even when the Japanese strategic predicament was hopeless, when resistance became—by Western lights—futile, their soldiers fought to the last. These desperate battles reflected, in some degree, the warrior ethic of *bushido*. Overlaid upon this, however, was a rational calculation by Tokyo. The superiority of American resources was manifest. If Japan pursued the war within the limits of conventional military behaviour, its defeat was inevitable. Its leaders' chosen course was to impose such a ghastly blood price for each American gain that this "nation of storekeepers" would find it preferable to negotiate, rather than accept the human cost of invading Japan's main islands. If such a strategy was paper-thin, and woefully underestimated American resolution, it determined Japanese conduct by land, sea and air until August 1945.

"No matter how a war starts, it ends in mud," wrote Gen. Joseph "Vinegar Joe" Stilwell. "It has to be slugged out—there are no trick solutions or cheap shortcuts." There was, and remains, no doubt that this was true of the war against Germany. But did it also apply to the war against Japan? The enemy was an island nation. If the U.S. Navy could secure sufficient Pacific footholds to provide air and naval basing facilities on the route to Japan, was it also necessary to fight a major ground campaign? It had been America's historic intention to conduct any war with Japan at sea and in the air, rather than by land battle. Whatever the achievements of U.S. ground forces since Pearl Harbor, the decisive victories had been secured by the navy—Midway and the progressive attrition of Japan's air and naval forces. While American strategic planning assumed eventual amphibious landings in the Japanese home islands, it remained the fervent hope of most commanders that blockade and air bombardment would render these unnecessary.

There was only one messianic advocate of a major campaign to retake the Philippines: MacArthur. While others varied their opinions in the face of changing circumstances, the general never did. It is possible that beyond ego, a worm of guilt gnawed about his own conduct in 1941–42. Albeit under presidential orders, he had abandoned his Philippines command to barbarous captivity, to flee with his personal staff, family, nanny and dubiously acquired fortune to safety in Australia. Now, when other commanders' eyes flitted between alternative objectives in the western Pacific, his own never wavered. King, an officer as imperious as MacArthur, favoured bypassing the Philippines, approaching Japan by way of its offshore island possessions, Formosa and Okinawa. Formosa presented a much smaller target than the mass of the Philippines, with the additional attraction of opening a gateway to the Chinese mainland.

The U.S. Army's War Plans Department concluded as far back as 1923 that, if America's Philippines bases were lost in the early stages of a conflict, their recapture would be "a long and costly undertaking." King complained that MacArthur was drawn to the islands solely by sentiment. Marshall likewise warned the general in June 1944: "We must be careful not to allow our personal feelings and Philippine political considerations to override our great objective, which is the early conclusion of the war with Japan . . . bypassing [is not] synonymous with abandonment."

On Hawaii, when Roosevelt expressed concern about the human cost of retaking the Philippines, MacArthur said: "Mr. President, my losses would not be heavy, any more than they have been in the past. The days of the frontal attack are over. Modern infantry weapons are too deadly, and direct assault is no longer feasible. Only mediocre commanders still use it. Your good commanders do not turn in heavy losses." This was self-serving bluster. It reflected MacArthur's disdain for the navy's conduct of the central Pacific thrust, and ignored the fact that Nimitz's forces met far stronger Japanese defences than his own had been obliged to face; in the course of the Pacific war, MacArthur's casualties in reality exceeded those of Nimitz.

But no significant opposition to MacArthur's Philippines ambitions was expressed. Six hours of meetings were dominated by Roosevelt and MacArthur. Nimitz merely outlined plans for an amphibious landing to establish bases on Peleliu, east of the Philippines, and described the progress of fleet operations. The main dish at the big formal lunch which punctuated discussion was the famous Hawaiian fish mahimahi, examined and approved as fit for presidential consumption by Vice-Admiral Ross McIntire, FDR's personal physician. MacArthur was able to say of his relations with the naval C-in-C: "We see eye to eye, Mr. President, we understand each other perfectly."

Robert Sherrod wrote of Nimitz, one of the greatest naval officers America has produced, that he "conceived of war as something to be accomplished as efficiently and smoothly as possible, without too much fanfare." The admiral was wholly without interest in personal publicity, and his Hawaiian headquarters was characterised by a cool, understated authority. When Marine general O. P. Smith went to report to Nimitz, he found him at his favourite relaxation facility, the pistol range. An aide "warned me that it was well to keep out of sight until the Admiral finished or otherwise he might challenge one to a match, the results of which might be embarrassing as he was a very good shot."

Born in 1885 into a German family who became successful hotelkeepers in Texas, Nimitz had intended an army career until offered a midshipman's place at the U.S. Naval Academy at Annapolis, Maryland. A former submariner who was among the pioneers of refuelling at sea, he was well-known for his skilful management of committees, and meticulous personal habits—he was irked by the unpunctuality of politicians. The admiral invariably travelled with his schnauzer, Mak, a mean little dog which growled. His staff, like most wartime service personnel, worked a seven-day week, but were encouraged to take an afternoon tennis break. They inhabited a sternly masculine world, for Nimitz insisted that there should be no women on the team. There was just one female intruder—a mine warfare intelligence officer named Lt. Harriet Borland, who for administrative purposes was deemed not to be a member of CINCPAC'S headquarters. The admiral and his wife, Catherine, entertained generously in their home at Pearl, often serving fruit delicacies flown from the Pacific islands.

A natural diplomat, sober and controlled, Nimitz strove to defuse tensions with MacArthur, even when—as sometimes happened—the general flatly refused to surrender control of shipping temporarily diverted to him from navy resources. In March 1944 the two men and their senior staffs met in Brisbane, for what promised to be a stormy encounter. "Nee-mitz," as MacArthur called the admiral sourly, opened the conference by telling a story of two frantically worried men pacing a hotel corridor. One finally asked the other what was troubling him. "I am a doctor," came the answer, "and I have a patient in my room with a wooden leg, and I have that leg apart and can't get it back together again." The other man said: "Great guns, I wish that was all I have to worry about. I have a good-looking gal in my room with both legs apart, and I can't remember the room number." Even MacArthur laughed, though it was unthinkable that he himself would have stooped to such perceived vulgarity. Carrier admiral "Jocko" Clark asserted reverently that Nimitz was "the one great leader in the Pacific who had no blemish on his shield or dent in his armour." This seems not much overstated.

Why, on Hawaii, did Nimitz not voice the navy's strong reservations about the Philippines plan? First, he found himself in a weak diplomatic position. Whatever MacArthur's private contempt for Roosevelt, at their meeting the general deployed the full force of his personality to charm the president, whom he had known since serving under him as army chief of staff. The undemonstrative Nimitz found himself perforce playing a subordinate role beside two showmen. More than this, naval commanders were themselves divided about future strategy. Admiral Raymond Spruance, commanding Fifth Fleet, favoured an advance on Okinawa by way of Iwo Jima, rather than taking Formosa. Despite King's order to plan for Formosa, Spruance instructed his staff not to waste time on it.

Nimitz himself, meanwhile, was more sympathetic to the Philippines plan than was King, his boss. Six months earlier, the Pacific C-in-C had been furiously rebuked by the chief of naval operations for advocating a landing on Mindanao rather than in the Marianas. While the navy certainly saw no virtue in protracted operations to recover the entire archipelago, Nimitz and his staff deemed it useful, indeed probably indispensable, to secure Philippines ground and air bases before advancing closer to Japan. Logistics would permit Mindanao-Leyte landings before the end of 1944, while no assault on Formosa was feasible before the spring of 1945. Furthermore, Japanese captures of U.S. air bases in China, and general disenchantment with Chiang Kai-shek's nation as an ally, made Formosa seem far less useful as a door into China than it had done a few months earlier. Nimitz almost certainly considered that the Hawaii meeting was symbolic and political, rather than decisive. The joint chiefs would arbitrate.

There was no purpose in attempting to translate a political showcase occasion into a strategic showdown.

Yet MacArthur, the man of destiny, believed that he had exploited the occasion to good effect. When he climbed back on his plane to return to Australia, barely twenty-four hours after landing on Hawaii, he declared triumphantly to his staff: "We've sold it!" He was justified in this assertion insofar as Roosevelt sailed home on 29 July, after a further two days visiting bases and hospitals, believing that the U.S. must retake the Philippines. Electoral considerations undoubtedly played a part in the presidential endorsement of MacArthur's wishes. Roosevelt knew that the general's political friends would raise a storm among American voters if they could claim that the suffering millions of the Philippines—America's dependents or colonial subjects, according to taste—were being wantonly abandoned to continuing Japanese oppression.

Even after Hawaii, however, for several weeks the U.S. joint chiefs of staff havered. Marshall had once described the MacArthur plan for the Philippines as "the slow way . . . We would have to fight our way through them, and it would take a very much longer time than to make the cut across." In north-west Europe, Eisenhower staunchly resisted pleas to liberate the starving Dutch people in the winter of 1944, arguing—surely rightly—that the welfare of the occupied peoples was best served by concentrating forces without diversion upon the defeat of Nazi Germany. Yet so great was the prestige of MacArthur, so effective was his emotional crusade for the Philippines' liberation, that to gainsay him would have required a vastly different supreme command in Washington.

From the late summer of 1944 onwards, America's difficulties in the Pacific related principally to the logistic challenges of supporting large forces at the limits of an oceanic supply chain. Moreover, in the early autumn, after MacArthur's cheap successes in Papua New Guinea, there was no anticipation of the intensity of resistance the Japanese would offer on Leyte and Luzon. U.S. air and sea power had lately overwhelmed the enemy's puny efforts wherever he accepted battle. Desperate courage and superior fieldcraft enabled Japanese soldiers often to inflict pain on American forces, but never to alter outcomes. For instance, a belated offensive at Aitape in New Guinea in July 1944 cost the Japanese 18th Army 10,000 dead, in exchange for killing some 440 Americans. U.S. forces paid with the lives of almost 7,000 men for the capture of the Marianas and later Peleliu—but the Japanese counted 46,000 dead. Such a dramatic balance in favour of the victors was small comfort to a Marine in a foxhole under mortar and machine-gun fire from an invisible enemy, with comrades bleeding around him. But it represented a reality which promoted optimism among American commanders in the autumn of 1944.

It was almost certainly the correct decision to undertake limited operations to straddle the Philippines with naval and air power, seizing bases, destroying Japanese aircraft and interdicting enemy shipping routes. MacArthur's plans, however, were vastly more ambitious. He was bent upon a campaign of progressive liberation which could contribute little to expediting America's advance upon the Japanese home islands. His first landing would be made in the south, on Mindanao. U.S. forces would then advance progressively via Leyte to the capture of the largest island, Luzon, which MacArthur assured the chiefs could be taken in a month. Nimitz, meanwhile, would prepare to capture the central Pacific island of Iwo Jima, and thereafter assault Okinawa.

Just as in Europe, where Eisenhower committed his armies to a broad-front advance, rather than favouring any one of his subordinate commanders' operations above those of others, so in the war against Japan the U.S. continued the twin-track strategy, sustaining both MacArthur's invasion of the Philippines and the navy's drive across the central Pacific. This represented a broadcasting of resources acceptable only to a nation of America's fantastic wealth, but it was the compromise adopted by the chiefs of staff, with the belated acquiescence of Admiral King. So assured could be America's commanders of forthcoming victory that it was hard for them to regard the Philippines as an issue of decisive importance—and indeed, it was not. It was in no one's interest to bet the ranch against MacArthur about rival routes to a final outcome which was not in doubt. In the late summer of 1944, the general began to gather land, sea and air forces for a November assault on his "second homeland."

CHAPTER TWO

Japan: Defying Gravity

1. *Yamato* Spirit

THOUGHTFUL JAPANESE understood that the fall of the Marianas in the summer of 1944 represented a decisive step towards their country's undoing. It brought the home islands within range of vastly more effective bombing. American submarines were already strangling the country's supply lines. U.S. ground forces would soon be assaulting Japan's inner perimeter. Yet the Japanese people had been at war for seven years, since their invasion of China. Domestic life became harsh long before Pearl Harbor. To most, outright defeat was still unthinkable. When twenty-one-year-old Masaichi Kikuchi graduated from army officer school in the summer of 1944, he went home to his tiny village north of Tokyo bursting with pride to show off his new uniform. In a community where everyone inhabited thatched cottages shared with their plough horses, chickens and silkworms, he was the only one of five brothers in his family, and indeed in the whole village, to secure a commission. "We grew up in a world where everyone who was not Japanese was perceived as an enemy," said Kikuchi, "Chinese, British, American. We were schooled to regard them all as evil, devilish, animalistic. Conflict was a commonplace for our generation, from Manchuria onwards. Everyone took it for granted. Even in 1944 when we knew things were not going well, that Guadalcanal and Guam and other places had gone, it never occurred to any of us that the whole war might be lost."

By contrast with the austerities of the home islands, throughout Japan's mainland empire from Manchuria to Siam, the privileged status of millions of Japanese as occupiers and overlords remained apparently secure, their routines deceptively tranquil. Kikuchi was posted to an airfield defence unit in Malaya, where he found life extraordinarily pleasant. There was he, a peasant's son, occupying a large British colonial house on Singapore's Caton Road, attended by two servants, with a beach a few hundred yards away "where on clear evenings I could look out upon the most beautiful moon I had ever seen." At the officers' club, though movies were no longer available and they were forbidden to play mah-jong, there were billiards, plenty of beer and *sake*, food and cheap Malacca cigarettes. "Even at that stage of the war, the life of an officer in the Japanese army in a place like that was incredibly privileged. I must confess that, when we knew so many others were out there fighting and dying in Burma and the Pacific, I often felt guilty about my own circumstances."

Petty Officer Hachiro Miyashita had seen too much action with the fleet to feel embarrassment about his "cushy" posting at Tenga airfield, also in Malaya, where his unit taught deck landing to trainee carrier pilots, because no fuel was available nearer home for such purposes. Miyashita revelled in the big bath with hot water at his billet in the old British officers' quarters, the golf course (though none of them knew how to play), and the absence of enemy activity: "It seemed like heaven." Miyashita was the twenty-six-year-old son of the owner of a Tokyo fruit shop, now defunct because there was no more fruit to sell. He had volunteered for the navy back in 1941, and experienced its glory days. He and the rest of the flight crews stood cheering on the deck of the carrier *Shokaku* as their aircraft took off for Pearl Harbor, and joined the rapturous reception on their return: "What passions that day fired!" Through the years which followed, however, their lives became incomparably more sober. After the 1942 Coral Sea battle, in which the ship was hit three times and 107 men died, each body was placed in a coffin weighted with a shell, and solemnly committed to the deep. The coffins broke open, however, and sprang to the surface again. The ship's wake became strewn with bobbing corpses, a spectacle which upset the crew. Thereafter, they tipped their dead overboard with a shell carefully lashed to each man's legs.

Miyashita lived through hours of frenzied firefighting when American bomb strikes tore open the flight deck, and endured the harrowing experience of clearing casualties and body parts. He never shrugged off the memory of picking up a boot bearing the name "Ohara," with a foot still inside it. In the Marianas battle of June 1944, aboard the carrier *Zuikaku*, he watched a pall of black smoke rise above the sea, marking the end of his old ship *Shokaku*, and of most of the shipmates he knew so well. He thought of close friends from the petty officers' mess like Ino and Miyajima, now among the fishes, and muttered to himself: "My turn next." *Zuikaku* lost almost all its aircraft. "As long as we were fighting, there was no time to think. Afterwards, however, as we sailed home, seeing the hangar decks almost empty, sorting out the effects of all the crews who were gone, gave us a terrible feeling. From that stage of the war, my memories are only tragic ones." Hitherto, Miyashita had prided himself on his steadiness in action. After three years of Pacific combat, however, "I found that I jumped when a hatch cover clanged shut. My nerves were in a bad way."

So were those of more exalted people than Petty Officer Miyashita, and it influenced them in strange ways. Thousands of Japanese civilians on Saipan chose to kill themselves, most by leaping from seashore cliffs, rather than submit to the American conquerors. Vice-Admiral Matome Ugaki, later commander of the navy's kamikaze units, wrote in his diary: "It's only to be expected that fighting men should be killed, but for women, children and old men in such large numbers on a helpless, lonely island to prefer death to captivity . . . What a tragedy! None but the people of the *Yamato* nation could do such a thing . . . If one hundred million Japanese people could display the same resolution . . . it wouldn't be difficult to find a way to victory."

Here was a vivid example of the spirit prevalent among Japan's leadership in 1944–45. Many shared a delusion that human sacrifice, the nation's historic "*Yamato* spirit," could compensate for a huge shortfall in military capability. In modern parlance, they committed themselves to asymmetric warfare. This was unconvincing in a death struggle between nations. In December 1941, Japan had launched a war against enemies vastly superior in resources and potential. Its leaders gambled on two assumptions: first, that the U.S. would lack stomach for a long contest; second, that Germany would triumph in Europe. Both were confounded. Indeed, far from Japanese accession increasing the strength of the Axis, it served to ensure Hitler's doom by making America his enemy. So dismayed were the Western Allies by their defeats in 1941–42 that they chose to perceive these as manifestations of their conquerors' prowess. They were correct, insofar as the Japanese displayed an energy and effectiveness then lacking among the British and Americans. Japan's early triumphs, however, reflected the local weakness of the vanquished, rather than the real might of the victors.

The Japanese people were far more enthusiastic about going to war in December 1941 than had been the Germans in 1939. Japan's mission to expand territorially into Asia, and to defy any nation which objected, had enjoyed popular support since the beginning of the century. After their country's 1941 intervention in French Indochina, many Japanese were bewildered, as well as embittered, by America's imposition of a trade embargo. The U.S. had swallowed Japanese colonisation of Formosa, Korea, Manchuria and eastern China. Washington acquiesced, albeit with distaste, in the huge British, French and Dutch empires in Asia. Why should Japanese imperialism be any less acceptable to American sensibilities? Although Japan's experience of war in China was painful, it also seemed successful. Few Japanese knew that military victories on the mainland had not been matched by economic gains of anything like the necessary magnitude. They possessed no national memory of slaughter in the trenches, such as many Germans retained from World War I, to check their rejoicing at Pearl Harbor.

Cultural contempt for the West was widespread. "Money-making is the one aim in life [of Americans]," asserted a Japanese army propaganda document. "The men make money to live luxuriously and over-educate their wives and daughters who are allowed to talk too much. Their lack of real culture is betrayed by their love of jazz music . . . Americans are still untamed since the wild pioneer days. Hold-ups, assassinations, kidnappings, gangs, bribery, corruption and lynching of Negroes are still practised. Graft in politics and commerce, labour and athletics is rampant. Sex relations have deteriorated with the development of motor cars; divorce is rife . . . America has its strong points, such as science, invention and other creative activities . . . [But while] outwardly civilized it is inwardly corrupt and decadent." If such descents into caricature of the enemy were often matched by Allied propaganda about the Japanese, they were unhelpful in assisting Tokyo's commanders realistically to appraise their enemy.

To an extraordinary degree for a nation which chose to launch a war, Japan failed to equip itself for the struggle. Its leaders allowed relative economic success woefully to delude them about their ability to sustain a conflict with the United States. Pre-war Japan was the world's fourth largest exporter, and owned its third largest merchant fleet. The nation's industrial production rose strongly through the thirties, when the rest of the world was striving to escape from the Depression, and amounted to double that of all the rest of Asia, excluding the Soviet Union. Japan's consumption index for 1937 was 264 percent of the 1930 figure. The country was still predominantly rural, with 40 percent of the population working on the land, but the industrial labour force grew from 5.8 million in 1930 to 9.5 million by 1944, much of this increase achieved by a hesitant mobilisation of women and the exploitation of a million imported Koreans.

Between 1937 and 1944, Japan achieved a 24 percent increase in manufacturing, and 46 percent in steel production. But these achievements, which seemed substantial when viewed through a national prism, shrank into insignificance alongside those of the United States. Between 1942 and 1945, the U.S. produced 2,154 million metric tons of coal, Japan 189.8; the U.S. 6,661 million barrels of oil, Japan 29.6; the U.S. 257,390 artillery pieces, Japan 7,000; the U.S. 279,813 aircraft, Japan 64,800. Overall Japanese industrial capacity was around 10 percent of that of the United States. Though Japan possessed some of the trappings, and could boast some of the achievements, of a modern industrial society, in mindset and fundamental circumstances it was nothing of the kind. In an Asian context it seemed mighty, but from a global perspective it remained relatively primitive, as the Japanese army discovered when worsted by the Russians during the Mongolian border clash of August 1939 at Nomonhan.

Japan was a military dictatorship, insofar as the army dominated decision-making. Popular dissent was suppressed as the country entered its *kurai tanima*—"dark valley"—from 1931 onwards, when the power of the nominally civilian elected government was progressively eclipsed by that of the military. The war minister, always a serving soldier, was the most influential cabinet member. Yet the direction of the Japanese war machine was feeble, fractious and inept. Rivalry between the army and navy, "star and anchor," was arguably no more bitter than that which prevailed in the U.S. armed forces. America, however, was rich enough to be able to afford this. Japan was not. Moreover, in the U.S. the president and in Britain the prime minister arbitrated on matters of prime strategic importance—for instance, to impose the doctrine of "Germany First." In Japan, no one could dictate effectively to either army or navy. To an extraordinary degree, the two services—each with its own air force—pursued independent war policies, though the soldiers wielded much greater clout. The foremost characteristic of the army general staff, and especially of its dominant operations department, the First Bureau, was absolute indifference to the diplomatic or economic consequences of any military action.

Mamoru Shigemitsu, successively Japan's wartime foreign minister and ambassador in China, was scornful of the army's faith both in German victory and in Japan's ability to induce Russia to remain neutral. Industry was never subject to the effective central control which prevailed in Britain, never mind the Soviet Union. In his analysis of Japanese and Western wartime attitudes towards each other, John Dower has observed: "Whereas racism in the West was markedly characterized by denigration of others, the Japanese were preoccupied far more exclusively with elevating themselves." In the early stages of the eastern war, many Asians were attracted by Japanese claims that they were liberating subject peoples from white imperial dominance. It soon became plain, however, that far from the conquerors purposing an Asian brotherhood, they simply envisaged a new world in which the hegemony of Westerners was replaced by that of another superior people—the Japanese. Japan had ambitious plans for colonising her newly won and prospective possessions. By 1950, according to the projections of Tokyo's Ministry of Health and Welfare, 14 percent of the nation's population would be living abroad as settlers: 2.7 million in Korea, 400,000 in Formosa, 3.1 million in Manchuria, 1.5 million in China, 2.38 million in other Asian satellites, and 2 million in Australia and New Zealand.

None of these immigrants would be permitted to intermarry with local people, to avoid dilution of the superior *Yamato* race. The British, French and Dutch had much to be ashamed of in their behaviour towards their own Asian subject peoples. Nothing they had done, however, remotely matched the extremes, or the murderous cruelty, of Japan's imperialists. Rigid segregation was sustained from all local people except "comfort women." Stationed at Indochina's great port of Haiphong, army engineer Captain Renichi Sugano "didn't really feel that I was in a foreign country, because I lived entirely among Japanese people. Even when we left the port to go into the city, we ate at Japanese restaurants and cafés, or in the officers' club." The nation's leaders urged Japanese to think of themselves as "*shido minzoku*"—"the world's foremost people." In 1940, Professor Chikao Fukisawa of Kyoto University wrote a booklet in which he asserted that the emperor embodied a cosmic life force, and that Japan was the true ancient cradle of civilisation. The government caused this thesis to be translated and distributed, for the enlightenment of English-speakers.

Here was a mirror image, no less ugly, of the Nazi vision for Hitler's empire. Its worst implication for the Japanese themselves was that many were taught to believe that their own inherent superiority would ensure victory, dismissing objective assessment of economic factors. They allowed themselves to be deluded, as at first were the Allies, by the significance of their 1941–42 victories. Japan's existence was dependent upon imported fuel and raw materials, most of which had to be transported thousands of miles by sea from South-East Asia. The country needed at least six million tons of petroleum a year, and produced only 250,000 in its home islands. The balance came from British Borneo, Burma and the Dutch East Indies. The navy, however, addressed neither mass-construction of escort vessels nor mastery of anti-submarine techniques, both indispensable to frustrating the American blockade.

The convoy system was introduced late in 1943, and became universal only in March 1944. So desperate was the shortage of anti-submarine vessels that thirty-two ships once waited ninety-five days in Palau harbour for lack of a single escort, and this was not untypical. Winston Churchill recognised the Battle of the Atlantic, the maintenance of Britain's supply lines, as vital to averting defeat, even if it could not secure victory. Japan's senior naval officers, by contrast, were obsessed with confronting the U.S. surface fleet. They treated the maintenance of their country's merchant shipping routes as unworthy of the attention of samurai until it was far, far too late, and no higher authority gainsaid them. The training of pilots and ground crews, the development of new combat aircraft, languished disastrously. No attempt was made to organise an effective air-sea rescue service to retrieve ditched airmen. Even if Japanese admirals scorned humanitarian considerations, their fliers should have been valued for their skills. Instead, hundreds were simply left to perish in the Pacific.

Japan's rival centres of power, the army, navy, and the great industrial combines—the *zaibatsu*—conducted separate wars in their own fashion, concealing the most basic information from each other as jealously as from the enemy. "To our distress, it became evident that our military and government leaders had never really understood the meaning of total war," wrote Masatake Okumiya, one of the foremost Japanese air aces. Allocation of materials was clumsy and arbitrary. Scientists and engineers addressing vital defence projects found themselves obliged to scavenge wherever they could get commodities, in the face of cumbersome and unsympathetic bureaucracies. When the group working on Japan's primitive nuclear programme wanted the wherewithal for a heating experiment, their request was deemed unconvincing: "We would like to obtain an extra ration of sugar to build an atomic bomb." Even when the scientists did obtain a little sugar, the stock was constantly depleted by the sticky fingers of passers-by. Japan's war effort was crippled by the amateurishness and inefficiency of its industrial and scientific direction.

In his post-war prison cell Gen. Hideki Tojo, prime minister until July 1944, identified a principal cause of defeat: "Basically, it was lack of coordination. When the prime minister, to whom is entrusted the destiny of the country, lacks the authority to participate in supreme decisions, it is not likely that the country will win a war." This was, of course, a self-serving half-truth. But it was indeed hard for a nation's chief executive to control its destinies when, for instance, he was told nothing of the navy's 1942 defeat at Midway until weeks after the event. Sixty years old in 1944, a short man even by Japanese standards, Tojo was the son of a famous general under the Meiji emperor. His notoriously sloppy personal appearance was at odds with his meticulous reputation as an administrator, which caused him to be nicknamed "Razor." He made his reputation running the military police in Manchuria, then became commander of Japan's mechanised forces in China. He served as deputy war minister in Prince Konoe's 1938 cabinet, and thereafter as air force chief. A psychopathic personality, Tojo had supposed that a mere forceful military demonstration in China would persuade Chiang Kai-shek to acquiesce in Japanese ambitions.

In October 1941, Tojo formed the government which led Japan to war with the West. He afterwards learned from painful experience how defective was his own country's machinery of government. As prime minister he accurately identified many of Japan's critical needs, but failed to induce colleagues to act effectively to meet them. Tojo, a supposed dictator, possessed far less authority in militarist Japan than did Winston Churchill in democratic Britain. When he sought to concentrate more power in his own hands, colleagues protested that many of Germany's difficulties derived from Hitler's relentless meddling in military detail. "Führer Hitler was an enlisted man," said Tojo dismissively. "I am a general." His superior qualifications proved insufficient, however, to reverse the tide of war. The loss of Saipan in July 1944 precipitated his fall from office, which was accomplished without much domestic upheaval. He was succeeded by Lt.-Gen. Kuniaki Koiso, a former governor of Korea and chief of staff of the Guandong Army in Manchuria. Koiso lacked Tojo's administrative abilities, and was notorious for his refusal to confront unpalatable realities. His only policy was to persevere, pursuing a fantasy of making terms for Japan through a bilateral deal with China.

If successive prime ministers were unable to wield effective authority, who could? The leaders of Nazi Germany existed in a gangster ethos. Most of the rulers of Japan, by contrast, were men of high birth, possessed of cultural and educational advantages which made the conduct of their wartime offices seem all the more deplorable, both practically and morally. At the lonely pinnacle stood the emperor, forty-three years old in 1944, denied by his throne the comfort of intimates, and by his choice any personal indulgences. A light sleeper, Hirohito rose at seven each morning in the Imperial Palace, breakfasted off black bread and oatmeal, then worked until a lunch of cooked vegetables and dumpling soup. He neither smoked nor drank. To an extraordinary degree, Hirohito's role in the origins and course of Japan's war remains shrouded in dispute, just as his precise powers in Japan's constitutional system mystified most of his own subjects during his reign. Historians lament the fact that MacArthur in 1945 made no attempt to exploit circumstances to have the emperor interrogated. Tojo's predecessor as Japanese prime minister, Prince Konoe, complained to an aide after his own fall from power in 1941: "When I told the emperor that it would be a mistake to go to war, he would agree with me, but then he would listen to others and afterwards say that I shouldn't worry so much. He was slightly in favour of war and later on became more war-inclined . . . As prime minister I had no authority over the army and could appeal [only] to the emperor. But the emperor became so much influenced by the military that I couldn't do anything about it."

For several decades after World War II, a legend was sedulously promoted, chiefly by the Japanese, of Hirohito's long-standing pacifism. This view is now discredited. The emperor shared many of the army's ambitions for his country, even if instinctive caution rendered him nervous of the huge risks which his generals embraced. Never until August 1945 did he speak or act with conviction against the excesses of "his" army. Hirohito indulged spasms of activism in vetoing appointments and initiatives.

For the most part, however, he remained mute while successive governments pursued policies which not only brought his nation to disaster, but also earned it a reputation for barbarism quite at odds with the emperor's own mild personality.

In a century of revolutions and falling monarchies, he was acutely sensitive to the vulnerability of his throne. During the inter-war years the palace frequently trembled as military fanatics attempted coups, murdered ministers and promoted ever more strident nationalism. The army and navy were nominally subordinate to the emperor. But if Hirohito had attempted to defy the hard-liners during the years before and after Pearl Harbor, it is likely that the palace would have been physically attacked, as indeed it was in August 1945. He himself might well have been overthrown. Like most surviving monarchs of his time, Hirohito perceived the preservation of the imperial house as his foremost duty. A belief in the precariousness of his own position, in a society dominated by unyielding samurai, does much to explain his passivity.

If this merits some sympathy from posterity, however, it cannot command admiration. While he deeply desired to be a conscientious monarch, Hirohito proved a fatally weak one, who cannot be absolved from the crimes of both commission and omission carried out in his name. He allowed others to wield executive authority in a fashion which wrought untold death and suffering, and he cannot have been unaware of the military's bloody excesses. Two of his brothers, for instance, attended screenings of an army film depicting Japan's biological warfare experiments on human subjects at Unit 731 in Manchuria. By the summer of 1944 the emperor yearned for a path out of the war, if only because he realised that his country was losing it. He did nothing effective, however, to advance this purpose. Until June 1945 he continued to believe that negotiation with the Allies should be deferred until Japan's hand was strengthened by battlefield success.

Most Japanese are reluctant to articulate unwelcome thoughts. Gen. Renya Mutaguchi described the difficulty which he suffered when discussing with his commander-in-chief an untenable battlefield situation in Burma: "The sentence 'The time has come to give up the operation as soon as possible' got as far as my throat," he said, "but I could not force it out in words. I wanted him to understand it from my expression." Faced with embarrassment, Japanese often resort to silence—*mokusatsu*. Such habits of culture and convention represented a barrier to effective decision-making, which grew ever harder to overcome as the war situation deteriorated. Power was dissipated within the ranks of Japan's officer corps, in a fashion which crippled effective executive action unless it was of an aggressive nature. Logical assessment of the nation's predicament demanded that peace should be made on any terms. Since such a course was unacceptable to the Japanese army, the nation continued its march towards catastrophe.

It may be argued, however, that such a policy in the face of adversity was not unique to Hirohito's people. Japan's options in late 1944, a Japanese might say, were not dissimilar to those of Britain in 1940. Winston Churchill's commitment to resist Nazi Germany after the fall of France was neither more nor less rational than that of Japan after losing the Marianas. Without allies, Britain possessed no better prospect of encompassing the defeat of Nazi Germany than did Japan of defeating the Americans. Britain's salvation was achieved overwhelmingly through the actions of her enemies in forcing the Soviet Union and the U.S. into the war, not by any military achievement of her own save that of defiance in the face of hopeless odds.

The leaders of Japan told their own people little less about the apparent hopelessness of their predicament in 1944 than Britain's prime minister had told his own nation after the fall of France. Churchill, indeed, had something of the samurai about him—a belief that will alone could achieve great things. In April 1940 he tried to insist that British units cut off by the Germans in Norway fight to the death or take to the mountains as guerrillas, rather than withdraw or surrender. "Commanders and senior officers should die with their troops," he urged passionately in February 1942, as Singapore stood on the brink of collapse. "The honour of the British Empire and of the British Army is at stake." Unlike some other prominent Conservatives, when Britain stood alone he judged it better to accept the likelihood of her defeat than to make terms with Hitler. Japan's leaders likewise believed that unconditional surrender would precipitate the loss of all they held dear. If the cause of Japanese militarism seems to posterity immeasurably less admirable than that of British democracy, it engaged its adherents with equal devotion.

Japan's leaders, like Churchill in 1940, perceived themselves as "buggering on," and their people seemed willing to accept the requirements of such a policy. Japanese captured in the Pacific in September 1944 asserted to U.S. interrogators that morale back home remained high, that civilians were "tightening their belts in preparation for a hundred years' war." Two officer prisoners claimed that America's public pronouncements caused Japanese people to believe that their society was doomed to extinction in the event of defeat. Only a few older captives admitted doubts about the civilian will to fight on.

In the last year of the war, some thoughtful and informed Japanese senior officers recognised that the defence of their country against economic blockade could not be sustained. In May 1944, for instance, Rear-Admiral Sokichi Tagaki of the navy's general staff reported: "Analysis of air, warship and merchant shipping losses, together with Japan's inability to import raw materials essential to industrial production and the prospect of air attack on the home islands, show that Japan cannot achieve victory and should seek a compromise peace." In 1944, Japan consumed 19.4 million barrels of oil, yet was able to import only 5 million. This shortfall would worsen in 1945. The Japan Planning Board estimated a requirement of 5 million tons of shipping for essential movement of supplies, but the merchant fleet had shrunk to 2.1 million, only half of this tonnage serviceable. Tanker capacity, especially, was much depleted. In June 1944, the army general staff's Conduct of War Section reported that there was "now no hope for Japan to reverse the unfavourable war situation . . . It is time for us to end the war."

However, the phrase "end the war" was fraught with equivocation. In the minds of almost every senior Japanese, it meant the pursuit of acceptable terms. At the very least, Japan must be permitted to retain hegemony over Manchuria, Korea and Formosa. Allied occupation of the home islands and war crimes trials of Japanese leaders were unacceptable, as was any Allied meddling with Japan's system of governance. Many Japanese in the summer and autumn of 1944 were discussing the possibility of ending hostilities. Virtually none contemplated accepting the Allied demand for unconditional surrender. So sclerotic was the national decision-making process that nothing effective was done to act upon the knowledge available to the nation's leaders.

There is little doubt that the death of Hitler before April 1945 would have precipitated a German collapse. By contrast, it is hard to believe that the removal of any prominent Japanese, including Hirohito or his successive prime ministers, would have hastened his nation's capitulation. The Japanese fought on, because no consensus could be mobilised to do anything else. A dramatic political initiative to offer surrender, even one supported by the emperor, would almost certainly have failed. Japanese strategy in the last phase of the war rested not upon seeking victory, but upon making each Allied advance so costly that America's people, as well as her leadership, would deem it preferable to offer Japan acceptable terms rather than to endure a bloody struggle for the home islands. If this assessment was fanciful, and founded upon ignorance of the possibility that a weapon might be deployed which rendered void all conventional military calculations, it offered a germ of hope to desperate men.

By late 1944, many Japanese civilians had become desperate to see an end to the war, which was ruining their lives and threatened to destroy their society. Even before Pearl Harbor, Japan was divided by widespread poverty, and by tensions between city and countryside, peasants and landlords, soldiers and civilians. For all the government's strident nationalist propaganda campaigns, conflict had deepened rather than healed domestic divisions. There was bitterness that the rich and the armed forces still ate heartily, while no one else did. The government's Home Ministry was dismayed by the incidence of what in the West would be called defeatism, "statements, letters and wall-writing that are disrespectful, anti-war, anti-military or in other ways inflammatory." There were reports of people making contemptuous references to the emperor as a *baka*, *bakayaro* or *bocchan*, "fool," "stupid fool" or "spoiled child."

There was substantial support for Communism, reflected in graffiti and street talk. Police reports cited cases of alleged industrial sabotage, of drunken workers shouting "Stalin *banzai*!" Industrial disputes and stoppages remained rare, but Japan's leaders were always fearful of revolution, as privations increased. A story enjoyed wide circulation in Tokyo's military and political circles of a Soviet attaché declaring jovially that when his country entered the eastern war and occupied Japan, the Red Army would need to undertake a serious anti-Communist propaganda campaign. Japan, however, never found it necessary to imprison dissenters in anything like the numbers detained in Germany or the Soviet Union. Arrests for "peace preservation law violations"—most of the accused being left-wingers, with a handful of religious zealots—peaked at 14,822 in 1933, then declined to 1,212 in 1941; 698 in 1942; 159 in 1943—of whom only fifty-two were prosecuted. While many Japanese were profoundly unhappy with their lot, they perceived no means of doing anything about it, save to maintain their personal struggles for existence.

For years, austerity had been a familiar reality. Inessential driving was banned eighteen months ahead of Pearl Harbor. Oil and iron ore were stockpiled, even plumbing fixtures were stripped from homes. Production of rubber-soled *tabi* shoes was halted to save raw material. There was no coffee. Neon lighting in Tokyo's Ginza district was extinguished, and a monthly family fast day introduced. It was no longer permissible to polish rice, which diminished its bulk. From 1940 this was rationed, along with sugar, salt, matches and suchlike, to enable the government to build up stocks in anticipation of siege. Women were forbidden to style their hair or wear smart clothes. Food was a preoccupation of every urban Japanese, which soon became an obsession. In August 1944, one factory reported that 30 percent of women and boys in its workforce were suffering from beriberi, brought on by malnutrition. "Observing a slice of funny little fish and two vegetable leaves which constitute a ration allowance," wrote Admiral Ugaki, "I contemplated the hardships of those who prepare a daily meal instead of the complaints of those who eat it." Absenteeism mounted, as factory workers spent more and more time searching for food for their families. Daily Japanese calorie intake, only 2,000 before Pearl Harbor, fell to 1,900 in 1944, and would descend to 1,680 in 1945. British calorie intake never fell below 2,800, even in the darkest days of 1940–41. An American GI in the Pacific received 4,758 calories.

Twenty-three-year-old Yoshiko Hashimoto was the eldest daughter of a businessman living in the Sumida district on the eastern side of Tokyo. Her father owned a small textile firm employing fifteen people, struggling to survive because he had lost access to raw material imports and depended on synthetics. Mr. Hashimoto had no son, so Yoshiko would inherit the business. To ensure that there would be a man around to run it, her father arranged her marriage to thirty-one-year-old Bunsaku Yazawa, whose family owned a shop opposite their house. "It would be nice to say that it was a love match," said Yoshiko, "but it wasn't. It was my father's choice." Yazawa had already spent much of his twenties as an unwilling draftee in Manchuria. Three months after his 1941 wedding to Yoshiko, he was shipped abroad again. On demobilisation from the army in 1944, he was posted to air-raid duties in Tokyo, based at a primary school not far from the Hashimoto home, where his squad was responsible for demolishing houses to make firebreaks. "He hated the war," said his wife tersely.

In addition to Yoshiko, three other daughters were living at home: Chieko, nineteen; Etsuko, seventeen; and Hisae, fourteen. In 1944 Yoshiko gave birth to a son, Hiroshi, who was now the apple of his grandfather's as well as his mother's eye. It was a hard time to rear a baby. Food was so short that Yoshiko, undernourished, found herself unable to breast-feed. In order to get a small ration of tinned milk, it was necessary to secure a certificate signed not only by a doctor, but by the neighbourhood committee. "It was always coupons, coupons, coupons and queues, queues, queues. Anyone who could afford extra food bought it on the black market. Everything hinged on who knew who." As in Germany, there was intense bitterness between town- and country-dwellers. City folk trekked to rural areas, to persuade farmers illegally to barter food for household possessions. Yoshiko's mother was reduced to surrendering her most cherished kimono in exchange for rice. Such bargains also demanded a struggle for a place on a train to a farming district.

The most dreaded government communication which most young people received was either a "red paper," consigning a man to the armed forces, or a "white paper," which committed every male and many females over seventeen to industrial labour. However, Chieko Hashimoto thought herself lucky to have a job in an armaments factory, because this entitled her to a ration of otherwise unobtainable noodles. "By that time, we were thinking merely of survival, of how to find the next meal," said

Yoshiko. "A baby could only cry about its hunger, but mothers like me had to try to do something about it. It's really hard to bear your child's sobs, when you have nothing to give him." In the Hashimoto household, as in most Japanese families, only men smoked. The women claimed to do so, however, in order to collect a cigarette ration. This was eked out by drying *itadori* weed, which was then rolled in scraps of dictionary paper. Gas and electricity were available only for a few hours a day. Soap and clothing were desperately short—an unwelcome consequence was that head lice became endemic. The local cinema near the Hashimoto home kept going, but since December 1941 its patrons had been deprived of Hollywood favourites like Shirley Temple. A few little music halls stayed open, featuring performances by local comedians. The young cherished irreplaceable jazz and tango records. Those wishing to amuse themselves of an evening were reduced to singing songs in the bosom of the family.

"We never talked about the war at home, and we knew very little about what was happening," said Yoshiko Hashimoto. "Even in 1944, the papers and radio still said that we were winning." Desultory efforts had been made to evacuate children and their mothers from cities, but these largely foundered, for the same reason as in Britain. Town and country children, thrown together by circumstances, disliked each other. Yoshiko spent several months with her baby son at the home of a rural uncle in the Chiba district outside Tokyo. But she hated the lack of privacy in the home of near strangers whose every word was audible through paper walls, and returned to the city.

Sixteen-year-old Ryoichi Sekine and his father lived together in the Edogawa district of eastern Tokyo, with a young rustic cousin named Takako Ohki helping with the housework. Ryoichi's mother and one sister had died some time earlier. A younger sister had been sent to live with relatives in the country. The teenaged Ryoichi found little to enjoy about the war. First, his ambitions to train as an engineer were stifled as schools devoted diminishing attention to learning, ever more to military training. By late 1944 his class spent most of their days working on an anti-aircraft-gun production line at the Seiko factory. Study of the English language was banned, except for technical terms. Young Ryoichi, like so many of his generation, felt that he "missed a chance of the thing which every teenager wants to enjoy." His father was an optical engineer who worked for Minolta and Fujifilm. Association with military technology caused Mr. Sekine to be well informed about the war, and very gloomy about it. The food shortage caused the family to spend hours haggling for beans and sweet potatoes with crusty farmers outside the city. Lacking soap, they scoured their dishes with ashes. One day, a large black object fell from an American plane overhead. They were frightened that it was a bomb, but it proved instead to be a drop tank jettisoned by a U.S. fighter. When Ryoichi strolled curiously over to examine it, he found himself savouring the stench of aviation spirit as if it was perfume, for petrol had become rare and precious.

The war progressively penetrated every corner of the lives even of children. Schools emphasised the destiny of young Japanese to become warriors. Ten-year-old Yoichi Watanuki, son of a Tokyo small businessman, suffered an embarrassing tendency to feel airsick when lofted on a swing in the playground. A teacher said to him scornfully: "You won't make much of a fighter pilot, will you?" Pupils were shown caricatures of their American and British enemies, whose defining characteristics appeared to be that they were tall, ugly and noisy. There were shortages of the most commonplace commodities. Celluloid covers for exercise books vanished; rubber-covered balls were replaced by baked-flour ones, which melted when it rained. Everything metal was requisitioned by the armaments factories: even spinning tops were now made in ceramic. Art classes drew military aircraft, music classes played military music—Yoichi did his part on an accordion. School outings stopped.

Every community in Japan was organised into neighbourhood groups, each mustering perhaps fifteen families. Yoichi Watanuki's father had always supported the war. His playmate Osamu Sato's father, a former naval officer, belonged to the same neighbourhood group. Mr. Sato was bold enough to declare from the outset: "Japan should not have started this war, because it is going to lose it." Now, Yoichi heard his own father say gravely: "Sato was right. Everything is turning out exactly as he predicted."

In the summer of 1944, as the threat of large-scale American bombing became apparent, evacuations of city children were renewed. One morning at Yoichi's school assembly, the headmaster demanded a show of hands from all those who lacked relatives in the country to offer them shelter. More than half fell into this category. They were informed that their education would thenceforward continue at a new school in Shizuoka Prefecture, south of Mount Fuji. A few days later, a bewildered and mostly sobbing crowd of children gathered at the station, while behind them on the platform stood their parents, likewise tearful, to bid farewell. Flags were waved, the train whistle blew, mothers cried "*Banzai! Banzai!*" in circumstances utterly different from those in which Allied soldiers were accustomed to hearing the word. The children departed for a new life.

It was not a happy one. They were billeted in a temple in densely wooded mountains, bitterly cold in winter. Water had to be carried from a nearby river, and the children were obliged to wash themselves and their clothes in the icy flow. Lice became endemic. Their teachers, all women or old men, were as unhappy as their charges. Yoichi and his companions discovered one day that a delivery of sweet cakes—by now a rare delicacy—had somehow reached the school. To the children's disgust, the teachers ate them all. They were constantly hungry, reduced to stealing corn or sweet potatoes from the fields. If they ventured into the nearby village, farmers' children broke their schoolbags and mocked them with cries of "*Sokai! Sokai!*" "Evacuees! Evacuees!" When Yoichi took a hand helping with the rice harvest, he felt shamed by his clumsiness in wielding a sickle, his own uncut row of plants lagging many yards behind those of deft rural companions.

His father made occasional visits, sometimes bringing food. When Yoichi's mother gave birth to a new baby, Mr. Watanuki bought a cottage near the temple in which his elder son's school was housed, where the family might be safer. This proved a sensible precaution. Soon afterwards their Tokyo house was burned out in an air raid, and the whole family adopted rural life. They were safe in the mountains, though shortages of food and fuel relentlessly worsened. For the people of Japan, apprehension represented wisdom. Worse, much worse, lay ahead.

2. Warriors

JAPAN'S CAREER soldiers and sailors professed astonishment at the "amateurishness" of other armies and navies, but themselves displayed reckless insouciance towards the technological development of warfare. The Japanese army was principally composed of infantry, poorly supported by armour and artillery. Japan built only light tanks. Soldiers carried a 1905 model rifle. In 1941–42 the navy and air arms were adequately equipped, but thereafter Allied weapons decisively outclassed Japanese ones. By late 1944, for instance, the legendary Zero fighter was at the mercy of the American Hellcat. As a young student at the Naval Technical Institute before the war, Haruki Iki gained a personal insight into his nation's resistance to innovation. Senior officers flaunted their contempt for the radar development programme. They said: "Why do we need this? Men's eyes see perfectly well." Japanese radar lagged far behind that of the Allies. "Before World War II, Japan's experience of war had been gained entirely against the Chinese, who possessed scarcely any artillery or other heavy weapons," observes Japanese historian Professor Akira Nakamura. "Japan had not participated in a land campaign during World War I. The Japanese army entered World War II quite unequipped to fight a modern enemy. From 1941 onwards, front-line soldiers urged the importance of developing more advanced weapons. Unfortunately, their voices were not heeded at the top." Likewise staff officer Maj. Shigeru Funaki: "We were far too influenced by our experience in China. There, we had no need of modern equipment and tactics. Because we kept beating the Chinese, we became over-confident."

Societies run by civilians proved vastly better able to organise themselves to fight the Second World War than those dominated by military men, of which Japan offered the most notable example. It is hard to overstate the extent to which Anglo-American wartime achievements were made possible by the talents of amateurs in uniform, fulfilling almost every responsible function save that of higher military command. Intelligence, for instance, was dominated by academics, many of startling brilliance. Montgomery's intelligence chief in north-west Europe was an Oxford don masquerading in a brigadier's uniform. In Japan, by contrast, authority and influence remained almost exclusively in the hands of career officers, who were reluctant to grant scope to outsiders even in such fields as scientific research. The Japanese army and navy never mobilised clever civilians in the fashion of the Western Allies. Intelligence was poor, because the Japanese mind-set mitigated against energetic inquiry, frank analysis and expression.

By 1944, said Shigeru Funaki, "people understood that we were poorly prepared and equipped for a long war. I saw how important fuel was going to be to us. Because I had always enjoyed American movies, I knew what an advanced society America was. Yet we told each other that Americans were too democratic to be able to organise themselves for war. Many military men supposed that victory could be gained by fighting spirit alone. Our intelligence was never good, because few officers acknowledged its importance. Commanders understood the need for battlefield information, but not for strategic intelligence about the big picture."

Maj. Shoji Takahashi was a staff officer in the intelligence department of South Asia Army HQ. "Only in 1944 did the war situation really begin to alarm us," he said. "The Japanese army did not take intelligence nearly seriously enough. At South Asia Army HQ, we had no proper system, no analytical section, no resources—that's how bad it was. Perhaps our attitude reflected Japan's historic isolation from the rest of the world. We had no tradition of being interested in other societies and what they were doing. It came as a shock to realise how powerful the Allies were becoming, and how much they knew about our actions and intentions."

"Intelligence became a backwater for officers who were perceived as unfit for more responsible postings," in the words of Japanese historian Kazutoshi Hando. "Strategic decision-making was concentrated in the hands of perhaps twenty people, military and naval. Even if our intelligence services had gained access to important information, it would have remained unexploited if it ran against the convictions of the decision-makers. They would not have wanted to know." MacArthur was sometimes accused of displaying a cavalier contempt for strategic deception, of the kind widely and often successfully practiced by the Allies in Europe. Yet such was the reluctance of Japanese commanders to heed evidence which did not fit their own convictions that the most tempting morsels of false intelligence would almost certainly have been wasted on them. The British launched some Byzantine schemes in Burma, such as planting dummy plans where the enemy must find them. The Japanese seemed not even to notice.

The gravest weakness of *bushido*, Captain Kouichi Ito believed, was that "no one was allowed to say what he really thought, so that we could not explore better ways to do things." The Western Allies possessed advantages not only of better direction and resources, but also of language. English, properly used, is a clear and powerful medium of expression. Japanese, by contrast, is fraught with equivocation. Tokyo's forces suffered chronic communications difficulties because signals were so vulnerable to misinterpretation.

THE MEN who fought for Japan displayed a courage and capacity for suffering which bewildered and sometimes terrified their opponents. The British general Sir William Slim called the Japanese soldier "the most formidable fighting insect in history," a phrase characteristic of the mood of his period. A British officer who thought better of Japanese rankers than of their commanders called them "first-class soldiers in a third-class army," which seems fair. Their virtues owed something to national culture, and even more to an ethos ruthlessly promoted from the top. Like the Waffen SS, many Japanese army officers were recruited from lower-middle-class backgrounds. They achieved in uniform a social status denied to them in civilian life, and paraded this in similar fashion.

From the day that a man joined the Japanese army or navy, he was subjected to conditioning more brutal even than that of the Russians. Physical punishment was fundamental. When Souhei Nakamura set off to report to his recruit depot in Manchuria, he carried a big flask of *sake* which his girlfriend had given him as a parting present. In a train otherwise crowded with Chinese, he fell into conversation with two Japanese soldiers. He told them about his *sake*. "You'd better not turn up at the barracks with that," they said knowingly, "or you'll be in real trouble." The three of them drained the flask. The soldiers slumped into happy unconsciousness, the boy stumbled out to seek fresh air at a window. He returned to find his baggage stolen by Chinese passengers. Reporting to his barracks, he was foolish enough to relate his experience to an NCO, who thrashed him on the spot. From that day, Nakamura hated military life. His view is a useful corrective for those who suppose that every Japanese recruit was eager to die for the emperor. "I thought of joining the army simply as a one-way ticket to the Yasukuni Shrine," he said laconically. Yasukuni is dedicated to those who fall in the service of the emperor.

The first year of military service was notoriously dreadful. "Personality ceased to exist, there was only rank," said Masaichi Kikuchi. "You became the lowest of the low, condemned to cook, clean, drill and run from dawn to dusk. You could be beaten for anything—being too short or too tall, even because somebody didn't like the way you drank coffee. This was done to make each man respond instantly to orders, and it produced results. If you want soldiers who fight hard, they must train hard. This was the system which made the Japanese army so formidable—each man was schooled to accept unquestioningly the orders of his group leader—and then took over a new recruit intake to boss around himself. Isn't that the way it is in every army?" Lt. Hayashi Inoue said: "The first year as a recruit was a terrible time for everyone. It was just something you had to get through, and accept. Most of our men were very simple, innocent, poorly educated fishermen, peasants and suchlike. They had to be taught the meaning of discipline." On border duty in Manchuria, Private Shintaro Hiratsuka was hit in the face by a sergeant for losing his overcoat. This caused him to become disaffected, and to embark on a career of petty theft. Caught and beaten again, he deserted, was arrested and executed.

The NCO commanding Iwao Ajiro's recruit detail disliked bruising his hand by beating offenders himself, and thus ordered them to beat each other. At first they did so without enthusiasm, causing the sergeant to shout in fury: "You are soldiers of the Imperial Japanese Army! When you hit a man, do it as if you mean it!" Once, after Ajiro missed a meal because he was running round the parade ground to atone for some crime, he crept into the cookhouse to claw a few mouthfuls of rice by hand from the pan—and was caught by his NCO. "You're a pig!" the man roared. "Get down on your knees and behave like one!" Ajiro was obliged to crawl across the messroom floor, snorting and snuffling. On another occasion, clearing his rifle in darkness in the midst of a Manchurian winter wilderness, he dropped a bullet. When he reported to the guardroom, his sergeant screamed: "You have lost valuable army property! You will stay out there until you find that bullet!" If such behaviour reflected a psyche common to most armies, the Japanese carried it to extremes unknown elsewhere.

During Japan's war in China, the practices of conducting bayonet training on live prisoners, and of beheading them, became institutionalised. Such experiences were designed to harden men's hearts, and they achieved their purpose. A South African prisoner of the Japanese on Java wrote: "I saw innumerable ways of killing people, but, most significantly, never by just shooting them. I say 'significantly' because this for me was the most striking evidence of the remote and archaic nature of the forces which had invaded the Japanese spirit, blocking out completely the light of the twentieth-century day."

Naval discipline was little less brutal. On the seaplane carrier *Akitsushima*, Leading Seaman Kisao Ebisawa was a senior rating charged with administering punishment at the weekly disciplinary muster. He beat the backsides of green seamen with a heavy stave employed throughout the service for this purpose, "to sharpen them up." Five strokes were customary. "After dealing with a score or two of men," said Ebisawa ruefully, "one's wrist got pretty stiff." When a destroyer's cutter rescuing survivors from a sunken battleship threatened to be swamped by struggling figures seeking to clamber aboard, those in the boat simply drew their swords and hacked off the hands of would-be intruders, Japanese like themselves.

Twenty-three-year-old Lt. Kunio Iwashita hailed from the mountain area of Nagano, where his father rather implausibly kept a French restaurant. To become naval officers, he and his brother had to overcome official doubts about whether scions of such a trade were socially eligible. The Iwashitas defeated prejudice by passing out at the top of their courses, including flight school. Kunio's adored sibling died in 1942 at the Battle of the Santa Cruz Islands, shot down after bombing the American carrier *Hornet*. His own entry into combat was delayed by a long stint as an instructor, which probably contributed much to his survival. Iwashita had flown over four hundred hours before he was posted to Iwo Jima, where he experienced a savage initiation. The first nine Zeroes of his unit, 301 Squadron, flew the 750 miles from their mainland base at the beginning of July 1944. By the time Iwashita arrived next day, three pilots including the squadron commander had already been shot down.

Next day, though suffering acute stomach pains which were afterwards diagnosed as appendicitis, he was scrambled with his squadron to meet a new American strike, from which bombs were already cascading down on the airstrip. Airborne, Iwashita found himself behind a flight of four Hellcats, and poured fire into the rear plane. Its wing broke off. The Japanese saw the American pilot, wearing a white scarf, meet his own glance for an instant before the Hellcat plunged towards Mount Suribachi. The other Americans swung in pursuit of the Zero. Iwashita's plane was badly hit before he escaped. After killing his first enemy, his reactions were those of novice warriors of every nationality. He found himself speculating about the American's girlfriend, mother, last thoughts.

Just as the army possessed many reluctant soldiers, the air force had its share of pilots who flinched from combat. Iwashita acknowledged that every squadron was familiar with the odd man whose aircraft suffered chronic technical problems, or who found reasons to turn back before completing sorties. One such pilot on Iwo Jima was summarily transferred to an anti-aircraft battery, where he was killed by American strafing. Awareness swiftly dawned of the shortcomings of their own weapons and technology. Iwashita said: "When I became a pilot, I didn't think anything could be better than the Zero. I was confident that I was flying the best fighter in the world. In combat, however, I came to understand that it was not as simple as that. American pilots were very good, and had a lot of kit we didn't, like radio intercommunication." On one sortie over Iwo Jima, thirty-one Zeroes took off and only seventeen came back. Four such battles reduced Iwashita's Zero wing from thirty-eight pilots to ten. Soon afterwards, with no planes left for them to fly, the survivors returned to Japan in a transport aircraft.

The life of a Japanese soldier was wretched enough before he entered combat. Many officers were shameless in allocating food to themselves even when their men were starving. A British historian has observed that the Imperial Army's frequent resort to rape reflected the fact that the status of women in Japan was low, while those of subject peoples possessed no status at all: "Right was what a soldier was ordered to do; to disobey was to do wrong. There was no moral absolute to set this against . . . For the ordinary soldier, rape was one of the few pleasures in a comfortless and deprived life in which he could expect to reap very few of the spoils of war."

Hayashi Inoue's closest friend was a fellow company commander in the 55th Regiment named Kazue Nakamura. When Nakamura was killed in northern Burma, his second-in-command withdrew without having retrieved the body, a grievous offence against the military code. Instead of facing court-martial, however, the delinquent was simply assigned missions on which he could expect to die. Inoue afterwards laughed at the memory: "It took ages for that man to get killed. Again and again, he was sent out—and came back. He got his deserts in the end, though." Inoue was a colonial administrator's son, drafted into the army in 1938 and commissioned in 1941. He accepted obedience without question: "If we were told to defend this position or that one, we did it. To fall back without orders was a crime. It was as simple as that. We were trained to fight to the end, and nobody ever discussed doing anything else. Looking back later, we could see that the military code was unreasonable. But at that time, we regarded dying for our country as our duty. If men had been allowed to surrender honourably, everybody would have been doing it."

If obedience was fundamental to the samurai spirit, the conduct of the Japanese high command was confused by the power and influence wielded by some younger staff officers of violently aggressive enthusiasms, empowered by political links to the top of the military hierarchy. These promoted the doctrine of "*gekokujo*"—initiative from below. The most notorious exponent was Col. Masanobu Tsuji, a fanatic repeatedly wounded in action and repeatedly transferred by generals exasperated by his insubordination. Tsuji once burned down a geisha house to highlight his disgust at the moral frailty of the officers inside it. His excesses were responsible for some of the worst Japanese blunders on Guadalcanal. He was directly responsible for brutalities to prisoners and civilians in every part of the Japanese empire in which he served. In northern Burma, he dined off the liver of a dead Allied pilot, castigating as cowards those who refused to share his meal: "The more we eat, the brighter will burn the fire of our hatred for the enemy."

Gen. Sosaku Suzuki, who commanded the defence of Leyte, wrote bitterly: "It is the Ishiwara-Tsuji clique—the personification of *gekokujo*—that has brought the Japanese army to its present deplorable situation . . . I tell you, so long as they exert influence . . . it can only lead to ruin." Paradoxically, in a culture dominated by obedience, some militant junior army officers exercised political influence out of all proportion to their ranks. It was unacceptable for subordinates to display intelligent scepticism. They were constantly indulged, however, in excesses of aggression.

For every four tons of supplies the United States shipped to its ground forces in the Pacific, Japan was able to transport to its own men just two pounds. A Japanese infantryman carried barely half the load of his American counterpart, because he lacked all but the most basic equipment. It is extraordinary to contemplate what Japanese troops achieved with so little. It became normal for them to fight in a condition of semi-starvation. Their wounded were chronically vulnerable to gangrene, because they possessed no anti-tetanus drugs. Signals equipment was never adequate, making it hard for units to communicate. Whereas U.S. and British armies were organised in balanced formations, composed of purpose-trained specialists—infantry, gunners, engineers and so on—in 1944–45 many Japanese positions were defended by improvised battle groups made up of whatever men could be provided with rifles and grenades. Service units, cooks, clerks were alike thrust into the line. In the circumstances, no great tactical skills were demanded of them. They were simply expected to fire their weapons, and die where they stood. The achievements of these patchwork Japanese forces matched or even surpassed those of Germany's battlegroups in Europe.

There were human similarities between Allied warriors and Hirohito's men which should not be neglected. A desperately wounded Japanese was as likely to cry out for his mother as any Marine or GI. It was a commonplace for Japanese soldiers starting an assault to say to each other:

"See you at the Yasukuni Shrine." If this reflected genuine fatalism, most were no more enthusiastic than their Allied counterparts about meeting death. They had simply been conditioned to accept a different norm of sacrifice. Above all, a chasm existed between the two sides' attitudes to captivity. American and British soldiers, sailors and airmen belonged to a culture in which it was considered natural and proper to surrender when armed resistance was no longer rationally sustainable. By contrast, it was driven into the psyche not only of every Japanese soldier, but of every citizen, that death must always be preferred. Gen. Hideki Tojo's *Instructions for Servicemen* proclaimed: "The man who would not disgrace himself must be strong. He must remember always the honour of his family and community, and strive to justify their faith in him. Do not survive in shame as a prisoner. Die, to ensure that you do not leave ignominy behind you!"

Among Tojo's people, surrender was deemed the most shameful act a man could commit, even if he was struggling in the sea after his ship had been sunk. Staff officer Maj. Shigeru Funaki asserted that this culture was rooted in the experience of the 1904–5 Russo-Japanese War. "A lot of our men in that conflict surrendered when their positions seemed hopeless. The army became determined that such things should never happen again. If it was acknowledged as honourable to be taken prisoner, then many men would make that choice." A Japanese POW named Shiniki Saiki told his American captors in the Pacific in September 1944, weeks before the word "kamikaze" was first heard: "All units are now considered to be suicide units."

When American and British troops became familiar with the Japanese preference for self-immolation, by means often designed to encompass Allied deaths also, they grew unwilling to accept risk or trouble to take an enemy alive. "The understandable reluctance of our troops to trust any Jap no doubt contributes to the difficulty of inducing the enemy to surrender," wrote an Australian officer on New Guinea. It is sometimes alleged that Western barbarism thus matched that of their foes. Yet it is hard to see why an Allied soldier should have risked a grenade from a Japanese soldier who, even when he made gestures of surrender, rejected the Western code whereby a prisoner contracted to receive humane treatment in return for forswearing further homicidal intent. After episodes in which Japanese taken aboard American submarines sought to sabotage their captors' highly vulnerable craft, such rescues were abandoned. This was prudent.

Until Japanese began to give themselves up in substantial numbers in the summer of 1945, their surrenders were likely to be accepted only by units which needed sample prisoners for intelligence purposes. Those who reached POW camps, by choosing survival, showed themselves unrepresentative. They were nonetheless the Allies' best sources of information about the mood in the ranks of the enemy. "We poor soldiers have to sacrifice our lives and fight with Type-38 rifles against Boeings, Consolidated B24s, North Americans and Lightning P38s," said an embittered private soldier who surrendered to the Americans. In the safety of a POW camp in Australia, he described himself as a Christian and a Communist, and offered to assist his captors by writing "a Formal Examination of Myself as a Japanese . . . I wish to sound the alarm to awaken the Japanese people." Private Sanemori Saito, taken on Bougainville, asserted that his commanding officer had gone mad, forcing the sick to report for duty, and sometimes calling parades at midnight. A construction unit officer captured while delirious with fever told his interrogators that "the Japanese possessed a blind faith in their leaders. Even though the military clique started war, the people were wholeheartedly behind it . . . PW thought the nearer hostilities came to Japan, the harder the people would fight."

One strange figure whom Americans plucked from the sea proved to be a mixed-race soldier, only a quarter Japanese, christened Andrew Robb by his parents, Shigeru Sakai by the army into which he found himself conscripted. Robb hailed from Kobe, where he had been educated at the English mission school. When captured, he was on passage to garrison duty as a sergeant interpreter in the Philippines. As an "impure Japanese" he claimed to have been victimised during recruit training, and was thus heartily grateful to be posted overseas. "His own reaction to Japan's chances had varied. Originally he had not thought her capable of overcoming the industrial power of the British and Americans combined, but Japan's earlier successes had led him to think that the Allies might be too involved in Europe to handle the situation in the Pacific." Robb said that he would like to inform his mother of his survival, but was fearful of "adverse public opinion" at home if his captivity became known.

This was a familiar sentiment among Japanese POWs. One suggested to his captors that the best means of encouraging defections would be, first, to avoid mention in Allied propaganda of the dreadful word "surrender"; and, second, to offer those who quit post-war resettlement in Australia or Brazil. An aircrew lieutenant captured while foraging in New Guinea in July 1944 found himself the only officer prisoner among five hundred other ranks. Aboard the ship taking them to a camp in Australia, he told interrogators, some of his fellow captives proclaimed that they had a duty to kill themselves. The lieutenant, who disagreed, responded contemptuously that anyone who wanted to jump overboard was free to do so. He would promise to deliver farewell messages to their families. No one jumped. But the stigma of captivity hung over every Japanese who succumbed, often long after eventual return to their own country. In this respect, the military code served Japan's rulers well. Without *bushido*'s terrible sanction of dishonour, in 1944–45 a host of Japanese would otherwise have given themselves up, rather than perish to prolong futile resistance. Refusal to face the logic of surrender was perhaps the most potent weapon Japanese forces possessed.

Japan's military commanders varied as widely in character and competence as their Allied counterparts. Gen. Tokutaro Sakurai, for instance, conformed to every caricature of Allied imagination. He was a China veteran notorious for ruthlessness and brutality. As an accessory to his uniform, he affected around his neck a string of pearls. His off-duty party piece was to perform a Chinese dance naked, with lighted cigarettes flaring from his nostrils. Some other officers, however, were both rational and humane. Masaki Honda, who commanded 33rd Army against Stilwell in Burma, was a passionate fisherman who often carried his rods in the field. A conscientious rather than gifted officer, he was among the few to show interest in the welfare of his men. He was fond of telling dirty stories to soldiers of all ranks. "Have you heard this one?" he would demand, already chuckling. He resisted assignment to Burma on the grounds that supplies of his beloved *sake* would be precarious.

The Allies sometimes supposed that Japanese readily embraced jungle warfare. In truth most hated it, none more so than Honda. Like many of Tokyo's generals, he was personally brave and tactically competent, but displayed little imagination. He once bewildered the Chinese and Americans by dispatching a personal message to Chiang Kai-shek, expressing regret that their two countries were at war, and commiserating on China's casualties: "I have witnessed with admiration for six months the conduct of your brave soldiers in north Burma, and am very gratified to feel that they, like us, are Orientals. I would like to congratulate you on their loyalty and commitment."

Gen. Kiyotake Kawaguchi had managed a prison camp holding Germans in the First World War, and prided himself on its civilised standards. In May 1942 he formally protested at the executions of senior Philippine officials. Once on Guadalcanal, where his forces were starving, he had to dispatch a man on a dangerous reconnaissance mission. Kawaguchi pressed into the soldier's hand the only pathetic consolation he could offer, a tin of sardines which he himself had brought from Japan. He was subsequently relieved of command, for denouncing the futility of sacrificing lives in impossible operations.

Dismissal was a common fate for senior officers who had either opposed starting the war against the Western Allies, or grown sceptical about the value of protracting it. Many thoughtful soldiers opposed Japan's long, debilitating campaign in China. "We felt that it was a mistake to be there at all, that Japanese strategy was ill-considered," said Maj. Kouichi Ito, "but senior officers who expressed this view were overruled." Maj.-Gen. Masafumi Yamauchi commanded 15th Division in Burma, without disguising a predilection for Western life acquired during a posting in Washington. Yamauchi was a frail, gentle soul. A tuberculosis sufferer, he subsisted on a diet of milk, oatmeal and newly baked bread until dismissed shortly before his death. His last recorded pronouncement about the war was "The whole thing's so silly . . ."

Masaharu Homma, son of a wealthy landowner, was recognised as a brilliant soldier, notable for his eccentricities. A romantic, impulsive, passionate man, in his off-duty hours he composed military songs and poems and was a familiar figure at Tokyo's smartest parties. As a young officer he made a disastrous marriage to a geisha's daughter named Toshiko, with whom he had two children. In 1919, while on an attachment in England, he received a cable from his mother announcing that his wife had become a professional courtesan. Consumed with misery, Homma invited a comrade, Hitoshi Imamura, to discuss his plight at the Sunrise restaurant high above London's West End. Inspired by liberal injections of whiskey, Homma suddenly said: "I don't want to go on living," and attempted to throw himself out of a window. Imamura restrained him. The story of two future Japanese army commanders wrestling in a London restaurant passed into legend. Imamura told Homma he must get a divorce, but instead the general wrote to Toshiko pleading for a reconciliation. A senior officer wrote scathingly to the heartsick young man: "What a sorry spectacle you are making of yourself! Are you really a Japanese officer? If you take back your wife, everyone will laugh at you." Homma replied miserably: "I don't mind being laughed at. I just want her with me again." It was at Toshiko's insistence that the couple parted. The general subsequently married a much younger woman, Fujiko, whom he also came to adore.

Homma led the 1942 assault on the Philippines. Despite Japan's victory, he was deemed to have bungled the campaign. Most significant, and reflecting a chronic weakness of the Japanese army, he was castigated for exercising excessive initiative, and disobeying orders which he considered unrealistic. In consequence, he never received another field command, and in 1944–45 his considerable abilities were denied to his country. The 1942 conqueror of Malaya, Tomoyuki Yamashita, likewise languished in Manchuria until October 1944, because his freethinking found no favour with successive governments. Less able men, willing to obey without question even the most absurd instructions, held key postings. The indispensable qualification for high command was a willingness to fight heedless of circumstances, and to avow absolute faith in victory. The result was that by the summer of 1944, many of those charged with saving Japan by their military endeavours possessed the hearts of lions, but the brains of sheep.

CHAPTER THREE

The British in Burma

1. Imphal and Kohima

The British and Japanese fought each other on the Burman front for forty-six months. Burma thus became the longest single campaign of the Second World War. It cost the Japanese only 2,000 lives to seize this British possession in 1942, but a further 104,000 dead to stay there until 1945. The largest country on the South-East Asian mainland, rich in oil, teak and rubber, Burma had been ruled by a British governor, with only token democratic institutions. Its population of eighteen million included a million Indians, who played a prominent part in commerce and administration. A host of Indian fugitives died in ghastly circumstances during the 1942 British retreat. Burmans had always been hostile to colonial rule. Many acquiesced willingly in occupation by fellow Asians, until they discovered that their new masters were far more brutal than their former ones. By 1944, they had learned to hate the Japanese. They craved independence and, ironically, now looked to the British to secure it for them. Yet Winston Churchill's government, and its servants in Asia, were confused about political purposes as well as military means. The poems of Kipling, the glories of the Indian Raj, the wealth and prestige which her eastern possessions had brought to Britain imbued old imperialists, the prime minister notable among them, with passionate sentiment. They yearned to restore the old dispensation. Some younger men recognised that the changes wrought by the war, and especially by Japanese triumphs in 1941–42, were irreversible. They perceived that most Indians were indifferent, or worse, to Britain's war. The enlightened, however, were not in charge.

The situation was rendered more complex by the involvement of the United States. The war with Japan exposed differences between London and Washington more profound than any which afflicted policy in Europe. Americans, from their president to soldiers and airmen who served in the China-Burma-India theatre, were almost universally antipathetic to the British Empire, and resented committing their country's resources to its resurrection. Where the British regarded Siam as an enemy, an ally of the Japanese, from 1942 the U.S. chose to see it merely as an occupied, victim country. This was partly because Washington harboured a conviction, which persisted through 1945, that London cherished imperialistic designs there. Americans shared with the British a commitment to undoing Japanese aggression, but would greatly have preferred not to restore the European powers' lost possessions to their former owners. So strong was this sentiment that most Americans, including the nation's leaders, would happily have forsworn British aid to defeat the Japanese, if they could thus have distanced themselves from the cause of imperialism. Only the most compelling global political imperatives persuaded the U.S. to cooperate with the British in the Japanese war. It is hard to overstate the mutual suspicion and indeed antagonism which prevailed between the Western Allies in Asia in 1944–45.

"I have noted a regrettable lack of any spirit of camaraderie between British and American sections," wrote a U.S. diplomat in India, "or any evidence of mutual frankness and trust." A British diplomat likewise reported: "The majority of American officers in this theatre . . . are pessimistic about the chance of any real Allied cooperation being achieved here, suspicious of British intentions, bitter over many real or fancied grievances, and convinced of the essential bad will and hopeless inefficiency of the Indian administration." If the British government was less troubled than it should have been by the deaths of three million Indians in the 1943 Bengal famine, precipitated by the loss of Burma's rice, those Americans aware of it were appalled. A growing proportion of British signal traffic on Asian matters was marked GUARD—not to be shown to allies.

"The Americans [in India] . . . have rather behaved as an Army of Occupation," wrote a senior British officer in December 1943, "or if that is too strong, much as we comport ourselves in Egypt *vis à vis* the Egyptian Army and Government." A British officer of the Indian Army wrote of the distaste for Roosevelt's people which pervaded his mess: "Our anti-Americanism probably stemmed from their reluctance to enter the war against Germany until 1941, their scornful attitude to any other Allied nations' efforts, and their ability to create huge material and massive air support for their war in the Pacific, while almost grudgingly offering us similar backing. Stories of men losing their wives and girlfriends to American forces in Britain, and films of gum-chewing, jiving, laconic groups of American soldiers and airmen, no doubt led us to the wrong message . . . We should have understood these things better, but we were young and often intolerant."

Such feelings were reciprocated. A sheaf of contemporary War Office reports complained of the reluctance of British and U.S. personnel to salute each other. Pollsters put a proposition to Americans at home: "The English have often been called oppressors because of the unfair advantage some people think they have taken of their colonial possessions. Do you think there is any truth in this charge?" Fifty-six percent of respondents answered: "Yes." The Office of Strategic Services, the American covert operations organisation whose missions operated out of India into South-East Asia, was rabidly anti-colonialist. OSS officers reported to Washington, entirely accurately, that many Indians thought well of Subhas Chandra Bose, the nationalist leader assisting the Japanese to raise an "Indian National Army" from the ranks of POWs to fight against the British. Even the governor of Bengal, Richard Casey, wrote in 1944 that he perceived no enthusiasm for the war among its people: "It would be a brave man who would say that the majority of Indians want to remain within the British Commonwealth."

Some 23,000 young Chinese Nationalists were "back-hauled" by air to India over the Himalayas for American training. They too were bemused and dismayed by their encounters with imperialism. Wen Shan, for instance, walked into Annie's Bar in Calcutta with a group of comrades, looking for a drink. British soldiers shouted: "Out! Out!" Wen remembered later: "We tried to say, 'We're just soldiers like you,' but they would not listen. Once, I saw a British soldier on a Hooghly bridge beating an Indian. This was the way I had seen Japanese soldiers treat Chinese people."

Wu Guoqing, a twenty-one-year-old interpreter from Chongqing, was thrilled to find that in India he had enough to eat, as he had never done in China. Indeed, he was translated overnight from a poor student into a privileged person with Indian "bearers" to clean his shoes and make his bed, like all Americans in the theatre. Wu recoiled from the poverty, however, which seemed to him worse than that of China, and from British behaviour towards Indians: "Some British people even hit them," he said wonderingly. "They treated them like animals." A British tank crewman from London's east end, John Leyin, was disgusted by the spectacle of two Tommies dangling strips of bacon fat from a train window, to taunt starving Indian passers-by. If such behaviour did not represent the entire reality of the Raj, it reflected the impression which it made upon many outsiders, especially American and Chinese, who saw India for the first time in those days.

For months following the expulsion of British forces from Burma in May 1942, they were merely deployed in north-east India to meet the threat of a Japanese invasion. As this peril receded, however, it was replaced by a dilemma about future strategy. Winston Churchill admitted to the British cabinet in April 1943: "It could not be said that the [re]conquest of Burma [is] an essential step in the defeat of Japan." Yet if this was acknowledged, what were British and Indian forces to do for the rest of the war? After the humiliations inflicted on them in 1941–42, the London government was stubbornly determined to restore by force of arms the prestige of white men in general, and of themselves in particular. If the Asian empire was not to be restored to its former glory, why should British soldiers sacrifice their lives to regain it? Herein lay uncertainties which afflicted strategy throughout the second half of the war, once the initial Japanese tide began to recede. What was Britain's Far East campaign *for*? And what would follow victory? No more convincingly than the French or Dutch—the other major colonial powers in Asia, though they contributed nothing significant to the war effort—did the British answer these questions.

In the latter part of 1942 and throughout 1943, Britain's operations against the Japanese were desultory, even pathetic. Led by feeble commanders against an unflaggingly effective enemy, and with scant support from the government at home, troops failed in a thrust into the Burman coastal region of the Arakan, and were obliged merely to hold their ground in north-east India. Embarrassingly, in the winter of 1943 the operations of six and a half British and Indian divisions were frustrated by just one Japanese formation. Americans like Lt.-Gen. Joseph Stilwell, senior U.S. officer in China, became persuaded that the British were no more willing energetically to grapple with the Japanese than were the Chinese armies of Chiang Kai-shek.

The only marginal success that year owed more to propaganda than substance: Orde Wingate's "Chindit" guerrilla columns, operating behind the Japanese lines and supplied by air, caught the imagination of the British public and especially of the prime minister, at the cost of losing a third of their number. At one rash moment, Churchill considered making the messianic, unbalanced Wingate C-in-C of Britain's entire eastern army. Deflected from this notion, instead he promoted the Chindit leader to major-general and authorised resources for him to mount large-scale operations behind the Japanese front in northern Burma.

Wingate was killed in a crash during the March 1944 fly-in. The Chindits' subsequent operations, like those of so many World War II special forces, cost much blood and produced notable feats of heroism, but achieved little. Wingate's death came as a relief to many senior officers, not least Slim, commander of the British Fourteenth Army, who regarded the Chindits as a distraction. Beyond such theatricals, more than two years were allowed to elapse between the ejection of the British from Burma in 1942 and their return across the Chindwin River. Stilwell's scorn for British pusillanimity was justified, insofar as Churchill opposed an overland campaign to regain Burma. The prime minister had seen British and Indian forces worsted in jungle fighting in 1942. He dreaded another torrid slogging match on terrain that seemed unfavourable to Western armies.

Against the implacable opposition of his chiefs of staff, who were prepared to resign on the issue, Churchill pressed for an amphibious assault on the great Dutch island of Sumatra, a concept which he rashly compared with his disastrous 1915 Dardanelles campaign "in its promise of decisive consequences." As late as March 1944 he revived the Sumatran scheme, causing the exasperated Alan Brooke, chief of the imperial general staff, to write: "I began to wonder whether I was in Alice in Wonderland." If a Sumatran operation was not feasible, the prime minister urged landing troops from the sea below Rangoon.

Churchill's lobbying for a grand South-East Asian amphibious adventure was futile, because Americans owned all the relevant shipping. They would commit their assets only to objectives favoured in Washington, which emphatically did not include Sumatra or Rangoon. Churchill fumed, on 5 May 1944: "The American method of trying to force particular policies, of the withholding or giving of certain weapons, such as carrying airplanes or LSTs [Landing Ships, Tank], in theatres where the command belongs by right of overwhelming numbers to us, must be . . . strongly protested against." By this stage of the war, however, Washington's control of Western Allied strategy had become almost absolute. "The hard fact is that the Americans have got us by the short hairs," wrote a senior British officer. "We can't do anything in this theatre, amphibious or otherwise, without material assistance from them . . . So if they don't approve, they don't provide."

Washington dismissed a British request for two U.S. divisions to join operations in Burma. The Canberra government likewise rejected a proposal that two Australian divisions in New Guinea should be transferred to British command in South-East Asia. If the British wanted to recapture Burma, they must do so with their own resources. "If our operations formed merely a part of the great American advance," cabinet minister Oliver Lyttelton warned the British chiefs of staff in March 1944, "we should be swamped. It [is] essential that we should be able to say to our own possessions in the Far East that we had liberated them by our own efforts."

Thus, the British government knew that a campaign to retake Burma would be difficult, and would not bring the defeat of Japan a day closer. But an army must march, British and Indian soldiers must die, so that Churchill's people were seen to pay their share of the price for victory in the Far East. Burma would be attacked overland from the north, because only the north interested Washington. Through its jungles and mountains ran a long, tenuous thread, the only land route by which American supplies could be shipped to China from India. Japanese troops occupied a vital section of this "Burma Road." If they could be dispossessed, northern Burma liberated, then the U.S. could pursue its fantastically ambitious plans to provide Chiang Kai-shek's armies with the means to become major participants in the war. At huge cost and despite chronic British scepticism, the road was being driven seven hundred miles north from India and south from China by 17,000 American engineers led by the brilliant U.S. Maj.-Gen. Lewis Pike.

From Churchill downwards, the British rejected the notion that China could ever play a part in the war remotely commensurate with the resources which the U.S. lavished upon her. When Roosevelt urged that a nation of 425 million people could not be ignored, the prime minister snorted famously and contemptuously: "Four hundred and twenty-five million pigtails!" Slim, commanding Britain's Fourteenth Army, deployed in north-east India, had some respect for Stilwell but never shared the American's belief that the Chinese could decisively influence the war against Japan. "I did not hold two articles of his faith," the British general wrote later. "I doubted the overwhelming war-winning value of this road and . . . I believed the American amphibious strategy in the Pacific . . . would bring much quicker results than an overland advance across Asia with a Chinese army yet to be formed."

If Britain could withhold respect for China, however, it could not deny this to the U.S. Some 240,000 American engineer and air force personnel were labouring in northern India and southern China to create and sustain the air and land links to which the U.S. government attached such importance. Washington indulged Britain's commitment to retake Burma only in pursuit of its own China ambitions. A million Indian labourers were deployed to create road, rail and airfield facilities to support a full-scale British offensive. Churchill still railed against what he perceived as the waste of it all. How could India, with more than two million soldiers, deploy as few as ten divisions against nine Japanese on the Burma frontier? "It is indeed a disgrace, that so feeble an army is the most that can be produced from the enormous expense entailed." In truth, an embarrassing number of Indian Army units were deployed on internal security duties. Churchill wanted Britain's eastern army to be profitably employed, but deplored the fact that "we are about to plunge about in the jungles of Burma, engaging the Japanese under conditions . . . still unfavourable to us, with the objective of building a pipeline or increasing the discharge over the 'hump' [the Himalayan air route to China]."

Allied operations in South East Asia were nominally subordinate to the supreme commander of South East Asia Command (SEAC), Admiral Lord Louis Mountbatten. "The interests in this theatre are overwhelmingly British," growled Churchill to the combined chiefs of staff when he imposed his protégé's appointment in September 1943. Mountbatten's meteoric elevation, from destroyer flotilla commander in 1941 to British chief of combined operations and then to SEAC at the age of forty-two, reflected the prime minister's enthusiasm for officers who looked the part of heroes. "A remarkable and complex character," Gen. Henry Pownall, Mountbatten's chief of staff, wrote of his boss. "There are so many paradoxes . . . his charm of manner . . . is one of his greatest assets; many is the time that I have gone in to him to have a really good showdown . . . he would apologise, promise to mend his ways—and then soon afterwards go and do the same thing again! [He] has great drive and initiative . . . He is however apt to leap before he looks . . . His meetings are overlong because he likes talking . . . And he likes a good big audience to hear what he has to say."

Mountbatten's many critics, who included Britain's service chiefs, regarded him as a poseur with a streak of vulgarity, promoted far beyond his talents on the strength of fluency, film-star good looks, and his relationship to the royal family. He was King George VI's cousin, and never for long allowed anyone to be unaware of it. Famously thick-skinned save where his own interests were at stake, of boundless ambition and limited intellect, his grand title as supreme commander meant little, for he was denied executive direction of either armies or fleets. The extravagant staffing of his headquarters in the sublime setting of the botanical gardens at Kandy, Ceylon, promoted derision.

Mountbatten was prone to follies. There was a 1943 episode in Quebec, where he fired a revolver at a chiefs of staffs' meeting to demonstrate the strength of "pycrete" as a material for a fanciful plan to build artificial iceberg aircraft carriers. The bullet ricocheted, narrowly missing the top brass of the Grand Alliance. Brooke fumed when Mountbatten solicited each of the commanders present for a souvenir tunic button: "I only quote this story, as an example of the trivial matters . . . that were apt to occupy Dicky's thoughts at times when the heart of the problem facing him should have absorbed him entirely." Mountbatten, however, endured endless disappointments and changes of strategy without losing heart. Once, when a scheme which he favoured was briefly approved, though it was evident to his staff that it would never be executed, Pownall wrote pityingly: "Mountbatten is in the seventh heaven of delight. He is so very simple-minded." "Dicky" was not a great man, but like many prominent actors in the dramas of the Second World War, he strove manfully to do his part in great events. He possessed two virtues which justified his appointment.

First, he was a considerable diplomat. He liked Americans, as so many British officers did not, and had a sincere respect for Asians and their aspirations. And the glamour of his presence, in a theatre where so many British soldiers felt neglected by their own nation, did wonders for morale. Almost every man who saw Mountbatten descend from a plane to visit them, in dazzling naval whites or jungle greens, was cheered by the experience.

As supreme commander, Mountbatten floundered when he sought to exercise authority, but distinguished himself as an ambassador and figurehead. Both he and his wife, Edwina, had a gift for regal informality. Peter d'Cunha of the Royal Indian Navy was once at his post in the wireless office of a patrol boat anchored in a creek off the Arakan, immersed in music from Radio Ceylon. Suddenly a pair of hands removed his headset. He turned in astonishment to perceive Mountbatten, who held it to his own ears for a moment. He then asked the operator's name, and said: "You seem to be very fond of English music." The supreme commander replaced the phones on d'Cunha's head and departed, saying: "Enjoy yourself; but just be a little bit alert. You never know who's coming!" The young man loved it, of course.

Yet Mountbatten could do nothing to undo his command's absolute dependence upon an American vision. Pownall wrote bitterly in his diary in February 1944: "If . . . we are relegated to mucking about in Burma, they may as well wind up this unlucky SE Asia Command, leave here if you like a few figureheads, a good deception staff and plenty of press men to write it up." If we recall Slim's scepticism about Stilwell's hopes for the Chinese—the British general's declared belief that the American advance across the Pacific would defeat Japan without an Asian land campaign—these strictures applied with equal force to anything which a British army might do in South-East Asia. Britain's field commander understood as clearly as her prime minister that the new Burma campaign would be launched to restore imperial prestige and to indulge American fantasies about China, not because British action could contribute substantially to victory over Japan.

In 1944, however, before the British could launch their grand offensive, the Japanese had one more throw to make. With extraordinary boldness, Tokyo's commanders embarked on an operation to seize the positions of Imphal and Kohima in north-east India. Even the Japanese at their most optimistic did not at this juncture suppose that they could conquer the country. Rather, they sought to frustrate the British advance into Burma. More fancifully, they hoped to precipitate a popular revolt against the Raj by showcasing during their advance units of the so-called Indian National Army, recruited from prisoners of war.

The Japanese high command's approach to the Imphal assault was recklessly insouciant. Gen. Renya Mutaguchi of 15th Army, whose concept it was, sacked his chief of staff for suggesting that the operation was impossible, mainly because of the difficulties of moving men and supplies in Assam, the wettest place on earth, with an annual rainfall that sometimes attained eight hundred inches. Mutaguchi, fifty-six years old, was a scion of an old but now somewhat diminished southern family. Like many Japanese generals self-consciously virile, he never wearied of proclaiming his enthusiasm for women and combat. He was an ambitious political soldier, prominent among those who had precipitated war in China. Belligerence, together with connections in high places, won him promotion to army command.

Mutaguchi found himself largely dependent on bullocks to move stores and munitions across some of the worst terrain in the world. Experiment showed that a laden beast could travel just eight miles a day. The Japanese army's supply line into Assam would be extraordinarily tenuous. A staff colonel was dispatched to Tokyo to secure endorsement for the operation from Prime Minister Tojo. A preposterous discussion took place while Tojo splashed in his bath. "Imphal . . . yes," said the prime minister, who had never displayed much interest in Mutaguchi's front. Japanese generals had a droll saying: "I've upset Tojo—it's probably Burma for me." They called the place "*jigoku*"—"hell." Now, the prime minister demanded: "How about communications? Have they been properly thought out? Eh? Eh? It's difficult country towards India, you know. What about air cover? We can't help him much. Does he realise that? Are you sure it will make things better rather than worse? What'll happen if the Allies land on the Arakan coast? Has anyone thought of that? Eh? Eh?" Mutaguchi's staff colonel outlined the plan while Tojo stood naked before him. At last, the prime minister said: "Tell Kawabe"—commander of the Burma Area Army and Mutaguchi's superior—"not to be too ambitious." Then he signed the Imphal operation order.

The battle which ensued became one of the British and Indian armies' proudest memories of the war, and decided the fate of Japanese arms in South-East Asia. Slim had expected an attack, but was caught off balance by its speed and energy. Japanese forces first hit the British in the Arakan coastal belt in February 1944, then moved the following month against Imphal and Kohima. The early weeks of the struggle were touch and go. "The whole time I had been in the theatre," wrote a cynical British officer, "the campaign had been conducted in an extremely leisurely manner by both sides. The only time I [saw] either protagonist hurry [was] when the Japs were heading for Imphal." Mutaguchi risked everything to move men fast through heavy country to gain surprise, and almost cut off an Indian division. The Japanese were successful in breaking land links to the British positions.

However, though the British faced Japanese troops on every side, the besiegers were in far more precarious condition than the besieged. Through the months of desperate fighting which followed, Slim's men held almost all the cards. Their numbers were much superior—albeit not locally at Kohima—and supported by tanks and artillery such as the Japanese were unable to deploy. They possessed command of the skies, and sufficient transport planes to achieve a feat unthinkable earlier in the campaign—the air supply of Imphal and Kohima. British and Indian troops were notably better trained and equipped for jungle warfare than in the past. They defeated the Japanese Arakan thrust so quickly that Slim, with the help of American aircraft secured by Mountbatten's intercession, was able to shift two divisions from that front to reinforce Imphal and Kohima.

Finally, the British were led by their ablest field commander of the war. Bill Slim—no one called him William—was born in Bristol in 1888, younger son of a hardware wholesaler whose business failed. The boy grew up in difficult circumstances. He always wanted to be a soldier, but spent the years before the First World War first as a pupil teacher, then as a clerk in a steel business. He wangled his way into Birmingham University Officers' Training Corps, and thence to a commission in 1914. He survived the bloodbath of Gallipoli, which killed or wounded more than half his battalion. Slim transferred to the Gurkhas and was serving with them when hit in the lung. In Mesopotamia he was wounded again by shrapnel and won a Military Cross. He finished the war as an Indian Army major.

Broad and burly, with a heavy jaw and much solid common sense, between the wars he advanced steadily in rank, assuaging financial embarrassment by the somewhat unexpected means of writing magazine stories under the pseudonym of Anthony Mills. It was Slim's misfortune to command Burcorps, the British force in Burma, during the disastrous retreat of 1942. It was generally acknowledged that he bore no personal responsibility for that defeat, but he himself liked to tell a story of his later return to Burma. One night he slipped unnoticed into Fourteenth Army's operations room, to perceive two staff officers standing before the map, one pointing confidently and proclaiming: "Uncle Bill will fight a battle *there*." The other figure demanded why. "Because he always fights a battle going in where he took a licking coming out!"

In contrast to almost every other outstanding commander of the war, Slim was a disarmingly normal human being, possessed of notable self-knowledge. He was without pretension, devoted to his wife, Aileen, their family and the Indian Army. His calm, robust style of leadership and concern for the interests of his men won the admiration of all who served under him. "Slim is a grand man to work for—he has the makings of a really great commander," enthused his chief of staff, Brig. John Lethbridge, in a 1944 letter to his wife. A soldier wrote of Slim: "His appearance was plain enough: large, heavily built, grim-faced with that hard mouth and bulldog chin; the rakish Gurkha hat was at odds with the slung carbine and untidy trouser bottoms; he might have been a yard foreman who had become managing director, or a prosperous farmer who'd boxed in his youth."

An Indian artillery officer told a typical "Uncle Bill" story. Suddenly summoned to order a full regimental shoot, the gunner dashed into his command post, knocking aside a big stranger who impeded his passage. Emerging shortly afterwards, he recognised his army commander, and began to stammer an apology for treating him so brusquely. "Don't bother about that, my boy!" said Slim cheerfully. "If everybody worked like you, we'd get to Rangoon a lot sooner!" The only people who seemed doubtful of Slim's merits were his superiors. Churchill never warmed to this bluff, understated officer, fighting a campaign with which the prime minister had no sympathy. Throughout Slim's career as commander of Fourteenth Army there were attempts to "unstick" him, even in his final glory days. His blunt honesty, lack of bombast and unwillingness to play courtier did him few favours in the corridors of power. Only his soldiers never wavered in their devotion.

In a lecture to the officers of 10th Indian Division, which he led earlier in the war, Slim voiced some of his thoughts about command: "We make the best plans we can, gentlemen, and train our wills to hold steadfastly to them in the face of adversity, and yet to be flexible enough to change them when events show them to be unsound, or to take advantage of an opportunity that unfolds during the battle itself. But in the end every important battle develops to a point where there is no real control by senior commanders. Each soldier feels himself to be alone . . . The dominant feeling of the battlefield is loneliness, gentlemen."

So it was through the bloody spring and early summer of 1944. On the plain at Imphal, and in the soaring Naga Hills where Kohima stood, British, Indian and Japanese troops struggled for mastery. "The scenery was superb," wrote one of the defenders, "the Highlands without heather, the Yorkshire fells without their stone villages, all on a colossal scale which made our trucks look very puny . . . On such an immense landscape, it felt like defending the Alps with a platoon." Ammunition consumption was prodigious. One battalion, 3/10th Gurkhas, expended 3,700 grenades in a single day's clashes. The Japanese, short of artillery support, likewise used showers of grenades to cover their attacks. Three British brigadiers died at Kohima. The tennis court of the former district officer's bungalow became the scene of some of the most brutal fighting of the war. Slowly, steadily, superior firepower told. Allied aircraft pounded the overstretched Japanese supply line. As well as losing ground, Mutaguchi's soldiers began to starve.

To the fury of the Japanese general, on 19 June, after eighty-five days, Kotuku Sato, his subordinate divisional commander at Kohima, abandoned the assault and began to fall back. The monsoon, which struck with exceptional force, reduced the tracks behind the Japanese front to mudbaths. "Despair became rife," said Iwaichi Fujiwara, a staff intelligence colonel. "The food situation was desperate. Officers and men had almost exhausted their strength after continuous and heavy fighting for weeks in the rain, poorly fed . . . The road dissolved into mud, the rivers flooded, and it was hard to move on foot, never mind in a vehicle . . . Almost every officer and man was suffering from malaria, while amoebic dysentery and beriberi were commonplace."

Still the Japanese army commander would not abandon Imphal. When Sato, back from Kohima, reported to Mutaguchi's headquarters on 12 July, a senior staff officer coldly offered him a short sword covered with a white cloth. Sato, however, felt more disposed to kill his superior than himself. He declared contemptuously: "15th Army's staff possess less tactical understanding than cadets." He recognised, as Mutaguchi would not, that the Japanese forces should have acknowledged failure and fallen back before the monsoon broke. Japanese often spoke scornfully of the long and cumbersome British logistic "tail." Now they discovered the cost of themselves having no "tail" at all.

Mutaguchi's hapless soldiers fought on at Imphal, being driven back yard by yard with crippling losses. Their commander's behaviour became increasingly eccentric. Having ordered a clearing made beside his headquarters in the jungle, he implanted decorated bamboos at the four points of the compass, and each morning approached these, calling on the eight hundred myriad gods of Japan for aid. His supplications were in vain. On 18 July the general bowed to the inevitable, and ordered a retreat. His ruined army began to fall back towards the Chindwin River, into Burma, Slim's vanguards pressing on their rear. "One battle is much like another to those who fight them," observed Captain Raymond Cooper of the Border Regiment, who was wounded at Imphal. This is indeed true. But the consequences of Imphal and Kohima far transcended any British achievement in the Far East since December 1941.

The campaign was a catastrophe for the Japanese. Of 85,000 fighting soldiers committed, 53,000 became casualties, five divisions were destroyed, two more badly mauled. At least 30,000 men died, along with 17,000 mules, bullocks and pack ponies, both sides' indispensable beasts of burden. The Indian National Army, in British eyes traitors, collapsed when exposed to action, and surrendered wherever Slim's soldiers would indulge them. Fourteenth Army suffered 17,000 casualties, but its spirits soared. "We knew we had won a great victory," said Derek Horsford, commanding a Gurkha battalion at the age of twenty-seven. "We were chasing Japanese up and down thousand-foot hills, finding everywhere their dead and abandoned weapons and equipment." An eyewitness with Fourteenth Army, advancing in the enemy's wake, wrote:

> The air was thick with the smell of their dead. The sick and wounded were left behind in hundreds . . . We saw dead Japs all along the road, some in their stockinged feet, and where the hills were highest and most exhausting, they lay huddled in groups. They carried only a mess-tin, steel helmet and rifle. Some lay as though asleep, while others were twisted and broken by the bombs which had rained down on them. Five hundred dead lay in the ruins of Tamu. The pagoda was choked with wounded and dying. They had crawled here, in front of the four tall and golden images, to die. Hand grenades littered the altar. In the centre of the temple was a dais, and carved into this was a perfectly symmetrical pattern on the foot of Buddha. It was littered with blood-soaked bandages and Japanese field-postcards.
>
> No men in this war can have been reduced to such a terrible condition. I saw two prisoners who were revived with hot tea. They were tiny men with matted hair which stood up like a golliwog's. One of them put his head in his hands and cried like a child. It was a disgrace for him to be alive. [Some Japanese] killed themselves where they stood with their own grenades . . . lousy, half-mad from hunger and explosions, and deserted by their officers. This is a picture of a shattered army . . . These small men with savage hearts and hands that can paint exquisite water-colours in the diaries which they leave lying in the red mud.

Lethbridge, Slim's chief of staff, wrote home:

> The Jap retreat must have been worse than Napoleon's retreat from Moscow. The whole jungle stinks of corruption. I counted twenty-five dead Japs on the side of the road, between two successive milestones. There must have been hundreds more who had crawled away into the jungle to die. In some places there are Jap lorries, with skeletons sitting in the drivers' seats, and a staff car with four skeletons in it. All these

> Japs had simply died of exhaustion, starvation and disease. I have never seen troops in such good heart as our people . . . I'm so delighted that the British Army has at last come into its own again, and shown the world how we can wage war. I really don't see how the old Hun can last much longer. Once we've finished him, we'll simply knock the hide off these little yellow swine.

On the Japanese line of retreat, correspondent Masanori Ito approached Renya Mutaguchi, architect of his army's disaster. "He seemed tired out," wrote Ito, who noticed that the general was shamelessly sipping rice gruel, even as starving survivors of his army stumbled past. "You want a statement?" Mutaguchi growled. "I have killed thousands of my men. I should not go back across the Chindwin alive." Mutaguchi did not kill himself, however, and lived to be sacked a few months later. Of all the Imperial Army's commanders, he had become the most detested and scorned by his own officers and men.

"Sometimes it is impossible to carry out very difficult orders, but even though the command recognise this, they will not admit their mistake until every man has died trying to carry them out," a Japanese officer prisoner told his British captors. "The unreasoning obedience of men in carrying out idiotic orders is pitiful to behold. It was often impossible for me to give the actual orders—sometimes I only passed on half of them. 'We get all the fighting but none of the food—why?' No one dared say this, but everybody thought it."

In the autumn of 1944, as Fourteenth Army began its own advance towards the Chindwin River and Burma, at first the Japanese could deploy only four very weak divisions, totalling some 20,000 men, against Slim's six, plus two independent brigades—a British ration strength of 260,000 men. In the north, Chinese divisions under Stilwell were making sluggish progress towards the clearance of the Burma Road between India and China. The only significant achievement of the second Chindit expedition was to assist the capture of Myitkyina, a vital link on the route, which finally fell on 3 August. It required the efforts of three Chinese divisions, aided by the American "Merrill's Marauders," together with several thousand Chindits, to achieve this success against the weak, poorly equipped Japanese 18th Division. But the prospect now beckoned of opening the China passage.

Slim's invaders were supported by forty-eight fighter and bomber squadrons and a total of 4,600 aircraft in the theatre, many of them American transports. The Japanese had just sixty-six planes. Though they were able to reinforce their ground forces before spring, the scene was set for Fourteenth Army to commence its recapture of Burma. Mountbatten's chief of staff, Gen. Henry Pownall, perceived an urgency about this task. Like others of his time, place and nation, he saw Britain engaged in a race between the recapture of her Asian colonies and American victory in the Pacific. If the British lost the contest, if they failed to secure physical possession before the Japanese flag came down, the Union flag might never again fly over this great region: "There's not much time to lose. The Yanks are going to have Japan beat by Xmas 1945. We have got a lot of cleaning-up to do by then. The Yanks are not going to wait for us (no reason why they should) but we really don't want our Far Eastern Empire . . . handed back to us entirely by American single-handed victory. So we aim at all Burma by next summer and Malaya not too long afterwards."

The twin battles of Imphal and Kohima had been essential to halt the Japanese advance westwards. British victory had crippled the fighting power of the enemy on the Burman front, where Japan no longer possessed resources to frustrate any significant Allied purpose. Slim's chief foes were now terrain, disease, weather, logistics. Mountbatten supported an important decision: to keep fighting through the monsoon, when in the past all significant operations were halted. Thereafter, Slim was called upon to move a modern Western army across hundreds of miles of the most inhospitable country in the world, devoid of road communications, to redeem the humiliations which Britain had suffered in 1941–42, and to keep alive a dream of empire which thoughtful men knew to be doomed. Churchill badly wanted to retrieve Burma and Malaya, but was determined, he told the chiefs of staff in September 1944, "that the minimum of effort should be employed in this disease-ridden country." Here was a prospect rich in pathos, tragedy or absurdity, according to viewpoint. As so often in wars, brave men were to do fine and hard things in pursuit of a national illusion.

2. "The Forgotten Army"

A British officer returning from home leave recorded gloomily: "In the UK . . . I found everywhere a dreadful ignorance about Fourteenth Army and also generally about Burma." But Slim's men had learned to take a defiant pride in their status as "the forgotten army." In the autumn of 1944 they advanced with spirits infinitely buoyed by victory at Imphal and Kohima. Some of the men who now began hacking a path towards the Chindwin River, sweating up the soaring hills and scrambling down the steep valleys towards its bank, had been fighting thereabouts since 1942. A young British signaller who joined 2nd Division was awed by the veterans with whom he found himself: "I was a pale white thing; they were tanned the colour of a mule's backside. I knew nothing; they knew everything and could say nothing." The same soldier, Brian Aldiss, wrote home as the advance to the Chindwin began: "The grand scenery here produces a great calm, and seems to reduce war to the useless squabble it really is." He was as moved as many other participants by the spectacle of Fourteenth Army negotiating the hills of Assam:

> When our lorry was labouring to the top of a crest, we could see the thread of vehicles far away behind us, below clouds; conversely, when we were in a valley, we could look up through clouds and see that thread continuing far ahead of us, climbing the next series of heights . . . To be part of this inset of war was most thrilling after dark. Dim headlights scarcely penetrated the muck we threw up. We could scarcely see the tail lights of the vehicle ahead. Speed was almost down to walking pace. The impression of an animal bent on traversing a strange planet was at its strongest. On either side, unknowable, thrilling, fearsome, stood the jungle, pale as a ghost jungle in its layers of dust.

The 1944–45 battle for Burma was the last great adventure of Britain's imperial army. It brought together under Slim's command British soldiers and Gurkhas, East and West Africans, above all Indians: Sikhs and Baluchis, Madrassis, Dogras and Rajputs, pride of the Raj. Only a fraction of those who fought for the Allied cause in Burma were British—two divisions—and just one in thirteen of all ground troops under Mountbatten's command in South-East Asia.

To a man, Britain's Indian troops were volunteers, many from the north, where soldiering was a traditional career. The dramatic expansion of the Indian Army between 1939 and 1945—from 189,000 to 2.5 million men—caused a dilution of quality, and especially a shortage of suitable leaders, which significantly affected its performance. Yet the exotic traditions, the romance and prowess of great regiments, still thrilled British officers who felt privileged to serve with them, usually on a scale of around twelve per battalion. "Gurkhas were wonderful chaps to command," said Derek Horsford, who made his military career with the little Nepalese soldiers. "They had a lovely sense of humour. You had to prove yourself, but once they liked you they would do anything for you." Gurkha riflemen ate goat and rice, their British officers sardines and bully beef. Slim enjoyed telling a story of encountering 17th Indian Division's famously feisty and colourful little commander, Pete Rees, leading a group of Assamese soldiers in the singing of a Welsh missionary hymn. "The fact that he sung in Welsh and they in Khasi only added to the harmony."

British officers were often much moved by the loyalty and courage of soldiers who were, to put the matter bluntly, mercenaries. A man of the 1/3rd Gurkhas said to his company commander one morning: "Today I shall win the Victoria Cross, or die." That Nepalese died sure enough, but his shade had to be content with the Indian Order of Merit. Such was the rivalry between two Indian officers of John Cameron-Hayes's gun battery that each declined to take cover on the battlefield within sight of the other. Personal honour—"*izzat*"—meant much. Captain John Randle was moved when his *subadar* Moghal Baz suddenly said as they ate one night: "I would like you to know, *sahib*, that with you I have served with great '*izzat*.'" Every man in Slim's army heard stories such as that of a Dogra *jemadar* badly wounded and taken to a dressing station. The NCO insisted on crawling back to his position, and fighting on until wounded three times more. As he lay dying, he repeated again and again the war cry "*Mai kali ki Jai!*" His British captain crawled to where he lay. The *jemadar* said: "Go back and command the company, *sahib*, don't worry about me."

Slim's chief of staff wrote to his wife: "One can't help feeling very humble when one deals with men like that. This army is truly invincible *given a fair chance*." Of twenty Victoria Crosses won in Burma, fourteen went to men of the Indian Army, three to a single unit, 2/5th Gurkhas. When a British officer met a Sikh colonel whose battalion he was relieving, he noted his immaculate turban, beard glistening in the monsoon rain: "I saw something in him that was new to me: relish for war. The Sikhs gave every impression of enjoying themselves."

It never occurred to the British government to consult Indian political leaders about the conduct of the war, any more than they sought the views of Burman exiles. Reports of dissension among the Allies about Asian policy, freely aired in the British and American media, were shamelessly censored from the Indian press. The subcontinent was treated merely as a huge reservoir of manpower. An army psychiatrist's report on Indian troops asserted that on the battlefield, most were "well-adjusted," as long as they were able to serve alongside men of their own racial group. "The sepoy," observed the report with imperialistic condescension, "accepts the army, its discipline, its customs and leaders uncritically. He is not greatly interested in the ideologies of the war, because he has a job which gives him a higher standard of living than before, an interest is taken in his welfare, and he gets leave fairly regularly. He does not ask a great deal more." Few British officers in Indian regiments perceived that the day of the Raj was done, or heeded the alienation of most Indian civilians from Britain's war. "We took it for granted that Burma and Malaya would remain parts of the British Empire. We never thought India might go," said Captain Ronnie McAllister of 1/3rd Gurkhas, whose stepfather was a senior officer of the Indian Police. "I remember dinner parties at my stepfather's house where there were police, Indian Civil Service people, Indians. Nobody even mentioned the possibility. We were cocooned against reality, you see, because the Indian Army was so staunch."

That army's cultural complexities aroused some bewilderment among newcomers. Pathans in John Cameron-Hayes's gunner unit not infrequently used their leaves to pursue tribal vendettas at home, before returning to the British war. John Randle, a company commander in the Baluchis at the age of twenty-two, was informed by his colonel of two taboos essential to maintaining respect for *sahibs*: an officer must never let himself be seen naked before his men, and should ensure that excretion was carried out in privacy on a "thunderbox," even in action. The officers' mess sweeper, a little man named Kantu whose broad grin never failed, thus sometimes found himself excusing the colonel's temporary absence from a battle, saying as he saluted: "*Command officer sahib, pot par hai*" "The CO's on the pot." Randle was so impressed by the spectacle of Kantu crawling out under fire to deposit the hallowed contents of the thunderbox in a latrine pit that he successfully submitted the sweeper's name for a Mention in Dispatches. Less happily, Randle was informed that a homosexual British officer had been making advances to sepoys. His soldiers, mostly Pathans, were plotting to kill him. Randle saved the man's life by having him removed for court-martial.

Once, an attached platoon of British troops arrived triumphant in the Baluchis' lines with the carcass of a wild pig they had trapped. Randle's *subadar-major* said firmly: "Sir, that thing is not coming into our position to defile us." The British sergeant said: "Sir, you know what the rations are like—we're all hungry and browned off to hell with bully and biscuits." Randle told the sergeant to remove the pig, dismember it and come back with the meat discreetly concealed in the men's haversacks, for transfer to their own cookhouse. The *subadar-major* acquiesced. Likewise when tins of mutton were delivered to the 4/1st Gurkhas, bearing labels which showed images of female sheep. The men declined to eat them. The battalion CO instructed his quartermaster to find a crayon and draw testicles on the beasts. The amended mutton was found acceptable.

There was rivalry between British and Indian units, with some disdain on both sides. Derek Horsford of the Gurkhas said: "We thought nothing of the British Army. They seemed to us terribly inefficient." War in Burma produced wild incongruities, such as the spectacle of the gunners of 119 Field Regiment singing "Sussex by the Sea" in honour of their native county as they heaved twenty-five-pounders across a jungle clearing. The culture and language of the Raj seeped into the veins of every man who served under Slim. Whether you were a Borderer or a Dragoon, tea was "*char*," the washerman a "*dhobi-wallah*," a mug a "*piyala*," food "*khana*," and so on. They smoked Indian "Victory V" cigarettes, packed in brown paper packets for European consumption, green for Indian and African. Soldiers found both "unspeakably vile."

The foremost tactical reality for both British and Americans fighting the Japanese was that when the enemy moved, he became vulnerable to their firepower, but while dug into his brilliantly concealed and meticulously protected bunkers, he was hard to see and harder still to kill. One of the more ridiculous documents produced by the wartime British Army, marked "Most Secret," was an August 1944 report from the Directorate of Tactical Investigation, summarising tests on bombarding simulated Japanese bunkers with infantry weapons. Researchers garrisoned a position with two cockerels, two goats and two white rabbits, "one somewhat dull in behaviour and suffering from mange." After a two-inch mortar barrage, reported the study, the animals were covered in dust, but otherwise little affected. "They appeared mildly surprised but in other respects were apparently normal. The goat was coughing slightly." PIAT anti-tank bombs caused the goat's pulse to slow and blood pressure to fall. On the battlefield, no doubt with scant help from the above study, "beehive" charges, tank gunfire, or an infantryman tossing a grenade into a bunker with one hand while firing a tommy gun through the slit with the other were found most efficacious.

But first it was necessary to find the enemy. A British officer noted that when his soldiers dug a foxhole, a pile of earth rose around it: "With the Japanese, you could never see that soil had been moved." A Borderer in Raymond Cooper's company was astonished to hear a "woodpecker"—a slow-firing Japanese light machine gun—chattering under his feet. Without noticing, he had stepped onto an enemy bunker. Cecil Daniels's platoon of the Buffs, advancing warily through the jungle, received their first intimation of the enemy "when there was a sudden bang and the sergeant who had been walking by the side of and slightly in front of me went down like a log. Firing seemed to break out all around. A shout of 'Stretcher-bearer' went out, but I shouted 'No need' as I could see that he was already dead, twitching in the throes of involuntary muscle convulsion. He wasn't breathing." The company runner, "Deuce" Adams, shouted: "Look out, there's a bloody Jap." Somebody shouted: "Take him prisoner." Someone else shouted: "Balls." Adams emptied a tommy-gun magazine apparently into empty ground, at point-blank range. The other men could see nothing. When they closed in on Adams, they found him peering into a foxhole containing a dead Japanese soldier. "He smelt pretty much, a sickly spicy smell such as all Japs seemed to have."

The suddenness and savagery of such encounters made a profound impression on every man who experienced them, especially at night. The 25th Dragoons, an armoured unit, never forgot a moonless moment in the Arakan when the Japanese broke into their main dressing station: "The screams of the patients, doctors and medical staff as they were shot and bayoneted, the blood-curdling yells of the attacking Japs through the night, was for all of us a nightmarish experience . . . This brutality and inhuman behaviour . . . affected us profoundly." Some British commanders favoured fighting whenever possible in daylight, because they acknowledged Japanese mastery of darkness. Maj. John Hill's men of the Berkshires were disgusted to find human body parts in the haversacks of dead enemy soldiers. They knew nothing of the cultural importance to every Japanese of returning some portion of a dead comrade's body to his homeland. "The war in Burma was fought with a savagery that did not happen in the Western desert, Italy or north-west Europe," wrote John Randle of the Baluchis. "I never once recall burying Jap dead. If there were sappers about, they were simply bulldozed into pits. Otherwise we shoved them into nullahs for the jackals and vultures to dispose of."

By the autumn of 1944, courage, ruthlessness and fieldcraft were the principal assets remaining to the forces of Nippon. The Allies were overwhelmingly superior by every other measure of strength. Yet a War Office report based on prisoner interrogation noted that "the Japanese still considers himself a better soldier than his opposite number on the British side . . . because [we] avoid close combat, never attack by night and are 'afraid to die.' " The author of this document recorded with some dismay that the Japanese thought less of British soldiers than of Indians or Gurkhas, and considered Fourteenth Army ponderous and slow-moving. They respected British tank, artillery and air support, but criticised their camouflage, fieldcraft and noisiness.

Since 1941, however, the British and Indian armies had learned a lot about jungle fighting. First, dense cover and chronically limited views made conventional European tactics redundant: "All experience . . . has demonstrated the utter futility of a formal infantry attack supported by artillery concentrations and barrages against Jap organised jungle positions," wrote Frank Messervy, commanding 7th Indian Division. "The dominating assets are good junior leaders and skilful infantry. The right answers . . . are infiltration and encirclement." In early encounters with the Japanese, the British repeatedly allowed themselves to be outflanked, and assumed a battle lost if the enemy reached their rear. By 1944, men understood that in jungle war there were no such comfortable places as "rear areas," nor such privileged people as non-combatants.

Every man of the support arms must be trained to fight, and all-round defence was essential. Units had to be untroubled by encirclement. At night, anywhere within enemy artillery or mortar range, each man dug a "keyhole," a slit thirty inches deep and six feet long, sufficient to protect him from anything but a direct hit. The British had a healthy respect for the enemy's skills: "The Jap selects the most unlikely line of approach . . . irrespective of the steepness of the slope or difficulties of terrain," noted General Gracey in tactical instructions to his division. "He hopes to overrun the forward edge of a position by surprise. To this end, he crawls up very quietly and patiently to our wire. His fieldcraft is excellent."

Movement was hampered by limited vision and poor maps. So much landscape looked alike. Patrols found themselves lost for hours, even days. Captain Joe Jack of 3/1st Gurkhas wandered fifteen miles at the head of his company before finding himself back where he started. In thick jungle, a mile an hour could represent good progress. Squads "froze" to verify the significance of every sound. In an advancing file, the first man was trained to look forward, the second right, the third left, the fourth to the rear. Rest was a luxury. Five hours' sleep in twenty-four, day after day, was not an unusual quota. The two commonest adjectives among British soldiers were "smashing" and "deadly," the latter often applied to their rations—soya sausages, baked beans, bully beef and Spam, "compo" biscuits, jam, tea and porridge, heated on meths blocks. Even if men seldom suffered serious hunger, food was always short. A rum ration was sometimes parachuted in, but in that climate beer would have been more popular. South African–made boots and Australian socks proved best suited to cope with jungle conditions.

Light artillery, often the only available fire support for Slim's infantry, was useful for keeping the enemy's heads down, but unlikely to kill. Short-range weapons such as tommy guns and grenades were most valued. Whereas in Europe artillery and automatic fire dominated the battlefield, in Burma marksmanship mattered. An unaimed bullet was likely to damage only vegetation. Communication was problematic, because portable radios seldom worked. It was hard to see hand signals from officers or NCOs. Intensive training was essential, to make men respond instinctively to emergencies.

"It seemed a terribly old-fashioned kind of war," wrote one of Slim's soldiers, "far closer to the campaign my great-uncle fought when he went with Roberts to Kandahar than to what was happening in Europe." Douglas Gracey, commanding 20th Indian Division, summarised differences between operations in Burma and Europe: lack of good road and rail communications, endless water, jungles and swamps which limited movement, "but NOT to such an extent as inexperienced commanders and troops think." Visibility was drastically reduced, and vehicles wore out fast. "*Every* Japanese in a defensive position must be dealt with. He will fight to the death even when severely wounded." Gracey concluded, however, with a fierce homily against allowing these considerations to induce defeatism: "Explode the Jap bogey and the jungle bogey. We are all round better than the Jap." By the winter of 1944 this was true, chiefly because Slim's men had more of everything.

Even when Fourteenth Army was winning battles, it never entirely conquered its other great enemy, disease. Many men disliked the marble-sized mepacrine tablets of which a daily dosage prevented malaria, at the cost of turning their skin yellow. In 1942–43, tablets were often discarded—not least by men who preferred malaria to combat—and perhaps also by a few who believed Japanese propaganda that they rendered a man impotent. By 1944, most units held parades to ensure that mepacrine was ingested as well as issued. Men were ordered never to expose more flesh than necessary after nightfall. In the conditions of the Burmese jungle, however, chronically inimical to human health, sickness caused more losses than gunfire. A six-month breakdown of 20th Indian Division's losses showed 2,345 battle casualties, and a further 5,605 non-battle hospital admissions. The latter included 100 accidents, 321 minor injuries, 210 skin diseases, 205 venereal, 170 psychiatric, 1,118 malaria and typhus, 697 dysentery.

Insects laid their curse upon man and mule. Fires were lit in bivouacs whenever security allowed, to keep mosquitoes at bay. A British surgeon described the difficulty of addressing patients: "One orderly was deputed to deal with the flies. He chased them off the instruments, the sterile dressing, the blood-soaked blanket, clothing and stretcher of the patient, the very wound itself, and swatted them as they tickled the defenceless, half-naked operator." Chronic skin and foot infections, hepatitis, water rendered distasteful by purifying tablets, clothing never dry or clean were the lot of every infantryman. Nor were tank crews more comfortable. In a steel box, sweat poured down men's torsos into the sodden waistbands of their shorts. Often it was impossible to clamber on the hot hull without using rags to protect skin, and especially knees. Crews were coated in dust, and breathed through handkerchiefs tied over mouths and noses. When a tank's main armament fired, the stink of cordite lingered in the turret. There was noise, perpetual noise. John Leyin's crew sang "The bells are ringing, for me and my gal" as their Lee lumbered into action, knowing that neither friend nor foe could hear the chorus above the roar of its engine.

Another tankman, Tom Grounds, described the aftermath of battle: "Back in harbour we faced the bleak task of getting the dead men out . . . I shall not forget the burned and wizened, half-crushed head of the loader. In shocked silence they were passed through the side-hatch and lowered to the ground. We dug two graves near the side of the hill . . . Padre Wallace Cox conducted a short service, and rough wooden crosses were put up. White ants would soon have eaten the crosses and the jungle grown over the graves."

Like every battlefield, Burma demanded instant decisions about life and death. One day Col. Derek Horsford of 4/1st Gurkhas found his medical officer bent over a casualty with half his intestines trailing out of his abdomen. In his agony, the man was clawing mud from the ground and stuffing it into the wound. "Has he got a chance?" Horsford demanded. The medical officer shook his head. "Give him an overdose of morphine." A year later, the man amazed them all by writing from Nepal not only to report his survival, but to thank his officers for saving him. In attacks, junior leaders learned to be ruthless about leaving wounded where they lay, to await designated stretcher-bearers: otherwise there were far too many volunteers eager to escape carnage by carrying casualties to the rear.

Discipline was summarily enforced. A saddler with an Indian Army mountain artillery unit asked for some grenades, to protect himself in the event of a Japanese night attack. Instead, however, he deposited one in the bunk of a sergeant-major, killing him, and threw a second which wounded a British officer. It emerged that the man had a grievance about pay. After a swift trial, he was shot by firing squad. When John Hill's company of the Berkshires was approached by Japanese who got alarmingly close before being challenged, it emerged that two sentries had been asleep. On waking and seeing the Japanese, they simply abandoned their position and fled. Hill had one man court-martialled and sentenced to two years' detention, because it seemed essential to drive home the message that such lapses cost lives.

Burma offered no châteaux or champagne to senior officers. Slim's chief of staff, Brig. John Lethbridge, described to his wife rats eating the soap in his "basha" and running over his bed at night; his sense of loneliness and remoteness; gnawing uncertainty about how long the campaign might continue. He begged for news of his garden in western England. "This place is vile in October. The sun is sucking up all the vile humours out of the stinking ground, and one sweats and sweats. I have ten GSO1s under me, and five are in hospital with malaria or dysentery, some with both!" Slim, paying a night visit to the headquarters map room, found himself almost stepping on a deadly krait. Thereafter, in that snake-ridden country, he used a torch fastidiously.

If such things were so for red-tabbed staff officers, conditions were infinitely harsher for men living, eating and sleeping within shot of the enemy. "Perhaps the reason why the old soldier is reputed to dramatise his story," wrote Raymond Cooper, "is because he cannot create for those who do not know 'the tiny stuffless voices of the dark,' nor can he fully explain the change in the vital values of the ordinary things of life. The contrast is too great." Victory at Imphal and Kohima had done much for the morale of Slim's army, but remoteness from home was a corrosive force. Private Cecil Daniels, a twenty-three-year-old former Kent shop-worker, began his military service as an Aldershot mess waiter in 1939, became an officer's batman, served in the Western Desert and Persia. By the winter of 1944 he had become an infantryman with the 2nd Buffs in Burma. Like so many others, this simple young man found himself bemused by the extraordinary experiences which befell him, so far from home. One night in his foxhole beside a pagoda, he lay awake gazing at the moon. "The thought went through my head that this same moon had been shining over the home of my family not so very many hours before, and I wondered what they were doing at this same moment, and what thoughts they were having of me."

Though the army's morale was high, said a War Office report dated 31 June 1944, "infidelity of soldiers' wives is still a grave problem." A company commander of 9th Borderers described an encounter a few minutes before an attack: "Waiting in the dark for reports to reach me that all were ready, I was approached by a man who blurted out in a hurried whisper that by that morning's mail his wife had asked for a divorce. 'I'll talk to you about it in the morning' seemed an inept reply to a man in his frame of mind, with five hundred Japs between him and the sunrise." The regular morale report on British forces overseas, compiled for the War Office by Brig. John Sparrow, asserted in November 1944: "Anxiety about domestic affairs is rife among the troops, particularly long-serving men. Nine times out of ten it is caused by selfish women. Few officers or men feel completely secure. In one unit both the CO and RSM asked privately for my advice about their matrimonial troubles."

Mountbatten told the army's Morale Committee that the average British soldier "does not like India or Burma, and never will. The country, the climate and people are alike repugnant to him." Sparrow's report noted continuing concern among British commanders overseas about "deliberate" desertions by some of their men—as distinct from drunken leave overstays and suchlike. "All seemed agreed," wrote Sparrow to the adjutant-general, "that re-introduction of the death penalty would be the only satisfactory deterrent . . . It was generally realised, however, at any rate by staffs and senior officers, that [this] is not practical politics." After a few months in Burma, John Hill of the Berkshires concluded that about 25 percent of his men were potentially brave, about 5 percent potential cowards, and the remainder neither. This seems a fair, indeed generous, valuation of most Allied units in the Second World War.

The strangest elements of Slim's army—in the eyes of posterity, if not of those who grew up amid the exotic panoply of Empire—were two divisions recruited from Britain's African colonies. The War Office, chronically short of manpower, was seized by a belief that jungle warfare would suit Africans; this though most had never seen such terrain in their lives. What can have been the thought processes of such men, some from the remotest bush country, who found themselves shipped halfway across the world, albeit as volunteers, to serve in a white man's war for less than half the pay a white man received, against an enemy with whom a Nigerian, Kenyan or Tanganyikan could have no conceivable quarrel? Non-Christians among them had sworn an oath of loyalty on cold steel, usually a bayonet, rather than upon the Bible.

The West African Division's commander, Hugh Stockwell, circulated an angry memorandum when he heard that some white officers had spoken scornfully of the men they commanded: "I get reports that certain officers and British ORs . . . have, in idle conversation, been considerably indiscreet in their remarks about the capability of the African soldier in battle . . . Any who talk in such a way merely 'foul their own nest.' I myself consider that it takes a great deal of moral courage to set the African the example he deserves or give him the leadership which is so necessary. I hope that you have the guts that your breeding as a Britisher should give you to overcome your difficulties."

Stockwell warned that he would court-martial any officer deemed guilty of "defeatism." In correspondence with higher commanders, however, he admitted that some of his units had performed poorly, especially when subjected to Japanese night attacks. The African, he wrote, "has not a fighting history, and as a rule therefore battle does not come naturally." Some men had proved very good soldiers, "but others are very, very 'bush' . . . [The African] moves stealthily when on patrol, but cannot react quickly to any sudden emergency, again due to an inherent dislike of the unknown and lack of intelligence which precludes quick thinking. He has a doglike devotion to his leaders he can trust and admire, and who respect him . . . The whole fighting potential of the Division is in the hands of the European officers and NCOs." Stockwell deplored the poor quality of many of these. Some units were officered by Polish exiles, who had been encouraged by Churchill to emigrate to West Africa. Most of these Poles spoke the same pidgin English as their men. Stockwell was obliged to report to 11 Army Group on 4 August 1944 that "a small outbreak of desertion or absenteeism among native West African troops has been found to be due . . . to a belief . . . that if they can get to Calcutta they will be able to join units of the USAAF as labourers or servants. Steps are being taken to refute this idea."

Col. Derek Horsford observed that though his Gurkhas had little regard for the unfortunate Africans as fighting soldiers—"they would go out on patrol only if you held their hands"—they were impressed by other attributes. "During the advance into the Kabaw valley, I found some of our chaps crouching behind a bush, watching a party of West African soldiers bathing. The Gurkhas were gazing fascinated, uttering exclamations of unwilling awe, at what they perceived as the extravagant dimensions of their black comrades' private parts." There was much bitterness after the war that in Slim's expressions of gratitude to his soldiers, he never mentioned the Africans. Some British officers evinced deep admiration for them. They cited examples such as that of Private Kewku Pong, a Gold Coaster wounded and left for dead when his unit was overrun by the Japanese. Pong found an abandoned Bren gun and kept firing until overcome by loss of blood. The British discovered him next day, just alive, still clutching the butt of his gun. He was awarded the Military Medal. A British chronicler wrote of Pong: "On his own, in the dark of the night, quite badly wounded, with . . . Japanese rampaging behind him. No Britisher to tell him what to do, no African NCO, no other African; he ought to have been hopeless and helpless, and no one probably would have blamed him if he had discreetly gone to ground until all was quiet . . . Did Slim ever hear of Kewku Pong?"

In November 1944, Sierra Leonean troops had to carry fifty stretcher cases over the Pidaung hill range. A British officer wrote: "Bamboo ladders were built to get the stretchers up the rock face . . . Nothing . . . will ever compare with the perilous descent from the 2,300-foot escarpment . . . The European and senior African NCOs went out with torches and guided the column in . . . By the light of bamboo flares the stretchers were passed hand over hand down the cliff faces, some Africans going on hands and knees to form a human bridge over the worst places. The last stretcher case was safely in the advanced dressing station by 9:30 that night, after fifteen hours on the march."

Radio Tokyo denounced the African divisions as "cannibals led by European fanatics." Yet perhaps the most convincing and passionate testimonial to their contribution is that of one of their officers, Maj. Denis Cookson: "Without a murmur of complaint they defended a country whose inhabitants they despised, in a quarrel whose implications they did not understand. They had volunteered to fight for the British, and if the British brought them to a wilderness, that was a sufficient reason. They squatted down in their trenches, polished the leather charms they wore next to the skin, prayed to Allah for his protection, and good-humouredly got on with the job." They deserved more gratitude from their imperial masters than they received.

Behind the infantry of both sides toiled one of the most extraordinary gatherings of pack animals ever mustered with a modern army. Only beasts could cover mountainous ground, especially during and after the monsoon. White bullocks were dyed green, to render them less conspicuous targets. British soldiers found themselves receiving special training as mule handlers, and many grew fond of their charges. All ranks had to be carefully instructed in packing saddles, for overloading caused girth sores, or worse. The four mules designated for an infantry rifle company headquarters, for instance, could carry 158 pounds apiece. A typical load was expressed in regulations as 1 signal pistol; 2 two-inch mortars plus 18 bombs; 500 rounds of .303 ammunition and 1,000 rounds of 9mm Sten. The Indian Army's mountain batteries' light guns were dismantled for mule portage. Their British officers were also issued with chargers, which rather than riding most used to carry personal effects—blanket, mosquito net, rifle in a saddle bucket. When supplies were air-dropped, these included corn in vast quantities for the pack train.

Beyond mules, Japanese and British alike exploited elephants. The animals and their local riders—"oozies," as they were known—had been employed before the war in Burma's teak forests. Slim's tusker supremo was Lt. Col. Bill Williams, a First World War Camel Corps veteran who had been handling elephants for the Burma-Bombay Trading Corporation since 1920. "Elephant Bill" adored his charges, and worked devotedly not only to make them serviceable to the British cause, but also to protect the animals' interests. In the winter of 1944 he led a force of 147 elephants across the Chindwin, reinforcing his herd with abandoned Japanese beasts as the army advanced. Although, surprisingly, each elephant could carry little more than a mule's load, their bridge-building skills were much in demand. It was an awesome sight, to see an elephant lift in its trunk a log weighing a quarter of a ton. The great animals built 270 crossings for Fourteenth Army. Men sometimes glimpsed, for instance, a broken-down amphibious DUKW being towed by a tusker. John Randle's unit was impressed by the elephants provided to carry its heavy mortars, but dismayed to find them eating their camouflage foliage.

The best "oozies" were what Williams called "real Burmans, the Irishmen of the East," inveterate gamblers who cared as much as he did for their animals. Some were careless, however, causing terrible suffering by allowing battery acid to leak from loads onto elephants' backs. Williams established a field veterinary hospital to care for the injured, but nothing could be done on the night when a horrified sapper officer drove into his camp to report that one of their favourite beasts, Okethapyah—Pagoda Stone—had trodden on a land mine. "I gave Alex a good tot of rum, told him I could not amputate an elephant's legs, and we could only do our best to prevent such accidents in future."

Williams scoured parachute drop zones for broken bags of salt, which his animals adored, and strove constantly to prevent the casual cruelty of soldiers. Once, an Indian Army Service Corps driver, enraged by an elephant blocking his road, simply shot it in the leg. In October 1944 Williams's favourite elephant, Bandoola, forty-eight years old, got loose in a pineapple grove and contacted acute colic after eating nine hundred fruits. Bandoola recovered from this experience only to be found dead a few months later with one tusk removed, and a wound inflicted by a British bullet. Romantic though the elephants were, they suffered grievously for their role in a struggle of which they knew nothing. Many used by the Japanese were wounded or killed by RAF strafing. Most of those recaptured had had their tusks sawn off for ivory. Some 4,000 elephants are estimated to have died in Burma between 1942 and 1945.

It was a strange world, that of Fourteenth Army, divorced from anything its soldiers had known in past life. "We had entered an enchanted zone—a place of evil enchantment, if you like," wrote Brian Aldiss. "You could not buy a ticket to get where we were . . . No women were allowed, or hairdressers, or any kind of extraneous occupation. Lawyers, entertainers, politicians—all were forbidden . . . To attend this show, you had to be young and part of the British Empire." There was no loot to be scavenged from the battlefield, such as the armies fighting in Europe enjoyed. There were only the enemy's swords and pathetic banners, though Aldiss was once bemused to see a man marching with an old Japanese typewriter lashed to his sixty-pound pack.

There were few illusions about the loyalties of Burmans, in whose country this bitter struggle was fought out. A 20th Division report described 10 percent of the locals—often tribesmen from minority communities, persecuted by the Burman majority—as pro-British, 10 percent as die-hard anti-British, and 80 percent as "lukewarm, assisting whichever superior forces they are forced or persuaded to." John Randle once entered a village to find a badly wounded Japanese, obviously dying, "with his left leg shattered, bloated and gangrenous." A group of Burmans surrounded him, one of whom was driving a stick up his anus. Randle shot dead both the Japanese and his Burman torturer.

Men learned to beware mist on the hills, which often persisted until mid-morning, screening enemy movements. They were respectful of Japanese 90mm mortars. At night, two green Very lights from the enemy lines usually signalled an attack. Officers found it prudent to dress indistinguishably from their men, to avoid attracting the attention of snipers. The first of 114 Field Regiment to be killed in action was John Robbins, a newly arrived young forward observation officer who went into action alongside the infantry wearing badges of rank, binoculars, and a map case prominently slung round his neck. One burst from a Japanese light machine gun removed Robbins.

In Indian and African units some British officers grew beards, to make their white skins less conspicuous. When Captain Ronnie McAllister joined 1/3rd Gurkhas at the beginning of 1945, he was warned to avoid exposing himself unnecessarily. One Gurkha colonel was notorious for making his white officers lead from the front, with the consequence that some twenty were killed within months. There had been a legendary 1/3rd incident in 1943, when in battle the CO himself started firing at the Japanese with a Bren gun. Afterwards, the *subadar-major* reproved him fiercely, saying: "This must never happen again. It is our job to fight, *sahib*, and yours to command." McAllister said: "The people who lived through 1944 had no illusions. They told us not to rush about too much, to stay alive."

Some of those who marched into Burma in the winter of 1944, including McAllister, had been waiting years to see action. Maj. John Hill was a pre-war regular soldier, now a company commander in the 2nd Berkshires, who had spent forty months on garrison duties in India: "The war took a long time to reach us." The Berkshires were shocked by their first sights of battle: "Jeep ambulances came slowly past us with the groaning, bloody, bandaged forms of three men. I remember saying to myself: 'So this is *it*,' and others must have thought the same. The ambulances passed the whole battalion slowly, as if to emphasise the moment. It seemed odd that, after five years of war, this was our first sight of casualties . . . To most of us, the next few short months would seem as long as years. To a few, they would be positive enjoyment; to most, a time when a job had to be done; to others, positive purgatory."

Men's battle careers were often brutally abbreviated. Charles Besly of the Berkshires was a twenty-six-year-old BSc, who before the war had worked in a circus and as assistant stage manager of a London theatre company. In Denmark when war broke out, he hitchhiked home to join the army. By January 1945 he had served for a year with his battalion as a platoon commander, without seeing action. Within days of his first contact with the enemy he won a Military Cross in a clash with the Japanese. He was severely wounded, however, almost losing a leg. Besly disappeared from the regiment, never to fight again.

Thousands of soldiers followed behind Slim's infantry, performing the myriad support functions of an army. Some maintained themselves in tiny cocoons of Britishness, upon which the war and foreign places scarcely impinged. Joe Welch was a south London joiner's son, working in a power station, who joined the army in 1939 and became a linesman in a signals company. He and a little cluster of comrades served successively in Iraq, Greece, Libya, India and Burma, without any of these campaigns leaving much mark upon them. They were awed by the scale of India, but Burma was simply "lots of trees . . . I once saw an elephant . . . There were all these monkeys and spiders that came up when we were eating. I never saw a Burman." The campaign, to chirpy little Joe Welch, was simply "rain, rain, rain and bully, bully, bully." He and his mates—a fellow Londoner named Joy, Garner from Manchester, Vince from Sheffield—carried their own little British world across the Chindwin in their Chevrolet truck with its wooden Indian-made body as composedly as they had rattled through Greece and the Western Desert. They laid their telephone lines from division to corps to army in the hills of Assam, then on the path to the Irrawaddy. What did the war mean to Joe Welch? "I didn't worry about it—just one of those things, innit?" That is how the 1939–45 experience was for millions of uniformed men, no poets they, yet all warriors of a kind.

Every man, whatever his rank or specialisation, was expected to turn a hand to anything. At the end of November 1944, the Berkshires found themselves road building just inside the Burma border. "Even the miners among us found it tough going," wrote Maj. John Hill, who wielded a pick with his men, "but it was all part of Fourteenth Army's philosophy of self-help and DIY, in modern jargon . . . blasting trees, bamboo roots, rocks and eternally digging and shovelling, digging and shovelling until we longed for knocking-off time at 1600."

During the advance from Imphal to the Chindwin, Slim's men met only sporadic Japanese resistance, for the enemy was in no condition to fight a serious battle. In consequence, beyond the strains of the march, among many units there was almost a holiday atmosphere. The long files marched each night for eight or nine hours, each man following a wooden tag dipped in phosphorus tied to his predecessor's backpack. Then, when morning came, they bivouacked. "Very soon companies would have settled down in their allotted areas on perimeters," recorded the History of the 3/1st Gurkhas. "Cookhouses and latrines would be built; the men, after consuming quantities of sweet tea, would make 'sun shades' for themselves and the *sahibs*, and everyone would settle down for a very pleasant day, which everyone could spend pretty much how he liked." When they reached the Chindwin one officer, John Murray, spent hours fishing vainly with rod and line. He was chagrined to hear a loud explosion, then to meet a triumphant party of his men clutching a large fish, secured by judicious use of a grenade. The Gurkhas enjoyed the spectacle of African soldiers potting monkeys with rifles, until stray bullets started to fly about their own heads.

Yet even when organised Japanese resistance was slight, almost every yard of the Burma war provided unwelcome surprises. John Cameron-Hayes was disturbed in the night by a weight descending on his mosquito net, which proved to be a cobra. When one of his men shot a boa constrictor, its falling corpse knocked him into a stream. During the hours of darkness, both sides employed "jitter parties," patrols whose function was to disrupt their opponents' repose. Beyond these, there were plenty of unscheduled encounters. One night a Gurkha NCO awoke from sleep to see seven figures standing together on the road just beside him, huddled over a map. He rose, challenged them, and was met by startled Japanese grunts. He smote one enemy soldier with a spade, while the others scattered and ran. A British officer, awakened by the racket, found two figures struggling hand-to-hand in the darkness beside him. Joining the fray, it was some seconds before he realised that he was fighting a fellow officer. There was a desultory exchange of fire, then silence fell. The camp returned to sleep, only to be wakened once more by a thunderous explosion. A Japanese officer had blown himself up on an anti-tank mine. The Gurkhas slept again. At dawn, but for the presence of four dead Japanese in their positions, they would have been tempted to dismiss the alarums of the night as mere fantasies.

Beyond casualties inflicted by the enemy, there was a steady trickle of accidents, inseparable from all military operations. The air-dropping of supplies became a dominant feature of Fourteenth Army's advance, and soldiers and pack animals were sometimes killed by loads falling upon them from the sky. As columns threaded up precipitous mountain tracks, at intervals a mule slipped, plunging into the valley below. A report noted wearily that the animal lost was invariably carrying a vital radio set—it was essential to ensure that some wirelesses were manpacked. A private of the Buffs performed a notable little feat of heroism, wiping out a Japanese machine-gun post with his Bren gun. Yet as he ran on forward, he tripped and fell. The spade protruding from his pack caught and broke his neck. In action shortly afterwards, a Buffs sergeant called to his runner, Cecil Daniels, for a bag of grenades. The NCO was infuriated when Daniels told him they were not primed. "I'm not carrying a haversack full of primed grenades," said Daniels firmly. He had been rendered cautious by seeing so many comrades fall victim to accidents with munitions.

"We seem condemned to wallow at half-speed through these jungles," Winston Churchill complained bitterly in October 1944, describing the progress of Fourteenth Army. Yet for those at the sharp end, every yard of movement meant pain and difficulty. Conventional fieldcraft demanded that men should avoid the few tracks, which were likely to be covered by enemy fire. Yet movement through thick cover was so desperately slow that only tracks and *chaungs*—riverbeds—offered any prospect of advancing at tolerable speed. Distances measured on the map were meaningless—what mattered was how far men had to march. They learned not to smoke or talk at night anywhere within reach of the enemy, for scent and sound alike carried far. They cursed the relentless damp, which misted the optics of gunsights and binoculars, rusted weapons overnight. Newly joined replacements often buckled under the weight of their packs. Training had not prepared them for the burdens men must carry in a country where vehicles were few and mules precious. Air-dropped artillery had to be manhandled into firing positions by sweating gunners.

If a man was lucky, every few months he was granted a brief leave in India. Soldiers resting from Burma were entitled to "convalescent scale" rations. A transport aircraft carried them to rear base, from which an Indian soldier still needed days of travel to reach his home. Wartime trains in the subcontinent were notoriously congested and slow. When a Tokyo propaganda broadcast on Christmas Eve 1943 asserted that Japanese forces would reach Delhi in ten days, a chorus of listening Punjabi soldiers, just returned from an irksome leave journey, chorused: "Not if they go by train, they won't!" Yet many of Slim's soldiers had no homes in India. On leave, they sought what pleasures they could discover. Sgt. Kofi Genfi of the Gold Coast Regiment described a touching experience: "Oh, the Indians were very kind to me. In Madras I went to dance—I am a ballroom champion dancer. I sat down, but I couldn't get a partner. I was shy. I didn't know how to engage a lady. A man came and said: 'Do you want to dance?' . . . He said 'Come, come.' He gave me his wife . . . We started to dance, and they all stopped and looked at me as if I was giving a demonstration. At the end, there was applause. Then every lady wants to dance with me!"

For the white as well as black soldiers of Fourteenth Army, there was a shameful divide between the luxuries offered to officers on leave in clubs and messes, and the pitiful delights available to other ranks. These focused upon bars and brothels of notable squalor. When John Leyin's tank gunner heard that he was to be repatriated to England, his joy was tempered by the misery of finding himself impotent, after repeated treatments for venereal disease. The British class system shaped the lives of the nation's soldiers overseas, even more in Asia than in Europe. Signaller Brian Aldiss wrote cynically: "Most rankers expected little from life, had been brought up to expect little. And received little." Few men returned content from leave. But the experience granted at least a brief reprieve from toil, sweat and fear.

THROUGHOUT THE BURMA CAMPAIGN, American transport aircraft, fighters and bombers provided vital support to Slim's operations. Chuck

Linamen, a twenty-year-old steelworker's son from Ohio, flew fifty-two B-24 Liberator missions from India to targets in Burma and Siam. The first that he and his crew knew of their posting to the Far East was when they opened sealed orders over the Atlantic en route to the Azores in August 1944: "I couldn't even pronounce the names of the places we were going." But from the moment he joined the 436th Squadron at Madagan, 130 miles north-east of Calcutta, he found himself one of the relatively small number of men who relished the task which war had imposed upon him: "I enjoyed every minute of it." He loved his crew, a characteristic all-American mix: Ray Hanson, "the best navigator in the world," from Minneapolis; Will Henderson, the co-pilot, from Montana; a Texan bombardier; Kentuckian radio operator; gunners from New York, Mississippi, Pennsylvania and Ohio. They mined Bangkok harbour, dropped bombs on railyards, bridges, Japanese positions. By the standards of Europe, all their missions were long-haul, cruising at 165 knots for a minimum of ten hours, a maximum of eighteen. By way of compensation, however, opposition from flak and fighters was slight. On some low-level missions they strafed Japanese positions like excited schoolboys from three hundred feet, gunners whose turrets would not bear shouting over the intercom: "Give me a shot! Give me a shot!"

This did not, however, make the assignment risk-free. Beyond the hazards of mechanical failure, the Japanese could spring unwelcome surprises. Over Bangkok, Allied aircraft weaved to avoid barrage balloons. At 6,000 feet above Karneburi on 3 April 1945, Linamen's Liberator was hit by enemy anti-aircraft fire which inflicted punishing damage on its systems, severed an aileron cable and removed the starboard wingtip. They fell 4,000 feet before the pilot regained control, and then he had to nurse the plane every mile of the way back, for seven and a half hours, to the RAF emergency strip at Cox's Bazaar. Over the base, he invited the crew to jump. A gunner asked: "What you doing, Curly?" "I'm going to ride her down," responded the pilot. The gunner said: "What are we waiting for, then?" The other nine men took up crash positions. Unable to slow the plane for landing without losing control, Linamen settled for a high-speed skid onto the beach, touching at 150 mph, frantically shutting down fuel, power, systems until they shuddered to a halt. The crew, terrified of fire, bolted out of the hatches. One man found himself lying on the sand inches from a propeller that was still windmilling and could have removed his head. "You laugh about these things afterwards, but any of them can cost a life."

Another day, over a target, the co-pilot suddenly shouted, "Yowie!" Linamen turned in bewilderment, demanding: "What's your problem?" A 20mm cannon shell had clipped off part of the man's leg, mercifully without damaging the aircraft systems. They hastened home, to deliver their casualty to the medics. If Linamen loved to fly, others did not: "A hell of a lot of people were pretty despondent. They didn't like India, they didn't like the job." One day, "The colonel leading the mission screwed up. The wing found the target fogged in, but farted around waiting for visibility to clear, and got a few shot down." Among the pilots lost was a Californian named J. C. Osborne, one of Linamen's closest friends.

During the monsoon, when the weather was unfit for bombing, the Liberators were transferred to transport duty, carting fuel over the Hump into China. One night on the ground at a Chinese airstrip, they found themselves in the midst of a Japanese air raid. The airmen crowded onto the roof of a revetment to watch the fireworks, until a stick of bombs landed a few yards away, driving the Americans hastily into cover. Linamen exclaimed: "My daddy always taught me that it is more blessed to give than to receive, and he sure was right!" Yet he felt no great animosity towards the Japanese: "They were just there, they were the enemy. I had volunteered to fly, I was doing a job." Linamen achieved some fame, as one of the airmen who attacked the bridge over the river Kwai, built by prisoners on the ghastly Burma–Siam railway. Yet they felt little emotion even about this mission. They knew that Allied prisoners were on the ground, but had heard nothing of their unspeakable sufferings. Bombing the bridge was just another mission.

Tactical air support was a critical force in the British advance, rendered even more formidable by the fact that Japanese fighters had almost disappeared from the sky. Day after day, Fourteenth Army situation reports—"sitreps"—recorded: "Enemy air activity: NIL." Hurribombers—Hurricanes adapted for ground attack—mounted over 150 sorties a day, aided by American Thunderbolts. Strafing was always hazardous. Even when enemy resistance was slight, the perils of the jungle and mechanical failure persisted. A Beaufighter crew of 211 Squadron once jumped from a damaged aircraft over their base in the Arakan, rather than risk a landing. Their parachutes drifted into a rain forest of 150-foot trees. Though within a mile of their airfield, the airmen were never seen again.

Beaufighters—big, tough, twin-engined aircraft which weighed ten tons and carried a two-man crew—flew long "intruder missions" of up to seven hours, usually against Japanese rear areas. They tried to time their attacks for dawn or dusk, racing in at fifty to a hundred feet, weaving to confuse the ground gunners. They carried a formidable armament—aimed by a reflector sight on the canopy, a red ring with a blade to direct rockets, a dot for the guns. The whole aircraft shook violently when the 20mm nose battery fired. Exploding cannon shells raised a dust cloud around a target, or sometimes prompted more dramatic effects when they hit river sampans loaded with fuel. "For an instant," twenty-one-year-old Anthony Montague Browne of 211 Squadron wrote lyrically of such a moment, "the flight of shells caught the sunlight, shimmering like a swarm of silver bees." His unit's "Beaus" usually attacked in flights of three or four, preferring to do so without their squadron commander, a devout Catholic who could be seen crossing himself before making a dive. Other pilots begged him to desist from this practice: "It looked doom-laden and distinctly disconcerting." Once, over the Irrawaddy, Montague Brown saw a string of boats carrying a brilliantly clad wedding party. Hapless guests sprang into the water as soon as they glimpsed the Beaufighter.

On the ground, at their airstrip, there were few comforts or diversions. Food was poor, the chief consolations a monthly ration of one bottle of whisky and four cans of Australian beer. When these were exhausted the pilots—a typical RAF mix of British, Australian, Canadian and New Zealand—had recourse to a local palm toddy arak, known as Rum, Bum and Broken Glass. Between operations every two or three days, they played a lot of poker. One squadron commander, with an implausible past as a ballet instructor, sought to raise the cultural tone by playing *Les Sylphides* on the mess gramophone before take-off. Beyond the airstrip, there was nowhere even to go for walks, amid unbroken swamps and jungle. The fliers had no contact with local people, except once when some aviation spirit was stolen. The British drove around the area in jeeps, pleading with rice farmers not to use the high-octane fuel as a substitute for paraffin in their lamps. The Burmans took no heed. "That night, the sky was red with flames from burning huts, and pathetic little queues formed outside the medical units for treatment," wrote Montague Brown.

The area was notorious for extremes of weather. Once, a tornado blew down all their huts. In the air, they met violent thermal currents and thunderstorms. A hailstorm could strip the camouflage paint from wing leading edges, leaving the aluminium shining like silver. When a crew was lost, the squadron usually had no notion of its fate. An aircraft literally went missing. It was an unglamorous existence, detached from the rest of mankind and the war, though by a quirk of communications they received airmail editions of the London *Times* only five days after publication. Montague Brown—who became Winston Churchill's private secretary a decade afterwards—wondered if the campaign would ever end. "Our progress to the liberation of Burma was extraordinarily lengthy," he wrote. "We had superiority in every arm, and after the early toe-to-toe slogging at Imphal . . . the terrain progressively improved for armour and transport . . . Why were we so dilatory? . . . Surely, we could have moved faster. I was later intrigued to find that Churchill shared this view." Hall Romney, a British POW on Japan's infamous Burma railway, wrote in his diary on 19 November 1944: "When one considers what the Americans have done in the Pacific, one cannot help thinking people have moved slowly in Western Asia."

This was a widely held view, even among those with less cause than Romney to yearn for haste. The Japanese army in Burma was crippled at Imphal and Kohima before Slim's army even left Assam. From that point onwards, the British invaders were overwhelmingly superior to their enemies. It would have been shameful indeed had Slim's forces been unable to crush a Japanese army which lacked tanks or effective anti-tank guns, possessed negligible air support and little artillery, was starved of supplies and ammunition, and heavily outnumbered. Logistics, climate and terrain, much more than the Japanese, determined the snail's pace of the Burma campaign until its last weeks. Scarcely any of the advanced technology used by the Allies in Europe for movement or bridging was available to Slim's army. His was a "make-and-mend" campaign, unloved by Churchill, barely tolerated by the Americans, woefully underacknowledged at home in Britain.

"This army is like Cinderella," Slim's chief of staff "Tubby" Lethbridge wrote ruefully, "and until the German war is over one can only wait patiently for all the things we want. One gets an awful feeling of frustration when every request, whether it be for equipment or individuals, is turned down." Fourteenth Army deserved more credit for its advance into Burma than sceptics such as young Flying Officer Montague Brown were minded to offer. In the early months of 1945, notable deeds and spectacular successes lay ahead for Slim's soldiers. What is remarkable, however, is not that the British prevailed, but that their Japanese foes sustained resistance for as long as they did. Victory in Burma was painfully long delayed.

CHAPTER FOUR

Titans at Sea

1. Men and Ships

As Slim always perceived, though his campaign engaged more men than MacArthur's, it was a sideshow. The critical struggles to defeat Japan were taking place far to the east, in conditions very different from those of the Kabaw Valley and Chindwin approaches. Most Americans in the Pacific theatre learned to regard salt water as their natural element. To be sure, scattered across the ocean there were pimples of rock and coral adorned with brilliant vegetation, barely visible on a hemispheric map. The value of these as unsinkable aircraft platforms caused their possession to be contested with terrible ferocity. Until the last months of the war, however, ground forces were relatively small. Navies dominated. From 1942 to 1945, hundreds of thousands of sailors grew accustomed to waking each morning to horizons of sky and sea interrupted only by ships and aircraft. The greatest fleets in history sailed the Pacific, yet shrank to nothingness in its immensity. When the American cruiser *Indianapolis* was sunk, it was four days before anyone noticed that she was missing, far less located her survivors. Many American, Japanese, Australian and—in the last phase—British sailors lived afloat for years on end. The U.S. carrier *Essex* once steamed continuously for seventy-nine days, during which she flew off her flight deck 6,460 planes, which dropped 1,041 tons of bombs, fired over a million rounds of .50 calibre machine-gun ammunition and consumed 1.36 million gallons of aviation gas.

The wartime expansion of the U.S. Navy was an extraordinary achievement, which should never be taken for granted. Between 1941 and 1945, its tonnage swelled from three million to almost thirty. Of the service's total war expenditure of $100 billion, more than a third went to ship construction. The pre-Pearl navy mustered 8,000 officers. Each war year thereafter, an additional 95,000 were granted reserve commissions, becoming "feather merchants" or "ninety-day wonders" at the end of their three months' training. The precipitous quality decline of the Imperial Navy contrasts starkly with the proficiency achieved by the Americans. As the Japanese lost experienced seamen and aircrew, those replacing them proved ever less competent. Suicide pilots might be brave enough, but in the battles of 1944–45 many of Tokyo's aviators and warship captains displayed astonishing diffidence. The U.S. Navy, meanwhile, grew better and better, in seamanship, gunnery, replenishment, submarine warfare, aircraft handling. This prowess was achieved mostly by men who, before the war, knew the sea only as a place to swim in. The fighter direction staff of the carrier *Langley*, for instance, included an advertising executive, a lawyer, a college teacher and an Atlanta architect who specialised in designing Methodist churches.

America's shipbuilding programme almost defies belief. President Roosevelt was always a committed supporter of a strong fleet. Following the 1940 Two Ocean Navy Act, Congress granted the navy the most generous open cheque in history. Admiral Ernest King, its profane, intemperate, womanising overlord, seized his opportunity and never let go. He set about creating an armada whose size owed little to rational assessment of the resources needed to defeat Japan, and almost everything to his own grandiose vision. By late 1943, the U.S. was building 7 battleships, 28 carriers, 72 escort carriers, 73 cruisers, 251 destroyers, 541 destroyer escorts and 257 submarines. These new hulls were destined to join 713 ships already in service. "The inescapable conclusion," an American historian has written, ". . . is that navy expansion goals had become completely divorced from strategic planning and were influenced more by political possibilities than any thorough reassessment of the fleet's long-term requirements."

King's programme prompted staggering growth in America's shipbuilding industry. Mare Island Navy Yard expanded from 6,000 employees in 1939 to 40,000 in 1944, Boston Yard from 8,700 in June 1940 to 50,000 three years later. Forty-two cruisers were ordered from a single private builder in New Jersey. By 1944 more than a million workers were building and repairing ships, 55 percent of them on the Atlantic coast, 27 percent on the Pacific, while a further two million served supporting industries. Most were working forty-eight-hour weeks on multiple shifts. Extraordinary ingenuity was deployed to maximise production. Many smaller vessels, submarines and escorts, were built in sections at plants as far inland as Denver, then transported to the coasts for completion. Thousands of landing ships were constructed on the Great Lakes and sailed to the sea—one imperfectly navigated LST approached within a hundred feet of Niagara Falls before being saved by grounding. Productivity increased dramatically, so that the man-hours required to build a destroyer halved from pre-war levels to 677,262; those for a light cruiser fell from 7.7 to 5.5 million. The consequence of this immense activity was that by late 1944 the American Pacific Fleet outnumbered the Japanese by four to one in ships, and overwhelmingly more in combat power. The USN was larger than the combined strengths of all the other navies in the world.

The navy made no attempt to consult with the army about the two services' respective needs. King merely declared magisterially that since the war cost his country $200 million a day, building ships saved money by hastening victory. He projected USN losses—and thus necessary replacements—for the period 1 May 1944 to 30 September 1945 (actual sinkings are given in parentheses): four battleships (none), nine carriers (one), twelve escort carriers (five), fourteen cruisers (one), forty-three destroyers (twenty-seven), ninety-seven destroyer escorts (eleven), twenty-nine submarines (twenty-two). By late 1944 the navy could call upon 3,000 carrier-based planes. Warships were coming off the slips faster than crews could be mustered and trained to man them. The navy never assessed its manpower needs, it simply enlisted every sailor it could get. In 1944, 8,000 new naval aviators entered training. On 2 July that year, King asked the joint chiefs for extra manpower to increase naval strength by June 1945 to 3.4 million men, a million of these at sea. Yet, to crew all the ships he had ordered, 4.1 million would have been needed.

All this reflected the fact that, with Pearl Harbor to be avenged, there was no political will to challenge the ambitions of the U.S. Navy. Americans had a historic, visceral scepticism about big armies, but since the late nineteenth century they had shown no such inhibitions about sea power. King served his country well by creating the greatest fleet the world would ever see, crewed by men who showed themselves worthy of it. But only a nation so absurdly rich could have built two hundred battleships, carriers and cruisers in the war years, as well as a thousand smaller ships. It may be argued that King's megalomania was no greater than that of Arnold and the air force, which also imposed a disproportionate drain on manpower. But the U.S. Army, always the Cinderella service, paid the price for both, with its chronic shortage of fighting infantrymen. Only late in the war did it dawn upon America's leaders that their monumental industrial mobilisation was generating far more ships and planes than it had conscripted men to serve them.

By the autumn of 1944, the principal American naval forces committed to the Pacific were submarine flotillas operating out of Pearl Harbor and Brisbane; Seventh Fleet, commanded by Vice-Admiral Thomas Kinkaid—a motley gathering of cruisers, escort carriers and old battleships which operated under MacArthur's orders in support of his land operations; and Nimitz's heavy units, dominated by fast battleships and carriers. These were led alternately by William "Bull" Halsey, whose belligerence had made him a popular legend, and Raymond Spruance, the cooler and cleverer hero of Midway. The rationale for this odd arrangement was that it was difficult to plan operations in the cramped conditions of a warship. Each admiral therefore took it in turns to work ashore at Pearl, preparing for the next phase, or to direct the task groups at sea. To increase confusion—not least among the Japanese—Halsey's command was known as Third Fleet; when Spruance took over, the same ships became Fifth Fleet. Under either designation, this represented the greatest concentration of naval power in the history of the world.

For those who served at sea, spasms of intense action served only to emphasise the dreariness of life between. "The thrills were brief and far apart," wrote a crewman of the carrier *Belleau Wood*. Except for its flight crews,

> day in and day out life at sea was pure monotony . . . Boilers, engines, bulkheads, decks, mess halls, offices and shops always look the same, no matter what goes on above. Every day was a duplicate of its predecessor and model for its successor: reveille in the dark to sit around battle stations for an hour until sunrise; launch aircraft for routine patrols which 90 percent of the time saw nothing save air, clouds and water; land aircraft; launch aircraft; land aircraft; three meals a day; scrub bulkheads; swab decks; run boilers and engines; then fade out with another hour after sunset at battle stations. "Relieve the watch. On deck section three. Relieve the wheel and lookouts." Relieve the watch, relieve the watch, day after day, week after week. The sea and sky rolled endlessly by from one port period to the next; our eyes became "waterlogged."

Many men chafed at their ignorance of the purposes of their ships' activities, beyond the obvious ones of bombardment and defence against air attack. "You never know where you're going from one island to the next," said Louis Irwin, a turret gunner on the cruiser *Indianapolis*. "My lasting regret was that I didn't know what the hell was going on, where we fitted into the big picture," said Lt. Ben Bradlee, a destroyer officer. Eugene Hardy served on the cruiser *Astoria* at Midway, but was unaware that he had taken part in a great battle until somebody told him afterwards. "Dear Mom and Dad," wrote a twenty-year-old to his family in New Jersey from the Pacific, "I really feel like writing a long letter because I have some time, but there isn't much to write about."

If routine often became oppressive, in many respects a naval rating's life was preferable to that of a combat infantryman. Death at sea was horrible, but actuarially much less likely than for a man in a "sharp end" role on land. Daily existence was softened by comforts unavailable to most ground troops. Yet in the Pacific, every seaman was prey to the unyielding heat. Temperatures above a hundred degrees were routinely recorded belowdecks. Ventilation was relatively crude and always inadequate. Senior ratings competed for prized bunk space near an air outlet. In rough weather, conditions grew much worse, for the blowers could not run. Heat rash was almost universal.

Many men slept on deck, so that warships at night were strewn with slumbering forms on gun positions and galleries, beneath the boats and in hammocks slung between rails on every corner of the superstructure. Prostrate figures crowded under the folded wings of aircraft on carrier flight decks. Lifejackets served as pillows. Locked into the unchanging routine of four hours on, eight hours off, overlaid with dawn and dusk calls to "general quarters," men learned to sleep in the most unpromising circumstances. James Fahey, a New Englander who served on the cruiser *Montpelier*, seldom occupied his bunk, instead lying down on the steel deck with his shoes for a pillow. If it rained, "you stand back under cover and hope it does not last very long." Some sought space as far as possible from explosives or fuel, but on a warship almost any refuge was illusory.

Naval forces often kept station in a given area for days on end, steaming circular courses rather than dropping anchor. Machinery was never silent, never still. There were always watches to be kept and duties to be filled; echoing broadcast announcements; hurrying feet on ladders; eyes and ears watching and listening at dials, screens, headphones. Everybody was tired almost all the time, yet so effective had this navy become that "there weren't many fuck-ups," in the words of a young reservist. "It was an exhausting life that discouraged reflection, introspection, or anything more intellectual than reading." A destroyer officer observed pityingly that two of his comrades, junior-grade lieutenants, were geriatrics of twenty-seven, "too old for the duty they had . . . The hours were too long and the physical demands too great. That's when I learned that war is for kids." Louis Irwin, a beer salesman's son from Tennessee, had joined the navy at seventeen in 1942, "for lack of anything better to do. I wanted a bunk to sleep in and not a foxhole." Irwin found himself most apprehensive not in combat, but on refuelling duty in heavy seas, facing the peril of being washed overboard.

During bombardment missions in the island battles, the big ships' guns fired hour upon hour, day after day, as long as forward observers pointed targets and ammunition held out. A novice sailor on the battleship *Pennsylvania* fell asleep under one of its vast gun turrets, then remained oblivious through general quarters and a piped warning that the main batteries were about to fire. Concussion almost killed him. A shipmate recorded: "Everyone had a new respect for the fourteen-inch guns after that." All 45,000 tons of a battleship shook when its main armament fired. Recoil thrust the vessel aside. Far below in the engine spaces, "it felt like being taken apart in the boiler rooms of hell. You could see motor mounts jump and steam lines move." Consequences became even more dramatic aboard smaller ships. Repeated concussions from the destroyer *Howorth*'s five-inch guns caused all the urinals in the heads to break free from their bulkheads.

Off-duty, in quiet times there might be a movie show, but mostly there was nothing to do save sleep and play cards. Machinist's Mate Emory Jernigan saw $20,000 on the table in a messroom poker game. Men played high, because they had nothing else to spend money on. Jernigan reckoned that 20 percent of the ship's gamblers ended up with 80 percent of the players' money. Ben Bradlee's commanding officer learned that the torpedo officer on their destroyer owed him $4,000 in card money. The captain ordered Bradlee to play his debtor double or quits until he lost.

Whereas ashore a combat officer's life was little better than that of an enlisted man, afloat those with commissions were privileged. Few ordinary sailors enjoyed war service, but some officers like Bradlee did, especially if they were fortunate enough to be able to use their brains, serving in small ships, less vulnerable to "brass and bullshit" than battleships and carriers. "I had such a wonderful time in the war," wrote Bradlee later. "I just plain loved it. Loved the excitement, even loved being a little bit scared. Loved the sense of achievement, even if it was only getting from Point A to Point B, loved the camaraderie . . . I found that I liked making decisions."

Emory Jernigan, by contrast, with none of the privileges of rank, wrote that "time and distance, plus loneliness, make a tasteless soup, hard to stomach for long periods of time, and ours was a long, long time." James Fahey wrote in his diary: "You want to be free again and do what you want to do and go where you want to go, without someone always ordering you around." It was a sore point in the navy that officers received a disproportionate share of medals—they accounted for less than 10 percent of personnel, but received almost two-thirds of all decorations. They were the ones in the spotlight if a ship was deemed to have done something good, while their men remained "bit players." On the destroyer *Schroeder*, for instance, Seaman Robert Schwartz dived into heavy seas one day to save a comrade who had fallen overboard—and received no recognition. Emory Jernigan hated seeing fried eggs being carried to the officers' quarters, while he and his messmates breakfasted off the powdered variety, always watery, together with powdered lemonade: "It was a constant, nagging reminder that we were first-class citizens caught in a third-class situation." One of the ship's black mess stewards revenged himself on a bullying captain by spitting or urinating in the wardroom coffee before serving it.

Some men, however, found the experience of naval service deeply rewarding. Carlos Oliveira was the immigrant son of Portuguese parents. He had never been to school and spoke no English. In 1941 the navy rejected him as a volunteer, but in the panic after Pearl Harbor he was enlisted direct into the fire room of the battleship *Wisconsin* and served three years before being released to attend boot camp. It was there that a young officer, a southerner named Betts, made a remark that impressed him: "Carlos, a lack of formal education is not an impediment if a man can read and will read. Books can take you anywhere you want to go." Oliveira said later that the war turned people like himself into real Americans.

Through his years at sea Emory Jernigan, a twenty-one-year-old farm-boy from a desperately poor home in Florida, missed more than anything the chance of a walk in the woods. He ate better as a sailor than as a child, but missed grits. At his battle station in a destroyer's forward engine room, as Jernigan and his comrades heard the concussions of battle over-head, they never forgot that if steam lines fractured, they would cook in seconds. At high speed, propeller shafts shrieked in protest, "a warping sound as if they wanted to leave the mounts. The rudders and hydraulic lines would moan in their labors, and underwater explosions would hit the hull just outside." After months of combat, nerves became frayed to the limits, "so that when a big pipe wrench fell very noisily on a grating behind me, it scared me half to death." They emerged after hours of such ordeals covered in stinking salt sweat. One of Jernigan's comrades, after experience of action below, jammed into an ammunition-handling room, successfully begged a station topside.

Some men found small-ship life intolerably uncomfortable and sought transfers, especially after experience of typhoons—three U.S. destroyers foundered with heavy loss of life in the great Pacific blow of December 1944. Conversely, however, life aboard escorts and submarines possessed an intimacy impossible to achieve on a big ship with a crew of up to 3,000, where no one man ever visited every compartment. "Each ship is like a city, large or small," wrote Emory Jernigan. "Even a tugboat is a little town all of its own." Personal relationships fluctuated dramatically among men living month upon month in enforced proximity: "You'd be playing checkers with a friend one day, and the next you couldn't stand him."

The quality and quantity of seamen's rations seemed to army personnel infinitely enviable. The official *Navy Cookbook* of the period included such gems as: "The following words . . . are defined for the benefit of those who may not be familiar with some of the terms used in cooking: CANAPE (KA-NA-PA) a slice of bread fried in butter, on which anchovies or mush-rooms are served. CAVIAR (KAV-I-AR) prepared or salted roe of the sturgeon or other large fish, used as a relish." Everything in big ships' galleys was on a heroic scale. The recipe for canned codfish cakes began: "Take 40 pounds of potatoes and 15 pounds of codfish . . ." And for beef chop suey: "30 pounds of beef, 30 pounds of cabbage, one pint Worcestershire sauce . . ."

A sample menu in the 1945 *Navy Cookbook* ran: "Breakfast—grapefruit juice, cornflakes, grilled sausages, french toast, maple syrup, butter, milk, coffee. Lunch: cream of vegetable soup, roast beef, brown gravy, buttered potatoes, harvard beets, carrot and celery salad, ice cream, rolls, butter, coffee. Supper: lamb fricassee, mashed potatoes, tossed green salad, french dressing, coconut jelly doughnuts, bread, butter, tea." "Tin can" sailors in destroyers never fed in such a fashion, but larger vessels offered astonishing fare save in combat, heavy weather or when operations delayed rendezvous with "reefers"—refrigerated ships. Messdeck menus then became reduced to Spam and beans.

Almost every human and mechanical need had to be met by shipment across thousands of miles of ocean. The south-west Pacific was known as the "goat and cabbage circuit," because so much unwelcome food came from Australia. The scale of logistics was staggering. In the five months from 1 September 1944, for instance, fleet tankers delivered to the fast carrier force 8.25 million barrels of fuel oil, 12.25 million gallons of aviation gas. In addition, they shifted thousands of drums of lubricating oil in fourteen grades, compressed gases, oxygen, spare belly tanks, mail, personnel and food. Fresh water was a constant issue. The heat caused tanks to become contaminated with bacteria, which necessitated draining them for cleaning. So desperate were some seamen for a serious drink that they built stills or drained alcohol from torpedo propulsion systems. The latter practice may have raised morale, but drastically shortened the torpedoes' range.

The mood of every ship was different, and strongly influenced by the personality of its captain. Some were admired, ever thoughtful for the welfare of their men. Others were not. The captain of *Franklin* once bawled out his stewards over the carrier's broadcast system: "You black messmen are the sloppiest bunch of mess attendants I have ever seen." A disgusted crewman said: "He . . . sounded just like a Georgia redneck—in front of 3,000 men. It was not right." Another carrier captain was described as "one of the most irascible and unstable officers ever to earn a fourth stripe, but a man with a slide-rule brain." Yet another was judged by a fellow officer "emotionally unstable, evil-tempered . . . He drank too much too often; had a capacity for insulting behavior, especially when drunk." A destroyer officer's diary recorded dismay about his skipper: "The old man is getting nastier all the time. There is something wrong with that guy mentally. The poor, pitiable old fool told us last night that none of us were any good and that professionally we stink." Doctrinal procedures standardised throughout the fleet did something, but not enough, to iron out unhappinesses created by mad or bad captains. Big ships were invariably commanded by regular officers. To run a cruiser or carrier, it was thought essential to possess at least six years' sea time. Many smaller vessels, however, were committed to the hands of reservists.

Ben Bradlee suggests that some reserve officers, civilians in uniform, performed better than their career counterparts: "We hadn't spent years learning all the stuff about how things worked, we simply knew what they did." One of Bradlee's own captains, a professional navy man, was notoriously inept at mooring ship, often causing lines to snap. Once he turned in disgust to a reservist lieutenant on the bridge and said: "Goddamn it, I can't stop this son-of-a-bitch. You do it." Because amateur sailors knew so little, navy manuals detailed the minutest aspects of each man's duties. The November 1944 *Organization and Regulations for U.S. Pacific Fleet* decreed, for instance: "Messmen shall keep themselves meticulously clean . . . cooks, bakers and butchers on duty shall wear the 'chef's cap.' Naked personnel will not be permitted in galleys or messing spaces . . . The use of profane and obscene language is prohibited."

Morale was much influenced by the frequency of letters from home. Cheers and whistles rang through a ship when mail call was piped. Emory Jernigan was ashamed to be summoned by his captain and rebuked for failing to write to his mother, who had complained. Rumour, scuttlebutt, was the breath of life: the Japs were ready to quit; the ship was headed for refit; the next target was Okinawa, or Leyte, or Peleliu. Good commanding officers broadcast frequently, telling their crews everything they knew about what the ship and the fleet were doing. This was especially important in action, to hundreds of men imprisoned in steel compartments far belowdecks. For their very sanity, they needed to know what a huge, unseen detonation meant; whether their team seemed to be winning; sometimes, whether damage to their own ship was as grievous as concussions, screams, smoke pulsing through ventilators made it seem.

By late 1944, even the biggest ships were overcrowded: with gunners for additional batteries of anti-aircraft guns crammed onto upper decks; up to 10 percent surplus personnel to compensate for those who habitually "missed ship" on sailing for the combat zone; and staff officers. Experts on one new specialisation or another—flak or human torpedoes or mine counter-measures—were shoehorned into messdecks, to the chagrin of those who had to make space. Commodore Arleigh Burke observed wryly that visitors left an aircraft carrier with an impression that "the most important thing was the battle for food and living room." Nor was overcrowding confined to men. Far more technology was now available than ships could readily carry. "Top hamper," excess weight on superstructures, threatened stability. A staff officer said ruefully: "Every time we bring out something new they [ships' captains] will not give up what they have on board, they want the new item also. We have got to saturation point now, so you can't put the stuff on."

Men yearned for a chance to stretch legs ashore, but this meant only a glimpse of some thankless strip of coral and palms. On Mongong Atoll, for instance—"Mog Mog Island," as sailors knew it—the genial Commodore "Scrappy" Kessing, an elderly officer who had escaped from hospital to join the war, provided R-and-R facilities which were once utilised by 20,000 sailors in a single day. In March 1945, before Okinawa, 617 ships were anchored there. James Hutchinson of the battleship *Colorado* joined his ship's boxing team simply for the excuse to get ashore on Ulithi to train. Ulithi, repair base for the fleets, was a miracle of logistics organisation, but offered few joys to tired sailors. Enlisted men queued for hours for places in a boat to the shore, where they might be allocated four cans of beer apiece. Their commissioned counterparts forced a passage into the most overcrowded officers' club in the western Pacific for a spasm of noisy drinking before recall to their ships.

Manus was reckoned to have much better facilities, but crews saw the island only when bombs and ammunition needed replenishment. Even this requirement was often fulfilled at sea. Sanctimonious post-war tributes were paid to the partnership between warships and civilian-crewed supply ships. In truth, however, the latter were often slothful and ill-disciplined, flaunting their higher pay in the faces of navy men. A cruiser captain off Leyte was disgusted to hear a supply ship crewman cry contemptuously across the water to his men: "Suckers! Suckers! I get twenty bucks a day, whadda youse guys get?"

Aboard a carrier, flight operations and aircraft maintenance demanded almost incessant activity. On other ships, however, weeks or months of monotony were only occasionally interrupted. There was seldom a sight of the enemy, only of the deadly projectiles which he launched. Lt. Ben Bradlee saw two Japanese in the whole war. Once he glimpsed a pilot whose frozen features were visible before he crashed into the sea a few yards off the ship's bow. The second time, from Bradlee's destroyer off Corregidor a solitary figure was spotted swimming, wearing what appeared to be a torn nightgown. Bradlee was dispatched in a boat to pick him up, while a raucous chorus of sailors lined the rail, jeering, "Throw him back."

Naval war imposed abrupt, drastic transitions from routine to mortal terror and back again, which contrasted with an even tenor of discomfort and fear for infantrymen in combat ashore. At any hour of day or night, a ship might be electrified by a broadcast call. "Of all the announcements none packs quite the wallop of 'GENERAL QUARTERS . . . GENERAL QUARTERS . . . ALL HANDS MAN YOUR BATTLE STATIONS!' ' wrote an officer. "Though you may have heard it fifty times before, the fifty-first still has the freshness of the first." A carrier officer, Ensign Dick Saunders, said: "When the action does come, it happens so quickly you are never quite ready for it. It's all over within a matter of seconds and then you wait, wait, wait again for some more."

2. Flyboys

FOR ALL the majesty of the big ships, the thrill of racing destroyers and PT-boats dancing over the waves, by 1944 every sailor in the Pacific knew that the fleet's airborne firepower was what counted: Avenger torpedo bombers; Helldiver dive-bombers; Hellcat and Corsair fighters. The fast fleet carriers operated in task groups of four, accompanied by appropriate escorts. Concentrating "flattops" economised on standing fighter patrols—CAPs, which covered their operations against Japanese air attack. The big ships sought to operate in open seas, offering maximum scope for manoeuvre, minimum exposure to surprise. They were screened by destroyer radar pickets, posted many miles out to provide early warning. A few years earlier, carrier-borne aircraft had been thought a poor substitute for land-based air support. In 1944–45, it remained true that heavy bombers could not operate from flight decks, but so vast was the U.S. Navy's aerial armada that it could deliver a devastating punch against any target afloat or ashore. Each fleet carrier carried a mix of around fifty fighters, thirty dive-bombers, a dozen torpedo-bombers. The chief limitations on the ability of Nimitz's fleets to support land operations were weather and the admirals' yearning to pursue their own strategic purposes, unencumbered by responsibilities to soldiers or Marines.

The men of the air groups wore uniforms which implied that they belonged to the same service as seamen, but the "flyboys" of the "brown shoe navy" thought of themselves as a separate breed. Their lives were almost entirely divorced from those of their parent ships' crews. Until the last stage of the war, around one-third of carrier airmen could expect to die, in combat or one of the accidents inseparable from high-pressure flight operations. A catapult failure, careless landing, flak damage which injured hydraulics or undercarriage—all these things could, and did, kill a crew or two most days—10 percent aircraft losses a month were factored into the planning of carrier operations.

Airmen were roused from their bunks two hours before take-off, to dress and eat—they were usually briefed for a dawn sortie the previous night. They received the order "Pilots, man your planes!" through bullhorns and the broadcast system, then ran through the hatches along catwalks to the flight deck, to be strapped into their seats by plane captains waiting on the wings. If it was dark or twilight, deck crews with illuminated batons pointed the way to the port side, where catapult rings and rigs were attached to the heavier torpedo-bombers—fighters usually took off unassisted—while pilots ran through their checklists. Then, on signal, at intervals of a few seconds, one by one they gunned their engines and were hurled forward into the air. Men took off from relative calm and comfort, flew into the heat of combat, experienced thrills and fears such as few seamen knew, then bounced back onto a heaving deck, to be violently checked by an arrester hook. They pulled themselves stiffly out of their cockpits after anything up to seven hours sitting on an unfriendly dinghy pack, went below for debriefing—and probably a shot of bourbon. Aircrew were the despair of many regular navy officers. Most cared nothing for the honour and traditions of the service, nor for ship's discipline. They reckoned that if they flew and fought, nothing else was anybody's business.

The rest of the U.S. Navy might be dry, but few air groups were. On the carrier *Makassar Strait*, for instance, commanding officer Herbert Riley—one of just two regulars aboard, a former naval aide to Franklin Roosevelt—wrote: "There was medicinal liquor aboard all the carriers to be used under supervision of flight surgeons. Their supply was generous . . . Liquor had its uses, believe me." After one of his air group's first missions, he found flight surgeons "dispensing liquor in water glasses . . . the pilots were high as kites."

Thereafter, Riley introduced rules. He ordered the vacant admiral's cabin to be converted into an aircrew club, complete with *Esquire* pin-ups and cocktail tables. Inside, any aviator was eligible for two drinks a night, provided he was not scheduled to fly. Cmdr. Bill Widhelm, operations officer of Task Force 58, complained bitterly about discrimination between officers and men in the allocation of alcohol: "There are men out there on those ships that haven't had a foot on shore for a year. I don't see why we can't do like the British, give those enlisted men a grog. Pilots get it. I had it. But those enlisted men never get it."

Cmdr. Jim Lamade of *Hancock* sought discretion to fine aviators for misdemeanours, because traditional navy punishments held no meaning for them: "These young pilots . . . are not naval officers as we know a naval officer. They're just flying because it's their job . . . Discipline . . . means nothing to them. If you say, 'We'll ground this pilot,' well . . . they don't want to go to combat anyhow, so they'd just as soon be grounded . . . they will lay around the bunk room all day and read . . . But if you take some money away from them, they will feel that."

Likewise Cmdr. Jim Mini of *Essex*: "The boys in a squadron these days don't have the navy as a career. There's a problem of leadership; you have to have the boys like you. You can't lean on being a commander and saying, 'You'll do this or else.' You have to present it to the boys in an attractive fashion . . . I can safely say that if [the tour] had been much longer, we would have had trouble, and the boys would have broken down more than they did." A high proportion of aviators caused disciplinary problems, declared a navy report: "The very exacting nature of flight duties has combined with the youth and frequent irresponsibility of flying officers to create difficulties which a special board was created to police." Fliers' letters home displayed carelessness about security; they broke the rules by keeping diaries; and "drink is often an issue."

Flying combat planes from carriers was one of the most thrilling, yet also most stressful, assignments of the war. Ted Winters remarked of some of their long, long sorties: "It isn't a question of how much gasoline, it's how long you can keep your fanny on that seat." It was an inherently hazardous activity to operate a plane from a cramped and perpetually shifting ocean platform, even before the enemy became involved. "We learned to listen for the slightest change in the sound of the engine which might reveal a loss of power," wrote a pilot. "We always welcomed a moderate wind which increased the air flow over the fightdeck. Five to ten knots made the difference between a comfortable take-off and 'sweating it out.' "

Beyond combat casualties, the log of a Marine Corsair squadron on *Essex* showed that during a typical fortnight, one plane "splashed" taking off on each of two successive days; on the second of these, another plane crashed on landing. Three days later, one Corsair was lost at sea. Thereafter, three more went into the sea at two-day intervals. Hard deck landings damaged airframes. Sherwin Goodman, an Avenger gunner, suffered a typical mishap one morning when the flight deck hydraulic catapult failed in mid-launch. His plane slumped into the sea. Seconds later, the huge ship passed close enough to strike the sinking Avenger a glancing blow. A destroyer retrieved the crew intact, however, collecting the usual six gallons of ice-cream ransom for returning them to their carrier, and to operations.

"Oh I'd rather be a bellhop than a flyer on a flattop," the pilots sang, "with my hand around a bottle not around the goddamn throttle." Unpredicted violent weather could write off whole squadrons of aircraft, because it made navigation problematic. Error meant a descent into the sea when gas ran out. As on shore, almost every aviator wanted to be a "fighter jock," with the thrill of engaging enemy aircraft in the war's best carrier fighter, the Grumman Hellcat. It is intoxicating to go into battle knowing that your own side possesses much better trained, and thus more proficient, pilots than the enemy. By late 1944, the average Japanese flier had just forty flying hours' experience before entering combat. His American counterpart had at least 525 hours, and it showed. In the last phase of the war, U.S. carrier fighters were inflicting amazingly disproportionate losses on their failing foes. Commander Winters: "Most of our kills were from the rear end. [The Japanese] are scared to death of the Grummans. Only when they outnumber you terrifically will they even stay near you. They will make passes, but stay far away and scram when you turn on them." Such cautious enemy behaviour seemed a long march from the kamikaze spirit, of which so much would be heard in 1945.

Flying became more hazardous, however, when planes were committed to ground strafing or ship attacks. Low-level dive-bomber and torpedo-carrier missions remained gruelling to the end. Lamade of *Hancock* was shocked by the intensity of the Japanese barrage as he and his men dive-bombed targets around Hong Kong. With unusual sophistication, enemy anti-aircraft gunners followed the American planes down almost to ground level, from 15,000 feet to 8,000, then 3,000. "From pull-out, I looked back and saw five planes of my group going down in flames. We're going to have to figure out some way to combat that AA," Lamade told navy debriefers. "After that attack, Admiral McCain said he was very sorry we had lost so many pilots. I told him we . . . can't go on fighting Japs continually without suffering some losses."

To beat flak, pilots learned to dive faster and more steeply than they had ever trained for. Cockpit glass fogged with the dramatic change of atmosphere as they pulled out of a descent and soared upwards after releasing bombs. As ever in combat, the men who survived were those who were determined but careful: "We had four or five pilots who were over-eager," Fred Bakutis of *Enterprise* told debriefers. "They were excellent boys, very energetic and hard to hold down. It is these people who generally don't come back, because they are so anxious to do damage to the Japs that they take risks beyond reason." Yet there were also shy pilots, content to release their bombs and swing away towards safety with a carelessness of aim that exasperated their commanders. And because these were very young, sometimes wild young men, they were sometimes reckless in the use of their lethal weapons. Senior officers were irked by the frequency with which American planes misidentified as Japanese were shot down by "friendly fire" from combat air patrols. A pair of bored pilots unable to identify an enemy target might work off their frustration on a Filipino fishing boat or lumbering cart ashore.

The job nobody wanted was night operations. Take-offs and landings in darkness were more hazardous, the monotony of patrols usually unrelieved by action. If a pilot made a poor deck approach in daylight, he was "waved off" to try again, but in darkness he had to land and take the consequences, rather than hazard the ship by having it switch its landing lights on again. "What the boys want to do," said a night-fighter squadron commander, Turner Caldwell of *Independence*, "is to get into a day fighter squadron or a day torpedo squadron and get to be aces and sink Jap carriers and that sort of thing. And so we have to give them inducements of various kinds because they are kids and they don't understand enough about the military life to know that this stuff has to be done. All they know is that they don't want to do it."

While the carrier crews might remain at sea for years on end, the men of the air groups knew that they were only passing visitors. If injury or death spared them, they were rotated ashore after six months' duty. After two combat tours, asserted a navy report, pilots "lose their daring . . . feel they have done their parts and other pilots who have not fought should take over the burden." One pool of replacement pilots was held ashore on Guam. A second group waited on fleet supply ships, condemned to weeks of crucifying boredom before being abruptly informed one morning that their turn had come, and transshipped by breeches buoy to join an air group. Some replacements idled at sea for months before reaching a carrier. "Upon arrival," complained a squadron CO, "they were practically worthless, because they had forgotten everything they had been taught." It was tough for a man to be pitchforked among strangers, beside whom within hours he was expected to fly and die. "All of a sudden," said Jim Lamade of *Hancock*, "they're expected to go ahead and hit the ball right smack on with a combat fighting squadron . . . those boys get discouraged and you can't blame them." Some such men reported sick. Flight surgeons felt obliged to be harsh. "Combat fatigue is a word we use continuously," said Lamade, "and nobody knows what it means. It covers a multitude of sins. I think it ought to be thrown out of our language."

Squadron commanders found that the strain of leading their men in combat left them little patience or energy for routine duties back on the ship. They complained about bureaucracy and paperwork. A CO was exasperated to find that after some of his men hit the airfield of neutral Portuguese Macao by mistake, a court of inquiry was convened. Planes, by contrast, were casually expendable. Salt corroded paintwork, yet the remedy was always in short supply, because nobody cared to store large quantities of notoriously flammable paint aboard a carrier. If an airframe was badly damaged, or a plane completed eight months' service, it was most often tipped overboard. With American factories producing new aircraft by the thousand, a worn one seemed worth little.

There were accidents, always accidents. When tired young men were pushing themselves and their equipment to the limits, mistakes were inevitable. The guns of aircraft parked on flight decks were triggered, injuring neighbouring planes and people. Badly battle-damaged planes were discouraged from landing on their carriers, to avoid messing up flight decks. Ditching in the sea was an almost routine occupational hazard. Destroyers shadowed carriers during flight operations, to retrieve waterlogged fliers. As long as pilots were lucky, and ensured that their cockpit hoods were locked open to avoid plunging to the bottom with their planes, they could expect to survive an ocean landing. Ninety-nine men in Jim Lamade's air group endured the experience, most with an insouciance conceivable only at such a time and place.

Fred Bakutis of *Enterprise* spent a week on a raft in the Sulu Sea after coming down in the Surigao Strait. Comrades dropped him a two-man life raft. "That plus my own one-man raft made my seven-day tour of duty out there pretty pleasant," he told his debriefers with studied nonchalance. "The weather was pretty good except at night when it rained pretty hard. I had lots of water, using my one-man raft as a water wagon. My food consisted of minnows, seaweed, candy rations. My main problem in the raft was to stay comfortable. The hands became very sore—and also my rear end." On Bakutis's seventh night adrift, he was wakened from a doze by the sound of diesels, and for a few heart-stopping moments feared that a Japanese vessel was approaching. Instead, however, to his infinite relief an American submarine loomed out of the darkness.

The submarine rescue service, often operating close inshore amid treacherous shoals or under Japanese fire, received the gratitude of every American flier. Together with "dumbo" amphibians and patrolling destroyers, the submarines achieved miracles in saving hundreds of precious aircrew from sea, sharks and the enemy. Cmdr. Ernie Snowden of *Lexington*'s Air Group 16 paid warm tribute to the submariners: "If they had wheels I think they would climb right up over the beach and pick us up. We have nothing but praise for them." On 10 October 1944, for instance, twenty-one aircraft were shot down attacking the Ryukyu Islands. Yet only eleven pilots and crewmen were lost, the remainder being rescued, six of them off Okinawa by a single submarine, *Sterlet*. When Lt. Robert Nelson crashed in Kagoshima Bay off Kyushu, his dinghy began to drift inshore. A tiny cruiser-based Kingfisher seaplane landed alongside him, and Nelson clung to its float while it taxied several miles across the water to rendezvous with a submarine—adding a torpedo-bomber crew to its burden on the way.

During an air battle off Iwo Jima, Japanese Zero pilot Kunio Iwashita was astonished when the surface of the sea was suddenly broken by a long black shape, as an American submarine surfaced to pick up a ditched pilot. An American flying boat, apparently bent on the same mission, was shot down by Japanese fighters. Iwashita said: "We were amazed to see the Americans taking so much trouble about their people. Nobody provided that sort of service for us." An extreme example of "force protection" was displayed on 16 September 1944, when Ensign Harold Thompson ditched three hundred yards off Waisile, while strafing Japanese barges in his Hellcat. A Catalina dropped a life raft which Thompson boarded, only to find himself drifting relentlessly towards a pier. Two other Hellcats were shot down trying to protect him by strafing the shoreline—one pilot was killed, the second rescued by a "dumbo." Thompson moored his raft to a chain of Japanese barges, and two American PT-boats raced in to rescue him. Their first attempt was frustrated by coastal gunfire, but after Avengers dropped smoke floats to mask their approach, a boat snatched Thompson just as the Japanese closed in on him. More than fifty aircraft were involved in the rescue, "which sure was a wonderful show to watch," said Thompson, back on his carrier *Santee*.

Destroyers traditionally extracted "ransom" for every flier they sent back. "Rescued pilots were prized possessions," wrote a destroyer officer. "Before returning them, we would strip them of all their fancy clothes—silk scarf maps, survival kits with great knives, compasses and magnifying glasses, and their pistol. Then we would ask the carrier to send over all the geedunk—ice cream—they had, plus a minimum of two movies our crew hadn't seen."

At sea in the Pacific, by the fall of 1944 the might of the U.S. Navy was unchallengeable. That is to say, no rational adversary would have precipitated a headlong confrontation with such forces as Nimitz now deployed. The summer clashes, the "Great Marianas Turkey Shoot," had fatally crippled Japanese air power. Only the Japanese navy, in the mood of fatalism and desperation which afflicted its upper ranks, could still have sought a "decisive encounter" against such odds. The struggle for the Philippines was to provide the setting not only for America's major land campaign of the Pacific war, but also for the largest sea battle the world would ever know.

CHAPTER FIVE

America's Return to the Philippines

1. Peleliu

MacArthur left Hawaii on 27 July 1944 confident that he had secured endorsement of his commitment to retake the Philippines. Nonetheless, when the American and British chiefs of staff met at Quebec on 11 September to open the Octagon strategic conference, plans were still on the table not only for landings in November on Mindanao, thereafter on Leyte and Luzon, but alternatively for seizing Formosa and the port of Amoy on the Chinese mainland. In the days that followed, however, the assembled U.S. leaders—for the British were not consulted about this exclusively American issue—found themselves confronted by new circumstances. During planning for Third Fleet's autumn operations, Halsey and his staff had agreed that in future, instead of merely addressing predetermined objectives, they would search for opportunities. In pursuit of this policy the fast carriers were now roaming the western Pacific, launching massive assaults on Japan's surviving air forces. Off the southern Philippines on 12 September, 2,400 American sorties accounted for some two hundred Japanese aircraft in the sky and on the ground.

At noon on the thirteenth the admiral signalled a report to Nimitz, who speedily forwarded it to Quebec, that Japanese resistance was feeble. Halsey, unaware that the enemy was deliberately husbanding resources for a "decisive battle" on the Philippines, urged fast-forwarding the strategic programme. He proposed cancelling all preliminary island landings, and staging a speedy assault on Leyte. This was Halsey's most influential intervention of the war. Such a change of plans was complex, but perfectly feasible in a theatre where every man and ton of supplies earmarked for shipment to one objective could be redirected to beaches elsewhere, by a nation which now possessed mastery of the ocean and the sky above.

MacArthur was at sea and observing wireless silence, but his staff immediately accepted Halsey's proposal as a means of foreclosing the Formosa-Philippines debate. The general, once back in communication, hastened to add his endorsement. He said nothing of his intelligence staff's well-justified belief that the Japanese defenders of Leyte were stronger than Halsey recognised. Much more serious, he made no mention of his engineers' opinion that it would be hard to build good airfields on the island, and almost impossible in the imminent monsoon months. Over the thirty months since he himself had escaped from Bataan, MacArthur's personal interrogations of every American who escaped from the Philippines "revealed the concern of a man whose yearning to get back to his beloved 'second homeland' had become virtually an obsession," in the words of a biographer. The general had no intention of advertising any impediment to its fulfilment.

In Quebec, after hasty consultation the American chiefs of staff set a target date of 20 October for a landing on Leyte. Admiral King's persistent arguments against following this with a move to Luzon, the main Philippine island, were overruled. The navy withdrew its support for attacking Formosa when it became plain that a landing there was logistically impossible before March 1945, and would require much larger ground forces than were available. The Philippines, by contrast, were immediately accessible. Planning for Leyte began at MacArthur's new headquarters on the banks of Lake Sentani, in the Cyclops Mountains above Hollandia, New Guinea. Once the decision was made to retake the Philippines, there was neither logic in nor resources for an early assault on Formosa. Since the seizure of Formosa was essential to any landing on the China coast that too was now ruled out. As the U.S. Navy's great historian Samuel Eliot Morison wrote, "The two rival roads were . . . converging on Leyte." All intervening operations were cancelled, save two. First, on 15 September almost 20,000 men landed on the island of Morotai, southeast of the Philippines, and secured its airfield against negligible opposition. By late October, Morotai was crowded with U.S. aircraft waiting to rebase on Leyte. Second, Nimitz and MacArthur shared a conviction that it was important to seize the tiny Palau Islands, of which Peleliu was the key, and to secure their airfields, before assaulting Leyte.

The Palau invasion convoys were already several days at sea, carrying Maj.-Gen. William Rupertus's 1st Marine Division 2,100 miles from Guadalcanal. The lumbering landing ships averaged a speed of only 7.7 knots, even slower than the 12.1 knots of the transports. Brig.-Gen. O. P. Smith, assistant commander of the division, passed the voyage reading a couple of novels from his ship's library: *A Yankee from Mount Olympus* and *The Late George Apley*. Tranquillity aboard was marred by the skipper's insistence on issuing orders and admonishments by loudhailer from the bridge. Smith failed to make friends with the ship's dog, "an aloof cocker spaniel who refused to notice anyone except the captain." Approaching the Palaus, even veterans of Pacific landings were awed by the size of the force assembled—some 868 ships, 129 in the assault element. Submarine chasers guided the fleet, destroyers guarded it, sweepers cleared mines in its path. Behind these came a great flock of command, survey, repair and hospital ships, anti-submarine net-layers, oilers, salvage vessels, tugs, floating dry docks, a dredger, PT-boats, a floating derrick, LSTs, DUKWs, LSDs, cargo ships and 770 small landing craft for 1st Marine Division, together with as many again for the army's 81st Division, joining the Marines from Pearl Harbor. Such was the scale on which the United States launched even a modest Pacific amphibious landing in the autumn of 1944.

On the morning of 15 September, amid a calm sea, a glittering array of brass watched from the command ship *Mount McKinley* as shoals of landing craft headed for the shore. Peleliu had received three days of intensive gunfire from five battleships, five heavy cruisers and seventeen other vessels, which periodically ceased fire only to make space for air attacks. Vice-Admiral Jesse Oldendorf, the bombardment commander, declared: "We have run out of targets." Nine miles offshore the cocky naval skipper of Col. "Chesty" Puller's transport enquired, as Puller's men clambered into their landing craft, whether the Marine would be returning on board for his dinner. The colonel responded testily that he expected to be fighting for several days. Surely not, said the sailor. The navy's bombardment would "allow the regiment to walk to its objective unmolested." If that proved so, said Puller, the captain should come ashore that afternoon, join the Marines for a meal, and collect some souvenirs. Rupertus, the operational commander, had no experience of a heavily opposed landing, and was himself blithely confident. Four days, he said, should suffice to clear the island. As the Americans approached Peleliu, smoke from the bombardment shrouded the higher ground inland. Rocket ships fired ripples of projectiles ahead of the infantry pitching in their landing craft, then turned aside to open the passage for the assault waves. AA guns on the ships fired airburst shells at rocks behind the landing places. "Chesty" Puller told his men with characteristic theatricality: "You will take no prisoners, you will kill every yellow son-of-a-bitch, and that's it."

The Marines hit the beaches at 0832. There were no Japanese in their immediate vicinity. Within minutes, however, the invaders found themselves under heavy shellfire, which wrecked dozens of amphibious vehicles, and made the men reluctant to forsake cover and advance beyond the beach. Medical corpsman Bill Jenkins's unit suffered its first casualty seconds after disembarking. It was "Pop" Lujack, the oldest man in the company, "a guy I thought a lot of, and it hurt me badly when I saw he was hit. I didn't know any better but he was hit in the head and practically the whole back of his head was shot off, and I was laying down there trying to fix him up. One of the guys came up and said, 'Doc, get out of there, he's dead.' "

More than 10,000 Japanese were defending the island. Rather than attempt to hold the coast under American bombardment, Col. Kunio Nakagawa had deployed his men inland, on a series of coral ridges which offered commanding views of the shore. The beach at Peleliu, flailed by enemy fire, became one of the Marines' most shocking memories of the Pacific war, and cost them over two hundred dead on the first day. Though the beach had been reconnoitred, Rupertus and his staff knew nothing of the terrain inland, which was ideally suited to defence. Peleliu had been a mining site. Each ridge was honeycombed with tunnels, in which the Japanese had installed electricity and living quarters, impervious to shells and bombs. Marine communications proved so poor that commanders were left struggling to discover their own men's whereabouts, and were thus hesitant about calling in close artillery support. Of the eighteen tanks landed with 1st Marines, three were knocked out before they reached the beach, and all but one were hit by shells thereafter. In the chaos, a senior officer landed to investigate why so many vehicles were blazing. He could discover little. Most of 1st Marines' headquarters had been wiped out, and 5th Marines' HQ was also badly depleted. A shell blast concussed a Louisiana-born staff officer so badly that he began to murmur in the French of his childhood.

A Japanese counter-attack in the afternoon, supported by light tanks, was easily repulsed, the enemy shot to pieces. When feeble little Japanese "tankettes" surrounded an American medium tank, it destroyed eleven in a circle, "like Indians round a wagon train," as O. P. Smith put it. Here was a pattern which would become familiar in all the late Pacific battles: when the Japanese moved, they were slaughtered; when they held their ground, however, they were extraordinarily hard to kill. Smith was sitting at his forward command post when a mortar bomb landed just short of its protecting bank. A Marine fell back onto the general, a small fragment lodged in the back of his head. Smith's aide bandaged him: "The boy was not badly hurt and was talkative. He was married and had been out of the States for two years. To him, the wound was a ticket home." American guns were getting ashore only slowly, because so many amphibious vehicles had been destroyed. Snipers provoked wild retaliatory fusillades, as dangerous to Americans as to Japanese. When Smith wanted to visit regimental command posts, he could find them only by tracking phone wires.

Nightfall brought no respite. There were 12,000 Americans onshore, crowded into a beachhead which granted each man a few square feet of coral, sand and insects. The Marines held no clearly defined perimeter, merely scrapes and holes between four and seven hundred yards inland, along more than a mile of coast. Most of the men were utterly bemused, conscious only of incoming fire. Japanese infiltrators crept into American forward positions, grenading and testing nerves. A man who found himself under friendly fire even after shouting the password resorted to singing a verse of the Marine Corps hymn. Some 7th Marines landed amid the shambles, and found themselves unable to locate their objectives. After being harried from place to place, out of radio contact with higher command, under heavy mortaring their amphibious tractors returned to the assault ship *Leedstown*. Alongside in darkness, the navy refused to let the men board, supposing that they had run away. Their colonel was reluctantly permitted to climb the side alone, to radio divisional headquarters for new orders. Eventually his men were grudgingly authorised to re-embark, but many boats' occupants spent the whole night lost at sea.

It took 1st Marine Division a week and 3,946 casualties to secure the key airfield sites, mocking Rupertus's four-day estimate. Even then the Japanese overlooked them from the Umurbrogol Ridge, and could sustain observed fire. After the Japanese shot down medics recovering wounded, heavy mortars laid smokescreens to protect stretcher-bearers. The whole island occupied only seven square miles. In O. P. Smith's words, "For the first few days, real estate was at a premium." The beach area was crowded with makeshift bivouacs. There was little scope for outflanking enemy strongpoints. These could only be assaulted headlong, each yard of progress costing blood. "The thousands of rounds of artillery shells, the mortar barrages, the napalm strikes and the bombs poured in . . . [These] undoubtedly killed many Japanese in exposed positions, but those in caves were untouched and there were always new relays of snipers and machine-gunners to replace those who had fallen on the peaks . . . For the concentrated fury of the fighting it was only exceeded by Tarawa and Iwo Jima," wrote a senior Marine. Reinforced concrete blast walls protected each tunnel mouth. When the Americans finally secured the largest cave system on 27 September, it proved to have housed a thousand defenders.

No place on the island was safe. Bill Atkinson watched a BAR gunner take up position behind a tank and start firing. To Atkinson's horror, the Sherman suddenly lurched backwards, crushing the man to pulp. Fifth Marine Virgle Nelson, hit in the buttock, hollered with glee: "Oh my God, I guess I get to go back now!" Bill Jenkins, a medical corpsman from Canton, Missouri, was awed by a tough machine-gunner named Wayley, who was hit four times. Told that he was to be evacuated, Wayley said: "No way." Jenkins asked his buddy Jack Henry to get a litter. The moment Henry moved, machine-gun fire caught his arms, and he came running back into the tank trap where they lay. "One arm [was] 99.9 percent off and the other almost as bad. I could have taken a scissors and clipped both arms off and buried them. I wasn't trained to try and set the cut-up, broken-up arms . . . all I did was just kind of put them together, both of them, and I wrapped them up the best I could with T-shirts and used tourniquets. I put his arms over his head to keep him from bleeding to death." Against the odds, Henry survived.

Another man begged Jenkins for medicinal brandy. The corpsman said sheepishly: "Gosh, I had some, but I got so damn scared I drank it myself." Seventeen-year-old Tom Evans landed as a replacement rifleman, but was immediately detailed as a litter-bearer. "I am carrying this guy on the stretcher and he's been dead maybe a day and a half but already his body is kind of oily and covered with flies and maggots. I slipped and fell as I was going downhill and naturally he comes sliding down and straddled my neck, and I had maggots on me—Ohh." Marines learned to race clouds of accursed blowflies to every meal, sliding a hand across a can top the instant it was opened. Men's lips and ear tops blistered in the sun. Commanders dispatched from the ships offshore fresh bread—"a great morale-builder"—and occasionally ice cream in milk cans. "Chesty" Puller asked his Marines if there was anything he could get them. Predictably, they asked for a drink stronger than water. Puller issued medicinal alcohol mixed with powdered lemonade. Others found a cache of Japanese *sake* and beer, and were briefly heard singing on line.

"Our troops should understand," a command report admonished waverers, "that the Japanese is no better able to go without food than we are, his stamina is no greater, the Jap gets just as wet when it rains and he suffers as much or more from tropical ills." All this, however, was often hard for Americans on Peleliu to believe. Seventeen-year-old medic Frank Corry had three platoon commanders killed The last was hit when he rashly stuck up his head to view a Japanese position. Corry watched wide-eyed as his platoon sergeant, big, tough Bob Canfield, cradled the dead man's head in his arms and burst into tears, saying: "Why did you do it?"

Snipers behind the lines caused chronic jumpiness, intensified by undisciplined rear-area troops firing weapons for the fun of it. After O. P. Smith investigated one panic, he found that it had been provoked by black stevedores on the shore shooting at an abandoned tractor: "They claimed no one had ever told them they were not to fire their rifles, which was probably correct." Nor was every alarm unjustified. When the exasperated divisional HQ commandant set off with a shotgun to suppress an outbreak of apparently needless firing near his headquarters, he found two dead Marines beside the corpses of three Japanese who had killed them. Until a well could be sunk, every American was desperately short of water. Emergency supplies were landed in oil drums which sickened those who sampled them. Temperatures sometimes reached 115 degrees. Scores of men succumbed to heat exhaustion, for which salt tablets proved an essential prophylactic. The jagged coral caused boots to wear out within days. A thousand new pairs and 5,000 sets of socks were flown in from Guam.

The army's 81st Division landed on neighbouring Angaur on 17 September. After an easy disembarkation, inland the invaders met thick, matted, almost impenetrable rain forest. The beaches were clogged with traffic. The soldiers, fresh to combat, readily panicked in encounters with even small numbers of Japanese. Angaur was only two miles long, and by 20 September it was secure, but the conquerors had not enjoyed their experience. They were still less happy to find themselves loaded back onto ships and transferred to Peleliu. Marines and soldiers were seldom comfortable fighting together. O. P. Smith wrote sceptically: "It is hard to put your finger on it, but there is quite a different atmosphere in an army command post as compared to the CP of a Marine outfit. Orders are given like the book says you should give them, but you have the impression they are not carried out." Rupertus was reluctant to enlist army aid. After a week of fighting and alarming casualties, however, he perceived no choice.

Long-range flamethrowers proved the most effective weapons against Peleliu's cave mouths, but each assault was painfully slow and costly. In October, gales and torrential rain added to the invaders' miseries. Marine Corsairs at last began to use the island's airstrip on 21 October, but organised resistance persisted for weeks more. Lt. Ilo Scatena of the 2/5th Marines kept a platoon roster. Of forty-two men with whom he landed, fourteen were killed and fourteen wounded. In all, the island's capture cost 1,950 American lives, and gave the invaders one of the most unwelcome surprises of the Pacific war. Almost all the defenders chose to perish rather than quit. A month after Peleliu's commander, Col. Kunio Nakagawa, committed suicide on 24 November, his surviving soldiers killed a group of souvenir-hunting American soldiers. The last five known Japanese surrendered on 1 February 1945. Statisticians afterwards calculated that it had taken 1,500 rounds of artillery ammunition to kill each member of the garrison. To capture this tiny outpost, Marine and army infantrymen also used 13.32 million .30 calibre rounds, 1.52 million of .45 calibre, 693,657 rounds of .50 calibre, over 150,000 mortar bombs and 118,262 grenades.

As so often in the Pacific, a marginal objective inflicted worse than marginal casualties. It is widely agreed today—as indeed it was in the winter of 1944—that the decision to occupy the Palaus was one of Nimitz's few bad calls of the war. The Japanese lacked means to exploit their remote island airfields. The defenders of Peleliu could not interfere on Leyte, or anywhere else. Its garrison could have been left to rot. American aircraft could use Morotai's strips as easily as those on the Palaus. Once the Peleliu operation was launched onto implacably hostile terrain, there was no shortcut by which firepower or technology could overcome resistance. Although the Marines had fought terrible battles on the Pacific islands, at Tarawa and Saipan they attacked before the defenders had completed the construction of their positions. Now, however, as Japan's Pacific perimeter narrowed, the enemy knew where to expect the Americans, and had been granted ample time to prepare to receive them.

In the Pacific there were no great battles resembling Normandy, the Bulge, the Vistula and Oder crossings, exploiting mass and manoeuvre. Instead, there was a series of violently intense miniatures, rendered all the more vivid in the minds of participants because they were so concentrated in space. Such contests as that for Peleliu were decided by the endeavours of footsoldiers and direct support weapons, notably tanks. This was a battle fought on Japanese terms. Like others that would follow in the months ahead, it suited their temperament, skills and meagre resources. The defenders of Peleliu possessed no means of withdrawing, even had they wished to do so. Their extinction therefore required a commitment of flesh against flesh, the sacrifice of significant numbers of American lives. The U.S., whose power seemed so awesome when viewed across the canvas of global war, found itself unable effectively to leverage this in battles of bloody handkerchief proportions, such as that for Peleliu.

2. Leyte: The Landing

THE STRUGGLE to regain the Philippines became by far the U.S. Army's largest commitment of the Asian war. MacArthur's long campaign on New Guinea had never caught the imagination of the American public as did the Marines' battles for the Pacific atolls. The general's grandeur was more imposing than his forces—until late 1944 he seldom controlled more than four divisions in the field, in Europe a mere corps command. His next campaign, however, would become the main event of America's conflict with Japan. More than 400,000 Japanese awaited the invaders. The Philippines represented a critical link on the sea route between Hirohito's South-East Asian empire and the home islands. Tokyo believed that a confrontation there would offer its best chance to bloody the Americans, if not to throw them back into the sea, before the "decisive battle"—a chorus reprised in all Japan's war plans—for Kyushu and Honshu. The Japanese difficulty was that their scattered forces lacked mobility in the face of American air and naval superiority. MacArthur could choose where to make his landings. It would be hard for the defenders swiftly to shift large bodies of troops in response.

On a map, the Philippine islands resemble a dense scatter of jigsaw pieces. Their combined mass is almost as large as Japan, rich in luxuriant vegetation and extravagant weather cycles. After the 1898 Spanish-American War, which ended European hegemony, U.S. senator Albert Beveridge spoke for many Americans when Washington decided against granting independence to the Filipinos. He cited "the divine law of human society which makes of us our brother's keeper. God has been preparing the English-speaking and Teutonic peoples to bring order out of chaos . . . He has made us adepts in government so that we may administer government among savage and senile peoples."

Filipinos resisted U.S. dominance, in the early days by violent insurgency, and never ceased to crave independence. Socially, the islands were dominated by a rich landlord class. The mass of peasants remained poor and bitterly alienated from the plantocracy. Two-thirds of Filipinos between twenty and thirty-nine were uneducated. Yet many Americans retained a romantic conviction that the virtue of their intentions made U.S. rule over the Philippines somehow more honourable than that of, say, the British in India. U.S. soldiers who served on the islands before 1942 regarded them as a leisure resort offering cheap comforts, servants and amenities of a kind they never knew back home, amidst a lazy Spanish culture. The 1944 U.S. armed forces' *Guide to the Pacific* noted: "For Isaac Waltons: The Philippines are a fisherman's paradise . . . Recommended for deep sea trolling is a split bamboo rod, a drag reel capable of holding 400 yards of 12 thread line, and a good gaff hook."

Japan's thirty-month-old occupation had been patchy in its impact: oppressive and brutal in some places—the most strategically important naturally including the capital, Manila—while scarcely felt in remote areas. In 1943 the Japanese granted the Philippines, along with most of their other occupied territories, notional self-government under a local puppet regime. Yet such was the mindless cruelty of Tokyo's soldiers that this gesture inspired little gratitude among Filipinos. Imperial General HQ reported in March 1944: "Even after their independence, there remains among all classes a strong undercurrent of pro-American sentiment . . . Guerrilla activities are gradually increasing." The Japanese fully controlled only twelve of the country's eighteen provinces. Elsewhere, guerrilla bands roamed widely, American-armed and sometimes American-led. Several U.S. officers, such as the legendary Col. Russell Volckmann, had survived in the hills of Luzon since the spring of 1942, and now directed forces thousands strong. The more idealistically inclined guerrillas inflicted four hundred casualties on Japanese occupation forces in 1944, a modest enough achievement. Others merely pursued lives of banditry.

The Japanese South Asia Army moved its headquarters to Manila in

April, when uncertainty persisted in Tokyo about whether the Americans would land in the Philippines at all. Its commander, Field Marshal Count Hisaichi Terauchi, had no such doubts. "If I was MacArthur, I would come here," he growled at a staff conference in the summer of 1944. "He must know how weak are our defences." Terauchi, once a candidate to replace Tojo as prime minister, was not held in high esteem either by the Americans or by most of his peers. His staff, however, respected the fact that, although a rich man, he succumbed to few personal indulgences. "He could have filled his headquarters with geishas if he wanted," said one officer admiringly, "but he never did. He was a really clean-living soldier." Terauchi was exasperated by the need to refer every detail of his deployments to Tokyo. The general staff only gave final endorsement to his defensive plan for Leyte two days before the Americans landed there.

Until the autumn of 1944, Terauchi's principal subordinate was the Philippines' occupation commander, Lt.-Gen. Shigenori Kuroda, a mild-mannered little man devoted to women and golf. Kuroda said cheerfully: "Why bother about defence plans? The Philippines are obviously indefensible." Such remarks caused Tokyo to conclude that he was a trifle ill-suited to confront an American amphibious assault. Two weeks before MacArthur's invasion, Kuroda was supplanted by Gen. Tomoyuki Yamashita, who assumed command of 14th Army under Terauchi. The newcomer summoned his staff and addressed them at his headquarters in Manila: "The battle we are going to fight will be decisive for Japan's fate. Each of us bears a heavy responsibility for our part in it. We cannot win this war unless we work closely and harmoniously together. We must do our utmost, setting aside futile recriminations about the past. I intend to fight a ground battle, regardless of what the navy and air force do. I must ask for your absolute loyalty, for only thus can we achieve victory."

In truth, there was no more chance of the rival services working harmoniously together in the Philippines than anywhere else in the Japanese empire. One day in September, a naval officer convinced himself that he saw American ships off-loading troops on Mindanao. A standing order of South Asia Army decreed that all signals on an issue of such gravity must be dispatched jointly by responsible naval and military officers. Ignoring this, the navy sent a flash message to Tokyo announcing an American invasion. Every Japanese formation in the field and at sea was alerted. Hours of alarm and confusion followed. Soldiers in Manila remained disbelieving, and of course their scepticism was justified. The army regarded the false alarm as further evidence of the navy's proclivity for fantasy, displayed daily in its wildly exaggerated claims of U.S. ships sunk and planes destroyed.

Yamashita himself, fifty-nine in 1944, had acquired three reputations:

first, as an intensely nationalistic political soldier; second, as an outstanding commander; third, as possessing the loudest snore in the Imperial Army, a vice which made his staff reluctant to sleep anywhere near him. The general had been sidelined from high command in 1936, following an equivocal role in an attempted coup against the Tokyo government, but his abilities and popularity among junior officers earned his recall in 1941. As commander of 25th Army in Malaya he achieved his greatest triumph, securing the surrender of a superior British force at Singapore. Yet the government, nervous of his new status as a national hero, once more sidelined Yamashita. Japan's ablest commander was serving in Manchuria when the summons to the Philippines arrived. He said quietly to his chief of staff: "So it's come at last, has it? Well, my going won't change anything. It's my turn to die, isn't it?" When his wife suggested that she should stay in Manchuria, the general said: "You'd better go home and die with your parents." The Manchurian puppet emperor Pu Yi claimed that Yamashita covered his face and wept at his official leave-taking before embarking for the Philippines. "This is our final parting," said the Japanese. "I shall never come back."

In Tokyo en route to Manila, at a series of meetings with the nation's leaders, "Hobun" Yamashita strove in vain to persuade them to share his own brutally realistic appraisal of the strategic situation. A clever and good-natured man who had travelled widely in Europe, he knew the war was lost. Admiral Mitsumasa Yonai, the navy minister, already privately committed to negotiating a way out of the war, merely shook his head sorrowfully in the face of the general's blunt words and said: "Do your best, Hobun, do your best." Yamashita attended a formal farewell ceremony with Hirohito, which he seemed to enjoy. He told an aide as he left the Imperial Palace that he felt as happy as he ever had in his life. Having saluted his emperor, he was ready to die.

In Manila, the general was unimpressed by the staff which he inherited, and even more dismayed by the quality of the troops he inspected, most of them rendered slothful by long occupation duty. Subordinates shared his misgivings. Lt. Suteo Inoue of the 77th Infantry Regiment, for instance, recorded in his Philippines diary: "Soldiers here lack comradely spirit. I have never seen such an undisciplined outfit as this one. To be strong, units need a sense of shared identity. This regiment is the worst in the Japanese army . . . It took a hundred men almost seven hours to cross a river 150 metres wide . . . due to lack of barges. I presume this reflects Japan's general lack of resources. We have underestimated the importance of material strength, and are now suffering the consequences. If this state of affairs continues for another year, Japan will be in trouble, and our withdrawal from Greater East Asia will become inevitable."

Yamashita ordered a supply officer to transfer service troops to combat duty, and to draft Filipino labour to shift stores in their stead. To his chagrin, he was told that local people could not be trusted in such a role. The commander of 14th Army now had only days in which to prepare for the coming of the Americans. He knew that months would not have sufficed.

LUZON, in the north, is the Philippines' principal landmass, seconded by Mindanao, in the south. Between lies a jumble of densely populated lesser islands, of which Leyte is among the easternmost. In October 1944 this was MacArthur's choice for a first lodgement. Some 115 miles long and 45 miles broad at its widest point, it was inhabited by 915,000 of the Philippines' 17 million people, in modest towns of sun-bleached stucco and villages of straw-thatched huts. Leyte Gulf lies open to the ocean, and thus to an invasion fleet. The immediate American objective after securing the beaches was the rice and corn belt of Leyte Valley. There MacArthur planned to build airfields to relieve his dependence on carrier air support. He would then dispossess the Japanese of the mountainous regions beyond the plain. When the island was secure he would address Luzon, and thereafter liberate the rest of the archipelago.

Once American forces had secured a firm foothold in the Philippines and achieved command of local skies and seas, piecemeal ground operations could contribute nothing towards the defeat of Japan. But the islands had been the general's home. He viewed their people with a paternalistic warmth as great as any British *sahib* felt towards Indians. Liberating them from Japanese rule was the most compelling objective of MacArthur's war. Around three-quarters of a million Filipinos, Japanese and Americans would pay with their lives for its accomplishment.

In the weeks preceding the landing at Leyte, American carrier aircraft struck again and again at Japanese airfields and shipping. On 10 October, 1,396 sorties were launched at the Ryukyu Islands, south of Japan, which destroyed significant shipping and a hundred enemy aircraft for the loss of twenty-one American planes. Two days later, Halsey's flattops dispatched 1,378 sorties to Formosa. Japan's Vice-Admiral Shigeru Fukudome, commanding 6th Base Air Force, described later how he watched the air battles, applauding as planes fell, until he perceived that most were Japanese. The struggle was not entirely one-sided—forty-eight American planes were downed on the twelfth. But next day the Japanese lost forty-one in futile attacks on Third Fleet. Over five hundred Japanese aircraft were destroyed between the twelfth and the fourteenth, an intensity of attrition dwarfing the 1940 Battle of Britain and indeed all air combat in the European theatre. Even Japanese aircrew being trained on Kyushu for carrier operations were thrown recklessly into the battles with Halsey's squadrons. Most were lost, and with them Japan's last chance of sustaining a seaborne air capability.

On 14 October, Admiral Soemu Toyoda reported to Fukudome that the U.S. Third Fleet was retiring defeated. A Japanese communiqué of 16 October announced American losses of eleven aircraft carriers, two battleships, three cruisers and one destroyer, besides eight carriers, two battleships and four cruisers damaged. The nation was urged to celebrate the "glorious victory of Taiwan." In truth, of course, Halsey had achieved overwhelming success. He departed to wreak havoc elsewhere. All the Japanese had to show for their efforts was severe damage to two U.S. cruisers. American carriers had demonstrated that they could range at will, inflicting overwhelmingly disproportionate injury upon any Japanese force they met at sea or in the sky.

Yamashita received his first indication of MacArthur's Philippines armada in a fatuous signal from his divisional commander on Leyte: "Enemy fleet approaching, uncertain whether they are sheltering from weather or fleeing from Formosa battle." At dawn on 20 October, the seven hundred ships of MacArthur's central Philippines attack force began offloading seven miles off the shore of Leyte Gulf. Almost 200,000 men of Sixth Army were mustered in the transports, commanded by Lt.-Gen. Walter Krueger. Krueger was born in Prussia in 1881. When his father died, in 1889 his mother emigrated to the United States. Her son began his military career ten years later, as a volunteer infantryman on Cuba. He rose to the rank of sergeant, then elected to seek a commission as a regular soldier. In the Pacific, to the mystification of officers who thought him a dull dog, slow and cautious, Krueger became MacArthur's favoured field commander, his primacy rewarded by the key role on Leyte.

American warnings had been broadcast to the local population to move inland to avoid the bombardment. Filipino guerrillas were alerted by radio flashes the day before the landing. It was widely believed at SWPA headquarters that the campaign would be easy. But MacArthur's staff intelligence estimates seriously underestimated Japanese strength, even if the Leyte garrison was not reinforced. Gen. George Kenney, MacArthur's air chief, predicted on 24 September: "The objective is relatively undefended—the Japanese will not offer strong resistance." He wrote likewise: "If my hunch is right . . . the Japs are about through." Kenney was an able air commander, but like all those who worked with MacArthur, his judgement was impaired by wishful thinking.

So practiced had become the art of amphibious operations that since 1942 the delay between a U.S. fleet's arrival offshore and its first landings had been cut from four hours to two. The Leyte bombardment force carried heavier metal than that which supported the 6 June D-Day landings in Normandy. For soldiers aboard transports, almost any peril seemed worth enduring to escape the crippling heat belowdecks. Some units, formerly earmarked to land on the island of Yap, had been at sea since 27 August. Now they clambered clumsily down the scrambling nets into their landing craft, which circled until signal flags gave the order to head for the shore. Men of four divisions began to land in two main bodies: one at the north end of the gulf near the capital, Tacloban; the second fourteen miles southwards. Conditions were perfect. There were no mines, no surf. Fires blazed along the shoreline in the wake of the naval bombardment. Desultory Japanese artillery, mortar and machine-gun fire began to harass the invaders only after the first waves had landed, for coastal defensive positions were weakly held. American casualties were concentrated in a few unlucky units, such as two companies of the 3/32nd Infantry which lost eight killed and nineteen wounded to machine guns in a matter of seconds. Several American tanks were knocked out by a nearby 70mm gun. It was mid-afternoon before tanks and infantry demolished the strongpoint and passed on westward.

In most places, however, resistance was negligible. Only 20,000 of Yamashita's 400,000 men were deployed on Leyte. They were deemed low-grade soldiers, mostly recruited from the commercial workers of Osaka and Kyoto. Terauchi decreed: "The navy and air force will attempt to annihilate the enemy on X-Day . . . The Area Army will at the same time annihilate the enemy on Leyte." Yet despite these grandiose phrases, Yamashita planned to make his principal stand on Luzon. On Leyte, the Japanese intention was to inflict pain and buy time, rather than to defeat Sixth Army. Thus, as landing craft shuttled to and fro, Krueger's four divisions were easily able to stake out positions inland. A few hundred yards behind the beach, in the deserted village of San José, men of the 7th Cavalry found several abandoned Japanese cars and crates of Japanese beer bottled in Manila. "Leyte, like most of the other islands we had landed on during the last three years, was better seen at a distance," wrote Private Bill McLaughlin. "Lying offshore the perfume of the land was exotic, but on close inspection about all that could be seen was mud and rotting vegetation. The only inhabitants lived in squalid huts of grass and thatch, and looked half-starved."

The first Filipino the Americans met was wheeling a bicycle between the tall palm trees, frantically waving his broad-brimmed hat. "As he approached, his face appeared to be composed entirely of smile," wrote correspondent Robert Shaplen. "It was impossible to understand what he

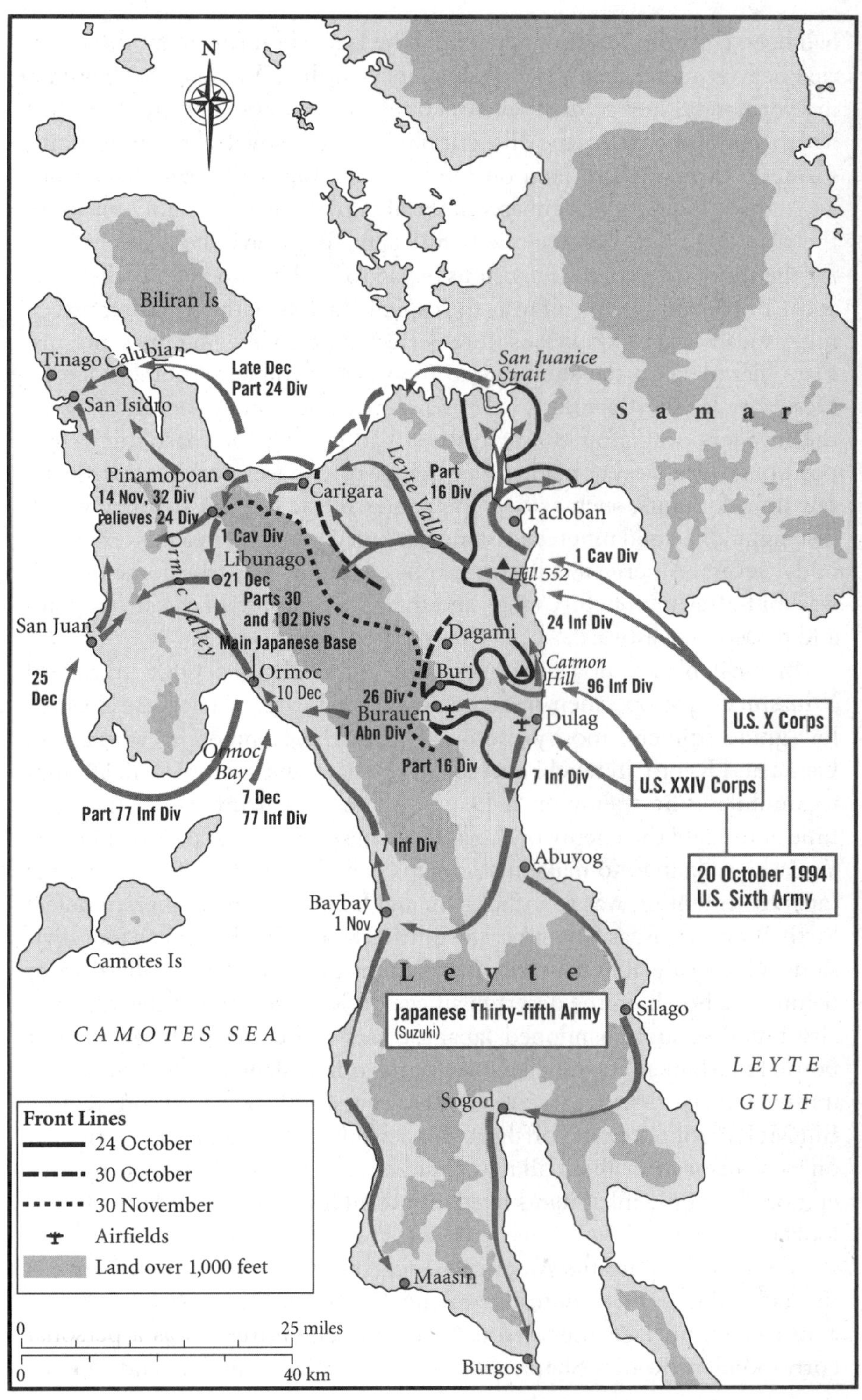
N
Biliran Is
Tinago
Calubian
San Isidro
Late Dec
Part 24 Div
San Juanice
Strait
Samar
Pinamopoan
14 Nov, 32 Div
relieves 24 Div
Carigara
Leyte Valley
Part
16 Div
Tacloban
1 Cav Div
Libunago
21 Dec
Parts 30
and 102 Divs
Ormoc Valley
Hill 552
1 Cav Div
24 Inf Div
San Juan
Main Japanese Base
Dagami
Catmon
Hill
25
Dec
Ormoc
10 Dec
Buri
96 Inf Div
26 Div
Burauen
11 Abn Div
Dulag
U.S. X Corps
Ormoc
Bay
Part 16 Div
7 Inf Div
U.S. XXIV Corps
Part 77 Inf Div
7 Dec
77 Inf Div
7 Inf Div
Abuyog
20 October 1994
U.S. Sixth Army
Baybay
1 Nov
Camotes Is
Leyte
Japanese Thirty-fifth Army
(Suzuki)
Silago
CAMOTES SEA
LEYTE
GULF
Sogod
Front Lines
24 October
30 October
30 November
Airfields
Land over 1,000 feet
Maasin
0
25 miles
0
40 km
Burgos

The American campaign on Leyte, October–December 1944

was saying, but it was easy to see that he was filled with an almost hysterical happiness. He grabbed the hand of every soldier he could reach and shook it ecstatically." This "first liberated Filipino," as he was dubbed, proved to be Isaios Budlong, a former Tacloban telegraph operator. Soon hundreds of local people were milling around the Americans, exuding holiday exuberance. One man presented a box of Japanese biscuits to the 7th Cavalry's colonel. An elderly villager kept fingering soldiers "as a woman would fondle a piece of silk."

The colonel commanding the 2/34th Infantry directed the attention of a 75mm tank gun onto a cluster of farm shacks which he feared might harbour Japanese. "The smaller building erupted in a flash of fire—lumber, chicken feathers, chickens and debris filling the area," wrote Captain Paul Austin, a Texan. "We waded the rice paddy waist-deep, and I walked past the farmhouse. A Filipino man and woman had appeared and were standing near the rear of their house. They smiled and bowed as we went past. They seemed so glad to see us that they did not mind that we had just blown their chicken house to smithereens."

All morning, from the cruiser *Nashville* MacArthur watched his men move ashore. Then, after an early lunch, the great man set forth to join them. This was his first visit to Leyte for over forty years, since he was a young army engineer, and he devoted intensive attention to its stage management. "Regard publicity set-up as excellent," he signalled to his public-relations staff shortly before the landings. "I desire to broadcast from beach as soon as apparatus can be set up. After I have done so you can use records made to broadcast to the U.S. and to the Philippines at such times and in such ways as you deem best." Now he stepped down the ramp of a landing craft a few yards off the beach, and waded serenely through knee-deep water and a cluster of photographers who immortalised this great symbolic moment of the Pacific war. He said to Richard Sutherland, his chief of staff: "Well, believe it or not, we're here."

Once on Philippine sand, he ignored distant small-arms fire and greeted a few soldiers. Then, standing beside the islands' new president, Sergio Osmena—who scarcely disguised the fact that he would have preferred to stay in America until the battle for his country was won—MacArthur broadcast a resounding proclamation: "People of the Philippines, I have returned! By the grace of Almighty God, our forces stand again on Philippine soil." His words fell on unsympathetic ears among some American soldiers and seamen who later heard them. More than a few recoiled from the fashion in which MacArthur treated this vast commitment of U.S. power and hazard of American lives as a personal affair. Yet what else save theatre might have been expected from a great actor? Yamashita, when told of the beach photographs of "*Maggada*," as

Japanese pronounced his name, assumed them to be faked. Yet they were no more the product of stage direction than everything else about Douglas MacArthur.

That first day, the Americans lost just fifty-five men killed and missing, 192 wounded. Most of the invaders' difficulties were created not by the enemy, but by nature. Along the landing frontage it was hard to move even a few hundred yards inland through dense cover and swamps, where heavily laden soldiers could plunge up to their necks. The landing of stores proved a nightmare. Many ships had been poorly loaded, so that the wrong equipment came off first. Far too few men had been allocated to handling parties. Terrain impeded transfer of rations, ammunition, medical supplies forward to combat units. Some 1.5 million tons of equipment, 235,000 tons of combat vehicles, 200,000 tons of ammunition and the same weight of medical supplies were scheduled for off-load in the first days, with 332,000 tons being added each month thereafter. Within hours the beaches became crowded with stores, vehicles, weapons, fuel drums, debris, piled anywhere and going nowhere in a hurry. Logistics, on an island almost bereft of metalled roads, would become a dominant issue of the campaign.

For ten days following the landings, most invaders found themselves advancing across swamp-ridden flatlands, meeting limited resistance. They gazed apprehensively at the steep, densely covered mountains in the distance. "The simple truth about war," a soldier who fought the Japanese has written, "is that if you are on the attack, you can't do a damned thing until you find your enemy, and the only way to do that is to push on, at whatever speed seems prudent, until you see or hear him, or he makes his presence known by letting fly at you." On the second day, "long before noon, the rate of the regiment's advance was measured by the ability of the infantry to overcome the terrain," wrote a historian of the 32nd Infantry. By the following evening, five miles inland, some men were succumbing to heat exhaustion, and all were drenched in sweat: "The cogon grass was so high that men smothered in its growth. Everywhere swamps and rice paddies had to be crossed." Sometimes the Japanese were rash enough to launch charges, which the Americans repulsed with much slaughter. One such suicidal rush against a company of the 32nd cost the Japanese seventy-five killed for one American wounded.

Much more often, however, the enemy exploited local conditions to inflict surprises as the invaders struggled through cover. A U.S. infantry platoon was emerging from a banana grove when a single machine-gun burst wounded eleven men. Japanese soldiers sprang out and bayoneted casualties, until driven back by automatic fire. Even in allegedly secure areas, infiltration by small groups of enemy, assisted by the dense vegetation, remained a hazard: one Japanese soldier crawled up to an American artillery piece and laid a satchel charge against its breech before being killed by a grenade. Advancing infantry suffered long waits, sometimes under mortar or artillery fire, while engineers repaired bridges for tanks and checked for mines. There were never enough engineers.

Private Jack Norman was a twenty-one-year-old from Chester, Nebraska, who had dropped out of college to become a hotel bellhop, "which made good money, but it wasn't all legal," as he observed wryly. Drafted at nineteen, he experienced a not unusual odyssey through the U.S. military system. He served in a dozen Stateside camps, first being exhaustively trained as a gunner, then as an engineer, finally becoming a most reluctant infantryman in the 96th Division. He and his comrades landed on Leyte in complete bewilderment about what was going on around them, and learned slowly through the days that followed: "You were wet all the time . . . There were spiders this big." He counted eagerly the Japanese whom he thought he killed with his BAR, and got to twenty-five. Once he found an empty gun emplacement, wandered over to it and suddenly saw two Japanese soldiers on the other side. Before bolting, they threw a grenade, fragments of which lodged in Norman's leg. These removed him from the line for a few days, until they were extracted. Private Norman did not like Leyte.

The Japanese too were scarcely enjoying their own experience. As soon as word reached Manila of the landings, Maj. Shoji Takahashi of South Asia Army's intelligence staff decided to discover for himself what was happening, though explicitly ordered to remain at headquarters. Takahashi, a thirty-one-year-old farmer's son and career soldier, with some difficulty begged a lift on an aircraft landing on Leyte, then hitchhiked to the forward area, under constant American shellfire. He spent his first night not uncomfortably, in a civilian house with two other staff officers. Next morning, however, they emerged to find themselves in the path of an American air strike. A bomb buried Takahashi in four feet of earth, killed one roommate and badly wounded the other. After digging himself out, he toured the perimeter under a storm of American shells and bombs. He reflected gloomily that if he was killed while acting in defiance of superior orders, his soul would be denied a resting place at the Yasukuni shrine, and offered his services to the local regimental commander. "Forget it," said the colonel. "You'll be much more useful if you get back to Manila and tell them just how rough it is down here." Takahashi escaped on a minesweeper to area army headquarters.

On 23 October, at a little ceremony in Tacloban, MacArthur and Osmena celebrated the restoration of civil government to the Philippines. Sixth Army struggled to grapple with the administrative problems of meeting the needs of local Filipino people, many of whom expected to be fed. Unruly bands of guerrillas and bandits—the two were indistinguishable—milled around the American columns, offering aid that was sometimes useful, often not. Most local people were in rags, and the Americans learned to mistrust those who looked more presentable. A grand figure in lavender trousers, yellow shirt and yellow hat introduced himself to the liberators as Bernardo Torres, former governor of Leyte Province. He said that he hated the Japanese, but proved to have served them as director of food production. A crowd at a town meeting in Tacloban shouted: "Long live Americans, lovely Americans!" Filipino assistance in humping supplies and casualties soon became indispensable to MacArthur's units. Senior officers were exasperated by the generosity of soldiers who gave rations to local people, because this made food a less tempting inducement for them to risk their lives as battlefield porters. "Filipino labor . . . performed manual labour with lassitude," an American official historian observed sourly.

Each day the invaders were killing substantial numbers of enemy, and gaining ground. Yet the Americans were dismayed to discover that on the northern and western coasts beyond the mountains, the Japanese were reinforcing strongly. Units from Luzon were being ferried to Ormoc and several lesser ports. Few ground-based U.S. aircraft could operate from Leyte, and it was weeks before carrier planes effectively interdicted supply routes. Meanwhile, thousands of enemy troops got through. On the plains, American infantry were strafed by Japanese aircraft, an experience that grew distressingly familiar: "Empty casings jingled down upon us like sleighbells," in the fanciful image of one soldier. Though Japanese squadrons flying against Leyte from Luzon were much mauled by U.S. fighters, their attacks on American airfields seriously hampered deployment of the air support MacArthur needed. To his chagrin, the general was obliged to demand continuing cover from the carrier aircraft of Halsey's Third Fleet.

Movement on Leyte was tough. An army report observed acidly: "It is foolish to land large numbers of vehicles if there are insufficient engineers to maintain the roads." Tanks and trucks chewed tracks into quagmires. There was dismay about service troops' lack of enthusiasm for deploying close to the front, or performing their duties when gunfire was audible: "It is essential that all units . . . be imbued with the spirit that when necessary they shall take the same chances as the infantry. Artillery may have to be placed close up to the front line, or to provide its own local defensive protection at night; engineers must often build bridges under fire; MPs, especially in the pursuit phase, must direct traffic under fire. Service units . . . must take their places in the defensive positions when troops are limited."

On 24 October a local Japanese regimental commander, Lt. Col. Takayoshi Sumitani, issued a defiant handwritten order to his men of the 24th Infantry: "The fate of the Empire depends on this decisive battle of the Philippines. This force will fight the decisive battle around Tacloban, and will smash the barbaric enemy. There is no greater glory and honour than this . . . Now, the rigorous training you have received will be put to the test . . . Every officer and man will unite to fight courageously in a spirit of self-sacrifice. Annihilate the enemy as his Majesty the Emperor expects, and show your respect for Imperial benevolence."

This was vain bombast. The Americans were now far too strongly established to be evicted from Leyte. What Sumitani and his kind could and did achieve, however, was to engage Sixth Army in much harder fighting than MacArthur and his staff had anticipated. And even as the invaders advanced across the island, offshore there now unfolded one of the most spectacular dramas of the Philippines campaign, indeed of the Second World War.

CHAPTER SIX

"Flowers of Death": Leyte Gulf

1. Shogo

THE LARGEST naval clash in history took place at a time when its outcome could exercise negligible influence upon Japan's collapse. It was inspired by a decision of Japan's admirals to vent their frustrations in a gesture of stunning futility. In October 1944 they found themselves stripped of air cover, and facing overwhelmingly superior American forces. They wished to concentrate their fleet in the home islands. Instead, however, most big ships were obliged to operate from anchorages where fuel oil was available, off Borneo and Malaya. The Imperial Navy still disposed a force which, a few years past, had awed the world. Of ten battleships in commission at the start of the war, nine remained. It seemed to Japan's admirals intolerable—worse, dishonourable—that capital units swung idle at their moorings while on shore the army fought desperate battles. The navy thus sought to precipitate an engagement, even though every projection of its outcome promised defeat.

The Americans were unprepared for such an initiative. As so often in north-west Europe, they credited their enemies with excessive rationality. MacArthur's headquarters thought a Japanese dash through the San Bernardino or Surigao strait approaches to Leyte Gulf unlikely. The enemy's ships would lack searoom, and would confront both Halsey's Third Fleet and Kinkaid's Seventh. Ever since the summer, however, Japan's commanders had intended to commit most of their surviving surface units to what they called Shogo—"Operation Victory." When Vice-Admiral Ugaki of the battleship squadron was shown a draft, he wrote: "Whether the plan is adequate or not needs further study, but at a time when we have been driven into the last ditch we have no other choice . . . It is essential still to hope for victory . . . and endeavour to attain it." In other words, it was preferable to do anything than to do nothing. Shogo would be a thrust comparable in its desperation with Hitler's Ardennes offensive three months later.

Even as Japan's commanders and staffs pored over charts through September and early October, their vital air squadrons were vanishing into the ocean. Day after day off Formosa, Halsey's planes inflicted devastating losses. "Our fighters were but so many eggs thrown at the stone wall of the invincible enemy formations," Vice-Admiral Fukudome wrote wretchedly. U.S. radar picket destroyers enabled the Americans to mass aircraft in holding patterns a hundred miles out from Third Fleet whenever Japanese attacks threatened. Fighter direction had become a superbly sophisticated art. So too had massed attacks on Japan's air bases and floating assets. On 10 October, 1,396 American sorties against Okinawa and the Ryukyus ravaged shipping and destroyed a hundred enemy aircraft for the loss of twenty-one. Between the twelfth and the fourteenth, the Japanese lost more than five hundred aircraft. Their combat casualties were matched by a steep decline in aircraft serviceability—to 50 percent, even 20 percent, compared with the Americans' 80 percent. Many Japanese ground crews had been lost in the Pacific atoll battles, and no trained replacements were available.

These setbacks were matched by extraordinary Japanese self-deceit about what had taken place. Vice-Admiral Ugaki rejoiced about a destroyer squadron's "tremendous feat" of sinking three aircraft carriers, a cruiser and four destroyers. In truth, in the action cited the Americans had lost one destroyer. Here was a high command forsaking that indispensable practice, honest analysis. Instead, in drafting the Shogo plan, Japan's commanders embraced a tissue of illusions. Most of the 116 planes left to the Japanese fleet were winched rather than flown aboard carriers in their Kyushu anchorage on 17 October, because the pilots were deemed too inexperienced to make deck landings. The fleet now relied upon land-based air cover. Japan's forty surviving aircraft in the Philippines were reinforced tenfold by 23 October, but remained subject to relentless attrition on the ground and in the air. At sea, the Japanese assembled forces of 9 battleships, 4 carriers, 15 heavy and light cruisers and 29 destroyers. This seemed impressive, until measured against the U.S. Navy's strength: 19 task groups around the Philippines comprised 9 fleet, 8 light and 29 escort carriers; 12 battleships; 12 heavy and 16 light cruisers; 178 destroyers; 40 destroyer escorts and 10 frigates. The United States now deployed more destroyers than the Japanese navy owned carrier aircraft. Third Fleet's 200 ships occupied an area of ocean nine miles by forty.

The objective of Shogo, complex as most Japanese operational plans, was to enable three squadrons, two sailing from Borneo and one from Kyushu, to rendezvous off Leyte Gulf, where the Combined Fleet would fall upon MacArthur's amphibious armada and its covering naval force, Seventh Fleet. Though the Japanese believed that their air attacks had already crippled Halsey's Third Fleet, operating north-east of the Philippines, they sought to decoy his carriers and battleships out of range of Leyte. For this purpose, Japan's four surviving carriers and skeletal complement of aircraft were to feint southward, making a demonstration the Americans could not fail to notice. The carriers' inevitable loss was considered worth accepting, to remove Halsey from the path of the main striking force. Shogo was scheduled for the earliest possible date after the expected American landing.

Most senior officers and staffs opposed the plan. They perceived its slender prospects of success and likely calamitous losses. They saw that, by waiting until the Americans were ashore, they would have missed the decisive moment in the Philippines. Shogo reflected the Japanese navy's chronic weakness for dividing its forces. Even the bellicose Ugaki wrote on 21 September that it seemed rash "to engage the full might of the enemy with our inferior force . . . committing ourselves to a decisive battle . . . There was little chance of achieving victory. Watching a Sumo wrestler taking on five men in succession, it was plain that he could not prevail if he expended too much effort grappling with each opponent in turn." Some officers said: "We do not mind death, but if the final effort of our great navy is to be an attack on a cluster of empty freighters, surely admirals Togo and Yamamoto would weep in their graves." Critics challenged a scheme which demanded daylight engagement. Only darkness, they believed, might offer a chance of success, of exploiting the Imperial Navy's legendary night-fighting skills. Even the army, itself so often imprudent, thought Shogo reckless.

Vice-Admiral Takeo Kurita, designated as operational commander, made the best case he could for the operation. "Would it not be shameful," he demanded at his captains' final briefing, "for the fleet to remain intact while our nation perishes? There are such things as miracles." Yet Kurita himself, though a veteran destroyer and cruiser leader who had seen plenty of action, was notoriously cautious. He had gained his flag by virtue of seniority, not performance. He was to execute a plan devised by Combined Fleet headquarters, which demanded extraordinary boldness. On the eve of sailing, only Kurita's rhetoric matched the demands of his mission. The fleet, he told his officers, was being granted "the chance to bloom as flowers of death." His audience responded as custom demanded, leaping to their feet to cry "*Banzai!*," but there was no eagerness in their hearts. Kurita and his captains then embarked upon one of the most reckless and ill-managed operations in naval history.

The series of actions which became known as the Battle of Leyte Gulf was fought over an area the size of Britain or Nevada. Following a Japanese naval code change, American intelligence gained no hint of the enemy's plan, but both of Kurita's southern squadrons were detected long ahead of reaching Leyte. Before dawn on 23 October, Halsey received one of the most momentous sighting reports of the war from the submarine *Darter*, patrolling the Palawan Passage with its sister ship *Dace*: MANY SHIPS INCLUDING 3 PROBABLE BBS 08–28N 115–30E COURSE 040 SPEED 18 X CHASING. This was Kurita's 1st Striking Force, en route from Brunei Bay. What a spectacle it must have been. No one has bettered Winston Churchill's imagery of twentieth-century dreadnoughts at sea: "gigantic castles of steel," prows dipping as they advanced in stately procession, "like giants bowed in anxious thought."

Five battleships and ten heavy cruisers steamed in three columns at sixteen knots, without an anti-submarine screen. This was all the more astonishing since the Japanese intercepted the American radio transmission, and thus knew submarines were at hand. At 0632, *Darter* fired six torpedoes at the cruiser *Atago*, Kurita's flagship, from point-blank range—980 yards—then loosed her stern tubes at the cruiser *Takao* from 1,550 yards. *Atago* was hit four times, *Takao* twice. *Dace*'s skipper, Bladen Claggett, whipped up his periscope to see "the sight of a lifetime": *Atago* billowing black smoke and orange flame, sinking fast by the bow. *Takao*, though hit hard in the stern, remained afloat. Claggett heard two huge explosions. "I have never heard anything like it," wrote the submarine skipper. "The soundmen reported that it sounded as if the bottom of the ocean was blowing up . . . Heard tremendous breaking-up noises. This was the most gruesome sound I have ever heard." The diving officer said: "We'd better get the hell out of here."

Admiral Kurita and his staff swam from the stricken *Atago* to the destroyer *Kishinami*, and thence transferred to the great battleship *Yamato*. Some 360 of *Atago*'s crew drowned, including almost all the admiral's communications staff. If Kurita's conduct thereafter was clumsy, no fifty-five-year-old could have found it easy to exercise command after suffering such a personal trauma. *Darter*'s sister boat *Dace* launched four torpedoes at the cruiser *Maya* and heard huge explosions, signalling her end. Belated Japanese destroyer attacks prevented either submarine from firing again. Kurita's ships increased speed to twenty-four knots to escape the killing ground. The first action of Leyte Gulf had inflicted substantial damage on the Japanese before they fired a shot. Some officers of "Centre Force," as Kurita's squadron was designated, expressed rueful admiration for the American submarines' achievement: "Why can't our people pull off a stunt like that?" Why not, indeed? This first American success was made possible by a tactical carelessness amounting to recklessness, which would characterise almost every Japanese action in those days. However gloomy were Kurita and his officers about the operation they had undertaken, it is extraordinary that they spurned elementary precautions. Japanese behaviour suggested a resignation to death much stronger than the will to fight. In this titanic clash, a once-great navy was to conduct itself in a fashion that would have invited ridicule, were not such great issues and so many lives at stake.

It was now plain to the Americans that Kurita's ships were headed for the San Bernardino Strait, at the north end of Samar Island. On reaching its eastern exit, they intended to turn south for the seven-hour run to Leyte Gulf, and MacArthur's invasion anchorage. The second Japanese squadron, under Admiral Shoji Nishimura, had also been spotted, steaming towards the same objective from the south, past Mindanao. Halsey dared not lead his own battleships into San Bernardino, which had been heavily mined by the Japanese. Instead, he ordered three fast carrier groups to close the range and launch air strikes. The Japanese, however, moved first. Three groups of fifty aircraft apiece, flying from Luzon, attacked the carriers of Sherman's Task Group 3. A long, bitter battle ensued. One Hellcat pilot, the famous Cmdr. David McCampbell, shot down nine Japanese planes, his wingman six; five other pilots claimed two each. McCampbell had initially been rejected for flight training back in 1933, because of poor eyesight. Yet the aggression indispensable to all fighter pilots made him one of the most successful of the navy's war. "It's competitive all the way through," he said wryly. On 24 October 1944, nearly all the prizes were won by the Americans. The Japanese attacking force was almost wiped out.

Just one Judy dive-bomber penetrated the American screen and landed a 550-pound bomb on the light carrier *Princeton*, crowded with planes preparing for take-off. Fuel caught fire, torpedoes exploded, hundreds of desperate men crowded the flight deck. At 1010, half an hour after the initial explosion, all crewmen save damage-control parties abandoned ship. The cruiser *Birmingham* steamed close alongside to help fight *Princeton*'s fires, sending thirty-eight volunteers aboard the stricken carrier. A jeep and a tractor slid from *Princeton*'s lofty deck onto the destroyer *Morrison*, which was taking off men while using machine guns to ward off sharks from survivors in the water. *Princeton*'s agony continued for 2½ hours, until a new Japanese air raid was signalled. *Birmingham* temporarily stood off. After *Lexington*'s Hellcats broke up the attackers, however, the heroic cruiser closed in once more, and tried to take *Princeton* in tow.

A huge explosion in the carrier's torpedo stowage put an end to the salvage attempt, and inflicted shocking damage on *Birmingham*. The ship's war diary recorded: "Dead, dying and wounded, many of them bloody and horrible, covered the decks . . . Blood ran freely down the waterways." The hulk of *Princeton* was sunk by American torpedoes. *Birmingham* retired from the fleet, "a dockyard case." Amazingly, thanks to the courage

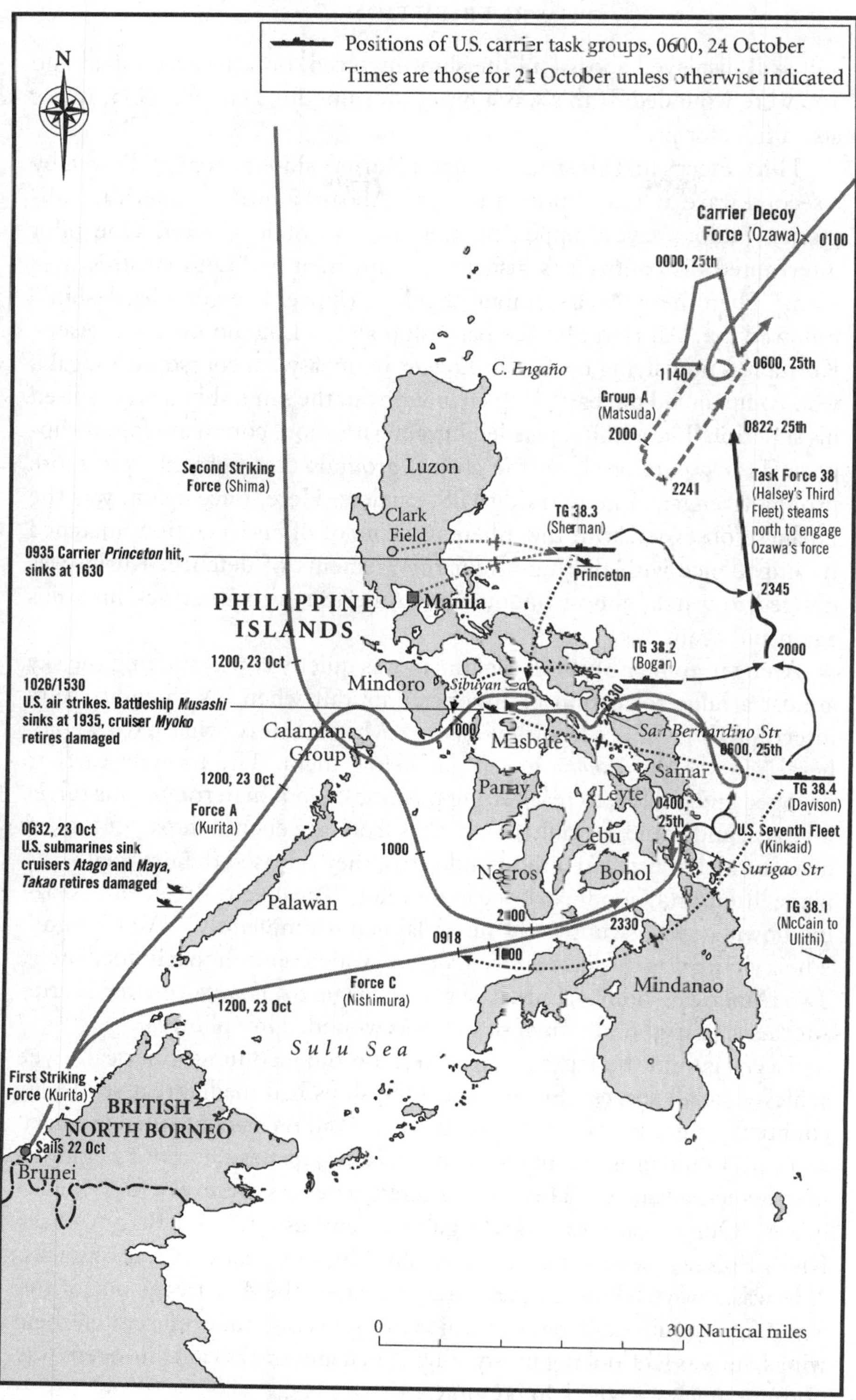
Positions of U.S. carrier task groups, 0600, 24 October
Times are those for 24 October unless otherwise indicated
N
Carrier Decoy Force (Ozawa)
0100
0000, 25th
0600, 25th
1140
Group A (Matsuda)
2000
0822, 25th
2241
C. Engaño
Luzon
Second Striking Force (Shima)
Task Force 38 (Halsey's Third Fleet) steams north to engage Ozawa's force
TG 38.3 (Sherman)
Clark Field
0935 Carrier Princeton hit, sinks at 1630
Princeton
2345
PHILIPPINE ISLANDS
Manila
TG 38.2 (Bogan)
2000
1200, 23 Oct
Mindoro
Sibuyan Sea
1026/1530
U.S. air strikes. Battleship Musashi sinks at 1935, cruiser Myoko retires damaged
2330
Calamian Group
1000
Masbate
San Bernardino Str
0600, 25th
Samar
1200, 23 Oct
Panay
TG 38.4 (Davison)
Force A (Kurita)
Leyte
0400, 25th
U.S. Seventh Fleet (Kinkaid)
0632, 23 Oct
U.S. submarines sink cruisers Atago and Maya, Takao retires damaged
1000
Cebu
Surigao Str
Negros
Bohol
Palawan
2300
2330
TG 38.1 (McCain to Ulithi)
0918
1000
Force C (Nishimura)
Mindanao
1200, 23 Oct
Sulu Sea
First Striking Force (Kurita)
BRITISH NORTH BORNEO
Sails 22 Oct
Brunei
0
300 Nautical miles

The Battle of Leyte Gulf, 23–25 October 1944

and skill displayed aboard all the ships involved, only 108 men died and 190 were wounded. If this was a bitter morning for Halsey's TG3, it was also a time for pride.

Third Fleet's first air strike fell upon Kurita's ships at 1026, followed by a second wave at 1245, another at 1550. Aboard a nearby American submarine, sailors eavesdropped on the airmen's radio chatter. One pilot interrupted his controller's instructions impatiently: "Let's get this over with." Then there was a clamour of yells: "Yippee! I've got a battleship!" followed by: "All right, let the battleship alone. Line up on the cruiser." Kurita was now flying his flag in *Yamato*, in uneasy concourse with Ugaki, who commanded the battleship element from the same ship, and despised his superior. The admiral pleaded in vain with shore command for air support. This was refused, on the absurd grounds that fighters were more profitably engaged in attacking U.S. carriers. Here, once again, was the Japanese obsession with the inherent virtue of offensive action, matched by impatience with the humdrum requirements of defence. Kurita was obliged to watch, almost impotent, as American aircraft struck his ships again and again.

Avenger gunner Sherwin Goodman was quietly contemplating the sky amidst a huge formation of American aircraft when his thoughts were interrupted: "It was a beautiful day . . . My goodness, what have we got here?" It was the *Yamato* group, far below them. The torpedo-carriers dropped and circled, to reach firing positions. Goodman rotated his turret forward, and could see only gun flashes from the enemy ships: "It looked like a tunnel of fire." At a thousand yards, they released their torpedo, the plane lifted, and Goodman cried at his pilot, "Break left! Break left!" Gazing down as they swung away, he exclaimed triumphantly: "We hit him!" Their victim was the light cruiser *Noshiro*, which sank almost immediately. Two American bombs caused slight damage to *Yamato*, giving Kurita another bad fright. His chief of staff was wounded by splinters.

Every gun in the Japanese fleet fired on the incoming Americans, yet achieved small success. Since 1942, U.S. ships had made great strides in countering air attack by radio fighter direction, radar-controlled gunnery and radio-guided proximity shell fuses. The Japanese had not begun to match such advances. Their anti-aircraft defences were woefully inadequate. "Our captain was a great gunnery enthusiast," said Petty Officer Kisao Ebisawa, who served on a warship through many U.S. air attacks. "He was always telling us that we could shoot the Americans out of the sky. After innumerable raids in which our guns did not even scratch their wings, he was left looking pretty silly. When air attacks came in, there was nothing much we could do but pray."

On 24 October, huge "beehive" shells from the battleships' main armament did more damage to their own gun barrels than to American planes, but pilots were shaken by the spectacle. "It's nerve-racking," said one, "because you see the guns on the ships go off. And then you wonder what in hell you are going to do for the next ten or fifteen seconds while the shell gets there." Amid the erupting black puffballs in the sky, again and again American torpedo- and bomb-carrying aircraft got through unscathed.

The Japanese navy's Lt. Cmdr. Haruki Iki commanded a squadron of Jill torpedo-bombers, based at Clark Field on Luzon. On the twenty-fourth, entirely ignorant of Shogo, they were ordered to launch a "maximum effort" mission in search of the American carriers. They could carry sufficient fuel only to reach Third Fleet. Early afternoon found Iki leading his formation of eighteen aircraft north-east over the sea. They received their first intimation of the desperate drama of the Combined Fleet when they saw far below the battleship *Musashi*, under American attack. They had scarcely absorbed what was happening when Hellcats fell on them. A massacre followed. As inexperienced pilots strove to jink out of American sights, within a matter of minutes fifteen Japanese planes were shot down. Two aircraft escaped back to Clark. Iki himself found refuge in cloud.

By the time he emerged, sky and sea were empty, his fuel exhausted. He turned south-east and ditched in shallow water a few hundred yards off the north shore of Leyte Island. He and his gunner stood on a wing waving at figures on the beach, who were plainly Japanese. Iki fired flares to attract attention. Eventually, a small boat approached. "We're navy!" cried Iki. "We're army," the occupants of the boat responded dourly. Familiar animosity between the two services asserted itself. The soldiers were alarmed to perceive that the plane's torpedo had fallen from the fuselage, and lay menacingly on the bottom, a few feet below. They pointed: "Can't you do something about that thing?" "Like what?" demanded Iki crossly. Eventually the soldiers were persuaded to close in and rescue the airmen. Once ashore, Iki begged the local commander to signal his base, report his survival, and provide him with transport to get back. No message was sent, and it was a week before he reached Clark. He arrived to find that a memorial parade had just been held for himself and the rest of his unit. His commander embraced him, back from the dead. "Somehow, I knew we hadn't seen the last of you," said the officer emotionally. With no planes and no crews, there was nothing more for them to do on Luzon. Iki was evacuated to Kyushu to organise a new squadron.

THE JAPANESE PILOT was by no means the only airman to land "in the drink" that day. There was also, for instance, twenty-two-year-old Joseph

Tropp from Cheltenham, Pennsylvania, gunner of a flak-stricken Helldiver. As his air group faded away to the east after making its attack on Kurita's ships, Tropp was left bobbing alone in a dinghy—his pilot had been fatally injured when their plane ditched. He found himself in the path of the entire Japanese fleet. Their battleships did not deign to notice him, but when a destroyer passed within fifty feet "a Jap sailor yelled and I could see others pouring out of their hatches talking, gesticulating. They lined up at the rail shaking their fists, yelling and laughing. One of them disappeared and came back with a rifle, and I was sure he intended to strafe me, but I could see and hear them yelling about something else that distracted their attention." More American aircraft were approaching, and Tropp was left to his own devices. After two days in the dinghy he landed on Samar, met guerrillas who delivered him to the Americans, and eventually returned to his carrier.

Far graver misfortunes now overtook Kurita. Cmdr. James McCauley, directing Third Fleet's torpedo-bombers, divided his planes between the three biggest Japanese ships. *Musashi* was struck nineteen times by torpedoes, seventeen times by bombs. This attack, declared pilot David Smith, was "absolutely beautiful. I've never seen anything like it . . . no bombs missed. The torpedo planes came in on a hammerhead attack, four on each bow, and you could see the wakes headed right for the bow. They all ran hot straight and normal, and exploded. Well, she stopped and burned like hell, and when I left her about thirty minutes later the bow was flush with the water."

Yamato and *Nagato* were also slightly hit. The heavy cruiser *Myoko* was obliged to turn for home with shaft damage. At 1930, the 67,123-ton behemoth *Musashi*, each of its main turrets heavier than a destroyer, the huge gold imperial chrysanthemum still adorning its prow, rolled over and sank. Some 984 of its 2,287 crew perished—it was four hours before Japanese escorts addressed themselves to seeking survivors. Ugaki afterwards composed a haiku about the death of *Musashi*'s captain, Rear-Admiral Toshihira Inoguchi. This ended winsomely: "Who can read the heart of an admiral brooding?" The weather—"Fair"—was the only aspect of 24 October about which Ugaki could bring himself to comment favourably in his diary. On this, "the first day of the decisive battle," he lamented how few American planes had been shot down. Anti-aircraft fire from Kurita's ships had accounted for only eighteen attackers. Inoguchi's last testament, scribbled as his ship foundered, recorded regret that he and his comrades had placed exaggerated faith in big ships and big guns.

Yet given the fact that Halsey's aircraft had been able to strike all day without interference from Japanese fighters, the results were far less comprehensive than the Americans might have expected, and than their pilots claimed. Halsey wrote after the war: "The most conspicuous lesson learnt from this action is the practical difficulty of crippling by air strikes alone a task force of heavy ships at sea and free to maneuver." This is wholly unconvincing. Far more relevant was the fact that the American fliers started their battle tired, desperately tired, after days of intensive action. The carrier *Bunker Hill* had already been detached to Ulithi because of the exhaustion of its air group, and other ships' pilots were in little better case. Fatigue diminished accuracy. A Hellcat commander, Lamade of *Hancock*, was especially critical of the Helldivers' performance during this period: "The dive-bombers are not hitting what they're aiming at—I don't think they're aiming at all." An analysis of one air group's operations on 24 October concluded: "Too many targets were attacked scattering light damage to many ships . . . radio discipline must be improved." That day, only around 45 of 259 U.S. strike aircraft achieved hits. This fell far short of the best performances by carrier pilots in the autumn of 1944. Despite the sinking of *Musashi*, American sorties on 24 October were relatively unsuccessful.

Yet they were enough to shake Kurita. At 1400 that afternoon, the Japanese force reversed course away from the San Bernardino Strait. The admiral signalled to naval headquarters: "It is . . . considered advisable to retire temporarily beyond range of enemy air attack, and resume our operation when the actions of [other] friendly units permit." Whatever Kurita did thereafter, his force could no longer achieve its scheduled dawn rendezvous off Leyte Gulf with the southern Japanese squadron. Ashore, the Japanese mood was already grim. One of the day's luckier men was Maj. Shoji Takahashi in Manila. When the Shogo squadrons sailed, the navy requested the presence of an army liaison officer, to sail aboard *Musashi*. Takahashi volunteered. He thought the trip sounded rather fun. That night, when South Asia Area Army learned that the great battleship and many of her crew lay on the sea bottom, the intelligence officer's colonel wagged a grim finger at him: "Lucky I wouldn't let you go, isn't it?" Admiral Halsey, hearing his pilots' reports, was convinced that Third Fleet had achieved a decisive victory, that Kurita's force was broken and in retreat.

Nishimura's "C" Force, comprising two old battleships, a heavy cruiser and four destroyers, was absurdly weak for independent action. A further element of the Combined Fleet, Shima's small squadron, was pursuing the same route as Nishimura, but lagging hours behind him. It was as if the Japanese high command was offering its enemies a feast in successive courses, each scaled to fit American appetites, with convenient pauses for the cleansing of palates. As "C" Force began its long approach to Leyte Gulf from the south on the morning of the twenty-fourth, it suffered one ineffectual American air attack before Halsey's carriers moved north to address Kurita. Thereafter, it was plain to Admiral Thomas Kinkaid, commanding Seventh Fleet, screening the Leyte beachhead, that it would be up to his ships to dispose of Nishimura; and that the Japanese would traverse the Surigao Strait during darkness.

Kinkaid was a fifty-six-year-old New Hampshireman who had spent much of his early service in battleships. He nursed some resentment that he had been removed by Halsey from a carrier group command earlier in the war, and was generally deemed a competent rather than an inspired officer. At 1215, he ordered every ship to prepare for a night engagement, signalling: "General situation: enemy aircraft and naval forces seem to be assembling . . . for an offensive strike against Leyte area . . . attack tonight by enemy striking group may occur after 1900. General plan: this force will destroy [by] gunfire at moderate ranges and by torpedo attack enemy surface forces attempting to enter Leyte Gulf through . . . Surigao Strait."

MacArthur demanded to be allowed to stay aboard the cruiser *Nashville* for the battle, and only under protest transferred his headquarters ashore. The twenty-eight supply and command ships in San Pedro Bay were left to be screened by destroyers. Admiral Jesse Oldendorf, commanding the force of old battleships and cruisers providing bombardment support for Leyte, deployed these in line across the mouth of the strait to await the enemy. The five destroyers of Captain Jesse Coward's Squadron 54 took station ahead as a skirmishing force, supported by six further destroyers of Desron 24 and nine of Desron 56, in readiness to launch successive torpedo attacks. A swarm of little PT-boats patrolled still further forward, riding easily on the glassy sea. The PTs' first, unfortunate engagement involved an American plane: they shot down a night-flying "Black Cat" Catalina which was searching for Nishimura.

The night was full of apprehension. Kinkaid, on his command ship *Wasatch* in San Pedro anchorage, was dismayed to hear of a Japanese bombing raid on Tacloban, which detonated a fuel dump. The American battleships at the entrance to Surigao heavily outgunned Nishimura's squadron. Because they did not expect to engage enemy warships, however, they carried little armour-piercing ammunition. A night action was always chancy, especially against the Japanese. It was most unlikely that Nishimura's feeble force could break through Seventh Fleet, but a few lucky Japanese shells might wreak havoc.

The battle began at 2236, as the little jungle-green-painted wooden PT-boats raced at twenty-four knots to launch the first attacks. One after another, amid foaming wakes and flickering Japanese searchlights, they strove to close the columns of advancing ships. Nishimura's secondary armament fired repeated salvoes at the fragile craft. In the course of skirmishes that lasted almost four hours, thirty boats fired torpedoes—and all missed. The PTs were the navy's special forces, chiefly employed for reconnaissance and rescue duty. Their torpedo training had been neglected. One craft was lost, three men killed. Nishimura's squadron surged on northwards.

The American destroyers fared better. These were almost new *Fletcher*-class ships, displacing 2,000 tons apiece. Their five-inch guns were irrelevant to a contest with capital ships. Coward ordered his turret crews to hold their fire, for muzzle flashes would only pinpoint them for the Japanese. It was the destroyers' torpedoes that mattered, launched from much stabler aiming platforms than the PT-boats, and capable of sinking anything. Even in darkness after the moon set just past midnight, visibility was better than two miles. The temperature on deck was eighty degrees, the heat below stifling. In combat information centres, anti-submarine sonars pinged monotonously. Five or six men crowded into the dark, sweaty space behind or below each ship's bridge, dominated by an illuminated, glass-covered plot on which a pinpoint of light showed the ship's position. On American radar screens, the sea slugs that represented Nishimura's ships were closing fast.

As those with a view watched the PT-boat actions, the captain of one destroyer, *Monssen*, broadcast to his ship's company at general quarters: "To all hands. This is the captain. We are going into battle. I know each of you will do your duty. I promise that I will do my duty to you and for our country. Good luck to you, and may God be with us." The harshest predicament was not now that of men manning the upper decks, but that of hundreds more sweating in their flashproof denims and anti-flash hoods at switchboards and ammunition hoists, machinery controls and casualty stations below, where they could see nothing of events until a ghastly moment when explosives might rip through thin plate, blood and water mingle with twisted steel. Such images were vivid in the imaginations of most sailors, as they drank coffee and ate sandwiches through the interminable wait to engage.

Nishimura's column was led by four destroyers. His own flagship, the old battleship *Yamashiro*, followed, with *Fuso* and *Mogami* at thousand-yard intervals behind. At 0240 *McGowan* reported "Skunk 184 degrees distant fifteen miles." Fifteen minutes later, Japanese lookouts glimpsed the distant enemy, but their huge searchlights failed to illuminate Coward's ships. Now the American destroyers began to close, thrashing down the twelve-mile-wide strait at thirty knots. Even with the Japanese slowed by an adverse current, Nishimura's ships and the Americans were approaching each other at better than fifty miles an hour. At 0258, with the Japanese in plain sight, Coward's squadron made protective smoke. He ordered the three ships in his own division: "Fire when ready." A few seconds after 0300, the Americans began loosing torpedoes at a range just short of 9,000 yards. To have gone closer, the destroyer leader believed, would have invited devastation from Nishimura's gunfire. A Japanese searchlight suddenly fixed *Remey* in its dazzling glare, making its crew feel "like animals in a cage." The battleships began lighting the sky with star shells, while striving in vain to hit American destroyers making a land speed approaching forty mph. In seventy-five seconds, twenty-seven torpedoes left their tubes. Coward swung hard to port, then zigzagged through their eight minutes of running time. At 0308, they heard a single explosion aboard a Japanese ship, probably *Yamashiro*.

The two ships of Coward's western group were much more successful. They fired at 0311, just as Nishimura ordered his ships to take evasive action, which turned them smartly into the tracks of the incoming torpedoes. *McDermut* achieved a remarkable feat, hitting three Japanese destroyers with a single salvo. One blew up immediately, a second began to sink, a third retired with the loss of her bow. Lt. Tokichi Ishii, forty-four-year-old engineer officer of *Asugumo*, suddenly found paint peeling from the deckplates above his head, in the heat from fires. A series of explosions rocked the ship as American gunfire detonated their own torpedoes. He saw pressure gauges crack, telephone wires burn. Smoke poured into the engine room. As the men coughed and choked, they strove in vain to close hatches and shut off ventilators. Finally, as conditions became intolerable, Ishii ordered his men topside. On deck, they worked frantically to douse the fires—and at last succeeded. Returning to the engine room, at 0345 he reported to the bridge that the ship had regained power. He was just descending the ladder to return to his post when another American torpedo hit the ship. The blast catapulted him into the sea. He clung to a plank, watching the ship settle by the stern under renewed American shellfire. Ishii swam to a raft with difficulty, for his leg had been gashed wide open in the torpedo explosion. Hours later he was washed ashore on Leyte, seized by guerrillas, and to his embarrassment delivered alive to an American PT-boat.

A torpedo from *Monssen* hit *Yamashiro*, now crippled. The next American destroyer attack, by Squadron 24, probably achieved two hits. It is still disputed whether battleship gunfire or torpedoes were responsible, but what is certain is that the battleship *Fuso*, laid down in 1912, caught fire and broke in two after a huge explosion. Bewilderment persists about how readily such a huge ship succumbed, but senility plainly rendered it vulnerable. At 0335 the last American destroyer squadron engaged, urged to "Get the big boys!," of which only two were left, one damaged. The "tin cans' " moment had passed, however. All Desron 56's torpedoes missed. Shells from the American battleships and cruisers began to straddle the Japanese. One of Desron 24's torpedoes may have hit *Yamashiro*, but she was already racked by the fire of American fourteen- and sixteen-inch guns. Some naval officers later criticised the destroyers' performance in the Surigao Strait, asserting that they erred in launching torpedoes 3,000 yards beyond optimum range. Technically, such strictures are valid. Torpedo-guidance technology was relatively unsophisticated. It required extraordinary luck and skill to score hits at distances of four or five miles, in the strong currents of the strait. But this was not a situation in which suicidal courage was needed. A close engagement would almost certainly have resulted in gratuitous American destroyer losses, when Nishimura's squadron was anyway doomed.

The American big ships sounded general quarters only at 0230, shortly before the flares of explosions from the destroyer actions became visible. A small black mess attendant who served belowdecks in *Maryland*'s ammunition supply pleaded emotionally for a post where he could do some shooting: "I want to be on the guns—I know I can hit them good. *I know I can*." With a nice touch of human sympathy, he was posted to a 20mm mount. In the shell decks below the turrets, men shifted charges for the ships' slender supply of armour-piercing ammunition—the battleships carried mostly high-explosive projectiles for shore bombardment. Warrant gunners checked temperatures: precision was indispensable to accurate fire. "We didn't know too much, but like all sailors, we could sure speculate," said Lt. Howard Sauer, in the main battery plot high in the foretop of *Maryland*.

All the odds were with the Americans, but in Sauer's words, "We remembered the *Hood*"—a 42,000-ton British battle cruiser which blew up in consequence of a single hit from the German *Bismarck* in May 1941. They watched red tracers converging on the skyline, then heard the order to Oldendorf's battleships: "All bulldogs, execute turn three." Barely maintaining steerageway at five knots, they thus presented their flanks and full broadsides to the enemy. As Nishimura's ships closed within range, the vast turrets traversed. Gunners pleaded for the order to fire: "Shoot, shoot, shoot." One by one, main batteries reported readiness: "Right gun turret 2, loaded and laid," and so on. On the command "Commence firing," the chief fire controller in each turret touched his left trigger to sound a warning buzzer, prompting upper-deck crewmen to close eyes and muffle ears. Then a right finger pressure prompted brilliant flashes, thunderous detonations: "On the way." Amid the concussions, Howard Sauer recalled, "we rode the mast as it lashed to and fro, just as a tree moves in a strong gale."

Jesse Oldendorf's flagship *Louisville* was so impatient to fire that the gunners failed to press the warning buzzer, causing the admiral to be temporarily blinded by muzzle flashes. He slipped into the cruiser's flag plot and gazed at the blips on the screen indicating Nishimura's ships. Soon, however, he became distracted by incessant voices echoing through the broadcast system, and returned to the flag bridge. The battleships fired their first rounds at 26,000 yards, the cruisers at 15,600. By an exquisite chance, four of the six capital ships under Oldendorf's command had been salvaged from the bottom of Pearl Harbor in the years following the "Day of Infamy." They were now deemed too old and slow to sail with Halsey, but three—*Tennessee*, *California* and *West Virginia*—were equipped with the latest fire-control radar, infinitely superior to anything the Japanese possessed. These monsters, taking their last bow in a contest between "ships of the line," fired sixty-nine, sixty-three and ninety-three rounds respectively from their main armament. The Japanese Vice-Admiral Ugaki once enquired sourly why, if battleships had become redundant as some people claimed, the Americans used so many. This night, they wreaked havoc. *Yamashiro*, flying Nishimura's flag, was soon blazing brilliantly. The heavy cruiser *Mogami* turned to flee. At 0402 a hit on the bridge killed all her senior officers. She continued to steam, heavily on fire. Seven minutes later *Yamashiro* capsized and sank, with the loss of the admiral and almost her entire crew. A cruiser and a destroyer, both badly hit, thus became the only survivors to escape. By contrast, three U.S. cruisers were straddled by Japanese fire, but no American heavy unit was hit. At 0405, after just fourteen minutes, Oldendorf ordered his battleships to cease firing. He knew that the Japanese squadron was devastated, and was alarmed by reports of American destroyers in the target zone.

The night actions were not yet ended, however. Twenty miles behind the main Japanese force, Vice-Admiral Kiyohide Shima led a further squadron of three heavy cruisers and escorts. Its first casualty was the light cruiser *Akubuma*, hit by a PT-boat torpedo aimed at a destroyer. At 0420, Japanese radar detected enemy ships, and Shima ordered his own captains to launch torpedoes. These were fired against the nearby Hibuson Islands, which survived undamaged, a nonsense that highlighted the pitiful limitations of Japanese radar. Shima then approached the two blazing parts of *Fuso*, and mistook them for separate ships. He was in no doubt, however, that disaster had befallen Nishimura. Turning south once more, he signalled naval headquarters: "This force has concluded its attack and is retiring from the battle area to plan subsequent action." Retreat merely presaged further humiliations. The cruiser *Nachi* collided with a fugitive from Nishimura's squadron, the burning *Mogami*. The two somehow limped away southwards. *Mogami* later suffered an American air attack, and was finished off with a Japanese torpedo. Another Japanese destroyer was sunk by land-based U.S. aircraft.

As Oldendorf's force advanced slowly down the Surigao Strait, the Americans saw only two burning Japanese ships, together with survivors in the water, most of whom declined rescue. By dawn, the stem of *Fuso* was the sole visible relic of Nishimura's squadron. *Louisville* catapulted a float-plane aloft, which reported no sign of enemy activity. It had been a ruthless slaughter, but this did not trouble Oldendorf. "Never give a sucker an even break," he said laconically. Hiroshi Tanaka, a bedraggled aircraft mechanic from *Yamashiro* who fell into American hands, observed bitterly that Nishimura had handled his squadron "more like a petty officer than an admiral." It is hard to disagree, and even harder to conceive of any other outcome of such an ill-matched encounter. Oldendorf made no attempt to pursue the surviving Japanese, urging Kinkaid to put carrier aircraft on the case. He had fulfilled his own executioner's role. Just one Japanese heavy cruiser, together with five destroyers, reached home. The Leyte anchorage seemed safe. American casualties from the Surigao Strait action numbered 39 killed and 114 wounded, almost all of these inflicted by "friendly fire" on the destroyer *Grant*, which had disobeyed orders to hug the shore when the American heavy guns opened fire.

What else could the Japanese conceivably have expected? The action's outcome reflected strategic folly, technological weakness and tactical incompetence. The Americans deployed overwhelming firepower under almost ideal circumstances. They were able to array their big ships broadside so that every gun could bear. The obliging enemy, who could use only his forward turrets, headed into the crossbar of Oldendorf's T. As dawn came on 25 October, America's veteran battleships could retire from the history of fleet warfare, having written a last memorable page. Yet the most bizarre action of Leyte Gulf was still to come.

2. The Ordeal of Taffy 3

JUST BEFORE sunset on the previous evening of the twenty-fourth, Admiral Kurita's fleet had turned once more towards the San Bernardino Strait, goaded by a signal from commander-in-chief Admiral Soemu Toyoda: "All forces will resume the attack, having faith in divine providence." A staff officer muttered cynically: "All forces will resume the attack, having faith in annihilation." Through the darkness, the Japanese pressed on eastwards, at every moment expecting to encounter American submarines. At first light, as they passed into open sea east of the Philippines, they waited grimly for a sighting of planes or ships from Halsey's Third Fleet, which would signal their doom. After intercepting a signal from a surviving destroyer, they knew that Nishimura's squadron had been destroyed: "All ships except *Shigure* lost to gunfire and torpedoes." Yet the minutes passed, and the horizon ahead of Kurita remained empty. Halsey's ships, the greatest assembly of naval might in the world, were not there. The American admiral had committed one of the most astonishing blunders of the war at sea.

Kurita has been so fiercely criticised for faintheartedness on the afternoon of 24 October, when he turned back, that the obvious point is sometimes missed: had the Japanese admiral maintained his course into the San Bernardino Strait, Halsey's aircraft would have renewed their assaults at dawn. American battleships would have awaited him as he approached the eastern exit. His fleet's destruction would have been inevitable. As it was, luck and American rashness offered Kurita a remarkable opportunity.

William "Bull" Halsey was the sixty-one-year-old son of a naval officer, a man of fierce passions whom wartime propaganda, a talent for quotable bombast and an unfailing eagerness to engage the enemy had made a national hero. Classmates at Annapolis used to say that he looked like a figurehead of Neptune, with his big head, heavy jaw and customary scowl. Single-mindedly devoted to the sea, he had no hobbies and no apparent interest in personal matters. Though he was obsessively neat and immaculately dressed afloat, ashore his wife found him clumsy: "If a man has a nervous wife he wants to get rid of, all he has to do is send for you. Five minutes after you've come in, bumping into sofas and knocking over chairs, she'll be dead of heart failure." His domestic life was notably dysfunctional. Like MacArthur, though in a very different, cruder fashion, Halsey acted and talked the warrior's part: "I never trust a fighting man who doesn't drink or smoke!" He cherished in his cabin a magnificent western saddle presented by an admirer, to assist fulfilment of the admiral's promise that he would one day ride Hirohito's white horse through Tokyo. Nimitz remarked that when he sent Spruance out with the fleet, "he was always sure he would bring it home; when he sent Halsey out, he did not know precisely what was going to happen." Halsey's boldness was in doubt seldom, his judgement and intellect often.

For four days, Vice-Admiral Jizaburo Ozawa had been flaunting his presence more than two hundred miles north of the U.S. Third Fleet. His carriers had only 116 aircraft, half their complement. On the morning of the twenty-fourth he launched seventy-six of these on a notably ineffectual strike against Halsey's ships. The surviving planes landed on Luzon, having achieved their only serious purpose, that of attracting American attention. Late in the afternoon, a U.S. reconnaissance aircraft at last sighted Ozawa's squadron. Halsey's reaction perfectly fulfilled Japanese hopes. He turned north to engage the empty carriers with every unit at his disposal. "As it seemed childish to me to guard statically San Bernardino Strait," he told Nimitz and MacArthur afterwards, attempting to justify his decision, "I concentrated TF 38 during the night and steamed north to attack the North Force at dawn. I believed that [Kurita's] Center Force had been so heavily damaged in the Sibuyan Sea that it could no longer be considered a serious menace to Seventh Fleet."

To the day of his death, Halsey never acknowledged that he had allowed himself to be fooled. On the map of the Leyte Gulf battle in his post-war memoirs, Ozawa's carriers are unequivocally identified as "Japanese main force." Halsey considered that Kurita's squadron had been crippled and repulsed by his aircraft on the twenty-fourth. American pilots' reports suggested that four battleships were sailing with Ozawa's carriers. Halsey chose wilfully to ignore overnight reports that Kurita was once again heading into San Bernardino. He wrote later, in self-exculpation: "It was not my job to protect the Seventh Fleet. My job was offensive, and we were even then rushing to intercept a force which gravely threatened not only Kinkaid and myself, but the whole Pacific strategy." Rear-Admiral Robert Carney, Halsey's chief of staff, said: "With the conviction that Center Force had been so heavily damaged that although they could still steam and float they could not fight to best advantage, it was decided to turn full attention to the still untouched and very dangerous carrier force to the north."

Halsey could argue that some intelligence assessments still credited the Japanese carrier force with far more formidable air capability than it possessed. Yet this does not explain his most culpable error of all: failure to ensure that Kinkaid and Nimitz understood that he was steaming away from Leyte with everything he had, soon putting the Philippines battlefield beyond range of his aircraft or battleship guns. Claims have been made that he believed a signal had been sent to San Pedro and Pearl, and that fault for its non-transmission lay with his staff. This is unconvincing. It is much easier to believe that Halsey simply acted recklessly, in pursuit of glory and a decisive victory. In almost three years of war, both sides had become obsessed with the importance of carriers, decisive units of Pacific combat. Shrewd intelligence analysts at Pearl had reported that, almost stripped of aircraft and deck-qualified pilots, Ozawa's ships were now mere hulks. They even suggested that these might be sacrificed as decoys.

Halsey spurned such assessments. He displayed a hubris unsurprising, perhaps, in a navy that now dominated the Pacific theatre. He ignored the fact that Kurita's ships, wherever they were, represented the most formidable naval force left to the enemy. Victory at Midway in 1942 had been achieved when Halsey was sick, and the much more measured Spruance commanded the U.S. fleet. Now, Spruance was ashore, and Halsey enjoyed full scope to blunder. Kinkaid's Seventh Fleet, essentially an amphibious support force, was left unshielded and oblivious in the path of Kurita. Even had Oldendorf's old battleships been in sight east of Leyte, rather than in the Surigao Strait, Seventh Fleet would have been dangerously outgunned by the Japanese.

The morning of 25 October found Rear-Admiral Thomas Sprague's sixteen escort carriers, mustered in three task groups designated as Task Forces—"Taffies"—1, 2 and 3, cruising in their usual operating areas, some forty miles apart and about the same distance east of Leyte. For the ships' crews, service with Seventh Fleet offered none of the glamour of offensive action under Halsey or Spruance. When one of the carriers' escorting destroyers, *Johnston*, was commissioned twelve months earlier, only 7 of its 331 officers and men had previous sea experience. The crew had since learned much about working their ship, but enjoyed precious little glory. "Well, Hagen," sighed Ernest Evans, *Johnston*'s captain, to his gunnery officer, "it's been an uneventful year." He was bitterly disappointed to have missed the Surigao Strait action, which his excited radio operators had eavesdropped on.

Escort carriers, workhorses of the war at sea, were crude floating runways, most converted from tankers and merchantmen. Their class acronym, CVE, was alleged by cynics to stand for "Combustible, Vulnerable, Expendable." They lacked the defensive armament, aircraft capacity and speed of purpose-built fleet carriers four times their tonnage. They were intended only to provide local air support, in this case for the Leyte Gulf amphibious armada and MacArthur's soldiers ashore. Each carried twelve to eighteen obsolescent Wildcat fighters and eleven or twelve Avenger torpedo and bomber aircraft. The previous day, the fighters had accounted for some twenty-four Japanese aircraft over Leyte.

That morning, Taffy 3's five carriers, three destroyers and four destroyer escorts had just secured from routine pre-dawn general quarters. It was the midst of the most unpopular watch of the day, 4 to 8 a.m., when, in the words of a jaundiced Pacific sailor, "the morning sun would be looking like a bloody bubble in a peepot." Most crews had gone to breakfast as the ships turned into the north-east wind and prepared to fly off the first sorties of the day. Lookouts suddenly reported anti-aircraft fire north-westwards, and radio rooms a gabble of Japanese voices flooding the ether. At 0647, in what one captain called "a rather frantic voice transmission," an anti-submarine-patrol pilot announced that four Japanese battleships, eight cruisers and accompanying destroyers were just twenty miles from Taffy 3. Momentarily, its commander, Rear-Admiral Clifton "Ziggy" Sprague—confusingly, two unrelated Admiral Spragues were off Leyte that day—believed these must be Halsey's ships. Then the Americans saw pagoda masts, and at 0658 the Japanese opened fire.

It was one of the great surprise attacks of the war. Despite all the technological might of the U.S. Navy, Kurita's ships had been able to sail almost 150 miles in seven hours, unnoticed by the Americans. Human eyes detected them before radar did. Admiral King, in Washington, blamed Kinkaid for failing to watch Kurita's movements. It can certainly be suggested that the admiral could have spared a few search planes of his own to monitor Kurita's movements alongside Halsey's aircraft. Richard Frank persuasively argues that, with the Japanese known to be at sea, Kinkaid should also have moved his Taffies further from San Bernardino.

Yet it seems impossible to dispute the fundamental point, that dealing with Kurita was Halsey's responsibility. Seventh Fleet was nicknamed, somewhat derisively, "MacArthur's private navy." Kinkaid's mission was to support Sixth Army. "Halsey's job," said Kinkaid later, "was to keep the Japanese fleet off of our necks while we were doing this." Halsey had already engaged Kurita, and possessed overwhelming firepower for the purpose. Kinkaid knew that Halsey had gone in pursuit of Ozawa, but it never occurred to him that he had taken his entire force. Given the strength of Third Fleet, there were ample heavy units for some to have guarded against the Japanese battle squadron—yet none was left behind. This, although on the night of the twenty-fourth Halsey was told that Kurita had turned back towards San Bernardino. Here were the painful consequences of divided command. Halsey was answerable to Nimitz, Kinkaid to MacArthur. At Leyte Gulf, failure to appoint an overall supreme commander for the Pacific theatre came closer than at any other time to inflicting a disaster on American arms.

Sprague and his officers, confronted by an array of impossibly mighty enemy ships, almost twice as fast as their own carriers, believed they faced a massacre as surely as any wagon train surprised by Sioux: "That sonofabitch Halsey has left us bare-assed!" exclaimed the admiral. "Our captain announced on the PA that the whole Japanese fleet was attacking Taffy 3," wrote Walter Burrell, a medical officer on *Suwanee* with Taffy 1. "I looked out on the forecastle and sure enough it looked like there were a hundred ships on the horizon." The nearest American heavy units were those of Jesse Oldendorf, sixty-five miles south. This represented almost three hours' steaming, an eternity in such circumstances. It was vividly apparent that the fate of Taffy 3 would be settled long before American big ships could reach the scene.

Yet Kurita, in his turn, was shocked—and wildly deceived. He had supposed that no significant American naval force lay between himself and Leyte Gulf, that his course was open to ravage Kinkaid's amphibious armada. A first glimpse of Sprague's ships persuaded him that he faced Halsey's Third Fleet and its huge carriers. Rather than organise a concerted movement led by his destroyers, he ordered a general attack, every Japanese ship for itself. In four columns, Kurita's squadron began to close on Sprague's task group, firing as they came. A cluster of pilots in a carrier ready room was broken up by the entry of an officer who said: "The Jap fleet's after us." This was received with disbelief. "Everybody was laughing and joking, couldn't believe it," said an aviator whose plane was unserviceable. "We went up on the flightdeck and about half an hour later, we began to hear things whistling and dropping astern of us, which turned out to be sixteen-inch shells. It was a kind of funny feeling to be on deck when you're under attack and don't have anything to fly."

Sprague's ships laboured to increase speed to 17½ knots and open the range, making smoke while sustaining an easterly course so that they could fly off aircraft. Rear-Admiral Felix Stump of Taffy 2 tried to reassure Sprague on voice radio: "Don't be alarmed, Ziggy—remember, we're back of you—don't get excited—don't do anything rash!" Yet Stump's tone conveyed his own dismay, and his words were unconvincing. Taffy 2 possessed no more firepower than Taffy 3. Sprague's six carriers were arrayed in a rough circle, with the destroyers beyond. In the first four minutes of action, *White Plains* was straddled four times by fifteen-inch gunfire. Her crew were fascinated by the vari-dyed water plumes, designed to enable Japanese gunners to distinguish each ship's salvoes: "They're shooting at us in Technicolor!" By a twist of fortune, a heavy rain squall now swept across the sea. For fifteen important minutes this masked the American ships from the Japanese, who were obliged to resort to radar-directed fire. Kurita signalled triumphantly home that his squadron had sunk a heavy cruiser. Yet so poor was Japanese fire control that at this stage their guns had hit nothing at all.

Here was one of the strangest melodramas of the Second World War. After more than two years of Pacific combat dominated by clashes between ships and aircraft whose parent fleets were often hundreds of miles apart, American seamen now watched with naked eyes as some of the largest warships in the world fired upon them at almost point-blank range, in the manner of the navies of Nelson and Decatur. Fevered activity on the carriers launched one by one into the air every plane that could fly, carrying whatever ordnance chanced to be fitted, to fulfil a simple mission: hit the Japanese. On *Gambier Bay*, Captain William Vieweg ordered the crew out of a plane already on the catapult, then deliberately fired it into the sea, for his ship was generating too little wind speed to launch. With only a few torpedoes and bombs loaded, many planes which did get off were reduced to strafing the Japanese warship decks with machine-gun fire.

Rationally, this was as useful as belabouring an armoured knight with a walking stick. Yet, from beginning to end of the Leyte battle, perverse psychological forces were in play. The Japanese had embarked on the Shogo operation anticipating the worst. At every turn they behaved with the fatalism of doomed men, convinced of their own inferiority to the enemy. Kurita and his captains expected to be attacked and sunk by carrier aircraft, and here indeed were carrier aircraft. They anticipated a disastrous encounter with the U.S. Third Fleet, and here it seemed to be. A weak and vulnerable American force, Taffy 3, was under assault by one of the most powerful battle squadrons in the world. Yet Kurita and his captains assumed that they faced defeat. It remains an enigma how by October 1944 the fighting seamen of the Japanese navy had been reduced to such poverty of thought, will and action. This was the force which conceived and executed the attack on Pearl Harbor, which destroyed the British capital ships *Prince of Wales* and *Repulse*, which performed miracles of skill and daring in the early years of war. Yet now the commanders of Japan's greatest warships revealed stunning ineptitude. On 25 October their ship recognition was inept, their tactics primitive, their gunnery woeful, their spirit feeble. None of this diminishes the American achievement that day, but it invites the bewilderment of history.

Besides the carrier pilots who threw themselves at Kurita's ships, the heroes of the morning were the U.S. destroyer crews. With an unflinching aggression that further alarmed the Japanese, they raced towards the enemy's battle line. "Prepare to attack major portion of Japanese fleet!" Ernest Evans of *Johnston* told his crew, in a pardonably histrionic moment. Evans, a short, barrel-chested, half-Cherokee Native American, steamed into action with all his five-inch guns firing. This was the gesture of an urchin pummelling a giant. Yet when he launched torpedoes, one struck the heavy cruiser *Kumano*, which fell out of line. An American cruiser officer described the experience of suffering a torpedo hit as "about the same as driving a car at high speed when you hit a pile of logs. You'd be knocked up in the air, probably sideways, and you'd come down on the concrete on the other side with all wheels flat."

At 0730, three fourteen-inch shells hit *Johnston*, which seemed to one of its officers "like a puppy being smacked by a truck." The ship's radar array collapsed onto the bridge, killing three officers. Evans lost his shirt and three fingers of one hand; scores of men below were killed or wounded. *Johnston*'s speed fell away to seventeen knots. Cmdr. Leon Kintenburger of *Hoel* had only skippered his ship for a fortnight. Its guns fired ten salvoes at the Japanese before incoming shells knocked out the directors. The ship received more than forty heavy-calibre hits, and stayed afloat as long as it did only because many huge armour-piercing rounds passed through the hull without exploding. Cmdr. Amos Hathaway of *Heermann* at first could not see the Japanese either visually or on radar, and merely obeyed Sprague's directional order. Confused about what was going on, "I told the crew this was either going to be the bloodiest, worst thing we had ever seen—or nothing. That is always an easy and good prediction to make."

When water spouts began to rise out of the surrounding sea, at first Hathaway scanned the sky in search of bombers, before realising he was being shelled. His ship dashed between the fleeing escort carriers, the bridge crew almost blinded when the rain squall struck. Then the sky cleared and Japanese ships loomed huge before them. Hathaway belatedly realised that he must do the unthinkable—launch a daylight torpedo attack on enemy heavy units. He turned to his navigator, Lieutenant Newcome: " 'Buck, what we need is a bugler to sound the charge.' He looked at me as if I was a little crazy, and said 'What do you mean, Captain?' I said that we were going to make a torpedo attack. Buck gulped." It is an important truth about war that soldiers on shore, and pilots aloft, almost always have some personal choice about whether to be brave. By contrast, sailors crewing a warship are prisoners of the sole will of their captain. On 25 October 1944, it is no libel upon the crews of Taffy 3's escorts to suggest that some must have been appalled. They were conscripted as heroes, borne at high speed towards an overwhelmingly powerful enemy.

Amid smoke and shifting squalls, even now Hathaway knew little of what was happening, nor that *Heermann*'s sister ships *Hoel* and *Johnston* were damaged. He simply fired seven torpedoes at the heavy cruiser *Chikuma* from a range of 9,000 yards, as Japanese shells began to straddle *Heermann*: "You could hear the express-train roar of the fourteen-inchers going over us." Then a Japanese eight-inch shell exploded on the bridge, leaving a shambles of fallen antennae, twisted steel and bloodied men. The helmsman, together with an aviator rescued the previous night and three other men, lay dead. Hathaway survived only because he had climbed to the higher fire-control position to get a better view of the battle. Quartermaster Jack Woolworth was badly hit in the buttocks, but said nothing and kept his post. *Heermann* suffered eight-inch hits in the engine uptakes, sonar dome and keel—and survived. Red, yellow, green splashes continued to land all around her. Hathaway marvelled that so many could miss: "Why they didn't get more hits than they did I don't understand."

The Americans were also bemused that the Japanese ships seemed to be advancing so slowly, some making as little as ten knots.

Heermann's five-inch guns fired at the battleship *Kongo*'s fire-control tower, but as soon as the ship's last three torpedoes were spent, Hathaway ducked into the pilothouse and radioed Sprague in plain language: "Exercise completed." He said later: "I don't know why I used these words. I had an idea the Japanese might be listening on the circuit, and I didn't want them to know I didn't have any more torpedoes." *Heermann* retired in such haste that Hathaway avoided ramming the carrier *Fanshaw Bay* only by giving an emergency full astern order. The destroyer likewise missed by inches the damaged *Johnston*. "As we cleared each other, a spontaneous cheer went up from each ship." When Commander Evans perceived that *Hoel* was hit, though his own ship was crippled, men were throwing body parts over the side and just two guns remained operational, he swung *Johnston* back into the fray. The destroyer could make only fifteen knots: "We were weaving back and forth," said gunnery officer Robert Hagen, "taking on whatever ship seemed to be closing the carriers the fastest, and we still stayed up with the Japanese cruisers, destroyers, while the Japanese battleships dropped aft . . . The captain fought that ship as no other man has ever fought a ship."

The American destroyers' attacks were uncoordinated, indeed chaotic. Almost all their torpedoes were launched from ranges too long to be effective. But *Yamato* chose to swing away sharply to avoid them, and so wide was the vast ship's turning radius that it fell far behind the rest of Kurita's line. The Japanese were alarmed by American aggression, even if Sprague's warship guns inflicted little damage. *Hoel*, hit repeatedly just before 0800, stayed afloat for a further hour, until sunk by Japanese battleships as they passed the hulk at close range. The destroyer escort *Samuel B. Roberts* lost 3 officers and 86 men, out of a crew of 178. Her captain told his men as they steamed into battle that the ship could not expect to survive, and he was right. By 0820 the Americans had expended all their torpedoes, and the survivors retired towards Sprague's carriers. Except one. The *Johnston* continued to fire on the enemy at close range until at 0945 its crew abandoned ship under a hail of Japanese shells. Of 327 men only 141 were saved, not including Evans, its fine captain.

Kurita dispatched four heavy cruisers to move fast around the Americans and cut them off. Sprague, perceiving this force, ordered that every plane should concentrate against it. It was a day for rhetoric and wisecracks which passed into legend, such as the chief's cry from his quad mount on *White Plains*: "Hold on a little longer, boys! We're sucking them into 40mm range!" *White Plains* scored hits on the cruiser *Chokai* with her single five-inch gun. After American dive-bomber attacks, *Chokai* blew up at 0930. The carrier *Kallin Bay* scored a hit on another cruiser's turret, just before she herself was struck at 0750, after flying off her aircraft. The frail ship survived thirteen eight-inch shell impacts and *Fanshaw Bay* a further four, partly because Japanese armour-piercing ammunition failed to detonate against the thin decks. Below, men laboured amid smoke and bursting steam pipes, plugging holes to keep out the sea, and sealing fractured mains.

Meanwhile, aircraft had hit and slowed another Japanese ship—the heavy cruiser *Suzuya*. Bombs and aerial torpedoes sank the cruiser *Chikuma*. One Taffy 3 pilot, Ed Huxtable, maintained passes at the Japanese battleships for two hours after expending his ammunition. "It takes a lot to go in there carrying nothing," said a profoundly admiring comrade. Some fliers expended their ammunition, rearmed ashore at Tacloban and returned to the charge. Captain John Whitney of *Kitgun Bay* felt pity for his 20mm and 40mm crews who had nothing to do but watch, impotent, while the ship's single five-inch gun lobbed shells at the enemy and Japanese projectiles straddled the carrier. Captain William Vieweg of *Gambier Bay* was baffled to see each Japanese ship firing slow salvoes alternately from forward and rear turrets, rather than in unison. He swung his carrier after glimpsing each set of gun flashes, then watched shells land where *Gambier Bay* would have been, had she not turned: "This process lasted, believe it or not, a half-hour during which the enemy was closing constantly." The enemy's first hit on the carrier at 0825 slowed its speed from 19½ knots to eleven. Thereafter, *Gambier Bay* was hit steadily for an hour, until it lay dead in the water. When a passing Japanese cruiser fired on the hulk from 2,000 yards, to the Americans' amazement its shells missed. The carrier was doomed, however. After it capsized and sank at 0907, Vieweg and his fellow survivors spent two days in the water.

Kurita's destroyers launched torpedo attacks from too long range to be effective, but one of his captains blithely claimed that "three enemy carriers and one cruiser were enveloped in black smoke and observed to sink one after another." Such fantasising was commonplace among junior aircrew on both sides, but becomes hard to excuse in ranking officers. By 0925, this extraordinary encounter had lasted 143 minutes. American aircraft were still hitting the Japanese with whatever they had. The planes of Taffy 2 launched forty-nine torpedoes and claimed several hits on battleships and heavy cruisers for the loss of twenty-three Wildcats and Avengers, slightly fewer than Taffy 3's aircraft casualties. When their fuel became exhausted, most American pilots landed ashore on Leyte. Halsey, at last grudgingly acknowledging the plight of Kinkaid's ships, had dispatched battleships and a carrier group southwards, but it would be many hours before these appeared. It is a measure of the chaos prevailing in the American high command that only at 0953 was Jesse Oldendorf ordered to start northwards with his battleships, desperately short of ammunition. There still seemed nothing to stop the Japanese ships destroying Taffy 3, possibly the other escort-carrier groups also.

Yet suddenly, Sprague and his stunned crews saw the Japanese do the unthinkable. They ceased fire, turned, broke off the engagement. "Goddammit, boys, they're getting away!" cried a signalman in comic disbelief. "At the end of two hours and twenty-three minutes under continuous fire, to my utter amazement and that of all aboard, the Japanese fleet turned around," said Whitney of *Kitgun Bay*. "We were within effective gun range for another fifteen minutes, but they did not fire another shot at us." Kurita claimed to have decided that the American carriers were too fast for him to catch. Two floatplanes catapulted from the Japanese ships to reconnoitre Leyte Gulf had failed to return. There was no word from Ozawa. Nishimura's squadron was known to be lost. Kurita's radio operators had heard Kinkaid call in plain language for fast battleships. "Japan was showing signs not only of fatigue, but of decay as well, and nowhere was this more apparent than in the fields of communications and intelligence," in the words of a Japanese historian. On 25 October 1944, such "decay" was startlingly displayed on the flag bridge of *Yamato*.

Kurita later produced a range of excuses for his disengagement decision: after three days and nights without sleep, "my mind was extremely fatigued. It should probably be called 'a judgement of exhaustion.'" He talked unconvincingly about a signal, of which no record was ever found, reporting American warships to the north, in his rear. He claims to have decided to regroup his diminished forces and resume his original mission—an assault on the amphibious shipping in Leyte Gulf. In reality, he havered for more than three hours, then set course for retirement through the San Bernardino Strait. Sprague watched the huge Japanese superstructures fade from the horizon. "I could not get the fact into my battle-numbed brain," he wrote later. "At best, I had expected to be swimming by this time." His command of six escort carriers, three destroyers and four escorts, supported by a job lot of aircraft, had mauled and frightened off most of the surviving Japanese battle fleet.

Sprague's subsequent report to Nimitz said that but for "the very poor decision of breaking off the action . . . the Jap main body could have, and should have, waded through and completed the destruction of this task unit, and continuing to the south would have found our naval opposition very low." Sprague found the enemy's poor gunnery "unexplainable," and attributed his force's survival to the "definite partiality of Almighty God."

Kinkaid signalled to MacArthur ashore: "Our situation has again turned rosy from black, black, black."

The naval action around the Philippines on 25 October was not confined to the attacks of Kurita's battle fleet. While recovering its own planes Taffy 1 was surprised by six Japanese aircraft and a submarine which damaged the carriers *Santee* and *Suwanee*. At 1050, while Taffy 3 was still recovering from the early-morning drama, a Zero crashed into the flight deck of *St. Lo*, setting off a series of bomb explosions which caused the ship to blow up at 1125. Some 754 survivors were rescued. Soon after noon next day, another plane hit *Suwanee*, inflicting 245 casualties and doing terrible damage. "The second explosion . . . buckled our bulkheads and ruptured water mains . . . so that we began to flood," wrote medical officer Walter Burrell.

> As the water rose to knee height in our compartment, the ship was listing uncomfortably and lying dead in the water without steerage because of destruction of the bridge and wheelhouse. Isolated from the rest of the ship with only the reflection from the gasoline fires above and a few flickering battle lamps for light, I saw my wounded partially covered with wreckage and already awash . . . with my corpsmen and stretcher bearers, we were able to move out wounded through the hatches from one compartment to the next . . . A sailor, apparently in panic, came running along the passageway screaming: "Everyone's going over the side! The captain's dead! Everyone on the bridge has been killed! Everyone's abandoning ship." Now, contagious panic and cold fear! The wounded . . . began struggling to get out, screaming hysterically, "Where's my lifejacket? Who took my lifejacket? Turn that loose! Gimme that! No, it's mine!" Some were shoving towards the entrance, fighting and scrambling over one another.

Burrell checked the panic, conspicuously taking off his own life jacket and hanging it on a hook. Small-arms ammunition began to explode, ignited by a gasoline fire, and prompting frightened men to jump overboard—a common occurrence when carriers were hit, cause of many needless deaths. The medical officer struggled to aid wounded lying on the forecastle, most "severely burned beyond recognition and hope. All that could be done for the obviously dying was to give the most rudimentary first aid consisting of morphine, a few swallows of water, and some words of companionship." Thanks to brilliant damage control, within an hour *Suwanee*'s fires were out, power and steerage restored, ruptured mains shut off. The ship survived, to limp home for repairs. Yet a submarine and a handful of suicidal pilots had inflicted on the Americans greater loss than the whole of Kurita's fleet had accomplished. Here was an ominous portent.

THE BADLY BOMBED CRUISER *Suzuya* sank at 1322 on the twenty-fifth. At about the same time, operating at extreme range, 335 miles, one of Halsey's carrier groups at last reached Kurita's ships. Of 147 aircraft which attacked, 14 were lost. Neither this mission nor another strike from Taffy 2 inflicted significant damage. Early on the morning of the twenty-sixth, three more American aircraft sorties sunk a light cruiser, *Noshiro*, and damaged the heavy cruiser *Kumano*, which limped into Manila. The crews of forty-seven USAAF Liberators which attacked Kurita's units claimed much, but accomplished nothing. The battered, forlorn, humiliated Japanese fleet regained Brunei Bay at 2130 on 28 October, most of its ships leaking oil and taking in water from near misses. Survival was its only significant achievement.

HALSEY began his dash north, after the sighting of Ozawa's carriers, at 2022 on the night of 24 October. Commander Dahl, the popular executive officer of the carrier *Belleau Wood*, broadcast to its crew: "Attention all hands. We are steaming north to intercept the Jap fleet which is coming out to fight. When the gong rings, move in a hurry. Be prepared for anything. That is all." Yet twenty-two minutes earlier, Ozawa had himself turned away north, on hearing of Kurita's retirement from the San Bernardino Strait. He assumed that Shogo was aborted. Only when naval high command insisted upon resuming the operation did Ozawa again set course towards the Americans who he was so eager should find him.

Most of Halsey's subordinates were amazed by his decision to take north every element of Third Fleet, leaving not a single destroyer to watch San Bernardino. Admiral "Ching" Lee in the battleship *Washington* signalled Halsey that he believed Ozawa's force to be a decoy. He received in response a perfunctory "Roger" from the flagship. Lee later sent another message to Halsey, asserting his conviction that Kurita would reappear. This was unanswered. More extraordinary yet, during the night Halsey ignored a new sighting report of Kurita's ships, heading east once more. Third Fleet's carrier commander, the famously taciturn Marc Mitscher, was woken with the news by staff officers, who urged him to speak to the fleet commander. Mitscher demanded briefly:

"Does Admiral Halsey have that report?"

"Yes."

"If he wants my advice, he'll ask for it."

Mitscher went back to sleep, and thus sixty-five American ships continued steaming north at sixteen knots, to engage just seventeen Japanese vessels of Ozawa's command. Halsey's task forces rendezvoused just before midnight: four *Essex*-class carriers and the old *Enterprise*, five light carriers, six battleships, two heavy cruisers, six light cruisers, forty-one destroyers. Halsey even recalled aircraft which had been shadowing Kurita's force. Not surprisingly, in view of Japanese contrariness, Third Fleet lost Ozawa for some hours during the night, then located his ships again at 0710 on the twenty-fifth, when Sprague's escort carriers were already in flight from Kurita, hundreds of miles to the south.

Around 0800, American Avengers which were orbiting a holding position some seventy miles from Ozawa were vectored onto their first attack of the day. With negligible interference from Japanese fighters, they launched torpedoes at point-blank range. *Chitose* was hit by a succession of bombs, three of which caused damage below the waterline, and sank at 0937. *Zuikaku* was crippled by a torpedo; a destroyer was sunk; nine Japanese aircraft shot down. The next wave of Americans arrived at 0945 to behold "a picture of wild confusion" on the sea below, with Japanese ships manoeuvring desperately. *Chiyoda* was soon hit, blazing and abandoned. A third wave struck the Japanese at 1310, most of its two hundred aircraft flown by crews on their second mission of the day. *Zuikaku* and *Zuiho* suffered multiple hits and caught fire.

Cmdr. Ted Winters, CO of *Lexington*'s Air Group 19, was a fascinated airborne spectator: "There wasn't any of this having the carriers blow up and roll over like I had thought when I went out. They took the first [hits] like somebody getting a slug in the stomach and then fires broke out . . . when a fish hits one of those ships it doesn't look like a big explosion like a bomb; it looks like someone running over a fire plug—a spurt straight up in the air. The fires didn't consume the entire ship, though. Finally after about three hours the carriers rolled slowly, finally rolled over and went down." Fourth and fifth waves of American aircraft failed to sink *Ise*. A sixth strike at 1810, delivered by tired aircrews, accomplished little. Four carriers and a destroyer had thus been destroyed by 527 bomb and torpedo sorties, supported by 201 fighters. Masanori Ito wrote with justice that Ozawa's "mission was to be defeated, and in being defeated he accomplished that mission."

Halsey had reluctantly ordered his battleships south at 1115, to support Seventh Fleet. He would have preferred to keep Lee's squadron to finish off the Japanese cripples. Captain Lewis Dow, Halsey's communications officer, afterwards adopted a contemptuous tone about Sprague's appeals for help: "We had frantic screams from the Seventh Fleet that they were being annihilated . . ." Only late that afternoon were American submarines alerted to concentrate on Ozawa's force, and their sole prey was the light cruiser *Tama*.

Ted Winters was flying back to *Lexington* when he saw the stricken Japanese carriers below him, "still smoking a little. Going back past this other Jap carrier dead in the water, I found a bunch of our cruisers steaming in a north-westerly direction. I thought at first they were Japs because they were so near. I called on the VHF: 'If you will change course forty-five degrees to the right, you will find a Jap carrier dead in the water with no destroyers or battleships around.' " The cruisers asked Winters to sweep north and check that no Japanese heavy units were in range. After reporting the sea clear, he spotted fall of shot for the cruisers, watching the alternating green, yellow and red splashes. With futile courage, a few Japanese gunners were still firing from the hulk. "It wasn't five minutes after they opened fire, and it looked like she just rolled over and went down in a cloud of smoke leaving her fanny sticking up in the air . . . The coordinator's job is a lot of fun."

Halsey described in characteristic terms the moment at which his fleet overran the scene of the Japanese sinkings: "We found no Jap ships, but Jap swimmers were as thick as water bugs. I was having breakfast when Bill Kitchell burst in and cried: 'My God Almighty, Admiral, the little bastards are all over the place! Are we going to stop and pick them up?' " Halsey replied: "Not until we've picked up our own boys"—downed American pilots. He signalled his destroyers not to be over-zealous about their rescue activities: "Bring in cooperative flotsam for an intelligence sample. Non-cooperators would probably like to join their ancestors, and should be accommodated."

Eleven of Ozawa's original seventeen ships were able to sail home. Halsey afterwards made much of the importance of his action off Cape Engano, in writing off the last of Japanese carrier capability. Yet it was Japanese, and not Americans, who scripted Halsey's battle, and he conformed to their design with embarrassing exactitude. The enemy had accepted that their carriers were no longer useful as aircraft platforms, but could serve one last function in luring Third Fleet from the path of Kurita's advance. Halsey accepted the bait. Only Kurita's feebleness prevented the Combined Fleet from inflicting serious destruction upon the Americans around Leyte Gulf. Had he lingered long enough to do so, his own ships would almost certainly have gone to the bottom, because Halsey and Oldendorf would have been given time to intercept their escape. But the Japanese could have inflicted a humiliation on the U.S. Navy before meeting their fate.

American victory in the battles of Leyte Gulf was overwhelming. The Japanese lost 285,000 tons of warships, their opponents just 29,000 tons. American casualties of 2,803 were no more than the Red Army lost every four hours of the war. Japanese losses were far greater than at Midway in 1942. Yet this was, of course, a much less critical encounter. Midway changed the course of the war, arresting the Japanese advance across the Pacific. Whatever might have befallen at Leyte Gulf, Japan's fate was sealed. Even if Kurita had broken through to MacArthur's anchorage, there were sufficient supplies and munitions ashore to ensure that loss of shipping need not threaten Sixth Army. Even if the Japanese had destroyed Taffy 3—or indeed all three Taffys—the Americans would have suffered embarrassment rather than disaster, as they had almost a hundred carriers in commission. In short, no course of action by Kurita would have altered the strategic balance around the Philippines.

Leyte Gulf, however, commands the awe of posterity. At Jutland in 1916, 99 German ships engaged 151 British; at Leyte, 216 American and 2 Australian ships met 64 Japanese. 143,668 American sailors and fliers—more than the combined strengths of the U.S. Navy and Marine Corps in 1938—met 42,800 Japanese. This was the last great clash between rival surface fleets. American setbacks reflected astonishing failures of command and control. Several critical messages between Third and Seventh Fleets and Pearl were two hours in transmission, via relay on Manus. Nimitz, a great commander, must share with Admiral King blame for the systemic failure which permitted Halsey to abandon the San Bernardino Strait and embark upon an adventure which carried risks of such magnitude.

Halsey blundered by dispatching one carrier task force, holding 40 percent of his huge air strength, to rest and rearm at Ulithi even after he knew that the Japanese were at sea. Richard Frank suggests that if he had left his battleships to cover the San Bernardino exit when he set off to chase Ozawa, prudence would have made it essential also to leave some carriers to provide air cover for them. Third Fleet's air component would have been dangerously depleted, when it sought to address the Japanese carriers. This seems a significant point. Yet the fundamental remains: Halsey critically misjudged the relative threats posed by Kurita and Ozawa.

The U.S. admiral's impulsive behaviour reflected the mood of a navy which had grown accustomed to overwhelming superiority. His defenders stress the fact that, at Leyte Gulf, Halsey was anxious to ensure that he would not face the charge of over-caution levelled at Spruance four months earlier, following the Battle of the Philippine Sea. Fifth Fleet's commander was alleged then to have allowed the Japanese carriers to escape destruction, by declining to pursue them. Rivalry with Spruance certainly influenced Halsey's decisions on 24–25 October, but these overwhelmingly reflected his temperament, together with a habitual carelessness about planning and staffwork. Had Third Fleet's commander not possessed such fame, he might have been relieved for his misjudgement at Leyte. The war was in its last phase, however. The Japanese navy was beaten. Though MacArthur privately believed that Halsey should be sacked, there was no appetite in the U.S. Navy for the humiliation of a celebrated admiral.

Among sailors, Halsey incurred much heavier criticism for another blunder two months later, when he kept his fleet at sea after a typhoon was forecast. When this came, it sank three destroyers, crippled many other ships, and drowned almost eight hundred men. By contrast, Halsey's Leyte Gulf blunder was redeemed by the follies of Kurita. The night action of Oldendorf's battleships, cruisers, destroyers and PT-boats in the Surigao Strait was a set piece in the best traditions of the U.S. Navy. Less spectacular, yet at least as significant, was the achievement of American damage-control parties. "Prosecute damage control measures with utmost diligence and tenacity. Don't give up the ship!" decreed the navy's 1944 *Tactical Orders and Doctrine*. The men of the USN fulfilled this injunction with extraordinary devotion and sacrifice. On ship after ship at Leyte, they achieved miracles amidst flaming fuel and twisted wreckage, dying men and choking smoke. Damage control was an outstanding aspect of U.S. naval performance, enabling vessels to be saved from destruction which, in other navies or at an earlier phase of the war, would have been doomed.

Only for the Japanese were the Leyte Gulf actions unredeemed by any morsel of glory. Their commanders had been ordered to seek "flowers of death." Yet the officers of the Combined Fleet displayed stoicism and passivity, rather than the verve and determination which their orders demanded. Even in the simplest battle manoeuvres, again and again on 24 and 25 October Japanese captains were found wanting. Contrast the development of the American and Japanese navies in the course of the Pacific conflict: the U.S. Navy expanded its strength tenfold, so that it was overwhelmingly officered and manned by amateur sailors. Yet the performance of these men proved remarkable. The Japanese navy, which at the start of the war displayed notable superiority in seamanship and gunnery as well as technology, by the end lagged hopelessly in these skills. Japanese officers and men who perished were replaced by newcomers of steadily diminishing competence. Between 23 and 26 October, the Japanese lost four carriers, three battleships, ten cruisers and nine destroyers. The Americans lost three small carriers, two destroyers and a destroyer escort. Some 13,000 sailors perished, most Japanese.

There might have been fewer U.S. fatalities but for an extraordinary failure of omission, for which blame attaches to Kinkaid. Amazingly, for a nation that devoted greater resources than any other combatant to rescue, in the confusion that followed Leyte Gulf, hundreds of American sailors—notably survivors from lost ships of Taffy 3—were left in the water for up to two days and nights before those who remained were located. They had suffered terribly, not least from sharks. "Fifty hours in the water," one of the destroyer *Johnston*'s survivors, Lt. Robert Hagen, reflected disbelievingly. "That's too long to wait before you're picked up!" It was a sorry postscript to the battle. Those men had deserved better from the commanders they had served so well.

Admiral James Clark returned from leave shortly after Leyte Gulf, and reported to Nimitz on Hawaii. "I guess I missed the best battle of the war," said Clark, in some chagrin. "Oh, no," replied Nimitz with a quiet grin. "The best battle will be the last battle."

3. Kamikaze

By a characteristic irony of war, American victory at Leyte Gulf exercised far less influence upon the last phase of the struggle than another, at first apparently marginal, series of events. On 15 October 1944, five days before MacArthur landed on Leyte, Rear-Admiral Masafumi Arima removed his badges of rank and clambered into the cockpit of a plane at Clark Field on Luzon. He then took off at the head of his fliers to attack Halsey's fleet off Formosa. The commander of 26th Naval Air Flotilla, Arima was an impeccably dignified figure who defied the clammy Philippine heat to wear full uniform at all times. A slender, gentle, soft-spoken warrior, he came from a family of Confucian scholars. He cherished a book on tactics written by his own grandfather, which had become a minor military classic. That morning of the fifteenth, he sought to make a personal contribution to the art of war by crashing his plane into an American aircraft carrier. He left Clark untroubled by the apprehension, common to most pilots, that he might not come back. He intended not to do so.

Arima's melodramatic gesture ended in bathos. He plunged into the sea alongside a carrier, without damaging it. But he was one among many desperate men who concluded in those days that new methods were required to offer the Japanese any possibility of overcoming their enemy's overwhelming might. Two army fliers based on Negros Island had already made a suicide attempt on 13 September, meeting the same fate as Arima before they reached a target. Several Japanese fighter pilots deliberately rammed American bombers in what were known as *tai-atari*—"body-bashing" attacks. Since the Marianas disaster, many Japanese officers, including a naval aide to the emperor, had discussed the possibilities of launching a systematic suicide campaign. Captain Renya Inoguchi, senior air staff officer of 1st Air Fleet on the Philippines, wrote gloomily in his diary: "Nothing is more destructive to morale than a belief that the enemy possesses superiority."

Conventional Japanese air forces were being devastated by the Americans. Haruki Iki and his squadron landed at Clark on 14 October to find that a sister unit which arrived only the previous day had already lost its commanding officer and most of its planes. "In the Philippines, every day was desperate," said Iki. "At night, the work of the ground crews preparing aircraft for next day's strikes was constantly interrupted by American bombing. Even when we drove from the mess up to the strip in darkness, if we showed headlights we were liable to be shot up by American night-fighters, which was no fun at all." Every time Iki flew out, he penned a last letter for his wife, Yoshiko, living with their two children at her parents' house on Kyushu. "If I did not leave a letter, she might never even have known where I died, because nobody would have told her," said the pilot. When the decision was made to launch suicide missions, Iki welcomed it: "At the time, this seemed the only option we had."

A Japanese instructor wrote of his efforts to train pilots: "Everything was urgent. We were told to rush men through. We abandoned refinements, just tried to teach them how to fly and shoot. One after another, singly, in twos and threes, training planes smashed into the ground, gyrated wildly through the air. For long, tedious months, I tried to create fighter pilots. It was a hopeless task. Our resources were too meagre, the demand too great." Before entering combat, American pilots had received two years of training and flown at least three hundred hours, often many more. In 1944, Japanese fliers' previous hundred hours of pre-operational experience was cut to forty. Navigation training was abolished. Pilots were told simply to follow their leaders. A Japanese after-action report on the poor performance of their fliers in the Marianas declared: "Chapter 49 of the *Combat Sutra* says that 'Tactics are like sandals. Those who are strong should wear them' . . . [The consequence of lack of pilot training, however, is that] it looks . . . as if good sandals were put on the feet of cripples."

Suicide attack offered a prospect of redressing the balance of forces, circumventing the fact that Japanese pilots were no longer capable of challenging their American counterparts on conventional terms. Instead, their astonishing willingness for self-sacrifice might be exploited. Here was a concept which struck a chord in the Japanese psyche, and caught the Imperial Navy's mood of the moment. Officers cherished a saying: "When a commander is uncertain whether to steer to port or starboard, he should steer towards death." An alternative aphorism held that "One should take care to make one's own dying as meaningful as possible." The suicide concept appeared to satisfy both requirements. Four days after Arima's death, Vice-Admiral Takijiro Onishi, new commander of 5th Air Base on the Philippines, held a meeting with Captain Inoguchi, his staff and some fliers. They agreed that Zeroes fitted with five-hundred-pound bombs and crashed headlong into targets could achieve much greater accuracy than conventional bombing. A one-way trip also doubled the range of a plane. Inoguchi proposed calling the movement *shimpu*, a word for "divine wind." Another word of much the same meaning, however, soon passed into the vernacular of the Second World War: *kamikaze*.

On 20 October, Onishi addressed men of the first designated "special attack" unit: "Japan is in grave danger. The salvation of our country is now beyond the power of the ministers of state, the general staff and humble commanders like myself. It can come only from spirited young men like you. Thus, on behalf of your hundred million countrymen, I ask this sacrifice of you, and pray for your success." A few months and several hundred suicide attacks later, genuine kamikaze volunteers became hard to find. But in those first weeks, a substantial number of Japanese aircrew eagerly embraced the concept, offering themselves for "useful death." When an officer flew to the Philippines base of Cebu and invited applicants for suicide missions, the entire unit came forward except two pilots in the sickbay. One flier, Uemura, had just written off a precious aircraft in an accident. He acknowledged miserably that he was the worst pilot in the squadron. His commander reassured him: "Don't worry, Uemura, I'll find a chance for you. Stop worrying and go to bed." The pilot bowed deeply, saying, "Thank you sir. I shall be waiting."

When Commander Tamai of the 201st Air Group put the idea to his twenty-three pilots, all professed enthusiasm. Lt. Yukio Seki said: "You've absolutely got to let me do it." Seki was just three months married, after a correspondence romance. He had received a random parcel from a girl, one of many dispatched by civilian well-wishers to Japan's soldiers, sailors and airmen. This one, unusually, contained the sender's name and address. The officer began exchanging letters with her. They met on his leave, fell in love, married. Before Seki left on his last mission, instead of asserting that he was sacrificing himself for his country, he told war correspondents: "I'm doing this for my beloved wife." To a Western mind, self-immolation in such circumstances is incomprehensible. To some Japanese of the time, however, it seemed intensely romantic.

On 21 October 1944, as the first suicide section took off from Luzon, their comrades stood by the flight path singing, "If duty calls me to the mountain, a verdant greensward will be my pall." The mission ended in anticlimax, for the planes returned without finding a target. But that day a Japanese aircraft from another field crashed into the cruiser HMAS *Australia* off Leyte, killing thirty men and inflicting major damage. On 25 October, in the aftermath of the Leyte Gulf naval battle, kamikazes led by Seki achieved their first important successes, sinking *St. Lo*, damaging *Santee* and *Suwanee*. The carrier *Intrepid* was struck off Luzon four days later. Onishi now secured the consent of his superior, Admiral Fukudome, to recruit kamikaze volunteers in large numbers. Fukudome had at first resisted, arguing that suicide missions would not play well with aircrew. Most of 2nd Air Fleet's 24 and 25 October attacks on the American fleet employed conventional tactics. Only after these resulted in further disastrous losses did suicide assaults become institutionalised.

Captain Inoguchi flew into Manila on 26 October to confer with Onishi about expanding "special attack" squadrons. The staff officer was dismayed by the squalor of the Philippines' capital: "People in the streets appeared haunted and nervous; many were leaving the city, carrying huge bundles on their shoulders. Heavy smoke . . . hung over the harbour. At AA positions along the waterside, soldiers were busy clearing shell cases and debris from the last raid . . . I was shocked to see so many sunken vessels, only their mast tips showing above the surface." The two Japanese officers found themselves meeting in an air-raid shelter. With bleak understatement, Onishi observed: "This is certainly an unorthodox command." A young suicide volunteer arrived at naval air headquarters to say farewell, greeting the admiral with the words: "Hello, uncle." In truth there was no blood relationship, but Onishi was his father's closest friend. In this strange, indeed ghastly little world, death was everywhere around them. Inoguchi's brother had been lost two days before, commanding the battleship *Musashi*. His nephew died a week later as a kamikaze.

Onishi's vision for achieving Japan's salvation through the "divine wind" soon attained demented proportions: "If we are prepared to sacrifice twenty million Japanese lives in 'special attacks,' " he said, "victory will be ours." Not all officers shared his enthusiasm. Lt. Cmdr. Tadashi Minobe, who led a night-fighter group in the Philippines, was transferred back to Japan after openly denouncing the kamikaze concept. Propaganda, however, immediately set about ennobling this new ideal. The last letters of suicide pilots passed into Japan's national legend. Petty Officer Isao Matsuo wrote on 28 October: "Dear parents, please congratulate me. I have been given a splendid opportunity to die. This is my last day."

Through the weeks that followed, as Onishi and Inoguchi mustered more volunteers, suicide attacks and American losses in the seas around the Philippines mounted dramatically. On 30 October, a hit on the carrier *Franklin* killed fifty-six men. Vernon Black, manning a .50-calibre machine gun on *Belleau Wood*, watched a green-nosed Japanese attacker diving on his own ship: "He was afire in the engine, then something hit me. Burning gasoline sprayed all over. It got awfully hot . . . my clothes began to burn." Black, like many others, leapt into the sea to escape the flames: "There was a lot of screaming in the water and whistles blowing." His life jacket immediately burst, burnt through. He scrambled onto a raft with a dozen other men, and forty minutes later was picked up by a "merciful can"—a destroyer. Down in *Belleau Wood*'s engine room, at first news of the strike "nobody got particularly excited as flight-deck fires were no novelty, and none of us up to that time had heard of the word 'kamikaze,' " in the words of Ensign Bob Reich. But the damage was grave: the carrier lost twelve planes, ninety-two crew killed and fifty-four seriously injured. Like *Intrepid*, *Belleau Wood* was forced to withdraw to Ulithi for repair.

Many Japanese attackers were shot down, but an alarming number broke through to the fleet. The balance of the air battle seemed to be tilting in favour of the enemy. Some U.S. carriers were obliged to leave station for rest and resupply. More Japanese planes arrived from Formosa and Kyushu. Tacloban airfield was still only marginally operational for U.S. fighters. Escorts began to take heavy punishment. When a kamikaze hit a destroyer's hull, a Brooklyn sailor said wonderingly: "You could of drove a Mack truck tru duh hole." "This type of attack is quite different from what we have been combating before," said Cmdr. Arthur Purdy of the destroyer *Abner Read*, lost at Leyte on 1 November. "This Japanese needs merely to get up there and get into his power dive with fixed controls to solve a very simple problem, because a ship's ability to turn during a thirty- or forty-second approach is so limited." Purdy argued that nothing smaller than five-inch gunfire could stop such a plane. He urged the need for increased fire protection on upper decks. Blazing fuel, rather than the initial explosion, doomed his own ship. Three other destroyers were damaged in the same series of raids.

The Americans quickly perceived that the attacks represented a systematic campaign, rather than the whim of individual pilots. The enemy was also mounting conventional fighter, bomber and torpedo attacks against troops, airfields and ships by day and night. A smokescreen was laid across the San Pedro anchorage whenever an air threat was identified—in 1945 this became a navy SOP, Standard Operating Procedure. The light cruiser *Honolulu* survived a torpedo hit which killed sixty men as a result of heroic exertions by her crew, but mechanic Leon Garsian found himself trapped alone far belowdecks in a radio compartment. Watertight doors protected his own position, but those above were flooded. Garsian used mattress padding to check water trickling in, and at last attracted attention by shouting through a ventilation duct. Rescuers had to cut through four inches of armour with acetylene torches before he was finally rescued, after sixteen hours in what he feared would prove his tomb. More Japanese raiders approached while the crew was labouring to save *Honolulu*. Reckless anti-aircraft fire from neighbouring ships killed a further six of the cruiser's men and wounded eleven. Off Leyte, promiscuous American shooting became almost as alarming a hazard as the Japanese, with thousands of nervous gunners striving to engage low-level attackers.

Admiral Kinkaid signalled Nimitz, asking for urgent carrier strikes against the kamikaze bases: "Air situation now appears critical." He also pressed Kenney, in a stream of messages: "If adequate fighter cover not maintained over combatant ships their destruction is inevitable. Can you provide the necessary protection?" No, Kenney could not. The lack of usable fields on Leyte, together with steady losses to Japanese strafing, rendered the U.S. Army's airmen incapable of deploying sufficient force to stave off attacks, as well as providing support for Krueger's ground forces. Before commencing the Philippines operations, MacArthur assured the chiefs of staff that Kenney's squadrons, together with the aircraft of Seventh Fleet under his own command, would easily be able to handle the air situation after the first few days ashore. Instead, in early November the general found himself obliged to ask for the return of Halsey's carriers. Third Fleet's aircraft rejoined the battle, and inflicted a level of attrition quite unsustainable by the Japanese. But in the first weeks of the Leyte campaign, the Americans suffered more heavily from enemy air power than at any time since 1942.

On 27 November, kamikazes struck the light cruisers *St. Louis* and *Montpelier* and the battleship *Colorado*. By some freak, as a Japanese plane on its death ride streaked between the foremast and forward stack of *Colorado*, blood from its wounded pilot showered down on sailors manning 20mm gun tubs. "I was standing in the open and was so scared I was paralysed," wrote James Hutchinson. "I couldn't come to my senses enough to move until it was all over." Two days later, kamikazes got to the battleship *Maryland* and the destroyer *Aulick*, inflicting major damage and casualties, and hitting another destroyer. Third Fleet's fast carrier force was attacked on 25 November. Two suicide aircraft inflicted fresh damage on *Intrepid*, another struck *Cabot*, yet another *Essex*. The Japanese sneaked in amidst a cloud of American aircraft returning from a mission, becoming indistinguishable on saturated radar screens.

Even when enemy planes were identified, their pilots were taught to veer constantly, so that American gunners remained uncertain which ship was targeted. "You just don't know which one's coming at you," said Louis Erwin of the cruiser *Indianapolis*, a turret gunner. A destroyer of Desron 53 rammed a sister ship while taking drastic evasive action, one of several such incidents. Crews learned to curse low cloud, which shielded suicide attackers from combat air patrols. "The first thing I saw that day was a plane with meatballs on the wings just rolling into a dive," wrote a destroyer crewman on 29 November. For a dismaying number of Americans serving in the ships off Leyte, such a sight was their last.

Fire, always fire, was the principal horror unleashed by a kamikaze strike on an aircraft carrier, laden with up to 200,000 gallons of aviation gas. An airman on *Essex* "rushed over to help get a man out of a 20mm gun mount. I tried to pull him out of the fire but part of his arm came off . . . I got sick." Another ran onto the flight deck: "I seen these fellows with short sleeves, the flesh hanging. I grabbed a big tube of Ungentine and tried to rub it on one guy's arms. The skin came off in my hands." In action, men learned to ensure that every possible inch of their flesh was covered by anti-flash hoods, rolled-down sleeves, denims. Yet still men burned. "We buried fifty-four people, mostly officers, the same day, and several each day for almost a week who died from burns," wrote Cmdr. Ted Winters of *Lexington*, which was hit on 5 November. "Seven of our bomber pilots were up there [on the bridge island] watching us come in and five were blown off the ship. Part of the Jap pilot was hanging from the radar . . . it was rugged."

For the loss of ninety aircraft, the Japanese had put three carriers out of action. Suicide missions inflicted far more damage upon the U.S. Navy in their first weeks than had been achieved by the Shogo operation of the Combined Fleet. The emperor was told of the "special attack force's" achievements. Hirohito said squeamishly: "They certainly did a magnificent job. But was it necessary to go to such extremes?" When his words were reported to Onishi, the admiral was crestfallen. He himself was now convinced that, because of the desperate shortage of planes and pilots, only suicide tactics could make a serious impression on the Americans, and he was surely right.

The kamikaze squadrons evolved procedures as they went, or rather as they died. Initially, commanders dispatched attackers in threes, each flight escorted by two fighters, which were intended to return to report results. Later, when sufficient planes were available, pack tactics were adopted, to swamp the defences. Fliers were urged to take time, to ensure that they impaled themselves on a suitable ship: "An impatient pilot is apt to plunge into an unworthy target." The forward elevator of an aircraft carrier was defined as the ideal aiming point. It was too dangerous for aspirant pilots to practice a steep dive onto their targets. They were invited to perform this manoeuvre just once, in the last seconds of their lives.

A squadron officer said: "There were new faces and missing faces at every briefing . . . The instructor and the mission remained the same, but the audience constantly changed . . . There were no theatrics or hysterics—it was all in the line of duty." Ground crews polished planes almost obsessively. "It was [one technician's] theory that the cockpit was the pilot's coffin, and as such should be spotless," said an officer. It was a point of honour among the suicide crews themselves that they should take off laughing. Tears were deemed appropriate for spectators watching take-offs, and the doomed pilots seemed to agree. One kamikaze wrote crossly in his diary how irked were he and his companions when they glimpsed staff officers exchanging jokes as planes started up.

The most difficult problem for the Japanese in the last months of 1944 was not to find volunteers for suicide missions, but to convey them alive to the Philippines despite American fighters and the poverty of trainees' airmanship. Of the first 150 homeland aircrew assigned to the islands, only half arrived. Among one group of fifteen, just three reached the battlefield. Planes remained desperately short. By mid-December, Inoguchi's unit possessed twenty-eight pilots, but only thirteen Zeroes. Crews worked day and night to make them more airworthy.

For the remainder of the war, kamikaze attacks represented by far the gravest threat faced by U.S. forces in the Pacific. In Samuel Eliot Morison's words, "The Japanese had perfected a new and effective type of aerial warfare that was hard for the Western mind to comprehend, and difficult to counteract." A British Royal Navy staff study, drafted in 1945, observed: "Logically, suicide attack in any of the forms, air or sea, practised by the Japanese, differed only in kind from the last-ditch defence enjoined upon the British after Dunkirk, and only in degree from such missions as the [RAF's 1943] air attack on the Moehne Dam." Yet Americans were bewildered, indeed repelled, by the psychology of an enemy capable of institutionalising such tactics. "I could imagine myself in the heat of battle where I would perhaps instinctively take some sudden action that would almost surely result in my death," wrote a destroyer officer, Ben Bradlee. "I could not imagine waking up some morning at 5 a.m., going to some church to pray, and knowing that in a few hours I would crash my plane into a ship on purpose."

It was never plausible that suicide attacks could alter the outcome of the war, but American casualties increased as tactics were refined. The Japanese noted that their own losses were no worse than those incurred by conventional bombing or torpedo missions. Between October 1944 and August 1945, 3,913 kamikaze pilots are known to have died, most of them navy pilots, in a campaign that peaked with 1,162 attacks in April. Around one in seven of all suicidalists hit a ship, and most inflicted major damage.

Some Japanese were deeply dismayed by the kamikaze ethic. The letters and diaries of more than a few pilots reveal their own reluctance. Yet the young men who agreed to sacrifice themselves became celebrated as national heroes. One day the wife of a high court judge, whose pilot son had fallen ill and died in training, appeared at Kijin base. She brought a lock of the boy's hair and a scarf, and asked that these should be carried as mementoes by a kamikaze on his mission. She had inscribed the scarf with the words: "I pray [that you will achieve] a direct hit." A group leader duly carried the relics to his own death. Mamoru Shigemitsu, one of the more rational among Japan's political leaders, nonetheless wrote in stubborn admiration after the war: "Let no man belittle these suicide units and call them barbaric."

The cultural revulsion which kamikazes inspired in Americans was intensified by sailors' bitterness at finding themselves exposed to increased peril of mutilation or death, when the war was almost won. "If you were below decks, you could tell when the fight moved in closer by the type of gunfire," wrote Emory Jernigan. "First the five-inch, then the 40mm, and then the 20mm would cut loose. When the 20mm fired all sixty shots and stopped for a second to reload, you could tell the fight was close and getting closer. There was nothing to do except suck your gut and, in my case, I would recite my own little motto from boyhood: '*I don't give a damn if I do die, do die; just so I see a little juice fly, juice fly*.' "

It can be argued, in the spirit of the Royal Navy's staff study, that only a narrow line separated the deeds of Japan's suicide pilots from the sort of actions for which the Allies awarded posthumous Medals of Honor and Victoria Crosses. A significant number of American and British sailors, fliers and soldiers were decorated after their deaths for hurling themselves upon the enemy in a fashion indistinguishable from that of the kamikazes. But Western societies cherish a distinction between spontaneous individual adoption of a course of action which makes death probable, and institutionalisation of a tactic which makes it inevitable. Thus, the Allies regarded the kamikazes with unfeigned repugnance as well as fear. In the last months of the war, this new terror prompted among Americans an escalation of hatred, a diminution of mercy.

Rear-Admiral Robert Carney, Third Fleet's chief of staff, shared Halsey's disdain for wasting humanity on the enemy: "We ran afoul of Japanese hospital ships, some were sunk, some couldn't be identified, some were adjacent to proper military targets and suffered as a result . . . It would seem to be an unnecessary refinement to worry too much over these incidents. The Japanese hospital ships have undoubtedly been used for illegal purposes and they are caring for Nips which we failed to kill in the first attempt. Every one who is restored to duty potentially costs the life of many of our people."

Captain Tom Inglis of the cruiser *Birmingham* glimpsed enemy sailors in the water off Mindanao: "I was somewhat puzzled as to the proper treatment to accord these Japanese. I suggested that some should be taken prisoner. The admiral told me that would be done after we were sure the ships had been sunk, and I understand that a destroyer did pick up at least two of these Japanese sailors as samples of the rest. I guess I asked a very embarrassing question in my action report, as I remarked that it would be helpful if a definite policy would be enunciated concerning the treatment of Japanese merchant sailors, suggesting that it should be stated whether they should be left swimming in the water or whether they should be taken prisoner or killed. I have received no answer to that question." A seaman wrote of his own attitude to the enemy: "We came to believe he was slime . . . not worthy of life; seeing dead Japanese in the water was like making love to a beautiful girl." As the kamikaze offensive intensified, the concept of offering quarter to an enemy who waged war in such a fashion came to seem to the Allies not merely inappropriate, but redundant.

CHAPTER SEVEN

Ashore: Battle for the Mountains

GEN. TOMOYUKI YAMASHITA had intended to fight his main battle for the defence of the Philippines on Luzon. Yet he found his judgement summarily overruled by his superiors. Field Marshal Terauchi allowed himself to be deceived by the navy, which asserted with shameless irresponsibility that its Leyte Gulf battles had ended in triumph. Japan's fliers likewise reported that they were inflicting crippling attrition on American air forces. Fortified with such illusions, Terauchi and his staff became convinced that an important victory was within their grasp, if only Japan's soldiers did their part to match the achievements of its sailors and airmen. In South Asia Army's perception, "the Navy succeeded in the operations by sinking most of the enemy's carriers (nine out of twelve), several battleships etc., in the Formosa Sea . . . It [was also] believed that the sea and air battle on the twenty-fourth and twenty-fifth resulted in a 70 percent victory for us. All information received at area army headquarters was favourable." The navy's recklessness in launching the Combined Fleet against Leyte Gulf was now, therefore, to be matched by that of the army, in the name of honour but in the service of folly.

Early in November, Lt.-Gen. Akira Muto arrived in Manila to assume the role of 14th Army chief of staff. "Nice to see you," said Yamashita. "I've been waiting for you a long time." Muto asked: "What's the plan?" The general responded: "I've no idea what we shall do. You'd better have a bath, then we'll talk." Muto said ruefully that every stitch of spare clothing he possessed, down to his underwear, had just been incinerated in an American air raid. "Borrow mine," said his commander generously. Yet even freshly clad, Muto felt no better when he learned of Field Marshal Terauchi's insistence on a fight to the finish for Leyte. As Yamashita talked, Muto perceived that the general was furiously angry. Transferring units to Leyte by sea meant that many would be ravaged in transit, while those that got through could not be adequately supplied and supported. No reinforcement of Leyte could alter an outcome that was now inevitable. Yet there was nothing to be done. Terauchi was in charge. Yamashita's orders to Gen. Sosaku Suzuki, his subordinate commander on Leyte, continued to pay lip service to that familiar Japanese expression of purpose, "annihilation" of the enemy. Yamashita knew full well, however, that the only forces destined for annihilation were his own.

Meanwhile, his orders were to throw every possible man onto Leyte, and he did his utmost to fulfil them. Between 20 October and 11 December, though substantial numbers died or lost their equipment, some 45,000 Japanese troops landed in the west and north of the island. Private Eichi Ogita of the 362nd Independent Battalion experienced the sort of nightmare passage familiar to many Japanese soldiers. He was dispatched from Luzon with his unit on a small wooden schooner, but on 25 October the vessel was sunk by an American submarine. Ogita and other survivors somehow struggled ashore on the north-west coast of Leyte. When daylight came, they found that their battalion commander was dead, while the adjutant, company commander and Ogita himself were among the wounded. They had salvaged a few weapons, but no food. For a time they squatted on a nearby hilltop, then realised that it was essential to get moving. A lieutenant and ten men went in search of Japanese forces. When they did not return, next day the remainder of the party set off towards their original destination, the port of Ormoc.

It proved a terrible journey. They wandered uncertainly, lacking maps and compasses. Most of their wounded died. When at last the survivors reached the town, they found it under air attack. "Enemy planes appear, but ours do not," Ogita wrote gloomily in his diary. "I wonder why." On 13 November, they had yet to fire a shot: "We have not received orders to start the attack because many of our troops have not yet landed." He whistled to keep his spirits up: "There are only thirty-four men in our company, but we have confidence enough to take on an enemy battalion."

This was typical of the manner in which Japanese reinforcements reached the Leyte battlefield, losing many men and much equipment before even encountering American troops. It is astonishing, in such circumstances, that they achieved as much as they did. MacArthur's Sixth Army faced an intensity of resistance beyond anything SWPA's supreme commander had anticipated. By 7 November the Japanese 16th Division, original garrison of Leyte, had lost all its battalion commanders and engineer officers, together with most of its company commanders and half its artillery. But much of 1st Division had arrived from Luzon, and more was coming. Suzuki was hopeful of driving the Americans back across the central plain.

Again and again, Krueger's units found themselves caught off-balance by Japanese entrenched on higher ground. The 1/382nd Infantry were in the midst of a rice paddy when they came under intense fire which killed or wounded every officer of two companies: "Men threw away their packs, machine guns, radios and even rifles. Their sole aim was to get through the muck and get onto solid ground once more. Some of the wounded gave up the struggle and drowned in the grasping swamp." Captain George Morrissey, a doctor with the 1/34th Infantry, wrote: "We had just begun to dig in when an artillery shell lit in the forward part of the perimeter. I ran up there to find three killed, eight seriously wounded. Just then the rain began to pour furiously and it got dark. The first man I saw was bleeding from a jagged hole in the neck. It was a hell of a thing there in the rain not being able to do anything but having to try anyway. This man died on the way in and another next day. No supper. Foxhole full of water. Our artillery thunders and cracks all night . . . I have never been so filthy before."

The campaign yielded its share of heroes. It is often the case that men distinguish themselves in combat who are an embarrassment everywhere else. Before the Leyte landing, infantrymen confined to the stockade for punishment had been returned to their units. The commander of G Company, 2/34th Infantry, strongly objected to accepting back Private Harold Moon, a persistent troublemaker. He got Moon anyway. On the night of 21 October, the regiment faced a series of violent, almost overwhelming enemy attacks. Dawn revealed foxholes surrounded by enemy dead. Several lay near the body of Private Moon, killed after fighting to the last with rifle and grenades. He received a posthumous Medal of Honor, which roused both admiration and bewilderment among his comrades. "I only knew him as a G Company screw-up," wrote Private Eric Diller wonderingly.

Diller was himself an interesting study—the son of German Catholic immigrants who fled to the United States in 1936 because of his mother's Jewish blood. In a machine-gun squad on Leyte, the twenty-year-old carried papers which still classified him as an alien—indeed, notionally an enemy one. Diller was squeamish about many manifestations of war in the Pacific. When comrades set about extracting gold teeth from dead Japanese, he declined to keep his own share. He felt unhappy about the treatment of the few enemy who became live captives: "I saw an undernourished, sick-looking, pathetic specimen brought into our perimeter, where a newcomer to the platoon proceeded to punch the helpless prisoner in the face. No one said anything but most felt, as I did, that kind of behaviour was nothing to be proud of."

Beyond grief inflicted by the enemy, there was that created by the weather. Within days of the landings, it began to rain. Deluges of tropical intensity persisted through the weeks that followed. Men grew accustomed to marching, fighting, eating, sleeping soaked to the skin. Roads and tracks collapsed beneath the pounding of heavy vehicles. Phone lines shorted. Tanks and trucks bogged down or were wrecked. Streams swelled and burst. Liver fluke rendered bathing in rivers hazardous. Batteries swiftly deteriorated. It was difficult for gunners to keep cordite dry. Howitzers had to be cleaned three times a day. Blankets became covered with mildew. Folded canvas rotted. Bolts on vehicles and machinery rusted irretrievably into place. Fungus grew in weapon optics. White phosphorus in shells melted in the heat, which also blew out the safety disks of flamethrower tanks. It proved necessary to keep vehicle fuel tanks fully filled, or moisture seeped in.

Airfield construction became a hopeless task. A minor typhoon on 29 October blew away tentage and created havoc at stores dumps. Many men found themselves on short rations, because the overstrained logistics system was obliged to prioritise ammunition. "The task of supply and evacuation of wounded soon assumed staggering proportions," the American official historian acknowledged later. Richard Krebs of the 24th Division described a blow which struck the island on 8 November: "Floods raced in almost horizontal sheets. Palms bent low under the storm, their fronds flattened like streamers of wet silk. Trees crashed to earth . . . The howling of the wind was like a thousandfold plaint of the unburied dead."

Though overall American casualties were not excessive, some units suffered severely in local actions. For instance, in three days at the end of October, the 2/382nd Infantry lost thirty-four men killed and eighty wounded, fighting for the town of Tabontabon. George Morrissey wrote on 5 November: "I saw the creek bed where the fighting had been yesterday, and we brought the bodies out. Thank God I'm not a rifleman. Near the scene were two sad heaps of humanity. In the first were five Filipino men, bound and bayoneted. In the second three women and three children, bound, bayoneted and partially burned."

Leyte Valley was secured by 2 November. After ten days ashore, SWPA headquarters announced that the Japanese had suffered 24,000 casualties for American losses of 3,221, including 976 killed and missing. MacArthur's staff persistently and grotesquely misjudged the campaign's progress. As early as 3 November, SWPA reports referred repeatedly to enemy "remnants" or "final remnants" in full retreat. "The end of the Leyte-Samar campaign is in sight," asserted a press communiqué. Yet five days later, a bulletin grudgingly acknowledged "sharp fighting . . . The enemy has rushed reinforcements into this sector." Two days later still, SWPA announced that Sixth Army had destroyed the entire original Leyte garrison—but added lamely that this had been replaced by reinforcements from Luzon. American intelligence throughout the battle was poor, partly because the Japanese seldom directed local operations by radio, partly because MacArthur and his subordinates were unwilling to heed what they learned. "Ultra," claimed Sixth Army's G3 Clyde Eddleman, discussing the role of enemy signal decrypts, "was of little value to Sixth Army directly. It gave some indication of Japanese morale but little else." There were notable disadvantages to fighting an enemy short of sophisticated communications.

Sixth Army now began the second phase of the Leyte battle: the struggle to clear the mountains which dominated northern and western areas of the island. By 8 November, the Americans had 120,000 men ashore, contesting possession with perhaps one-third that number of Japanese. On the densely covered hills, the enemy could exploit to the utmost his tenacity, fieldcraft and small-unit tactical skills. Krueger's operations were bedevilled by ignorance of the ground, which was poorly mapped. The Americans suffered two months of pain and frustration, which imposed a serious delay upon MacArthur's planned landing on Luzon. Names such as Bloody Ridge and Breakneck Ridge became etched into the consciousness of thousands of his soldiers as they strove to dislodge the Japanese from their positions, then to hold these against counterattacks. Private Luther Kinsey of the 382nd Infantry expressed a bewilderment common among Krueger's men: "I'm surprised it isn't going faster. I knew they were camouflaged and dug in, but I didn't know so few of them would hold up so many of us."

The phrase which dogged the experience of every American commander on Leyte was "pinned down." "The 1st battalion made little progress," says a typical account, describing the 128th Infantry's attack on a position named Corkscrew Ridge. "Company A was immediately pinned down by machine-gun, mortar and rifle fire." A unit could legitimately declare itself to be in this condition if it suffered substantial casualties, then incurred more by every attempt at movement. Yet all too often, the words merely indicated that a force had come under fire, taken to cover and stayed there even before suffering significant loss. Footsoldiers hoped that support arms—artillery, aircraft or tanks—would discover a means of silencing resistance without need for those "pinned down" to expose themselves to a further advance under fire.

A battalion commander in the Philippines described a typical combat conversation with a fresh second lieutenant: "The new john radioed back to battalion requesting reinforcement—he was pinned down. I took the radio mike . . . and asked the lieutenant if he had anyone hit. He answered that he had not, and then I asked: 'How then do you know you are pinned down?' He replied that they were being shot at and couldn't move. I told him that I was not convinced, and he would have to get out on his own. When the patrol returned, without a single casualty, I found him an unhappy and resentful 2nd john. I admonished him to face up to the facts of life, for combat was a serious business. He had to do his job, which meant not calling for help unless he truly needed it." Much of the story of the Leyte campaign, and indeed of infantry action in World War II, was of commanders struggling to make men move forward, when those at the sharp end feared that to comply would prove fatal to their welfare.

The CO of the 307th Infantry sent a brusque, ungrammatical circular to his regiment: "I don't want this business of when someone calls 'litter-bearers,' for everyone to stop fighting. You must not attack without your bayonets fixed. The Corsairs will not support us unless we stop firing on them . . . Right now we are not aggressive enough, although we are getting lots of experience." Everything hinged on what a few bold men would do. On 15 December 1944, Sgt. Leroy Johnson of the 2/126th Infantry led a nine-man patrol to reconnoitre a ridge near Limon. Spotting an enemy machine gun, Johnson crawled to within six yards of it, then returned to report. He was told to destroy the gun, and advanced with three other men. They found themselves in a grenade duel with the Japanese, which continued until Johnson saw two grenades land close to his comrades, and threw himself on them before they exploded. Johnson was awarded a posthumous Medal of Honor for his sacrifice, but it would have been unrealistic to expect many men of Sixth Army to emulate it. Aggressive junior leadership is what makes things happen on battlefields, and there were never enough Sergeant Johnsons.

One of the epic actions of the campaign was fought by the 1/34th Infantry, under Lt. Col. Tom Clifford. Early on the morning of 10 November, his battalion was shipped seven miles along the north coast in landing craft, to a beach in the midst of Carigara Bay. There, they off-loaded without opposition, and began marching into the hills. Three days later they took up position on Kilay Ridge, a nine-hundred-foot elevation which commanded much of the surrounding countryside, and provided vital flanking support for American operations on Breakneck Ridge. The battalion remained on Kilay until 4 December, in almost continuous contact with the Japanese. Clifford's men were isolated, dependent for supply on Filipino porters and spasmodic airdrops. They suffered much, but held their ground. During one firefight, Clifford himself was visiting a company headquarters where he found a man wounded in the thigh, unable to walk. The colonel carried the casualty a mile on his own back over a mountain trail to his command post. On leave in the U.S. shortly before, Clifford was detained by military police without his dogtags, and accused of impersonating an officer. Now he received a Distinguished Service Cross for outstanding leadership.

Conditions on Kilay Ridge were never less than dreadful. "Rained all night and still raining hard," medical officer George Morrissey wrote on 20 November ". . . The ground is a deep gooey churned mixture of mud, urine, faecal matter, garbage. The floor of our aid station is three inches deep with caked mud." He described the terror of his helpless patients when shooting came close. It became especially hard to treat men when mud-stained fragments of clothing were blown into their wounds. So tenuous were the battalion's communications that it took three days to move each casualty to a first-surgery facility. Some did not make it, despite the devotion of their Filipino carriers. Morrissey noted bleakly that the yearning to go home, common to every man in the Pacific theatre, was replaced in those days by a much more modest ambition—to get off Kilay. On 26 November, he wrote: "No loud talking or laughing around here these days. People converse in low voices, as at the bedside of a sick patient . . . Platoons have twelve to fifteen men at most . . . The mortality among our good non-coms has been very high . . . These are jittery days."

They drank from potholes of milky water, and in the deep darkness of the nights cursed the bats which flew in thousands around their heads. There was no mail, and often they felt abandoned by their higher formation. Clifford explained by radio his difficulties with sick and hungry men, the Japanese crowding them. Corps headquarters shrugged: "You are in a tough spot." The colonel was finally reduced to threatening: "Either you give us artillery or I'm going to pull my men off the ridge and leave the Japs looking down your throat." The battalion got its gunfire support. Each morning, Morrissey viewed with disgust the heap of soaked, slashed, stinking clothing and dirty bandages lying outside the aid station to be burned. A sick call produced a queue of a hundred men, most suffering inflamed feet or fever. The doctor grew wearily accustomed to the cry: "Will you look at my feet? Will you look at my feet?" The 1/34th was relieved on 4 December, and made its weary way down to the coast. Clifford had lost 28 killed and 101 wounded, but his battalion could boast one of the most impressive performances of the campaign.

Other units suffered almost as badly in the November actions. "These bearded, mud-caked soldiers came out of the mountains exhausted and hungry," said a 24th Division report on the experience of the 2/19th

Infantry. "Their feet were heavy, cheeks hollow, bodies emaciated and eyes glazed." When they left the line 241 officers and men—about a third of the battalion—were immediately hospitalised with skin disorders, foot ulcers, battle fatigue and exhaustion. "The men looked ten or fifteen years older than their ages," wrote Kansan Captain Philip Hostetter, medical officer of the 1/19th Infantry. "They spoke little and moved slowly. There was no joking or horseplay." Hostetter consigned three exhausted company commanders to hospital.

It sometimes seemed, to commanders and footsoldiers alike, that the Leyte campaign was being conducted in slow motion. "The infantry policy was to avoid battle unless great force could be brought to bear on that particular point, and never to substitute courage of men for firepower," wrote Philip Hostetter. "This meant a long war with much maneuvering." It became a matter of bitter debate whether blame for American sluggishness lay with Walter Krueger of Sixth Army, or with those under his command. The general circulated a highly critical report detailing his units' perceived failings: poor junior leadership; an instinct to seek cover in the face of modest resistance, and to call down artillery fire to suppress it. "How many officer casualties?" Krueger once demanded after an operation on New Guinea. "Good," he said, when told that they had been high. He thought stiff losses an indication that junior leaders had been doing their jobs properly.

On Leyte, the general asserted that units were too roadbound, and relied on frontal attack, rather than attempting envelopments. Patrols withdrew as soon as they glimpsed Japanese rather than linger to assess enemy strength and pinpoint defensive positions. Some U.S. officers, Krueger claimed, were shockingly inattentive to their soldiers' welfare, failing to ensure that they received regular hot food, leaving them to sleep in wet foxholes even when no enemy was within range. In his view, "many commanders were indifferent to such matters"—a damning indictment. "If more than minor resistance was encountered, the troops frequently fell back and called for fire from supporting weapons," claimed Sixth Army. "On one occasion a company called for artillery fire upon a roadblock and then withdrew 350 yards while the concentration was delivered." By the time the infantry resumed their advance, the Japanese had reoccupied their positions: "The natural reluctance of American infantrymen to engage the enemy in close quarters had to be overcome. There were several instances in which the American attacking force simply felt out the Japanese position and then sat back to wait it out. In one area no progress was made for four days." Several unit commanders, including the regimental CO of the 21st Infantry, were dismissed for being "insufficiently aggressive."

The 1944 edition of the U.S. War Department *Handbook on Japanese Military Forces* described the enemy with something close to contempt:

> To the Japanese officer, considerations of "face" and "toughness" are most important, and they are therefore prone to indulgence in "paper heroics." Despite the opportunities presented during six years of active combat, the Japanese have continued to violate certain fundamental principles of accepted tactics and technique . . . such violations are based . . . upon their failure to credit the enemy with good judgement and equal military efficiency. Whether or not they have profited from recent experiences remains to be seen . . . The defensive form of combat generally has been distasteful to the Japanese, and they have been very reluctant to admit that the Imperial Army would ever be forced to engage in this form of combat.

On Leyte, such assertions were recognised as nonsense by every American from Krueger downwards. Sixth Army reported with respect on the enemy's tactical skills: "The Japanese . . . displayed superior adeptness, and willingness to go into the swamps and stay there until rooted out . . . The most notable characteristics exhibited were the excellent fire discipline and the effective control of all arms. Without exception individual soldiers withheld their fire until it would have the greatest possible effect." It is interesting to contrast the manner in which the two sides used weapons. An analysis of 519 Sixth Army fatal casualties showed that 1 man died of bayonet wounds, 2 from blast, 170 from fragments—mortar or artillery. Ninety-seven proved unclassifiable; the remaining 249 were victims of small-arms fire. In other words, in contrast to the World War II battlefield norm, on Leyte the Japanese relied chiefly upon rifles, machine guns and mortars. Short of artillery and lacking tanks, they had no choice. The Americans, meanwhile, inflicted an estimated 60 percent of Japanese ground losses with their artillery, 25 percent with mortars, only 14 percent with infantry weapons, and 1 percent with aircraft. Military operational researchers rated nine rifles as possessing the value of one machine gun, and a medium mortar as matching the destructive capability of three machine guns. On Leyte, the U.S. Army sought as usual to exploit its overwhelming firepower, under most unfavourable conditions; the Japanese were obliged to make the most of the humble rifle—and did so.

The frustrations of Sixth Army persisted through November. Krueger's divisions were gaining ground, and killing many Japanese. But it was all happening painfully slowly. Hodge, commanding XXIV Corps, wrote: "The difficulties of terrain and weather were fully as difficult if not more so than was the enemy . . . Supply problems ranged towards the impossible." An alarming number of Sixth Army soldiers succumbed to combat exhaustion and disease. The 21st Infantry, for instance, reported 630 battle casualties and 135 losses to "other causes." Replacements were nowhere near keeping pace with such a drain, either in quantity or quality. By 12 November, Sixth Army was short of a thousand officers and 12,000 men—almost the equivalent of a combat division. These deficiencies were, as always, worst in infantry rifle companies. Some platoons were reduced from forty to twelve or fifteen men.

Shoestring Ridge, a few miles inland and south of Ormoc Bay, was so named by the Americans because it was the scene of a desperate defensive action, fought with slender resources against six Japanese attacking battalions. To support 6,000 Americans on the line, the 32nd Infantry could muster just twelve trucks and five DUKWs, with access restricted to a single narrow mountain track. Each vehicle journey required crossings of fourteen precarious bridges and fordings of fifty-one streams. To sustain a single infantry regiment required thirty-four tons of supplies a day. It took 3½ days, for instance, for stores shipped from the beaches to reach forward units of 12th Cavalry. Rainstorms impeded airdrops. Somehow, the fighting men were sustained in action, the position was held; but Sixth Army could never fully exploit firepower on Shoestring, because of ammunition shortages.

The pattern of American activity was grimly monotonous. Each dawn a unit moved out, advancing up some precipitous hill until the enemy was encountered. Companies rotated the dubious privilege of taking point. Captain Paul Austin, leading F Company of the 2/34th Infantry, learned to dread his CO's phrase, "It's your turn in the morning." The first intimation of meeting Japanese was a burst of fire, often fatal to the leading Americans. The rest hugged cover until stretcher-bearers were summoned, artillery called in, a set-piece attack organised in company or battalion strength. This required hours, sometimes days. When the assault closed in, Japanese survivors withdrew—to do the same thing again a few hundred yards back.

Often, before the Americans consolidated on new positions, the enemy counter-attacked. Important ground left untenanted was swiftly seized by the enemy. There was a black comic moment on Shoestring Hill in early December, when a runner shouted an order for a three-man picket of the 2/32nd Infantry to pull back. Wilfully or not, the whole of G Company took this as a cue, climbed out of its foxholes and streamed away downhill. By the time the movement was halted, Japanese had occupied the American positions. Huge exertions were required to win them back next day.

The terrain's steepness almost defied belief. On 6 December, a company of the 1/184th Infantry was working its way along a trail beside a clifftop. Japanese machine guns opened fire, hitting twenty men, of whom all but two fell over the precipice. Eight wounded survivors crawled into the battalion aid station that night, but the remainder died. One night in late November, in bright moonlight Sgt. Marvin Raabe of 7th Division led thirty men in three successive bayonet charges to dispossess Japanese of vital ground, a feat for which he received a field commission. Dug in once more, some men were exasperated by the noisiness of Japanese wounded in front of their positions. "One enemy soldier, about thirty-five yards in front of the platoon position . . . had delivered a regular little ritual," wrote an infantryman. "First he would moan and wail for a few minutes, then sing in Japanese, then string out a long line of epithets, decidedly uncomplimentary, at the defenders." An NCO, George Parked, endured the racket as long as he could, but finally climbed out of his foxhole, marched down the hillside and fired three shots. "Now sing, you bastard," he said, returning to his post.

At night on the coast, fireflies swarmed around the coconut palms, "giving them the appearance of Christmas trees," in the words of a Marine officer. In the hills, Japanese sustained intense activity through the hours of darkness, probing and raiding Sixth Army positions. Little damage was done, but such "jitter parties" kept tired men from sleeping, precipitated barrages of illuminant flares and often promiscuous American shooting. There were many "friendly fire" casualties on Leyte, but these were never quantified. It was thought kindest to relatives to report all fatalities simply as "killed in action," and so it probably was. Krueger's artillery sustained harassing fire, shooting occasional blind rounds at likely-seeming places on Japanese-held ground. The enemy responded by creeping close to the American lines, sometimes within twenty-five yards, to gain safety from shelling. Private Jack Norman became so exhausted that he once fell asleep during a barrage. In the morning, his companions in the foxhole announced that at one point he had woken, declared angrily, "If they don't quit this shooting, I'll get up and go home," then gone smartly back to sleep. He recollected nothing of this.

Norman got his ticket out one morning shortly afterwards, during an advance to clear a canyon of Japanese. They moved cautiously, shooting into each rock opening, following up with flamethrowers and grenades. "We thought we'd cleaned out those caves—but we hadn't." Shots suddenly echoed across the canyon, one of them hitting Norman in the shoulder, holing his collarbone and puncturing his lung. He remained coherent enough to point to his companions where the gunfire had come from, to watch a flamethrower team address the cave mouth, and hear the screams which followed. Then an unknown Samaritan helped him over a log bridge across a creek, and onto a jeep ambulance. After that, he remembered only a succession of operating tables until he glimpsed the Golden Gate Bridge.

Airmen based on Leyte found compensations immeasurably remote from the experience of the fighting soldiers: "It was pleasant to have houseboys around quarters and laundry services, even if the native women did pound garments destructively upon rocks in muddy streams to 'clean' them," in the words of the air force historians. "Barter with the natives produced wooden sandals, mats, knives and other trinkets for souvenirs, while cockfights, a national Filipino institution, became a fad." When Eric Diller was posted from a rifle company on Leyte to a motor pool, "for the first time in my army career, I enjoyed every moment of it . . . No one was shooting at me. I was fed three hot meals daily in a mess hall. We lived in tents with wooden floors. Showers were available. Movies were shown on a regular basis. The working hours were reasonable and enough time was left to play volleyball daily . . . It absolutely reconfirmed my opinion that infantry does not receive nearly adequate recognition."

It was a common delusion among MacArthur's riflemen that they were the principal victims of the Leyte experience. Yet for the Japanese, matters were infinitely worse. On 26 November, a battalion commander of the 77th Infantry Regiment gave a bleak briefing to his officers: "The tactics we have been using against an enemy with superior firepower only increase our losses. Our cherished night attacks lose their potency when the enemy can illuminate the battlefield. The most effective tactical methods are to stage raids in small groups." Lt. Suteo Inoue of the same regiment wrote in his diary for 3 December: "Soldiers have become very weak, and only half the platoon are physically fit . . . the majority are suffering from fever."

Bill McLaughlin, a reconnaissance scout, was once exploring his unit's frontage with another man when, to their horror, they found that they had blundered into Japanese positions. "As we crouched there hardly daring to breathe, listening to their jabbering, it came to both of us at once that we were listening to some pretty scared Japanese boys looking for reassurance that they were not alone. It was so absurd, a couple of frightened Yanks playing Indians and crawling around on one side of the grass screen and a bunch of frightened Japs crouching on the other." The two Americans crawled thoughtfully away.

Krueger's men took few prisoners on Leyte: 389 before 25 December and a further 439 thereafter. If this was partly because not many Japanese wished to surrender, it was also because few Americans were willing to accommodate them. A U.S. divisional commander, Maj.-Gen. William

Arnold of the Americal, was asked after the war if he encouraged surrenders. His response was ruthlessly pragmatic: "No . . . for the simple reason that an average Japanese prisoner knew nothing whatever about anything . . . and I doubt whether an officer would know anything." Arnold rejected "emotional talk of war crimes" committed by either Japanese or Americans: "You've got soldiers with no brains at all, some of them, and they'd kill you just as soon as look at you. You have them everywhere. The Americans are just as bad as anybody else as far as that's concerned. In the heat of combat, you shoot people who would have probably surrendered."

One of the small number of Japanese who survived in American hands was a twenty-two-year-old private named Sumito Ideguchi, who successfully deserted from his unit. A former truck driver, he had endured a familiar sequence of miseries. His transport was sunk en route to Leyte. Rescued by a minesweeper, he was eventually sent into the line. Ideguchi found himself serving alongside strangers from unfamiliar regions of Japan, whom he could not relate to. Perceiving himself banished from home, he told his captors that he would like to settle in the United States.

An unusual perspective on the American soldier's experience can be gained from letters home which were intercepted in transit by U.S. military censors, and still repose in their old files. All references to atrocities, looting or other forms of unsoldierly behaviour were deemed inappropriate, and caused men's letters to be confiscated. For instance, Private George Hendrikson of the 21st Infantry wrote to his wife in Dallas, Oregon: "One of my buddies and I went out on a souvenir hunt one day up there and we capture 1 Jap and two Philippines that were helping the Japans I got a good fountain pen off of them and my buddy got a good Cig lighter which he sold for $20 and he got a watch also so we were luckily [*sic*]."

Staff Sergeant G. Gionnarli of the 34th Infantry described a Japanese attempt to surrender: "One came out with his hands up. One of my men shot him through the arm." Lt. William Spradlin wrote: "If one [Japanese prisoner] gets to our rear area alive it's only because we . . . can't afford to shoot." Private Rex Marsh's letter, recalling how he cut off the head of a dead Japanese with a bolo knife, went undelivered, likewise that of a soldier who described his withering contempt for Filipinos. Sgt. Leonard Joe Davis of the 34th Infantry was rash enough to confide his misery in writing to a former comrade now living in Waterloo, New York: "The Japs have been giving us hell, Monty, even worse than any yet. I'm sure glad to get out of the fight for a while, we have replacements twice since you left and now, guess how many we have in the company—50. I would have shot myself in the foot if I would have had to stay much longer, I have been trying to for a long time, you know how you feel. Lots of the boys did it."

· · ·

In the Philippines, the landmasses being contested were much larger than the islands or atolls on which the Americans had been fighting for so long, save Papua New Guinea. Since the Japanese had nothing like enough men to defend everything, Krueger possessed much more scope for manoeuvre than American attackers on Saipan or Peleliu. Yet, just as Sixth Army's commander criticised his subordinates for missing chances to bypass Japanese strongpoints, so Krueger's critics complained of their general's lack of drive and imagination. In particular, he was accused of lacking an eye for terrain—failing to identify key features and secure them ahead of the Japanese. Reality probably lay somewhere between the two claims: the high command was without flair, and many infantry units were slow. Whatever the causes, the protraction of the campaign bred recrimination.

Most serious of all for MacArthur was the frustration of his fundamental justification for taking Leyte: its exploitation as an aircraft and logistics base. The waterlogged plains were wholly unsuitable for intensive aircraft usage, and even for stores depots. Kenney's Fifth Air Force, charged with supporting and protecting Sixth Army, possessed 2,500 aircraft, yet two months after the invasion hardly any of these could operate from Leyte's landing grounds.

It is a shocking indictment of MacArthur and his staff that they chose to ignore forecasts of these difficulties, submitted long before the landings. On 10 August 1944, Col. William J. Ely, executive officer of Sixth Army's engineers, delivered a report in which he highlighted the "soil instability" of Leyte Valley, and the impossibility of accomplishing vital engineer tasks—above all airfield construction—with the troops available, at the height of the rainy season. "Perhaps we can mud and muddle through again on a shoestring," wrote the colonel gloomily, "but the shoestring must be frayed by this time and if it broke we may lose our shirt as well as our shoe." Ely's commanding officer strongly concurred with this report, which was forwarded to SWPA HQ—and dismissed. The rejection of prudent professional advice about the shortcomings of Leyte as a forward air base reflected reckless irresponsibility by the supreme commander and his staff.

By 21 November, the appalling weather infected even MacArthur's notoriously bombastic communiqués with gloom. "Another tropical typhoon with continuous rains is lashing Leyte," declared one bulletin. "Bridges are washed out, streams are torrents and roads have become waterways. All traffic air, ground and sea is fraught with great difficulty and hazard and battle conditions are becoming static." Almost twenty-four inches of rain fell on Leyte in November, double the customary monsoon dose. Few of the men on the mountains, Americans or Japanese, had effective shelter. That winter of 1944, providence was ungenerous to the Allied armies both in Europe and Asia, subjecting Eisenhower's and MacArthur's forces alike to weather which crippled their operations. In adverse conditions, it is vastly easier for defenders to hold ground than for attackers to advance.

Engineers exercised heroic ingenuity to overcome the airfield problem. The Japanese had never laid hard surfaces on their strips. The Americans scoured the island for suitable material. At Tacloban, it was found that a naval dredger's mighty 2,800-horsepower pumps could move solid substances a mile through hoses. Coral was shifted directly from the seabed offshore to the airfield. Yet still it proved a massive task to create serviceable landing grounds: "A battalion [of engineers] could accomplish no more in a month than a platoon could have carried out in a week under good weather conditions." Two airfields had to be abandoned, and a third did not become operational until 16 December.

The Japanese were unaware that Kenney's aircraft could scarcely fly out of Leyte. Ironically, therefore, on 27 November and 6 December they lavished scarce resources on launching commando and paratroop landings against the American strips. These attacks caused panic in Krueger's rear areas—air corps service personnel fled one position, abandoning all their weapons, which the Japanese promptly turned on the Americans. The intruders were soon killed or dispersed, order restored, but Leyte never became a significant USAAF base. The difficulties of stockpiling and shifting stores increased, rather than diminished. MacArthur had allowed the geographical convenience of the island to blind him to its unsuitability for every important strategic purpose.

An amphibious landing south of Ormoc on 7 December enabled the Americans three days later to seize the port, and cut off the Japanese from further resupply or reinforcement. Troops entering the ruined town found "a blazing inferno of bursting white phosphorus shells, burning houses, and exploding ammunition dumps, and over it all hung a pall of heavy smoke from burning dumps mixed with the gray dust of destroyed concrete buildings, blasted by . . . artillery, mortar, and rocket fire." In the week 15 to 21 December, western Leyte's Ormoc Valley was secured. MacArthur announced the formal completion of operations across the entire island on Christmas Day, 1944: "The Leyte-Samar campaign can now be regarded as closed except for minor mopping-up," said a SWPA communiqué. "General Yamashita has sustained perhaps the greatest defeat in the military annals of the Japanese army."

In Manila, the Japanese high command sought to preserve formalities, somewhat hampered by American air raids. On 23 December, Yamashita held a sumptuous full-dress dinner in honour of the local naval commander, Vice-Admiral Mikawa. The power supply failed in midfeast, plunging a glittering array of officers into darkness until a young staff officer bustled round, distributing candles. Two days later, Mikawa returned the compliment on a ship in Manila harbour. Yamashita limped aboard, having been injured by metal fragments during demonstrations of a new weapon. His chief of staff murmured to Mikawa that it might be wise not to give the invalid too much wine. "Rubbish, you damn fool!" exploded Yamashita, who overheard. "I drink what I like." The general had plenty to forget, and indulged freely. That same day, 25 December, he had signalled General Suzuki that thenceforward Japanese troops on Leyte must fend for themselves. There could be no further reinforcement or resupply. The battle for the island was lost. Suzuki's remaining elements dispersed into the mountains.

But as many as 20,000 Japanese remained. Even though they now adopted guerrilla tactics rather than fighting as regiments with support weapons, for four more months they sustained the struggle. A communiqué from MacArthur asserted that 117,997 enemy troops had been killed on Leyte, at least double the real total. MacArthur's soldiers were infuriated by his public announcement of a victory which was still far from secure. Though Krueger's Sixth Army was withdrawn from combat to prepare for the Luzon landing, Eichelberger's Eighth Army endured hard fighting to accomplish the "mopping up" of which their supreme commander spoke so carelessly. "MacArthur's communiqués are inaccurate to a disgusting degree," wrote Lt. Gage Rodman of the 17th Infantry. "We who were on the spot knew we were only beginning to fight when he made his ridiculous announcement that our objective was secured."

The capture of Leyte cost some 15,500 American casualties, including 3,500 dead—almost 700 of the latter, a battalion's worth, after MacArthur proclaimed his "victory." Japanese losses were confused by uncertainty about how many troops were drowned in transit to the island when transports were sunk by U.S. aircraft or submarines, but the total approached 50,000. Eighth Army claimed a "body count" of 24,294 Japanese merely for the period from Christmas 1944 to May 1945. Even if this figure was much exaggerated, it reflected the severity of continuing operations. From January onwards, the surviving Japanese on Leyte were dependent on local food taken from civilians, and even on growing their own crops.

They lacked salt, radio batteries, ammunition. Many of the stragglers had had enough. Whether they were fortunate enough to be able to surrender, however, depended upon escaping the eyes of their own superiors—and then meeting Americans willing to take them alive. One soldier who did so was a certain Private Saito, who lingered in hiding for weeks after being wounded, and kept a diary. "A year ago tomorrow I was inducted," he wrote.

> That was an unhappy day, for I left behind everything worthwhile. Today I experienced the first stage of a new life. I heard the voices and footsteps of American soldiers, and my heart leapt. Instead of fear, I find that I feel a certain warmth towards them. I cannot help but think that those voices have come to save me. Though I wanted to go out to meet them, the wound in my foot prevented it.
>
> For forty-three days now, I have been grateful for this hut because of my gangrene. I feel deeply grateful to my friend Nakata, for without him I would have died on 7 December, under that terrific naval bombardment. He saved me at the risk of his own life. To lose one's life in a war of this kind is extremely regrettable. I could not teach him that the conflict arose from the greed of the military and capitalist clique. My hatred for the army hierarchy is stronger than I can express. I must survive and tell this story to the [Japanese] people, or my soul will never rest. The things that we did in China are being done to us. Japan will soon be defeated. We have learned from this war how inferior are our science and industry to those of the enemy. From the outset, I never thought that we could win.

Private Saito was fortunate enough to be taken alive on 13 January, by men of the 17th Infantry. It is unknown whether he survived to return to Japan.

At Clark Field on Luzon, navy fighter pilot Kunio Iwashita and his comrades knew the war was going very wrong indeed. "The longer one fought, the more sobered one was by the reality of so many friends being killed. One morning in November 1944 when we were escorting twelve bombers on a mission to attack American transports at San Pedro, I saw below on the sea the whole array of their carriers, battleships, transports, destroyers. I realised what very bad trouble Japan was in—and I thought that looked like my own day to die." Iwashita survived, but around 70 percent of his fellow aircrew at Clark were lost on operations in the Philippines. Just four of thirty-five fighter pilots who graduated in his flight-training course survived the war.

Some Japanese senior officers from Leyte reached other islands in a series of night dashes, spending their days hiding in the jungle behind deserted beaches in a fashion uncommonly like that of Allied fugitives from Japan's great offensive of 1942. General Suzuki, Leyte's commander, was killed in April, when a launch in which he sought to escape was strafed by American aircraft. Some of his men survived, to join other island garrisons. Yamashita dispatched fanciful orders to surviving elements which reached Mindanao and Cebu: "The army will attempt to drive back the advancing enemy . . . reduce [his] fighting capability . . . and hold the area as a foothold for future counter-offensives by Japanese forces."

While the Americans had prevailed in their largest ground campaign of the eastern conflict thus far, few of those who fought had relished the experience. "Perhaps the best way to describe life in the Pacific war would be to say we endured," wrote Private Bill McLaughlin, a recon scout with the Americal Division. ". . . The heat, the insects, disease, combat and the boredom in between . . . We came to expect little, and to be satisfied with little in the way of comfort: a few candles, some playing cards, a little hard candy." American soldiers felt that they had suffered much, to gain possession of a few thousand square miles of swamp and mountain, peasant huts and ruined towns. "This theater has been a victim of over-optimism almost as much as the European one," wrote Lt.-Gen. Robert Eichelberger of Eighth Army on 8 January, soon after accepting responsibility for "mopping up" Leyte.

Only senior officers, privy to the airfields fiasco, understood that MacArthur had landed Sixth Army on the wrong island. It was fortunate that this American strategic error was partially redeemed by a matching Japanese one. Terauchi's folly in compelling Yamashita to reinforce failure enabled Krueger's formations to inflict heavy losses, to destroy units which would otherwise have been awaiting the Americans on Luzon. In Japan, the fall of Leyte precipitated the resignation of the government of the prime minister, Lt.-Gen. Kuniaki Koiso. Koiso had proclaimed this to be "the decisive battle"—so often a doom-laden phrase for his nation. Now it had been lost. Koiso paid the price, unlamented by his own people. He was replaced by a deeply reluctant Admiral Kantaro Suzuki, seventy-seven years old, deaf and ill, bereft of a coherent vision of his own purpose in power, save to preside over the cabinet.

If U.S. casualties in this first Philippines campaign seemed painful, they were in truth modest, either by the standards of the Japanese or by those of the European war. It was impossible to beat such a formidable enemy without suffering some attrition. Leyte proved a worse defeat than the Japanese need have suffered, a more substantial victory than MacArthur deserved.

CHAPTER EIGHT

China: Dragon by the Tail

1. The Generalissimo

YAMASHITA in the Philippines recognised that his struggle against MacArthur's armies could have only one outcome. If the Americans found the campaign tough, they were always advancing. Even during this last phase of the Second World War, however, in one theatre Japan's armies continued to gain ground, and to win victories. In China, a million Japanese soldiers sustained and even enlarged their huge, futile empire. Neither Mao Zedong's Communists in the north nor Chiang Kai-shek's Nationalists in the west and south proved able to frustrate Japanese advances. The killing and dying, the rape and destruction which Hirohito's armies had unleashed in Manchuria in 1931, persisted and even intensified on the Asian mainland in the last months of the war.

Thirty-six-year-old John Paton Davies, a U.S. Foreign Service officer born in China, the son of missionaries, knew that country's vastnesses as intimately as any man. He witnessed the Japanese seizure of Manchuria. For much of the war he served as political adviser to Lt.-Gen. Joseph Stilwell, until October 1944 Allied chief of staff to Chiang Kai-shek. Afterwards, with the bitterness of a man whose diplomatic career was destroyed by Senator Joseph McCarthy for his alleged role in the American "loss" of China, Davies described the country as "a huge and seductive practical joke, which defeated the Westerners who tried to modernise it, the Japanese who tried to conquer it, the Americans who tried to democratise and unify it—and Chiang and Mao." He likened China's condition in the 1940s to that of fourteenth-century Europe. He was an intimate observer of twentieth-century America's titanic and wholly unsuccessful attempt to impose its will upon a society impossibly remote in circumstances as well as geography.

China's wartime sufferings, which remain unknown to most Westerners, were second in scale only to those of the Soviet Union. It is uncertain how many Chinese died in the years of conflict with Japan. Traditionally, a figure of fifteen million has been accepted, one-third of these being soldiers. Modern Chinese historians variously assert twenty-five, even fifty million. Ninety-five million people became homeless refugees. Such estimates are neither provable nor disprovable. Rather than being founded upon convincing statistical analysis, they reflect the intensity of Chinese emotions about what the Japanese did to their country. What is indisputable is that a host of people perished. Survivors suffered horrors almost beyond our imaginings. Massacre, destruction, rape and starvation were the common diet of the Chinese people through each year of Japan's violent engagement in their country.

Historians of Asia assert that the Second World War properly began in China, rather than Poland. In 1931 Japan almost bloodlessly seized Manchuria—the north-eastern Chinese provinces, an area twice the size of Britain, with a population of thirty-five million people, ruled by an old warlord—to secure its coal, raw materials, industries and strategic rail links. The Nationalist government based in Nanjing was too weak to offer resistance. The following year, Tokyo announced Manchuria's transformation into the puppet state of Manchukuo, nominally ruled by the Manchu Emperor Pu Yi, in practice by a Japanese-controlled prime minister, and garrisoned by Japan's so-called Guandong Army. The Japanese perceived themselves as merely continuing a tradition established over centuries by Western powers in Asia—that of exploiting superior might to extend their home industrial and trading bases.

As a sixteen-year-old in 1941, Souhei Nakamura was dispatched by his family from Japan to work for an uncle's motorcycle-repair business in Manchuria, where he was introduced to the delights of colonial mastery. "It was wonderful there—an easy life with lots of good food, much better than being at school. All I had to do was keep an eye on the Chinese doing the real work." He had money in his pocket, and used it to pleasant purpose. After being sent packing by the first local brothel he visited—"You're much too young"—he was introduced to a twenty-four-year-old geisha, who solaced the teenager's life for the next four years. "In Manchuria in those days, every Japanese was a privileged person. I will tell you just how privileged. One day in town, I watched a Chinese policeman book a Japanese woman for crossing a road against a red light. A Japanese soldier who saw them told the Chinese to release the woman and apologise. When the policeman refused, the soldier shot him dead." There was a frontier atmosphere about Manchuria, soon overflowing with Japanese peasant immigrants who were supposedly obliged to buy land from local Chinese, but who in reality sequestered what they wanted without payment.

The Japanese annexation of Manchuria, and their progressive advance into China thereafter, involved rapacity and brutality on a scale which shocked the world, and inflicted untold misery on those in their path. "For me, the war started on 18 September 1931, when the Japanese seized my home town," said Wen Shan, a Manchurian lawyer's son who fled south to Yunnan to escape the occupation. "We were victims of those gangsters for the next fourteen years." He was reared on Nationalist propaganda about Japanese barbarities, much of it true. In 1937 Japan extended its mainland empire, occupying most of the Chinese coastline with its ports and industrial cities, chief sources of wealth in a chronically starving land. "The Japanese forced my father to become a traitor, by joining one of their business syndicates and working for them," said Jiang Zhen, a landlord's son from Shanghai. "When he would no longer do so, they made him a slave labourer, and when he became too sick to work, they sent him home to die."

As the Japanese armies moved inland, millions of Chinese fugitives fled west, including the Nationalist government of Chiang Kai-shek. He abandoned his capital, Nanjing, in favour of Chongqing. The Nationalist army's resistance to the invaders cost much blood and achieved little success. Xu Yongqiang, an engineer's son who lived in the British concession at Tianjin, south-east of Beijing, a precarious island of safety amid the rising Japanese tide, said: "Every morning we watched corpses drifting downriver to the sea. Out in the countryside, the Japanese were using peasants to build pillboxes for their positions. When the pillboxes were completed, they shot the peasants."

China is larger than the United States, and characterised by extreme variations of climate and topography. In 1944 only around 12 percent of its surface was cultivated, because the remainder was too high, dry or steep—around half the country lies more than a mile above sea level. Hundreds of millions of Chinese eked out primitive lives in conditions of chronic misery. Zhu De, for instance, commander of Mao Zedong's Communist armies, was born fourth among thirteen children of his parents. He was the last one to survive, for his younger siblings were drowned at birth in the absence of means to feed them. Although there were frequent outbreaks of plague—some deliberately propagated by the Japanese through their biological warfare Unit 731—there were no medicines. It became a commonplace prophylactic against infection to tie a live cockerel to the chest of a convenient corpse, to ward off spirits. Most of the population lived in huts built of mud and rubble. The average farm was less than four acres. Foreigners who visited China were enchanted by places of extraordinary beauty, "of lacquerware and porcelain, embroidered silk and bridges over still pools, courtyards pierced by moon gates." The dominant images, however, were of tragedy and destitution.

Japanese policy in China was determined overwhelmingly by the army, often against the strong wishes of Tokyo's civilian politicians. By 1941, at a

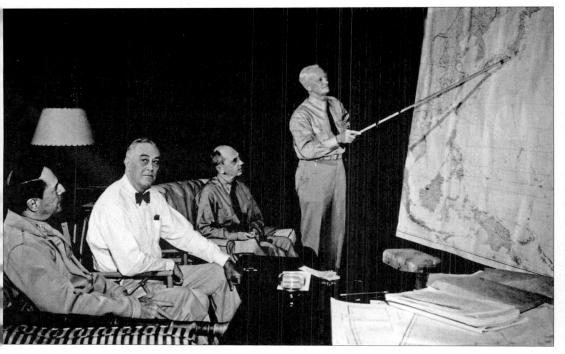

The president as U.S. commander-in-chief: in July 1944, in the midst of his re-election campaign, Roosevelt summoned MacArthur and Nimitz to meet him on Hawaii, allegedly to expound their plans for victory over Japan.

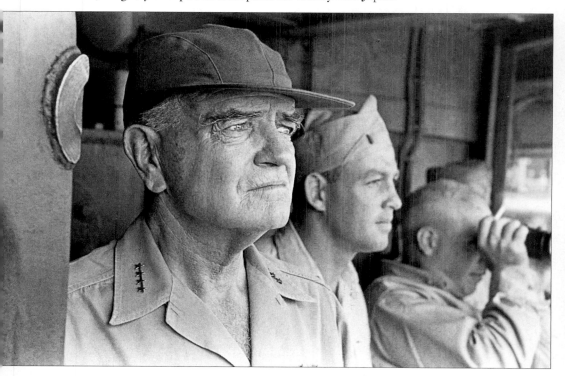

Admiral William "Bull" Halsey on the flag bridge of the battleship *New Jersey* as he led his Third Fleet towards the Philippines in September 1944.

Sikhs charge a foxhole.

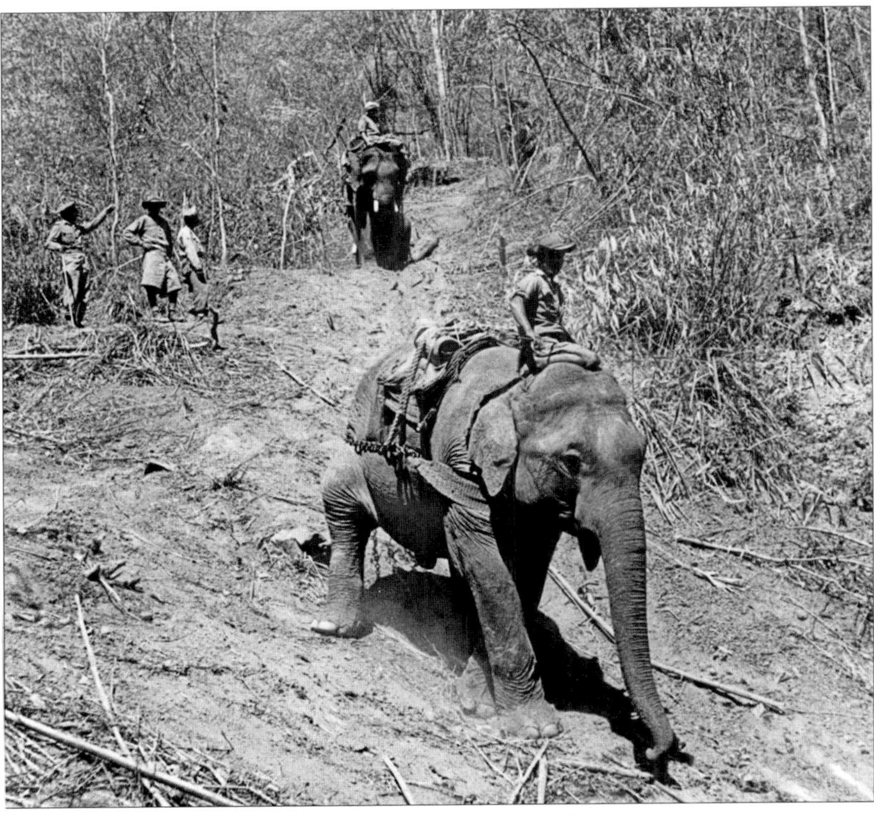

Elephant transport played a significant role in enabling the Fourteenth Army to build bridges and move supplies amid some of the most intractable terrain on earth.

ABOVE: One of thousands of river crossings during the 1944–45 campaign.

RIGHT: The indomitable Bill Slim, probably the ablest and certainly the most sympathetic British field commander of the Second World War.

War in China, where at least fifteen million died. Scenes during the Japanese invasion, which inflicted untold suffering and destruction without giving Tokyo a decisive victory.

Chinese Leaders

ABOVE LEFT: Mao Zedong and Zhou Enlai. ABOVE RIGHT: The puppet emperor Pu-Yi. BELOW: Chiang Kai-shek.

ABOVE: A snatched glimpse of the Japanese Combined Fleet on its passage towards destruction in September 1944. BELOW: USS *Gambier Bay* bracketed by Japanese fire during the Battle of Leyte Gulf.

ABOVE: The cruiser *Birmingham* aids the stricken *Princeton* after a crippling air attack. BELOW: Commanders Nimitz, King and Spruance photographed aboard the cruiser *Indianapolis*.

Commanders

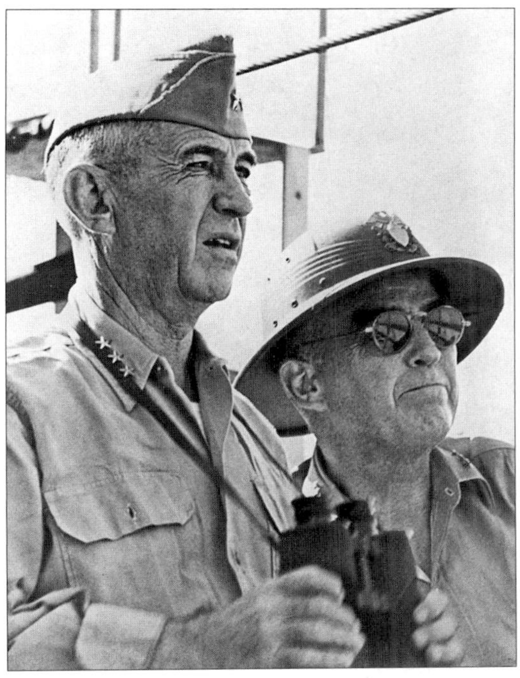

ABOVE: Krueger and Kinkaid.
BELOW LEFT: Kurita. BELOW RIGHT: Ugaki.

ABOVE: Men crouch, tensed aboard a landing craft.
BELOW: Marine amphibious vehicles approach Peleliu.

A task group led by some of almost one hundred U.S. carriers at sea in late 1944.

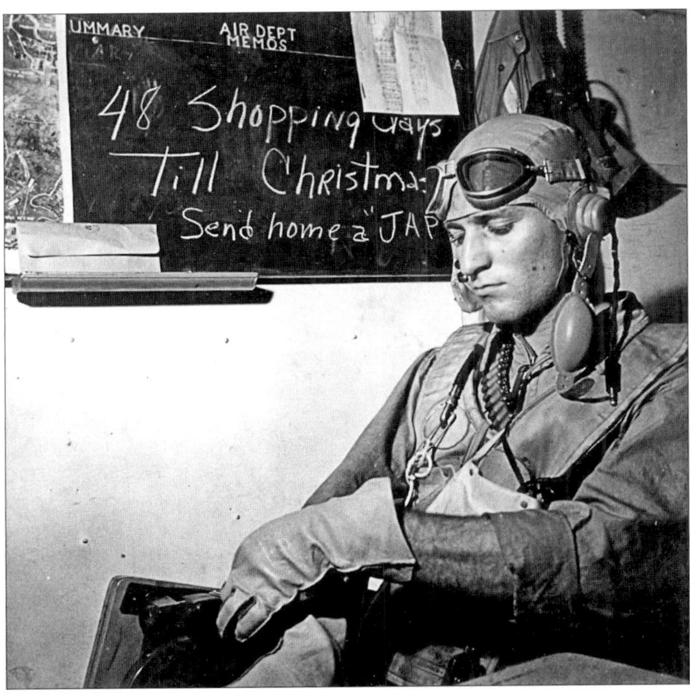

A pilot in the "ready room."

Launching a Hellcat.

One of the U.S. Navy's foremost Pacific aces, Commander David McCampbell.

above: U.S. soldiers taking cover on Leyte in November 1944, and *(below)* fighting through the wreckage of Manila in February 1945.

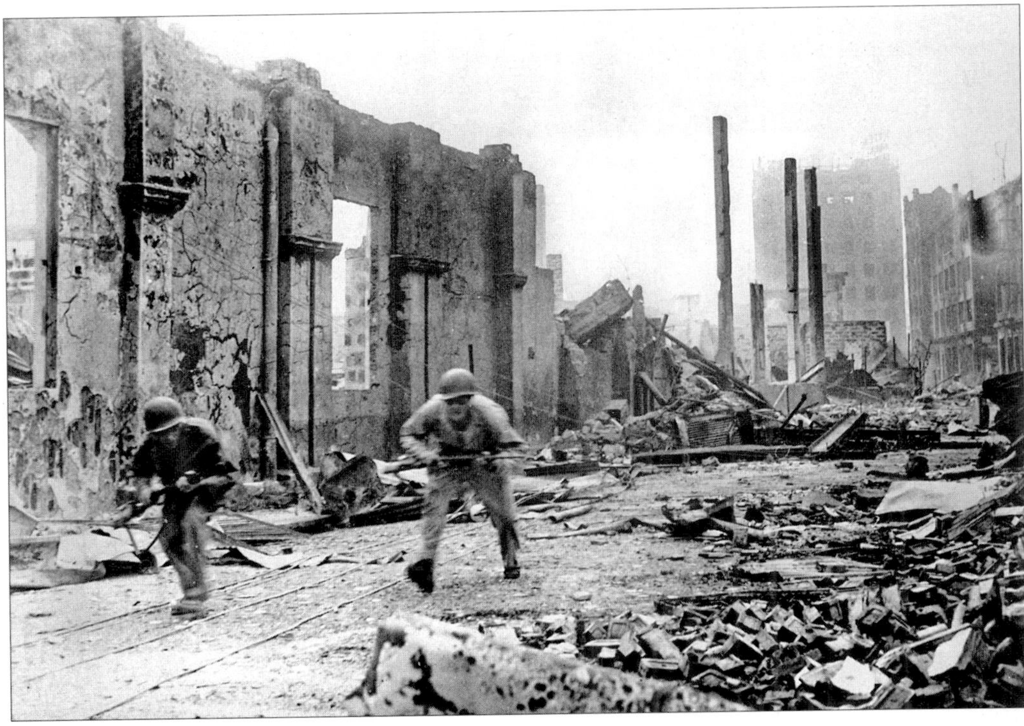

ABOVE: The Marines land on Iwo Jima. BELOW: Only a handful of Japanese, such as these men, chose surrender rather than death in the last stages of the bloody struggle for the island.

MacArthur.

Bill Bradlee.

Lieutenant Philip True.

Emory Jernigan.

Rear-Admiral Clifton Sprague.

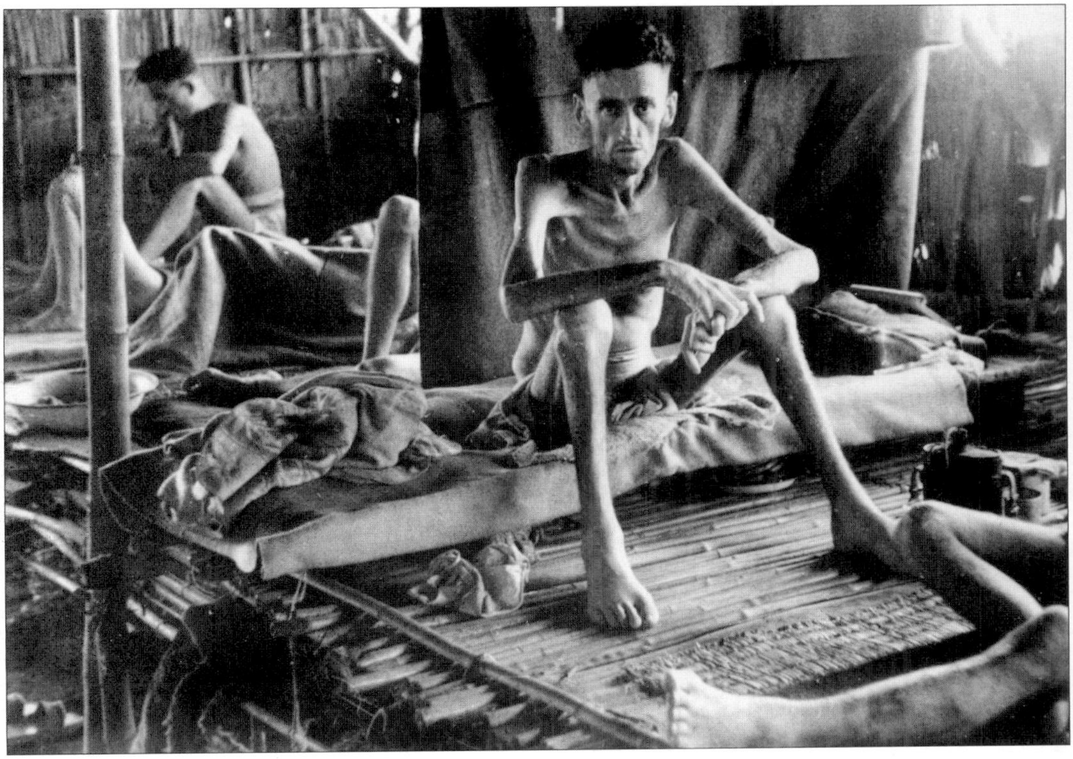

ABOVE: A British survivor at Nakhon Pathom, Siam, in 1945. BELOW: Four Australians drag themselves to the U.S. submarine *Pampanito*, which had sunk the transport taking them to Japan. Most of their companions perished.

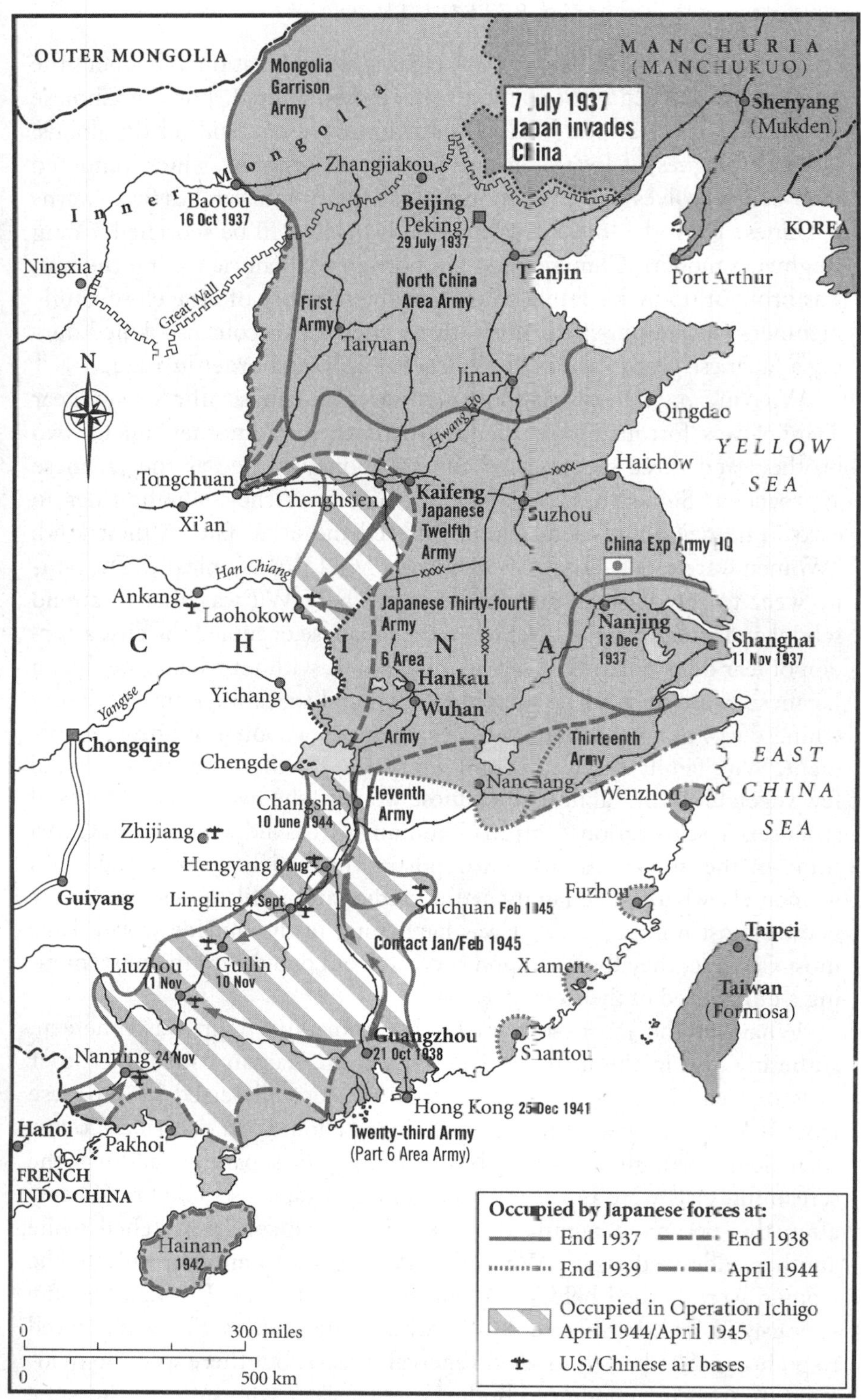
OUTER MONGOLIA
MANCHURIA
(MANCHUKUO)
7 July 1937
Japan invades
China
Shenyang
(Mukden)
Mongolia
Garrison
Army
Inner Mongolia
Zhangjiakou
Baotou
16 Oct 1937
Beijing
(Peking)
29 July 1937
KOREA
Ningxia
Great Wall
Tianjin
Port Arthur
North China
Area Army
First
Army
Taiyuan
N
Jinan
Qingdao
Hwang Ho
YELLOW
SEA
Haichow
Tongchuan
Chenghsien
Kaifeng
Japanese
Twelfth
Army
Xi'an
Suzhou
China Exp Army HQ
Han Chiang
Ankang
Laohokow
Japanese Thirty-fourth
Army
6 Area
Nanjing
13 Dec
1937
Shanghai
11 Nov 1937
C H I N A
Hankau
Wuhan
Yichang
Yangtse
Chongqing
Army
Thirteenth
Army
EAST
CHINA
SEA
Chengde
Nanchang
Wenzhou
Changsha
10 June 1944
Eleventh
Army
Zhijiang
Hengyang 8 Aug
Guiyang
Lingling 4 Sept
Suichuan Feb 1945
Fuzhou
Contact Jan/Feb 1945
Taipei
Liuzhou
11 Nov
Guilin
10 Nov
Xiamen
Taiwan
(Formosa)
Guangzhou
21 Oct 1938
Shantou
Nanning 24 Nov
Hong Kong 25 Dec 1941
Hanoi
Pakhoi
Twenty-third Army
(Part 6 Area Army)
FRENCH
INDO-CHINA
Occupied by Japanese forces at:
End 1937
End 1938
End 1939
April 1944
Occupied in Operation Ichigo
April 1944/April 1945
U.S./Chinese air bases
Hainan
1942
0
300 miles
0
500 km

The Japanese occupation of China, 1937–45

cost equivalent to 40 percent of Japan's annual national budget, the invaders had gained most of the territory they wanted. For the Chinese people, the miseries of a brutal occupation were overlaid on the floods, famines, plagues of locusts and other natural disasters which rendered their ordinary lives wretched enough. "If the city gate catches fire," warns a Chinese proverb, "the fish in the ponds below will be scorched." Yang Jinghua, a modern Chinese historian born in Manchuria during the war, was brought up by his father to cherish the memory of nine close family members—two sisters, two aunts, three uncles, two cousins—killed during a Japanese visit to their village near the Korean border in 1944.

Wu Yinyan, twenty-year-old daughter of an official in a village near Tianjin, was fortunate. Her family—parents, grandmother, uncle, two brothers and three sisters—had enough money to flee as the Japanese approached. Sometimes they walked, sometimes they bought rides in carts. The neighbours left behind suffered the usual fate of their kind: "Women were raped, houses were burned," said Wu laconically. The family went to stay with an aunt in Beijing, where Wu was able to attend school and later university. Yet when the Japanese occupied the city, a curtain of fear descended. "I never went out alone, without friends, because a Japanese could do what he wanted to anyone. I was always afraid." Every Chinese was obliged to bow to every Japanese, a source of bitter resentment. Wu's family survived mainly on maize, for there was no meat and few vegetables. Like almost all Chinese women, she lived in conditions of strict sexual segregation. Only in Communist areas did war bring to China some of the new freedoms and opportunities which it conferred upon women elsewhere. The family had no radio, and until August 1945 they knew almost nothing of what was happening in the outside world. Like most Chinese, they focused upon survival from one day to the next, nursing a dull hatred of their occupiers.

Whatever the Japanese wanted, they took. Lin Yajin was nineteen, gathering rice in the fields near her village in Hainan with three other girls one day in October 1943 when they were all seized by Japanese troops. At first they were merely questioned about local guerrilla activity, then held overnight in a hut. Next evening, in separate buildings the screaming girls were raped by a succession of Japanese soldiers. Thereafter, this became a nightly routine. Often, one soldier watched while another addressed a girl. When the unit moved to another village, the women were herded behind. By the summer of 1944, Lin had become seriously ill, and therefore of less interest to the soldiers. She was allowed to go home. She had contracted venereal disease, but there were no medicines to treat her condition. Both she and a sister who suffered the same fate were mocked by their neighbours, and indeed became near outcasts in the years that followed. She never married or had children. In 1946 she learned that the other three girls seized with her three years earlier had died of disease in Japanese hands.

Chen Jinyu was only sixteen when the Japanese army took her to become a "comfort woman," together with every other available girl in her village in Baoting district. "Because I was pretty they used me more often than the rest. After a month I couldn't bear it any more. One day I and some other girls were bathing in the river. I slipped over to the far bank and had started running when a Japanese guard saw me. He blew his whistle. Soldiers caught me, beat me pretty badly, then locked me up. Next morning, in heavy rain, I was forced to crawl across the ground in front of everyone, then beaten till I was a mass of cuts and bruises. In the end I couldn't move any more, and just lay there in the mud and the water. The other girls begged the Japanese officers to spare me. If they hadn't intervened, I doubt that I would have survived." She remained a comfort woman until June 1945, when in desperation she escaped to the mountains, where she scavenged until the war ended.

Jiang Fushun, a boy of thirteen in 1944, was one of eight children of a peasant who worked as a water carrier for the Japanese at Hutou in Manchuria. They knew nothing of the outside world: "We were conscious there was a war—that was all. We knew the Japanese expected to fight, because they were building all these fortresses." They never saw the hapless slave labourers who toiled underground for months behind the Japanese perimeter wire, then were killed in their thousands to ensure that the secrets of Hutou's defences were kept. Fields behind the town became the property of some of Manchuria's 300,000 Japanese immigrants. The new landowners' ventures into agriculture met with little success, however. To crop rice, many were obliged to enlist the labour of dispossessed locals. There was no social contact between occupiers and occupied.

One day the Japanese announced that the garrison was holding an exercise. All Chinese must remain indoors with their windows closed. It was a hot afternoon. The uncle of Zhou Baozhu opened his window. He was beaten half to death by Japanese police. Other offenders were thrashed with iron bars or thrown into boiling water. For local children, there were no games, no play with friends, no schooling, for all association was forbidden. In return for labouring all day beside his father, carrying water on their shoulders from the river to the garrison huts, Jiang's family received a monthly ration of cooking oil and twenty-four pounds of corn, which somehow kept them alive, supplemented by wild vegetables from the nearby forest.

Liu Yunxiu, twenty-year-old daughter of teachers in Changchun, Manchuria, found herself obliged to learn Japanese in school, and to attend Japanese-sponsored classes in the arts of housewifery—cleaning, cooking, sewing: "This sort of thing was not at all the Chinese style." Liu would have liked to train as a doctor, but such options were closed to a woman. Like Wu Yinyan, she knew nothing of the war, save as "noises off." For instance, a friend's brother ran away to join Communist guerrillas. His family heard long afterwards that he had been killed. Another classmate left the school to make an arranged marriage to the puppet emperor Pu Yi. Liu remembered the girl's parents sobbing at her departure, because thereafter they were forbidden to see her.

Liu's chief awareness of the war derived from chronic shortages, especially of food. She and her family were sometimes reduced to eating the bitter greenstuff *xiang shan*. One morning, her grandmother opened the door of their house to see corpses lying in the street. A typhus outbreak had struck the city, and her sister-in-law contracted the disease. In the absence of medicines, folk remedies revived. They bathed the girl's body in a mix of egg white and rice wine. She lived. Liu's parents, like Wu Yinyan's, were intensely strict, "indeed, feudal." She was forbidden to leave the house alone, or to have any contact with boys. As for the Japanese, "My parents felt that the only choice was to obey. They told me not to join or take part in anything. There was never any talk of politics in our house. That is how things were."

In such a way did many Chinese survive the Japanese occupation—and the twentieth century. Collaboration with the Tokyo-imposed puppet government in Nanjing was widespread. "The Japanese made everyone spy on each other," says historian Yang Jinghua. "If one family offended against the regime, ten were punished." Many stories of resistance to the Japanese lacked heroic endings. Xu Guiming was born into a peasant family in Ji Lin Province, Manchuria, in 1918. In his early childhood there was some money, and he attended a Confucian school. But the family's fortunes declined into abject poverty. At the age of thirteen he joined a local guerrilla group named the Red Guard Union, 5,000 strong, operating around the Songhua River. He shared their battles through two years that followed, until he was wounded by a bullet in the stomach in a clash with a Japanese-sponsored Manchukuan unit. For three months his father tended him in the guerrilla camp, then transferred him to the care of local Buddhist nuns. Soon after he recovered, the guerrillas became locked in a series of battles with local collaborators and supporting troops, determined to secure the area for planting opium. After weeks of skirmishes and hasty retreats, only two hundred guerrillas remained, encircled by Manchukuan troops and police posts. One night when they were sleeping in a local temple, Xu was taken aside by the chief monk.

"You are much too young to be involved in this bloody business," he said. "Go home."

Back in his own village, however, Xu found no sanctuary. Local collaborators called. They told his family there was a choice. Everyone knew that their son had been a guerrilla. They must pay "squeeze," or the Japanese would reward informers handsomely. The only member of the family who had money was Xu's brother-in-law. He raised 120 silver yuan to pay off the blackmailers, but they knew this would not be the end of the matter. Xu needed to disappear. He made his way to the city of Jilin. There, through the next few years of occupation and unyielding hardship, he strove to acquire a training, or at least some education. He was apprenticed for a time to a sock maker, then to a bicycle repairer. He spent six years working in a rice factory, then became manager of a Korean-owned grocery store. At twenty-one he acquired an unsatisfactory wife with an expensive taste for mahjong and an irritating one for gossip.

Yet, as Xu observed wryly, he achieved a sort of success. He became a bourgeois who could write, count and speak some Japanese. Much as he hated the occupiers, they represented the best, if not only, source of employment. In 1944 he obtained work as a clerk in the Japanese propaganda bureau at Aihni, beside the Russian border on the Amur River. He worked there until August 1945. By definition, he became a collaborator. Yet how else were a host of Chinese to sustain existence? "Even when the Japanese were obviously losing, they behaved as arrogantly as ever," said Xu. "In such a job, at least I was safe from the army and police. We were in the business of survival. I needed the money."

Li Fenggui, born in the countryside near Shanghai in 1921, grew up in abject peasant poverty, his childhood landmarked by natural disasters, even before the Japanese entered the stage. There were two years of Yangtse floods, when everything which his family grew was submerged and ruined. In one year their landlord, "a very cruel man," permitted them to keep only 160 pounds of corn from the harvest, to feed a family of fourteen. Once Li remembered the whole family being taken by their father to a nearby town to beg in the streets. In March 1940, the Japanese descended. Some 140 people were herded away from his hamlet and its neighbours to become slave labourers. In the next village to their own, just two miles away, twenty-four houses were burned, three people were killed, seven women raped, all the rice and grain taken. One of those killed was a fifty-eight-year-old woman who was bayoneted after being raped. Such experiences, multiplied a millionfold, explain the passion of the Chinese people towards the Japanese invaders. "In 1942," said Li, by then a Communist guerrilla, "when the Americans had entered the war, we were so happy to have allies! We felt a surge of hope that Japan would be defeated very quickly. That soon died, and we grew more realistic. We knew that we must win sometime. But we had no idea when."

CHINA'S PRINCIPAL RULER, Generalissimo Chiang Kai-shek, was born in 1887, son of a modestly successful trader near Ningbo in eastern China. He received much of his military education in Japan, and rose to prominence as a protégé of Dr. Sun Yatsen, who led the 1911 revolution which overthrew imperial rule. By the time Sun died in 1925, Chiang was his chief of staff, enjoying the support of some of the most powerful secret societies in China, of much of the army, and—more surprisingly—of the Soviets, who identified him as a coming man. Chiang shared with Mao Zedong an absolute ruthlessness, vividly exemplified by his destruction of the Yellow River dikes in the path of a Japanese advance, exposing six million people to flooding and starvation. He was indifferent to his own armies' casualties, save where these threatened his power base. He gained control of China for his Kuomintang movement—abbreviated as the KMT—through a progressive series of advances north from Canton between 1925 and 1931, sweeping aside such lesser aspirants as Zhang Zongchang, the "dogmeat general" of Shandong, who was said to have "the physique of an elephant, the brain of a pig and the temperament of a tiger."

Political power in China was attainable only with the support of bayonets. Chiang exploited his skills as a military organiser to become the most powerful of all warlords, also having pretensions to a revolutionary ideology. "Fascism is a stimulant for a declining society," he declared in an address to his "Blue Shirt" followers in 1935. "Can fascism save China? We answer: 'Yes.' " He described liberal democracy as "a poison to be expelled from the country's body politic." Yet his professed Christianity and enthusiasm for the West caused many Americans to overlook the absolutism, brutality and corruption of his regime. Thus, for instance, former China medical missionary Congressman Walter Judd in 1944, comparing Americans and Chinese: "The two peoples are nearer alike, we are nearer to the Chinese in our basic beliefs, our basic emphasis on the rights of the individual, and in our basic personal habits of democracy, than we are to most of the countries of Europe."

Indian political leaders admired Chiang as a nationalist, and applauded his outspoken opposition to colonialism. Nehru and the Congress Party described him as "the great leader." Many modern Chinese scholars are far less dismissive of Chiang than might be expected. Yang Jinghua, a historian of Manchuria who has been a Communist Party member for more than thirty years, today regards the generalissimo as a great man: "We say about Mao that he was 30 percent wrong, 70 percent right. Despite the fact that Chiang was a profoundly corrupt dictator, I would say the same about him." Such assertions do not signify that Chiang Kai-shek was a successful or admirable ruler; merely that some of his own people retain respect towards his aspirations for a modern, unified China.

Many Japanese politicians and soldiers learned to regret their entanglement in China as they struggled to stem the American tide in the Pacific. Occupation delivered nothing like the economic benefits which the invaders had expected. Had the huge Japanese forces committed in China—amounting to 45 percent of the army even in 1945—been available for service elsewhere, they might have made an important contribution. That year, Hirohito and army chief of staff Field Marshal Hajime Sugiyama held a conversation which became legendary. The emperor enquired why the China war was taking so long to finish. "China is bigger than we thought," said Sugiyama. Hirohito observed: "The Pacific is also big." In 1943 or 1944, Tokyo would have been happy to withdraw from most of China if the Nationalists had been willing to abandon hostilities and concede Japanese hegemony in Manchuria. This, however, Chiang would never do. And as America's commitment in China grew, the Japanese could not permit U.S. forces or their Nationalist clients to gain control of the coastline. They perceived no choice save to use a million soldiers to hold their ground.

The occupation of Manchuria and eastern China was mercilessly conducted. Unit 731, the biological warfare cell based near Harbin, was its most extreme manifestation. Beyond hundreds of Chinese prisoners subjected to experiments which invariably resulted in their deaths, often by vivisection, the unit sought to spread typhus, anthrax and other plagues indiscriminately among the Chinese population, sometimes by air-dropping of germ cultures. Post-war Japanese claims that reports of atrocities were exaggerated, and that soldiers' misdeeds were unauthorised, are set at naught by the very existence of Unit 731. Its activities matched the horrors of some Nazi concentration camps. The surgical evisceration of hundreds of living and unanaesthetised Chinese, under the official auspices of the Japanese army, represented the nadir of its wartime conduct.

For an ordinary Japanese soldier, China was a miserably uncomfortable, as well as perilous, posting. "Your parents have got four other sons, so they shouldn't miss you too much," an NCO declared callously as he detailed Private Iwao Ajiro for service on an airfield an hour from Beijing. Ajiro hated everything about China, and that airfield. There were no facilities except a brothel staffed by Chinese and Korean comfort women, whom no one much cared for. Their Japanese counterparts were described euphemistically as "nurses," or, in modern parlance, "paramedics." "A man's pay was only seven yen a month," Ajiro complained, "and one of those women cost a yen." The hoary old soldier said in 2005:

> Nowadays the media go on and on about what terrible things Japan is supposed to have done in China. It's a joke. They only tell one side of the story. What about all the Japanese who got killed out there? What do you think it was like for us in a signals section, who had to go out on patrols in parties of four or five, looking for line breaks? If you found a lot of cable missing and went to look for it in the nearby village, there'd be a hundred people there who could kill you—and sometimes did—if you pushed them too hard. They'd steal the cable not to "do their bit" against Japan, but because they were so dirt-poor they needed the stuff.
>
> We Japanese take a bath every day. Those "*chankoro*"—"chinks"—were so desperate they only got a bath twice a year, at New Year and on their birthdays. They had no running water, only wells. Their houses were made of mud that melted in the rain. In the war, we sometimes ran short of toilet paper, but they never used anything but leaves—leaves, for heaven's sake! Outside the great east gate of Beijing, you'd see pigs snuffling about. We used to argue about why they were so poor. We decided they were just lazy. Those Chinese would never do a thing more than they had to. The cleaners in our barracks would sit down and take a smoke as soon as they'd done exactly what orders laid down. Japanese, now, are different—we get on with things without being told to. Chinese water was always filthy, but they were so inured to it that they didn't get ill. Ours had to be filtered before a Japanese soldier could drink it. We'd try to teach the Chinese how to do things properly. They just shook their heads and said: "We have our own way." They'd never learn, never learn.

Ajiro's testimony represents a vivid exposition of the cultural contempt which pervaded the occupying army in China. A modern Japanese historian observes laconically: "More than a million Japanese soldiers served in China, and not one of them troubled to learn its language."

Yet Americans in the country suffered their own fatal illusions and frustrations, founded upon a romantic vision which had been a century in the making. "If the American way of life is to prevail in the world," thundered a prominent member of the "China lobby," novelist Pearl S. Buck, in 1942, "it must prevail in China." The U.S. sought to make Chiang's nation a major force in the Grand Alliance, an objective which proved wholly beyond the powers of both sponsor and protégé. Churchill was exasperated by what he perceived as a U.S. fixation with China—"an absolute farce"—which appeared to extend even to a willingness to grant

Chiang a voice in the post-war settlement of Europe. The prime minister wrote to his foreign secretary, Anthony Eden, in August 1944: "I have told the president I would be reasonably polite about this American obsession. But I cannot agree that we should take a positive attitude . . ."

The war efforts of both the Allies and Japan were drained by their respective China commitments, though the U.S. was vastly better able to bear its share. China was too crippled by its own burdens and dissensions to wage effective war against a foreign power. The Nationalist army sometimes fought hard in the early years following the invasion, killing 185,000 Japanese between 1937 and 1941 in exchange for the loss of vastly more of its own men. By the time the Western powers engaged, however, the best of Chiang's soldiers were dead, and the survivors were exhausted. Hatred of the Japanese did more to unite the Chinese people than any other force in their history. Yet their puny efforts to resist the invader brought upon them death and destruction out of all proportion to any military accomplishment.

Chongqing, Chiang's wartime capital, was detested by almost all those obliged to serve and live there: servants of the regime, foreign missions overwhelmingly dominated by that of the U.S., refugees from all over China, carpetbaggers, Japanese spies, black marketeers, swindlers, merchants, influence-peddlers, beggars—the flotsam of a continent. An old imperial city standing on cliffs at the junction of the Yangtse and Jialing rivers, Chongqing lay in the south-east of Sichuan, China's largest province. Its squalor was notorious. Sewage ran down open ditches, even in thoroughfares renamed with grandiose Kuomintang pretension the Road of the National Republic or Street of the People's Livelihood. Many universities and armament manufacturers, refugees from the coast, had established themselves around the city. Six cinemas served the cultural requirements of exiles from all over China, who swelled the local population from 300,000 to a million. Restaurants learned to serve ham and eggs for Americans. Movie-makers from Hankau made propaganda films for the China Film Corporation. The *Hankow Herald*, now published in Chongqing, offered English-language news, while foreign listeners to the Voice of China heard bulletins read in English by Ma Binhe, a six-foot Chinese in a skullcap who was once a Dubliner named John McCausland.

Rickshaws and sedan chairs plied the streets, but carried scant romance. It was a dank place of fogs and Japanese bombings. Two enormous red paper lanterns, set on poles on nearby hilltops, warned of imminent attack; a green stocking was hoisted to signal the "all-clear." "The streets were full of squealing pigs, bawling babies, yelling men, and the singsong chant of coolies carrying loads up from the river," recorded American correspondent Theodore White. John King Fairbank, another

U.S. visitor, claimed that the city resembled "a junk heap of old boxes piled together . . . There is no colour. Nothing grows out of the rock, the stone is all gray and slightly mossed; people, houses, pathways all blend into gray, with the gray river swirling between." As in every Chinese city, the streets of Chongqing were densely populated with beggars, sometimes whole families together. Educated mendicants saved face by dispatching letters to solicit money, rather than doing so in person.

Chiang wielded power alternately from a villa headquarters and a residence, situated on opposite sides of the river. He and his remarkable wife sometimes serenaded each other as they crossed the Yangtse by launch. Meiling, forty-seven in 1944, came from a powerful mercantile family and had been educated at Wellesley College, Massachusetts. She was said to speak English better than Chinese. After becoming the generalissimo's third wife in 1927, she was sometimes described as the most powerful woman in the world. For years she served as her husband's deputy, patron of a galaxy of organisations, honorary commander of Gen. Claire Chennault's American Volunteer Group—"the Flying Tigers"—and a formidably energetic propagandist for the KMT in the United States. "She can become at will the cultivated, Westernised woman with a knowledge of literature and art," the British writer Christopher Isherwood wrote admiringly, "the technical expert, discussing aeroplane engines and machine guns; the inspector of hospitals; the president of a mothers' union; or the simple Chinese wife. She could be terrible, she could be gracious, she could be businesslike, she could be ruthless; it is said that she sometimes signs death warrants in her own hand."

When Gardner Cowles, publisher of *Look* magazine, prevented Madame Chiang from flying to the U.S. with Republican presidential candidate Wendell Wilkie after his 1942 tour of China, she gouged her nails into his cheeks. In her tumultuous progresses across America, this startling beauty charmed reporters and addressed both houses of Congress, but created unpleasantness by clapping her hands to summon White House servants. Stafford Cripps, the British Labour politician who met the Chiangs in 1940, enthused with characteristic foolishness that he found them "perfect dears, so kind and simple and natural." This was perhaps because Cripps never encountered the KMT's notoriously brutal secret police, or maybe because the generalissimo offered him a job. Madame Chiang's close alliance with Gen. Claire Chennault, whose buccaneering flying exploits had made him a national hero in the United States, served the regime well until at least 1944, when Chennault's star waned in Washington, as American leaders came to understand that he was a wildly over-promoted adventurer.

2. Barefoot Soldiers

After Pearl Harbor, Chiang's armies began to receive massive American support in kind and in cash, much of which the generalissimo and his supporters pocketed. Since there was no overland link between British-ruled India and Chiang's territories between 1942 and early 1945, all supplies had to be flown five hundred miles "over the Hump" of 15,000-foot mountains to Kunming, the nearest accessible landing ground in China, at staggering cost in fuel, planes and American pilots' lives. In December 1942, the Hump air shuttle shifted a mere thousand tons a month. By July 1944 it was carrying 18,975 tons. This was an extraordinary logistical achievement, but remained a negligible contribution to the Chinese war effort; especially so as most of these supplies were stolen and sold long before they reached Chiang's soldiers. Much of the matériel which remained was absorbed by the needs of the U.S. air forces in China. It was simply not feasible to airlift arms and ammunition on the scale needed to equip a Chinese army. From beginning to end, Chiang's formations lacked indispensable heavy weapons to match those of the Japanese. For all the strivings of American generals, diplomats and military advisers, most of the fourteen million men drafted into the Nationalist army between 1937 and 1945 served as hapless victims rather than as effective combatants.

Xu Yongqiang, in 1944 an interpreter with the Nationalists, watched new intakes of men herded in from the provinces: "Most recruits came simply as prisoners, roped together at bayonet point. They had so little training that it was easy to see why they were no match for the Japanese, who for years had been schooled to kill. It was inhuman! Inhuman! There were no such things as civil rights in China. For eight years, it was the peasants who had to fight the Japanese, both for the Communists and the Kuomintang. The middle class stayed at home and made money. The big families did nothing at all." Chiang Kai-shek once encountered a column of recruits roped together. With his own cane he beat the officer responsible, and later summoned the general in charge of conscription to beat him also. The episode highlighted one of Chiang's many weaknesses. He identified problems, but failed effectively to address them. Recruitment remained chronically corrupt. The rich always escaped. Press gangs waylaid wanderers. Gunner officer Ying Yunping said bitterly: "If only more people had been willing to fight! There were all those intellectuals, who spoke endlessly about how much they loved their country, but wouldn't themselves lift a finger to defend it. They just talked a good game."

The war in China baffled foreign observers, because it bore so little resemblance to conventional military operations. Huge bodies of soldiers straggled hither and thither across great tracts of landscape. Guns were sometimes fired. Towns and villages were occupied or abandoned. Chinese movements, however, seemed to be conducted without reference to those of the enemy. Officers treated their men as mere beasts of burden or sacrifice. Gen. Dai Li, known to Westerners as "Chiang's Himmler," headed the Nationalists' huge and effective intelligence network. Dai detested foreigners without distinction, and employed his energies against Chiang's domestic enemies rather than against the Japanese. It became progressively apparent to the Western Allies' representatives in China that they were witnessing a grotesque tattoo, rather than a campaign capable of causing serious trouble to the Japanese.

A characteristic January 1945 report to London from the British military attaché in Chongqing declared: "It is difficult to give you detailed reviews of Japanese operations . . . since we do not have the necessary information . . . Chinese . . . reports are usually vague and unconvincing . . . This is not surprising, since Chinese are usually retreating and are often, as at present, not really in contact with the enemy . . . They are prone to exaggerations to cover up their own reverses." Rhodes Farmer, an Australian eyewitness, noted that many Japanese "offensives" were dismissed by Westerners as "rice bowl operations." Farmer said: "The campaigns the Japanese waged between 1938 and 1944 were foraging expeditions rather than battles. They had no greater strategic objective than to keep the countryside in terror, to sack the fields and towns, to keep the Chinese troops at the front off-balance, and to train their own green recruits under fire." When Chiang Kai-shek's communiqués asserted that his armies were "fighting strongly" to defend a given position, the usual reality was that the Japanese had not chosen to take it.

Thirty-year-old Maj. Shigeru Funaki was the youngest of five sons of a retired Japanese army officer. His father made it plain that, since his elder siblings had declined to continue the family's military heritage, it was Shigeru's duty to do so. He was commissioned into the Imperial Guard in 1935, and thereafter became an unfashionable thing in the Japanese army—an armoured specialist and devotee of the British strategic guru Basil Liddell Hart. Funaki spent two of the war years in China commanding a tank unit: "As the Chinese had no weapons capable of stopping tanks, they were useful things for us to have." He was no more impressed than any other Japanese soldier by the Nationalist army: "One Japanese division was worth four or five of theirs. They had no heavy artillery, no armour, and were very poorly organised. Whenever you pressed a Chinese army, it simply pulled back. They were always happy to give ground, because they had so much of it. They kept retreating and retreating." Lt. Hayashi Inoue, who served in the theatre for eighteen months, said:

"The Chinese were poor soldiers. Their weapons and equipment were not up to much, and they were virtually untrained. We were always winning victories. Wherever we went, we won. The difficulty was that although you beat the Chinese in one place, they were still everywhere else. Every night, we were liable to be harassed by guerrillas."

Most of the pain inflicted by each side's operations fell upon the civilian population. When either Japanese or Nationalist soldiers approached, peasants and townspeople buried their clothes and valuables and fled into the hills, driving pigs and cattle before them, taking seed grain and even furniture. Rhodes Farmer reported a conversation with the inhabitants of a ransacked town: "One man slowly put four fingers on the table and then turned the hand over. I understood his meaning . . . the [Chinese] 44th Army had looted the city completely. He told me in a low voice that the army raped, plundered, set incendiary fires, and murdered . . . They [the local people] all said that the enemy was better than the Chinese troops . . . [Yet] on their retreat, the enemy [also] burned and killed on a large scale." Though Farmer was an enthusiastic propagandist for the Communists, such a story was entirely credible.

Yan Qizhi, a small farmer's son from Hebei, became a Nationalist infantry soldier at sixteen, and fought his first actions with a locally made Wuhan rifle which always jammed after four shots. His ambition was to arm himself with a sub-machine gun. In one of his regiment's first battles as part of Chiang's 29th Army, it lost almost half its sixteen hundred men. There were only rags to bandage the wounded. "The Japanese had so much more of everything," Yan said, "and especially aircraft. By 1944, life was pretty wretched. We had just enough to eat, but the food was very poor. We went through the whole winter with only summer uniforms. Most of us, like me, simply had no idea what had happened to our families." His only notable compensation for service in 29th Army, he said, was that he received his pay. In many of Chiang's formations, senior officers stole the money. "I hated the war: so many battles, so many dead and maimed friends. When I close my eyes, I can see them now. An army is not just weapons and equipment, it is spirit. The Kuomintang army lost its spirit."

The lives of Nationalist soldiers—notionally some two million of them in 1944, organised in two hundred divisions—were relentlessly harsh. Bugles summoned them to advance, to retreat, to die. Their weapons were an erratic miscellany: old German or locally made pistols and rifles; a few machine guns, artillery pieces and mortars, invariably short of ammunition, often rusting. They had no tanks and few vehicles. Commanders might have horses, but their men walked. Only officers had boots or leather shoes. Fortunate soldiers possessed cotton or straw sandals, but were often barefoot beneath the long cotton puttees which covered their legs. If they had a little kerosene, they used it to bathe chronic blisters.

Gunner captain Ying Yunping found himself walking more than two hundred miles during an epic retreat to Mianyang. One night, accompanied only by his batman, he staggered into a village and begged shelter and food. He was grudgingly given a few salted vegetables. His suspicions were roused, however, when he noticed that many of the people around him were carrying guns. His batman finally muttered: "They're bandits. They want your sub-machine gun. They say they hate the Kuomintang, and they're going to kill you." Ying's skin was finally saved by the eloquence of his batman, who parleyed with the bandits for the officer's life, saying: "He's not one of the corrupt bastards. He's not a bad fellow." Finally, a villager came to Ying and said: "Forgive us." The captain shrugged: "There's nothing to forgive. You have given me my life." Next day, he and his batman trudged onwards, away from the Japanese, towards Mianyang. When they rejoined the army, officer and soldier were separated. "In wartime, it was very hard to stay in touch. I never saw him again. But in my thoughts, for the rest of my life he has been 'my Mianyang brother.' "

Off-duty, officers drank the fierce *maotai* spirit, played mahjong, visited brothels or attended the occasional show put on by a "comfort party" of actors and singers. Few rankers enjoyed such indulgences. Soldiers smoked "Little Blue Sword" cigarettes when they were fortunate enough to be able to get them. John Paton Davies described the pathetic pleasures on which Chiang's men depended to relieve a life of otherwise unbroken hardship and oppression: "a cricket in a tiny straw cage, a shadow play manipulated by an itinerant puppeteer, gambling a pittance on games of chance, or listening to the fluted tones of flights of pigeons, each with a whistle tied to a leg—any one of these was enough to make an off-duty afternoon."

Among Nationalist soldiers leave was unknown, desertion endemic. Eight hundred recruits once set off from Gansu to join a U.S. Army training programme in Yunnan. Two hundred died en route, and a further three hundred deserted. Tuberculosis was commonplace. Wounded men often had to pay comrades to carry their stretchers, for otherwise they were left to perish. In battle or out of it communications, mail, tidings of the outside world, were almost non-existent. Ying Yunping, a thirty-year-old born in Manchuria the son of a salt merchant, was a married man with a baby daughter. During the early battles for Nanjing, his wife left him to return to her family. Ying never saw or heard of her and their daughter again.

If men received their rations, these might consist of fried pancakes, pickles, soup. The fortunate carried a sack of dried fried rice. In a town, in the unlikely event that a man possessed money, he might buy from a street seller a bowl of "congress of eight jewels," or *youtiao*—a stick of fried batter. More often, desperate soldiers were driven to seize whatever they could extort from hapless peasants or townspeople. The official ration allowance of twenty-four ounces of rice and vegetables a day was seldom issued. GIs laughed to see Chinese soldiers carrying dead dogs on poles to their cooking pots. Yet what else was there to eat? "Even junior officers could not survive or feed their families without corruption," said Xu Yongqiang, who served in Burma. Luo Dingwen, an infantry platoon commander with 29th Army, saw peasants lying by the roadside as his regiment marched past, dying or dead of starvation. "We usually relied on what food we could find in villages in our path," he said. Despairing American military advisers reported that many Chinese soldiers were too weak even to march with weapons and equipment. Most were clinically malnourished. Not even the U.S. could feed two million men by air over the Hump.

A prominent American soldier in China wrote of his Nationalist counterparts: "Senior officers were suspicious of all foreign officers, totally callous to their subordinates and would not voluntarily assist other Chinese units in trouble." General Sun in northern Burma refused to loan mules to take food and drugs to another formation, even though he knew its men were starving. A Chinese divisional finance officer casually asked an American: "How are you getting yours?" He was curious about his U.S. colleague's route to "squeeze."

There is no dispute—outside modern Japan, anyway—about the atrocities carried out by the Japanese in China, merely about their scale: for instance, Japanese historians make a plausible case that "only" 50,000 Chinese were killed in the 1937 Nanjing massacre, rather than the 300,000 claimed by such writers as Iris Chang. Yet the overall scale of slaughter was appalling. In 1941 the Japanese launched their notorious "Three All" offensive, explicitly named for its purpose to "Kill All, Burn All, Destroy All." Several million Chinese died. The survivors were herded into "protected areas" where they were employed as slave labourers to build forts and pillboxes.

It was an extraordinary reflection of the cult of *bushido* that many Japanese soldiers took pride in sending home to their families photographs of beheadings and bayonetings, writing letters and diaries in which they described appalling deeds. "To the Japanese soldier," an American foreign service officer reported to Washington, "the resistance from armed peasants . . . and the unmistakable resentment or fear of those whom he does not succeed in 'liberating' are a shocking rejection of his idealism . . . The average Japanese soldier . . . benightedly vents the conflict in vengeful action against the people whom he believes have denied his chivalry."

The Japanese argued that the Chinese were equally merciless to foes, and it is true that the Nationalists frequently shot prisoners. The Communists, at this period of the war, sought to spare the peasantry and customarily recruited KMT prisoners into their own ranks, even if officers were unlikely to survive. But beheadings of political enemies were familiar public spectacles in China. Most Japanese soldiers were no more willing to accept captivity in Chinese hands than in those of the Western Allies. "Once in 1944, we had a Japanese post surrounded," said Communist guerrilla Li Fenggui of 8th Route Army. "The defenders fought until their ammunition was gone. Even then, one man ran towards four of us, brandishing his rifle. This Japanese and one of our men went at each other with bayonets. They thrust and parried until I managed to get behind the Japanese and give him a stroke which took his arm off. He fell to the ground quick enough, but we had to keep stabbing again and again until he lay still and died. That was a brave man!"

A Nationalist soldier found his unit unexpectedly under fire while escorting sixty Japanese POWs. "At such a moment [our commander] was in no position to consider his orders to treat prisoners well. He had to take resolute action. At the word, our machine gunners opened fire, and we rid ourselves of the encumbrance." Rural areas feared the depredations of the Nationalist army at least as much as those of the Japanese. Peasants had a saying: "Bandits come and go. Soldiers come and stay." Modern Chinese historians argue, however, that the fact that their own people inflicted atrocities upon each other was, and remains, a domestic matter of no rightful concern to foreigners; that nothing done by Chiang or Mao mitigates the crimes of the Japanese.

At the cost of deploying a million men, the occupiers maintained almost effortless military dominance over the forces of Chiang, and never sought to challenge Communist control of Yan'an Province. At the November 1943 Cairo Conference, President Roosevelt insisted upon anointing China as one of the four great Allied powers, assisted by Stalin's acquiescence and in the face of Churchill's contempt. Yet Roosevelt's crusade to make China a modern power languished in the face of poverty, corruption, cruelty, incompetence, ignorance on a scale beyond even U.S. might and wealth to remedy. It was characteristic of the cultural contempt which China harboured towards other societies that even in the darkest days of the Japanese war, almost all Chinese retained a profound disdain for the Americans and British. Additionally, as Christopher Thorne has argued, the U.S. never satisfactorily resolved its purpose. Did it seek to help China win its struggle against the Japanese? To create a strong China? Or to support the regime of Chiang Kai-shek? These objectives were probably unattainable, and certainly irreconcilable. Thorne omits a fourth, which weighed far more heavily with the U.S. chiefs of staff than any altruistic desire to aid the Chinese people. Just as in Europe Soviet soldiers were doing most of the dying necessary to destroy Nazism, Washington hoped that in Asia the expenditure of Chinese lives might save American ones.

All these aspirations foundered amidst the chaos and misery of China, and the inability of Chiang Kai-shek to fulfil the role for which Washington cast him. In 1944, Chiang's economic recklessness and a Japanese initiative which flooded southern China with $100 billion of counterfeit money created catastrophic inflation, which ruined the middle class. A quarter of the population of Nationalist areas were by then refugees, victims of the forced mass migrations which characterised the wartime period. A drought in the south is thought to have killed a million people. Some American personnel were making fortunes running a black market in fuel and supplies. Even as Chinese people were dying of starvation, some Nationalist army officers sold food to the Japanese.

A visiting American intelligence officer delivered a devastating report to the War Department in May 1944:

> Chinese troops are underfed, improperly clothed, poorly equipped, poorly trained, lacking in leadership . . . Because of "squeeze," men are lucky to get 16 oz of their 22 oz daily rice ration. Almost all are illiterate. Motor maintenance is a problem, as they run a vehicle until it stops before any inspection is conducted. Trucks are usually overloaded 200%. Most drivers operate at an excessive rate of speed at all times. Along the Salween river, I was informed that not a shot had been fired since last November . . . that not over 2000 Japanese opposed fifteen Chinese divisions. Most of the troops appeared to be loafing. A Chinese army subsists locally and lives off the country . . . During the first week of February 1944 Lt. Budd, railhead officer at Kunming, dispatched 250 trucks for Kweiyang. Of this number 192 trucks failed to report and were either hijacked or stolen outright by Chinese drivers.

In the first quarter of 1944, 278 American trucks in southern China simply disappeared. The report asserted that a section assessing the performance of Chinese commanders was endorsed by all long-serving U.S. officers in China, but the relevant pages of the National Archive copy are missing, marked "Removed on orders of the War Department." It is reasonable to guess that this excision was made in 1944, because the report's verdict was so damning.

In the spring of 1944, when elsewhere in Asia and the Pacific their fortunes were in relentless decline, amazingly the Japanese found the will and the means to launch "Ichigo," an ambitious operation which swept across central and southern China, vastly enlarging Japan's area of occupation. Ichigo was provoked by the American air threat. B-29 bombers had begun to operate from bases in China. The Japanese initiated Ichigo to deprive the Americans of these. Half a million men, 100,000 horses, 800 tanks and 15,000 vehicles swept across the Yellow River and into Henan Province on a 120-mile-wide front. Some thirty-four Nationalist divisions simply melted away in their path. The Japanese killed forty Chinese for every loss of their own. Nationalist resistance was almost entirely ineffectual. Chiang invariably overstated his own difficulties, to extort additional aid from the Allies. But the British director of military intelligence in India reported on 17 May 1944:

> It has been the lowest common denominator of appreciation of China's prospects that, however much conditions depreciated, China would not capitulate . . . There is now a distinct possibility of China's collapse . . . Conditions in occupied territory are said to compare favourably with those in KMT areas . . . [Its] collapse would render the Burma campaign a waste of effort . . . The plight of the common people is so bad that they would be apathetic and do nothing . . . There would be no regret for the Allies, as anti-foreign feeling is always just below the surface. The disaffection in the provinces is so great that their leaders would take a purely opportunistic view. The Generalissimo, faced with a crumbling structure, has no machinery with which to save it.

On the Japanese rolled into Hunan Province, crossing the Miluo River, killing casually as they went. Hunan had already been suffering famine for two years. Now matters grew much worse. For the Chinese people of the rice-producing regions between Hunan and Guangdong, in Guangxi and Guizhou provinces, Ichigo meant hundreds of thousands, perhaps millions, of new deaths from famine and disease. Peasants were reported to have revolted, disarming as many as 50,000 Nationalist soldiers, who were willing enough to abandon the war. American special forces teams from the Office of Strategic Services strove to deny the Japanese the great supply dumps and airfield facilities established at such cost. Some 50,000 tons of matériel were destroyed at one base, Tusham, by Maj. Frank Gleason and fifteen Americans, together with their Chinese cook and orphan mascot. The Nationalist retreat was punctuated by occasional stands, notably at Hengyang in June and July. The American correspondent Theodore White joined 62nd Army, which was seeking to dislodge the Japanese from the southern hills beyond the town:

> It was dawn when we fell into the troop column, but the cloudless skies were already scorching. As far as we could see ahead into the hills and beyond were marching men. They crawled on foot over every footpath through the rice paddies; they snaked along over every ditch and broken bridge in parallel rivulets of sweating humanity. One man in three had a rifle; the rest carried supplies, telephone wire, rice sacks, machine-gun parts. Between the unsmiling soldiers plodded blue-gowned peasant coolies who had been impressed for carrier duty. There was not a single motor, not a truck . . . not a piece of artillery . . . The men walked quietly, with the curious bitterness of Chinese soldiers who expect nothing but disaster.

White watched pityingly as lines of men in their yellow and brown uniforms, feet broken and puffed, heads covered not by helmets, but instead by woven leaves for protection from the sun, sought to claw a way up the hills towards the Japanese positions. For three days he awaited the trumpeted Nationalist counter-offensive. Then he understood: he had witnessed it. On 8 August, Hengyang fell. Later that month, when the Japanese had reorganised their supply lines, they resumed their advance. Chiang's 62nd Army melted away in their path. Logistics, not resistance, was the chief force determining the enemy's pace. "Even in late 1944," one of Chiang's biographers has written, "the Japanese army could still march where it wished and take what it wanted." Allied intelligence officers expressed surprise that the Japanese were advancing only forty miles a week, "despite facing nil opposition."

Chiang ordered that commanders who retreated should be shot, but this did not noticeably improve his armies' performance. Added to the miseries of war were ghastly accidents such as one at Guilin, where a locomotive ploughed into a crowd of refugees standing on the railway tracks, killing several hundred. Chiang and Meiling chose this moment to hold a press conference at which they denied rumours that their marriage was in difficulties. Madame Chiang and her sister then set off for Brazil, exploring a possible haven for their family fortune if events at home continued to go awry. Even the most committed Americans came close to despair. China resembled a vast wounded animal, bleeding in a thousand places, prostrate in the dust, twitching and lashing out in its agony, inflicting more pain upon itself than upon its foes.

The only Chinese divisions which performed with some competence were five—equivalent in strength to two American—serving in northern Burma. These were the creations of the U.S. general "Vinegar Joe" Stilwell. He flew tens of thousands of men for training in India, where they were quarantined from Nationalist corruption and incompetence, then deployed them for an offensive aimed at reopening the land route into China. Equipped, fed and paid by the Americans, often receiving the benefit of U.S. air support, these units proved notably more effective than their brethren in China.

"Chinese soldiers showed what they could do if they were properly trained and given American equipment," Wen Shan, a lawyer's son who served in Burma as a truck driver, said proudly. "We had officers who did not steal men's food, as they did in China." Wen, like many young Chinese who served with Americans, was boundlessly impressed by their wealth and generosity, though shocked by the way white GIs treated their black counterparts. Jiang Zhen, a twenty-three-year-old landlord's son from Shanghai who drove trucks on the Ledo road, said of his time there: "I was very lucky. I had a great opportunity, and it became an important experience in my life."

Wu Guoqing, an interpreter at 14th Division headquarters in Burma, enjoyed his entire experience with the army. In India and on the battlefield he marvelled at the openness of the Americans with whom he served: "They said what they liked. They criticised their own government. That's what they call democracy. In China we are not like that, not open in the same way." Yet it would be mistaken to over-idealise either the Chinese-American relationship in Burma, or the performance of the Nationalist divisions there. Wu witnessed a bitter row between a young U.S. military adviser and a Chinese colonel. The American officer pressed the Nationalists to display more aggression, especially about patrolling. The KMT officer flatly refused. Likewise, when British troops in Burma began to operate with Stilwell's force, they were unimpressed by Chinese passivity. The British official historian wrote contemptuously: "It might be said that never had such an army remained so inactive before so small an enemy force for so long." The modest achievements of Stilwell's divisions in northern Burma counted for little, set against the strategic paralysis prevailing in Chiang's own country.

3. The Fall of Stilwell

IN THE LATE summer of 1944, the Japanese Ichigo offensive precipitated a crisis in the relationship between Chiang Kai-shek and the American government. As the Nationalist armies fell back, ceding great tracts of territory, leading figures in the U.S. leadership at last perceived that China was incapable of fulfilling Washington's ambitions. It could not become a major force in the struggle against Japan. Stilwell signalled to Marshall, chairman of the joint chiefs of staff: "I am now convinced that he [Chiang] regards the South China catastrophe as of little moment, believing that the Japs will not bother him further in that area, and that he imagines he can get behind the Salween [river] and there wait in safety for the U.S. to finish the war." This was an entirely accurate perception, but one of little service to the relationship between China's leader and America's senior military representative in his country.

Personal antagonism between Stilwell and Chiang, festering for many months, attained a climax. Few Americans knew more about China than "Vinegar Joe." After serving in France in 1918, where he rose to the rank of colonel, he spent most of the inter-war years in the East, and learned the Chinese language. A protégé of Marshall, who admired his brains and energy, Stilwell was appointed in February 1942 to head the U.S. Military Mission to Chiang, and to direct lend-lease. He also accepted the role of chief of staff to the generalissimo. From the outset, it seemed bizarre to appoint to a post requiring acute diplomatic sensitivity an officer famously intense, passionate, intolerant, suspicious, secretive. Stilwell praised subordinates as "good haters," and cherished his feuds as much as his friendships. During the 1942 retreat from Burma he took personal command of two Chinese divisions, sharing with them a gruelling 140-mile march to sanctuary in India. Sceptics said that such adventures showed Stilwell's unfitness for high command: he had no business indulging a personal predilection for leading from the front, putting himself with the men in the line, when his proper role was at the generalissimo's side, galvanising China's war effort.

Roosevelt delivered homilies about the importance of treating Chiang with respect, writing to Marshall: "All of us must remember that the Generalissimo came up the hard way to become the undisputed leader of four hundred million people . . . and to create in a very short time throughout China what it took us a couple of centuries to attain . . . He is the chief executive as well as the commander-in-chief, and one cannot speak sternly to a man like that or exact commitments from him the way we might do from the Sultan of Morocco."

This, of course, was nonsense. Roosevelt's remarks reflected naïveté about the mandate of Chiang, as well as about the character of Stilwell. The general was incapable of the sort of discretion the president urged. Famously outspoken, he flaunted his contempt for the incompetence of Chiang—"the peanut"—and for the British, whose military performance impressed him as little as their governance of India. Roosevelt urged U.S. commanders to display greater respect for the ruler of China, but American policy reflected a colonialist vision. It was absurd to suppose that an American general could impose on Chinese armies standards which their own officers could not; that Nationalist soldiers could be incited by a few thousand Americans to achieve objectives which Chiang and his followers refused to promote. American adviser Maj. E. J. Wilkie complained that even Stilwell-trained Chinese troops were hopelessly casual in their use of firearms: "I saw a machine gunner firing his weapon with one hand while eating with his other."

Stilwell's most notable military achievement was to direct the advance of Chinese troops on Myitkyina, the northern Burmese town whose liberation was critical to opening the Burma Road. Aided by a small force of Americans—the legendary Merrill's Marauders, who endured hardships comparable with those of Wingate's Chindits—Stilwell's forces triumphed at Myitkyina in August 1944. Yet the British, whose forces contributed significantly to that operation, remained highly sceptical of the Chinese performance, and of Stilwell's claims for it. Success at Myitkyina owed much more to Japanese weakness than to Allied genius. A shrewd judgement on Stilwell was offered by the British Bill Slim, who liked the American, and thought his post-war published diaries did him a disservice: "He was much more than the bad-tempered, prejudiced, often not very well-informed and quarrelsome old man they showed him to be. He was all that, but in addition he was a first-class battle leader up to, I should say, Corps level, and an excellent tactician, but a poor administrator. At higher levels he had neither the temperament nor the strategic background or judgement to be effective."

Stilwell and Chiang Kai-shek were divided on one irreconcilable issue. The bespectacled American sought to run a campaign to defeat the Japanese. The haughty, implacable Chinese warlord, by contrast, addressed the demands of his own nation's politics. He needed to maintain the support of his generals, frustrate the rise of the Communists, husband his military strength for the moment when Nationalist armies must reoccupy Japanese-ruled China, and crush Mao Zedong. By the autumn of 1944, Stilwell's patience with Chiang's military inertia was exhausted. The generalissimo's fury at Stilwell's perceived presumption could no longer be contained. Chiang rejected out of hand a request from Roosevelt that Stilwell should be given direct command of the Nationalist armies. This was indeed fanciful. Americans were savagely critical of British conduct in India. Yet Americans in China, from Stilwell downwards, behaved with comparable insensitivity and matching condescension. GIs referred to Chinese as "the slopies," Chiang as "Chancer Jack." In Kunming, the northern terminus of the Hump air route, Chinese servants were so abused that it was found necessary to post notices: "U.S. personnel will not beat, kick or maltreat Chinese personnel." Wen Shan, a supply driver on the Ledo road, said ruefully: "Americans considered a Chinese life to be worth a great deal less than an American one." U.S. Captain Medill Sarkisian, in the same area, submitted a formal protest when told that his Chinese troops could not feed alongside Americans: "From any point of view, I believe that inferior treatment of Chinese soldiers is prejudicial to our best interests . . . when in their own country to treat them as unworthy to eat with our own men."

Sgt. Wade Kent was one of thousands of American engineers labouring to complete the road and fuel pipeline from Ledo through northern Burma into China. An accountant's son from Richmond, Virginia, Kent was appalled by India, "the most terrible place I had ever seen. I wasn't born into the lap of luxury, but to see human beings in that condition was terrible." In Burma, the first man his unit lost was washed away in a foaming river. They worked in the jungle, "hot, miserable, damp . . . those damn leeches, one pulled off one's boots to find them full of blood," in teams of three GIs with each crew of Burmans. One of Kent's comrades was killed when he drove his bulldozer over an old Japanese mine, but mostly they worked in a huge silence broken only by jungle noise. When at last the path into China was opened, they welcomed the coolness of the mountains, but encountered new hazards. Chinese villagers punched holes in their fuel pipeline, then attempted to use the gas they stole for their lamps. "They sometimes set fire to whole villages—then blamed the Americans." Fuel leaked into the paddies, killing precious rice. Trucks plunged into ravines. For almost two years, there was no R and R, precious little news of the outside world: "It was a strange assignment."

Kent and his comrades achieved a technical triumph which proved a strategic cul-de-sac. A kind of madness had overtaken the American war effort in China, to which many men posted to the theatre succumbed, in this alien Oriental world where leopards and tigers were known to kill U.S. soldiers, who in turn hunted them with carbines. At the Hump airlift's forward HQ in Kweilin, "the most lovable and abandoned town in the Orient," some of the most skilled prostitutes in Asia had set up shop after fleeing from Hong Kong. Here, "silken clad girls with ivory bodies and complete devotion to their art" practiced it to the satisfaction of visiting Americans, but doubtful advantage to the war effort. Edgar Snow, no friend to either the Nationalists or the U.S., was nonetheless right to suggest that "the one abiding sentiment that almost all American enlisted personnel and most of the officers shared was contempt and dislike for China." It was a rich irony of both national policy and personal behaviour that Americans perceived themselves as anti-colonialists, yet conducted themselves in wartime China at least as autocratically as the British in South-East Asia.

In October 1944, Stilwell became the most prominent casualty of American frustration and failure. Emily Hahn describes the general as "incapable—surely to an abnormal degree?—of appreciating that there are more points of view than one's own, and that the world is appreciably larger than America." Stilwell refused to acknowledge that, whatever the limitations of Chiang's regime, he must work through its agency. Rationally, of course, his view was correct. If the Nationalist army was to play a useful role in the war, it must purge itself and reform, in the manner of the Chinese divisions airlifted to India beyond reach of Chiang's dead hand. Had the generalissimo reformed his forces as Stilwell urged, the destiny of the Nationalist regime might have been different. However, to imagine that Chiang Kai-shek could forsake absolutism and corruption was akin to inviting Stalin to rule without terror, Hitler without persecuting Jews. Stilwell's demands represented an assault on the very nature of the Chongqing regime. It was futile to yearn for Nationalist China to be what it was not, to suppose that an American could override Chinese leaders, however base.

In the autumn of 1944, Roosevelt made one of his most bizarre, indeed grotesque, appointments. He dispatched as his personal emissary to China one Patrick Hurley, a rags-to-riches Oklahoman ex-cowboy who had risen to political prominence as President Hoover's secretary of war. Hurley was a buffoon, loud-mouthed and verging on senility. An ardent Republican, he was also a prominent figure in the "China Lobby," precious little though he knew of China. He came, he saw, he addressed Chiang as "Mr. Shek." Finally, he reported to Roosevelt: "Today you are confronted by a choice between Chiang Kai-Shek and Stilwell. There is no other issue between you and Chiang Kai-Shek. Chiang Kai-Shek has agreed to every request, every suggestion, made by you except the Stilwell appointment [to command China's armed forces]."

On 13 October, Hurley recommended Stilwell's sacking. Roosevelt, who had earlier favoured replacing the general as director of lend-lease and chief of staff while retaining him as battlefield commander in Burma, acceded. Stilwell wrote to his wife of his delight in "hanging up my shovel and bidding farewell to as merry a nest of gangsters as you'll meet in a long day's march." He said to John Paton Davies: "What the hell. You live only once and you have to live as you believe " He quit immediately, without waiting even to brief his appointed successor, Lt.-Gen. Albert Wedemeyer, who had been serving as deputy chief of staff to SEAC commander Lord Louis Mountbatten. Wedemeyer arrived in Chongqing on 31 October, with a much more restricted mandate than his predecessor. He was to manage U.S. air operations out of China, "advise and assist the generalissimo," but remain aloof from politics.

Chiang rejoiced. He perceived the removal of Stilwell as a triumph for his own authority. Yet after just ten days, Wedemeyer signalled Marshall in Washington: "The disorganization and muddled planning of the Chinese is beyond comprehension." After a month in his new role, the U.S. general reported on the condition of Chiang and his armies in terms which matched or transcended Stilwell's histrionic dispatches:

> Generalissimo promised would fight hard to hold [Guilin-Liuzhou] area for at least 2 months, as it was it fell without a fight. The troops that melted away so quickly . . . were by Chinese standards well equipped and fed . . . I have now concluded that G and his adherents realize seriousness of the situation but they are impotent and confounded. They are not organized, equipped and trained for modern war. Psychologically they are not prepared to cope with the situation because of political intrigue, false pride and mistrust of leaders' honesty and motives . . . Frankly I think that the Chinese officials surrounding the G are actually afraid to report accurately conditions . . . their stupidity and inefficiency are revealed and further the G might order them to take positive action and they are incompetent to issue directives, make plans and fail completely in obtaining execution by field commanders . . . efficiency of Chinese combat units . . . is very low.

Wedemeyer was fearful that the Japanese planned to take Kunming, terminus of the Hump air route, and strove to concentrate Chinese forces to defend it. To the dismay of Mountbatten and Slim, he withdrew from Burma the American-trained Chinese divisions, the best troops in the Nationalist order of battle, and airlifted them to the Yunnan front. Yet they arrived there as the crisis passed. The Japanese halted. They had achieved their aim—to open a land link to their own forces in Indochina, at a time when the sea passage was threatened by American blockade. In the Allied camp, it was recognised that the closure of Ichigo was the result of a policy decision by Tokyo, owing nothing to the Chinese Nationalist army's powers of resistance. After almost three years of herculean effort by the United States, the employment of a quarter of a million Americans on the Asian mainland, Washington was obliged to confront the fact that the Japanese could do as they chose in China; that the country was as much a shambles as it had been in 1942, save that thanks to American largesse the regime's leader and principal supporters, together with a few U.S. officers, were incomparably richer. None of this constituted a case for retaining Stilwell in his former role. Hurley was thus far correct, that it was absurd for the most senior American soldier in China to be entirely alienated from the man endorsed by the U.S. as its national leader. Washington belatedly realised what Chiang had always understood—that America was stuck with him; that no threats of withdrawing support unless conditions were met had any substance, because the U.S. administration had no other Chinese card in its deck.

For the rest of the war, Wedemeyer suffered familiar frustrations about the shortcomings of America's huge, hopeless ally. If Stilwell's successor managed to avert a showdown with Chiang, he saw nothing to diminish his contempt for Asians. Stilwell recorded an earlier conversation with Wedemeyer. "Al stated that he thought the British and we should permit the Germans and the Russians to beat each other into pulp . . . that Britain and the United States were the guardians and legatees of the only civilisation worth preserving."

Through the winter of 1944, Allied diplomats and soldiers speculated freely that Chiang's regime might collapse, that by default Tokyo might find all China at its mercy. "In about six months the Japanese have advanced . . . a distance of roughly 500 miles over comparatively poor l[ines] of c[ommunication] against a considerable concentration of Chinese troops, supported by the American/Chinese air force operating from well-prepared forward bases," reported Mountbatten's intelligence chief in a gloomy appreciation on 2 December 1944. "Economically they have secured adequate rice to maintain their forces but, of greater consequence, they have denied to the Chinese the resources of these areas . . . It appears probable that one of the main aims of Japanese mil strategy is to prolong the war in the hope that war-weariness, assisted possibly by disagreement between the Allies after the defeat of GERMANY, may enable her to secure a negotiated peace."

Wedemeyer persisted with ambitious plans to rebuild the Nationalist armies. He had sufficient tact and discretion to sustain a relationship with Chiang, at the cost of quarrelling bitterly with the British. As the Chinese predicament worsened, acrimony increased between U.S. officers committed to Chiang and Mountbatten's people, wearied to despair by what they regarded as a grand American futility. Americans believed that British strategy was driven chiefly, if not exclusively, by a preoccupation with resurrecting their own empire. On 9 December 1944, Mountbatten's chief political adviser, Esler Dening, reported to the Foreign Office in London: "General Wedemeyer told me with conviction that there would not be a British Empire after the war . . . At present the question was whether to prop up a tottering China with props which may not hold, or to hit the Japanese hard where we have the forces to do it. [This] seems already resolved in favour of the former. If props hold, America will get the credit and if they do not, we shall get the blame."

The only happy man in all this was the generalissimo. He deluded himself that he had gained all his objectives. Supplies flowed up the Burma Road in ever-increasing quantities. Yet Chiang would pay a heavy political price for his military failure. The U.S. no longer deluded itself that Japan's forces in China could be defeated by the Chinese. Washington thus turned to the only other power capable of doing so—the Soviet Union. Through the winter of 1944–45, with increasing urgency Washington solicited Russian participation in the war against Japan. Chiang believed that he had played his cards with brilliant skill, by preserving American support for his regime on his own terms, without conceding any scintilla of domestic reform. Yet the consequence would be a great Russian army's descent upon Manchuria, with the endorsement of the United States.

"Nineteen forty-four was the year in which Chiang Kai-shek's policies completely collapsed, along with his defence of China," says a modern Chinese historian, Professor Niu Jun of Beijing University. At a period when elsewhere in the world Allied arms were decisively ascendant, in China alone did the Japanese remain victorious. It is mistaken to dismiss the generalissimo as an absurd figure. He knew his own country better than did the Americans. He understood that no Chinese army could defeat the Japanese. His willingness to surrender territory, of which China possessed so much, rather than to confront the enemy on terms which suited Tokyo, was more realistic than the grandiose visions of Stilwell, Wedemeyer or Roosevelt. "Chiang did some big things for China," says a historian of Manchuria, Wang Hongbin. "He ended the domination of the warlords, and he fought the Japanese. He was criticised for failing to oppose the Japanese takeover of Manchuria, but what else could he realistically do? He lacked the military means to resist. His strategy was simply to wait for a chance to engage the enemy on favourable terms. Is not that what the Americans and British also did in the Second World War? The Americans did not understand China. They wanted this country to do much more than it was capable of."

Chiang's regime was ultimately doomed by its corruption, and by the generalissimo's inability to translate some shrewd conceptions into any sort of reality. He liked to proclaim sonorously: "I am the state." But, by surrounding himself with thieves and sycophants, he denied his government the services of subordinates who might have rendered it sustainable. The generalissimo would ultimately discover that his achievement in forcing the Americans to indulge his regime on his own terms merely ensured its collapse. John Paton Davies wrote: "Stilwell's big mistake, in which I sometimes went along with him, was to think that he could strike a bargain with the generalissimo . . . Had Chiang been able and willing to do what Stilwell asked, China might well have emerged from the war a great power . . . As Chiang could no more reform his power base than overcome his idiosyncrasies, the bargain was doomed—as was Chiang." U.S. ambassador Clarence Gauss, who was replaced by Hurley shortly after Stilwell's sacking, wrote perceptively in the autumn of 1944: "Time is on the side of the Chinese Communists . . . as time goes on, the Kuomintang's influence and control in free China is deteriorating if not yet disintegrating; and . . . if the Soviet Union should come to make war upon the Japanese . . . defeat of the Japanese continental armies would probably leave the Communist forces and their regime in a strong political and military position."

From the winter of 1944 onwards the war effort in China, which had never synchronised with events elsewhere, lapsed into a pattern wholly at odds with them. While in Europe and the Pacific the Allied march to victory gained momentum, in Chiang Kai-shek's land the enemy retained power to advance at will. The occupation of swathes of new territory did nothing to mitigate the hopelessness of Japan's wider circumstances. "Ichigo was a success in a narrow sense," said Japanese staff officer Maj. Shigeru Funaki, "but it did not help our overall strategic position. We still had a million men in China who were denied to the Pacific campaign. Our success in overrunning the B-29 airfields in China simply meant that the Americans moved their bases to the Marianas."

The Japanese advance made a mockery, however, of Washington's claims that China was a serious partner in the Grand Alliance. The country was like some dowager stricken in years and heavy with rheumatism, unwillingly obliged to dance at a ball. The effort was painful, the achievement pitiful. The Japanese had no wish to extend their Asian perimeter until American assertiveness forced them to do so. The principal consequence of the huge Allied commitment was to intensify the miseries of China's people. Li Fenggui, a Communist guerrilla from a peasant family in Shandong Province, was one of eighty-nine young men who left his village to fight. Afterwards, just four returned. The community's experience was mirrored throughout China. The Chinese people paid a terrible price for participation in the Second World War, while contributing almost nothing to Allied victory.

NINE

MacArthur on Luzon

1. "He Is Insane on This Subject!": Manila

THE LARGEST CAMPAIGN of the Pacific war, second phase of MacArthur's drive to recapture the Philippines, began on 15 December 1944. Elements of Sixth Army landed on Mindoro, just south of Luzon. The island was of comparable size to Leyte, but the Japanese mounted no significant ground defence. The operation became, in the words of an American engineer, "just a maneuver for shore party units." Within a fortnight, airfield construction teams accomplished on Mindoro what had proved so difficult on Leyte—the creation of strips from which large numbers of aircraft could operate.

The Japanese knew that a landing on Luzon would not now be long delayed. On 2 January 1945, Yamashita moved his headquarters to the pine-clad summer resort town of Baguio, 7,400 feet up in the mountains of the north. From there, he planned personally to direct the "Shobu" group, 152,000 strong, one of three such commands into which he divided his army. The second "Kembu" force on Bataan and around Clark Field had 30,000 men, the third "Shimbu" group another 80,000 south of Manila. Staff officers described Yamashita in those days as possessing a mellow, fatalistic calm. He spent hours reading the essays of a Buddhist priest. In the evenings, he often wandered into the staff mess and gossiped to whichever officers were on hand. He was not above chatting to his private soldiers. His mind seemed much on the past. He expressed concern about the welfare of Allied prisoners on Luzon, and told his superior Field Marshal Terauchi that he intended to relinquish these to the Americans as soon as they landed. Terauchi sternly dissented, but Yamashita told the officer responsible to surrender the POWs anyway.

At MacArthur's headquarters at Tacloban, the general and his staff nursed a delusion that the Japanese army in the Philippines had been largely destroyed on Leyte. During a conference before the Luzon operation, Sixth Army intelligence asserted that large Japanese forces remained in the Philippines. MacArthur, sucking on his corncob pipe, interrupted:

"Bunk." Brig.-Gen. Clyde Eddleman, Krueger's G3, laughed and said, "General, apparently you don't like our intelligence briefing." "I don't," responded MacArthur. "It's too strong. There aren't that many Japanese there." Eddleman said: "Most of this information came from your headquarters." Maj.-Gen. "Sir Charles" Willoughby, MacArthur's intelligence chief, one of the courtiers least admired by outsiders, leapt angrily from his chair. "Didn't come from me! Didn't come from me!" he exclaimed. Eddleman sighed: "General, may I skip the intelligence portion and go on to the basic plan?" "Please do."

Afterwards, MacArthur called Eddleman to follow him into the bedroom of his quarters in the old Palmer House, almost the only coconut planter's house still standing in Tacloban. "Sit down," said the general. "I want to give you my ideas of intelligence officers. There are only three great ones in history, and mine is not one of them." Sixth Army asserted that there were 234,000 Japanese troops on Luzon. MacArthur preferred his personal estimate—152,000. Krueger's officers were much more nearly correct. Nothing, however, including substantial Ultra intelligence, would persuade the commander-in-chief to believe that his forces would face important resistance. Herein lay the seeds of much distress to come.

MacArthur spent hours at Tacloban pacing the verandah in solitary state or with a visitor. "We grew to know his mood from the way he walked, how he smoked," wrote one of his staff. "There would be times we would see him racing back and forth, an aide at his side, talking rapidly, gesticulating with quick nods, sucking his pipe with deep, long draughts." Those who once questioned the general's courage—the "dugout Doug" tag—were confounded by the calm with which he endured frequent Japanese bombings, and indeed near misses. His paranoia, however, had worsened. He attributed Washington's supposed lack of support for his operations to "treason and sabotage." He was an unremitting critic of Eisenhower's campaign in Europe, and indeed of everything done by the supreme commander who once served under him as a colonel. When the U.S. Treasury forwarded a draft of a proposed advertisement promoting War Bond sales on which his own name appeared below Ike's, he wrote angrily that unless he was listed before his former subordinate, he refused to feature at all. Later, in July 1945, he was enraged to discover that Eisenhower was briefed on the atomic bomb before himself. More seriously, his confidence in his chief of staff had been fatally weakened by the scandal about the presence of Sutherland's Australian mistress at Tacloban. Sutherland kept his title, but for the Luzon campaign MacArthur relied increasingly on the counsel of Brig.-Gen. Courtney Whitney, an ambitious officer much given to bombast, neither liked nor respected by anyone else.

On 9 January 1945, MacArthur's Sixth Army landed at Lingayen Gulf, halfway up the western coast of Luzon. Kamikazes provided fierce opposition. MacArthur had reproached Kinkaid for his allegedly excessive fear of suicide planes, but now the admiral's apprehension was vindicated. Again and again during the days before the assault, suicide pilots struck at the invasion armada. Fortunately for the Americans, the Japanese as usual focused attacks on warships rather than transports crowded with troops. One escort carrier and a destroyer escort were sunk, twenty-three other ships damaged, many severely. The enemy's pilots seemed more skilful than before, their tactics more sophisticated. They approached at deck level, often baffling American radar, and provoking a storm of reckless AA fire which killed men on neighbouring ships—the battleship *Colorado* suffered significant casualties. The British admiral Sir Bruce Fraser, designated commander-in-chief of the Royal Navy's embryo Pacific Fleet, was a guest of Jesse Oldendorf's on the *New Mexico* when a kamikaze crashed into its superstructure. Lt.-Gen. Herbert Lumsden, Churchill's personal representative on MacArthur's staff, was killed, along with the ship's captain and other officers. Fraser escaped only because Oldendorf had beckoned him across the bridge moments before: "This thing came down just where we had been standing."

During the seaborne approach to Luzon 170 Americans and Australians were killed and five hundred wounded by kamikaze attacks. The strain on men's nerves became acute. They found themselves obliged to remain alert every daylight hour for a guided bomb that could hurl itself into their ship's upperworks, mangling steel and flesh. Aboard the heavy cruiser *Australia*, Pierre Austin was one of many sailors aggrieved by the enemy's madness: "At this late stage, after all one had survived, the feeling was: 'Not now—please, not now!' We knew it was going to be our war; we were going to win." On 8 January, a Val dive-bomber crashed into *Australia*'s foremast, killing thirty men and wounding sixty-four, including Pierre Austin. His war ended in a hospital.

Oldendorf, commanding the naval force, warned MacArthur that he lacked sufficient air cover to hold off the kamikazes unless Third Fleet's carrier aircraft could be diverted from attacking Japan to provide support, which of course they were. In the month beginning 13 December 1944, the cumulative toll from Japanese air assault was alarming—twenty-four ships sunk, sixty-seven damaged. Yet to the astonishment of the Americans, as MacArthur's troops drove inland from Lingayen, the kamikaze offensive stopped. The Japanese had lost six hundred aircraft in a month.

N
Yamashita's headquarters
Held by Japanese remnants up to end of war
0
100 miles
0
150 km
Camigun
23 June
Part 511 Para Inf Regt
Aparri
Gonzaga
Laoag
Cordillera Central
0930hrs, 9 January 1945
U.S. Sixth Army (Krueger)
26 June
Contact
Tuguegarao
25 June
Vigan
19 Apr
Sierra Madre
I Corps (Swift)
6 Div and 43 Div
Ilagan
19 June
Bontoc
XIV Corps (Griswold)
37 Div and 40 Div
Luzon
San Fernando
Bauang
Baguio
Bayombong
Agoo
Damortis
Rosario
Bambang
Tayug
Japanese Fourteenth Area Army (Yamashita)
Lingayen
17 Jan
Carmen
Zambales Mts
San Jose
13 Feb
Tarlac
Cabanataun 24 Jan
PHILIPPINE SEA
21 Jan
Iba
Bamban
Gapan
Clark Field
29 Jan
XI Corps (Hall)
Porac
Del Carmen Field
San Fernando
San Antonio
Dalupihan
Calumpit
Olongapo
5 Feb
Manila
4 Feb/3 March
Battle for Manila
15 Feb
Regt of XI Corps
Bataan Peninsula
Manila Bay
Nielson & Nichols Fields
21 Feb
Bataan cleared
Cavite
Lamon Bay
Corregidor
Laguna de Bay
31 Jan
Majority 11 Abn Div
Mauban
10 April
Daet
Nasugbu
Atimonan
3 Jan
Remainder drop by parachute. Light opposition
Tagayta Ridge
Tiaong
Catanduanes
Lucena
Siain
Calauag
Balayan Bay
Batangas
Naga
Lubang Is
Calapan
Boac
2 May
Contact
Command boundary
U.S. Sixth Army
U.S. Eighth Army, 1 Jan 1945
1 April
158 Regt CT
Legaspi
Mindoro
Burias
Irosin
Sibuyan Sea
San Bernardino Str
San José
15 December 1944
Western Visayan Task Force (Dunckel) lands. Light opposition. Other landings between 21 December and 22 January

The American invasion of Luzon, January–June 1945

Only fifty remained on Luzon. Japanese fighter pilot Kunio Iwashita was at Clark Field, Manila, on 9 January when he was ordered to lead his squadron's three surviving aircraft to a new strip. Some five hundred personnel, most of them ground crew, were left to join the retreat of the Japanese army, and face months of attrition and starvation. Just four of these men were afterwards recorded alive. A few minutes after Iwashita and his fellow pilots arrived at their new base, American aircraft struck, destroying all three fighters. The Japanese airmen escaped by sea to Formosa. On Luzon thereafter, neither the U.S. Navy nor Sixth Army faced significant air attack. Tokyo husbanded its remaining planes to defend Formosa, Okinawa and the homeland.

Krueger's troops met only spasmodic artillery and mortar fire as they advanced inland, and there were soon 175,000 Americans ashore. While most of the Leyte fighting had engaged only four divisions, Luzon would ultimately involve ten, in addition to huge numbers of support troops. At first, climate slowed the advance more than the enemy. On 16 January alone, forty-nine men of the 158th Infantry were evacuated with heat exhaustion. Water was short. Five thousand tons of supplies were landed each day, but shifting them forward proved a nightmare, only marginally assisted by jury-rigging stretches of Luzon's battered rail system. I Corps drove north and eastwards.

In the first three days ashore, the Americans lost just 55 dead, 185 wounded, while claiming 500 enemy killed. Krueger and his staff were bemused by the desultory resistance. When the Americans reached the hills, however, Yamashita's plan became apparent. Knowing that he could not prevent the Americans from achieving a lodgement, he had instead concentrated most of his forces in the island's mountain areas. Experience on Leyte had shown how effectively steep uplands could be defended. Fourteenth Army's commander believed that he could inflict pain and delay on MacArthur by exploiting Luzon's wildest terrain. He had no thought of victory. "What is wanted of us," he told his officers, "is to get in one good blow at the Americans, to strengthen the government's hand in negotiations at the conference table."

The Japanese held positions prepared with their usual skill, and were soon killing Americans. "This is terrible country to fight in, jungle thicker than Biak, heat is prostrating . . . There is an awful lot of combat hysteria among the new recruits and heat exhaustion among all hands," wrote Captain Paul Austin of the 34th Infantry. On board the transports to Luzon, his regiment had suddenly received an intake of eight hundred replacements: "They had no chance to learn their duties or who their non-coms were. They had a high incidence of hysteria and caused deaths of many of our old men by freezing under fire."

In the south, however, at first there was less resistance. XIV Corps advanced towards Manila under relentless goading from the theatre commander. "General MacArthur visited Corps CP," Gen. Oscar Griswold of XIV Corps wrote in his diary on 14 January. "Said he expected little opposition, that the battle of the Philippines had already been won on Leyte. I do not have his optimism." As late as 23 January, MacArthur was raging against "Sir Charles" Willoughby for allegedly overestimating Japanese strength. The general said petulantly: "I don't see how I have gotten as far as I have with the staff I have been surrounded with." Eichelberger of Eighth Army reported this remark to his wife, adding with relish: "So you see, they all have their troubles."

Griswold's men reached the forward defences of Clark Field a week later. Around the air base they fought a sluggish series of battles to secure the commanding heights. These provoked bad-tempered recriminations between elements of Sixth Army. The 129th Infantry, for instance, protested at the flight of its supporting tanks, which refused to return to the line even when the regiment found itself facing a Japanese armoured attack at Tacondo. MacArthur accused the 37th Division of "a notable lack of drive and aggressive initiative." Krueger wrote angrily to Kenney, the air chief: "I must insist that you take effective measures to stop the bombing and strafing of our ground forces by friendly planes."

XI Corps made a new beach landing at San Antonio, north-west of Manila, on 29 January, and on 31 January two regiments of 11th Airborne Division came ashore at Nasugbu, some forty-five miles south-west of the capital, and began their own advance on the city, soon joined by a third regiment which parachuted in. By 4 February, the first airborne units were on the outskirts of Manila, facing the main southern defence line. A glider infantry company commander famously radioed his battalion: "Tell Admiral Halsey to stop looking for the Jap fleet. It's dug in here on Nichols Field."

Meanwhile, in the north, the 37th and 1st Cavalry Divisions raced each other for Manila, slowed by difficult terrain and increasingly stubborn resistance. As the Japanese retreated, they lit the fuse on demolition charges at the only bridge over the Tulihan River. This was snuffed out by a gallant navy lieutenant, James Sutton, attached to 1st Cavalry, who dashed forward alone and pitched a clutch of mines over the parapet into the water. MacArthur had identified the internment camp at Santo Tomas University as a key objective. On the evening of 3 February, a P-38 flew low overhead and dropped a message to its 3,400 inmates, almost all American civilians: "Roll out the barrel. There'll be a hot time in the old town tonight." A relief column pushing towards the camp met two Filipino guerrilla officers who offered to show the way to the camp. After overcoming initial American wariness, the guerrillas clambered aboard the lead tank. They met few Japanese until there was a brief skirmish outside the internment centre, in which one of the Filipinos was killed.

At 2100 "Battlin' Basic," a Sherman of 1st Cavalry Division, crashed through the camp gate with its searchlight blazing. A trooper burst into the main building, demanding: "Are there any goddamn Japs here?" An elderly American woman touched him: "Soldier, are you real?" The prisoners broke into hysterical screams and cheers, snatches of "God Bless America" and "The Star Spangled Banner." A Japanese officer, one of the most detested in the camp, suddenly ran out in front of the tank brandishing a sword and pistol. He was shot in the stomach. "Groaning and writhing on the ground, he was seized by the legs and dragged to the main building clinic, internees kicking and spitting at him, one or two men even slashing him with knives, and some women burning him with cigarets [*sic*] as he was pulled past them." The wounded man eventually received American medical aid, but died a few hours later.

Most of the Japanese staff barricaded themselves into the education building, with 275 Americans as hostages. After a parley, in exchange for the prisoners' freedom the guards were allowed to leave. Santo Tomas was in American hands, but the compound was soon beset by enemy gunfire, which killed some internees who had survived almost three years of hunger, disease and confinement. One woman, Mrs. Foley, lost an arm at the shoulder when a shell exploded in her room. She was taken to the emergency hospital with her fifteen-year-old daughter, Mary Frances. "Mrs. Foley kept asking about her husband, and Mary Frances told her he was fine," said American nurse Denny Williams. "She knew he was dead, but she did not want to tell her mother when she was facing surgery for her amputated arm. Kids grew up fast in Santo Tomas."

Then, inevitably, MacArthur came, to take his bow in the midst of a frenzied throng of his fellow countrymen. "They seemed to be using their last strength to fight their way close enough to grasp my hand," he wrote mawkishly. "They wept and laughed hysterically, and all of them at once tried to tell me 'thank you.' I was grabbed by the jacket. I was kissed. I was hugged. It was a wonderful and never to be forgotten moment—to be a life-saver, not a life-taker." Next day, 4 February, MacArthur sought to enter Manila. Griswold of XIV Corps wrote sourly: "He is insane on this subject! With just a handful of scouts we passed along a road where our dead and enemy dead could often be seen . . . Finally prevented from getting in by enemy action. Why we didn't all get killed I don't know! This, in my opinion, was a most foolhardy thing for a C-in-C to attempt." South of Manila, Eichelberger of Eighth Army wrote warily: "We met more resistance around Nichols Field than we expected. We had hoped to get in without resistance, and I do not recall any G-2 reports that predicted the Japanese would try to hold in the city." MacArthur's headquarters announced the imminent fall of the capital. The enemy disagreed.

American intelligence was correct in supposing that Yamashita did not wish to defend Manila. He knew that his forces could neither hold a long perimeter around the city, nor feed its 800,000 people. He had thus ordered the local commander, Gen. Shizuo Yokoyama, to destroy the harbour installations and bridges over the Pasig River, then pull out. Humanitarian sentiment about Manila's civilians also seems to have played a part in Yamashita's thinking. Such scruples were not, however, shared by Rear-Admiral Sanji Iwabuchi, who commanded 16,000 naval personnel in the city. The army had no authority over Iwabuchi, and he was determined to fight. Though his sailors possessed no infantry training—most, indeed, were survivors of lost vessels including the battleship *Musashi*—they were plentifully supplied with automatic weapons and munitions salvaged from ships and planes.

In the weeks before Sixth Army arrived, they fortified key areas of Manila to formidable effect. General Yokoyama persuaded himself that since the navy intended to fight, honour demanded that the three army battalions left in the city should do likewise. As MacArthur's troops approached, the Japanese withdrew across the Pasig River, blowing bridges and making demolitions which started huge fires in residential areas.

For centuries visitors had been inspired by Manila, from the old Spanish city of Intramuros with its narrow cobbled streets, churches and fort built on the site of an old Muslim stockade, to the broad avenues and Luneta, a great greensward where fiestas were held. By 1945, however, Manileros had little scope for partying. The price of rice had soared. Almost everyone was hungry, including the Japanese, some of whom were reduced to supplementing their rations with wild grasses. Dysentery and typhus were rife. The city's Mayor Guinto urged the starving to take to the countryside, and some did so. Repression intensified: there were roundups of suspected American agents, identity parades at which "secret eyes"—hooded informers from the *makapili*, the 5,000-strong quisling militia—denounced hapless people who were removed to Fort Santiago's old Spanish dungeons.

Manila's Europeans were prime suspects. On 28 December 1944 the Japanese *kempeitai* descended on the Malate Church, arrested Fathers Kelly, Henaghan and Monaghan, and took them away. What was left of the priests after torture was eventually returned. The people of Manila had plentiful warning of the occupiers' intention to turn their city into a battlefield, which makes it all the more curious that no such intelligence reached MacArthur. Sailors laboured at building strongpoints and barricades, felling the palm trees on Dewey Boulevard so that aircraft could land there. Artillery was manhandled onto the upper floors of office buildings. Mines improvised from shells and bombs were laid at road junctions, machine guns emplaced to cover them.

The American advance was repeatedly checked by cheering crowds of local people. Troops entering northern Manila were greeted with flowers, fruit, beer. Some Filipinos doffed their hats and bowed. Progress was delayed when troops found that the Japanese Balintawak Brewery was undamaged. For several hours, GIs filled and emptied helmets again and again, until the beer vats ran dry. "Throngs of Filipinos filled the streets as though celebrating a jubilee," wrote Captain Bob Brown of the 5th Infantry. "In places they were so many I could not pick out my men. When Jap mortar shells came in they disappeared like mist in hot sunshine, but when the firing stopped they returned just as quickly to resume the celebration."

"The fighting became a shoot-out, Wild West style," said Captain Labin Knipp. "Japs popped out of alleys and buildings trying to escape the fires. We were ready and shot first." There were strange encounters. Maj. Chuck Henne of the 3/148th Infantry found himself invited into a house by an immaculately dressed Chinese woman, who offered refreshments in perfect English, clapping her hands for a servant despite the fires and detonations only a few streets away. "Not many men were ever privileged to sit on a balcony with a beautiful woman, partaking of tea and cakes and looking out on a burning city," marvelled Henne.

The stage was now set for one of the ugliest battles of the Pacific war, the only one in which American forces found themselves contesting possession of a conurbation. For the next month, Sixth Army found itself committed to a street-by-street, often house-by-house struggle against suicidal Japanese resistance. American encirclement denied General Yokoyama the option of withdrawal, even had he been able to persuade his naval counterpart to accede to this. The Japanese knew they were trapped, and fought accordingly. The battle's principal victims were not combatants, but the civilian population, which suffered appallingly. Instead of a triumphal parade through the streets for which MacArthur had made elaborate preparations, he found himself presiding over Manila's martyrdom.

As so often in his campaigns, the general was slow to perceive the gravity of the struggle. "Our forces are rapidly clearing the enemy from Manila," announced a bulletin from his headquarters on 6 February, followed next day by another: "The 37th Infantry and 1st Cavalry Divisions continued mopping-up operations in north Manila, while the 11th Airborne did the same in south Manila." MacArthur himself declared on

6 February that the capital had been secured at 6:30 that morning. *Time* magazine, swallowing the general's assertion and adding a cliché to taste, said that the city had fallen "like a ripe plum." In reality, its ordeal had scarcely begun.

"MacArthur has visions of saving this beautiful city intact," wrote Griswold of XIV Corps on 7 February. "He does not realise, as I do, that the skies burn red every night as [the Japanese] systematically sack the city. Nor does he know that enemy rifle, machine gun, mortar and artillery fire are steadily increasing in intensity. My private opinion is that the Japs will hold that part of Manila south of the Pasig river until all are killed." Griswold added two days later: "Army commander [Krueger] dissatisfied with progress, *as usual*. Damndest man to serve with I ever saw!" American intelligence about enemy deployments was almost non-existent. Some fifteen hundred Japanese were killed in clashes north of the Pasig, but these were only an overture. As Krueger's men began to force the river crossings on 7 February, they discovered how hard the enemy was willing to fight.

The 3/148th Infantry crossed the river in amphibious tractors and assault boats. "Leaving the near bank," wrote an officer, "the I company boats were making good progress, moving in a ragged crescent, when the Jap fire stormed through them—machine guns and cannon. This fire, coming from the west, ripped through the formation scattering boats, turning the move into a mad dash for the cover of the far bank. It was spellbinding to watch pieces of paddles and splintered chunks of boat plywood fly through the air while men paddled with shattered oars and rifles. On reaching the far bank, the men jumped out of their boats and scrambled up the bank taking their dead and wounded comrades with them. What seemed to last for hours was over in ten minutes."

"The sky was a copper-burnished dome of thick clouds," wrote a senior officer of the 37th Division, an Ohio National Guard formation. "So great was the glare of the dying city that the streets, even back where we were, were alight as from the reflection of a reddish moon. Great sheets of flame swept across the rooftops, sometimes spanning several city blocks in their consuming flight . . . We saw the awful pyrotechnics of destruction, spreading ever faster to encompass and destroy the most beautiful city in the Far East."

The U.S. Army in the Philippines possessed none of the extensive experience of street fighting acquired by Eisenhower's forces in Europe. In Manila, they learned hard lessons. The city's principal buildings were designed to be proof against earthquakes. Paco police station, for instance, defied repeated assaults by infantry supported by artillery and heavy mortars. Two tanks were lost to mines before the armour suppressed Japanese fire sufficiently to allow a final assault: "Even then," declared a Sixth Army report, "the Japanese did not withdraw and the last of them were destroyed in sandbagged emplacements dug deep in the floor of the basement." Against large public buildings, it proved necessary to use 155mm howitzers firing at point-blank range, six hundred yards. Assaulting the Finance Building, 155s and tanks bombarded lower floors only, lest high-trajectory shells burst in civilian areas beyond. Shells systematically demolished the structure until the defenders retreated to its basement. Americans fighting their way up the stairs of the Manila Hotel found the enemy reoccupying the lower storeys behind them. Some two hundred Japanese were finally driven into its basement air-raid shelter, which became their sealed tomb.

Guards fled from Bibilid Prison, leaving behind 447 civilian and 828 military prisoners, most American. Some were men whom MacArthur had left behind on Corregidor in 1942. It was a merciful surprise that they were left alive, but beyond their emaciation, all the prisoners liberated in the Philippines proved traumatised. The world had changed so much, while they were isolated from it. Col. Bruce Palmer described seeing POWs freed at Cabanatuan: "I'll never forget the bewildered look on these men. They just could not believe they had been released. Our equipment—everything we had—helmets and everything else were so foreign to them. They just thought we were men from Mars." Krueger's staff officer Clyde Eddleman visited liberated POWs in their hospital tents. A sergeant was "sitting there on a cot, sort of dazed, and he looked at me and said: 'Didn't you command HQ Company the 19th Infantry back in 1938?' Yes, I did. 'Well, I was Corporal Greenwood who fought in the lightweight class.' " Now, NCO and officer met as men from different universes.

Block by block, ruin by ruin, dash by dash across streets swept by enemy fire, the Americans advanced through Manila. After the first days, Japanese senior commanders could exercise little control. Their improvised battle groups simply fought to the death where they stood. The baseball stadium was ferociously defended—Japanese sailors dug in even on its diamond. They held the post office until it was reduced to rubble. On Provisor Island in the Pasig, American soldiers played a deadly game of hide-and-seek amid the machinery of a power station. Maj. Chuck Henne reflected: "Such . . . are lonely, personal times during which the presence of other troops counts for little. Relaxing is impossible, for uncontrollably muscles tighten and teeth are clenched. The blast of a heavy shell is unforgettable, as is the dud that goes bouncing overhead down a cobblestone street. The close ones leave a chalky taste in one's mouth. Being bounced in the air and stung by blasted debris gets a trooper counting arms and legs and feeling for blood."

Americans were amazed by the fashion in which civilians wandered across the battlefield, apparently oblivious of the carnage. A company commander inspecting foxholes was disconcerted to discover some of his men clutched in the embraces of Filipino women. He sighed: "I hope they don't get VD." The streets crawled with destitute children. A boy named Lee attached himself to the 3/148th Infantry, then after some days tearfully confessed to being a girl named Lisa. She was delivered to a Catholic orphanage.

Again and again, advancing troops suffered unwelcome surprises. When a jeep struck a mine dug into the street, not even body parts of its occupants were recovered—only the chassis of the vehicle reposed at the base of a crater. While a group of men was being briefed to fall back to a rest area, one of their number standing on a mound suddenly rolled to the ground, stone dead. A stray bullet, fired probably a mile away, had struck him without warning. A colonel from a reserve battalion visited a forward command post. Stepping up to a window, he fell dead to a Japanese bullet. "It was . . . so common in combat," said an eyewitness. "One mistake and you're dead." Though there was much talk of snipers, in reality there were few marksmen among the Japanese navy contingent. They relied overwhelmingly on machine guns, for which they possessed almost unlimited quantities of ammunition.

Private Dahlum of the 3/148th was point man of a patrol moving down an alley when a Japanese officer and six men sprang out. Before any American could react, the officer swung his sword and delivered a fearsome, mortal blow at Dahlum's head. The patrol then shot down all the Japanese without further loss. The incident was over within seconds, leaving the survivors scarcely believing that it had taken place. "Suspecting that every closed door and dark window screened a lurking Jap was nerve-racking," wrote an American officer, "and all too often the Jap was there. Once across the street and into a building the job seemed less risky as the men turned towards the offending emplacement using demolitions to open 'doors' through fences and building walls. The final move would be fast shooting to cover a demolition team which could close and blast the position using grenades or satchel charges."

The most repellent aspect of the Japanese defence of Manila was their systematic slaughter of the city's civilians. The Japanese justified this policy by asserting that everyone found in the battle area was a guerrilla. Over a hundred men, women and children were herded into Paco Lumber Yard along Moriones and Juan Luna Avenue, where they were bound, bayoneted and shot. Some bodies were burned, others left rotting in the sun. Japanese squads burst into buildings packed with refugees, shooting and stabbing. There were massacres in schools, hospitals and convents, including San Juan de Dios Hospital, Santa Rosa College, Manila Cathedral, Paco Church and St. Paul's Convent.

Some civilians found themselves herded out of their homes by Japanese who asserted that shellfire made them unsafe. They were taken to an assembly area on Plaza Ferguson, where there were soon 2,000 under guard. Young girls were then separated and removed first to the Coffee Pot Café, then to the Bay View Hotel, where brothels were established. The Japanese sought to give their men who were soon to die a final exalting sexual experience. One twenty-four-year-old named Esther Garcia later gave evidence about the experiences of her fifteen- and fourteen-year-old sisters, Priscilla and Evangeline: "They grabbed my two sisters. They were in back of me. And we didn't know what they were going to do. So my two sisters started fighting them, but they couldn't do anything. So they grabbed my sisters by the arm and took them out of the room. And we waited and waited and waited and finally my younger sister came back and she was crying. And I asked her, 'Where is Pris? Where is Pris?' And she said: 'Oh! They are doing things to her, Esther!' So everybody in the room knew what was going to happen to us. When Priscilla came back, she said: 'Esther, they did something to me. I want to die. I want to die!' " A Japanese soldier had cut open her vagina with a knife.

At night, Americans on the line were bemused to hear sounds of chanting and singing, shouts and laughter, as Japanese conducted final carouses. These were sometimes succeeded by grenade explosions, as soldiers killed either themselves or hapless Filipinos. Some of the worst Japanese atrocities took place, ironically enough, at the city's German Club, where five hundred people died, five of them Germans. Twelve members of one family, the Rocha Beeches, were bayoneted and then burned alive, along with their nursemaid. A fifteen-year-old was raped in the street amid gunfire and screaming people. The Japanese responsible then rose and used his bayonet to open her body from groin to chest. Twelve German Christian Brothers were killed in the chapel of La Salle College. Doctors, nurses and patients at the Red Cross centre were all massacred on 9 February. The Irish fathers at the Malate Church who had been tortured earlier in the month were now rearrested, and never seen again.

A pregnant woman, Carmen Guerrero, walked into the American lines, clutching a child in her arms. She had seen her husband tortured before her eyes, then removed to be shot. She had neither eaten nor slept for a week. She wrote later: "I had seen the head of an aunt who had taught me to read and write roll under the kitchen stove, the face of a friend who had been crawling next to me on the pavement as we tried to reach shelter under the Ermita Church obliterated by a bullet, a legless cousin dragging himself out of a shallow trench in the churchyard and a young mother carrying a baby plucking at my father's sleeve—'Doctor, can you help me? I think I'm wounded'—and the shreds of her ribs and her lungs could be seen as she turned around."

The big villa of Dr. Rafael Moreta on Isaac Pearl Street had become a sanctuary housing sixty people. At midday on 7 February, twenty Japanese sailors burst in with fixed bayonets, led by a short, stocky officer with a heavy moustache. Men and women were separated, searched for arms and stripped of their valuables. The men were then forced into a bathroom, and grenades tossed in with them. Those who remained alive heard the screams of women, the sobbing of children. When silence descended and the Japanese had gone, the surviving men stumbled out to find thirty women, all of whom had been raped, dead or dying, along with their children in like condition.

It quickly became plain that murders on such a scale represented not spontaneous acts by individual Japanese, but the policy of local commanders. If their own men were to perish, the victors were to be denied any cause for rejoicing. A captured Japanese battalion order stated: "When Filipinos are to be killed they must be gathered into one place and disposed of in a manner that does not demand excessive use of ammunition or manpower. Given the difficulties of disposing of bodies, they should be collected in houses scheduled for burning, demolished, or thrown into the river." Oscar Griswold of XIV Corps was bewildered to read a translation of a diary found on a dead Japanese, in which the soldier wrote of his love for his family, eulogised the beauty of a sunset—then described how he participated in a massacre of Filipinos during which he clubbed a baby against a tree.

It seems purposeless further to detail the slaughter, which continued until early March. The incidents described above are representative of the fates of tens of thousands of helpless people. A child emerging from a hospital saw a Japanese corpse and spat on it. His father said gently: "Don't do that. He was a human being." By now, however, few Manileros were susceptible to such sentiments. In considering the later U.S. firebombing of Japan and decision to bomb Hiroshima, it is useful to recall that by the spring of 1945 the American nation knew what the Japanese had done in Manila. The killing of innocents clearly represented not the chance of war, nor unauthorised actions by wanton enemy soldiers, but an ethic of massacre at one with events in Nanjing in 1937, and with similar deeds across Asia. In the face of evidence from so many different times, places, units and circumstances, it became impossible for Japan's leaders credibly to deny systematic inhumanity as gross as that of the Nazis.

Yet the U.S. Army took little pride in its own role. To overcome the

Japanese defences, it proved necessary to bombard large areas of the city into rubble. Before the Philippines landings, MacArthur dispatched a message to all American forces, emphasising the importance of restraint in the use of firepower. Filipinos, he wrote, "will not be able to understand liberation if it is accompanied by indiscriminate destruction of their homes, their possessions, their civilization, and their lives . . . this policy is dictated by humanity and our moral standing throughout the Far East." In consequence, and much to the dismay of his subordinates, MacArthur refused to allow air power to be deployed over Manila. Only after the 37th Division suffered 235 casualties in one day on 9 February did the theatre commander reluctantly lift restrictions on the use of artillery. "From then on, to put it crudely, we really went to town," said the 37th's commander. A hundred American guns and forty-eight heavy mortars delivered 42,153 shells and bombs. The U.S. official historian shrugged: "American lives were undoubtedly far more valuable than historic landmarks."

One post-war estimate suggests that for every six Manileros murdered by the Japanese defenders, another four died beneath the gunfire of their American liberators. Some historians would even reverse that ratio. "Those who had survived Japanese hate did not survive American love," wrote Carmen Guerrero. "Both were equally deadly, the latter more so because sought and longed for." Artillery killed four hundred civilians around the Remedios Hospital. A local man, Antonio Rocha, approached a U.S. mortar line and told its officer that his bombs were falling on civilians, not Japanese. The American impatiently gestured him away. The columns of the neoclassical Legislature Building collapsed into heaps of rubble. On 14 February, MacArthur's headquarters announced: "The end of the enemy's trapped garrison is in sight." Yet death and destruction continued unabated as Krueger's men approached the last Japanese stronghold, the old Spanish city.

Oscar Griswold of XIV Corps wrote on 28 February: "C-in-C refused my request to use air on Intramuros. I hated to ask for it since I knew it would cause death of civilians held captive by Japs. We know, too, that the Japs are burning large numbers to death, shooting and bayoneting them. Horrid as it seems, probably death from bombing would be more merciful . . . I fear that the C in C's refusal to let me have bombing will result in more casualties to my men . . . I understand how he feels about bombing people—but it is being done all over the world—Poland, China, England, Germany, Italy—then why not here! War is never pretty. I am frank to say I would sacrifice Philipino [*sic*] lives under such circumstances to save the lives of my men. I feel quite bitter about this tonight."

In the last days of February, the Americans began the final and most brutal phase of the struggle to overcome the defenders of the old city.

Griswold wrote: "The assault upon Intramuros was unique in modern warfare in that the entire area was mediaeval in structure, and its defense combined the fortress of the Middle Ages with the firepower of modern weapons." Granite walls twenty feet thick were breached with heavy artillery. The 145th Infantry then attacked, supported by a company of medium tanks, a company of tank destroyers, an assault-gun platoon, two flamethrower tanks and self-propelled artillery. Once inside Fort Santiago, American demolition teams sealed deep recesses, dungeons and tunnels, after throwing in white phosphorus grenades or pumping down gasoline and igniting it. To its end, the battle remained fragmented, confused, pitiless.

Only on 3 March could Manila be deemed secure. Some 3,500 Japanese escaped across the Marikina river. Weary and exasperated, Oscar Griswold wrote: "General MacArthur had announced [Manila's] capture several days ahead of the actual event. The man is *publicity crazy*. When soldiers are dying and being wounded, it doesn't make for their morale to know that the thing they are doing has been officially announced as finished days ago." MacArthur picked a path through the debris of his old quarters in the penthouse of the Manila Hotel, where he found his library destroyed, a dead Japanese colonel on the carpet: "It was not a pleasant moment . . . I was tasting to the acid dregs the bitterness of a devastated and beloved home," he wrote later. It seems bizarre that he paraded his own loss of mere possessions in the midst of a devastating human catastrophe. He wrote to his wife, Jean, reporting the good news that he had recovered all the family silver. He took over a mansion, Casa Blanca in the smart Santa Mesa district, established residence, and defied widespread criticism by summoning Jean to join him there.

American soldiers were not merely exhausted, but also deeply depressed by all that they had seen, done and suffered in Manila. The 3/148th Infantry, for instance, had lost 58 percent of its strength. Many of the casualties were veterans of the Solomons campaigns. Among new replacements there was an outbreak of self-inflicted wounds, which caused the perpetrators to be court-martialled. To relieve his men's gloom, the battalion's colonel ordered an "organised drunk." Two truckloads of Suntory whiskey were procured, and issued at a rate of three bottles per man. One day was devoted to drinking, a second to "healing." This may not have been a good answer to the battalion's morale problem, but its officers were unable to think of better ones.

The victors counted 1,000 American dead, together with 16,665 Japanese—and 100,000 Manileros. In those days, other Luzon cities also suffered massacres by the occupiers: 984 civilians were killed in Cuenca on 19 February; 500 in Buang and Batangas on 28 February; 7,000 civilians were killed in Calamba, Laguna. In all, a million Filipinos are estimated to have died by violence in the Second World War, most of them in its last months. There was intense debate about whether MacArthur should have bypassed Manila, rather than storm it. What is certain is that he was mistaken in his belief that he could serve the best interests of the Philippine people by committing an army to liberate them. Whatever Filipinos might have suffered at the hands of the Japanese if the Americans had contented themselves with seizing air bases for their advance on Tokyo, and held back from reoccupying the entire Philippines archipelago, would have been less grievous than the catastrophe they suffered when MacArthur made their country a battlefield. And in March 1945, the struggle for the islands was far from ended.

2. Yamashita's Defiance

EVEN AS the battle for Manila was being fought, senior U.S. officers speculated about the looming end of the war in Europe, and its implications for the defeat of Japan. Lt.-Gen. Robert Eichelberger of Eighth Army wrote on 16 February: "I believe the BC [Big Chief] would fight against any attempt to bring the European crowd over here, even if they should desire to do so. I personally hope that the Japanese will quit if and when Stalin begins to push down along the Manchuria railway. They will realize they cannot hope to stand against that pressure . . . If we ever get Russia on our side out here the Japanese will be in a horrific position and therefore I think they will quit before having their towns bombed out." Eichelberger added on 5 March: "I never expect the BC to change. He will never want anybody on the stage but himself."

While three American divisions were fighting for Manila through February, others recaptured the great symbolic place-names of Bataan and Corregidor. Zig-Zag Pass, on the approaches to the Bataan Peninsula, became the scene of some of the most painful fighting of the campaign. Before the area was secured several senior officers, including a divisional commander, were sacked for alleged inadequacy. An American parachute assault on the fortress island of Corregidor surprised the Japanese defenders in advance of an amphibious landing, but cost heavy jump casualties, and days of bloody mopping-up. A tank fired into the Malinta Tunnel, hitting munitions which exploded, blasting the vehicle bodily fifty yards backwards and overturning it. On the islands of Corregidor and nearby Caballo, the Americans disposed of the most stubborn underground defenders by pumping oil into their bunkers, then setting this ablaze. "Results," said the divisional report, "were most gratifying." Some Japanese chose to end their ordeal by detonating underground ammunition stores, killing Americans unlucky enough to be standing above. It was a messy, horrible business. Even MacArthur felt unable to display much triumphalism about the recapture of these famous symbols, though he led a flotilla of PT-boats to a ceremony on Corregidor.

Sixth Army's drive north and eastwards meanwhile continued, in the face of dogged resistance. Through the months that followed, Yamashita conducted a highly effective defence of the mountain areas in which he had fortified himself. Japanese units fought; inflicted American casualties; caused days of delay, fear and pain; then withdrew to their next line. Krueger's engineers toiled under fire to improve steep tracks sufficiently to carry tanks and vehicles. Disease took its toll of attackers and defenders alike. Japanese soldiers endured hunger always, starvation latterly. "Of the forty-nine men who are left, only seventeen are fit for duty," wrote Lt. Inoue Suteo of the Japanese 77th Infantry on 19 March. "The other two-thirds are sick. Out of fourteen men of the grenade discharger section, only three are fit . . . 43rd Force [to which his unit belonged] is called 'the malaria unit' . . . The quality of Japanese soldiers has fallen dramatically. I doubt if they could carry on the fight. Few units in the Japanese army are as lacking in military discipline as this one."

Private Shigeki Hara of the 19th Special Machine-Gun Unit described the misery of retreating in a column of sick men. They abandoned all personal possessions, though Hara sought to sustain the custom of taking home to Japan some portion of every dead fellow soldier: "After daybreak, removed arm from the dead body of a comrade and followed the main body . . . was attacked by a company of guerrillas and suffered one casualty. Killed one enemy with the sword." In addition to the usual tropical afflictions, men discovered that scrub typhus was carried by a small local red mite. Its symptom was a high fever, which inflicted heart damage from which some victims never recovered. "Practically every day two or three men fall out and [are] instantly shot by the officers," said Private First Class Bunsan Okamoto, a twenty-four-year-old apprentice salesman serving with the 30th Recce Regiment. He was fortunate enough to be captured by the Americans and kept alive for intelligence purposes. A U.S. officer met an attractive young Filipino woman who said she had been in flight for weeks with three Japanese soldiers. "The last few days," she reported, "they were in tears most of the time." Americans found a pencilled note among supplies abandoned by the enemy, signed by a despairing Japanese: "To the brave American soldier who finds this—tell my family I died bravely."

All over the Philippine archipelago in the early spring of 1945, Japanese garrisons waited with varying degrees of enthusiasm for Americans to come. On Lubang, for instance, an island some eighteen miles by six within sight of Luzon, 150 of Yamashita's men shifted supplies into the hills, in readiness to maintain a guerrilla campaign. "They all talked big about committing suicide and giving up their lives for the emperor," said their commander, Lt. Hiroo Onoda. "Deep down they were hoping and praying that Lubang would not be attacked." A small American force landed on 28 February, inflicting a slight wound on Onoda's hand as he and his men retreated. Thereafter, hunger and sickness progressively worsened their circumstances. One day, high in the hills, a pale young soldier came to Onoda from the sick tent, asking for explosives. He said: "We can't move. Please let us kill ourselves." Onoda thought for a moment, then agreed: "All right, I'll do it. I'll set a fuse to the charges." He looked into twenty-two faces, "all resigned to death," and did his business. When he returned after the explosion, there was only a gaping crater where the sick tent had been.

In those months, more Japanese in the Philippines died from hunger and disease than the U.S. Army killed. In some degree, this must be attributed to a psychological collapse, overlaid upon physical weakness. Onoda, whose life on Lubang became that of a hunted wild animal, prowled the mountains struggling for survival, rather than making much attempt to injure the enemy. One day he glimpsed American gum wrappers beside a road, and found a wad stuck to a weed. He felt a surge of bitterness and frustration: "Here we were, holding on for dear life, and these characters were chewing gum while they fought! I felt more sad than angry. The chewing gum tinfoil told me just how miserably we had been beaten."

A military surgeon in the Philippines, Tadashi Moriya, ate bats:

> We tore off the wings, roasted them until they were done brown, flayed and munched their heads holding them by their legs. The brain was delicious. The tiny eyes cracked lightly in the mouth. The teeth were small but sharp, so we crunched and swallowed them down. We ate everything, bones and intestines, except the legs. The abdomen felt rough to the tongue, as they seemed to eat small insects like mosquitoes . . . Hunger is indeed the best sauce, for I ate fifteen bats a day.
>
> An officer reported that he saw a group of soldiers cooking meat. When he approached, they tried to conceal the contents of the mess tins, but he had a peep at them. A good deal of fat swam on the surface of the stew they were cooking, and he saw at once that it couldn't be *karabaw* [animal] meat. Then I had the news that an officer of another unit was eaten by his orderly as soon as he breathed his last. I believe

the officer was so devoted to his orderly that he bequeathed him his body. This loyal servant fulfilled his lord and master's final wishes by burying him in his belly instead of the earth.

Col. Russell Volckmann, an American officer who had been leading guerrillas against the Japanese on Luzon since 1942, provided a report to Sixth Army assessing the enemy's tactical strengths and weaknesses. He admired Japanese powers of endurance, skill in moving men and equipment over harsh terrain. He thought well of their junior officers and NCOs. More senior commanders, however, impressed him little with their "absurd orders, assignment of impossible missions in relation to a unit's strength, utter disregard for the lives of subordinates, refusal to admit defeat or even face the fact that events are going against him [*sic*] and inability to adjust to a changing situation, proneness to exaggerate success and minimize failure causes higher echelons to get a false picture. Jap small unit tactics are tops but there is seldom any coordination between units. To sum it up—the Jap officer generally has no idea of modern methods of fighting in large mass." This seems fair. The Japanese showed themselves superb soldiers in defence, yet often failed in attack because they relied upon human spirit to compensate for lack of numbers, firepower, mobility and imagination. When the Japanese counterattacked, they were almost always repulsed with heavy loss. But when they merely held ground, as did Yamashita's men for most of the Luzon campaign, they performed superbly.

To the dismay of Krueger's Sixth Army, after the fall of Manila MacArthur launched the five divisions of Eichelberger's Eighth Army on the progressive recapture of the lesser Philippine islands. Strategically, this decision had nothing to recommend it. American forces struggling to defeat Yamashita on Luzon were left grievously shorthanded. Eichelberger's formations, which carried out fourteen major and twenty-four minor amphibious landings in forty-four days all over the Philippines Archipelago, thereafter spent weeks pursuing small Japanese forces which hit and ran, inflicted casualties, then retreated, day after day and month after month, with worsening weather and American morale. Samuel Eliot Morison notes that the joint chiefs of staff in Washington strongly questioned the necessity for the further extension of ground operations in the Philippines. "It is still something of a mystery," the great naval historian remarks acidly, "how and whence, in view of these wishes of the JCS, MacArthur derived his authority to liberate one Philippine island after another." The simple explanation is that MacArthur's manic will to fulfil his personal mission was stronger than that of the chiefs of staff to stop him doing so.

In this second phase of the Luzon campaign, the general's behaviour became bizarre. During the advance on Manila he had assumed personal command of American forces and repeatedly risked his life in forward areas, hustling his generals on. When the capital fell, however, he seemed to lose interest in subsequent operations, only once visiting a Sixth Army front before the war's end. He constantly criticised Krueger for sluggishness, but successfully recommended his subordinate to Washington for promotion to a fourth star. Most senior Americans on Luzon thought it would have been more appropriate to sack Krueger. It was the familiar story. MacArthur was loyal to his own, right or wrong, competent or otherwise. Promotion for Krueger represented an endorsement of his own performance.

Robert Sherwood of the Office of War Information visited MacArthur on 10 March and reported in some alarm to Roosevelt: "There are unmistakable evidences of an acute persecution complex at work. To hear some of the staff officers talk, one would think that the War Department, the State Department, the joint chiefs of staff—and, possibly, even the White House itself—are under the domination of 'Communists and British Imperialists.' " Sherwood thought the atmosphere at SWPA headquarters profoundly unhealthy. While MacArthur's demeanour became ever more autocratic, his interest in accepting responsibility for military operations in the Philippines diminished. The clearance of Luzon was a mess, because he and Krueger showed themselves far less competent commanders than was Yamashita.

"It was a long, slow and costly operation," said Maj.-Gen. William Gill, commanding the 32nd Division. "Morale was poor, because the men were tired—they'd been in there in combat for months . . . We killed a lot of [Japanese], of course, killed many more of them than they killed of us, but we lost too many . . . Our engineers that were building roads often came under machine gun fire." On the steep mountains, progress was painfully laborious. Gill watched admiringly one day as a soldier driving a bulldozer worked under fire beside a sheer precipice, manoeuvring his blade to deflect bullets which whanged off the steel. The fruits of such labour were often doubtful. "We sometimes reported enemy losses as ten times our own when we did not know the correct number," admitted an American officer.

By April, some infantry regiments were reduced to half strength. Salvatore Lamagna returned late from a home furlough in Thompsonville, Connecticut, an offence for which he found himself busted from sergeant to private. When he reached his old unit, he sought out his comrades from the New Guinea campaign: "I looked around to see if I could find anyone I knew. Most of the guys were new to me. 'Where's Tietjen?' 'He was killed by a Jap artillery shell,' Farmer says. I felt bad. I asked if any of the original 4th Platoon guys that left from Hartford, Ct. were left. 'Just you and I,' he says."

Discipline lapsed badly in some units. Maj. Chuck Henne was walking beside a train one day in April when he heard shooting from the cars. Soldiers were firing at buffalo in the fields. He identified himself as a battalion executive officer: "They laughed and kept on shooting . . . I then shouted up to the men and told them to get their asses back in the car or I would shoot them off the roof . . . They came off the roof handing their rifles down butt first . . . I asked the lieutenant if he could now control his men . . . He sulked and vowed he could handle his troops. If he had been mine, I would have relieved him on the spot."

The struggle to cut and hold Yamashita's principal supply route, the Villa Verde Trail, became one of the most bitter of the campaign. "The price that the . . . trail cost in battle casualties was too high for value received," said Gill of the 32nd Division. There was heroism. Lt. Van Pelt and a platoon of the 3/148th Infantry tried to work forward to deal with a Japanese 150mm gun. Pelt fell mortally wounded by machine-gun fire, which also hit two others beside him. One of these, Private Fred Ogrodkick, dragged himself into a cave, then realised that his buddy still lay in the open. He struggled out again, braved the fire to drag his friend into shelter, then sat trying to bandage both their wounds. Private Melvin Kidd, a K Company truck driver, saw what had happened. He jumped onto the engine deck of an M4 tank, rode forward under fire, jumped down and began to treat the wounded men in the cave. A Japanese shell blew down the entrance, trapping all three inside. An American infantry squad followed the tanks forward, and hacked open the cave mouth with bayonets and entrenching tools. Others rushed the Japanese positions. An officer later asked Kidd why he had joined a fight that was not his business. He shrugged: "It seemed the right thing to do."

Higher commanders had worries of their own. Col. Bruce Palmer, chief of staff of 6th Division, was dismayed by the conduct of his general, Edwin Patrick, who behaved recklessly when sober, and worse when drunk, which was alarmingly often. A Japanese machine gunner solved this problem by killing Patrick when he exposed himself while visiting a battalion observation post. Soldiers were startled to discover how cold it became at night, when the sun dropped behind the mountains. There were mornings when they found water buckets covered with ice—and nights when the heavens opened. "With the torrents of rain beating down only a few were able to sleep," wrote Chuck Henne. "Helmets were large enough only to keep the rain out of one's eyes. The issue poncho held back the flood for a time and then became nearly as wet on the inside as on the outside. Worst of all, as the torrent continued, foxholes and slit trenches started to fill, and when bailing failed to keep up . . . a man could choose between sitting in a water-filled hole or getting out to sit in the mud. It was a bad night, and no doubt the Japs were as miserable as we were."

Yamashita held out until the end of the war in his mountain fastnesses on Luzon, though the Americans had destroyed most of his forces. By August 1945 his Shobu group had been driven back into a forty-two-square-mile redoubt near Bontoc, and its supplies were almost exhausted. In the last six weeks of the war, these remnants killed some 440 American soldiers and Filipino guerrillas—but themselves lost 13,000 men. The general gave an interview at his headquarters to the Domei News Agency, in which he said—surprisingly to those who suppose all Japanese commanders to have been brutes: "I think Japan has made a big mistake, in the way it has conducted foreign occupations. We lack any experience of this, and it is one of our weaknesses. We simply haven't tried to understand other societies. Relatively speaking, Japan is poor. We can't compete scientifically with the West. Nor do we use the skills of our women as we might. They should be educated, albeit differently from men." For Yamashita and his comrades, however, such revelations of sensitivity came too late. He himself was burdened with the appalling crimes of the Japanese occupiers of the Philippines, and would soon be called to account for them.

It is a striking feature of the Second World War that the populist media of the democracies made stars of some undeserving commanders, who thereafter became hard to sack. MacArthur's Philippines campaign did little more to advance the surrender of Japan than Slim's campaign in Burma, and was conducted with vastly less competence. Its principal victims were the Philippine people, and MacArthur's own military reputation. Before the landing at Leyte, this stood high, probably higher than it deserved, following the conquest of Papua New Guinea. The early blunderings of that campaign were forgotten, and the general received laurels for the daring series of amphibious strokes which achieved victory. In the Philippines, however, instead of achieving the cheap, quick successes he had promised, his forces became entangled in protracted fighting, on terms which suited the Japanese. MacArthur's contempt for intelligence was a persistent, crippling defect. On Luzon, where he sought to exercise personal field command, his opponent Yamashita displayed a nimbleness in striking contrast to the heavy-footed advance of Sixth Army. Stanley Falk has written of MacArthur: "On those occasions when the Japanese faced him with equal or greater strength, he was unable to defeat them or to react swiftly or adequately to their initiatives." "The . . . South-West Pacific commitment was an unnecessary and profligate waste of resources, involving the needless loss of thousands of lives, and in no significant way affecting the outcome of the war."

Japanese barbarism rendered the battle for Manila a human catastrophe, but MacArthur's obsession with seizing the city created the circumstances for it. The U.S. lost 8,140 men killed on Luzon. Around 200,000 Japanese died there, many of disease. If the exchange ran overwhelmingly in America's favour, those same enemy forces could have gone nowhere and achieved nothing had the Americans contented themselves with their containment. SWPA's supreme commander compounded his mistakes by embarking upon the reconquest of the entire Philippines Archipelago, even before Luzon had fallen. MacArthur presided over the largest ground campaign of America's war in the Pacific in a fashion which satisfied his own ambitions more convincingly than the national purposes of his country.

TEN

Bloody Miniature: Iwo Jima

PLACE-NAMES which pass into history often identify locations so unrewarding that only war could have rendered them memorable: Dunkirk and Alamein, Corregidor and Imphal, Anzio and Bastogne. Yet even in such company, Iwo Jima was striking in its wretchedness. The tiny island lay 3,000 miles west of Pearl Harbor and less than seven hundred south of Japan. It was five miles long, two and a half wide. Dominated at the southern tip by the extinct volcano of Mount Suribachi, five hundred feet high, in the north it rose to a plateau, thick with jungle growth. Iwo had been claimed by Japan in 1861, and desultorily employed for growing sugarcane. A Japanese garrison officer described it sourly as "a waterless island of sulphur springs, where neither swallows nor sparrows flew."

The perceived importance of this pimple derived, as usual, from airfields. During the last months of 1944 and the early weeks of 1945, American aircraft pounded Iwo Jima on seventy-two days. As fast as Japanese squadrons reached the island, their planes were destroyed in the air or on the ground. The usefulness of the base to Tokyo thus shrank to the vanishing point. Yet, in the boundless ocean, the U.S. Navy coveted Iwo as one of the few firm footholds on the central axis of approach to Japan. In the autumn of 1944 the joint chiefs mandated the island's seizure. After various American hesitations and delays, which served the defenders' interests much better than those of the invaders, an armada was massed. Even as MacArthur's soldiers battered their way across the Philippines, three Marine divisions were embarked.

One of the island's garrison, Lt.-Col. Kaneji Nakane, wrote to his wife a few weeks before the U.S. landing, with the banality common to so many warriors' letters: "We are now getting enemy air raids at least ten times a day, and enemy task forces have struck the island twice. We suffered no damage. Everybody is in good shape, so you don't have to worry about me. The beans brought from our house were planted and are now flowering. Harvest time is approaching, and the squashes and eggplants look very good. Yesterday we had a bathe, and everybody was in high spirits. We get some fish, because every time the enemy bombs us a lot of dead ones are washed ashore . . . We have strong positions and God's soldiers, and await the enemy with full hearts."

Another Japanese on Iwo Jima was a teenager named Harunori Ohkoshi. The youngest of five children of a Tokyo roofing contractor, he had cherished illusions about the glories of service life. In 1942, at the age of fourteen, he applied to the navy to become a boy sailor, forging a letter of parental consent, for which he sneaked access to the family seal. When all was revealed, his mother was distraught, his father supportive. Less than two years later, at sixteen, he was serving as flight engineer on a navy transport plane, carrying engine parts from Kyushu to Saipan, when it was bounced by Hellcats. Easy meat, the transport ditched in the sea. Four men died, but Ohkoshi and two others were retrieved by a passing fishing boat, and eventually deposited on Iwo Jima. When the local command found that the survivor was a qualified engineer, he was posted to a maintenance unit.

Ohkoshi and his comrades grew accustomed to being strafed by American P-38s, which approached too low and fast to offer warning. They were also bombed from high altitude by B-24s, and shelled by warships. Comrades taught the teenager to lie across the line of attack when he prostrated himself before machine-gunning fighters claiming that he thus presented a smaller target. By February 1945, because length of service counted for more than age, at seventeen he found himself a technical sergeant—and no longer an aircraft mechanic. Every man on Iwo Jima was pressed into combat infantry service. Ohkoshi was given command of a fourteen-man group. They were issued with helmets and equipment, together with a makeshift assortment of weapons ranging from machine guns to hunting rifles and pistols. Along with 7,500 other naval personnel, the teenager was trained to address tanks by thrusting pole charges into their tracks. Ohkoshi's group dug bunkers deep, deep into the hills and rock of Tanana Mountain, at the centre of the island. He covered his own hole with the wing of a wrecked Zero, overlaid with timber and camouflage. On 16 February 1945, as the final American bombardment began, Ohkoshi was sent with a patrol to view the coast. He returned awed, saying: "You can hardly see sea for ships." Then he and his squad took up positions which they scarcely left through the next seventeen days.

Watching from offshore the devastation wrought by the bombardment, Marine lieutenant Patrick Caruso felt a stab of pity for defenders like Ohkoshi: "I . . . thought of the helpless feeling those poor Japanese must have had on that island." Another lieutenant bet Caruso, whose unit was in reserve, a bottle of brandy that they would not need to land.

William Allen of the 23rd Marines "couldn't understand why we needed three divisions to take this piddling island." Private First Class Arthur Rodriguez, a BAR man, offered a tortured figure of speech: "My first impression of Iwo Jima was that it looked like a termite nest in the shape of a turkey drumstick with Suribachi as its kneecap." What followed became the most famous, or notorious, battle of the Pacific war.

Some of the men who began to land along the south-east coast on the morning of 19 February had been six weeks at sea, on passage to an objective initially identified to them only as "Island X." Others had embarked at Saipan a few days earlier. When word came to "saddle up," the Marines of 4th and 5th Divisions found it hard to climb the ships' ladders, each of them being weighed down with at least fifty pounds, sometimes a hundred pounds, of weapons, kit and ammunition. The clumsy clamber down scrambling nets from a ship's side to an assault craft pitching on the swell was an alarming experience even for veterans. One man itemised his own load: clothing and helmet, backpack and entrenching tool, poncho, three light and three heavy rations, two packs of cigarettes in a waxed paper sack, leather case of weapon-cleaning kit, extra socks, gas mask, cartridge belt, pistol and two clips, sterile canned compress, two water canteens, one GI knife, two fragmentation grenades, binoculars—and a Browning Automatic Rifle weighing thirty-six pounds. Men bent under such burdens made hard landings in the boats. James Shriver crushed his fingers in a hatch, and was nursing the pain as he looked towards Suribachi and thought miserably: "They expect me to get up that fucking mountain!" Shriver was an eighteen-year-old assistant BAR man from Escondido, California. His original gunner was removed by military police just before embarkation, having been discovered to be only fourteen. Now, with a substitute, Shriver prepared to land with the 28th Marines.

As amtracs splashed forth from the hulls of their parent transports, correspondent John Marquand likened the spectacle to "all the cats in the world having kittens." The first wave of sixty-nine hit the beach at 0902. From his landing craft, James Vedder glimpsed wrecked planes on the airstrip, terracing inland, and further south the sheer rock walls of Suribachi. Under the thunder of the bombardment, debris flew skywards, great clouds of smoke drifted across the shore. Vedder, a surgeon with the 3/27th Marines, watched as two Zeroes struggled off the ground, only to collide with the bombardment and plunge into the sea. As he touched the shore and stumbled through the clogging black ash underfoot, the first human he saw was a dead Japanese, obviously burnt by a flamethrower. The doctor noted curiously that half the corpse's moustache was scorched away.

As soon as the invaders began to scramble up the steep terrace behind the beach, shells and mortar bombs fell in dense succession, maiming and killing with almost every round among the crowds of heavily laden Marines. Pillars of ash erupted into the air. Burning vehicles, dead and stricken men, unwounded ones hugging the earth, created traffic chaos. Some braver souls pressed on inland, but as these were cut down, the assault's momentum faltered. One of Vedder's corpsmen had been tasked to carry his instruments ashore. In a moment of panic, the man simply ran forward, leaving the surgeon's bag on their boat. Vedder found fragments of hot steel smouldering on his clothes, and brushed away a splinter that was stinging his backside. Within seconds of landing he was at work, removing a large fragment of jawbone wedged in the back of a Marine's throat, to enable him to breathe freely again. He could do nothing, however, for the ruin of his face: "I wondered how our plastic surgeons would ever restore this man's identity."

The bombardment had destroyed Japanese defences close to the beaches. The Marines were quickly able to stake out positions three hundred yards inland. Yet the entire perimeter remained within easy range of the enemy. When armour began to land, tracks thrashing for a grip in the ash, most was swiftly knocked out by anti-tank guns. Some 361 Japanese artillery pieces, together with plentiful heavy mortars and machine guns, were dug into Iwo Jima's defences. An ordeal began which persisted through the days and nights that followed. Shelling, mortar and small-arms fire inflicted casualties and relentless misery on every American unit from the shoreline to the foremost positions.

Lt.-Gen. Tadamichi Kuribayashi, the slender, elegant, fifty-three-year-old commander of Iwo Jima, had no illusions about the outcome of the struggle to which he was committed. He had served in Canada and the U.S. in the 1930s, and knew the relative weakness of his own nation. "This war will be decided by industrial might, don't you agree?" he mused to a staff officer. Kuribayashi had opposed the conflict, because he did not think it winnable. Yet fatalism did not impair his meticulous preparations to defend Iwo Jima. He had no faith in the survivability of positions on the beaches or airfields, though he could not prevent the navy contingent, beyond his authority, from devoting heavy labour to such entrenchments. He concentrated upon defence in depth, exploiting rocky heights. In the months before the American landing, some fifteen hundred natural caves were sculpted and enlarged into an intricate system linked by sixteen miles of tunnels, centred upon Kuribayashi's command bunker, seventy-five feet underground.

If such burrowing represented a primitive response to the technological might of the invaders, it was also a formidably effective one. Most

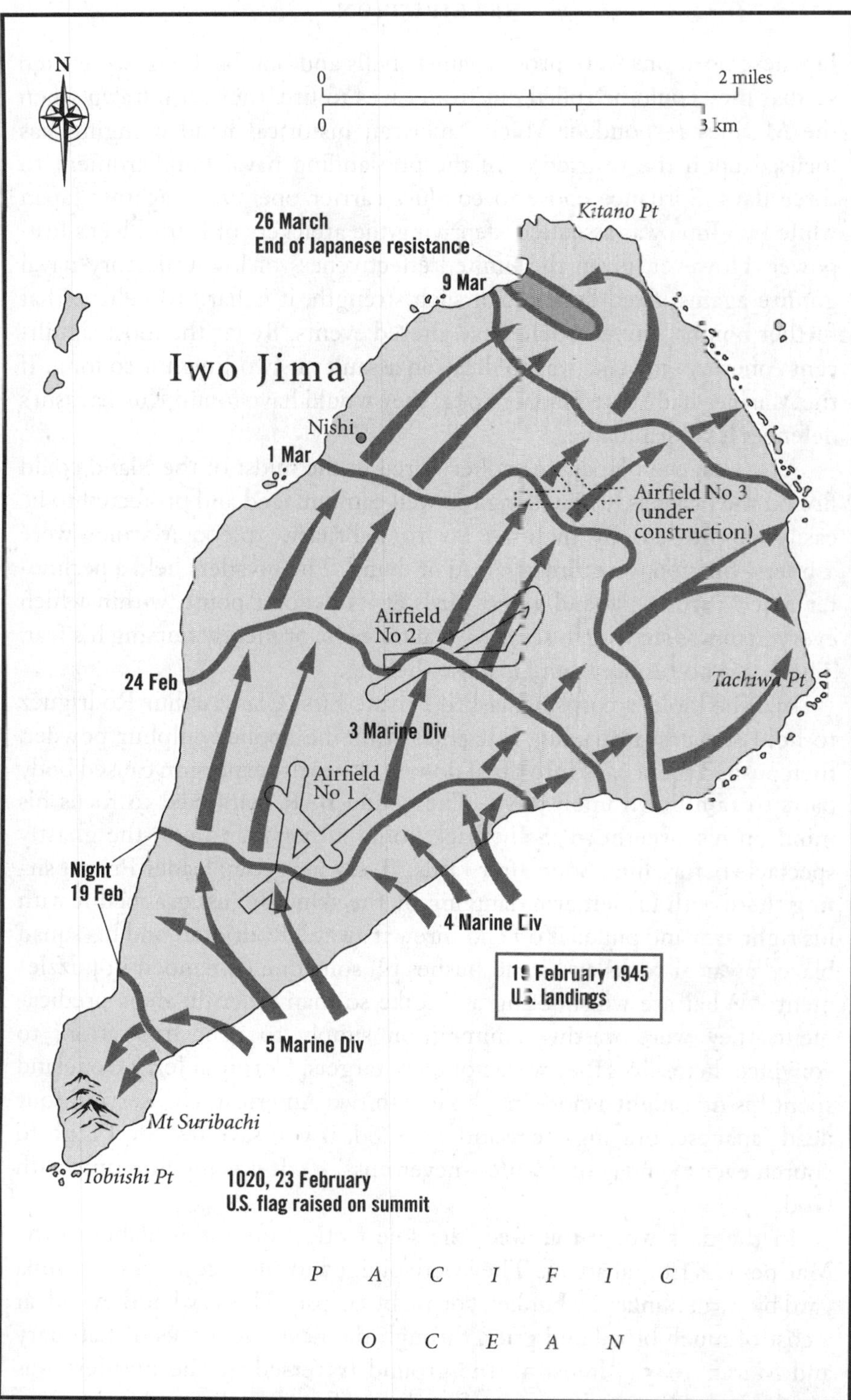
N
0
2 miles
3 km
26 March
End of Japanese resistance
Kitano Pt
9 Mar
Iwo Jima
Nishi
1 Mar
Airfield No 3
(under
construction)
Airfield
No 2
24 Feb
Tachiwa Pt
3 Marine Div
Airfield
No 1
Night
19 Feb
4 Marine Div
19 February 1945
U.S. landings
5 Marine Div
Mt Suribachi
Tobiishi Pt
1020, 23 February
U.S. flag raised on summit
P A C I F I C
O C E A N

Iwo Jima, February–March 1945

Japanese positions were proof against shells and bombs. Guns were sited so that they could be rolled out from caves to fire, then withdrawn when the Marines responded. Much American historical hand-wringing has focused upon the restriction of the pre-landing naval bombardment to three days. Spruance chose to conduct carrier operations against Japan while Iwo Jima was assaulted, depriving the attackers of Fifth Fleet's firepower. However, given the limited effectiveness of low-trajectory naval gunfire against fixed defences of such strength, it is hard to believe that further bombardment would have altered events. By far the most significant American mistake was to delay an assault on Iwo Jima for so long. If the Marines had landed in late 1944, they would have found Kuribayashi's defences less formidable.

As it was, even Japanese artillery sited in the midst of the island could fire on the beaches, while being too well camouflaged and protected to be easily suppressed. By nightfall on 19 February, 30,000 Marines were ashore—but 566 were already dead or dying. The invaders held a perimeter 4,400 yards wide and 1,100 yards at its deepest point, within which every man was striving to scrape a shallow hole, or merely nursing his fear. There was no respite from Japanese shelling.

In a shellhole, a corpsman asked Private First Class Arthur Rodriguez to hold a man's protruding intestines while he applied sulphur powder, then pushed them back into his abdomen. A nearby explosion caused body parts to rain down upon them. The young BAR man tried to focus his mind on his sweetheart, Sally, back home rather than upon the ghastly spectacle before him. Soon afterwards, "I saw my group leader Privett sitting there with his left arm dangling by the skin. He just grabbed it with his right arm and pulled it off and threw it away." Rodriguez and his squad blazed away at rocks and small bushes till someone demanded in puzzlement: "What are we shooting at?" Like so many men in their predicament, they were wasting ammunition simply to vent frustration, to convince themselves they were not mere targets. Corporal Jerry Copeland spent his first night ashore in a hole with two American corpses and four dead Japanese, praying incessantly: " 'God, if you save my life I'll go to church every Sunday of my life—never miss' . . . It was my first time with God."

In the days which followed, the sole tactical option available to the Marines was frontal attack. They were obliged to advance across Iwo Jima yard by yard, bunker by bunker, corpse by corpse. This is what they did, at a cost of much blood and grief, through the next five weeks of February and March 1945. Almost all the ground traversed by the invaders was overlooked by the Japanese. Battalion after battalion, the Marines launched open-order assaults. Most petered out after one or two hundred yards, because so many participants fell. True, the application of technology helped. Armoured bulldozers hacked routes uphill for tanks. Flamethrowers proved invaluable, lancing cave mouths to make way for explosive charges. Warship and artillery fire did something to suppress Japanese fire. But to occupy Iwo Jima, to stop the mortar bombs and shells scouring every American position back to the beaches, the Americans could discover no effective substitute for sending men forward again and again, to prise each cluster of rocks piecemeal from shockingly dogged defenders.

The more exposed Japanese positions around the airfields were overrun in the first days, as Kuribayashi had anticipated, but their navy occupants accounted for significant numbers of Americans before perishing. Mount Suribachi fell on the fifth day, 23 February, after a savage struggle with its 1,500 defenders. Lt. Harold Schrier led forty men of the 5th Division onto the summit. When crews on the ships offshore witnessed the Stars and Stripes rising on the volcano's summit, many raised a spontaneous cheer, as did the American people when they saw the legendary photograph of a second flag raising. Yet American triumph in the south left most of the 22,000-strong Japanese garrison still entrenched in the north, with an overwhelming advantage. Since they were neither willing nor able to leave Iwo Jima alive, their immobility conferred priceless invisibility. The defenders were told: "Each man should think of his foxhole as his own grave, fighting to the last to inflict maximum damage upon the enemy." The Japanese held a small area in which even infantry bunkers were impervious to anything less than a direct hit, and in which there was no scope for outflanking manoeuvres. The onus was entirely upon the Americans to move, and thus to expose themselves.

"We had a gross misconception of the enemy before we encountered them," wrote Patrick Caruso. "They were not jokes; they were not inept. We hated them enough to kill them, but we did respect their ability. I often thought that if we had to go to war again, I would want them on our side." The Marines were surprised to find that many Japanese corpses were those of large men, for they had always thought of the enemy as pygmies. They were bemused to see some sprouting heavy black beards, such as never featured in American propaganda images.

After several days of combat, wrote Arthur Rodriguez, "we had not seen any of the enemy to shoot at. It made us feel frustrated and angry, because we had almost nothing to show for all our casualties." The U.S. Marine Corps was a formidable fighting force, but on Iwo Jima the sight of so many men dying if they attempted to move created a popular bias in favour of hugging cover. This was natural, but militarily crippling. "The terrain was most favourable to the defense . . . The uncanny accuracy of enemy rifle fire caused many casualties," wrote Lt. Col. Joseph Sayers. He thought Japanese artillery poorly directed, but noted that the defenders did not squander men in futile charges, as they had done in earlier Pacific battles. "The enemy is a much improved fighter." Sayers delivered a bleak after-action verdict on a typical day for the 2/26th Marines on Iwo: "Low morale, fatigue, an average strength of 70 men per company," and next evening: "Morale was very low, and the strain of many days in the line was evident. It was noted that the men became more careless, and exposed themselves more to fire when fatigued." He urged a halt to the practice of dispatching replacements to join units on the line, for there was no opportunity to instruct them in even the basic skills of survival. Ten out of seventeen replacement medical corpsmen sent to his battalion were killed or wounded within days simply because, in the view of their commander, they were ignorant of fieldcraft.

As an operations officer with the 24th Marines, Maj. Albert Arsenault was responsible for making a nightly situation report, characteristically exemplified as: "Progress a hundred yards, casualties thirty-seven. Tied in for the night." Regimental headquarters demanded: "How many Japanese did you kill?" "None that we could be sure of." "None! Thirty-seven casualties and you haven't killed any Japanese! You've got to do better than that." Arsenault thereafter projected Japanese losses at least double those of his own unit: "One day was pretty much like another: small advances, heavy casualties."

Warrant-Officer George Green, an artillery forward observer (FO) with 3/21st Marines on Airfield 2, kept seeing a bespectacled Japanese popping his head up. When he urged a nearby rifleman to shoot him, the man replied crossly: "He's in I Company's sector—let them get him." A captain radioed Green, demanding to know why he was not firing. The FO answered that he could see no targets. "Pick some prominent landmark and fire anyway," said the officer. Two grenades suddenly arched through the air, and fell nearby. Green shouted to a nearby BAR man, who rashly walked towards the bushes from which the bombs seemed to have come. There, he toppled dead. A fire team eventually silenced the Japanese with grenades. Amid endemic nervousness in the perimeter, a Navajo Native American "code-talker" who spoke poor English was mistaken for a Japanese by a group of Marines. The man sat paralysed with well-merited fright until he was identified by another Navajo.

The 3/9th Marines landed on 23 February in tearing high spirits, eager for battle. Languishing on the ships in reserve through the first days, they and the rest of 3rd Division were fearful of missing the action. The tinny, echoing ship's PA system informed them that 4th and 5th Divisions had met only "light resistance." Within minutes of reaching Airfield 1, however, they found themselves under shellfire. Oklahoman Lieutenant Clyde McGinnis, at thirty the oldest man in K Company, urged his nearest companions to follow him into a crater, where they found a freshly decapitated Marine, still holding a smouldering cigarette in his hand. McGinnis said: "Damn, this is a hot place," and started singing "Take Me Back to Tulsa." He called back to the men behind: "I'll be all right here, but I do think those guys are trying to kill me."

Firepower alone was incapable of destroying Japanese positions. "The most discouraging thing was, right in the middle of this tremendous barrage you'd hear the damned enemy open up their machine guns," wrote Lt. Col. Robert Cushman, twenty-nine-year-old commander of the 2/9th Marines. "It wasn't knocking out those bunkers. So it was just a painful, sluggish business with tanks, H.E. and flame-throwers. And then the infantry with their flame-throwers and grenades and pole charges, digging them out." Cushman's battalion went through two complete changes of platoon leaders. Once, when his battalion was reduced to two hundred men and he ordered a charge, "nobody got out of their foxholes. So I picked up a rifle and bayonet and went round and got everybody out the hard way, and eventually they got moving along with the tanks."

"At times, it appeared that the only sure way of leaving Iwo Jima alive was to be wounded," said Patrick Caruso. For almost every man who was hit, comrades had a word of consolation. Corporal Robert Graf, however, noticed that when his platoon encountered an intensely unpopular officer prostrate on a litter, the whole file of men passed without speaking. Graf's own turn came a few days later. A shell fragment struck him in the buttock—the "million-dollar wound." As he was carried back to the beach for evacuation, "not only alive but leaving this godforsaken island . . . so many prayers of joy and happiness sprang to my lips."

It was often hard to tell how bad a wound was. Lt. John Cudworth of 9th Marines saw his close friend Bill Zimmer, a former Marquette University baseball and football player, ride past on top of a tank, smoking a cigarette. Zimmer told him: "I got hit in the balls and I guess I'm doing OK. Can you get me a couple more cigarettes?" Cudworth handed up half a pack and waved "So long." Next morning the doctor told him: "Zim didn't make it." Men especially feared the hours of darkness, because they knew that if they were hit, it was unlikely that any help could reach them before dawn. Some cracked. Combat fatigue cases mounted alarmingly. "Before getting on the ship in Guam, and on passage to Iwo, little 'Oiky' Erlavec was all excited, he was going to get to shoot some Japs," wrote John Cudworth. "After seeing dead Marines on the island and having artillery land near us, he blew higher than a kite and had to be sent back. A sorry event for such a young kid."

For the defenders, of course, each day of the battle was as terrible an ordeal as for the Americans—worse, because they were far more meagrely provided with food, water, medical supplies, or hopes of victory. Harunori Ohkoshi's naval unit was spared the early attentions of the invaders, but the heat in their bunkers was almost unendurable: "If you put a bare hand on that volcanic rock, it was scorched." Through the first ten days, cooks and water carriers made circuits of their positions before dawn and at dusk, but thirst remained a chronic problem. During the long, tense time of waiting, with the thunder of the battle a few hundred yards distant, they made desultory conversation, mostly about home.

Ohkoshi shared his hole with three other men. He felt closest to his runner, Hajime Tanaka, a Tokyo type like himself in a unit of farmboys: "He was a good bit older than me, maybe twenty-five, a real family man, and wonderfully steady whatever was happening." At intervals they were dispatched in small groups on reconnaissance or fighting patrols. These were nerve-racking affairs. On terrain where rocks and vegetation restricted visibility to a few yards, as they crept forward they knew their lives hung upon whether they spotted Americans first. Only once did they clash directly, with a small group of Marines whom they surprised and wiped out with grenades and bayonets. One American got close enough to hit Ohkoshi with the barrel of his pistol before the Japanese killed him.

Each day, American battalions lunged forward, sometimes gaining a few hundred yards, more often declaring themselves pinned down after suffering substantial casualties. The usual quota of brave, sacrificial Marines paid with their lives for being willing to force themselves forward just a little further, inducing others to follow where they led. The combination of thirst, rain, filth, cold food and fear ate into the spirits of even the best. Lt. Ken Thomson, a former sergeant commissioned following heroic performances on Guam and Bougainville, said: "Once I get back home to Minnesota and marry my girl, I'll never leave." He was killed a few days later. Sometimes, when Japanese perceived their own positions as hopeless, or simply grew weary of enduring bombardment, a handful of screaming figures hurled themselves at the Americans, to be cut down. But most of Kuribayashi's men obeyed orders to hug their positions and die where they lay. All battles break down into a host of tiny, intensely personal contests, but this was especially true of Iwo Jima. Each man knew only the few square yards of rock, vegetation and stinking sulphur springs where he sheltered, crawled, scrambled and fought with a shrinking handful of companions.

For the men aboard the ships offshore, it was a harrowing experience to find themselves so close to and yet so remote from the horrors which their fellow Americans were enduring. True, a handful of kamikaze aircraft broke through to the fleet, sinking the escort carrier *Bismarck Sea* and damaging *Saratoga*, but for the most part sailors were embarrassed by the comfort and safety in which they witnessed the battle. Coastguard Lt. Paul George, a twenty-two-year-old from Vinings, Georgia, never experienced personal fear on his LST, because he had no cause to, "other than feeling sorry for the guys who were ashore." Surrealistically, from a distance of a few hundred yards "we could just watch the war going on. Through the glasses I could see tanks trying to get through the sand and not having a whole lot of luck, Marines diving into foxholes."

Dr. Robert Watkins was operating shipboard: "Sometimes we were so close to shore that we could see the infantry and tanks fighting as though they were in our backyards. Some days were clear and lovely; on others the chill wind and fog whipped across the scudding whitecaps, raising waves that almost wrecked our landing boats. Some days the sun shone and I did not know it. Some nights the moon was bright, but not for me. Some sunrises I watched through the portholes as I washed the blood of the night's work from my hands and clothes."

Watkins hated operating on men with stomach wounds, because each case took at least four hours, together with many more hours of post-operative care, and half died anyway: "In the time that one belly wound is being operated on, I can save half a dozen lives and limbs with other wounds. And I am a lousy belly surgeon." A man being prepared for the operating table protested as a chaplain removed his watch. "You don't need my watch . . . You've got a watch," he said feebly. Corporal Red Doran, an Iowan BAR gunner from 3/9th Marines, lost his sight to blast. Evacuated, his bedmates had to endure the ghastly experience of hearing Doran join two other young men in similar plight, singing "Three Blind Mice." The captain of an attack transport was named Anderson. One day, his own Marine son was brought aboard, hopelessly mangled. The boy said: "Dad, I sure hope you've got some good doctors aboard." They were not good enough, for young Anderson died. His father buried him in the American cemetery ashore.

The faces of forward observers, directing naval guns alongside the infantry, remained unknown to ships' crews, yet their voices became intensely familiar down the radio. An FO's voice called "Fire!" Shipboard, there were deafening concussions, a pause, then a voice again: "Fan-fucking-tastic," or perhaps, "Bull's-eye," or sometimes, "That was a little close, friends. Back off a blond one." When one destroyer's FO at last paid a visit to the ship, its crew cheered him aboard. Ben Bradlee, the gunnery officer, wrote of the Marine: "He turned out to be my age, and even younger-looking, all jerky gestures and haunted eyes . . . I didn't know how to tell a man I loved him in those days, but I sure loved him." The visitor ate so much ice cream that he threw up.

The concentration of tens of thousands of men fighting over a few square miles of blasted rock and blackened vegetation created all manner of unwelcome problems. Radio nets became entangled. When phone wires were cut, it was often too dangerous to ask linesmen to search for the breaks. "It was necessary for officers to expose themselves constantly in order to maintain control," wrote Lt. Col. Joseph Sayers. Within days, excrement, abandoned equipment and debris lay everywhere. Few men found it necessary to dig their own holes, because of the mass of craters and foxholes which pockmarked the battlefield. Armour was vital to forward movement, yet dangerous to nearby infantrymen. The lumbering monsters crushed foxholes and drew Japanese fire. When surgeon James Vedder found tanks halted by his aid station, he told them angrily to go away.

John Lane, a New York jeweller's son, joined the 2/25th Marines in the midst of the battle. "We replacements were despised and perhaps hated by the survivors of the company," he wrote, "because we were so green, untrained and innocent, hated because we were there because their buddies had been killed or wounded . . . All were so bearded, dirty, dusty and exhausted that at first I couldn't tell them apart." Lane, a company runner, became famously lucky. He never saw a live Japanese, nor fired his rifle, nor was hit, though it sometimes seemed to him that everyone else was. "You'd come across little piles of dead Marines, waiting to be collected. Six or seven guys piled up, turning greenish-gray, then black. Dead Japanese, some hit by flame-throwers, eyes boiled out, lips burned away, white teeth grinning, uniforms burned away and sometimes the first layer of skin, too, so the muscles would show as in an anatomical sketch. Penis sticking up like a black candle stub. Napalm boiled the blood, causing an erection, some said."

Patrick Caruso found himself succumbing to silent reveries in the wary hours of darkness: "My mind traversed the spectrum of my past: school and college, and how final exams were so critical—until Iwo; why making the football team was so essential—until Iwo; how making a good impression on a date was so important—until Iwo; how getting a job during summer vacations was so significant—until Iwo; what's in store for my future. My future? Iwo is my present and future . . ." Marine Jack Colegrove had written home on 26 February: "Dear Mom, finally got time to sit down and write a few lines. I know you must be pretty worried about me by now, no doubt you heard that I am on Iwo Jima. I have come through the battle thus far without a scratch, so did my friend Pentecost, I cant write to everybody so can you just tell all my friends I'm okay, all my love Jack."

Three weeks later, however, Colegrove was obliged to report: "Gosh, sweetheart, I'm sorry I haven't written for such a long time. However I have a very good excuse—I have been wounded and all that sort of stuff. Two days before I got hit, Pentecost was hit in the stomach, tho the fellows say it wasn't too bad. At present I'm in a hospital in the Marianas, no telling how long I'll be here, might be quite a while. Has our little island grown very popular back there? Man o man, that sure was a rugged place, wasn't very nice at night, either. Sure did lose a lot of swell buddies . . . Think I'll have to come home soon—for good. Guess I'm washed up as a Marine . . . I was thinking today that it's a good thing I or you won't have to pay my hospital bill. It must be quite a bit. Lets see—150 shots of penicillin, hundreds of sulfa pills, blood plasma and whole blood, dressing, chow etc. Today I managed to get into a wheelchair . . ."

As gently as he could, Colegrove was breaking terrible news to his mother. He sent another letter to a friend in Detroit named Torbet: "I wanted to ask you a favor. You see I lost my left leg on Iwo Jima. I don't know if I should tell mother now, or wait until I get an artificial leg and start walking again. If you think it best to tell her, I wish you would. I don't know what the matter is with me, but I can't seem to tell mom myself. I sure am getting tired of laying around in these damn hospitals." Next day Colegrove made the effort to write to his mother himself: "You wanted to know how bad I was hit, well, here goes, stand by!! one piece of shrapnel in left elbow, another piece in my right leg, last and not least—no left leg. Better let that idea of me getting married ride for a while. Don't worry cause I'm getting along swell. Lately I've been tearing up & down the ward in a wheelchair—whee! Bye now and take it E-Z, love and kisses Jack."

Most men on Iwo Jima felt a dull, bitter loathing for the enemy who inflicted such horrors upon them. Lt. Robert Schless expressed uncommonly sensitive emotions when he wrote to his wife, Shirley: "I was never once sore at the Japs. The more I learned of them, the more I could understand their motives. They were scrupulously clean, despite living underground. They carried photos of their families with them, and those families had a nobility which would be difficult to match. Many of their personal objects—their fans and swords and other things—are of great beauty. If Japan is at present going through a Victorian period of bad taste nevertheless there is taste among all her people. I believe the symbol of the rising sun has for them a great beauty of a pristine, virginal nature."

More commonplace was the attitude of the group of Marines whom eighteen-year-old Corporal Jerry Copeland encountered poised over an oil drum in which they were boiling Japanese skulls, which earned them $125 apiece. Copeland, who described himself as a San Francisco juvenile delinquent until he joined the Marines, had loved training on Parris Island, South Carolina, and was among the few who now found the experience of combat rewarding: "The first guy I ever killed, I got so much joy, so much satisfaction out of it . . . Flame-thrower's great to get guys out a cave, but boy, the guy who's got to approach the cave has a problem. You don't move too well with a flame-thrower."

In the first days of March, just as MacArthur's men were completing the capture of Manila, the Marines on Iwo Jima started direct attacks on the positions of Harunori Ohkoshi's naval group. Incoming fire was devastating. Ohkoshi and his companions found that in daylight they dared not raise their eyes to the weapon-slits of their bunkers. They were forced to fire their heavy machine gun blind, pulling a lanyard from beneath. After two days of American assaults, the navy men were ordered to withdraw into the dense network of tunnels and bunkers at the summit of the position. On 8 March, they were told that they were to sortie for a mass night attack, to regain the lost summit of Mount Suribachi.

It was plain from the outset that this was suicidal, and initiated by officers disobeying the stringent orders of General Kuribayashi. Their objective was more than two miles distant. Every Japanese movement provided the Americans with the opportunity for a massacre. Yet some of the navy's officers, knowing they must face death anyway, chose to indulge themselves by doing so on their own terms. They sprang from tunnel entrances at the head of their men, into the path of overwhelming fire. Darkness offered the Japanese no protection, for flames and American flares lit the battlefield. By the time Ohkoshi and his group emerged, the ground was piled with bodies. "The attack was a shambles," said the young sailor. "The whole thing never had a chance." Not every Japanese sought martyrdom eagerly: "We had to push a lot of men out of the tunnels, because they knew what was waiting for them on top." Around eight hundred navy personnel perished, for negligible American losses.

One senior soldier, Lt. Col. Baron Takeichi Nishi, tried in vain to dissuade the naval officers. Nishi was a legendary figure who had won an equestrian gold medal at the 1932 Los Angeles Olympic Games. Ohkoshi had glimpsed him a couple of times before the battle, riding by on a horse as he and his comrades dug trenches. Now, Nishi commented contemptuously on the navy men's futile action: "Anyone who wants to die can do it any time. It's only fifty metres to the American positions." Uncertainty shrouded Nishi's end. Some said that he shot himself, others that he was led into an attack by his orderly, having been blinded by blast. He left behind a fine collection of photographs of himself in Olympic playboy days, beside such Hollywood stars as Douglas Fairbanks, Mary Pickford and Spencer Tracy.

Though most of the navy men died running forward towards the American positions, a few survivors remained in the open. Harunori Ohkoshi and his group crawled some three hundred yards, inch by inch, attempting to regain their tunnels under the American fire raking the battlefield. At intervals the seventeen-year-old called softly to those behind him, checking who was left. Each time, fewer voices answered, as machine guns silenced them one by one. Dawn found Ohkoshi pinned down with just three others, amid a jumble of Japanese bodies. They adopted desperate expedients, smearing handfuls of human debris onto themselves to simulate convincing corpses. "The blood and guts of the dead kept us alive," said Ohkoshi. They lay in the open for forty-eight hours, in plain sight of the Americans. When their water was gone, they sucked blood. Days and nights were alike punctuated by the screams of dying Japanese, their cries of "Mummy, mummy!" or the names of loved ones. The noise of firing was deafening, scarcely ever stilled. At last, American activity in their vicinity seemed to slacken. The battle had moved on. The four Japanese crept back into the tunnel system.

Underground, they found a few medics and other survivors such as themselves, perhaps fifty men in all. Day after day they lay in stifling heat, and at night crawled out to search the battlefield around their positions for water bottles or food. A steady trickle of men failed to return from these scavenging missions, having been shot by the enemy, or fallen foul of booby-trap wires. A core of survivors like Ohkoshi lingered, however, long after the Americans declared victory, and most had left the island.

By the time K Company of the 3/9th Marines reached Iwo's north beach, about 50 men remained of the 230 who had landed less than three weeks earlier. On the afternoon of 10 March, when some had thought their battle over, they were ordered to carry out a local reconnaissance. Sgt. Gordon Schisley said to Patrick Caruso: "You know, Lieutenant, the men who are here now have come all the way. Wouldn't it be hell if someone were to get hurt on a little patrol like this?" Caruso nodded. His two platoons advanced perhaps a hundred cautious yards without glimpsing the enemy. Each cave mouth they passed received a flamethrower's kiss. The sun shone brilliantly, and there was a welcome breeze off the ocean. Suddenly, they were under fire. Caruso's men scrabbled for cover. The battalion commander called on the radio: "King 2, bring the men back." But Caruso could not withdraw until he could pass word to his scattered Marines. Sergeant Schisley fell, hit in the neck. Sergeant Henry, a Nebraskan who saved every cent of pay for improvements to his farm, collapsed. Caruso was shocked by the anguished look of appeal on Henry's face as he died. Everywhere men were being hit, and soon the lieutenant himself fell with a bullet in the leg. He crawled behind a rock, and was eventually evacuated with the other survivors. His combat career had lasted twelve days. The 3/9th Marines lost all twenty-two company officers who originally landed on Iwo Jima. Ten were killed, the rest wounded.

U.S. headquarters declared organised resistance on Iwo Jima ended on 14 March. Most surviving Japanese were thereafter fugitives like Harunori Ohkoshi rather than combatants, though they continued to harass American mopping-up operations with small arms and occasional wild, hopeless charges. In his underground headquarters, General Kuribayashi found time to send a signal to the general staff in Tokyo, offering advice gleaned from the Iwo Jima experience: "However strongly you build beach defences, they will be destroyed by battleship bombardment. It is better to erect dummy defences on the shoreline. It is essential to maintain eavesdropping watches, since the enemy communicates in plain language. The violence of enemy fire is beyond description. It can take more than ten hours for a junior officer to move a single kilometre to pass information. Where telephone links are used, cables must be buried. Radios should be located at a distance from headquarters, to protect these from bombardment following enemy radio location. Enemy headquarters are often noisy, and sometimes use lights at night. Defence against armour is critically important—anti-tank ditches must be dug. It is essential to stockpile ammunition, grenades and mortar bombs on isolated islands which are to be defended. The enemy's ground control of aircraft is very good. Snipers should regard flame-thrower operators as priority targets."

Neither then nor later did the Americans perceive much useful to be learned from Iwo Jima and its notorious killing grounds—Turkey Knob, the Amphitheater, Charlie-Dog Ridge, the Meat Grinder—save about man's capacity to inflict and endure suffering. The experience renewed the usual fierce criticism from the army about the Marines' allegedly sacrificial tactics. Maj.-Gen. Joseph Swing of the 11th Airborne Division, for instance, wrote an angry letter home on 8 March in response to rumours that Nimitz rather than MacArthur was to command the invasion of Japan. Swing regarded the admiral as standard-bearer for Marine methods which he held in low esteem: "It makes me sick when I read about the casualties on Iwo Jima. It can be done more scientifically. We laugh at the fruitless method of the Jap in his banzai attacks and yet allow that fanatic"—he referred to Lt.-Gen. Holland Smith of the Marines—"to barge in using up men as if they were a dime a dozen."

There were those, including Holland Smith, who persuaded themselves that a longer preliminary bombardment of Iwo Jima would have made the early days, especially, less costly. There was agreement that more heavy artillery was needed, especially eight-inch howitzers. Yet there is no reason to suppose that any alternative tactical method would have changed anything, in that close and densely fortified area. Many Marines argued that the only effective means of shortening the battle would have been to pump poison gas into the Japanese underground complexes. They derided the brass in Washington for being squeamish about such methods. Even Nimitz later expressed regret that gas was not used.

Though it often seemed to the Americans that the battle would never end, they prevailed at last, occupying the entire wretched island. A Marine had fallen for every Japanese, a most unusual balance of loss in Pacific battles. On 26 March, some 350 Japanese staged a final banzai charge in the north-west. Startled Americans found themselves fighting hand-to-hand with swordsmen. The assault was broken up, the Japanese killed. General Kuribayashi emerged from his headquarters bunker one night, marvelling to see that the trees and foliage which had once covered the hillside were all gone, leaving only blackened rock and scorched stumps. He sent a last signal to Horie, his staff officer on neighbouring Chichi Jima: "It's five days since we ate or drank, but our spirits are still high, and we shall fight to the last." Then, on 27 March, he and his staff killed themselves. The senior naval officer, Admiral Toshinosuke Ichimaru, walked at the head of sixty men into the path of American machine guns outside his cave—yet survived, probably to his own disappointment. Having failed to get the enemy to kill him, he shot himself soon after Kuribayashi's death.

In the struggle for Iwo Jima 6,821 U.S. Marines and 363 navy men died. A further 17,372 were wounded. Such a toll would have seemed negligible to the Red Army, fighting the Germans in Europe, but represented an extraordinary intensity of loss for a battle conducted over an area only a third the size of Manhattan Island. More than one in three of the Marines committed became casualties, including nineteen of the original twenty-four battalion commanders. In Maj. Albert Arsenault's battalion, 760 men were killed or wounded. The 5th Division had required twenty-two transports to bring its men to the island, but was carried away in just eight. All but a few hundred of the 21,000 defenders perished.

It was six weeks before American troops addressed themselves systematically to clearing the caves in which such survivors as Harunori Ohkoshi clung on. First, they tried teargas. Then they sent captured Japanese to broadcast by loudspeaker, who sometimes called on men by name to come out. One POW approached Ohkoshi's tunnel entrance, bearing water and chocolate, only to be shot by the occupants. "We were doing him a favour," claimed Ohkoshi laconically. "His honour was lost." On 7 May, in bright sunshine, men of the army's 147th Infantry poured a hideous cocktail. They pumped 700 gallons of salt water into one of the biggest tunnel complex entrances, then added 110 gallons of gasoline and 55 of oil. The deadly flow, ignited by flamethrower, raced through the underground passages, starting a string of ammunition fires, incinerating many Japanese and causing others to kill themselves amid the choking, clogging smoke. Some men embraced each other, then pulled pins on grenades held between their bodies. Ohkoshi finished off several dying men with his pistol. Yet after three months of subterranean animal existence, he decided that he himself would rather die in the sun. The Americans had sealed the tunnel entrances, but by frenzied labour some Japanese clawed passages to the surface. Ohkoshi was the first to burst forth, like a shaggy, blackened mole. He was at once seen and shot by an American, and fell writhing with two bullets in the leg. His surviving companions were more fortunate—or not, as the case might be—and were captured uninjured. Nursing shame and exhaustion, they were taken away into captivity. When Ohkoshi saw his own features in a mirror on Guam, he did not recognise the skeletal ruin of a human being which he represented. A U.S. officer's report on the episode concluded dryly: "Fifty-four were eventually taken into custody with some difficulty. Two of these subsequently committed suicide."

Captain Kouichi Ito, an army officer who remained a lifelong student of Japan's wartime campaigns, believed that Iwo Jima was the best-conducted defensive operation of the Japanese war, much more impressive militarily than the defence of Guadalcanal, or the subsequent action in which he himself participated on Okinawa. Yet it would be mistaken to suppose that most Japanese defenders of the island found their experience, or their sacrifice, acceptable. A survivor from the 26th Tank Regiment, Lieutenant Yamasaki, wrote afterwards to the widow of his commanding officer, in a letter which reflected a sense of the futility of what he and his comrades had endured: "In ancient times our ancestors said: '*Bushido*, the way of the warrior, is to die.' This may have sounded wonderful to knights of old, but represents too easy a path. For both the living and the dead Iwo Jima was, I think, the worst of battlefields. Casual words about '*bushido*' did not apply, for modern war does not make matters so easy. Unfeeling metal is mightier than warriors' flesh. Where, when, how, who died nobody knew. They just fell by the wayside."

When Marine veterans got back to Hawaii, one group marched triumphantly down the street waving a Japanese skull and taunting local Japanese-Americans: "There's your uncle on the pole!" The experience of Iwo Jima had drained some survivors of all human sensitivity. Was the island worth the American blood sacrifice? Some historians highlight a simple statistic: more American aircrew landed safely on its airstrips in damaged or fuelless B-29s than Marines died in seizing it. This calculation of profit and loss, first offered after the battle to assuage public anger about the cost of taking Iwo Jima, ignores the obvious fact that, if the strips had not been there, fuel margins would have been increased, some aircraft would have reached the Marianas, some crews could have been rescued from the sea. Even if Iwo Jima had remained in Japanese hands, it could have contributed little further service to the homeland's air defence. The Americans made no important use of its bases for offensive operations.

Yet to say this is to ignore the fact that in every campaign in every war, sacrifices are routinely made that are out of all proportion to the significance of objectives. Unless Nimitz had made an implausible decision, to forgo land engagement while the army fought for the Philippines, to await the collapse of the enemy through bombing, blockade, industrial and human starvation, the assault on Iwo Jima was almost inevitable. Whether wisely or no, the enemy valued the island, and took great pains for its defence. It would have required a strategic judgement of remarkable forbearance to resist the urge to destroy the garrison of the rock, a rare solid foothold in the midst of the ocean. If some historians judge that America's warlords erred in taking Iwo Jima, the commitment seemed natural in the context of the grand design for America's assault on the Japanese homeland.

ELEVEN

Blockade: War Underwater

By early 1945, Japan's ability to provide raw materials for its industries, and even to feed itself, was fatally crippled. The nation could import by sea no more than a fraction of its requirements. An invisible ring of steel extended around the waters of the home islands, created by the submarines of the U.S. Navy. In the course of 1944, a large part of Japan's merchant shipping, and especially of its tanker fleet, was dispatched to the sea bottom by a force which gained less contemporary prominence, and indeed subsequent historical attention, than the Marines on Iwo Jima or Nimitz's carrier task groups. Yet it imposed economic strangulation on Japan in a fashion Germany's U-boats had been unable to inflict on Britain. An April report by MacArthur's staff concluded: "The entire question of Japanese merchant shipping requirements may soon be academic, if losses continue at anything like the present rate. That this possibility has occurred to the Japanese is indicated by a Tokyo broadcast on 17 February, in which the Japanese forces in China and other overseas garrisons were warned that they might have to operate without help from the homeland." Only 1.6 percent of the U.S. Navy's wartime strength—16,000 men—served in its submarines. Yet these accounted for 55 percent of all Japan's wartime shipping losses, 1,300 vessels including a battleship, eight carriers and eleven cruisers, a total of 6.1 million tons. The achievement of America's submarines reached its apogee in October 1944, when they sank 322,265 tons of enemy vessels.

For those who manned the navy's crowded, stinking underwater torpedo platforms, the exhilaration of hunting prey was matched by the terrors experienced when they themselves became the hunted. Cmdr. Richard O'Kane's experience of forty-eight hours off the Philippines in October 1944 was not untypical. His submarine, *Tang*, on its fifth war patrol, was operating alone in the Formosa Channel. Off Turnabout Island in the early hours of the twenty-fourth, first day of the Leyte Gulf battle and fourth after MacArthur's landing, he spotted a Japanese reinforcement convoy: four freighters with planes on deck, a transport, a destroyer and some smaller escorts. In a few devastating minutes, O'Kane fired torpedoes which sank three freighters. The surviving freighter and destroyer closed on the surfaced submarine in an attempt to ram. *Tang* slipped between them—and the two Japanese ships collided. O'Kane fired four more torpedoes from his stern tubes, which missed, then cleared the area at full speed.

The next night, in the same hunting ground, he encountered the largest convoy he had ever seen, "a solid line of pips across the screen." An escort rashly switched on its searchlight, illuminating a transport. O'Kane sank this, together with a tanker which blew up, leaving the surviving vessels milling in chaos. Two hours after midnight, however, *Tang*'s luck changed drastically. One of its torpedoes fired at a transport ran amok, circled, and by fantastic ill-luck struck the surfaced submarine abreast of the aft torpedo room. Following the explosion, O'Kane himself and two sailors with him in the conning tower were thrown alive into the water, and retrieved by the Japanese. *Tang*, mortally damaged, plunged 180 feet to the sea bottom. The men in the hull somehow succeeded in closing the conning-tower hatch. Some thirty surviving officers and men reached the temporary safety of the forward torpedo room, where choking smoke from burning documents soon rendered half of them unconscious.

For the next four hours, Japanese escorts depth-charged ineffectually. At 0600, some men began to escape using Momsen Lung breathing apparatus, of whom eight reached the surface. Five were still clinging to a buoy when a Japanese ship picked them up four hours later. The surviving Americans were trussed and laid on deck, then kicked and clubbed by burnt and injured enemy sailors who had suffered grievously from their torpedoes. Statistics may help to explain such behaviour: in the course of the war 116,000 of 122,000 seamen serving Japan's pre-war merchant fleet were killed or wounded, most by American submarines. Yoshio Otsu, a survivor of a stricken merchantman, was enraged to find himself under fire from American planes: "Seeing no one on board, they strafed those in the water. The swine! Not satisfied with sinking the ship, they must kill those swimming in the sea! Was this being done by human beings? We were utterly helpless." Seven officers and seventy-one men were lost with *Tang*, which had accounted for 22,000 tons of Japanese shipping.

EVERY NATION'S soldiers instinctively believe that wars are won by engaging the armies of the enemy and seizing terrain. Yet the most critical single contribution to the American defeat of Japan was made far out of sight of any general, or indeed admiral. The Japanese empire was uniquely vulnerable to blockade. Its economy was dependent upon fuel and raw materials shipped from China, Malaya, Burma and the Netherlands East Indies. Yet, unlike the British, who faced a similar threat to their Atlantic lifeline, the Japanese failed to equip themselves with a credible anti-submarine force to defend their commerce. Here was one of the major causes of Japan's downfall. The admirals of the Imperial Navy fixed their minds almost exclusively upon power projection by surface and air forces. Vice-Admiral Inoue Shigeyoshi was one of the few pre-war Japanese naval officers who urged dismissing the concept of "decisive battle" between surface warships. Instead, he proposed planning for a submarine war against commerce, together with a long amphibious and air campaign in the central Pacific. His views were thrust aside. With extraordinary myopia, the Japanese failed to address the obvious likelihood that their enemies might also project naval power through a submarine offensive. Japan possessed only a tiny force of anti-submarine escorts, whose technology and tactics remained primitive.

At the outbreak of war, the United States possessed the finest submarines in the world, the 1,500-ton *Tambor* class, later refined as the *Gato* and *Balao* classes. These had air-conditioning—a priceless virtue in the tropics—a top speed close to twenty-one knots, a range of 10,000 miles, and the ability to crash-dive in thirty-five seconds. Yet for almost two torrid years their effectiveness was crippled: first, by chronic torpedo technical failure; second, by over-cautious commanders—30 percent were removed by the end of 1942; and third, by a doctrinal preoccupation with sinking enemy warships which almost matched that of the Japanese. Ronald Spector has remarked on the irony that the U.S., which joined World War I in large measure out of revulsion towards Germany's policy of unrestricted submarine warfare, entered World War II committed to wage such a campaign. Yet while the U.S. Navy had no moral scruple about sinking unarmed merchant ships, until relatively late in the war it regarded these as a lesser target priority than the Japanese fleet.

In February 1944, the U.S. Navy's submarine operational textbook *Current Doctrine* was extensively rewritten. The new manual devoted much more attention than earlier editions to the blockade of commerce. Yet a remarkable number of its pages still concerned procedures for submarines operating in support of surface warships, in a fleet action. The cult of the "decisive battle" exercised a febrile influence on American as well as Japanese naval imaginations. "It is the opinion of most submarine officers that any combatant ship is worth a full nest torpedo salvo," declared page 51 of the 1944 *Doctrine*—implying that a merchant ship might not be. To the end of the war, submarine captains' accounts of their successes dwelt most proudly upon sinkings of warships, rather than cargo vessels. Only in 1944, after more than two years of American involvement in the war, were submarine captains explicitly directed to target enemy tankers.

Even at this relatively late stage, *Doctrine* included oddly anachronistic passages: "In battle, submarines may, through threat or actual attack, serve as the anvil against which own battle line may attack enemy battle line." Here was an injunction which sounds more relevant to Nelson's navy than Nimitz's. *Doctrine*'s foreword asserted grudgingly: "During probable long periods before fleet action occurs, submarines may usefully be employed in the following tasks: (a) Patrol (including commerce destruction) (b) Scouting (c) Screening," and so on. Yet, while America's carrier-led surface forces turned the tide of the Pacific war at Midway and the Coral Sea, then progressively destroyed the Japanese fleet, it was the undersea flotillas which struck at the heart of Japan's war-making capacity. If the U.S. Navy had addressed itself earlier in the war to systematic blockade, Japan's collapse might have been significantly accelerated. As it was, only in 1944 did America's commerce campaign begin in earnest, after torpedo shortcomings had been belatedly addressed, and deployments were better directed.

This became the submarines' year of triumph. In 520 war patrols, 6,092 torpedoes were fired. The Japanese merchant fleet lost 212,907 tons of shipping in July; 245,348 in August; 181 363 in September. Sinkings declined to 103,836 tons in December, only because the enemy began to run out of ships to attack. In 1944 as a whole, American submarines dispatched over 600 Japanese ships, totalling 2.7 million tons—more than the combined totals for 1942 and 1943. Japan's bulk imports fell by 40 percent. A hundred American submarines operated out of Pearl Harbor and advanced bases at Eniwetok, Majuro and Guam, a further forty from Australia. Pearl's boats worked patrol zones around Japan and the Philippines with such nicknames as "Hit Parade," '*Marus*' Morgue" and "Convoy College." Fremantle- and Brisbane-based boats operated in the South China Sea and off the Netherlands East Indies.

Submariners complained that the navy library at Pearl would never lend its best movies to their boats, because these were either kept out for the sixty-day duration of a patrol, or never returned at all. In the course of the war, Germany lost 781 submarines, Japan 128. By contrast, the Japanese navy sank only 41 American submarines, 18 percent of those which saw combat duty. Six more were lost accidentally on Pacific patrols. Even these relatively modest casualties meant that 22 percent of all American sailors who experienced submarine operations perished—375 officers and 3,131 enlisted men—the highest loss rate of any branch of the wartime U.S. armed forces. Yet there was never a shortage of volunteers for the submarine service, with its extraordinary pride and buccaneering spirit. It was not merely extra money—a 50 percent increase on base pay, matching the premium paid to aviators—which kept crews coming. It was their just conviction that they were an elite. It is a tribute to the quality of personnel that, by August 1945, almost half of all surviving enlisted men from the December 1941 U.S. submarine service had been commissioned.

The long passage from home base to a patrol area, cruising on the surface at fifteen knots, was seldom hazardous, and gave crews a chance to shake down. A quarter of the eighty-odd sailors in a boat on each mission were newcomers, replacing experienced hands sent on leave, transferred to training duties or assigned to new commissions. Freshmen had to master the delicate art of using submarine toilets inside a pressure hull: "It was hard to flush below a hundred feet and keep a clean face," wrote one. Even submariners sometimes got seasick, as did aviators whom they rescued. Overcrowding was worst in the early days of a patrol, because every square inch of space, including sleeping spaces and shower stalls, was crammed with supplies. Submarine food was famously the best in the navy, and some boats carried a baker as well as a cook. Crews needed every small indulgence that could be provided, to compensate for the discomforts of two months aboard a giant sealed cigar tube packed with machinery, fuel and explosives, dominated by the stench of the "three Fs"—Feet, Farts and Fannies. "We were essentially a steel bubble, with only one small hole left for the furiously probing fingers of the sea—the conning tower hatch," in the words of a submarine officer.

Once they reached their appointed operational areas, boats awaited either radio intelligence of an enemy shipping movement, or a chance visual sighting. American submarines in the Pacific not only spent almost every night on the surface, but could also take risks in daylight. The Japanese never matched the Allies' formidable radar-equipped anti-submarine air forces. "We had almost disdain for the threat which aircraft posed for submarines," wrote an American captain. "This was more a mark of Japan's inferiority in anti-submarine warfare, of her poor airborne electronics, than a tribute to our boldness."

Japanese pilot Masashiko Ando agreed. He flew anti-submarine patrols out of Cam Ranh Bay, Indochina. Only once in all their years of patrolling did his crew sight an American submarine. Flying at 6,000 feet off the coast of Indonesia one day in May 1945, they glimpsed a wake far below. As they descended, with intense excitement they identified a submarine proceeding heedless on the surface. They fell steeply from the sky behind it, closing fast until the conning-tower lookouts spotted them, leapt for the hatches, and began a crash dive. At 600 feet, Ando released his depth charge. Triumphantly, he and his crew watched a great spout of water ascend from the explosion point, close to where the submarine had disappeared. They flew home to report that they had achieved a sinking. Only after the war did they learn that the American vessel had suffered merely superficial damage. This was a characteristic experience for Japanese anti-submarine patrols.

On the boats, hour after hour, often day after day, lookouts scanned empty horizons, while in the hull the crew went about their domestic routines. Watchkeepers at the hydroplanes maintained trim, technicians performed maintenance, off-duty men played chess or cribbage, or more often slept. Even when there was no enemy in sight, conning a submarine was a relentlessly demanding activity, especially in shallow waters. Diving officers and planesmen ended their watches exhausted by the strain of maintaining the boat's delicate balance in swells or stiff currents. In the engine and battery compartments, amazing feats of improvisation were performed by electricians and engineers. When *Pampanito* sprung a "squeaking leak" in her forward trim tank, two men made a hazardous entry into the tank. A third, an amateur diver, finally repaired the leak underwater using a face mask. Without such ingenuity, on a sixty-day patrol glitches and breakdowns were liable to render a boat toothless, or even doomed.

Informality was the rule in all things save operational disciplines. Men manned their stations in shorts, affected beards if they chose. They ate when they could, or when they felt like it: submarines operated an "open icebox" policy. There was a little authorised drinking. Each boat was issued six bottles of medicinal alcohol, which one unpopular captain reserved for himself. Some crewmen smuggled liquor aboard, or made their own. *Pampanito* suffered an engine-room fire when a raisin-jack still overturned. Most radio operators monitored the daily news transmitted in Morse by RCA, and compiled a ship's newspaper. Some captains imposed their own whimsical disciplines: for instance, Sam Dealey of *Harder* prohibited pin-ups, and would allow no "dirty talk" among his crew.

After hours or days of monotony and discomfort, routine would suddenly be interrupted by the heart-stopping moan of the klaxon, "*Aa-oo-gah, aa-oo-gah*," and the broadcast order: "Clear the bridge! Dive! Dive!" War is full of exclamation marks, and submariners experienced more of them than most. A sudden descent might be prompted by a sighting of an enemy aircraft, or a glimpse of funnel smoke. Since a submarine could move more swiftly than most convoys, it was normal procedure to shadow enemy merchant vessels until they could be engaged in darkness. Once night fell, it was often possible to attack on the surface, the preferred option. A submarine manoeuvred to achieve a position ahead of the target, which was tracked on the control-room TDC—Torpedo Data Computer, an early analogue computer resembling a vertical pinball machine.

In a submerged attack, the captain bent over the periscope lens below the conning tower, while clusters of sweat-streaked figures watched their dials in the control room, calling off details of target and orders for the approach: "Angle on the bow, starboard thirty-five. Mark the range! Down periscope! All ahead two-thirds! Steer two six five." Submarine captains were taught: surprise is fundamental. Use the periscope as little as possible, and remember that the higher your underwater speed, the more conspicuous a periscope's wake. Always pick a ship, rather than "firing into the brown" at a convoy or formation. Set a salvo of torpedoes to run in a spread which will cover 80 percent of a vessel's length. The straighter the firing angle, the better the chance of a hit. The bane of every attacking skipper was a target's sudden alteration of course, which was why every prudent surface ship zigzagged. So poor were Japanese sonar and radar, however, that it was rare for an escort to interrupt an attack before it was launched.

It was a curiosity of the war at sea that the Japanese, so often extravagantly bold, showed themselves far less aggressive submariners than the Americans. Many Japanese boats were diverted from attacking U.S. ships to transporting supplies to beleaguered Pacific garrisons. The Imperial Navy had better torpedoes than the Americans, yet its operations against the USN were seldom better than halfhearted. By contrast, many of Nimitz's captains were tigers. America's submarine admirals had no patience with timidity. They sacked every captain who seemed to lack aggression, which meant those who came home without sinking ships. In 1943, 25 out of 178 skippers were dismissed for the cardinal sin of "non-productivity." Even in 1944, 35 out of 250 were transferred out.

Crews held good commanders in deep respect. Radioman Artie Akers of *Angelfish* wrote: "I don't believe that any officer in the armed forces has a more difficult assignment than a good submarine commander." Few captains achieved more than two hours' consecutive sleep in operational areas. A patrol skipper had absolute responsibility for the key decisions of when, where and how to attack. Akers's first two commanding officers, pre-war Annapolis graduates, survived only one patrol apiece before being relieved. He wrote of the second: "This man seemed to know how to attack. He did not seem to be scared. He simply would not attack." He held his submarine submerged and passive, even when sonar indicated a tanker or freighter above—and was sacked on returning to Pearl. An excess of imagination was thought a handicap to good submarine commanders, as indeed it is to all successful warriors.

By 1944, many attacks were carried out by American wolfpacks, three or more boats working in concord. When this technique was first introduced, few captains relished the sacrifice of independence which it entailed. Yet once the Japanese abandoned lone sailings and dispatched almost all ships in convoy, submariners recognised that group tactics, so skilfully exploited by the Germans since 1942, were the logical response. In the Pacific, Cmdr. George Donaho's pack eliminated 64,456 tons of enemy shipping during a single patrol in the autumn of 1944. Of this total, *Spadefish* alone accounted for 26,812 tons, sinking three or four merchantmen from one convoy.

A key factor in submarine operations, as in so much else, was the flood of information gathered by intelligence, through enemy signals decrypted at the magnificent Naval Joint Intelligence Center on Hawaii—"the Salt Mines," or "the Zoo," as it was known to its 1,800 staff. By 1944, working seven days a week, in three shifts around the clock, JICPOA was monitoring and translating a high proportion of key Japanese naval and military signal traffic. Most movements of enemy warships and merchantmen were known at Pearl within hours, and were passed to American boats within range. The Japanese submarine *I-29* provided a spectacular example of target tracking. In July 1944, U.S. signals intelligence located *I-29*, on the last leg of a long passage from Germany carrying scientific instruments, moving from Singapore through the South China Sea. Three American submarines took up ambush positions, and *I-29* was dispatched by *Sawfish*. "It was an impersonal war," wrote Cmdr. Pete Galantin, skipper of *Halibut*. "Naval warfare had evolved to the point that sailors no longer saw their enemy as people; they saw only the steel or aluminum vehicles in which their enemy sailed or flew, trying to bring their own weapons to bear . . . In war at sea, only rarely does one see the human flotsam marking the scene of battle: the oil-soaked survivor, the burned seaman, the scalded boiler tender, the drowned soldier."

After the surge as a salvo of torpedoes left the tubes, there was an agonising wait, an officer monitoring a stopwatch, until crews heard either the thud of distant explosions, the horrible sounds of a ship breaking up underwater, or the silence which indicated failure. By 1944, American submarines were sinking a ship for every ten torpedoes they fired. Old compressed-air types travelled at forty-five knots. Their Mark 18 electric successors were slower, but emitted no telltale streams of bubbles. Occasionally, the firing submarine experienced the nightmare of a "hot run," a live torpedo jammed in its tube, which demanded immense delicacy to unload.

When an attack went right, it was extraordinary how much havoc a single boat could wreak. For instance, on 8 January 1945, *Barb*'s Cmdr.

Eugene "Lucky" Fluckey tracked a big convoy for five hours in the north Formosa Strait. After destroying several cargo ships in his first attack, he hastened preparations for a second: "Can feel aggressiveness surging through my veins, since the escorts are more scared than we are," wrote Fluckey. ". . . Destroyer suddenly turned towards us! . . . Aggressiveness evaporated. Assumed deep submergence at 140 feet." *Barb* finally surfaced to launch a second salvo, with Fluckey on the bridge: "Three hits observed, followed by a stupendous earth-shaking eruption. This far surpassed Hollywood, and was one of the biggest explosions of the war. The rarefaction following the first pressure wave was breathtaking. A high vacuum resulted in the boat. Personnel in the control room said they felt as if they were being sucked up the hatch." A little cluster of men on the bridge gazed at the carnage they had wreaked upon the Japanese: "We alternately gawked and ducked."

After an attack, a submarine either fled at full speed or, if in danger of being pinpointed by escorts, went deep. A destroyer could move at least fifteen knots faster than a submarine using its diesels on the surface, more against a submerged vessel dependent on electric motors. Submarine captains were told: never try to fight it out on the surface. A single manually trained deck gun was woefully inadequate against almost any Japanese warship. The slightest hull damage could make it impossible to submerge. In September 1944, the surfaced *Growler* launched torpedoes head-to-head with a Japanese destroyer attacking at full speed—the chanciest shot of all, because angles were so tight. Miraculously, the submarine scored a hit, and the Japanese warship sank two hundred yards short of the American one. Navy opinion held that *Growler*'s captain had taken a suicidal risk. If the "fish" had missed, his boat would have been rammed seconds later.

Being depth-charged was a terrifying experience for all those who experienced it, hearing detonations unleashed by warships which might spend hours groping for their unseen victim. The Japanese, however, never addressed the critical issue, that of throwing charges in geometrically schemed patterns. An American boat would seek refuge far beneath the surface, if possible in a friendly thermal which deflected sonar signals, with all non-essential equipment closed down to reduce the submarine's sound profile. Without air-conditioners, the atmosphere in the hull grew relentlessly more foul. Perspiration poured down men's bodies. Under attack, more than anything Pete Galantin found himself craving a cold shower.

A pattern of charges sent dull thuds echoing through the boat: *brr-oomp, brr-oomp, brr-oomp*. The radioman of *Angelfish*, Artie Akers, recorded that during ten war patrols he was depth-charged forty times, albeit sometimes briefly. When obliged to stay deep for long periods, crews scattered air-purifying powder on bunks, a feeble means of mitigating the stench. Vice-Admiral Charles Lockwood, submarine commander at Pearl, was enraged by a government official's indiscretion to the press in 1943, asserting that American boats cared nothing for Japanese depth-charging, because the enemy always used shallow settings, which exploded above their quarry. Thereafter, claimed Lockwood, the Japanese began to detonate charges deeper, and sank more boats.

Under depth-charging, which often continued for hours, submariners envisaged with hideous clarity the implosion of their frail hull, the crushing of the thin steel that held out the ocean. The father of a newly joined *Halibut* officer had once visited the boat at San Francisco, and observed sagely that he thought "submarine duty would be a good experience for a young man." A few weeks later, as chlorine gas leaked through the boat during a depth-charge attack, the young man wryly repeated his parent's words to the control room. Pete Galantin wrote: "Heads ached, lungs burned, and eyes smarted from the hours trapped in stagnant, foul air." Men sniffed for the scent of burning insulation in the vital electrical control cubicle, sought to guard against leaks of oil or air from the hull which might provide deadly clues for the enemy. When a depth charge exploded nearby, the shock rendered a boat's interior a shambles of falling cork, loose gear, sprung pipes, with oil or water spurting forth until leaks could be staunched.

If a charge came closer than that, there was simply a devastating crash as the hull burst open, the sea surged in, and the crew experienced a few seconds of horror before oblivion overtook them. The crews of stricken submarines were seldom granted an opportunity to escape. When they were, some declined to take it. In a legendary 1943 episode, Cmdr. John Cromwell refused to quit his boat, *Sculpin*, lying fatally damaged on the surface. A second officer, Ensign Fiedler, sat down at the wardroom table and began to lay out a solitaire hand. In a manner a Japanese would have respected, Cromwell told shipmates: "I can't go with you. I know too much." As the boat foundered, forty-two others from *Sculpin* were picked up by an enemy destroyer. Most of those men survived the war as prisoners, but others were less fortunate. Four submariners who swam from a sinking boat to reach the shore at Robaloto in the Philippines were summarily executed by their Japanese captors.

As always in war, luck was a decisive factor in submariners' survival. William Soczek served nine Pacific patrols, first as fire controlman, then as chief of boat on *Growler*, before being transferred ashore. *Growler* was lost soon after. A seaman on *Trout* became due for Stateside leave. When he received a letter from his wife demanding a divorce, however, he chose to stay with the boat—and perished when it was sunk on its next patrol.

Seawolf, one of the most famous and successful of all U.S. submarines, was lost with all hands on 3 October 1944, after an attack by an American destroyer.

The overwhelming majority of submarines sunk met their fates west of the Philippines or around Japan, in the sea-lanes where they engaged shipping. Retribution by enemy escorts was not the only hazard crews faced. On 31 October 1944 off western Luzon, *Guitarro* torpedoed an ammunition ship "which must have gone in the air almost as far as Manila." Nineteen hundred yards away, the submarine was hurled aside by blast and driven fifty feet underwater, with vents springing and fuel oil spraying through the boat's working spaces. Several boats were sunk in the same fashion as *Seawolf*, by "friendly fire" from U.S. ships or aircraft. Some grounded in shallow water, as did *Darter* following its triumph against Kurita's fleet during the Leyte Gulf battle. The boat was scuttled after its crew was rescued by *Dace*. Others experienced horrors in minefields. Manuel Mendez of *Pampanito* said: "Many will tell you that depth-charging is the most frightening experience, but unless you have found yourself submerged in a minefield and heard the cable lines scraping along the hull, you haven't lived." *Harder*, commanded by the legendary Texan Sam Dealey, was sunk by a Japanese patrol boat on 24 August 1944, after sinking sixteen Japanese ships totalling 54,000 tons. The fate of some lost boats was never known.

Salmon defied the odds off Kyushu on the night of 30 October 1944, and miraculously survived. After torpedoing a tanker, the submarine was crippled by depth charges, and descended five hundred feet before her dive could be checked. The captain decided the boat must take its chance on the surface. At first they found the surrounding sea empty, the nearest enemy vessel 7,000 yards away. The submarine's crew worked furiously in the darkness to plug holes and pump the bilges. After almost four hours, an enemy frigate approached. *Salmon* raked the Japanese with fire from its deck gun before escaping into a rain squall. Having radioed for aid, with the help of nearby sister boats and air cover, the submarine eventually reached Saipan.

A TRAGIC side effect of the submarine war was that it cost the lives of around 10,000 Allied prisoners, indeed perhaps as many as one-third of all those who perished in captivity. Nimitz's captains had no means of identifying transports carrying POWs, on passage to become slave labourers in the Japanese home islands, though in the latter part of the war Magic decrypts did indicate that certain convoys were carrying prisoners. The

U.S. Navy adopted a ruthless view, that destruction of the enemy must take priority over any attempt to safeguard POW lives. It is hard to see how commanders could have done otherwise: if the Japanese had perceived that prison ships were spared, they would certainly have started to carry Allied personnel as hostages. Most of the hapless victims simply vanished, their fates unknown to their attackers. In a few cases, however, there were survivors to tell terrible stories. The Japanese guard commander on the old tramp *Shin'yo Maru* told prisoners being transported from Mindanao that if the ship was attacked, he would kill them all. On 7 September 1944, *Shin'yo Maru* was indeed sunk by the submarine *Paddle*. As promised, guards mowed down all those who tried to flee the wreck. Some twenty POWs were mistakenly rescued by Japanese craft picking up their own people, but when the prisoners were taken aboard another vessel, each in turn was shot. One man jumped overboard and got ashore on Mindanao, as did a handful of others from the wreck, who were cared for by local people until picked up by *Narwhal*.

Two 10,000-ton freighters were carrying 1,800 British and 718 Australian POWs in a convoy from Singapore when one was sunk by the submarine *Sealion* on 12 September 1944. On the sinking vessel and in the water afterwards, some prisoners seized the opportunity to kill such Japanese as they could lay hands on. Their behaviour was shown to be prescient when Japanese escorts returned to pick up their own survivors, abandoning the prisoners to drown. "Gentlemen, I am sorry," a Japanese officer told his desperate neighbours in the water before he himself accepted rescue. "This is the way of my people. May you be spared." Next night, *Pampanito* sank a tanker and the second freighter. Six hundred more prisoners were left in the sea, dying in scores by the hour. An Australian was deeply moved to hear a cluster of British feebly singing "Rule, Britannia, Britannia rules the waves!" as they waited their turn to perish.

Three nights later, *Pampanito* returned to the area, and glimpsed a cluster of men on a raft. Assuming they were Japanese, the boat closed in to collect a sample captive for intelligence purposes. Confronted instead by Allied prisoners in the most desperate state, the Americans picked up seventy-three, radioed *Sealion* to join the rescue, and headed for Saipan: "It was heartbreaking to leave so many dying men behind," said the skipper. Thirty-two more POWs were recovered by the second submarine, of whom seven died on the passage to Saipan. The oddest feature of these rescue operations was that the U.S. submarines made no attempt to provide food or water for the men whom they were obliged to leave in the sea. Perhaps it was thought that quick deaths were more merciful. Of 1,518 prisoners who left Singapore, just 159 survived. It is hard to regard the

POWs' fate as anything save a tragedy of war, compounded by the customary inhumanity of the Japanese.

GOING HOME at the end of a patrol, most submarine captains allowed their tired, pallid crews to sunbathe on deck. At Pearl, the much-beloved Admiral Lockwood, "Prince Charley," personally greeted each of the boats under his command when it returned from patrol, while a band on the dockside played "Happy Days Are Here Again." Crews clambered a little unsteadily ashore. After something between five and ten Pacific war patrols, most of those who survived were transferred to less demanding Atlantic postings, or to shore jobs. Those who landed at Pearl and were destined to sail again retired to the Royal Hawaiian Hotel at Waikiki Beach for R and R. After a week or two ashore, replenishment and maintenance, they went back to do it all again.

"By the fall of 1944," wrote Cmdr. Pete Galantin, "the mood in headquarters at Pearl was almost euphoric." In November, patrol skippers found the supply of targets shrinking, but submarines continued to wreak devastation upon such ships as they met. On the sixth, a four-boat wolfpack attacked the heavy cruiser *Kumano*, escorting a convoy to Japan. *Guitarro* fired nine torpedoes and scored three hits. Two further torpedoes from *Bream* exploded against the cruiser's hull, as did three more from other submarines. The big ship was able to beach herself on Luzon, where she was finished off by carrier aircraft three weeks later. On 15 November, a wolfpack led by Cmdr. Charles Loughlin of *Queenfish* attacked a convoy transporting the Japanese 23rd Division from Manchuria to Luzon. One ship, carrying two battalions and the divisional artillery, was immediately sunk. Two days later, Loughlin's group again caught the same convoy in the Yellow Sea, sinking a second transport and damaging a tanker. Shortly afterwards, *Spadefish* hit an escort carrier, the 21,000-ton *Jinyo*, and watched her planes slide into the sea as she listed and foundered.

On 21 November, *Sealion* sank the battleship *Kongo* with a single torpedo hit. *Archerfish* was on lifeguard duty a hundred miles south of Tokyo Bay, when she was released for attack operations because no air force sorties were scheduled. The submarine promptly sighted and sank the aircraft carrier *Shinano*, a 59,000-ton converted battleship—of the same class as *Yamato* and *Musashi*—which had been commissioned only ten days earlier. The most successful of all Pacific submarines was *Flasher*, which achieved twenty-one sinkings, totalling over 100,000 tons. On its fifth war patrol in December 1944, it accounted for four tankers and two destroyers between the Philippines and Indochina. Each carried 100,000 barrels of oil. Only 300,000 barrels finally reached Japan that month. Thus, this one action by *Flasher* cut December's Japanese oil imports by two-thirds. On the same patrol, off Indochina on the night of 22 December, the submarine dispatched three more tankers. Such was the extraordinary impact of blockade.

Yet the campaign was now tailing off. This was not due to any decline in the intensity of submarine effort, but because the Japanese merchant fleet had shrunk so dramatically. Japan's commanders were unwilling to expose their remaining tonnage on suicidal deep-sea passages. "It had become an aviator's not a submariner's war," said Cmdr. Pete Galantin. The submarines had almost completed the isolation of Japan's home islands from her shrinking empire. Undersea craft could not operate in the shallow waters of the Yellow Sea and the Sea of Japan. Long-range Liberators and carrier aircraft took over the task of attacking Japanese shipping beyond reach of the submarines. The USAAF devoted only a small number of B-29 sorties to mining Japanese inshore waters, but these made an extraordinary impact. January 1945 became the first month for more than two years in which American planes sank more Japanese ships than did submarines.

It was the strong opinion of submarine officers that in the last months of the war the carrier armadas devoted excessive attention to impotent or immobilised Japanese warships, when they could more usefully have completed the destruction of the enemy's merchant fleet. Here was the U.S. Navy's old problem—an instinctive perception of a battle fleet as the foremost objective of any dashing commander, rather than dirty old coasters and tramp steamers, plying their frightened courses around the shores of Japan.

The Imperial Navy now lacked ability to influence the course of the war. The duration of Japan's resistance would be far more importantly affected by deprivation of fuel, food and raw materials. Only 4 percent of American naval air sorties were directed against merchant shipping, yet these destroyed 16 percent of Japanese merchant tonnage—an average of just nine sorties and four tons of bombs per thousand tons sunk. If American carriers had cruised south of Java and Sumatra, they might have achieved extraordinary results. That they did not do so reflected the preoccupation of Nimitz's commanders with engaging enemy warships and—in the last months of the war—hitting the Japanese home islands. It does not diminish the extraordinary wartime achievement of the U.S. Navy to assert that some of its admirals should have studied economics as well as tactics.

There were never more than fifty boats on operational duty in the Pacific at any one moment, of which twenty-two were on passage to or from their patrol areas. By comparison, the German navy at its zenith deployed over a hundred U-boats, and achieved peak sinkings in November 1942 of 636,907 tons of Allied shipping—106 vessels. This was far higher than the best American performance against the Japanese, yet the Allies were better able to sustain their losses. When the war was over, Japan's ruined cities constituted a more conspicuous testament to Allied destructive power than did the mass of her shipping invisible on the ocean floor. Yet maritime losses brought the Japanese economy to the brink of collapse even before the USAAF's bomber armadas began their work in earnest. The U.S. Strategic Bombing Survey, which was unlikely to reach conclusions biased in favour of the navy, declared in its 1946 report: "The war against shipping was the most decisive single factor in the collapse of the Japanese economy and logistic support of Japanese military and naval power. Submarines accounted for the majority of vessel sinkings." No other combatant force as small as the U.S. Navy's submarine flotillas and their 16,000 men achieved a comparable impact upon the war anywhere in the world.

TWELVE

Burning a Nation: LeMay

1. Superfortresses

POPULAR PERCEPTIONS of the Second World War identify the August 1945 atomic bomb attacks on Japan as a unique horror. Yet the fate of Hiroshima and Nagasaki can only properly be understood against the background of the air campaign which preceded the nuclear explosions, killing substantially larger numbers of people before the grotesque nicknames of "Little Boy" and "Fat Man" imposed themselves upon the consciousness of the world. In the early years of the Pacific war, save for the single dramatic gesture of the April 1942 Doolittle raid, launched from aircraft carriers, Japan was not bombed because it could not be reached. Meanwhile, in 1942 and 1943 the U.S. Army Air Forces in Europe devoted itself to precision attacks on industrial and military installations. This was partly because these were deemed the most useful targets; partly because America's political and military leadership proclaimed fundamental moral objections to area bombing, as practiced by the British.

As the war advanced, however, scruples faded. Dismissing "psywar ops" against the Japanese, Admiral Leahy, personal chief of staff to Roosevelt and later Truman, said: "The best psychological warfare to use on these barbarians [is] bombs." Likewise a contributor to the British *Spectator* magazine, writing in September 1944: "No Archbishop is likely to cry out against the bombing of Japan when it comes, for it will be difficult to ask mercy for an enemy that shoots airmen unfortunate enough to bale [*sic*] out over its sacred soil, and perpetrates atrocities of revolting perversity in China." It was the Japanese people's ill-fortune that it became feasible to bomb them just when American squeamishness about killing civilians was eclipsed by ruthlessly pragmatic assessments of how best to exploit available technology to injure the enemy and enhance the credibility of strategic air power.

Such critics as John Dower suggest that racial hatred towards the Japanese people caused them to receive harsher treatment at Allied hands, especially in the matter of aerial bombardment, than the Germans. This view seems to represent a misreading of events in Europe in 1944–45. A large proportion of all German civilians killed by Allied bombing perished in the last months of the war, when huge air forces operated with advanced technology against negligible defences. American airmen knew perfectly well that the effects of USAAF radar bombing of precision targets in urban areas was no more discriminatory than British area attacks. The destruction of Dresden is widely seen as a unique example of "frightfulness." In truth, of course, every day the Allied air forces aspired to inflict similar destruction, even if Americans enfolded themselves in a mantle of public regret about civilian casualties. Britain devoted almost one-third of its entire war effort to the strategic air campaign, while the USAAF's bomber forces consumed 10 percent of comparable American expenditure. War in some degree blunts the sensibilities of all those engaged in waging it. This was certainly true of those who made Allied bombardment policy.

It has been suggested above that few belligerents in any conflict are so high-minded as to offer to an enemy higher standards of treatment than that enemy extends to them. In the last phase of World War II, impatience overtook the Allies at every level. From presidents and prime ministers to soldiers in foxholes, there was a desire to "get this business over with." The outcome was not in doubt. The Axis retained no possibility of averting defeat. It therefore seemed all the more irksome that men were obliged to continue to die because the enemy declined to recognise the logic of his hopeless predicament. Any means of hastening the end seemed acceptable. In Europe, despite the misgivings of some senior officers, the USAAF participated in explicitly terroristic air operations against civilians, such as Operation Clarion in February 1945, designed to persuade the German people of their absolute vulnerability by attacking small communities and road traffic, military and civilian alike, killing many thousands.

The Japanese people found themselves at last within range of American bombers at a time when Allied moral sensibility was numbed by kamikaze attacks, revelations of savagery towards POWs and subject peoples, together with general war weariness. Joined to these considerations was the messianic determination of senior American airmen to be seen to make a decisive contribution to victory, to secure their future as a service independent of the army. The U.S. acquired the means to do terrible things to the Japanese people many months before "Little Boy" reached Tinian.

Claire Chennault, former freelance leader of the "Flying Tigers" translated into a U.S. general commanding the Fourteenth Air Force in China, was among the early advocates of intensive bombing of Japan. With five hundred aircraft, claimed this considerable charlatan, he could "burn out the industrial heart of the Empire with fire-bomb attacks on the teeming bamboo ant-heaps of Honshu and Kyushu." U.S. air chief Gen. "Hap" Arnold responded sternly that "the use of incendiaries against cities was contrary to our national policy of attacking military objectives." By 1943, however, visitors to the Dugway Proving Ground in Utah beheld the incongruous sight of a small Japanese village, faithfully reproduced in wood, each of two dozen houses with its *tatami*—straw-matting floor—and furniture. This phantom community was razed to the ground by bombers, demonstrating how easily the feat could be emulated and multiplied in the cities of Japan, where housing was of the flimsiest construction.

At about the same time, air staff identified eight priority industrial target systems in Japan, Manchuria and Korea. An October 1943 study noted that just twenty Japanese cities contained 22 percent of the nation's population. In June 1944, the bleakly named Joint Incendiary Committee assessed six urban areas on Honshu. It subsequently reported that if 70 percent of these six could be destroyed, 20 percent of Japanese production would be lost and 560,000 casualties inflicted. Arnold was told that it would be "cheap" to test the concept. The humanitarian issues involved, shrugged the researchers, were for national policy-makers to address.

It had always been a matter of course that the enemy nation which wrought the attack on Pearl Harbor should be bombed. Only the means were in question. In September 1942 the B-29 Superfortress, largest bomber the world had ever seen, made its maiden flight. This was the aircraft designated to wreak havoc upon Japan. Its size and sophistication, indeed the hubris of its very creation, represented monuments to American wealth and ingenuity. Each aircraft cost over half a million dollars, five times the price of an RAF Lancaster. The construction of a B-29 required 27,000 pounds of aluminium, over a thousand pounds of copper, 600,000 rivets, nine and a half miles of wiring, two miles of tubing. It was the first pressurised bomber in the world, with an operating radius of sixteen hundred miles, a crew of twelve and a battery of defensive armament.

The hundredth B-29 was accepted from its makers in January 1944, and a thousand were built by November of that year. Yet Tokyo was 3,900 miles from Hawaii. Until America possessed bases in the western Pacific, the only runways from which B-29s could operate against Japanese-held territory had to be constructed in India and China. The first squadrons reached India in the early summer of 1944, to encounter unwelcome squalor. "As we piled out of the airplane, anxious to see our new base," wrote a crewman, "my heart sank. This was not the civilized war we had expected to fight, for there were no barracks, no paved streets, nothing but insects, heat and dirt." Their first raid, on 5 June, against Japanese railway workshops in Bangkok, was farcical. Of 122 aircraft, 10 proved unserviceable, 14 failed to take off, 2 crashed immediately, 13 returned early. Of the remainder, in poor weather 77 attacked the primary target from heights between 17,000 and 27,000 feet. Just four tons of bombs even came close. One B-29 was hit by enemy fire. Another crashed on landing. Through the months that followed, with huge exertions and lamentable accuracy, further small loads of bombs and mines were dropped, making slight impact on the Japanese.

Meanwhile, extraordinary doings were afoot in China. Half a million labourers laid B-29 runways with rock crushed and hauled to the sites by human sweat, then levelled by giant rollers, each dragged by five hundred men and women. Scores of coolies died in accidents. The airstrips never properly matched the bombers' requirements. In April 1944, however, the first B-29 landed in China. By August, modest numbers were attacking Japan from the new fields. The logistics were amazing, and appalling. Each B-29 sortie required 20 tons of fuel, munitions and supplies. These were carried to the Chinese bases by B-29 transports, each of which burnt 28 tons of fuel to shift a 4.5-ton payload. The shuttle was soon taken over by C-109 aircraft, to spare the bombers. Flying the Hump airlift to Kunming was one of the most dangerous and unpopular missions of the war, involving a cumulative loss of 450 aircraft. Crew efficiency and morale were notoriously low. Airmen obliged to bail out found themselves in some of the wildest country in the world, populated by tribesmen who sometimes spared their lives, but invariably seized their possessions. One crew walked 250 miles in twenty-nine days before reaching friendly territory.

This Herculean effort enabled B-29s to attack Japan out of China, but at mortal risk and with negligible results. At that time it was not the enemy's fighters and flak guns which posed the major threat to crews' survival, but their own aircraft. In the words of their best-known commander, the B-29 "had as many bugs as the entomological department of the Smithsonian." Hydraulics, electrics, gun turrets, and above all power plant proved appallingly fallible. The four Curtis Wright R-3350 engines were "a mechanic's nightmare," prone to burst into flames during flight. Magnesium parts were liable to burn and fuse, alloy components to fail. "The airplane always felt like it was straining every rivet to be up there when you had it over 25,000 feet," recorded one flier, Jack Caldwell. Added to the B-29s' problems were the inexperience and shortcomings of their crews. The USAAF acknowledged that the problems of training men to fly this "battleship of the skies" were "monumental." On a typical raid on 19 August 1944, 71 aircraft set out for the Yawata steelworks, 61 by day, 10 by night. Five were destroyed by enemy action; 2 crashed before or during take-off; a further 8 were lost due to technical failures. Just 112 tons of bombs were delivered, for the loss of $7.5 million worth of aircraft, together with their precious crews.

Maj. Richard McGlinn and his crew of the 40th Bomb Group became unwilling protagonists in an extraordinary adventure. Flak damaged an engine just after their aircraft bombed. The flight engineer reported that they could not hope to reach base. They threw out everything loose and headed for Russia—America's ally in the war against Germany, though still neutral in the conflict with Japan. With radar and navigational equipment malfunctioning, McGlinn's aircraft became lost in clouds and darkness. They glimpsed below a city which they could not identify, flew northwards for a further forty minutes, then bailed out. All eleven Americans landed safely in tundra. They began to march north in three groups, each man carrying sidearm, survival manual and equipment. Mosquitoes plagued them in the swamps. Emergency rations were soon gone. They resorted to a diet of mushrooms, frogs, grouse, snails, mice, berries, leaves and moss.

One party, reaching a river, built a small raft. Its three strongest members set off downstream to find help, braving white waters and logjams. On 10 September they met a child, who took them to her village. Its inhabitants proved to be Russian, sure enough. By sign language, the bedraggled Americans communicated their plight. Over the days which followed, Soviet aircraft located the other fliers and dropped them welcoming notes: "Good day, comrades, you are in the USSR," together with supplies and instructions. When boats finally reached the desperate men, one rescuer described them as "emaciated and bearded, wearing ragged and tattered overalls that hardly covered the knees. One wore a leather jacket and battered shoes while the other had a foot covered by rags while the other foot was tied into a pistol holster. Their faces and bodies were so lacerated by midges that sores and contusions had formed." The Russians interned McGlinn and his men, along with the crews of thirty-six other American aircraft which landed in Siberia. The first fliers were returned home only in January 1945. The Soviets retained all U.S. aircraft which fell into their hands.

The USAAF was embarrassed by the deluge of Stateside publicity accorded to the new giant bombers, which caught the public imagination. Commanders knew how little, in reality, the planes were achieving. So did their British allies. In August Gen. Henry Pownall, Mountbatten's chief of staff, urged withdrawal of the B-29 groups from China. He pointed out that two and a half tons of supplies could be sent to the Chinese Nationalists for each ton being delivered to support the USAAF, "but they continue with these futile operations on a scale of attack that can't affect the course of the war at all." Radar bombing, in chronic poor weather over Japan, was accurate only to two miles. Enemy action accounted for a third of B-29 losses; the remainder were technical or self-inflicted. On 14 December, before a mission against a Bangkok bridge, pilots questioned the risks of dropping mixed loads of five-hundred- and thousand-pound bombs, which seemed liable to overtake each other and collide in the air. They were overruled and threatened with court-martial if they did not fly. Over the target, bombs indeed exploded amid the American formations. Four aircraft were lost. On other occasions, gun blisters blew out, engine failures persisted. Aircrew morale plumbed new depths.

It was evident that matters could not continue in this way, and they did not. On 29 August 1944 Curtis LeMay, youngest major-general in the service, flew to India to assume direction of the XXth Bomber Command. On 8 September he accompanied a B-29 mission as an observer. Fresh from Europe, where he had established a formidable reputation, he was dismayed by what he now saw. He quickly reported to Washington about the XXth. "They are very poor as a combat outfit," he wrote to Arnold's chief of staff on 12 September. ". . . They lack combat experience. Everyone is working like hell on the wrong things. In other words, they are finding out how to fight the same as our first outfits did at the beginning of the war, by the trial and error method. I don't think we can afford to operate our B-29s in that manner." In another letter a week later, he lamented the poor quality of both aircrew and staff officers, and demanded combat-experienced personnel: "The B-29 outfits are being filled with people who have spent the war behind a desk in the U.S." He noted that crews were far more frightened by the perils of overladen take-offs from poor strips than by those of meeting the enemy. With key airfields in China lost to the Japanese Ichigo ground offensive, LeMay concluded: "The operations of this Command under the conditions existing in this theater are basically unsound."

Initially, senior officers recoiled from accepting the blow to U.S. prestige involved in abandoning B-29 missions from China. Not until late in December did Gen. Albert Wedemeyer bow to the inevitable. Only in March 1945 did the XXth Bomber Command begin to pack up in India to move, with its aircraft and cargoes which included pet monkeys and a black bear cub, to join other units of the Twentieth Air Force already operating out of the Mariana Islands. At last the U.S. possessed Pacific bases from which the Japanese mainland was accessible.

LeMay had gone ahead of them. On 9 December Arnold wrote to him: "The B-29 project is important to me, because I am convinced that it is vital to the future of the Army Air Forces." In January 1945 the young general was transferred from the XXth to XXIst Bomber Command, taking over its headquarters on Guam. It was in this role that he launched the offensive against Japan which thereafter would be indelibly associated with his name.

Curtis Emerson LeMay was born into a modest family in Columbus, Ohio, where he worked his way through college. He displayed remarkably precocious technical skills, which persisted into his later life—while air force chief of staff, he built a colour television set with his own hands. He gained an army flying cadetship in 1928, and became recognized in the ensuing decade as a master of the techniques of pilotage, engineering and navigation, a tough trainer and strict disciplinarian. The coming of war brought him swift promotion. He was effective, fearless, driven, tactically innovative. In Europe he established a reputation as one of the most brilliant officers in the Eighth Air Force, who led from the front. He was respected rather than loved: aloof in manner, coldly focused in approach, precise and blunt in speech. Rueful pilots christened him "Iron Ass." LeMay's men cherished a legend that he once halted his jeep beside an aircraft being refuelled, causing a sergeant timidly to remonstrate about the trademark pipe clamped in his jaw: "Sir, it could ignite gas fumes." LeMay responded: "Son, it wouldn't dare." His chilling demeanour was not softened by the paralysis of one side of his face, the result of Bell's palsy. His ruthless assessment of the XXth Bomber Command in India, together with his rapid introduction of new training programmes and tactical methods, convinced Arnold that LeMay was the man to grasp the daunting challenge of running the USAAF's campaign out of the Marianas.

This too had languished. As the Marines seized island after island of the group through the summer of 1944, close behind them came excavators and graders to create runways and hardstands out of rock and coral. The first wing of 180 B-29s, together with 12,000 air and ground crew necessary to operate them, arrived on Saipan while Japanese stragglers were still at large. On the day of their first mission, three Japanese were killed trying to infiltrate a chow line. After the shock of spotting an enemy soldier shooting at a sentry, one airman was sent home with "combat fatigue." In January 1945, forty-seven Japanese were taken prisoner a thousand yards from the XXIst Bomber Command's headquarters. For the fliers, living conditions were primitive. One wrote in dismay of his arrival on Tinian: "I had hoped to find brown-skinned native girls, hula skirts, coconut trees and warm sea breezes . . . Instead, I found sunburned GIs swarming over a desolate coral rock. I wasn't on a paradise island—I was on a prison island."

Lt. Philip True's tour as a navigator with the 9th Bomb Group started badly, when his pilot halted their plane on the stands at Tinian. "Where's the whiskey?" demanded a half-naked ground technician. "Whiskey?" exclaimed the fliers in bewilderment. There was no whiskey. Their tough, correct Iowan commander, Maj. Dayton Countryman, had vetoed illicit liquor-smuggling from California. Yet on Tinian, they discovered, almost all good things had to be purchased with crates of whiskey—Schenley's "Black Death" being the preferred brand—shipped in the bomb bays of arriving aircraft.

They lived amid cloying humidity: "Leather began to get mouldy after the first few days, and most everything took on a musty odor," wrote a pilot. Men slept in Quonset huts, ten or twenty together. Officers found themselves digging field latrines. Ground crews were unable to work on aircraft in shorts, for the metal burnt their skins. As everywhere in the Pacific, there was resentment of the navy's superior food, quarters and facilities. The Japanese mounted night harassing raids, which caused widespread grief, besides inflicting a total of 245 casualties, destroying eleven aircraft and damaging forty-nine. One Japanese aircraft crashed onto a shelter, injuring forty men. "Everyone was on edge the rest of the day and many days to come," wrote Captain Stanley Samuelson. After each raid, scores of Americans were treated for cuts and bruises, having dashed for cover in the darkness, usually naked, across the sharp, unyielding coral. It was a cruel business for aircrew to face the strain of flying operations when they received so little respite on the ground.

The first American aircraft to overfly Tokyo since the Doolittle raid carried out a photo reconnaissance mission on 1 November 1944. It was followed on the twenty-fourth by 111 bombers. They flew at 2,000 feet until they were 250 miles out from Japan, then climbed to 27,000 feet for the bomb run. Navigation and bomb aiming proved poor. Through the winter of 1944, just 2 percent of attacking aircraft dropped their ordnance within a thousand feet of aiming points. Crews struggled against four hazards: inexperience and inadequate training; continuing aircraft mechanical failures; the stresses of take-off, exceeding the manufacturers' recommended all-up weight of 132,000 pounds; finally, most serious of all, at high altitude over Japan they encountered unprecedented headwinds, a "jet stream" exceeding a hundred knots, which played havoc with all estimates of scheduling and fuel requirements.

The appointed targets for the XXIst Bomber Command were Japanese aircraft manufacture, war industry and shipping. By January 1945, B-29s had achieved a negligible impact on any of these. Morale slumped. A pilot, Lt. Robert Copeland of the 500th Bomb Group, recorded in his diary bleak verdicts on operations out of Saipan. "3 Dec: The boys are beginning to crack. Captain Field started for the cliff last night before he was stopped and taken to the hospital . . . He'll probably be sent home"; "22 December: We bombed at 32,000 feet by radar and I have my doubts as to the results. I was scared to put it mildly"; "28 December: Yesterday's raid was really screwed up. They missed the primary and tried to make a 180-degree turn and hit it again but didn't succeed and dropped their bombs in Tokyo with dubious results"; "14 Jan: The mission to Nagoya yesterday seems to have been a flop . . . Hiat's ship got in the prop wash over Tokyo and was flipped over on its back and split S'd from 32,000 ft to 25,000 feet and their airspeed went to 380mph."

Another officer, Stanley Samuelson, had attended art school in his home state of Maryland before enlisting after Pearl Harbor. He flew fifty B-17 missions in the Mediterranean theatre, came home in 1943 and got married, then volunteered for B-29s. Why would a man offer himself a second time for sacrifice, after "doing his bit"? It is impossible to know, but a surprising number of pilots found that they enjoyed flying, even in combat, and were reluctant to abandon it. Samuelson, twenty-four years old, exploited his artistic skills to develop a useful sideline on Saipan, painting "nose art" caricatures on some of the wing's B-29s, at $50 apiece.

He flew his first Superfortress mission in October 1944. In the early days of the tour he experienced some euphoric moments, such as this one approaching Japan on Thanksgiving Day: "When the clouds broke, Mt. Fujiyama stood out on the horizon like a beautiful painting done by a master. It was a beautiful sight, and one that very few people will ever witness during this war. It was hard to believe that below us lay one of the rottenest countries that ever existed."

This brief idyll ended abruptly, however, a few minutes later when an engine failed. By the time it restarted, Samuelson's plane *Snafufortress* had fallen behind the formation. He tried to jettison his bombs, only to find them frozen in the racks. The bomb doors refused to close, causing drag which reduced speed still further. The intercom began to buzz with terse warnings of enemy aircraft from the gunners: "Three pursuit—five o'clock low. Four pursuit two o'clock high. Two pursuits twelve o'clock level." Samuelson wrote: "Things got hotter than hell, and the guns began to crackle in all directions." Enemy fighters attacked persistently for thirty minutes, terrifying the crew. It took them seven lonely, unremittingly tense hours to nurse the plane home, 1,400 miles across the Pacific. The bombardier crawled down the fuselage to the bomb bay and ditched their ordnance by hand. After landing, Samuelson slept for twelve straight hours.

This experienced combat pilot found himself, like most of his comrades, bitterly dismayed by the experience of operating B-29s. "There is no getting around it," he wrote in December, "we are all scared and scared plenty. This stuff of losing crews on every mission is a hard pill to swallow. It wouldn't be quite as bad if our losses were just because of the enemy, however planes ditch out in the middle of the Pacific because of engine failure and other mechanical troubles. The thought of landing a $600,000 plane and twelve men on a rough ocean at night, a thousand miles from nowhere, makes men out of boys and puts gray hairs on the men . . . One day is like another round here . . . no one has or wants a calendar. We all just live from day to day and raid to raid. There was some talk about Christmas being only two days away, however no one seemed to get too enthusiastic about it." A gunner wrote in his diary in January 1945: "We're all of us poor soldiers . . . too full of personally staying alive and wishing we were working in a defense plant."

In some theatres of war, aircrew were pampered. In the Marianas, no comforts were to be had. Joseph Majeski, a nineteen-year-old gunner with the 6th Bomb Group on Tinian, found himself living in a pup tent, queuing among a hundred other naked men for a shower—and always hungry. He persuaded his father to mail him jars of Gerber's baby food—apple sauce, pears and peaches—because these were nutritious and portable. Majeski contrived an illicit visit to an uncle aboard a ship anchored offshore: "I showered with hot water for the first time in months," he wrote. "The food served on the ship was great. Compared to the garbage we were eating on Tinian, I was sorry that I had not joined the Navy." Ashore, men washed their own clothes in aviation gas, or devoted leisure hours to building primitive washing machines with windmill propellers set in barrels. Gardens sprang up between huts. Many fliers found inactivity almost as distressing as combat. They lay under the unyielding sun, nursing dreams about when it was all over. "I had a nice talk with Wray and Cutter," Stanley Samuelson wrote on 4 January, recording a gossip with two of his crew. "Wray is a very smart lad and has his ambitions. He intends to get an International Harvester Agency in his own town and go into business for himself. Cutter just plans to get out of the army and tell everyone to go to hell if he so pleases."

On mission days, there was little talk in the open trucks on the way to the flight line. A Red Cross van came round, distributing coffee and doughnuts as crews waited for the word to go. Pilots talked to the ground crew chief, who had almost invariably worked all night with his men, readying the aircraft. They checked the 41B maintenance book. Then fliers helped mechanics pull down the props, two men per blade, to clear accumulated oil from the lower cylinders. Little "putt-putt" generators in the aircraft were started, to provide electricity for engine turn-over. One by one, in the order 3, 4, 2, 1, the Wrights coughed, spewed smoke, settled to a steady roar. Most take-offs were made to the east, because of the prevailing wind. Crews found these unfailingly frightening, as co-pilots called out the rising speed: "70–80–95–110–135." Each laden monster took fifty seconds to get airborne, from the moment a pilot posted halfway down the runway flashed a green light, indicating the way clear for the next plane to go. "Take-off seemed to run on for ever," said Fred Arner, "and those engines ran so damned hot."

Crews began to relax only when the first power reduction came, maybe two minutes after leaving the ground. Cabin pressure was set to 8,000 feet. Bombardiers clambered aft, to arm the incendiary clusters in the bomb bays. Many crews tuned to Armed Forces Radio, to alleviate the boredom of the seven-hour run to Japan. The loneliness of rear gunners, in particular, was notorious. Most left their posts to share the companionship of those clustered forward in the cockpit, though because of the engine roar they could converse only through the intercom. Pacific weather extremes created moments of terror, sometimes also extraordinary visual effects. "I became aware of the sky above me just beginning to be light—the dimmer stars disappearing as the dawn began to break, barely illuminating the tops of the mountainous cumulus build-ups towering above us to 30,000 or 40,000 feet," wrote one pilot:

> The sea below was black and the lower bases of the clouds a dark, dull gray. Then, almost as if in response to a drum roll, there was an explosion of color: streaks of red and orange began to shoot heavenward into a pale, azure canopy high above. The intensity built to a crescendo; a silent cacophony of color until the whole eastern sky was aflame, backlighting and illuminating the cumulus. I touched the intercom button, alerting the crew, and, after a couple of moments, quietly said: "Everybody . . . look out the left side of the airplane." There was a muffled response or two: "Jesus!" or "Christ!"

Throughout the flight, the navigator worked harder than any other crew member. Each aircraft was issued with a "flimsy" giving pre-set headings, position points and scheduled timings. To maintain these in darkness required taking celestial fixes, checking drift, peering into the APQ13 radar screen; in daylight, the sun was "shot" by sextant from the Perspex astrodome. It took sixteen minutes to work out where the aircraft had just been, and good navigators never let up. Iwo Jima below marked the halfway point. Thereafter, an hour out from the target, every man went to his post, donning big, heavy flak jackets. They circled an appointed assembly point until the entire formation was mustered, aided by identification symbols painted on aircraft tails—squares, circles, triangles—then began the run towards the enemy's country. "Dear Mom," Robert Copeland wrote home,

> the thing about combat that is beginning to impress me most is the appreciation I now have for the finer things of life. The love one has for friends, the love and need for a woman and the things one wants to do with this dream girl when this thing is all over. A woman somewhere seems to be the driving force behind all men in combat. You're so scared even 400 miles an hour doesn't seem fast enough. The bomb run is only four or five minutes long, but it seems like hours. The bomb bay doors are only open for one or two minutes, but that seems like an eternity. It's more like a wild horrible nightmare from which it is impossible to awaken, but nevertheless we do make it once more.

The songs which Superfortress crews wrote for themselves reflected the melancholy that afflicted most:

Oh I get that lonesome feeling
When I hear those engines whine
Those B-29s are breaking up
That old gang of mine
There goes Jack, there goes Bill
Down over Tokyo.
We all hope it's home we go,
How soon we do not know.

On the bomb run, planes were often buffeted by flak explosions. The worst mission that gunner Fred Arner flew was his crew's ninth. Delayed on the strip by a mechanical problem, they approached the target twenty minutes behind the main force, and fifty miles north of Tokyo found themselves meeting B-29s hurtling past in the opposite direction, "like getting the wrong way onto the beltway." In the nose was a "guest" bombardier, flying the last mission of his tour. He yelled aloud in terror each time a plane approached. There were other hazards. At least one B-29 shot itself down when over-excited gunners fired into their own engines. Attacking a fogged-in Osaka one day, Arner's crew could find only one other plane with which to formate for the bomb run. "At high noon we were over the target, but it could have been Pittsburgh as far as I was concerned. We bombed by radar, using Osaka Castle as our checkpoint." Sometimes they hit thermals which bounced the huge planes violently, throwing everything movable about the fuselage. In Arner's crew, the radar counter-measures man became known as "Pisspot" Smith, after a thermal doused him in the contents of the plane's potty.

When their loads fell away, noses lifted and aircraft surged forward, at least three tons lighter. However, on navigator Philip True's first mission, just after bombing, "a terrible rumble and chatter startled and shook me." Immediately behind his navigator's seat, the four-gun upper turret began firing. True glimpsed Japanese fighters, which attacked repeatedly for ten minutes. Then the guns fell silent, and the crew relaxed. They saw the Pacific below again, and settled for the long run home. Their relief was premature. True glimpsed the altimeter. They were down to 12,000 feet, and descending. Peering out at the starboard wing, True perceived two engines dead. Fuel was streaming from a tank ruptured by gunfire. The strain on the surviving port engines was acute. They were losing about a hundred feet a minute. The pilot announced that if their fuel would not hold out to Iwo Jima, they must jump. True was terrified: "The Pacific looked ominous, gray and ugly, swirling with swells and occasional white-caps."

Yet an hour later, they were still holding 4,000 feet. Soon after, they found themselves approaching Iwo Jima, among a gaggle of other aircraft with problems. "We circled Mount Suribachi, our starboard wing with the two dead engines pointing down, a view that produced in me a feeling of teetering on the edge of a cliff." The landing gear dropped. Then, to their horror, on final approach another B-29 cut recklessly across them. They lurched upwards and circled again. The pilot said: "If we can't get in this time, I'm going to pull up and drop you guys in the ocean. Be ready to go." In heavy cloud and rain, once again they lunged towards the strip, and heard a merciful thump as the wheels touched. They stopped with a few yards of runway to spare, clambered out, and examined the hole in their wing. They were down to their last ten minutes of fuel. A truck carried them through torrential rain to a holding area. True, like hundreds of others who felt that they owed their lives to Iwo, thought of the Marines "who had inched and crawled their way over this eroded hunk of volcanic debris . . . so that we could land and live." They got back to Tinian late that night, exhausted. Nothing seriously bad happened on any of their eleven subsequent missions.

Those who made it to the Marianas, after another seven hours over the unfriendly ocean, sometimes nursing a damaged plane, bumped heavily onto the runway, taxied in and cut engines. Somebody took out the "honey bucket" for emptying. Crews stretched stiffened limbs, and climbed unsteadily out of the fuselage. Even then, the ordeal was not always over. Ground engineer Bob Mann saw a plane land with bombs still hung up in its bay. Armourers refused to touch the lethal ordnance, saying that their job was to arm aircraft, not disarm them. With infinite care, the plane's bombardier and another crew member unscrewed the fuses.

Crews were given a slug of whiskey before debriefings, from which gunners were quickly excused, because they knew so little. Returning fliers understood that they had achieved only a brief reprieve. Stanley Samuelson wrote in January: "At present, no one knows how many missions we will have to pull. Some fellows will crack, and it is likely to be most anyone." A thin but steady stream of men decided that too much was being demanded of them. "After about ten missions," wrote Joseph Majeski, "our right gunner went to the colonel and said: 'I don't care if you shoot me but I will never set foot in that airplane again.' " The man was stripped of his rank and given a ground assignment. Most aircrew persisted, however, recognising that war service as a flier was less dreadful than as an infantryman. "We knew how rough it was on the ground," said Philip True. Ben Robertson, who started a tour out of Guam in February, decided after gossiping with some Marines about their experience on Iwo Jima that he was better off: "In our situation, it was pretty much a case of returning from a mission or not—there usually was not much in between." A steady drain of bomber losses continued. Stanley Samuelson's B-29 went down over Japan on 19 February. "Every day I get to hate this stinking rotten war more," he wrote, the week before he died. Robert Copeland was killed when his plane crashed near Kobe on a mission on 17 March. Just two of his crew survived as prisoners.

HERE, then, was the force which Curtis LeMay inherited in January 1945 from Maj.-Gen. Haywood Hansell, who had led the XXIst Bomber Command for five months. Hansell declined an offer to remain on Guam as LeMay's deputy. He was harshly treated, for his efforts had begun to improve the command's performance. But the ruthless replacement of unsuccessful officers was characteristic of American wartime policy, and by no means mistaken.

LeMay's initial verdict on his new appointment was even less indulgent than had been his view of the XXth Bomber Command in India. He wrote to Washington: "Maybe the road ahead always looks worse than the road behind, but after 10 days here this job looks much tougher than the one I just left . . . The staff here is practically worthless." He submitted a long list of requests for named officers to join his headquarters. He complained that some unit commanders might be competent aviators, but lacked leadership skills. Robert Ramer, who arrived in the Marianas in January with a replacement crew for the 497th Bomb Group, recorded: "Morale was terrible . . . Nothing worked." LeMay introduced a stringent training programme, and also threw himself into devising new tactical methods, focusing especially on the use of incendiary bombs. In his first few weeks, the XXth Bomber Command flew eight missions against Japan, including two experimental incendiary attacks. On three of these, not one bomb hit the primary target, though he increased each aircraft's load to three tons by dumping armament and equipment. It was evident to LeMay, though not immediately to his men, that the weak Japanese defences were the least of the Americans' problems; that the huge weight of guns fitted to the Superfortresses was almost redundant. An airman wrote laconically: "General LeMay has taken over the Bomber Command, and he is going to get us all killed." On 3 March, the new commander wrote to Arnold's chief of staff: "I am working on several very radical methods of employment of the force. As soon as I have run a few tests, I'll submit the plans to you for comment."

2. Fire-Raising

Long before Pearl Harbor, Japan's greatest strategist, Admiral Isoroku Yamamoto, predicted that when war came, "Tokyo will probably be burnt to the ground." While LeMay seized upon the potential of using incendiary bombs to destroy Japanese cities wholesale, he did not invent the concept. Before he had even taken up his post in the Marianas, a USAAF report declared: "vulnerability of Japanese cities to fire is still a tempting point for argument . . . That cities are a valid important military objective is certain . . . because of the heavy dispersal of industry . . . within the most congested parts of them." As early as September 1944, at a meeting of the Committee of Operations Analysts in Washington, Cmdr. William McGovern of OSS argued strongly for exploiting incendiary attack: "The panic side of the Japanese is amazing . . . [Fire] is one of the great things they are terrified at from childhood." McGovern, like most of his colleagues, was "all in favour of Japanese area bombing."

The fire-raisers got their way. The six-pound M-69 incendiary bomb, dropped in clusters packed into cylinders primed to burst open at a predetermined height, contained slow-burning napalm designed to spread on impact. It proved one of the most deadly weapons of the Second World War. Gen. Lauris Norstad, Arnold's chief of staff, wrote to LeMay: "It has become necessary to conduct a test incendiary mission for the purpose of determining the capabilities of our weapons and our tactics against Japanese urban industrial areas . . . This attack does not represent a departure from our primary objective of destroying Japanese airpower . . . it is merely a necessary preparation for the future."

By March 1945, the higher ranks of the USAAF were obsessed with the urgency of being seen to strike a decisive blow with B-29s. "It is air power that this Country has *after the War* that we must think of, as well as now," a senior USAAF officer wrote to MacArthur's air chief, George Kenney. The airmen sought to justify the huge resources committed to the B-29 programme, to prove the capabilities of independent strategic air power before the navy and army accomplished the defeat of Japan. The USAAF's leadership was almost as traumatised by the failures of the first six months of B-29 operations as had been the RAF in 1941 by the ineffectiveness of its precision-bomber attacks on Germany. The American answer was the same as the British one had been. A USAAF report of 6 December 1944, pre-dating by months LeMay's fire-raising operations, asserted blandly: "To date the Twentieth Air Force has not been capable of effectively bombing small precision targets by radar. Long-range forecasts indicate that weather will get progressively worse over the homeland of Japan until mid-summer . . . With the present status of radar, in order to get maximum utilization of the forces available, it may be necessary to accept area bombing for a major portion of the effort."

If striking at cities was the best means of inflicting damage upon the enemy's industrial base with available navigational and bomb-aiming technology, then this was what the XXth Bomber Command would do—and what American aircraft had been doing in Europe for months, albeit maintaining a notional commitment to destroying specified industrial targets. As when Britain's Bomber Command introduced area attack against Germany in 1942, the USAAF's new policy in the spring of 1945 was driven as much by a perception of operational necessity as one of strategic desirability. The transformation of the Pacific bomber offensive was the work of LeMay, but he faced no opposition from the USAAF's chiefs in Washington. They simply wanted results, and were not disposed to quibble about how these were achieved. "Whereas the adoption of nonvisual bombing techniques in Europe signified that civilian casualties were a matter of decreasing concern," Conrad Crane has written, "by the time such methods were applied against Japan, civilian casualties were of no concern at all."

LeMay laconically described his policy: "Bomb and burn 'em till they quit." His most famous—or, in the eyes of critics, most notorious—stroke was the pioneering fire-raising raid on Tokyo, Operation Meetinghouse, launched on the night of 9 March 1945. For the first time he instructed crews to attack at low altitude, where aiming accuracy was much more readily attained, and strong headwinds could be avoided. Four B-29s were designated as "homing aircraft"—what the RAF called "master bombers"—orbiting the city to direct the 325-strong main force. Crews were assigned loads of between 10,000 and 14,000 pounds, according to experience. LeMay had concluded that Japanese fighters were so ineffectual that a ton of defensive armament could be stripped out of each plane. The men briefed for the raid were appalled: "A sort of cold fear gripped the crews . . . Many frankly did not expect to return from a raid over that city, at an altitude of less than 10,000 feet." There was intense anger towards LeMay. "There were a lot of unhappy campers when they announced that we were to hit Tokyo—at night—individually and at an altitude between 6 and 9,000 feet," wrote pilot Robert Ramer. "We thought they had gone mad." LeMay afterwards claimed to have anticipated the possibility that his experiment would go disastrously wrong: "We might lose over three hundred aircraft and some 3,000 veteran personnel. It might go down in history as LeMay's Last Brainstorm."

Take-offs were staggered between 1736 and 1930. In consequence, later crews saw the flames over Tokyo long before they reached the city. George Beck, a B-29 gunner, recorded in his diary "black, stinking clouds of smoke up to 20,000 feet." All their commander's hopes were fulfilled. "Suddenly, way off at about 2 o'clock, I saw a glow on the horizon like the sun rising or maybe the moon," wrote Robert Ramer. "The whole city of Tokyo was below us stretching from wingtip to wingtip, ablaze in one enormous fire with yet more fountains of flame pouring down from the B-29s. The black smoke billowed up thousands of feet causing powerful thermal currents that buffeted our plane severely, bringing with it the horrible smell of burning flesh." Although the Japanese claimed to have put 312 single-engined and 105 twin-engined fighters into the air, only forty American crews reported even glimpsing an enemy aircraft. They began bombing at 0100, and the attack continued through the succeeding three hours, unloading 496,000 incendiaries on Japan's capital. By the time the bombers landed back in the Marianas they had been in the air fifteen hours, double the length of an average European sortie. The bellies of many aircraft were coated in soot from the fires of Tokyo. Just twelve bombers were lost, most destroyed by updrafts from the blazing city. Forty-two were damaged by flak, and two more crashed on landing. Unsurprisingly, the least experienced crews accounted for a disproportionate share of casualties.

General Arnold wrote to LeMay: "I want you and your people to understand fully my admiration for your fine work . . . Your recent incendiary missions were brilliantly planned and executed . . . Under reasonably favourable conditions you should . . . have the ability to destroy whole industrial cities." Perhaps the most astonishing aspect of the new policy is that it was implemented without reference to the political leadership of the United States. When Secretary of War Henry Stimson expressed belated dismay about media reports of non-discriminatory bombing of Japanese cities, Arnold assured him mendaciously that urban areas had become targets only because Japanese industry was widely dispersed among the civilian population: "They were trying to keep [civilian casualties] down as much as possible."

Stimson professed himself satisfied. He cautioned only that there must be no attacks on the ancient city of Kyoto. The further destruction of Japan and mass killing of its people was left entirely to the airmen's discretion. There is no documentation to suggest that either Roosevelt or Truman was ever consulted about LeMay's campaign. Here was an extreme example of the manner in which the higher direction of America's war was left overwhelmingly in the hands of the service chiefs of staff. Here also was a precedent, establishing the context in which the later dropping of the atomic bombs was carried out—with the acquiescence of the U.S. government rather than by its formal initiative.

Comment about the Tokyo raid in the U.S. press was overwhelmingly favourable. The implausibly named *Christian Century* suggested that the attack had "blasted large cracks in the myth by which a weak and inoffensive little man had become a conquering god." Raymond Moley in *Newsweek* expressed the hope that "through intensified bombing, the panicky streak in the Japanese mentality may be set off." No moral doubts were expressed, though many commentators acknowledged that the deliberate destruction of a city represented a new departure for the USAAF. The Twentieth Air Force clung to fig leaves, warning its senior officers: "Guard against anyone stating that this is area bombing." A XXIst Bomber Command report sought to clarify the nature of what had been done to Tokyo: "The object of these attacks was *not to* indiscriminately bomb civilian populations. The object *was* to destroy the *industrial and strategic targets* concentrated in the urban areas." In a narrow, absurdly literal sense, this was true. The nuance was meaningless, however, to those who lay in the path of the storm.

The sporadic American air raids which preceded that of 9 March had caused the Tokyo municipal authorities to evacuate some 1.7 million people, almost all women and children, from the capital to the countryside. On the night, six million remained in the city. One of these was Haruyo Wada, nine-year-old daughter of a spice wholesaler living in Joto-ku, a densely populated industrial and housing district networked with canals, near the Arakawa River. In addition to herself and her parents, a sixteen-year-old brother, Soichiro, and a five-year-old sister, Mitsuko, lived in their little two-storey wooden house. By that spring of 1945 they had grown very conscious of the threat of bombing, and nervous about it. Japanese knew how readily their houses burned. At school, children seemed to spend more time practicing air-raid drills than studying. Soichiro Wada spent most evenings on firewatching duties.

At a time when many Tokyo people were hungry, the war had hitherto dealt relatively kindly with the Wadas. The family spice business sustained enough friendly connections to keep them fed. Yet at home they slept lightly and uneasily, the family all together in the downstairs living room, ready for flight. Haruyo's father was a kindly man, whom she always felt safe with. He took the bomber peril very seriously. One day he came home and presented each family member with a pair of leather shoes—at that time, luxury items. They were designed to replace the wooden clogs which had become almost universal. "Your feet will not get burned so easily in these," Mr. Wada said gravely.

On the evening of 9 March, Haruyo played in the street as usual with her little friends: the Futami children, Yukio and Yoko, whose father made *sake* flasks; Hisayo Furuhashi, daughter of a decorator; Yuji Imaizumi, whose family were papermakers. Then she was called in to supper. Afterwards, as usual the Wadas sat around the radio for a while, listening to a programme of songs for children. They were in their beds when the air-raid warning sounded. Their father went outside, investigated, and returned to report that all seemed quiet. They relapsed into sleep for a time, then were wakened once more by a rising tumult. Their father slipped out, and returned looking troubled: "Something unusual is happening," he said. "You'd all better get your clothes on." Haruyo sat up "like a clockwork doll." Dressed, they went out into the street, and joined a throng of people already gathered, gazing in fear at the sky, where searchlights probed and flickered uncertainly. Aircraft droned overhead, and there was a reddening horizon in the south. Most disturbing for the fate of Tokyo, a strong north-westerly wind was blowing. No one said much, but Mr. Wada pushed his wife and daughters into the shallow shelter they shared with the Furuhashi family. The boy Soichiro disappeared to his fire-watching post.

As the family sat crammed into their hole with the Furuhashis, heat and noise progressively intensified. Beyond the thunder of concussions, ever closer, there were children's screams and a patter of running feet. Haruyo jammed her fingers into her ears, to deaden the terrifying sound of explosions. She felt sick. Then her father put his head in and said: "Come out of there—you'll roast if you stay." Her mother and sister hastened to obey, but Mrs. Furuhashi seized Haruyo's coat and tried to hold her back: "Stay here! Stay!" she cried hysterically. "You'll die out there." The child broke free, and crawled out into the street.

The entire horizon was now deep red. The wind seemed to have risen to the force almost of a typhoon. Blazing embers were hurtling through the air, bouncing like balls of fire over roofs and people. Clay tiles flew past, glowing fiercely. People were running, running—then burning, burning. Wide-eyed, Haruyo saw mothers in flight, apparently oblivious of the fact that the babies on their backs, the children whose hands they grasped, were on fire. The great flight of people seemed impelled by the gale, rather than by their own limbs. The Wadas seized their daughters tightly, and led them a few yards to a nearby railway embankment. They clambered up onto the tracks, and stood among thousands of others, in temporary safety. Almost all were too stunned to speak, as fire swept through the nearby houses, including their own.

For Yoshiko Hashimoto's family, living in the Sumida district of east Tokyo, until that night awareness of bombing had been slight. They felt no great fear in the face of spasmodic raids from small numbers of planes, which they described sardonically as "our regulars." "There was a strange feeling of detachment until the March raid," said Yoshiko, the twenty-four-year-old mother of a three-month-old baby boy, Hiroshi. "Even if someone quite close by got hit, you never thought it would happen to you." The family's principal concession to air-raid precautions was that they always slept in their clothes, and kept by the beds a *furoshiki*—a cloth square—with a few necessaries for parents and children tied up in it, together with baskets containing some clothes and a little food.

When the bombs began to fall on 9 March, at first only Yoshiko, her mother and the baby took to their shelter. Very quickly, amid the thunder and tumult of explosions, they understood that what was happening was on a scale beyond their experience or imagination. Their father called down to the shelter for the women to come out. He realised that a hole barely three feet below ground offered negligible protection. They emerged into a sea of flame. Yoshiko, clutching her baby, ran with her sister Chieko to the water tank a few yards beyond the house. Showers of incendiaries were falling around them. The sky over the city was a deep, cruel red. They piled their most precious possessions, above all bedding, onto a little cart. The girls' father shouted that they must flee before the approaching flames.

Thousands of people "almost mad with terror" thronged the streets. The Hashimotos had not gone far before they discovered that Chieko, pushing their cart, was falling behind. The little family saw that they were beside a railway. "We've got to go on," cried their father. "The line will be a target for the planes." He and his wife each clutched one of Etsuko's hands. Yoshiko, the baby on her back, tried to keep hold of fourteen-year-old Hisae. However, the child was encumbered by a cooking pot full of precious rice. In the desperate, pressing throng, the two girls found themselves dashed apart. "Wait for me! Wait for me!" cried Hisae. Then her plaintive voice faded. As the mob surged on towards the Sanno Bridge over the Tate River, Yoshiko lost her sister.

At the riverbank the Hashimoto family paused, desperate to recover their two missing daughters. But now the fires were upon them. A blast of unbearable heat overtook the fugitives. Flames seized baggage, nearby warehouses, then the heads of the terrified fugitives. Yoshiko saw people shrivelled by fire "like dead leaves," others holding up hands that were ablaze. On Yoshiko's back, the baby Hiroshi was screaming. Flaming fragments blew into the child's mouth. "Get him off your back! Get him down!" cried Yoshiko's mother. The girl took the boy in her arms, plucked a glowing ember from his lips, then sought to shield him from the flames and the terrible wall of heat. Her mother took off the hood covering her own head and put it on her daughter's, some of whose hair was already burned away. On the bridge, the panic-stricken crowd fleeing towards Fukagawa on the south bank came face to face with another mob seeking to escape fires on their own side. The two masses of people collided, creating new scenes of horror. "I watched people die before my eyes. I saw people burning."

"Jump in the river!" Yoshiko's father shouted, shaking her shoulders urgently. "It's your only chance!" She hesitated, from fear for her baby in the icy winter water. "Go on!" cried her mother. "You've got to do it!" Her parents and sister Etsuko stayed on the bank, for her mother could not swim. Yoshiko jumped.

In the Edogawa district, sixteen-year-old Ryoichi Sekine stood with his father and cousin watching the reddening sky in the west, listening to the thunder of bomb explosions, anti-aircraft fire and the rising wind. Ryoichi sought shelter as shrapnel fragments began to fall among them. Then fireballs were added, blazing embers and fragments that struck houses, held, and spread fire in seconds. The heat was growing. Instinctively, they ducked as a B-29 flew overhead so low that they could see flame reflections flickering on its silver underbelly. So fierce was the gale that it began to blow gravel across the road, checking the progress of anyone attempting to run against it. The fires were gaining ground fast, and it became plain that the Sekines must join the surging mob of fleeing people. Those in the worst case were the old, and mothers with children. Ryoichi's father, with rare presence of mind, gave an improvised banner to his young niece Takako Ohki, telling her to use it to lead all the mothers and old people she could find towards safety. The girl set off, holding aloft her emblem, followed by a column of fugitives.

Mr. Sekine, his son and a friend began a hasty tour of neighbouring houses, to ensure that everyone had got out. By the time they finished their check, not only was the path taken by the mothers and old people blocked by flames, but it had become impossible to stand upright in the gale of smoke. Choking and gasping, the three men crawled westward until they reached an open space, already burnt out. They saw corpses everywhere, the living frenziedly beating at flames on their own bodies. In the Naka River corpses floated in dense clusters, some obviously killed by flaming debris. The two Sekines struggled on towards a cluster of trees, which they recognised as the approach to the Suwa Shrine. Hundreds of people, dead and alive, lay in the shallow lake nearby. Corpses in the water did nothing to deter the living, in their desperation, from drinking and splashing their own scorched bodies.

Until the moment Yoshiko Hashimoto jumped into the river, she had been almost comatose with fear and the pain of the intense heat. The water revived her. She saw a tangle of lumber, partly ablaze, floating past. Seizing this with one hand, with the other she managed to push her baby onto the flimsy raft. He lay traumatised into silence as they drifted downstream. Even in the river, the heat was overpowering. Yoshiko ducked her head beneath the surface every few moments to cool her skin, and splashed the baby. Others were likewise struggling in the water, and Yoshiko found herself facing a new peril. Desperate men and women seized the timber, rocking and spinning it as they thrashed.

Yoshiko had been drifting perhaps half an hour when she saw a miraculous sight: a boat, rowed by two men. She cried out to them to take her baby, and with her failing strength pushed Hiroshi over the thwart. The rowers took pity on the mother also. She was dragged on board. They found that they could make little progress downriver, because their passage was blocked by flaming debris. On shore, they could see only a ring of fire. As the first light of dawn appeared, the boatmen lay on their oars and gazed at the stricken city. They and their two passengers were too shocked to speak. They merely wondered at the sight of a sun that looked more like a moon, a sickly yellow disk masked by pillars of smoke which towered over the landscape.

Slowly, very slowly, the heat began to diminish. Everything around Haruyo Wada which was susceptible to fire had succumbed. The first glimmerings of day appeared. Haruyo crawled out from beneath the cluster of humanity which had sheltered her—and found that all were blackened corpses save one, who took her hand. Providentially, it was her father. He had left his wife and other daughter at the station, and come back to search for her. Before she could even murmur, "Daddy," he said urgently: "Don't move from there," and disappeared again up the track. Minutes afterwards, he returned with her mother and sister. They stood in a scene of total desolation, wisps of white smoke lingering above the ashes, occasionally shot with blue flame as an ember met some vestige of material still unburned.

Haruyo could not grasp what had happened, and kept murmuring to herself: "Where am I? What has happened?" They began the search for her brother. Her parents were badly burned, their eyes almost closed by blisters, so that the children had to lead the way, picking a path between blackened corpses. Haruyo was fascinated by the number of dead mothers and infants; by the sight of one girl whose entire upper body was black and shrivelled, while by some freak her lower limbs were untouched. Five-year-old Mitsuko whimpered quietly, saying again and again: "My leg hurts." They recognised the site of their own home only when Haruyo glimpsed a fragment of much-loved family china. An iron pipe alone protruded aboveground. To their amazement, its tap delivered a feeble trickle of water, with which they sought to wash away the oily blackness which coated their faces and bodies.

Then there was another miracle. They saw a ragged, forlorn figure standing before them. It was the boy Soichiro. He was uninjured. He had crawled into a sewage pipe and lain in its shelter through the hours of destruction, soaking his body in damp filth. Mr. Wada sighed with passionate emotion: "We're all together again." In the shelter where, a few hours earlier, Mrs. Furuhashi had tried to hold back Haruyo from flight, they found their neighbours' family heaped, charred corpses. Indeed, every one of Haruyo's street playmates had perished. Among the Futamis, just two adults survived of a family of nine.

After a time, as the flames died, Yoshiko Hashimoto and the two boatmen who had saved her life steered their boat to the riverbank, and ventured ashore. They were stunned to behold the emptiness of a great urban landscape denuded of all buildings save a few lonely concrete survivors. The other landmarks were iron safes, standing forlorn amid the ashes of the homes and offices to which they once belonged. The only discernible colour in the scene was a dull, dead brown. Fallen phone and power lines hung like spiders' webs over the debris. Yoshiko was bewildered to perceive how little human life was visible. The great mobs which had thronged the streets during the night had vanished. Only a few lonely figures plodded through the desolation. Her rescuers, the boatmen, set about delivering her and her child, both exhausted and badly burned, to a hospital. They found a cart—or rather, its iron frame and wheels, for all the woodwork was gone. They laid mother and child upon it, and somehow dragged them through the ruins, the passengers frequently falling to the ground as Yoshiko lost her feeble purchase on the iron skeleton. Later, when she recovered her wits in hospital, she found that her saviours had vanished. "They saved our lives," she said in wonderment, "but I never knew their names. All I could tell from their talk was that one was a postman, the other a rice-seller."

Ryoichi Sekine, at the Suwa Shrine, was dimly aware that the overhead sound of aircraft was receding. Violent noise made by falling debris persisted, but there was little screaming, because people's breath was too precious. The injured sometimes groaned; that was all. The Sekines lingered perhaps two or three hours before moving. When they dared to rise, they perceived that most of those around them were dead. Ryoichi noted with blank curiosity the phenomenon of flickers of flame rising from corpses, fuelled by their body oils. While it was still dark, the Sekines tried to pick a path towards their home, but found the heat underfoot too great. They lingered awhile longer, then set off. Around dawn they reached the site, a ruin. For the first time, the smoke cleared sufficiently to reveal a glimpse of blue sky. It was around 7 a.m. Their eyes were swollen and bloodshot. They found a few mouthfuls of water to assuage their painful thirst, and some rice in their abandoned shelter, which they shared with grateful neighbours.

With absurd, ironic perversity, father and son said to each other: "Thank goodness we don't need to worry any more about the house burning down." Ryoichi's cousin Takako appeared. She said that the banner she had carried to lead the old people had proved useful for beating out the flames on their bodies. By the sort of fluke that pervades all great tragedies, they found that almost all their own neighbours survived, while in the main street a few yards distant every inhabitant had perished. The Sekines went to live in a temple whose chief priest had been a schoolmate of Ryoichi's, until that too was burned out in the great raid of May 1945. The family was unlucky in its choice of destinations. After quitting the ruins of Tokyo in favour of taking refuge in Osaka, they had to abandon their train en route, when it was strafed and wrecked by American fighters. Mr. Sekine said: "We should have ended this war a long, long time ago."

Two days later, Yoshiko Hashimoto and little Hiroshi made their way to the primary school where her husband's air-raid post had stood, and found him alive, together with her sister Chieko. Etsuko also came. She was hideously burned, but had survived after jumping into the river. Hisae and their parents were never seen again. Yoshiko mused long after: "Who did I blame for it all? The Americans? The Japanese had done the same thing to people. It was the war. Mine is the generation which allowed the war. We did nothing to stop it."

The Wada family fled from the remains of their old lives, and found refuge in the mountains of the Nagano Prefecture, with friends who ran a factory making armaments. Space was found in a workers' dormitory for the traumatised refugees. The former spice seller worked on a production line until the end of the war, while his wife took a job in the factory canteen. Japan's foreign minister, Mamoru Shigemitsu, a long-standing opponent of his nation's militarists, wrote later about the profound public bitterness generated by attacks such as that of 9 March: "Most of my mail consisted of questions why enemy prisoners, guilty of inhuman conduct, should receive favoured treatment when they burned people to death together with their homes, while those who escaped had nowhere to live and nothing to eat." Shigemitsu described the air attacks as "the most frightful experience the Japanese people have ever undergone." Even the Japanese military suffered no illusions about the impact of the Tokyo raid on civilian morale. On 15 March, a Japanese army general staff circular warned that "elements of the population have given way to a spirit of unrest. Throughout the homeland there are elements which we shall have to watch carefully, lest they jeopardise the prosecution of the war." Navy pilot Masashiko Ando said: "After the war, people would sometimes say to me: 'It must have been really tough out there, flying combat operations.' But when I had seen the bombed cities of Japan, I said: 'The toughest place to be was Tokyo.' "

George Beck, a B-29 gunner, wrote in his diary after landing back in the Marianas on 10 March: "An unforgettable mission . . . Squadron CO told us we were starting a new phase of the war in which we were going to burn down Japan's major cities. I took it with a grain of salt—but he was right."

The 9 March 1945 American bomber attack on Tokyo killed around 100,000 people, and rendered a million homeless. Over 10,000 acres of buildings were destroyed—16 square miles, a quarter of the city. A hundred of the capital's 287 fire stations and a similar number of its 250 medical facilities were wiped out. Over the weeks that followed, the XXth Bomber Command launched a succession of further raids, designed to achieve the same result elsewhere. On 11 March, B-29s went to Nagoya, Japan's third-largest city. Here, damage was much reduced by lack of a wind such as fanned the fires of Tokyo. Only two square miles of the city burned. On the thirteenth, Osaka was much more successfully attacked. Three thousand died, eight square miles of buildings were destroyed, half a million people were made homeless, for the loss of two American aircraft and thirteen damaged. On 16 March it was the turn of Kobe, population one million. Three square miles were destroyed, 8,000 people killed, 650,000 made homeless. Three bombers were lost and eleven damaged, all as a result of operational problems rather than enemy action.

After five such missions in a fortnight, a temporary halt to "burn jobs" became necessary. Air and ground crews were exhausted, supplies of incendiaries were running low. Yet the spirits of LeMay's command soared. In just five operations they had inflicted upon Japan eight times the damage done to San Francisco by the great 1906 earthquake. The enemy's cities had suffered in a few short days a scale of destruction which it had taken years to achieve in Germany, because Japanese buildings burned so much more readily. With the benefit of reports from its staff in Tokyo, Soviet naval intelligence reported: "Frequent bombings, particularly night attacks, have made a major impact on Japanese civilian morale. Exhaustion, sleeplessness and general strain have resulted in large-scale absenteeism which is affecting Japanese war production and causing acute anxiety in Japan's ruling circles."

The vulnerability of Japanese air defences had been laid bare. They lacked good anti-aircraft guns—on 9 March, flak accounted for just three American aircraft. Their radar sets were based on captured 1941-vintage U.S. and British technology, and were highly vulnerable to jamming. Their fighter pilots were poorly trained and ill-equipped either to locate bombers or to destroy them. Pursuing B-29s was a nightmare mission for Japanese fliers. Even those who knew their business found high-altitude engagement with the huge aircraft a gruelling experience. Ten minutes after taking off from the summer heat of Kyushu, Kunio Iwashita noticed ice forming around his oxygen mask. The Zero's machine guns were almost useless against the Superfortress. Iwashita himself scored just one success, on 29 April—a date he always remembered, because it was his wedding anniversary. After making no impression on his American victim with guns, he took up position some three hundred yards behind and just above it, then launched a guided bomb, which exploded beside the American's wing. The Japanese pilot followed the spinning wreck all the way down to the sea.

Again and again in the course of the Superfortress campaign, American aircrew expressed bewilderment at the poor showing of Japanese fliers, which seemed to accord so little with the enemy's general conduct in the last months of the war. "It was easy to see that the Nip pilots were plenty scared of us," wrote a U.S. flier as early as January 1945, "for out of thirty fighters spotted only ten attacked." Weather caused far greater difficulties for the B-29s than anything the enemy did. Japanese defences accounted for an average of just two American aircraft per attack. When American POW Mel Rosen saw the first bombers over his camp, "they looked like they were on a Sunday ride." "*B-nijuuku! B-nijuuku!*"—"B-29! B-29!"—cried the Japanese guards in anger, fear and bewilderment.

The B-29s' technical problems were progressively solved, aided by the dramatic diminution of engine strain at the lower operating altitudes mandated by LeMay. Propellers bit more effectively into the thicker air, enabling bomb loads to be doubled. Tremendous efforts were made to strengthen air-sea rescue. Up to fourteen "life guard" submarines were routinely deployed between Iwo Jima and Japan. By late summer, 2,400 U.S. personnel were committed to air-sea rescue, and were achieving dramatic results. If a B-29 landed successfully on the sea, it floated for ten to fifteen minutes. Of rescued crews, 45 percent were picked up in less than five hours, 36 percent in five to twenty-four; 13 percent in one to three days; 6 percent in three to seven days.

And if survivors, instead of drifting at sea, found themselves on one of the Pacific's uninhabited islands, they could turn to the wryly named *Castaway's Baedeker* in their survival kits, which described how to make the most of the least promising circumstances. Just under half of those who tried to ditch got home sooner or later. Air-sea rescue teams displayed extraordinary courage, persistence and determination. The only B-29 crews denied sympathy were a few who chose to land in the sea because, almost incredibly, they found this ordeal less terrifying than completing a mission.

Bombing Japan never became a routine assignment. For instance, on the night of 4 June 1945, when crews of the 9th Bomb Group were told at briefing that they would be attacking Kobe next morning at 14,000 feet, a storm of furious protest erupted: "Mess kits were banged on the wooden benches and all around me crew members were yelling, booing and shaking their heads," wrote a navigator. The twenty-nine-year-old group commander, Col. Henry Huglin, suppressed the uproar only by explaining that the attack height was dictated by a thick overcast to 16,000, and that it could be raised if the skies cleared over Japan. Yet back in the huts, some veteran crews were still predicting gloomily: "They'll be out waving flags and yelling 'Banzai.' " In the event, the mission proved relatively uneventful, but the apprehension was real enough. That same month, LeMay called for a special effort to curb the incidence of aircrew refusing flying duty. Up to 1 June, eighteen men from the XXth Bomber Command and sixty-nine from the XXIst had been relieved of operations for "anxiety reactions," and this was deemed too many.

Facilities on the Marianas slowly improved, to make their 100,000 USAAF campers less uncomfortable. With a hundred B-29s a month arriving from the factories, the Twentieth Air Force was now poised to impose a steady rhythm of pain and destruction upon the land of the enemy. Accuracy improved dramatically. Between January and June 1945 the number of bombs landing within a thousand feet of their aiming points rose from 12 percent to 40 percent. LeMay said: "The only thing the Japs have to look forward to is the total destruction of their industries." Arnold wrote to him on 21 March, praising the Tokyo raid as "brilliantly planned and executed." So heady was the climate of euphoria within the air force and outside it, fed by massive publicity in the U.S., that LeMay felt obliged to calm the frenzy, telling correspondents: "The destruction of Japan's industry by air blows alone is impossible." This prompted a rebuke from Arnold's chief of staff, Lauris Norstad: "Personally I have no quarrel with that thesis . . . But there is a War Department policy, stemming from last year's orgy of predictions that the war would end before Christmas, which prohibits predictions or speculations of any kind by General Officers." LeMay was warned to abstain in future from public forecasting, either positive or negative.

Yet the general had achieved an ascendancy which he sustained for the rest of the war. Enthusiasm was boundless for what his command had begun to do to Japan, and for the lustre which its deeds were deemed to have brought upon the air force. "Mission Number 40, the incendiary attack against Tokyo . . . on the night of 9–10 March is probably one of the most important ever flown by the Army Air Forces," asserted a post-war USAAF report. "Never before or since has so much destruction resulted from any single bombardment mission . . . it pointed the way to revolutionary new tactics." Air force chiefs hastened to endorse LeMay's attacks. "More than ever I am convinced of the importance of the bombs dropped on Japan between now and say, three months after the fall of Germany," Norstad wrote to him from Arnold's office on 3 April, following the issue of a new urban target list:

> This period will certainly be Japan's hour of decision . . . Results of the incendiary attacks have been tremendous. The first areas assigned were selected on the basis of a compromise between industrial importance and susceptibility to fire. With a greater respect we now have for our fire-making ability and the greater weight we are able to lay down, these new areas which have just been sent to you represent more nearly the top industrial areas. They also appear to be most susceptible to fire attack . . . If we are successful in destroying these areas in a reasonable time, we can only guess what the effect will be upon the Japanese. Certainly their war-making ability will have been seriously curtailed. Possibly they may lose their taste for more war. I am convinced that the XXIst Bomber Command, more than any other service or weapon, is in a position to do something decisive . . . You and your command have the respect, admiration and unqualified confidence of this headquarters. Keep up the good work.

Today, when many people in the West as well as in Japan recoil from the horrors inflicted by the 1945 bomber offensive, Norstad's words evoke a chill which is intensified by LeMay's post-war rationalisation of what his command did: "We were going after military targets. No point in slaughtering civilians for the mere sake of slaughter . . . All you had to do was visit one of those targets after we'd roasted it, and see the ruins of a multitude of tiny houses, with a drill press sticking up through the wreckage . . . The entire population got into the act and worked to make those airplanes or munitions of war . . . men, women, and children. We knew we were going to kill a lot of women and kids when we burned that town. Had to be done." As for the aircrew, few were troubled by the carnage they wreaked upon Japan. "I don't think we thought much about it," said Lt. Philip True. "At briefings, we were told we were bombing industrial areas, and that a lot of sub-assembly was located in surrounding residential areas. I don't think anybody enjoyed it. It was just a job that had to be done. By the time it was over I was ready to go back to school." True was indeed almost a schoolkid—as were they all. Some post-war critics have adopted the absurdly unrealistic view that aircrew should have refused to participate in firebombing. In truth, if the destruction of Japan's cities and massacre of its civilians were deemed inappropriate objectives for the USAAF, the onus rested squarely upon the media and the political leadership of the U.S.A. to demand that the campaign be prosecuted differently. They never did so.

After 1945, neither LeMay personally nor the air force as an institution welcomed the overwhelming evidence that Japanese industry was already being strangled to death by the American naval blockade when B-29 bombs began to fall upon it; that aerial bombardment in the last five months of war contributed little towards the destruction of Japan's war-making powers, though much towards punishing the Japanese people for their nation's aggression, if this was an appropriate occupation for the USAAF. As so often in the Second World War, especially in Asia, a campaign evolved out of synchronisation with the pace of events elsewhere, having missed a decisive place in the context of the struggle. If U.S. bombers had been able to strike hard at Japan in 1942 or 1943, even 1944, they might have achieved a dramatic impact upon Japan's industrial capability. As it was, however, by the time the Twentieth Air Force achieved the strength and competence to inflict major damage on the industrial cities of the enemy, Japan's war-making powers were in terminal decline from blockade.

Intelligence was a cardinal weakness of the B-29 campaign. Astonishingly little was known about the Japanese economy, industry, its choke points and weaknesses. In Albert Speer's anxiety to please his captors in May 1945, the Nazi armaments minister explained to American interrogators how they might bomb Japan more effectively than they had Germany. He stressed the importance of attacking the transport net, together with basic industries such as chemicals and steel: "It is much easier to dam up a river near the source than near the delta." When the war ended, LeMay was indeed preparing a great assault on Japanese transport links, though there is no evidence that he took his cue from Speer.

The U.S. Navy pressed relentlessly for air force assistance in tightening its blockade, calling for the B-29s to be diverted from attacking cities to laying mines in Japan's home waters. As in Europe, the airmen resisted any "distraction" from their independent strategic mission. Only grudgingly were some of LeMay's aircraft committed to mining at the end of March, prompted by fear that otherwise the navy would demand its own force of long-range aircraft. Some nine hundred mines were laid in Operation Starvation. Its impact was dramatic. The Japanese were as short of minesweepers as they were of everything else. The Shimonoseki Waterway was closed to shipping for a fortnight, prompting a 50 percent fall in imports. This crisis eventually induced the Japanese naval command to order supply ships to brave the channel, which caused a spate of sinkings. In all, B-29s dropped 12,000 sea mines, which accounted for 63 percent of all Japanese shipping losses during the period of their participation. Had LeMay's force been instructed to spend the rest of the war tightening the blockade, it would almost certainly have made a more useful contribution than by continuing the incineration of cities.

But it was not. In April, LeMay's men attempted some daylight raids on aircraft factories, which provoked heavy air battles. One formation was met by 233 Japanese fighters. Yet American losses from all causes remained between 1.3 and 1.6 percent, low by European standards. The B-29s returned to firebombing. On 13 April 352 aircraft attacked the "Tokyo arsenal area," as briefers designated the capital. A further 13.2 square miles of the city were burnt out, for the loss of eight aircraft. A week later, bombers attacked airfields on Kyushu, to assist the Okinawa campaign. Crews resented the diversion from their "real" task. Bombing was insufficiently accurate to make much impact on runways. For April as a whole, LeMay's planes devoted 31 percent of their effort to cities, 25 percent to aircraft plants, 37 percent to airfields.

Following the capture of Iwo Jima, P-51 Mustang fighters with long-range fuel tanks began to fly escort missions for the bombers. Their commanders hoped to inflict heavy attrition on the enemy's fighters in the air, as they had done against the Luftwaffe in Europe. Yet the fighters were notably less successful over Japan, partly because they met so few enemy aircraft. They were reduced instead to strafing "targets of opportunity," which proved relatively costly. Single-seat aircraft also proved alarmingly vulnerable to bad weather, and consequent blind navigation. On 1 June, a formation met a thunderstorm and violent turbulence, which inflicted a disaster greater than Japanese defences ever achieved: a B-29 tried to reverse course with its accompanying fighters, and met the following formation head-on. A shocking twenty-seven aircraft and twenty-four pilots were lost.

The Mustangs were plagued by misfortunes. Iwo Jima's alternating dust and mud created technical hazards. There were bewildering parachute failures—fifteen out of seventy-five pilots who tried to bail out suffered fatal malfunctions. Though the fighters possessed sufficient fuel endurance to reach Japan, many of their pilots found the long haul from Iwo intensely stressful. The VIIth Fighter Command began to rotate fliers out of combat after a mere fourteen or fifteen missions. Few airmen managed even that many. By May, some 240 Mustangs were committed to supporting bomber operations. The squadrons claimed to have shot down 221 Japanese aircraft, but the Americans lost 114 Mustangs in combat and 43 from operational causes, along with 107 pilots. This was a much less favorable exchange than had prevailed in the European theater. Given that the B-29s had shown themselves extraordinarily resilient to the Japanese defences, and that there was so little enemy air force left to fight, the fighter deployment proved a mistake.

On 25 May, 464 B-29s returned to Tokyo, destroying a further nineteen square miles of urban area with 3,258 tons of incendiaries. Of 26 bombers lost, only 4 or 5 fell to enemy action. A further 110 aircraft returned with damage, 89 from flak, 10 from fighters, 11 from a combination of the two. During May, LeMay's planes dropped 15,500 tons of bombs on three cities. On 1 June, 458 B-29s hit Osaka from high altitude. Ten aircraft were lost, 5 to enemy action. A raid on Kobe four days later marked the last occasion on which the bombers glimpsed significant numbers of enemy fighters. On the night of 15 June, another raid on Osaka killed a host of people and destroyed 300,000 houses. By now, the Twentieth Air Force was running out of targets. Bombers began to hit smaller cities. They attacked some refineries, not a profitable exercise when the Japanese had little oil left to process. In July, on nine nights of operations, they bombed thirty-five urban areas. Most burned satisfactorily.

JAPAN'S fighter pilots found the experience of combating the B-29s deeply depressing, because they achieved so few successes. It was not merely a question of making an interception; the undergunned Zero found it extraordinarily difficult to shoot down these armoured monsters. "We would try to get 2 or 3,000 feet above them, then dive steeply into attack, sometimes by coming up from beneath them," said Lt. Toshio Hijikata, commanding a flight whose only collective accomplishment was to shoot down a single B-29, tail-end Charlie of a formation, over the sea south of Kyushu. "Again and again we hit them with machine-gun fire, yet seemed to make no impression at all."

The lives of Japan's fighter pilots closely resembled those of the RAF's Battle of Britain fliers, five years earlier. Each day, they lolled in flying gear and parachutes on the grass beside their planes, ready for the electrifying order to scramble, as American planes were identified on radar. Then there was a rush to start up, taxi, and begin the long struggle to high altitude, which alone offered a chance of engaging the bombers. Fuel was available only for operational missions—there was none for replacement pilots to train. The young men were increasingly conscious of the futility of their efforts, the inevitability of defeat. If they escaped death, most shared Toshio Hijikata's expectation of "a lifetime as slaves of the Americans."

Like many Japanese, Hijikata blamed the army for everything: "We should have ended the war much sooner. Once we lost the Marianas, there was nothing to be gained from fighting on." Yet, like almost all his generation of young Japanese, he continued to do his own part, because he was unshakeably convinced that it was his duty to do so. Most pilots imbued their struggle with an aura of romance. For instance, Hijikata's much-admired comrade Tetsuzo Iwamoto was nicknamed "Koketsu," after the sword of a samurai warrior, to which Japanese literature attributed powers matching those of Excalibur in Western mythology.

On the ground, Hijikata shared a billet with five other pilots a few miles from the airstrip. Most nights he and his roommates played bridge, "for pretty high stakes, because we had nothing else to spend money on." The gramophone played music which might sometimes be popular Japanese, but was as likely to be that of Beethoven or Mozart. Their taste in music, like their enthusiasm for bridge, reflected the Japanese navy's pride in its European connections. While the rest of Japan was by now half-starved, pilots continued to receive good rations, because commanders knew that their men must eat to fight. Food also had to be the right kind. If aircrew were given sweet potatoes as a substitute for rice, such as many civilians received that summer, at 15,000 feet they suffered the agonies of stomach cramps.

Maybe once a week, and especially after a tough battle, the pilots piled into a truck and headed for the Ryotei restaurant on the main street of Kagoshima, to eat and drink with the geishas. Japanese fighter pilots, like those of every nationality, never had much trouble getting girls. Hijikata still cherished the memory of a typical brief wartime affair with a divorcée in Wonsan, whose house he visited to thank her for giving house room to some of his flight trainees. They found themselves listening to Tchaikovsky, then falling into bed.

There was a strange little drama at Kagoshima that summer, when a Hellcat pilot was obliged to bail out over the airstrip, his plane on fire. He landed with bad burns to his face and hands, and was taken to the medical quarters for treatment. He lay in bed there for two days before being removed to a POW camp. When the Japanese pilots heard about his presence, they could not resist an opportunity to behold the human face of the enemy they hated so much. Four curious young Japanese crowded into the American's room, and stood by his bed conversing as best his condition and their fragments of English allowed. His name was Murdoch. He was a college graduate, he said, who had been at university before he joined the navy. "Like me," said Hijikata brightly—"I was a trainee teacher."

Then came a moment which caused the Japanese much embarrassment. With difficulty because of his bandages, Murdoch tugged at his finger, removed and proffered a ring. Would the Japanese see that it reached his wife? They felt unable to accept, because they knew they would never be allowed to fulfil such a request. They wondered afterwards why he had made such a gesture of finality. Did he expect to die? To be shot? Probably. They never knew his fate, for next day he was taken away. But the Japanese fliers were moved by a sense of freemasonry with their adversary, once they met him face to face rather than at collision speeds.

LeMay's force now began to play with the enemy. B-29s dropped leaflets listing eleven Japanese cities and urging: "Read this carefully as it may save your life or the life of a relative or friend. In the next few days, four (or more) of the cities named on the reverse side will be destroyed by American bombs." These would be aimed at military installations, but "unfortunately, bombs have no eyes . . . You can restore peace by demanding new and good leaders who will end the war." In the words of an American historian, "this use of psychological warfare really made the generation of terror a formal objective of the fire raids."

One day, walking alone in the forest in the Honshu country district to which he had been evacuated, ten-year-old Yoichi Watanuki heard a thunderous crash among the trees. Investigating, he found a container burst open on the ground. It contained bale upon bale of American propaganda bills, which had failed to spread as intended. The boy peered curiously at drawings of Roosevelt and Churchill in a rickshaw being pulled by a hapless Japanese emperor, above the simple slogan: END THE WAR. Yoichi was impressed by the quality of the paper, better than anything he had seen for years. Seizing a huge armful of the leaflets, he carried them triumphantly home, where they served as fuel to heat a delicious hot bath.

The outcome of the war was now plain to most of the Japanese people, though diehards clung to hope. Among these was one of Yoichi's teachers. Early in 1945, when a B-29 crewman parachuted into their district, for some reason the man was led through the village only half-clad. "You see!" announced the teacher triumphantly. "This shows that the Americans are running short of clothing!" But Yoichi and a cluster of friends were much more impressed when an American fighter flew so low overhead one day that its wings almost touched the treetops. They saw the pilot's grinning features in his open cockpit as he gave the children a careless wave, and were awed by such an insouciant display of power.

U.S. bomber losses fell to 0.3 percent per mission. LeMay himself was rewarded for his achievements by further promotion as well as decorations. When Gen. Carl Spaatz, old and ill, was appointed overall supremo of Pacific strategic bomber forces in July, LeMay retained executive control as his nominal chief of staff. By August 1945 the Superfortresses had attacked sixty-six Japanese cities. Firebombing had made homeless a quarter of the nation's urban population, and killed at least 300,000 people—all statistics are unreliable. The Twentieth Air Force had lost 414 aircraft on combat operations: 148 of these to enemy action, 151 to "operational causes," 115 "unknown." A further 87 were lost in training accidents. 2,822 aircrew were killed or missing, of whom 363 eventually returned from Japanese imprisonment. The $4 billion cost—double that of the Manhattan Project, which developed the atomic bomb—paled in comparison with the $30 billion which the United States spent on European bomber operations, or with the $330 billion total cost of America's war effort.

THE HISTORY of the Twentieth Air Force's campaign reflects some critical truths about modern conflicts in general, and the Second World War in particular. First, the U.S. in 1945 was a prisoner of great industrial decisions taken years earlier, in quite different strategic circumstances. In 1942, the commitment to build the B-29 long-range bomber was entirely rational. The programme reached technological maturity and large-scale production too late to make a decisive impact on the war. Yet it was asking far too much of the U.S., never mind of its senior airmen, to forgo the use of these aircraft, at a time when the enemy was still resisting fiercely, and killing many Americans. *In the circumstances then prevailing*—an essential caveat for any historian to emphasise—the B-29s were bound to be employed. When precision bombing failed, as continued to be the case even when attempted under LeMay's direction in the spring of 1945, the cities of Japan were doomed to suffer the same fate as those of Germany. Rather than the will of commanders, it was the existence of a specific weapons system, the B-29 Superfortress, which impelled the incineration of several hundred thousand Japanese.

And so to LeMay himself. His name is forever associated with the fire-bombing of Japan, just as the RAF's Air Chief Marshal Sir Arthur Harris is identified with the area bombing of Germany. It seems quite mistaken to nominate either officer as a sin eater for the mass slaughter of civilians, a policy for which responsibility rightly belongs to their superiors. LeMay was a much more innovative and technically dynamic commander than Harris, not least because in Europe the American had acquired much experience of leading a bomber force in the air. Yet in character they had more than a little in common, including remarkable powers of leadership and determination, carried to the point of obsession. Neither was a cultured man. Their brutal choice of words, contempt for human suffering displayed during and after the war to justify their commands' actions, taste sour, even foul, to later generations.

But much of the criticism which has fallen upon LeMay and Harris ignores the qualities indispensable to those who fight wars on behalf of any nation, whether democracy or tyranny. In one of his letters home from the Pacific, Lt.-Gen. Robert Eichelberger cautioned his wife against badmouthing commanders merely because they did not seem nice men: "I imagine if one knew Napoleon or Julius Caesar, or any of the great leaders of history, there would have been a good many personal characteristics one would not have liked." Relatively few successful warriors are sensitive men or congenial fireside companions. Most possess an elemental commitment of an intensity happily unusual in civilised societies. They must daily give orders which bring death upon their own people, as well as the enemy. It is understandable that generations reared in peace, in the privileged circumstances of our twenty-first-century lives, should feel a revulsion towards the personal characters of Harris and LeMay. Yet such men are useful, indeed indispensable, in a war of national survival. Not every successful warrior needs to be an Attila, but he is unlikely to be Chaucer's "parfit gentil knight."

The key point about the roles of both Harris and LeMay is that they were subordinate officers, not supreme commanders. Each was the servant of a democracy, and of its elaborate military and political hierarchy. The Washington administration was scarcely oblivious of what American bombers were doing to Japan. At a press conference on 30 May, LeMay asserted that a million Japanese had already been killed in fire attacks. The U.S. secretary of war, Henry Stimson, was appalled, saying fiercely that he "did not want to have the U.S. get the reputation for outdoing Hitler in atrocities." Yet the only outcome was that LeMay was urged to curb his tongue, not his planes. No one suggested that he should change policy. If Churchill, Roosevelt or Truman, together with their respective chiefs of staff, perceived it as morally wrong to slaughter the civilian populations of Germany and Japan, then it was their function to decree otherwise, and if necessary to change the responsible commanders. They did not choose to do this. They acquiesced in, even if they did not enthuse about, what was done to the enemy in the names of their nations. They, rather than LeMay or Harris, must bear historic responsibility.

One of the most remarkable aspects of the Twentieth Air Force's 1945 campaign was the degree to which LeMay, a mere major-general of thirty-eight, was permitted to run his offensive out of the Marianas almost untrammelled by higher authorities. Washington sometimes interposed tactical advice or instructions—for instance, about the importance of diverting some aircraft from hitting cities to mining Japanese inshore waters—but never about strategic direction.

After Arnold's fourth serious heart attack of the war in January 1945, he was a sick man. The USAAF was haunted by apprehension that Nimitz might be given control of its operations from the Marianas: "Fear of losing control of the B-29s to the navy was paramount," in the words of the air force official historians. Conrad Crane, among others, has speculated about the possible consequences, had Nimitz or MacArthur been given authority over LeMay. Nimitz would have insisted that much more effort should be devoted to support of naval and ground operations. MacArthur, who perceived himself as a gentleman soldier, was implacably hostile to bombing civilians. In a staff memorandum of June 1945, one of MacArthur's closest aides, Brig. Bonner Fellers, described American air raids on Japan as "one of the most ruthless and barbaric killings of non-combatants in all history." Whatever the general might have ordered LeMay to do, he would not have permitted him systematically to raze enemy cities.

As it was, however, the Twentieth Air Force pursued its fire-raising campaign until the very last day of the war, with overall campaign losses of only 1.38 percent. Dr. Crane has written: "The course and conduct of the air campaign against Japan were primarily a product of one innovative air commander who took advantage of vague direction and a disjointed chain of command to apply his own solutions . . . Even today, viable alternatives to the fire raids seem unclear." There is no evidence that Arnold was ever less than wholly satisfied with his young star's conduct of what he allowed to become LeMay's private air force.

At the July 1945 Potsdam Conference, which Arnold attended, Stalin proposed a subsequent meeting in Tokyo. The airman delivered a jocular comment: "If our B-29s continue their present tempo, there [will] be nothing left of Tokyo in which to have a meeting." Arnold asserted proudly in those days: "The war with Japan is over as far as creative work is concerned. The die is cast." On 15 August 1945 he dispatched a teletype to LeMay congratulating him on his personal contribution to Allied victory: "one of the outstanding personal achievements of this war. You and the men under your command have indeed made clear to the world the full meaning of strategic bombardment. Your imagination, resourcefulness and initiative reflect credit on the entire army air forces. We are intensely proud of what you have done."

The official USAAF post-war history of LeMay's command was unstintingly triumphalist:

> Highlight of the entire Twentieth AF blitz against Japan was the last five months of dynamic operations. In reaching this fiery perfection, which literally burnt Japan out of the war, the Twentieth came a long way from its meager 77-plane, 368-ton shakedown strike against Bangkok . . . on June 5, 1944 . . . In its climactic five months of jellied fire attacks, the vaunted Twentieth killed outright 310,000 Japanese, injured 412,000 more, and rendered 9,200,000 homeless . . . Never in the history of war had such colossal devastation been visited on an enemy at so slight a cost to the conqueror . . The 1945 application of American Air Power, so destructive and concentrated as to cremate 65 Japanese cities in five months, forced an enemy's surrender without land invasion for the first time in military history. Because of the precedent-shattering performance of the Twentieth Air Force, no U.S. soldier, sailor or Marine had to land on bloody beachheads or fight through strongly-prepared ground defense to ensure victory in the Japanese home islands . . . Very long range air power gained victory, decisive and complete.

This passage seems worth quoting at length, because it highlights the extravagance of the airmen's claims for their contribution to victory, as well as their absence of moral reservations. The U.S. Strategic Bombing Survey estimated that air attack of all kinds had destroyed 36.8 percent of Japan's cars, 34.2 percent of machine tools, 20.6 percent of furniture and household goods. Some 15 million people, one-sixth of the population, had been rendered homeless, 13.2 million were unemployed, most because their places of work had ceased to function. A total of 2.51 million houses had been destroyed by bombs, a further 600,000 by the Japanese themselves, in the creation of firebreaks.

Back in 1941, the brilliant British scientific civil servant Sir Henry Tizard questioned the likelihood that, even with a massive force of bombers, the RAF could inflict damage upon German industry commensurate with the scale of aircrew lives and resources committed—ultimately almost one-third of Britain's entire war effort. Tizard did not dispute, he said, that bombing could inflict *catastrophic* damage upon Germany. He simply questioned whether this would also prove *decisive*, surely the essential criterion to validate a bomber offensive on the scale Britain eventually conducted. Tizard lost that argument to the airmen, but the historical evidence suggests that his scepticism was prescient.

The material damage inflicted upon Japanese industry by LeMay's offensive was almost irrelevant, because blockade and raw-material starvation had already brought the economy to the brink of collapse. Many raids burnt out factories where production was already flagging or halted. Yet no nation could regard with indifference the destruction of a large proportion of its urban housing, whatever the protestations of the Japanese military to the contrary. It seems essential to acknowledge the psychological impact of the B-29 campaign. No human being of any culture could fail to be impressed, indeed awed, by such a display of the enemy's might and his own nation's impotence. It seems impossible to doubt that, when Japanese surrender eventually came, it was influenced in some degree by the U.S. bomber offensive which preceded and indeed followed Hiroshima. It remains unlikely that the Twentieth Air Force's contribution justified its huge moral and material cost to the United States. It seems absurd, however, to deny its contribution to the collapse of Japan's will to resist.

For posterity, perhaps most important is to perceive LeMay's campaign as setting the stage, creating the moral and strategic climate, for Hiroshima and Nagasaki. A recent study has observed: "Nobody involved in the decision on the atomic bombs could have seen themselves as setting new precedents for mass destruction in scale—only in efficiency." Like Sir Arthur Harris, Curtis LeMay remained impenitent to the end. After the war, he shrugged: "Nothing new about death, nothing new about deaths caused militarily. We scorched and boiled and baked to death more people in Tokyo on that night of 9–10 March than went up in vapor at Hiroshima and Nagasaki combined." He claimed to regret nothing.

THIRTEEN

The Road past Mandalay

JAPAN'S 1944 DISASTERS in Assam and Burma prompted a wholesale sacking and replacement of its generals. The new commander-in-chief, Gen. Hoyotaro Kimura, set about painstakingly rebuilding his forces in readiness to meet the British Fourteenth Army, advancing south-eastwards. He offered no challenge to Slim's crossings of the Chindwin in November and December. As the British advanced, they encountered pitiful relics of their 1942 defeat: a column of thirty-eight Stuart tanks, blown up when they could not be evacuated, together with scores of rusted civilian vehicles, some still occupied by skeletons. Slim snapped at a man who decorated his jeep with a skull, telling him to take it off: "It might be one of our chaps, killed on the retreat." In northern Burma, shortly before Christmas men of 19th Indian Division joined hands with advanced elements of Stilwell's Chinese divisions at Banmaux. By the end of January, the Burma Road into China was at last open all the way to Kunming, and the first truck convoys of supplies began to move north. To acute British dismay, Chiang Kai-shek, having gained what he wanted from the campaign, ordered his Nationalist divisions back to their homeland, leaving Slim's forces to pursue unaided the advance towards Rangoon.

It seemed to the Japanese inevitable that the invaders would now drive south towards Mandalay, that city of temples beside the Irrawaddy, a lyrical rendezvous in British imperial folklore. Kimura's plan was to allow the British deep into Burma, where their lines of communications would become extended, while his own remained short. He then intended that the ten divisions of his 15th and 33rd Armies would smash Slim's forces as they sought to cross the Irrawaddy north of Mandalay.

Unfortunately for Kimura, however, Slim anticipated his foe's intention. In addition to notable powers of generalship, the British commander also possessed the luxury of strength, not only in infantry numbers but also in overwhelmingly superior air, artillery and armoured forces. He was able to support his advance with supplies air-dropped on an unprecedented scale, a facility which went far to counter the difficulties of terrain. Most of the Japanese formations, by contrast, lacked half their men and were desperately short of guns. Slim dispatched one British corps to make a noisy feint in the north—19th Division crossed the Irrawaddy at Thaneikkyin on 11 January 1945. This was where Kimura expected an assault, and the Japanese launched exactly the big counter-attack Slim wanted to provoke. Next, the British XXXIII Corps staged another demonstration north-west of Mandalay, before beginning river crossings at Ngazun on 12 February. This prompted Kimura to commit the bulk of his forces. Yet all the northerly activity masked Slim's real purpose: to push another corps across the Irrawaddy fifty miles to the south-west at Pakokku, and then drive east to the vital road junction of Meiktila, far behind Kimura's front, cutting off most of the Japanese formations in Burma from their supply lines. By St. Valentine's Day 1945, the southerly British force, IV Corps, had secured an Irrawaddy bridgehead against negligible opposition, and was poised to launch the decisive coup of the campaign, the seizure of Meiktila.

A soldier of 17th Indian Division, George MacDonald Fraser, wrote wryly of Operation Cloak, Slim's deception to confuse the Japanese: "He confused 9 Section, too; we dug in at no fewer than three different positions in as many hours, Grandarse lost his upper dentures on a sandbank, little Nixon disturbed a nest of black scorpions in the dark . . . the general feeling was that the blame for the whole operation lay at the door of first, Winston Churchill, secondly, the royal family, and thirdly (for some unimaginable reason) Vera Lynn . . . We did not know that 'Cloak' had worked brilliantly; we were footsore, hungry, forbidden to light fires, and on hundred percent stand-to—even although, as Grandarse . . . pointed out, there wasn't a Jap within miles."

Deception on this scale was only possible when the Japanese had lost the capability to conduct air reconnaissance, indeed possessed negligible intelligence-gathering capability. They lacked transport swiftly to change deployments, and firepower to hit hard even when they did so. The open country suited British armoured and mobile forces. This does not diminish Slim's achievement, however, in wrongfooting his enemy and masterminding an offensive which now began to inflict devastating casualties upon the Japanese, at small cost to Fourteenth Army. There was hard fighting in Burma between February and May 1945, when the British entered Rangoon. But the energy of Japanese defensive actions and counter-attacks reflected despair, rather than any realistic expectation of reversing the tide.

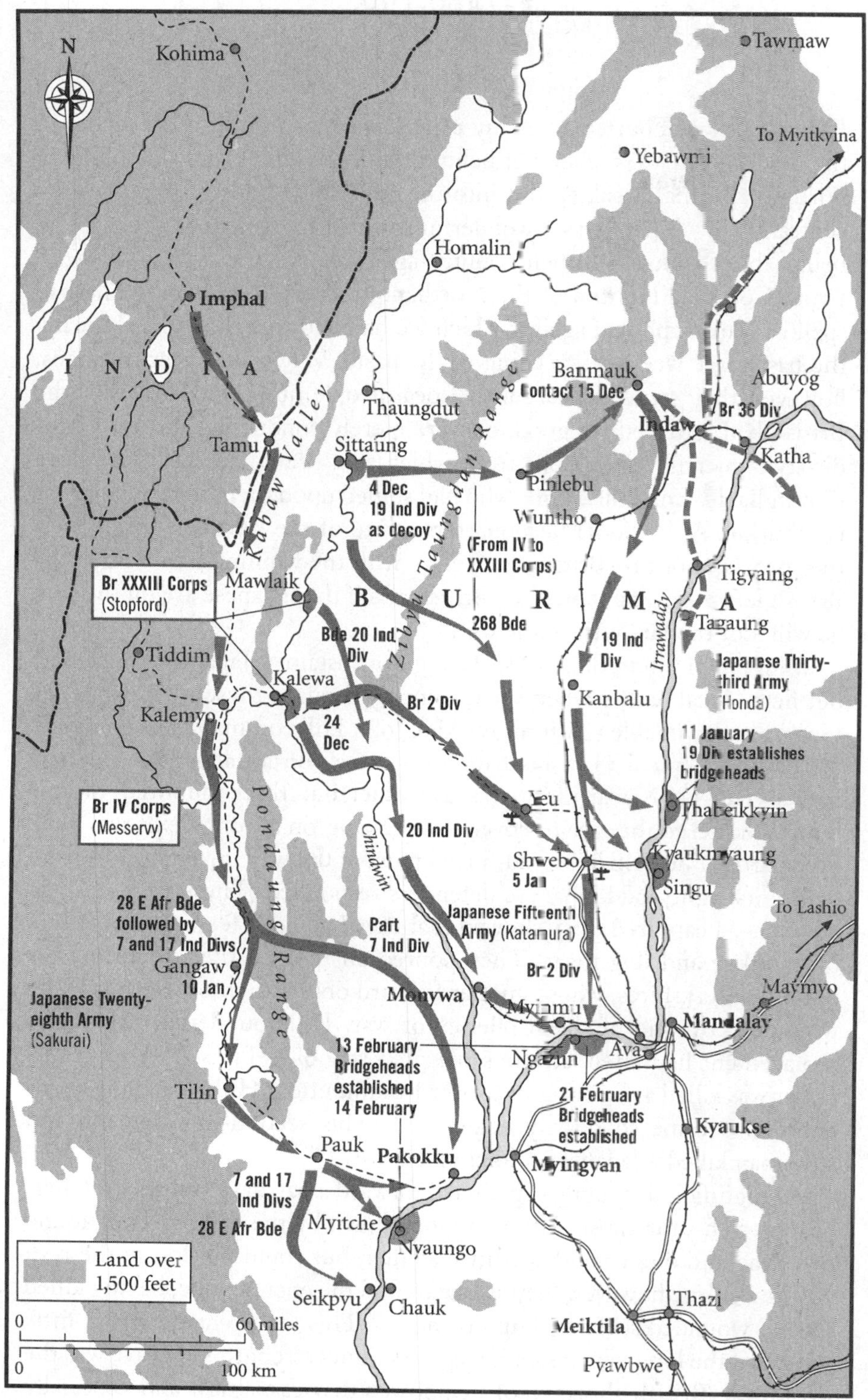

Fourteenth Army's advance on Mandalay, November 1944–February 1945

. . .

EVERY MAN of Fourteenth Army experienced a surge of relief when, in the first days of 1945, they left behind the thick jungle and steep hills of northern Burma, breaking out into the flat paddy fields of the country's central plain. "There was a wonderful spirit of freedom and sheer joy at being able to move in open country again, to see tracks and villages," wrote Col. Ted Taunton of the Northamptonshire Regiment. "The bad spell of claustrophobia against which we had had to fight so hard during the past three weeks was a thing of the past." When they met Burmans, however, they sensed uncertainty. Local people questioned whether the British had returned for good, or were merely conducting further Chindit-style guerrilla operations from which they would retreat once more into India, leaving inhabitants who had smiled upon them to face Japanese retribution. A divisional headquarters wrote of the Burman: "He is neither pro-Jap nor pro-British, he will go with the winning side. When the British left Burma he looted the British and if the Japanese are on the run, he will loot the Jap in the same way."

Slim's men found themselves facing not sustained Japanese resistance, but fierce local battles wherever the enemy thought these worthwhile, or found himself unable to withdraw. Maj. John Hill commanded a company of the 2nd Berkshires in his battalion's attack on an abandoned village named Kin-U. No artillery was available, but three hundred mortar bombs plastered the area to cover their assault, on a frontage of two hundred yards. The British had advanced most of the way through the village before its eighty-odd Japanese defenders responded. These were desperate men—a captured diary showed that they had been feeding themselves on monkey and dog meat. They poured all the fire they could muster upon the Berkshires, whose gunner forward observation officer was badly wounded. By one of the drolleries of war, Hill found that this man's replacement had attended the same prep school as himself. A sergeant-major was killed as he brought forward ammunition. Hill's company headquarters became so heavily engaged that his second-in-command and storeman killed a Japanese soldier apiece.

At nightfall, the young captain led forward a patrol of Indian stretcher-bearers to his foremost platoon, pinned down by the enemy. They found two dead and one wounded British soldier, but could not locate the rest. Next morning, however, they awoke to find the enemy gone, having killed six and wounded seven of Hill's company. This was a characteristic little action, of the kind which steadily eroded Slim's strength. So grave was the worldwide British shortage of manpower that casualties, and especially junior leaders, could seldom be replaced. Fourteenth Army's numbers shrank with every step that it advanced southwards.

From an early stage, though the invaders sometimes met tough resistance, they also found evidence that the Japanese lacked the skills and determination of earlier times. Their patrolling seemed halfhearted, and they sometimes exposed themselves carelessly. The familiar Japanese savagery towards prisoners was undiminished however. After a battle on 21 January, the Berkshires found dead British soldiers beaten, stripped of their boots and suspended by electric flex upside down from trees. This encounter sharpened the battalion's sentiment against their enemy. "Very few of us, whether professional soldier or conscript or volunteer, felt any twinges of remorse when one either saw a dead Japanese or killed a live one," wrote John Hill. "We had, after all, spent the whole war learning how to kill the enemy—and he us. No one expected any mercy." At Kabwet, on the Irrawaddy north of Mandalay, Hill's battalion lost nine officers and ninety other ranks, twenty-five of these in his own company, during operations to destroy a Japanese bridgehead. Gazing upon the enemy's dead after the battle, one of his men said with a twinkle in his eye: "None of them surrendered then, sir?"

Slim's feint in northern Burma has been hailed by posterity as a brilliant stroke, but for those at the sharp end, the price was hardship and fear. When the British 2nd Buffs began to cross the Shweli River near Myitson with 36th Division on 1 February, they were cruelly punished. Private Cecil Daniels reached the Japanese bank unhurt, and lay under its lee with other men, watching the sufferings of those caught by fire in midstream. "One of our chaps was calling, 'Please help . . . I've got it in the guts.' I felt so sorry for him . . . to be all alone and dying on a sandbar miles away from home tugged at my heartstrings but common sense got the better of me, I thought of my parents at home who had already lost one son. I was still cogitating whether to put one's life at risk when his cries got fainter and he slowly slipped beneath the water and floated away."

That night in the precarious British bridgehead, Daniels was eating his rations in a foxhole when the darkness was rent open by gunfire and the cries of his platoon sergeant: "They've broken through, get out, every man for himself!" The soldier wrote: "Then came the pounding of boots and silhouettes of men in flight, rushing past me kicking sand and dirt in my face as they ran down the bank, jumping into the swirling water. I sat in my hole quite bewildered by the rush of events, still eating my K ration." Daniels was reluctant to quit his hole for the river, but in the chaos he saw no choice save to abandon helmet and pack, and join the panic-stricken throng wading back to the British bank of the Shweli. At dawn "a scene of absolute misery met our eyes—the rest of the company (what remained of it) were morosely sitting or wandering about in a daze, very downhearted. Each one seemed to be asking others: 'Have you seen so-and-so?' " A lavish rum ration was issued.

Most men had lost their watches. Daniels had given his to a mate to mend. Now, he discovered that the mate was dead. Gazing at the brown water of the river, he saw the body of another company's sergeant-major lying bloated in the current: "Although he wasn't much liked in the battalion, it was a shame to see him like that." Though Daniels's company commander received a Military Cross for the action, it had cost the Buffs 114 dead and wounded. During the fortnight which followed, the river was successfully bridged elsewhere. It was fortunate for the spirits of Daniels and his comrades that they remained oblivious that they suffered in pursuit of a mere diversion.

The Shweli was a modest obstacle, beside the Irrawaddy. Slim staged Fourteenth Army's crossings of one of the biggest rivers in Asia with a ramshackle armada of assault craft, pontoons and rafts which Eisenhower's armies in Europe would have viewed with disbelief. There were no amtracs here. Slim himself observed ruefully: "I do not think any modern army has ever attempted the opposed crossing of a great river with so little." The "big picture" at the Irrawaddy was of overwhelming British success. Yet some units suffered severely. The Northamptons, crossing at Kyigon with 20th Indian Division on 13 February, found some of their boats foundering and others drifting far downstream from their objectives. In rough and rising water, craft overturned, precipitating overburdened infantrymen into the current. While scores crawled through the shallows to duck incoming fire, Bombardier Lees of 114 Field Regiment splashed upright for five hundred yards in full view of the enemy. He was carrying a gunner forward observer team's radio, and refused to get the set wet.

Fifty miles southwards at Myitche, where 7th Indian Division crossed the Irrawaddy on its way to Meiktila, Slim's men were assisted by another diversion, which drew off the most effective local Japanese formation to meet a threat from an East African brigade at Seikpyu. So successful was this, asserted the British official historian blandly, "that it was counterattacked and driven back to Letse, thereby drawing away from the main battlefield the only formidable striking force the Japanese had in the area." This account was a trifle disingenuous. In truth, Fourteenth Army was dismayed by the precipitate flight of the East Africans. An apologetic signal from their commander sought solace in the fact that one unit had retained its cohesion when the remainder fled: "Despite recent bad behaviour bulk 28 EA Brigade, 46 KAR (Nyasaland) remained unaffected . . . and have stood firm. Consider this fine performance especially in view behaviour remainder brigade." Yet, while it was true that one significant Japanese unit went in pursuit of the East Africans, sufficient enemy remained at 7th Division's crossing point, four miles above Nyaungu, to cause much grief to the South Lancashire Regiment.

Its men undertook the longest opposed river crossing of World War II. The Irrawaddy at this point was over 2,000 yards wide, which rendered it an alarming obstacle for heavily laden infantrymen in frail boats, even if the enemy was weak. The first of the South Lancs successfully rowed their boats across in silence and darkness during the early hours of 14 February. They established a bridgehead on the far bank without alarming the enemy. Then two Japanese were spotted swimming, apparently for pleasure. The enemy soldiers were shot, and thereafter a firefight developed. The rest of the South Lancs were late reaching the riverbank, and began the passage in daylight. Many of their boats' chronically unreliable outboard engines puttered to a stop in midstream. Japanese machine guns began to rake them, killing two company commanders and wrecking wirelesses. The commanding officer's boat was sunk. He and his companions with difficulty swam to safety back on the British bank.

The current began to sweep boats downstream, in a deadly parade past Japanese guns. A battalion of Punjabis which followed the South Lancs faced the same ordeal. Col. Derek Horsford and his Gurkhas watched the melodrama with mounting horror: "The South Lancs' CO eventually staggered into the presence of the brigade commander stark naked, and collapsed before his eyes, totally exhausted by his own and his unit's ordeal." Yet matters were not as bad as they briefly seemed. Horsford's Gurkhas made the crossing almost unscathed.

"With maddening sluggishness the boats nosed their way across the water," wrote an eyewitness. "Two boats grounded on a submerged and treacherous sandbank, but the men, quite undaunted, waded shoulder-deep in the swift current up to the beaches. At last all the boats grounded and the men swarmed up the cliffs and nullahs to their objectives on the high ground. More and more boats followed, heavily laden with troops, until boats were going both ways in an almost continuous stream while the air and artillery curtain of fire moved gradually downstream, and then back again behind the cliffs and beaches."

Once the British and Indian vanguards were ashore, they met little serious resistance. Some Japanese scuttled into tunnels, in which Slim's men entombed them with explosive charges. In one place, astonished British soldiers saw Japanese survivors form up in full equipment, then march into the river to drown themselves. Other defenders proved to be halfhearted members of the renegade Indian National Army, who surrendered or melted away into the countryside. Within days, the British striking force was concentrated on the east bank of the Irrawaddy, with no Japanese capable of stopping the dash on which it now embarked, sixty miles eastward to Meiktila.

The Japanese were soon being forced back from the river everywhere Slim's forces crossed. On 8 March, north of Mandalay the 19th Indian Division reported, "Opposition encountered appears very disorganised." Its senior staff officer, Col. John Masters, wrote exultantly:

> We rumbled down the cattle tracks in the heavy dust, past strands of jungle where the crackle of small arms fire showed that we had caught some Japanese. The tank treads clanked through villages blazing in yellow and scarlet conflagrations, palm and bamboo exploding like artillery, grey-green tanks squatting in the paddy round the back, ready to machine gun any Japanese who tried to escape before our advancing infantry . . . trudging along the sides of the road plastered with dust and sweat . . . The light hung sullen and dark overall, smoke rose in vast writhing pillars from a dozen burning villages, and spread and joined to make a gloomy roof. Every village held some Japanese, every Japanese fought to the death, but they were becoming less and less organised.

Even at this late stage, the Japanese commanders refused to acknowledge the British push towards Meiktila as more than a feint. Thus, when 17th Indian Division reached the town, its spearheads met only a ragtag defence, which was swept aside in the first days of March. The Japanese 15th and 33rd Armies in the north were now cut off. At last, Kimura understood how disastrously he had been outmanoeuvred. He perceived no alternative save to throw everything into an attempt to regain Meiktila. As the British poured reinforcements into the town by road and air, one of the most desperate battles of the Burma campaign began, while further north Slim's forces closed on Mandalay. Each side deployed some six divisions. The Japanese, however, were obliged to do most of the attacking. Wherever they moved, they exposed themselves to British aircraft and artillery. While the units of Fourteenth Army were well-fed, heavily armed and equipped, those of their opponents were in sorry condition. There were around 3,200 Japanese in Meiktila itself, but most were service troops. Allied tanks moved boldly, because the Japanese were poorly supplied with anti-tank weapons and mines. Indeed, given the state of their formations, it is astonishing that Kimura's soldiers put up the fight they did.

The 1/3rd Gurkhas, who were flown into Meiktila, fought their first action in defence of its airstrip. The battle proved "fairly traumatic," in the words of its adjutant, Captain Ronnie McAllister. "The tanks took a pasting because we advanced across open ground, unreconnoitred. It was a general shambles. The Japanese did not open fire until our chaps were twenty-five yards away." In earlier years back in India, McAllister, a career soldier, worried that he would be left out of the war. Now, however, he and his comrades found themselves in a nightmare predicament. They were led into battle by an old "dugout" North-West Frontier colonel named "Badger" Spaight, who was utterly confounded by the experience. To the relief of his men, after the first days Spaight was sacked, to be replaced by his second-in-command, Robert O'Lone, "who thoroughly understood what he was doing, after three years in the job." Thereafter matters went much better, though in Burma the battalion suffered a total of four hundred casualties, almost half its strength. "The Japanese still had the reputation from 1944, and we were very scared of falling into their hands, but by now we had much more of everything than they did. It was obvious we were winning."

On 16 March, 17th Division signalled insouciantly to Fourteenth Army: "Jap suicide squads dug in Meiktila airstrip, temporarily delaying today's fly-in . . . clearing north end airfield proceeding merrily situation quickly developing slaughter." For the Japanese, the battle was a ghastly experience. Gen. Masaki Honda, the eager fisherman now tasked to retake Meiktila, told his commander-in-chief bitterly: "There aren't twenty serviceable guns left among the two divisions. It's quite hopeless to go on." When ordered to hold his ground to enable the remnants of 33rd Army to escape, Honda asked for the order in writing, but said: "My army will keep fighting to the last man." So it did. Lt. Hayashi Inoue said: "Meiktila was a place where almost everyone died. There was nothing we could do. The British were so much stronger. Our anti-tank weapons simply bounced off their armour. We could only entrench ourselves behind the embankments of rice paddies. We were simply in the business of clinging on."

Ronnie McAllister, like every British Gurkha officer, deeply admired the courage of his little Nepalese soldiers, especially when acting as artillery observers, often three or four hundred yards in front of the infantry positions. Naik Dhanbahadur Limbu of the 3/10th Gurkhas was once manning an observation post, alone in a tree in front of his battalion position, taking muzzle-flash bearings of Japanese guns. He reported by phone that a big enemy attack was developing, and was told to clear out: within five minutes a British barrage would start falling around him. He chose instead to stay put. When a Japanese officer and several men assembled under his tree, Limbu dropped a clutch of grenades on them, killing three and wounding the officer. The Japanese never realised whence their nemesis came. All that night, Limbu calmly reported the enemy's movements as British salvoes bracketed his tree.

Further north, British and Indian soldiers driving down from the Irrawaddy were awed by their first sighting of Mandalay Hill, surmounted by its temples gleaming gold in the dusty haze. "Here before us," wrote John Hill, "was our first real goal at last: a recognisable place on the world's maps, not just an unknown village or a tangle of jungle." By 11 March, Fourteenth Army's daily situation report described "house-to-house and pagoda-to-pagoda fighting" taking place in Mandalay city. By the twentieth, the city was largely secured. Maj.-Gen. "Punch" Cowan, commanding 17th Indian Division, learned that among the British dead in its streets was his own son.

Everywhere, the Japanese were cracking. "We just overran them and killed them and killed them and killed them," said Lt. Col. Derek Horsford without sentiment. On 8 April John Sandle led his company of Baluchis to seize an objective named Point 900, west of Pyawbwe. A sepoy was shot as the Baluchis went in. When the defenders crumbled, Randle shouted to take prisoners. His *subadar* cried in response: "It's no good, *sahib*! They won't listen." Randle wrote: "They were in a blood lust . . . baying in high-pitched screams, with their lips drawn back over their teeth which gave them a ghastly wolflike insane grin. I found myself both exhilarated and appalled by this sheer animal lust to kill. In about ten minutes of grenade work, tommy- and bren-gun fire and the bayonet the whole Jap company was wiped out, with no prisoners taken. They put up little resistance, and I only had one other man killed." This was the only moment of the war at which Randle saw a Japanese officer turn and flee—to be shot for his pains. The bodies of 124 Japanese were dumped in a convenient ditch. Gunner Lt. John Cameron-Hayes said: "We felt it was going to be over pretty soon. The Japanese were on the run. Their corpses lay everywhere. They were much less aggressive than in the past."

For the men of Slim's army advancing, winning, was a wonderfully rewarding experience after the past years of pain and defeat. "I'm afraid I enjoyed the campaign," said Captain Ronnie McAllister afterwards. "It was great fun. We never thought of Burma as a sideshow, but as splendid theatre. We were tremendously proud of the regiment and the division." In those last weeks, British commanders found themselves hampered by lack of provost personnel to direct traffic, as tank and truck convoys jammed the few roads. Whole artillery units had to be diverted to this humdrum task.

Yet the visible rewards of the Burma campaign seemed pathetically drab. Slim wrote: "It was always a disappointment . . . to enter a town that had been a name on the map and a goal for which men fought and died.

There was for the victors none of the thrill of marching through streets which, even if battered, were those of a great, perhaps historic, city—a Paris or a Rome. There were no liberated crowds to greet the troops. Instead, my soldiers walked warily, alert for booby traps and snipers, through a tangle of burnt beams, twisted corrugated iron, with here and there, rising among the squalid ruins, the massive chipped and stained pagodas of a Buddhist temple. A few frightened Burmans, clad in rags, might peer at them and even wave a shy welcome, but at best it was not a very inspiriting welcome, and more than one conquering warrior, regarding the prize of weeks of effort, spat contemptuously."

Though the men of Fourteenth Army perceived themselves as winning a great victory, American scepticism persisted about almost everything the British did. A U.S. military observer group reported on an action of 23 April 1945: "Again in typical fashion the enemy held the initiative . . . 19 Division seldom knew where the enemy was . . . the enemy again proved himself able to conceal his movements, and to deny to the British any knowledge of his strength."

By the end of March, Slim had gained control of Burma's road and rail net. The orders received by Japanese units became increasingly fanciful, demanding the occupation of positions already irretrievably lost. One day in April, Honda's army headquarters in a garage on the outskirts of Pyawbwe found itself under fire. Every truck, car and radio was destroyed. The general lay writing his will while the position was defended by three hundred men, of whom a third were medical orderlies and other noncombatants. The Japanese received an unexpected deliverance when British tanks veered away northwards, unaware of the prize at hand. When darkness came, carrying only a cane and a handful of salvaged possessions in a pack, Honda led his survivors on foot towards Yamethin. The general was seen at his best in the days of flight which followed, still dispensing to his exhausted men the brothel jokes for which he was notorious. A few of his units were fortunate enough to possess transport. Maj. Mitsuo Abe described the Japanese 53rd Division's retreat: "Among the stream of vehicles, men of all manner of units commingled, many of them wounded. Some had their arms in improvised slings . . . some were bandaged with towels or strips of shirt. Some had lost eyes, others cried aloud for their mangled limbs to be cut off, others again raved in malarial fever. There were those who pleaded with friends to make their wills, and younger soldiers moaning 'Mother . . . mother.' Some cried out for their commanders as they struggled on, supported by a comrade on each side. It was hell on earth."

Slim's purpose was now to drive hard and fast for Rangoon, Burma's first city, 320 miles south of Meiktila, then turn back and mop up enemy remnants on both sides of the road. The chief impediments to the British advance proved to be logistical—weary men, worn-out tanks and trucks which had travelled almost a thousand miles since the campaign began. On 27 April, Fourteenth Army signalled to Mountbatten: "Leading troops now only 72 miles from Rangoon port . . . spirit of competition of leading troops in race south now intense. Since capture MANDALAY 20 March [Fourteenth] Army troops have advanced 352 miles in 38 days."

British commanders emphasised the need to minimise losses in this last phase of the campaign, when the outcome was decided: "Men are the most precious thing we've got," warned 20th Indian Division's commander, Douglas Gracey. "Use them with the greatest care." The dash for Rangoon, in the first days of the monsoon, which came a fortnight early, represented the high peak of Britain's war in the Far East. The Japanese were broken, even if some soldiers still possessed their familiar, terrifying will to fight: "I turned to see a Jap racing across in front of the bunker, a sword flourished above his head," wrote a soldier of 17th Division south of Meiktila. "He was going like Jesse Owens, screaming his head off, right across my front; I just had sense enough to take a split second, traversing my aim with him before I fired; he gave a convulsive leap, and I felt that jolt of delight—I'd hit the bastard!"

A Cumbrian soldier said: "If thoo wez a Jap, an' saw this lot coomin'—Goorkas, an' Pathans, an' Sikhs, an' them bloody great black boogers frae th' East African Division—fookin' Zulus, or suumat—aye, an' us, an' a—wouldn't *you* pack it in?" For the last time in its great history, Britain's Indian Army rode to the charge, triumphant after more than three years of defeat and disappointment. Slim himself was almost killed overflying Rangoon. Japanese fire hit his aircraft, wounding an American liaison officer. On 1 May, 25th Indian Division staged an amphibious landing on the coast south of the capital. Two days later, after killing four hundred of their own wounded who could not be moved, the Japanese abandoned Rangoon, and retreated eastwards. Prisoners at the city's jail painted a huge sign on its roof for the RAF: JAPS GONE. EXDIGITATE. The British marched in.

The Japanese retreat from Burma was marked by systematic atrocities against Burmans and Indian civilians, who were tortured and casually killed until the very end. The vanquished vented their bitterness on any victims to hand. Through the months that followed, Fourteenth Army fought on against broken Japanese units striving to retreat eastwards into Siam—there were still more than 60,000 enemy at large—but Slim's forces dominated the battlefield. The main campaign was ended. The British Union flag flew once more over Burma. The scale of loss on both sides highlights the fact that the decisive battles had been fought in 1944.

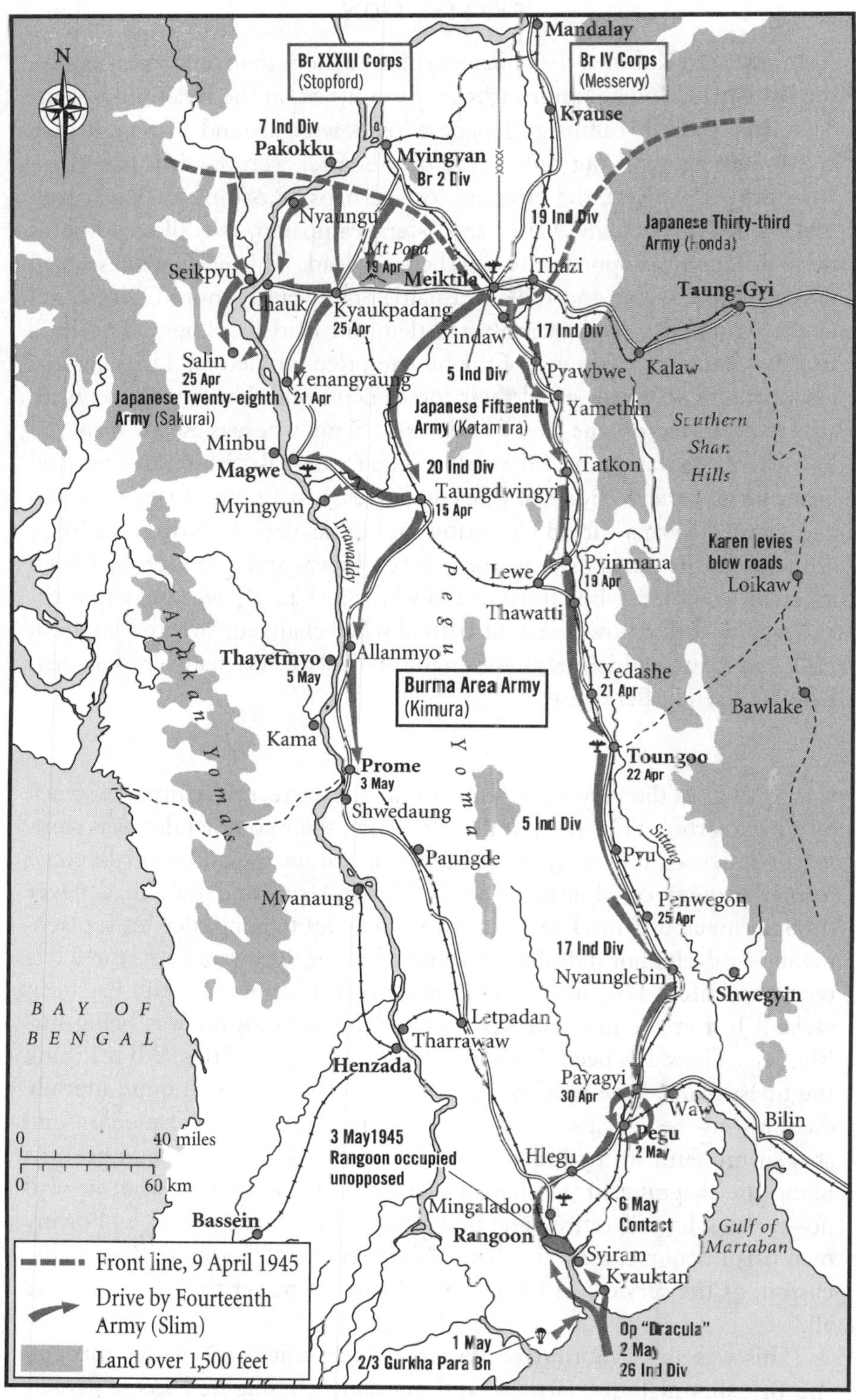

N
Mandalay
Br XXXIII Corps
(Stopford)
Br IV Corps
(Messervy)
Kyause
7 Ind Div
Pakokku
Myingyan
Br 2 Div
XXXX
19 Ind Div
Nyaungu
Japanese Thirty-third
Army (Honda)
Mt Popa
19 Apr
Seikpyu
Meiktila
Thazi
Chauk
Kyaukpadang
25 Apr
Taung-Gyi
Yindaw
17 Ind Div
Salin
25 Apr
Pyawbwe
Kalaw
5 Ind Div
Yenangyaung
21 Apr
Japanese Twenty-eighth
Army (Sakurai)
Japanese Fifteenth
Army (Katamura)
Yamethin
Southern
Shan
Hills
Minbu
Magwe
20 Ind Div
Tatkon
Taungdwingyi
15 Apr
Myingyun
Irrawaddy
Karen levies
blow roads
Pyinmana
19 Apr
Loikaw
Lewe
Thawatti
Arakan Yomas
Pegu Yoma
Allanmyo
Thayetmyo
5 May
Yedashe
21 Apr
Burma Area Army
(Kimura)
Bawlake
Kama
Toungoo
22 Apr
Prome
3 May
Shwedaung
5 Ind Div
Sittang
Paungde
Pyu
Myanaung
Penwegon
25 Apr
17 Ind Div
Nyaunglebin
Shwegyin
BAY OF
BENGAL
Letpadan
Tharrawaw
Henzada
Payagyi
30 Apr
Waw
Bilin
0
40 miles
0
60 km
3 May 1945
Rangoon occupied
unopposed
Pegu
2 May
Hlegu
Mingaladoon
6 May
Contact
Bassein
Rangoon
Gulf of
Martaban
Syiram
Kyauktan
Front line, 9 April 1945
Drive by Fourteenth
Army (Slim)
Land over 1,500 feet
1 May
2/3 Gurkha Para Bn
Op "Dracula"
2 May
26 Ind Div

Slim's drive on Rangoon, April–May 1945

At Imphal and Kohima, the Japanese suffered more than 60,000 casualties, the British and Indian armies 17,587. By contrast, in the Irrawaddy, Mandalay and Meiktila campaign Japanese losses were around 13,000, British and Indian 18,195—but only 2,307 of the latter were fatal. In the final, "mopping-up" phase, the Japanese lost perhaps 28,000 men, Fourteenth Army 435 killed. As in every Far Eastern campaign, overall loss figures mask a huge disproportion in numbers of dead. Thirteen Japanese died for each fatal British and Indian casualty. Significantly more Chinese fell in the struggle to reconquer Burma than did British soldiers. The Raj's Indian volunteers paid most of the human price for victory. The Japanese lost around two-thirds of all their forces deployed. The remainder were able to escape across the land frontier into Siam, whereas escape from the Pacific islands was almost impossible. The modest British figures masked heavy losses suffered by some rifle companies. Just 12 out of 196 men who had entered Burma with B Company, 2nd Berkshires, in November 1944 remained in its ranks in June 1945. Five officers and 107 men had been killed or wounded, while the unit as a whole lost 24 officers and 374 men. "I began to realise how much the battalion had changed," wrote Maj. John Hill. "So many had left us and so many arrived . . . We had very few men left who lived in Berkshire."

On 9 May, in the very hour of its triumph, Fourteenth Army was struck by a thunderbolt. The hero of the campaign, their commander, was summarily relieved. The supremo of Burma operations, Gen. Oliver Leese, a former protégé of Montgomery's in North Africa and Italy, had never thought much of Slim. Leese chose this moment to announce his replacement. Slim's chief of staff, Brig. "Tubby" Lethbridge, wrote a stunned letter to his wife: "The most incredible thing has happened—Bill has been sacked! Just at the moment when this masterpiece of his was being finished . . . There has been, I suppose, a clash of personalities. Bill is I think the finest man I have ever met, and every one of us would quite literally die for him—he is that sort of chap. The whole thing has sickened me and shaken my faith in my fellow man. He of course took it magnificently, being the magnificent gentleman that he is. I don't know what he will do—I think he will retire. The thing just doesn't make sense . . . For my own part of course, it means that as his chief of staff I go too. That is the custom of the service, so I fear darling I shall not get that division after all."

This was an extraordinary episode, which sent shock waves through the British and Indian armies, and permanently blighted Leese's reputation. "We were infuriated," said Captain Ronnie McAllister of 3/1st

Gurkhas. "Slim's sacking impinged on everyone." Within a few days, both Brooke in London and Mountbatten in Kandy understood that a blunder had been made. Leese's decision was reversed. Slim stayed. Leese himself was relieved shortly afterwards. Yet the commander of Fourteenth Army never received from either Brooke or Winston Churchill the laurels which were his due for his triumph in Burma. It is a measure of British priorities that in the whole of Brooke's voluminous wartime diaries there are only fifty-four references to Japan, amid countless concerning Germany. Montgomery is mentioned 175 times, Slim just 5. On 6 April 1945, Churchill wrote to his wife from Yalta: "Dicky [Mountbatten], reinforced by Gen. Oliver Leese, has done wonders in Burma." This seems akin to paying tribute for the triumphs of a football team to its owners rather than the manager. Slim received only three perfunctory, albeit respectful, mentions in Churchill's war memoirs. His name is unnoticed in Martin Gilbert's multivolume biography of the prime minister. Whether or not Fourteenth Army was "forgotten," Britain's leaders seemed content that its commander should be. It is unlikely that either Churchill or Brooke harboured any personal animus towards Slim. More plausibly, their attitude reflected disdain for the whole Burma commitment.

Remnants of Japan's broken armies trickled south-eastwards into Siam across the Sittang and Salween rivers through the early summer of 1945. Col. John Masters, senior staff officer of 19th Indian Division, described how he and his commander deployed their men along the Sittang in blocking positions to receive Kimura's broken forces:

> Pete and I drove up and down [the line], making dispositions as though for a rabbit shoot. We were ready to give mercy, but no one felt pity. This was the pay-off of three bitter years . . . Machine guns covered each path, infantry and barbed-wire protected the machine guns. Behind, field guns stood ready to rain high explosive shells on every approach . . . Tanks stood at road junctions. Fighters and bombers waited on the few all-weather airfields . . . The Japanese came on . . . The machine guns got them, the Brens and rifles got them, the tanks got them, the guns got them. They drowned by hundreds in the Sittang, and their corpses floated in the fields and among the reeds.

Lt. Hayashi Inoue of the 18th Division led ten men and two oxcarts on an epic march south from Meiktila to the sea. They reached the bridge at Sittang, the path to safety, after two months, having lost two men killed by guerrillas of the Burma National Army. "The Burmans were very friendly to us when we were victorious," said Inoue bitterly, "but when we started losing, they turned on us." In the last weeks of the campaign, the so-called Burma National Army raised by the Japanese changed sides and fell on its former sponsors. Captain Renichi Sugano was managing a railway supply depot at Moulmein, troubled only by British bombing which killed ten of his men, until in June 1945 soldiers of Japan's defeated forces began to trickle through his area. "They looked like beggars," he said in wonderment. He was even more shocked when immaculately uniformed commanders and headquarters staff officers, refugees from Rangoon, arrived at Moulmein. "When those men began to come, for the first time I realised that our army was in very serious trouble," said Sugano. "It was a terrible shock. We all wondered: 'What happens to us now?' " There was disgust within the Japanese army that whereas its commanders in the Pacific island battles chose to perish with their men, during the retreat from Burma many senior officers scuttled ignominiously to safety.

Japanese soldiers became as angered as their Western counterparts by the comfortable lives sustained by base units. In hospital in Bangkok, Hayashi Inoue requested the use of a vehicle to take six wounded men for an outing. He was turned down. "Petrol is as precious as blood here," shrugged a transport officer. Yet the same night, Inoue saw a staff car disgorge a laughing cluster of junior officers at a local restaurant. "It made me sick," he said, "to watch our people in places like Singapore and Saigon, taking out girls and living it up, while in Burma our soldiers were starving and fighting to the death."

THAT THE JAPANESE had suffered a massive defeat was not in doubt. But what had the British won? Although some Indian units fought with distinction in Iraq and Italy as well as with Fourteenth Army, Churchill was surely correct that the reconquest of Burma represented a slender return for the mobilisation of an Indian army of two and a half million men. A former British district officer who returned to the country in 1945 wrote: "The old unquestioning confidence had gone—on both sides. We had been driven out of Burma. The Burmans had seen this happen. In the trite phrase, things could never be the same again."

Although the renegades of the Indian National Army had fought poorly against the British, in captivity their interrogators were dismayed by the recalcitrance sustained by some. A report to the War Office on 5,000 INA taken in Rangoon warned that if these men were sent back to their old regimental depots, they would be obedient on parade, but "in their leisure time they will talk among themselves and to their comrades about Netaji Subash Chandra Bose, the Dream of Independence, the hardships they bore to make that dream a reality, and of the glory of an Indian Army officered solely by Indians . . . Source considers that no form of rehabilitation for the men of the INA can be successful unless it is based on the fostering of a national rather than a religious or provincial spirit." Though such men were vastly outnumbered by the Indian soldiers who fought loyally for the British, the renegades' spirit reflected the fact that the sands were fast running out for the Raj.

A British ranker, Brian Aldiss, wrote afterwards of the Burma campaign: "Exactly what purposes it served, except for the political one of convincing the Americans that their enemies were our enemies, is hard to say." He himself, a signaller who had seen only corpses, never watched a man die, ended the campaign with an odd regret: "I realised that I had longed to kill a Jap, just one Jap, riddle him with bullets and see him fall." Few of those who did the killing would suggest that Aldiss missed a rewarding experience. Without great enthusiasm, British forces in Burma and India prepared for their next operation, a huge amphibious landing to restore to Malaya, also, the tarnished glories of imperial rule.

FOURTEEN

Australians: "Bludging" and "Mopping Up"

One day in January 1945 an Australian company commander on the island of Bougainville, where his battalion had relieved an American unit two months earlier, telephoned his colonel. The men, he said, were "too tired" to carry out an attack which had been ordered. The colonel, named Matthews, insisted that the assault must be made. Half an hour later, the company commander telephoned again, to say that his men had refused to leave their positions: "They said they were all too tired, they were cut off from the world and could not get casualties back and weren't prepared to get any anyway." Matthews told the officer he must make his men obey their orders. "He said he knew they wouldn't, but would give it a go." Shortly afterwards the company second-in-command rang to report that the officer had broken down in tears. He was relieved and sent to the rear. Next day, another of Matthews's companies wilfully broke off contact with the enemy. A platoon commander reported that his men were "frightened." A third company commander told Matthews that his men lacked all confidence in him, the CO. The feeling was mutual. A month later Matthews wrote contemptuously about another battalion's similar experiences, observing laconically that they "must be no better than some of my companies."

If these episodes seem astonishing, they were by no means uncommon during the unhappy travails of Australia's forces in the south-west Pacific in the last phase of the war. From October 1944 to July 1945, Australian soldiers participated in a series of island campaigns. The evident futility of these embittered many men, drove some to the edge of mutiny and beyond. The last year of the war proved the most inglorious of Australia's history as a fighting nation. In the Mediterranean during 1941–42, Australian troops forged a reputation second to none. In 1943, many of the same soldiers fought a harsh, vital campaign in New Guinea, while America gathered its forces in the south-west Pacific. Australian soldiers performed as splendidly at Milne Bay and on the Kokoda Trail as they had done at Tobruk. Thereafter, however, the Australian Army seemed to disappear from the conflict. A trauma overtook the nation which divided its people, demoralised its forces and cast a lasting shadow over its memory of the Second World War.

The country had suffered deeply in the thirties' Depression, and greeted the outbreak of hostilities in 1939 without enthusiasm. Military conscription was introduced for home service only. Two divisions of volunteers were sent to the Middle East, and a third was lost at Singapore in 1942; Australian aircrew served with distinction in every theatre, and the Australian navy made a valuable contribution. But most Australian soldiers chose to stay at home, languishing idly in the ranks of militia units. The country was racked with labour disputes, many fomented by Communist-dominated trades unions. The Communist Party was banned in Australia until Russia entered the war. The leaders of its 20,000 membership, thereafter legitimised once more, professed to support the war effort. But strikes persisted, above all in the dock labour force.

Remoteness had made Australia a parochial society, but this is an inadequate explanation for the behaviour of some of its people. The refusal to adapt to participation in a war of national survival, when Japan aspired to make them subjects of its empire, was extraordinary. Public alarm about home defence prompted the Australian government in 1942 to insist on the return of all its soldiers from the Middle East. Churchill with difficulty retained the famous 9th Australian Division in Montgomery's Eighth Army until El Alamein in November, but this provoked anger in Canberra. When the Middle East formations returned home, they were committed to action in Papua New Guinea. There, through late 1942 and 1943, Australian troops under MacArthur's command fought some of the fiercest actions of the war against the Japanese.

With every month of the campaign, bitterness mounted among those volunteers for overseas service towards the host of their fellow citizens who refused to leave home. Their own country, they said, had become "a bludgers' paradise." "Bludger" is a word denoting a parasite, loafer or scrounger. The country seemed burdened with a depressing number of all three, many in uniform. The government responded to the unpopularity of military service by cutting the army's size by 22 percent in the last two years of the war, but its bloated officer corps meanwhile grew by 14 percent. War Minister F. W. Forde reported to Prime Minister John Curtin on the "deterioration in the morale of the Australian Fighting Forces that had obviously taken place . . . It would appear that this is largely due to their enforced stay on the mainland of Australia with no clearly defined indication as to when and where they may be likely to be called upon to take part in active operations."

American and British officers arriving to serve in Australia were stunned by the industrial anarchy which prevailed, the difficulties of getting ships offloaded or repaired. "Many . . . laborers refused to work in the rain or handle refrigerated food and many other types of cargo," an American official historian noted with dismay. "They objected, with some success, to the utilization of mechanical equipment." U.S. Army quartermaster details had to be kept on standby at docksides, lest rain suddenly halt off-loading by civilian labour. Absenteeism among the workforce at Townsville, on the north coast of Queensland, for instance, averaged 18 percent. Some dock labourers reported for work only at weekends, when double or triple pay was available, until such practices drove the U.S. Army to halt weekend supply movements. An Australian docker handled just a quarter of the average daily cargo shifted by an American soldier.

In September 1943, after a succession of outrageous dockside incidents, MacArthur wrote to Curtin, Australia's Labor prime minister, asserting that the Seamen's Union "was directly obstructing the war effort . . . Fifth column activities may be behind these occurrences." Following a mutiny on board an American cargo vessel, the union displayed solidarity by refusing to allow another crew to board the vessel until the mutineers were freed from confinement. Australian meatpackers haggled shamelessly about wage rates for producing rations for the U.S. Army, and rejected streamlined working practices proposed by the Americans. Industrial absenteeism reflected what a Sydney polling organisation described to the government as "apathy amongst large sections of the people towards the war effort." The black market, a feature of all wartime societies, achieved special vigour in Australia. Empty whiskey bottles with labels and seals intact were sold for five shillings apiece, to be refilled with adulterated spirit. Buying provisions "on the black" became a way of life.

Almost a million days' production was lost through strikes in 1942 and the first half of 1943, many of these in the docks and mines. Coal output fell substantially. By November 1943, no Japanese submarine had launched an attack in Australian waters for five months, yet Australian ships' crews refused to put to sea without naval escort, and downed tools to enforce their point. Americans were increasingly disgusted by what they perceived as Australian pusillanimity. MacArthur said: "I tell you, these Australians won't fight." The U.S. minister in Canberra, Nelson Johnson, wrote to the State Department in June 1944: "The Department may be surprised to know that the Legation has no record of even so much as a telephone call of congratulations from any official or private Australian following on the news of an American victory." In September 1944 the *Sydney Morning Herald* published a dispatch from India, saying that British and American servicemen were asking whether Australia was "pulling right out of the war." This report provoked a question in the Senate in Canberra on 13 September, demanding "whether the Australian Army was to take any further part in the war." In October 1944, the Sydney *Daily Telegraph* suggested that industrial strife in the country had reached "civil war or very near it."

In some degree, Australian behaviour reflected a crisis of national purpose and identity. Beyond this, there was frustration that, while their country's men were expected to fight, its leaders were denied a significant voice in Allied decision-making. "The Australian government tried to force an entrance into the higher councils of war, but had limited success," in the understated words of an Australian historian. The 1941–42 British débâcle in Malaya and Burma prompted a major political and cultural swing in Australian allegiances. "I make it quite plain," said Prime Minister Curtin on 27 December 1941, "that Australia looks to America, free of any pangs as to our traditional links or kinship with the United Kingdom." Australians' theatre of war was overwhelmingly dominated by, and dependent upon, the United States. Their historic British mentor and protector had been found wanting in the hour of need. With notable abruptness, they embraced the United States. In the case of their womenfolk, this was not merely figurative. American servicemen, of whom a million staged through Australia, were delighted by the warmth of their welcome from Australian girls, to whom the war granted a new sexual freedom. U.S. Navy crews were amazed to perceive crowds of teenagers—"pogey-bait"—waving in frenzied welcome as their ships approached Sydney harbour.

Yet, as the war advanced, grateful as were the Allies for Australia's huge contribution towards feeding their soldiers, there was sourness about the limited combat contribution being made by this country of seven million people. In January 1943, Curtin with difficulty steered through the Australian Parliament a militia bill, which made all Australian troops liable for overseas service—but only in the south-west Pacific, the theatre in which the nation's interests were directly threatened. This was the best that a weak government could do, with political and social stresses racking the nation. "The mainspring of Curtin's leadership . . . was a conception of the welfare of the Australian people which was limited to their life at home," wrote an Australian official historian.

In the course of the entire war, some 691,400 men were conscripted into the Australian Army. In 1944, however, almost all of these languished in barracks at home—bored, fractious, in an almost intractable condition of indiscipline. It is hard to overstate the contrast between the superb performance of 9th Australian Division in the Western Desert in 1941–42 and the shameful condition to which the national army was reduced two years later, absent from any significant land battlefield. The question of where Australian troops might be deployed was bitterly contested. MacArthur, who had become a national hero in 1942, never reciprocated Australian warmth. Australian forces were under his command, but he had lost faith in them. He had no desire to make his major thrust in the Philippines with any save American soldiers. Australian militia units—the "Chockos," or "chocolate soldiers," as they were known—were plainly unreliable. MacArthur's solution was to employ Australian troops to replace American units "mopping up" surviving Japanese garrisons where these still held out, on Bougainville, New Britain and parts of Papua New Guinea.

"Mopping up" was immediately identified as a thankless task, similar to that delegated by Eisenhower to Free French units in 1944–45, besieging German garrisons isolated in the French ports. On 18 October, Gen. Vernon Sturdee, commanding the Australian First Army in New Guinea, wrote to his commander-in-chief: "The Jap garrisons are at present virtually in POW camps but feed themselves, so why incur a large number of Australian casualties in the process of eliminating them?" Why, indeed? As early as August 1944, MacArthur had asserted: "The enemy garrisons which have been bypassed in the Solomons and New Guinea represent no menace . . . The actual time of their destruction is of little or no importance and their influence as a contributing factor to the war is already negligible." If this was so, if it was deemed unnecessary for American soldiers to engage these impotent but savage remnants, why now should it be desirable for Australians to do so, when the enemy had grown six months hungrier and more desperate?

The *Melbourne Herald* wrote in January 1945: "American public opinion, which is inclined to write off Australia as a fighting force for the remainder of the Pacific War, now sees the Digger in the humblest of secondary roles—mopping up behind the real fighting, slogging Yank." There was Australian anger, as well as bewilderment, that MacArthur insisted on deploying far more Australian troops for "mopping up" than their own commander-in-chief, Thomas Blamey, thought necessary. There was speculation that the Americans were embarrassed by Australian proposals that tasks which had occupied six U.S. divisions should now be fulfilled by the same number of Australian brigades.

Japanese garrisons on the disputed islands still numbered some tens of thousands, but possessed no power to injure the Allied cause. They were cut off from home, woefully understrength, racked by starvation and disease. Any rational strategic judgement would have left them to their own devices, screened by token Allied forces until their nation's defeat enforced their surrender. The notion that Australian soldiers should risk their lives merely to achieve a body count of impotent yet dangerous Japanese disgusted their commanders—and soon, also, soldiers on the ground.

After much debate, however, in October 1944 three Australian divisions were committed to Bougainville, in the Solomons; New Britain; and New Guinea. There they passed the last eight months of the war in frustration and discomfort, sometimes misery and fear. There was special dismay that while the Americans in these areas had pursued a passive strategy towards the surviving Japanese, Blamey decided that instead the Australians should actively pursue the enemy. He believed that offensive action would enhance morale. The Australian government also wished its troops to be seen to liberate territories under Australian colonial guardianship. This was a policy which might win some headlines, but was certain also to cost lives.

As commander-in-chief of the Australian Army, Gen. Thomas Blamey inspired little confidence within his own society, and less outside it. Argument persists in Australia today about whether Blamey bears responsibility for some of the army's worst wartime misfortunes, or merely faced difficulties which reflected the schisms besetting his nation. He was a conceited, corpulent, devious autocrat, sixty in 1944. Like most of those who served under him, he was a citizen soldier. He started life as a teacher and lay preacher, then found his way into the First World War through service in cadet and militia units. With the dramatic wartime expansion of the Australian Army, by 1918 he was a thirty-four-year-old brigadier, chief of staff to a corps commander. Between the wars he served as commissioner of the Victoria Police. In this role he earned an ugly reputation for corruption and politicking, which prompted his sacking in 1936. In a small world, however, this small man secured the appointment of army commander-in-chief in 1939, and kept it to the end. The legendary Australian war correspondent and historian Chester Wilmot wrote of the troops' attitude: "Knowing that Blamey had the reputation of being a crook, they did not serve happily under him."

Blamey's reputation was further diminished as deputy to Wavell during the 1941 débâcle in Greece. Not only was he himself accused of cowardice—a charge levelled by his own chief of staff—but he earned bitter enmity by securing the safety of his son, a staff officer, who was flown to Egypt from the stricken battlefield while a host of other men were left behind to the Germans. Sir Arthur Tedder, then senior British air commander in the theatre, described Blamey as "a rather unpleasant political soldier . . . a tubby little man with a snub nose and expensive complexion, high blood pressure and a scrubby little white moustache. He has a certain amount of common sense and 20 years ago may have been fairly useful, but—!" Likewise Auchinleck, writing from the desert: "He wasn't a general I should have chosen to command an operation." Sir Alan Brooke found him "not an impressive specimen. He looks entirely drink sodden and somewhat repulsive." Yet Blamey kept his job, returning to Australia as C-in-C, and riding stubbornly on the waves of controversy about the Australian Army's deployment. His conspicuous enthusiasm for women and alcohol even in combat zones disgusted many officers.

So unpopular did Blamey become that a demonstration was staged against him in the streets of Sydney. His willingness to commit forces to futile operations which cost hundreds of lives earned him the lasting animosity of many Australians. "On his head descended perhaps the strongest vituperation to which any military leader in that war was subjected by people on his own side," the Australian official historian wrote later. The best that can be said for Blamey was that his government deserved the real responsibility for tolerating his weakness, incompetence and self-indulgence, when he provided a host of reasons to justify dismissal.

The Australian Army's operations in the south-west Pacific became a wretched experience for those reluctantly obliged to take part. A private soldier named J. H. Ewen wrote from his Pacific island: "We are all just about had. Living on your nerves in mud and rain, sleeping in holes in the ground wears a fellow down. I have watched the boys' faces get drawn and haggard, and their movements slow and listless." There were long, nerve-racking patrols, on which monotony and discomfort never suppressed fear of an ambush or booby trap. The Japanese might be shattered strategically, but to the end their survivors retained the power to steal men's lives. Peter Medcalf described a man who broke down before a patrol on Bougainville: "A feeling of terrible sadness and compassion touched all of us. We gently helped him up and led him to Perce the Boss, holding his hands and guiding him like a small and helpless child. Among us were men of many backgrounds, hardened men who had seen the worst in their fellows; but the same feeling affected all of us—there but for the doubtful grace of God or providence go we."

"The political and grand strategic elements of the 1945 campaigns . . . drew the ire of Australian participants, who soon became aware of the dubious value of the operations, and that lives lost were wasted," wrote an Australian historian. "Consequently, they tried to minimise risks. In this, they were strongly encouraged by most commanders." A deep divide persisted between units of the old Australian Expeditionary Force and those of the despised militia. One soldier wrote home describing allegations of large-scale theft against militiamen, who he asserted were "capable of anything except fighting the enemy." For small units, these jungle deployments were desperately lonely. A platoon commander in New Guinea, thirty-five-year-old Victorian schoolteacher A. H. Robertson, wrote to his wife: "When you get into action, you don't see much of any troops except those of your own company, and very little of those not in your own platoon." They suffered chronic equipment shortcomings, not least boots. "Cross two rivers and what have you?" an Australian chaplain demanded bitterly. "A pair of uppers."

On 21 March 1945, Col. G. R. Matthews recorded that a senior officer had complained to him about the conduct in action of some militia units: "Troops when fired on rush back in disorder leaving their officers. They are frightened to move out of their perimeters. Patrols go out and do not complete tasks; sit in jungle and wait for time to elapse and then come in." That April, Private Ewen recorded a mutiny in the 61st Battalion: "Today 9 from D Coy and 3 from B refused to go on patrol . . . If they send us in again the Coys are going to refuse to go. So things are in a very bad state. Already two officers have been sent back for standing up for the men. Nearly all the boys have a vacant look in their eyes and look dazed." After coming out of action Ewen served three months' field punishment for refusal to obey an order: "75 of us refused to go into action until we were again given our leave." Defiant to the end, the soldier asserted that it was worth accepting court-martial to escape combat.

Back home, criticism of the military operations to which Australian troops were committed persisted to the end of the war, feeding off the testimony of those serving in the field, and intensifying their rancour. On 26 April 1945, as opposition leader Robert Menzies told the House of Representatives in Canberra: "I happen to entertain the strongest possible view that it is wrong to use the Australian forces . . . in operations . . . which seem to me to have no relation to any first-class strategic object in this war." More than a thousand Australians died in New Guinea in the last year of the war, along with 516 on Bougainville. Each loss was bitterly resented. Australian forces killed some thousands of Japanese, but to what end? "In both Australian and Japanese history the offensives of 1945 [in New Guinea] will endure as examples of splendid fortitude, but whether they should have happened seems likely always to be in dispute," wrote the Australian official historian long afterwards.

In the final months, two Australian divisions were deployed in an amphibious assault on Borneo. There, too, dissension focused upon whether an operation ordered by MacArthur served any useful purpose. The nominal objective was to regain control of the Dutch East Indies' rich oil fields. Yet it never seemed plausible that these could be made serviceable in time to assist the Allied war effort. The American blockade already ensured that Borneo's oil was doing little good to the Japanese. The view was widely held that the only purpose of the operation was to keep other Allied forces off America's pitch for the last round of the Pacific war.

On 1 May 1945, an Australian brigade group landed on Borneo's offshore island of Tarakan. This was garrisoned by 1,800 Japanese, and possessed an airfield thought likely to be useful for Allied operations on the mainland. Rugged fighting followed. By the end of July, three hundred Japanese remained at large on Tarakan, and the Australians had suffered 894 casualties. The prized airfield proved beyond repair. Ninth Australian Division landed in Brunei Bay on 10 June, and secured the immediate coastal area by the end of the month, for the loss of 114 killed. On 1 July, 7th Australian Division carried out the last significant amphibious landing of the war at the Dutch oil port of Balikpapan, in the south-east of Dutch Borneo. Over the week that followed, the Australians secured twenty miles of coastal territory around the port, leaving special forces and guerrillas to hunt Japanese through the inland wildernesses. Some 229 Australians died, and 634 were wounded. Once more, it was impossible to believe that anything worthwhile had been achieved—and every man at Tarakan and Balikpapan knew it.

The Australian Army lost 7,384 dead fighting the Japanese in the Second World War. This was fewer of the nation's warriors than died as prisoners having been captured in Malaya and at Singapore in 1942; slightly more deaths than the U.S. Marines suffered on Iwo Jima. For a people whose soldiers, sailors and airmen won such admiration in other theatres, it was a tragedy that in their own hemisphere the wartime experience was poisoned by domestic strife and battlefield frustration. Churchill bore a significant responsibility for his cavalier treatment of a nation which he continued to perceive as a colony, and for whose domestic difficulties he had no sympathy. Whatever the mitigating circumstances, however, it seemed perverse that, having won so much honour far away in the Mediterranean, Australia's share of the Pacific war ended in rancour and anticlimax.

FIFTEEN

Captivity and Slavery

1. Inhuman Rites

WHEN BRITISH PRISONERS released from Japanese confinement began to return to England in the late summer of 1945, each one received a printed letter, signed by a government minister. "Welcome home," it began. "You have suffered a long and bitter ordeal at the hands of a barbarous enemy." Much has been written in recent years about the climate of racial hatred which distinguished the conduct of the Western Allies' war with Japan from the conflict with Germany. Yet it was not until its ending that most of the revelations were forthcoming which have poisoned British, and in much lesser degree American, relations with Japan ever since. These related, of course, to the treatment of Allied POWs who fell into the hands of the Imperial Army between 1941 and 1945.

Throughout the war, a trickle of former prisoners reached Britain and the United States. Most were escapees from the Philippines, or survivors picked up by submarines from Japanese ships sunk while carrying POWs to Japan. They told their stories, and dreadful indeed these were. The U.S. government suppressed for months the first eyewitness accounts of the 1942 Bataan death march, on which so many surrendered survivors of MacArthur's army perished, and news of the beheadings of captured Doolittle raid aircrew. The British foreign secretary, Anthony Eden, gave a graphic account of some POW experiences to the House of Commons in January 1944, and the public was shocked by what it was told. Yet, in a curious reversal of the usual wartime propaganda inflation of the bestialities of the enemy, in official circles a reluctance persisted to believe the worst.

The few Japanese captured in Burma or the Pacific who had been in contact with Allied POWs were quizzed by Allied interrogators about their welfare, prompting the sort of response given by a twenty-five-year-old naval technician on 19 September 1944: "American PWs appeared to be in good health," said the Japanese. "About 60 British PWs quartered in same area . . . seemed to have an easy life, rising at 0800, doing a little exercise, then working in the gardens till 1100hrs. After dinner they again worked in the gardens till 1700, when they had supper and played games or went fishing." As late as January 1945, the British Foreign Office Political Warfare (Japan) Committee reached quite sanguine conclusions about the treatment of Allied captives. "There was evidence," the committee minuted, "that prisoners of war in Japan itself and in the more accessible regions are treated reasonably well, according to Japanese standards, and that reports of serious ill-treatment come from outlying areas where the Japanese government has little control over local military officers in charge of the camps. The Japanese while they were being everywhere victorious might have thought they could safely disregard the opinion of the rest of the world, but now . . . they must realise that . . . their future will largely depend on their external relations with other Great Powers. From motives of self-interest, therefore, they are more and more likely to realise that they had better treat prisoners of war well."

In the spring of 1945, such wishful thinking was discredited. Substantial numbers of British and Australian POWs were freed by Slim's victorious army in Burma, likewise Americans by MacArthur's men in the Philippines. Their liberators were stunned by the stories they heard: of starvation and rampant disease; of men worked to death in their thousands, tortured or beheaded for small infractions of discipline. An urgent signal was sent from Mountbatten's headquarters to the Foreign Office, asking for guidance about the treatment of atrocity stories. SEAC was told that they should be censored. If the British public learned before hostilities ended what had been done to its soldiers, sailors and airmen, outrage was inevitable. The Japanese, in their desperation, were capable of imposing even more terrible sufferings upon tens of thousands of POWs who remained in their hands. Prisoners were themselves haunted by an expectation that the Japanese would slaughter them in the rage of defeat.

When the war ended, it became possible to compare the fates of Allied servicemen under the Nazis and the Japanese. Just 4 percent of British and American POWs had died in German hands. Yet 27 percent—35,756 out of 132,134—of Western Allied prisoners lost their lives in Japanese captivity. The Chinese suffered in similar measure. Of 41,862 sent to become slave labourers in Japan, 2,872 died in China, 600 in ships on passage, 200 on the land journey, and 6,872 in their Japanese workplaces. These figures discount a host of captives who did not survive in Japanese hands on the battlefield, or after being shot down, for long enough to become statistics.

Of 130,000 Europeans interned in the Dutch East Indies, almost all civilians, 30,000 died, including 4,500 women and 2,300 children. Of 300,000 Javanese, Tamils, Burmans and Chinese sent to work on the Burma–Siam railway, 60,000 perished, likewise a quarter of the 60,000

Western Allied prisoners. There seemed no limit to Japanese inhumanity. When a cholera epidemic struck Tamil railway workers at Nieke in June 1943, a barracks containing 250 infected men, women and children was simply torched. One of the Japanese who did the burning wrote later of the victims: "I dared not look into their eyes. I only heard some whispering '*Tolong, tolong*'—'Help, help.' It was the most pitiful sight. God forgive me. I was not happy to see them being burnt alive."

To give a British illustration: when the Royal Navy destroyer *Encounter* was sunk in the 1942 Battle of the Java Sea, 123 of its crew lived to enter captivity. Of these, 41 were lost when a transport carrying them to Japan was sunk by an American submarine; 30 died in POW camps; just 52 returned to England in 1945. This represented a saga of systematic deprivation and brutality, overlaid upon the hazards of war, of a kind familiar to Russian and Jewish prisoners of the Nazis, yet shocking to the American, British and Australian publics. It seemed incomprehensible that a nation with pretensions to civilisation could have defied every principle of humanity and the supposed rules of war. The saga of Japan's captives has exercised a terrible fascination for Westerners ever since.

The overwhelming majority of Allied service personnel and civilians in Japanese hands were captured during the first months of the Far East war: Americans in the Philippines; Dutch in their East Indies colony; British, Australians and Indians in Hong Kong, Malaya and Burma. Thereafter, only small numbers were added: a few soldiers from battlefields, survivors of sunken ships, airmen shot down over Japanese territory. Even if detail was lacking, a powerful message filtered down through the ranks of all the Allied forces: it was worth taking pains to avoid capture. More significant, the Americans and British were no longer retreating and surrendering, but at worst holding their ground, more often advancing.

It is hard to overstate the trauma suffered by more than 100,000 American, British, Australian and Indian servicemen taken prisoner during the early Allied defeats. They had been conditioned by their culture to suppose that surrender was a misfortune which might befall any fighting man, especially those as poorly led as had been the Allies in the early Far Eastern campaigns, and as lamentably supported by their home governments. As crowds of disarmed personnel milled about awaiting their fate in Manila or Singapore, Hong Kong or Rangoon, they contemplated a life behind barbed wire with dismay, but without the terror which their real prospects merited. "In the beginning," said Doug Idlett, a twenty-two-year-old USAAF enlisted man from Oklahoma captured in the Philippines, "we thought: 'A couple of months and our army will be back.' " In the weeks which followed, however, as their rations shrank, medicines vanished, and Japanese policy was revealed, they learned differently. Officers and men alike, dispatched to labour in sweating jungles, torrid plains or mines and quarries, grew to understand that, in the eyes of their captors, they had become slaves.

"The Burma railway was a very difficult engineering challenge," said Captain Renichi Sugano, who commanded a section of No. 9 Railway Company, which supervised much of the construction work on this most terrible of all projects to which Allied prisoners were committed. "At the beginning, when we did the surveying, we were working in virgin jungle, where you could not even see through the trees to make measurements with a theodolite." Almost all Japanese army railway personnel developed malaria and fever. In the two months between wet and dry seasons, it was impossible to use either road transport in the mud, or boats on the falling rivers. Rations ran very short even for Sugano's men. "The further we got from the railhead, the worse things were. It was a very hard time."

Sugano and his colleagues much preferred the services of Allied POW labour to those of locally conscripted people. "From our viewpoint, the POWs were good workers," he said. "Having been soldiers, they were used to obeying orders. Local people did not understand discipline. Even when you told them they must boil water before drinking it, they drank from the river anyway, and got cholera. They were very troublesome people." Asked his views on the host of deaths among POW railway workers, Captain Sugano said cautiously: "Another unit was responsible for the care and custody of POWs. We simply borrowed them for labour, and returned them to their camp each night." Quite so. In the eyes of the Japanese, prisoners possessed no rights, were protected by no laws. Not only had they lost their honour by the warrior code of *bushido*, they had forfeited fundamental human respect. A Japanese war reporter, Ashihei Hino, observed without enthusiasm American prisoners on Bataan: "men of the arrogant nation which sought to treat our motherland with unwarranted contempt . . . As I gaze upon these crowds of surrendered soldiers, I feel as if I am watching dirty water running from the sewers of a nation whose origins were mongrel, and whose pride has been lost. Japanese soldiers look extraordinarily handsome, and I feel very proud to belong to their race."

As prisoners' residual fitness ebbed away, some abandoned hope. They acquiesced in a fate which soon overtook them. "There is no doubt that many men just 'dropped their bundle' and died," wrote Hall Romney, a forty-one-year-old former journalist who had been captured serving as a sergeant-major in the Singapore Volunteers, "whereas in similar circumstances men who retained a will to live survived . . . A feeling of loneliness has been a contributory factor in the deaths of many men, particularly some of the younger ones." Stephen Abbott, captured in Malaya as a subaltern of the 2nd East Surreys, wrote of their early imprisonment as a time of almost complete self-absorption, overwhelmed by a feeling of inferiority to those who had vanquished them: "The most junior soldier felt some sense of personal responsibility. However much we blamed our leaders we were . . . members of a team which had let Britain down . . . This sense of failure seemed to permeate Changi camp. Most conversations seemed centred around grievances, blame, and attempts at self-justification."

Among the most corrosive consequences of imprisonment was the collapse of loyalties, obligations to rank and peer groups. "I saw discipline go down the toilet very fast," said U.S. Captain Mel Rosen, taken on Bataan. Behind the wire, only a minority of officers such as the Australian Brig. Arthur Varley, retained the respect of their men. This no longer depended upon position in a military hierarchy, but solely upon the conduct of an individual leader. Bombardier Alex Young, an anti-tank gunner from Argyll, wrote contemptuously of his camp senior officer on Batavia: "Major D— was about as useful as a dead cat! His interests and motives were selfish. He looked on all sick (or so it seemed) as just so much encumbrances—they were better dead and out of the way. I saw him go off the train and never raise a finger to help those . . . who were too sick to move." Australian Don Moore spoke of one officer known as "the white Jap," who ran a canteen for his own profit in the camp which he commanded. In Aomi prison camp on Japan, where fifty-three of three hundred men died in the first months, Stephen Abbott was recovering from malaria and dysentery when an Anglo-Indian sergeant came to him and said: "I know you've been terribly ill, sir, but there are many dying men around. You're the commanding officer and I think it's now time you forgot yourself and got on with the job."

Hall Romney and his comrades on the railway in Siam despised their senior officer, Colonel Knights, never more so than when a visiting Japanese general asked whether the prisoners were satisfied with their conditions, and Knights answered: "Yes, very." The colonel, wrote Romney bitterly, "seems to accept everything the Japs propose without daring to protest or suggest alterations." Flying Officer Erroll Shearn, a forty-nine-year-old RAF administrative officer, was disgusted when the padre in his camp on Java, a non-smoker, persuaded desperate men to exchange their bread for his cigarette ration. Many British officers endorsed documents presented by the Japanese, promising not to escape. "You are signing away your honour, gentlemen!" cried a mocking British private soldier as most of his former commanders scribbled their names in Rangoon Jail. One of the most senior British captives, Maj.-Gen. Christopher Maltby, testified later about his shame that he had given such a promise, and had encouraged subordinates to do likewise: "During the early months a number of parties and individuals succeeded in escaping. In the light of after events it is to my lasting regret that I did not encourage larger parties to make the attempt."

In few camps did Allied solidarity prevail. When a hundred Americans suddenly arrived in the camp where Stephen Abbott had become senior British officer, there were immediate tensions. One American said: "Get this straight, Limey. We gotta look to the Nips, but we're not taking orders from any f—ing Britisher!" Abbott wrote that he thought these GIs the most frightening group of people he had ever met, Japanese not excluded. In almost all camps there was friction between Dutch prisoners, who were accused of selfishness on behalf of their own people, and POWs of other races. Erroll Shearn hated the Dutch in his camp on Java, and later scornfully dismissed the books written about their mutual experience by the South African Laurens van der Post: "The grandiose picture he draws is very much a figment of his extremely fertile imagination." Dr. Marjorie Lyon, an internee on Sumatra, was shocked that the Dutch refused to admit British casualties to their hospital: "The Dutch doctors I met were all ignorant and obstinate . . . [they] had given our men very shabby treatment." Doug Idlett, an American who worked at Yoshioka in a mixed-nationalities camp, said: "There was no love lost between certain nationalities, especially between us and the Dutch. The Dutch and Javanese had got there first and had all the best jobs, in the kitchens and suchlike."

Most men agreed that the key to survival was adaptability. It was essential to recognise that this new life, however unspeakable, represented a reality which must be acknowledged. Those who pined for home, who gazed tearfully at photos of loved ones, were doomed. "There was a weeding-out thing," said Corporal Paul Reuter of the USAAF. "The ones who cried went early." Andrew Cunningham, a former Hastings accountant captured with an air-sea rescue unit in Singapore at the age of twenty-four, spent almost two years building an airfield on Surabaya. "My life was a nonentity, a blank," he said later. "It was a mistake to look at photographs. It made people melancholy. I made a conscious decision that this was the new life, and I had to get on with it. I just dismissed the old one, as if it didn't exist. The tragedy was that so many people couldn't accommodate themselves. If anything plunged a dagger into me, it was seeing people give up. I saw some really nice guys just disintegrate, and throw themselves into boreholes. I could never understand how a person could sink so low. What a way to commit suicide! In a hole full of sewage!" Doug Idlett of the USAAF was bemused by the manner in which some men resigned themselves to death, even embraced it. He himself, by contrast, "wanted to survive, intended to survive. I felt it was up to me."

Some men could not bring themselves to stomach unfamiliar and indeed repulsive food. "They preferred to die rather than to eat what they were given," said Idlett. "I knew some that would not eat rice. Most died of inanition—loss of the will to live. At one time in the Philippines, we were burying fifty to sixty a day. I volunteered for the burial detail to get away from working on a farm in that Philippine sun—and to get an extra slice of bread. I don't like rice—but I ate it." American prisoners in the Philippines suffered grievously from the fact that, after enduring the siege of Bataan, most were half-starved when they entered captivity. "The ones who wouldn't eat died pretty early on," said Paul Reuter of the USAAF, a twenty-four-year-old miner's son from Shamokin, Pennsylvania. "I buried people who looked much better than me. They just crawled under a building. I never did have any thoughts of not living. We were a bunch who'd been through the Depression. I never turned down anything that was edible—and I guess I just had the right genes."

In Reuter's camp, "anything that was edible" meant whale blubber or soya meal, occasionally dried fish, "which we ate bones and all." Australian Snow Peat saw a maggot an inch long, and said, "Meat, you beauty!" "One bloke sitting alongside me said, 'Jeez, I can't eat that.' I said, 'Well tip her in here, mate, it's going to be my meal ticket home. You've got to eat it, you've got to give it a go. Think they're currants in the Christmas pudding. Think they're anything.' " Vic Ashwell, captured on the Sittang River in Burma as a twenty-two-year-old lieutenant with the 3rd Gurkhas, agreed with Peat: "I was prepared to eat anything. I volunteered for anything to get out, to keep body and mind ticking. When I saw younger officers just lying there, I'd urge them: 'Come on, get on your feet!' " Ashwell noted that the first to die were private soldiers from humble backgrounds, malnourished in childhood during Britain's Depression. Such men possessed few bodily reserves.

Squadron-Leader David Grant, at Mitsushima in Japan, wrote bitterly of "twelve hours of coolie labour on three cups of coarse rice and barley." The chronic shortage, cause of many deaths, was that of green vegetables. In Rangoon Jail, prisoners were permitted gardens, manured with human excrement, where they raised spinach, cucumbers, aubergines, sweet potatoes and carrots. They were forbidden to grow maize, on the grounds that guards would not be able to see their charges through the crop. In the coal mines of Fukuoka, by contrast, Don Lewis and his companions received only two hundred grams of rice thrice daily, with a bowl of soup twice. On Shikoku Island, Japan, British airman Louis Morris became obsessed with food, spending countless hours recording in minute handwriting English, American and Asian recipes, which he planned to use to start a catering business after the war. Like more than a few captives, he also wrote painfully sentimental verses:

I've missed the sunshine after rain
And England's garden from a train;
Of crowds I've missed the friendly touch—
I did not dream it meant so much;
I miss the downlands rolling free,
The wrack where shingle meets the sea.

In the shipyards near Osaka, where American Milton Young worked, two starving British prisoners ate lard from a great tub used for greasing the slipway. It had been treated with arsenic to repel insects. They died.

Every Allied POW was entitled to receive International Red Cross food parcels, which were delivered in large quantities, but were withheld or issued to prisoners according to local Japanese whim. Most were systematically pillaged by prison staff. Hundreds of tons of Red Cross supplies were belatedly released to camp inmates only after Japan's August 1945 surrender. While the war lasted, Paul Reuter received just three and a half parcels in forty months. Milton Young once offered to swap his tea ration for the coffee in a British prisoner's pack. "I've never tasted coffee," said the Englishman. Young made him some. After trying it, the other man would have nothing to do with a swap.

Tens of thousands of family parcels were also dispatched, but the Japanese seldom troubled to deliver them. Paul Reuter received in 1945 a package dispatched by his parents three years earlier, containing cookies and chocolate that had turned white with age. U.S. artillery captain Mel Rosen got a family parcel on Luzon in 1944 which he found wonderfully sensibly chosen: a carton of cigarettes, a sweater, a jar of candy and some vitamin pills. He was thrilled. Other men, by contrast, raged at the folly and insensitivity—in truth, tragic ignorance—which caused their loved ones to ship trifles. "Some men swore they would divorce their wives when they got home, for sending such stupid things," said Rosen wonderingly. "One sent a football. Here was her husband starving—and he got a football!" When Lt. Eunice Young, a U.S. Army nurse held among more than 3,000 mostly civilian internees at Santo Tomas, Manila, received a parcel from home, it contained a swimsuit: "Guess my mother thinks I'm vacationing out here!"

Around two-thirds of the prisoners at Santo Tomas were American, a quarter British. In the early war years, their circumstances were relatively privileged. As food dwindled and cash ran out, however, in 1944 their condition became parlous, deaths commonplace. During the fight for Bataan, U.S. Army nurses were told to destroy their money before surrendering. Within weeks, they bitterly regretted this. Behind the walls of Santo Tomas they survived only by signing IOUs to local representatives of big U.S. companies such as General Electric, whose credit was deemed good. After liberation, Lt. Rita Palmer and others found themselves called upon to pay up, to the tune of $1,000 or more apiece. "We were so hungry that when we ate a banana, we ate the skin too," said Hattie Brantley. "Anything to fill up our empty stomachs."

Most Santo Tomas prisoners rejected dried and salted dilis fish when first this was offered to them, partly because of its overpowering stench. By the last months, however, they ate the fish and were grateful. Thefts of food by prisoners became a worsening problem—women cleaning vegetables carried off peelings, men scoured the garbage dumps. "It was becoming very apparent to what degree plain honesty, ordinary decency, self-respect, community feeling, and all the higher values are dependent on the maintenance of the narrowest margin between having enough to eat and not having enough to eat." By December 1944, six or seven prisoners a day were dying of malnutrition in Santo Tomas. Through a characteristic eccentricity of Japanese management, two months before the camp's liberation, formal instruction was imposed to teach all prisoners the correct method of bowing in unison to their captors, "to show respect" at roll call.

Most British families at home were no better informed than Americans about the hideous circumstances of the prisoners. It is doubtful whether thirty-three-year-old RAF Aircraftsman Phil Sparrow gained much pleasure from this letter, when it reached him on Batavia:

> My Dear Philip, I am hoping you will get these few lines & to know you are well. Everyone at home are well and we hope soon to get a card from you. Say what you are needing most and we will try and get it sent through the International Red Cross. Victor has the distribution of tomatoes in this district and could do with his clerk back. Mother & Auntie was here to tea Sunday. They are both well. Esmee and Ivor were here for a week, both were well. We are expecting Cousin Edie and daughter-in-law. Her son is in Malaya like yourself. Keep a stout heart & may God bless and bring you safely back. Ernest joins me in love & the best of health your loving Aunt Ada.

Prisoners were bereft of possessions. Mel Rosen owned a loincloth, a bottle and a pot of pepper. Many POWs boasted only the loincloth. Even where there were razor blades, shaving was unfashionable, shaggy beards the norm. Few made use of what might ironically be called their "leisure hours." Paul Reuter claimed that he never did much, but never remembered being bored, "because the mind doesn't generate many thoughts when you're that hungry. I'm always angry with having wasted those years." In Aomi, Japan, prisoners took it in turns to give each other lectures on such themes as "Letters," "My Dog Rufus," "World Government," "The Virtue of Modesty," "The American War of Independence." In some camps, educational courses flourished. Andrew Cunningham took the opportunity to get coaching from a fellow prisoner in accountancy, his chosen career. In Rangoon Jail, British prisoners possessed some books. One officer, Bruce Tothill, kept a list of titles which he read. They included *As We Were* by E. F. Benson, *Frenchman's Creek* by Daphne du Maurier, *Crime and Punishment*, *Robinson Crusoe*, *Mansfield Park*, *Eminent Victorians*, *1000 Beautiful Things Selected by Arthur Mee*, *The Fair Maid of Perth* by Walter Scott. Pocket editions of Dickens were especially valued, because their thin paper made them ideal for rolling cigarettes.

In Milton Young's camp, when prisoners made a deck of playing cards they were thrashed by the Japanese for "presumption," but in most places chess and bridge were tolerated. In Rangoon in 1944, Maj. Nigel Loring had just called "Six spades" when Allied bombs began to fall around the jail. Amid deafening explosions which killed or wounded several prisoners, the cards scattered in all directions. When at last peace was restored, Loring exclaimed ruefully: "Goddammit! That was the best bridge hand I ever had!"

In almost every POW camp, drugs to treat disease were scarce or nonexistent. Superimposed upon a grossly inadequate diet, sickness carried off many men. In Burma and Malaya, beriberi was the principal killer, caused by a lack of vitamin B. Its symptoms began with chronic diarrhoea. Thereafter, a victim's body either swelled, or shrank to skeletal dimensions. In Rangoon Jail, doctors had a thermometer and a stethoscope, which enabled them to diagnose a man's condition, but they lacked drugs to ameliorate it. Guards were bribed to bring in poppies from which an opiate could be made. Working parties collected "blue stones"—copper sulphate—which could be crushed and stirred into water to form an antidote for jungle sores. Old razor blades were stolen for surgery. The ubiquitous flies provoked a cholera outbreak, which after killing ten prisoners was checked by skilful isolation of patients. Blood and mucus in a man's stool indicated dysentery, another ruthless killer. Jaundice, dengue fever and of course malaria took their shares. Alf Evans, an RAOC wireless mechanic, observed laconically that his Malayan camp was "not a bit like Butlin's at all. We had here ulcers, boils, crabs, malaria, blackwater fever, dingy, beriberi, sores, bugbites, Changi feet and depression." In sapper Edward Whincup's camp on the railway, open wounds were treated by scraping out pus with a spoon, then spraying the infected area with a saline solution or permanganate of potash with an RAF stirrup pump. When the British were joined by Tamil workers, unfamiliar with hygiene discipline, cholera struck.

An American Liberator crew was brought into Rangoon Jail in 1944, every man badly burned. As "war criminals" by Japanese definition, they had been granted no medical treatment whatever. When British doctors were belatedly allowed to see them, the airmen's wounds crawled with maggots. "With one exception," wrote a British officer, "they died screaming in agony as they had done since their arrival." Doctors found themselves grimly fascinated by the variety of illnesses which it became their lot to treat. For instance, prisoners working on an airstrip off Java developed "coral blindness." Poor diet generated many cases of vision deterioration. "Burning feet" exactly described symptoms of the condition. It became worse at night, so that men unable to sleep in their agony paced compounds through the hours of darkness. One of many post-war medical reports described the case of Private Barton of the 2nd Loyals, sentenced to five years' solitary confinement for an attempted escape from Changi in July 1942. Barton served three years, during which he received a daily allowance of "1/2 pint rice pap for breakfast, 1/2 pint dry rice and 1/2 pint green soup for tiffin and supper. Developed scrotal dermatitis, burning feet, glossitis, weakness of the legs, deafness and retro-bulbar neuropathy. When examined in October 1945 Barton showed bilateral nerve deafness, posterior column degeneration and severe memory defect."

In the midst of all this, prisoners were occasionally permitted to dispatch cards to relatives at home, couched in terms which mocked their condition, and phrases usually dictated by their jailers. "Dear Mum & all," wrote Fred Thompson from Java to his family in Essex, "I am very well and hope you are too. The Japanese treat us well, so don't worry about me and never feel uneasy. My daily work is easy and we are paid . . . We have plenty of food and much recreation. Goodbye, God bless you, I am waiting for you very earnestly, my love to you all." Thompson expressed reality in the privacy of his diary: "Somehow we keep going. We are all skeletons, just living from day to day . . . This life just teaches one not to hope or expect anything . . . I cannot explain my emotions, they are just non-existent."

In the face of institutionalised barbarism, some prisoners displayed unselfishness and nobility. In Rangoon Jail, a Gurkha *subadar* invited by the Japanese to compose an essay on the British wrote simply in block capitals: THE BRITISH ALWAYS HAVE BEEN AND ALWAYS WILL BE THE FINEST RACE IN THE WORLD. He was sent to solitary confinement. The Australian prison camp surgeon "Weary" Dunlop became a legend in his country. Others behaved less well. Corporal Paul Reuter of the USAAF slept on the top deck of a three-tier bunk in his camp at Hirahato on Japan. When disease and vitamin deficiency caused him to go blind for three weeks, no man would change places to enable him to sleep at ground level. "Some people would steal, no matter how much they were punished," said Reuter. "There was a lot of barter, then bitterness about people who reneged on the deals. There were only a few fights, but a lot of arguing—about places in line, about who got a spoonful more."

Sapper Edward Whincup, in a camp on the Burma railway, was shocked by the prevalence of pilfering by comrades, especially of blankets, their most precious possessions, which were sold to Thais in exchange for food. Two Australians caught stealing drugs in Hall Romney's camp were forced to parade outside the guardroom through thirty-six hours of blazing sun and chill night. "No one has any sympathy with them," wrote Romney. "They merit most severe punishment." Australians showed themselves both the best and worst of POWs. Their finest possessed extraordinary courage, endurance and tribal loyalty. Their basest were incorrigible thieves and ruthless bullies. This was a world in which gentleness was neither a virtue which commanded esteem, nor a quality which promoted survival. Philip Stibbe, a former Chindit officer in Rangoon Jail, wrote: "We became hardened and even callous. At one time bets were laid about who would be next to die. Everything possible was done to save the lives of the sick, but it was worse than useless to grieve over the inevitable."

Self-respect was deeply discounted. Every day, in every way, prisoners were exposed to their own impotence. On the Bataan death march, Captain Mel Rosen watched Japanese soldiers kick ailing Americans into latrine pits: "You don't know the meaning of frustration until you've had to stand by and take that," said Rosen. Some British officers in Rangoon Jail remained morbidly sensitive to their status as representatives of the power which claimed hegemony over the Burmans. They were thus ashamed to find themselves pushing carts of manure through the streets of the city in their loincloths, watched without sympathy by local people. "I wonder what the Poona Club would think!" muttered one British officer gloomily.

They strove to preserve tatters of "face" and discipline. For instance, when a working party was caught in the streets during an Allied air raid, their senior officer kept them marching in formed ranks. It seemed essential "that the Japanese, contemptuous of us anyway for being prisoners, should not be given any reason to despise us further," wrote Lt. Charles

Coubrough. This was, he said, "one of the few examples of firm leadership I was to meet during my captivity, and I responded gladly." Almost every prisoner afterwards felt ashamed that he had stood passively by while the Japanese beat or even killed his comrades. In logic, what could bystanders have done? To survivors, however, logic offered little comfort.

Each man chose his own path towards a relationship with the Japanese. Coubrough believed that it was essential never to show fear or seem to condescend. He sought to be cheerful and friendly: "It was pointless to maintain a defiant attitude for years." Prisoners hated the necessity to bow to every Japanese, whatever his rank and whatever theirs. In any case, no display of deference shielded them from the erratic whims of their masters. Japanese behaviour vacillated between grotesquery and sadism. In Ted Whincup's camp on the Burma railway, the commandant, Major Cheetah, insisted that the prisoners' four-piece band should muster outside the guardroom and play "Hi, ho, hi, ho, it's off to work we go"—the tune from *Snow White*—each morning as a column of skeletal inmates shambled forth to their labours. "Nobody looked or felt like the seven dwarves," noted Whincup grimly. If guards in his camp took a dislike to a prisoner, they killed him with a casual shove into a ravine. The Japanese seemed especially ill-disposed towards tall men, whom they obliged to bend to receive punishment, usually administered with a cane. Airman Fred Jackson, working on an airfield on the coral island of Ambon, found himself diverted to build a tennis court for the commandant, under the supervision of a pre-war Wimbledon umpire. When prisoners began to die, at first the Japanese commandant attended their burials. There were soon so many corpses, however, that he ceased to trouble himself.

One day, for no discernible reason six British officers were paraded in line, and one by one punched to the ground by a Japanese warrant officer. A trooper of the 3rd Hussars, being beaten beside the tea bucket by a guard with a rifle, raised an arm to ward off blows and was accused of having struck the man. After several days of beatings, he was taken outside the camp, tied to a tree and bayoneted to death. The commandant proclaimed the execution "a necessary exercise of discipline." The prisoner was not shot, he said, lest the sound of gunfire unsettle local natives.

At Hall Romney's camp on the railway, a soldier who struck a Japanese was placed at attention in the sun outside the guardroom. Whenever he moved, he was kicked in the stomach until his screams rang through the compound. The man was then dragged onto a lorry and taken away by a guard detail equipped with rifles and spades. Next day, his identification card was removed from the files in the camp office. An officer of the Gordons who protested against sick men being forced to work was taken into the jungle and tied to a tree, beneath which guards lit a fire and burnt him like some Christian martyr. At a camp in Japan, days before the end of the war five British officers were shot when a radio receiver was discovered in their barracks.

"The ordinary Japanese has the mind of an adolescent," Philip Stibbe wrote contemptuously. "His cruelty to animals, his attitude to sex matters, his ability to swallow the direst propaganda, his childish irritability and petty attitude to life all indicate this . . . [For a prisoner] ignorance of a rule or failure to understand an order, even when it was in Japanese, was never considered an excuse. If they were in a good mood, you had your face slapped; if they were feeling just a bit liverish they struck you with a clenched fist; on bad days they would use a rifle butt and kick you on the shins. But whatever they did the victim was supposed to stand perfectly still at attention."

WESTERN CIVILIANS who fell into the hands of the Japanese in China, the Philippines and South-East Asia were technically interned rather than imprisoned, often crowded into clusters of former colonial homes. In a few places, notably Shanghai, such communities came through the war worn, strained and wretched, yet almost all alive. In Shanghai's Chapei camp, the Japanese left families intact. Inmates complained of confinement and lack of privacy, but none starved. It was noted ruefully that deprivation of alcohol improved the fitness of some adults. They enjoyed the doubtful benefit of two pianos. Schoolchildren sat school exams. The Japanese seldom interfered with the monotony of life inside the compound. A British "Judicial Committee" imposed its own rules and punishments. A schoolboy watched curiously as a certain "Mr. M" scythed grass as a penalty for theft, while "Mr. R" served two weeks' solitary confinement in a tiny room under a stairwell for "sneaking to the Japanese."

Such temperate regimes were, however, exceptional. Across most of the Japanese empire, internees suffered almost as grievously as military POWs. Deprivation of food and lack of drugs for medical treatment killed large numbers, especially in the Dutch East Indies. Nini Rambonnet was the daughter of a Dutch colonial official, born in Batavia in 1920 and brought up in consequent comfort and ease. She had a personal maid at the age of thirteen, and as a young woman lived in a social whirl punctuated by a lot of golf and not much work. By the end of 1943, however, her golf clubs had been sold to Japanese naval officers to buy food, her mother tortured as an alleged British spy. Her twenty-two-year-old brother was working in the coal mines of Japan, and her father was dead of starvation and dysentery. She herself was confined among 1,200 women and children in Tijdeng camp, and found it difficult to master rudimentary domestic tasks: washing and ironing clothes, pulling a rubbish cart in shafts designed for an absent horse, sharing a lavatory with thirty others. The Japanese orders at roll call became imprinted on her brain: "*Kiotsuke*"—"Attention"; "*Keirei*"—"Bow"; "*Naore*"—"Stand at ease."

They lived on rice, offal and vegetables. One night a fox dumped a half-eaten chicken behind their bungalow: "I cooked it slowly and the smell was heavenly," Nini wrote. "In the morning I took it to the nurses' houses and we all shared a cupful each. The patients were complaining that they could only smell it, but we told them they were not allowed to eat it as they had dysentery." Like POWs, internees were victims of sudden Japanese whims. One day at Tijdeng, an order was issued that all dogs must be rounded up and killed. Lacking any other means, boys had to club the pets to death. Infractions of discipline were punished by hours kneeling on the street in full sun: "The hot asphalt was incredibly painful." When the camp commandant asked for women volunteers to work in his house, the first draft was rejected as insufficiently pretty.

During the original Japanese onslaught in 1942 there were many cases of rape, notably of Allied nurses, and vast numbers of Asians suffered sexual assault by their occupiers. In the camps, few Western women suffered in this way. Faced with starvation, however, a significant minority—estimated at around 10 percent by an Australian nurse on Sumatra—were happy to trade sex for food. Dr. Marjorie Lyon described a bitter fight in her camp on Sumatra when a thousand women forcibly resisted a 1942 attempt by the Japanese to remove some girls "to work for Nippon"—and won. In her later camp at Banginang, "no one was raped, and no one went to work for Nippon against their will . . . quite a few women and girls did go out to live with Japanese in their 'comfort houses.' But they were anxious to do so to get better conditions, and we could not prevent them. None of our British people did so."

Guards routinely struck the women: "I had a reputation for being able to handle Japanese, but sometimes it did not work, and then I got knocked about a bit, though I never had a formal beating-up. Only one girl was . . . given a real Gestapo beating, and that was because she was alleged to have been overheard saying that the Japanese were stupid to have blackouts in the camp when the street lights were blazing.' In Marjorie Lyon's group of 114 internees, 15 men and 4 women—the latter aged between fifty and seventy-two—died. One of the British women who died in a camp on a derelict rubber estate at Loebeck Linggan was a 1942 fugitive from Singapore named Margaret Dryburgh. Miss Dryburgh was a devout Christian, who cherished the captives' hymn:

Give us patience to endure
Keep our hearts serene and pure,
Grant us courage, charity,
Greater faith, humility,
Readiness to own Thy will,
Be we free or captive still.

On 21 April 1945, less than four months before the war ended, Margaret Dryburgh lay on a sickbed trying to say her favourite Twenty-third Psalm. A friend understood what she wanted, and stumbled through the words on her behalf. When it was over and a silence fell, the old woman smiled, said simply, "That's what I wanted," and died. At the same period in the hospital where Nini Rambonnet nursed, patients were expiring from malnutrition at the rate of ten a day. Corpses were laid in crude coffins of coconut leaves, on each of which the Japanese laid a bunch of bananas. The living attempted any expedient to assuage hunger. Nini ate toadstools, which made her very sick indeed. One of the girls, in that time of despair, asked a guard who spoke Malay when they would be released. He answered: "Not until your hair is grey and your teeth have fallen out."

2. Hell Ships

ALTHOUGH LABOUR on the Burma railway represented the worst fate that could befall an Allied POW, shipment to Japan as a slave labourer was an ordeal which also proved fatal to many. On 17 June 1944, prisoners were paraded in Hall Romney's camp on the railway. The commandant announced that they were being transferred to Japan. "Looking back on the past year and ten months since camps were first established in Siam," said the Japanese officer benignly,

> you have worked both earnestly and diligently and produced a great achievement in the construction of the Siam–Burma railway . . . For this we wish to express sincere appreciation. Your work in Siam having finished, you are being transported to the Land of the Rising Sun, an island country joyously situated and rich in beautiful scenery. From time immemorial our Imperial Nippon has had the honour of respecting justice and morality . . . They are men and women of determination, generous by nature, despising injustice in accordance with the old Nippon proverb "The huntsman does not shoot the wounded bear." In spring the cherry blossoms are in full bloom. In summer fresh breezes

rustle over the shadow of green trees. In autumn the glorious moon throws its entrancing light on sea and river . . .

After many more minutes of such lyrical rhetoric before his audience of half-dead men, the Japanese commandant concluded: "I wish you '*bon voyage*.' " The prisoners were sent on their way.

Conditions in the holds of transport ships were always appalling, sometimes fatal. Overlaid on hunger and thirst was the threat of U.S. submarines. The Japanese made no attempt to identify ships carrying POWs, of whom at least 10,000 perished following Allied attacks. RAOC wireless mechanic Alf Evans was among 1,500 men in the holds of the *Kachidoki Maru* on the night of 11 September 1944, when the ship was hit by four torpedoes. Evans was lucky. Suffering malaria, he was sleeping with other sick men on a hatch cover on the forward deck, instead of being battened below. As the ship began to settle, he asked a gunner officer: "What do I do? I can't swim." The gunner said: "Now's the time to learn." Evans jumped, and dog-paddled to a small raft to which three other men were already clinging. One had two broken legs, another a dislocated thigh. They were all naked, and coated in oil. A Japanese soldier hung on for a while, reciting repeatedly in English: "I am large sick, I am large sick." Evans, desperately cold, saw a Japanese tunic floating by. He seized this and put it on. Aboard the sinking hulk, the Japanese had been shooting their own wounded and pushing women into boats. One British POW, Ralph Clifton, saved a baby from the sea, for which a Japanese officer later rewarded him with ten cigarettes.

A destroyer arrived, and began to pick up survivors—but only Japanese survivors. The prisoners were left to the sea. Alf Evans paddled to a lifeboat left empty after its occupants were rescued, and climbed aboard, joining two Gordon Highlanders. They later hauled in other men, until they were thirty strong. After three days and nights afloat, they were taken aboard a Japanese submarine chaser. The captain reviewed the bedraggled figures paraded on his deck, and ordered them thrown over the side. The POWs were astonished to find that their own guard, Tanaka, a notoriously brutal character, dissuaded him. The vessel's captain satisfied his feelings by administering savage beatings all round. Eventually the prisoners were transferred to the hold of a whaling factory ship, in which they completed their journey to Japan.

Almost naked and coated in filth, they were landed on the dockside at Moji and marched through the streets, between lines of watching Japanese women, to a cavalry barracks. There they were clothed in sacking and dispatched to work twelve-hour shifts in the furnaces of a chemical works in the town of Omuta: "Life consisted only of work and sleep." Of the fifteen hundred men who had embarked with Alf Evans, just six hundred survived to become slave labourers.

On 13 December 1944, Captain Mel Rosen was among a detail of 1,619 American POWs marched through the streets of Manila to the docks. In earlier times, Filipinos sometimes gave V signs to prisoners, or kids called out "We're with you, Joe!" By that last winter of the war, local people had learned the price of such gestures. Most were silent and impassive. Next day the Americans left for Japan on the freighter *Oryoku Maru*, a voyage that was to become one of the most notorious of the war. Water and tea were periodically lowered to the prisoners in kegs. Those closest to the ladders drank. Others did not. Some men congratulated themselves on grabbing a few mouthfuls of boiled seaweed, but later regretted these, for they became violently sick. The ship was dive-bombed several times by U.S. carrier planes. The attacks ended at dusk. The prisoners were desperate with thirst. Doctors urged them not to drink their own urine, but some did so anyway. "That night was terrible, the worst thing I can imagine," said Rosen. "Discipline went to hell, especially among the newer arrivals. I did not myself see anyone biting a man's throat and drinking his blood, but I've heard of it happening from lots of others." Some prisoners wilfully killed others, in the demented struggle for water and food. Next day, they were again subjected to air attack. This time, they were hit.

The Japanese crew and guards abandoned ship. The prisoners forced their way on deck to find the superstructure on fire. They took to the sea, and for a few brief minutes revelled in its warm wetness: "It was such a wonderful feeling as one jumped off that ship into the water." Those who could not swim pushed hatch covers over the side and clung to them. The prisoners found themselves only a short way offshore from Luzon, and with little choice save to make for it. On the beach, they were welcomed by armed Japanese. As survivors struggled ashore, they were herded onto a tennis court on the old American naval base. Out of 1,619 men who had boarded the ship, some thirteen hundred remained. In the blazing sun, for some days they were not fed at all, merely given a little water. On the fourth and fifth days, each man received a spoonful and a half of raw rice. When they demanded aid for the sick and injured, a truck was brought to take them away. These men were never seen again, and were assumed to have been shot.

On Christmas Eve the survivors were put aboard another ship, the *Enoura Maru*, which took them to Formosa. It was deep winter. The Americans possessed only their shorts or G-strings. "People literally froze to death," said Rosen. Yet still there was wretchedly little to drink: "You could have got an IOU from any man for a cup of water—and he would have paid up after the war." When American Helldivers attacked again, Rosen was struck by steel fragments in the ankle, thigh and upper body. "There were dead and dying men everywhere. Steel deck supports fell, killing everyone underneath. After a few days, the Japanese lowered nets into the holds, to take away the dead. Then they took survivors off the hulk, and loaded us onto yet another ship the *Brazil Maru*. We buried dozens of men every day." On 29 January 1945 they arrived at Moji on Kyushu. Just 193 men landed, out of more than a thousand who left the Philippines. Rosen weighed eighty-eight pounds. The survivors were issued clothing from a stack of old British uniforms. An American doctor excavated bomb fragments from Rosen's armpit with a penknife, before they were taken to Fukuoka to start their labours.

Working conditions in Japan were in no way preferable to those in South-East Asia. Many prisoners' feet were so swollen by beriberi that in the desperate cold of winter, they could not wear shoes. Even under such blankets as they had, men shivered at night, for there was no heating in their barracks. At Stephen Abbott's camp at Aomi, when prisoners begged for relief, the commandant said contemptuously: "If you wish to live you must become hardened to cold, as Japanese are. You must teach your men to have strong willpower—like Japanese." Abbott demanded bitterly: "Men tortured by hunger, disease, bitter cold, and the daily fear of death?" Yet by 1944 the death rate in most Japanese camps had declined steeply from that of 1942 and 1943. The most vulnerable were gone. Those who remained were frail, often verging on madness, but possessed a brute capacity to endure which kept many alive to the end. In Hall Romney's camp, just six men died in July 1944, compared with 482 in the same month of 1943.

THE CULTURAL chasm between captives and their jailers often seemed unbridgeable. Stephen Abbott recorded an exchange with a guard named Private Ito on a ship taking them to Japan. Ito had been consistently brutal. The POWs had no inkling that he spoke English until suddenly he addressed a terse question to Abbott: "Homesick?" The Englishman shrugged. Ito said: "I've been homesick for six years—first in China, then the Philippines and Timor, most lately in Singapore. I shall now at last see my family and I am happy." Abbott said coldly: "That will be nice for you." Ito revealed that he had an economics degree from Tokyo University. He asked curiously what Abbott thought of the Japanese, and received a cautious reply: "I don't know them very well, so I cannot answer your question." The guard persisted: "How do you think of what you know? How do you think of me?" Abbott said: "In our army, we do not strike and beat people as punishment. Ito is always doing so, and this blackens my thoughts about him." The eyes of the little Japanese widened in amazement. He asked how the British Army punished wrongdoers. Abbott explained that physical chastisement was unknown. Ito never hit a prisoner again.

An enormous amount has been written about Japanese cruelty to prisoners. It should be noticed, nonetheless, that conditions varied widely in different camps. For instance, 2,000 British POWs in Saigon lived not intolerably until late 1944, sometimes even able to slip under the wire to visit local shops and brothels. It seems important also to record instances in which POWs were shown kindness, even granted means to survive through Japanese compassion. A British bugler, Corporal Leader, found himself in a Singapore hospital in 1942. Back home in Norfolk he had been a Salvation Army bandsman. Now, he was amazed to be visited by a Japanese who announced that he too had been a "Sally Army" member in Tokyo. He wanted to help the sick Briton. The Japanese contacted a local Malay Salvationist, who sent Leader letters, eggs and biscuits. Interned on Sumatra, Dr. Marjorie Lyon was able to keep many of her sick companions alive thanks to an officer named Mizusawa, who gave her drugs from the military hospital in Padang—and sometimes left her alone in the dispensary, to enable her to steal more: "He was a really kind-hearted Japanese."

When Erroll Shearn was digging air-raid shelters outside the Kempeitai headquarters in Batavia, two young Japanese officers emerged. Speaking in Malay, they applauded his gang's work. Shearn asked them cautiously: "How do you like winning the war?" They answered: "We don't like war. We are engineers, not soldiers, and we would much rather be back at Tokyo University." Shearn said: "I don't like war either. I am a lawyer, not a soldier." One of the Japanese pulled out a cigarette case, said, "You and I are friends. Have a cigarette," and gave the Englishman the packet. At lunchtime Shearn's benefactor returned, and asked if the prisoners had enough to eat. Told that they had not, he brought them food and tea.

Little old Mr. Yogi, civilian interpreter in Stephen Abbott's Aomi camp, had learned his indifferent English in an earlier career as a ship's purser. "Are you contented, Abbotto?" he asked one day. The British officer shrugged. Yogi himself always looked miserable. Now, he said: "Some of my people are not worried by trouble. They are young people accustomed to bullying from superiors. I am made unhappy by it because, perhaps, I am too proud. I am older and have seen things different in Japan. You understand? I am proud of being Japanese, but I also know something of how Western peoples live. I am not ashamed of real Japanese customs—but the war has changed the real Japan. We were much as you are before the war—when the army had not control. You must not think our true standards are what you see now."

Abbott wrote: "I realised that Yogi longed for peace as much as any of us. As a civilian he was treated with contempt by the soldiers . . . Above all things he wanted to regain his self-respect." Yogi told the Englishman that his wife was sick with beriberi and needed meat: "I have made decision that our cat must be killed to give meat for my wife." This unwilling samurai could not face killing the family pet himself: "Will you please ask your cook-sergeant to do this and make stew? I will bring cat tonight. Please do not tell other Japanese. They would laugh at me."

The terror of Aomi camp was its commandant, Captain Yoshimura. Every prisoner lived in fear of the screamed summons from a guard: "Number one to office—*speedo*! Yoshimura-San waits!" This officer was "small, stout, effeminate and twenty-six years old. He walked with a Napoleonic strut and his cruel, spiteful eyes blinked at you through thick glasses. He had a high-pitched voice and, when he raved, this rose to a scream which in other circumstances might have been amusing. His power was enormous—extending way beyond our prison camp. In Aomi town everyone, from the mayor to the most humble peasant, obeyed his commands. He was the only army officer for miles around and, as such, took precedence over all civilians." Yoshimura liked to draw his sword and swish it above the heads of prisoners, shouting contemptuously: "What are the lives of a hundred captives when thousands of brave Japanese are dying each day for the Emperor?"

Then came a day when there was an accident at the quarry where the prisoners worked, and which had already witnessed the deaths of forty of their number. This time, by a happy quirk of fate, it was the turn of Yoshimura to perish. The camp's senior NCO, Sergeant Sumiki, demanded of Stephen Abbott how he felt about the news. Abbott murmured something about "a terrible tragedy." Sergeant Sumiki burst out laughing, thumped the Englishman on the shoulder and cried out: "You lie! You very pleased. Me, too, very pleased!" The Japanese guards hated the tyrant as much as the British did.

One day at Doug Idlett's camp in the Philippines, there was a call for volunteers to work at Japanese headquarters for a month:

> I had beriberi. I was sitting holding my foot and typing with one hand. A Japanese interpreter named Sekiyawa asked what was wrong with me, and I told him. Next day he handed me a bottle of Vitamin B. I never saw him again, but I felt that he had contributed to me being alive. Later, at the coalyards in Japan where we worked, there was a shunting engine driver named Yoshioka. One day he was resting by his

can when we saw a *daikon*, a big Japanese radish, floating in the water by the tracks. We bent down and pulled it out. I stuffed it in my pants. Yoshioka asked: "What are you going to do with that?" I said: "Eat it." He said: "You cannot. It's dirty. Give it to me." Later, he gave it back to us cleaned, sliced and cooked. From that day on, he always arrived with his leggings full of corn or something else for us to eat.

Lt. Masaichi Kikuchi, commanding an airfield defence unit in Singapore early in 1945, was allotted a labour force of three hundred Indian POWs from the Changi compound. The officer who handed over the men said carelessly: "When you're finished, you can do what you like with them. If I was you, I'd shove them into a tunnel with a few demolition charges." Kikuchi was told of the standing order that any prisoner who disobeyed orders or attempted to escape was to be executed out of hand, "and I knew that this was being done." However, when two of his Indian POW detail broke out and were returned after being betrayed by local Chinese among whom they had sought refuge, Kikuchi handed them over to their own officer, a captain of the Indian Army, for punishment. He often asked himself afterwards why he had not killed them, as so many others were killed. A cynic would suggest that it was because Japan's defeat was plainly so close. Kikuchi himself simply claimed to regard executions in such circumstances as unjustified: "I told myself after the war that the only reason I had been allowed to survive was that I had done nothing bad to others." Likewise, in 1945 American and Dutch doctors at Kobe POW hospital signed a joint testimonial to its Japanese medical supervisor, Dr. Hiyajiro Ohashi, praising the extraordinary efforts of himself and his staff to assist Allied prisoners.

The point of such stories is not that they contradict an overarching view of the Japanese as ruthless and often wilfully sadistic in their treatment of despised captives. It is that, as always in human affairs, the story deserves shading. All the Japanese described above showed nuggets of courage, in defying a pattern of behaviour towards prisoners which their culture encouraged, even demanded. There is another issue. Because the Allies won the war, much was heard about the maltreatment of prisoners in German or Japanese hands, almost nothing about the reverse of the coin. There is ample anecdotal evidence that some American, British and Australian guards in POW camps behaved inhumanely towards their charges.

Some German prisoners—sensationalists claim tens of thousands—died in Allied hands in north-west Europe in the summer of 1945, chiefly because the administrative machinery was overwhelmed by their numbers. This was an argument advanced to justify some POW deaths in

Japanese hands in 1942. Nobody in London or Washington, however, troubled to investigate the fate of abused German or Japanese prisoners, far less to frame indictments against Allied personnel. In the nature of military affairs, those selected to guard POWs are among the least impressive material in every nation's armed forces. None of this represents an attempt to suggest moral equivalence between Japanese treatment of Allied POWs and the other way around; merely that few belligerents in any war can boast unblemished records in the treatment of prisoners, as events in Iraq have recently reminded us.

WHAT ENABLED some men to survive the unspeakable experiences of captivity, while others perished? Mel Rosen attributed 5 percent to self-discipline, 5 percent to optimism—"If you didn't think you were going to make it, you didn't"—and 90 percent to "pure luck." Milton Young, a carpenter's son from Rhode Island who spent an orphan childhood working on a chicken farm, believed that an uncommonly harsh upbringing helped him to survive Japanese captivity. He was even grateful not to have a home to think about: "I didn't have much of a family, and that helped."

At the end of the war, British private soldier Don Lewis of the 1/5th Sherwood Foresters recorded the fate of his battalion, almost a thousand strong when it went into action in Malaya at the end of 1941. Thirty-five men were killed in battle, and a further 11 died of wounds. In captivity, 50 died of "complaints unknown"; a further 1 of diphtheria; 17 of malaria; 9 of beriberi; 11 of cardiac illnesses; 31 of dysentery; 21 of malnutrition; 1 was killed by a falling tree; and 1 by an Allied bomb; 45 were lost on Japanese convoys; 24 were merely recorded as "missing." Lewis was among 287 men known to have returned to Britain.

Since 1945, pleas have been entered in mitigation of what the Japanese did to their prisoners in the Second World War. First, as mentioned above, there was the administrative difficulty of handling unexpectedly large numbers of captives in 1942, for whom no provisions of care or supply had been made. This has some validity. Many armies in modern history have encountered such problems in the chaos of victory, and their prisoners have suffered in consequence. Moreover, food and medical supplies were desperately short in many parts of the Japanese empire. Western prisoners, goes this argument, merely shared privations endured by local civilians and Japanese soldiers. Such claims might be plausible, but for the fact that prisoners were left starving and neglected even where means were available to alleviate their condition. There is no record of POWs at any time or place being adequately fed.

It is thus hard to dispute that the Japanese maltreated captives as a matter of policy, not necessity. They flaunted the cultural contempt with which their soldiers were taught to regard inferiors of their own society, never mind enemies who preferred captivity to death. A people who adopt a code which rejects the concept of mercy towards the weak and afflicted seem to place themselves outside the pale of civilisation. The casual sadism of the Japanese towards their prisoners was so widespread, indeed almost universal, that it must be considered institutional. There were so many cases of arbitrary beheadings, clubbings and bayonetings in different parts of the empire that it is impossible to dismiss these as unauthorised initiatives by individual officers and men. The indifference which the Japanese navy showed towards prisoners in its charge who found themselves struggling in the sea after their ships sank was shameful by any standard.

Japanese sometimes justify such inhumanity by suggesting that it was matched by equally callous Allied bombing of civilians. Japanese moral indignation caused many U.S. aircrew captured in 1944–45 to be treated as "war criminals." For instance, eight B-29 crewmen of the 29th Bomb Group were killed in 1945 by suffering unanaesthetised vivisection carried out in front of medical students at a hospital in Fukuoka on Kyushu. Their stomachs, hearts, lungs and brain segments were removed. Half a century later, one doctor present, Dr. Toshio Tono, said: "There was no debate among the doctors about whether to do the operations—that was what made it so strange." Many captured American airmen were beheaded, not only in the last days of the war, but even in the period immediately following the Japanese surrender.

Any society which can indulge such actions, whether or not as alleged acts of retribution, has lost its moral compass. Much Japanese behaviour reflected the bitterness of former victors about finding their own military fortunes in eclipse, becoming the bombed instead of the bombers. More than sixty years later, there still seems no acceptable excuse. The Japanese, having started the war, waged it with such savagery towards the innocent and impotent that it is easy to understand the rage which filled Allied hearts in 1945, when all was revealed. The ambivalence of post-war Japan about its treatment of captives is exemplified in the 1952 memoirs of wartime foreign minister Mamoru Shigemitsu, one of the more rational of the country's leaders. He wrote: "After the war many instances were recorded of kindly treatment by Japanese in individual cases, and a number of letters of thanks were received from ex-prisoners of war and persons who had been in concentration camps." Shigemitsu tarnished his own reputation by penning such pitiful stuff. War is inherently inhumane, but the Japanese practiced extraordinary refinements of inhumanity in the treatment of those thrown upon their mercy.

SIXTEEN

Okinawa

1. Love Day

THE U.S. ARMED FORCES' *Guide to the Pacific* briefed visitors to the Ryukyus, of which Okinawa is the main island, with unfailing facetiousness: "Those who wish a good memento of a stay in *Nansei Shoto* should get a piece of the lacquerware for which the islanders are famous." In the spring of 1945 some 12,000 Americans and up to 150,000 Japanese found death rather than porcelain amid Okinawa's sixty-mile length of fields and mountains, or in the waters offshore. The island was home to 450,000 people, who possessed Japanese nationality while remaining culturally distinct. Before an invasion of Japan's main islands could be attempted, it was evident to both sides that this southern outpost was likely to be contested. Its airfields, rather more than midway between Luzon and Kyushu, would have to be denied to the Japanese, secured by the Americans. At the time Operation Iceberg was launched in the spring of 1945, it was perceived in Washington only as a preliminary to the decisive battle that must follow, for Japan's home islands. Likewise in Tokyo, the defence of Okinawa was deemed vital to Japan's strategy for achieving a negotiated peace. If the U.S. could be made to pay dearly enough for winning a single offshore island, reasoned the nation's leaders and indeed its emperor, Washington would conclude that the price of invading Kyushu and Honshu was too great to be borne. They were correct in their analysis, but utterly deluded about its implications.

Twenty-five-year-old Captain Kouichi Ito was the son of a naval officer, brought up at the great Yokosuka naval base. Ito passionately wanted to be a warrior. He was embarrassed to find himself disqualified from service as a pilot or sailor, because he was prone to both air- and seasickness. Instead, he became a soldier, and passed out near the top of his 1940 military academy class. Anticlimax followed, however. For almost four years this fiercely ambitious young man found himself fulfilling garrison duties in Manchuria. While Japanese legions stormed triumphantly across Asia and locked themselves in combat with the Americans and British, Ito sat in his quarters reading endless books on the history of conflict—above all, about the First World War. Not until August 1944 did his unit, the 32nd Infantry, at last sail for an undisclosed destination. Only on their arrival did he and his comrades discover that they had joined the garrison of Okinawa.

The regiment, composed mostly of Hokkaidans, found the island strange and somewhat exotic, with its fields of sugarcane, unknown back home, its people's unfamiliar dialect. Okinawa is celebrated for a powerful local rice brew, *awamori*, which proved most acceptable to tens of thousands of soldiers who now began to fortify themselves there. Likewise, when cigarette rations ran short, it proved useful that Okinawan farmers grew illegal tobacco. Month after month the garrison laboured, enlarging and exploiting a great network of natural caves, preparing slit trenches and bunkers. The work was done with their bare hands. "We had no machines," said Kouichi Ito laconically. He himself, having walked the length of the coast, was sure that no invader would land on his regiment's rocky coastal sector in the south-west; and that entrenching this wasted precious resources. Orders were orders, however.

By the spring of 1945, Ito had become a battalion commander. His unit was better equipped than most of those deployed on Okinawa, having brought a full inventory of weapons from Manchuria. There was still some debate in command messes about whether the Americans would assault their island or Formosa, further south, but the 77,000 defenders recognised the likelihood that they would fight a great battle. The young officer Ito understood that the war was going badly: "After Saipan fell, I realised that we could lose." His regiment had left behind in Manchuria one-third of its complement of Hokkaidans. Like other units, it was now made up to strength with locally recruited Okinawans, who inspired little confidence, but added 20,000 unwilling conscripts to the garrison's strength. Ito took comfort from his father's judgement. The old sailor had seen something of Americans during convoy escort service in World War I, and asserted scornfully, "They have no idea of discipline." His son said: "I understood that the U.S. possessed enormous industrial resources, but I did not believe that in combat their soldiers could match the resolution of our men." After five years as a mere spectator of the war, the ambitious young warrior was eager to fight: "It seemed good to have a chance to take part in a real showdown with the enemy."

At last came a March morning when they awoke to behold on the sea before them a squadron of American warships, which soon began to bombard their positions. "Well, now we know," they said to each other. "It's us." Through the hours and days which followed, they sat passive in their caves while the earth shook with relentless concussions. The Americans were shelling everywhere, to sustain uncertainty about their intended landing place. As the Japanese grew accustomed to the barrage, Ito periodically emerged from his headquarters bunker into the dust-clouded daylight. Having never before been under fire, he wanted to test himself. When his unit joined battle, he was determined not to be seen to flinch. He was pleased with his own resolution, and waited confidently for the Americans to venture ashore.

After D-Day in Normandy, American landings on Okinawa represented the greatest amphibious operation of the war. More than 1,200 vessels transported 170,000 U.S. soldiers and Marines of Gen. Simon Bolivar Buckner's Tenth Army, with 120,000 more providing logistics and technical support. The island's seizure was to be a navy-run operation, under Nimitz's auspices, though soldiers were playing a substantial role. Four divisions would make the initial assault, with three more in reserve. Vice-Admiral Richmond Kelly Turner's 5th Amphibious Force was supported by Admiral Raymond Spruance's Fifth Fleet, mustering more than forty carriers, eighteen battleships and almost two hundred destroyers. "We bombarded all day long," wrote James Hutchinson of the battleship *Colorado* on 31 March. "We fired the sixteen-inch main battery about every three or four minutes all that time. It really gets to be a strain on a person's nerves after a while." Meanwhile, American units set about seizing several small offshore islands, preliminaries to the main assault.

On one of these, Tokashiki, twenty-two-year-old Lt. Yoshihiro Minamoto waited with his Shinyo suicide-boat unit. Minamoto was one of 2,200 cadets who graduated from Zama military academy in July 1944. As an engineer, he had completed three years' training—much more than American and British officers received at that time. Yet the most curious aspect of his ceremonial passing-out parade was the distribution of assignments which followed. Many newly minted lieutenants were promptly ticketed not merely for the possibility of death, but for its certainty. Some 450 were dispatched to train as kamikaze aircrew. Minamoto was among a further eighty posted to a seaborne special operations unit, whose mission was also explicitly suicidal. They were to man small boats laden with explosives, deployed to meet American amphibious landings. Minamoto, like his comrades, claimed to be untroubled: "At that time there was no choice." Suicide was now the pervasive theme among Japan's armed forces.

Unblooded in combat, Minamoto was imbued with an instinctive condescension towards his foe, which did not long survive his Okinawa experience: "The naval bombardment was terrifying. It seemed to go on and on. The sound of those shells in flight frightened me very much." Yet the

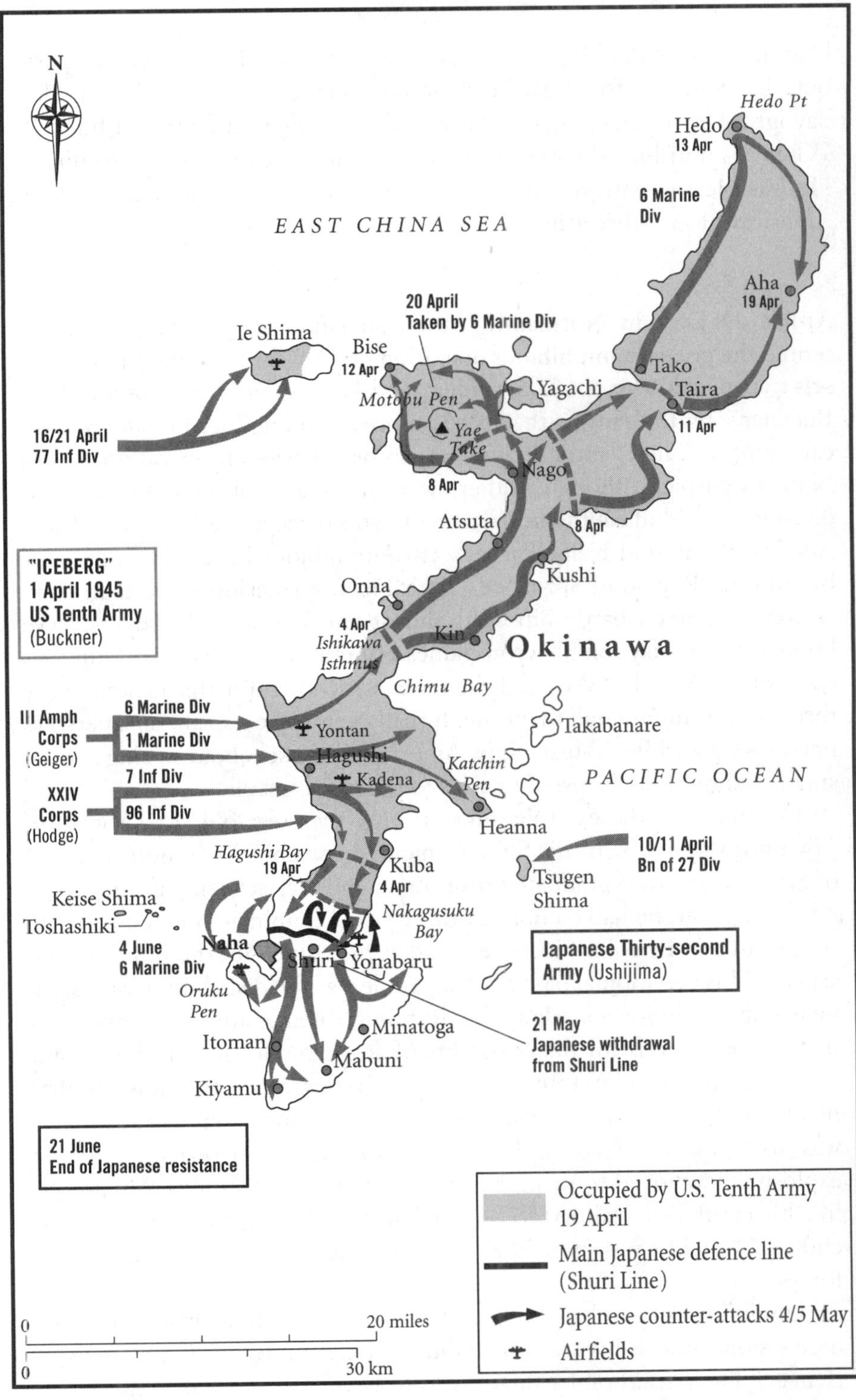
N
EAST CHINA SEA
Hedo Pt
Hedo
13 Apr
6 Marine
Div
Aha
19 Apr
20 April
Taken by 6 Marine Div
Ie Shima
Bise
12 Apr
Tako
Taira
11 Apr
Yagachi
Motobu Pen
Yae
Take
16/21 April
77 Inf Div
Nago
8 Apr
Atsuta
8 Apr
Kushi
"ICEBERG"
1 April 1945
US Tenth Army
(Buckner)
Onna
4 Apr
Ishikawa
Isthmus
Kin
Okinawa
Chimu Bay
III Amph
Corps
(Geiger)
6 Marine Div
1 Marine Div
Yontan
Takabanare
Hagushi
Katchin
Pen
PACIFIC OCEAN
XXIV
Corps
(Hodge)
7 Inf Div
96 Inf Div
Kadena
Heanna
Hagushi Bay
19 Apr
Kuba
4 Apr
10/11 April
Bn of 27 Div
Tsugen
Shima
Keise Shima
Toshashiki
Nakagusuku
Bay
4 June
6 Marine Div
Naha
Shuri
Yonabaru
Japanese Thirty-second
Army (Ushijima)
Oruku
Pen
Minatoga
21 May
Japanese withdrawal
from Shuri Line
Itoman
Mabuni
Kiyamu
21 June
End of Japanese resistance
Occupied by U.S. Tenth Army
19 April
Main Japanese defence line
(Shuri Line)
Japanese counter-attacks 4/5 May
Airfields
0
20 miles
0
30 km

Okinawa, April–May 1945

invaders' demonstration of naval and air power made little physical impact on the defenders, sheltering underground. Minamoto emerged from his cave on 25 March to a scene of devastation—"Trees were torn apart, the ground blackened, all our quarters flattened along with the local civilian houses." However, the suicide boats which he commanded were safe in laboriously dug bunkers along the shoreline. Glory and death seemed at hand for the two officers and thirty NCOs of his company, designated to pilot their explosive-laden craft against American ships.

But the crews on Tokashiki and its neighbouring islands never attacked. They were fifteen miles offshore, and U.S. escorts protected every route to the invasion armada. The Japanese had expected the Americans to anchor further south, allowing the suicide crews to strike them from the rear, on their seaward side. Now, instead, the vexed young commanding officer sought radio guidance from headquarters at Shanri Castle on the mainland, which was swiftly forthcoming: "Scuttle your craft." The order provoked a moment of hysteria among the crews. Many men burst into tears, denouncing their commanders: "Surely we haven't been through all this, to quit now!" The order was baffling, but was obeyed. Minamoto kept two boats intact, in case there was a new opportunity to launch them. The rest, almost a hundred craft scattered among three islands, were sunk in shallow water. Only a few of those on Okinawa itself were launched, to small effect.

On the morning of 27 March, American troops landed on Tokashiki. The suicide crews now lacked means to resist the invaders beyond swords, pistols and a few grenades. Minamoto ordered the coxswains to withdraw immediately to the north end of the island, to preserve them for future actions. He himself led the maintenance crews, around a hundred strong, in a brief defensive action. The Americans made short work of them. After losing nine dead in the first half-hour, Minamoto ordered his survivors to retreat northwards. He rejected the notion of self-immolation: "I felt that I wanted to fight to the death with the enemy, rather than merely bring death on myself." In the event, he did neither. Minamoto became a passive spectator of the first of the ghastly human tragedies which disfigured the Okinawa campaign.

Around nine hundred civilian farmers and families inhabited Tokashiki. As Minamoto and his men withdrew northwards into a jumble of rocks and caves, villagers left behind began to use grenades to kill themselves. Today, a revisionist movement among Japanese historians and nationalists seeks to argue that such civilian suicides were spontaneous acts, neither ordered nor condoned by the military. This is impossible to accept. Munitions had been supplied to many inhabitants, though it remains conjectural what orders accompanied them. On 28 March 1945 and in the days that followed, on Tokashiki 394 men, women and children immolated themselves. "Their actions reflected the spirit of the time," said Minamoto. "It was the consequence of all the reports about the fate of Japanese civilians on Saipan. Those islanders should not have been so hard on themselves. It wasn't as if the invaders were Chinese or Russians." This, however, was a sentiment of 2005 rather than of 1945. By a bleak irony, Minamoto and his fellow suicide crewmen survived in hiding, while more than a third of the civilians on Tokashiki perished. To the Americans, this little action represented only a skirmish, a minor objective seized at negligible cost. Yet for the Japanese, it was a foretaste of much worse to follow.

AT DAWN on 1 April, Sunday, code-named "Love Day," thousands of men of the two Marine and two army divisions which were to lead the assault on Okinawa crowded the decks of their ships, listening to distant automatic fire. Information about the landing beaches had been obtained from an eighty-year-old conchologist named Ditlev D. Thaanum, who collected shells there before the war, and possessed a collection of photographs. An almost equally elderly colleague of Thaanum named Daniel Boone Langford was flown to the Pacific to share his expertise with Turner's 5th Amphibious Force. Langford described, for instance, the deadly *habu* snakes on the island. Every soldier and Marine was briefed about them, though there was no subsequent record of any man seeing one. When the U.S. armada began the bombardment of Okinawa in the days immediately preceding the landing, navy frogmen cleared debris and obstacles from the beaches under the eyes of Japanese outposts. The enemy made no attempt to intervene.

The invaders were to land across a six-mile front on the south-west coast. Wallowing in the big transports, most men anticipated the worst. Spotter planes circled above, directing the naval guns. Wariness was essential to their pilots to avoid being caught by shells, especially from the high-trajectory five-inch destroyer armament. On the ships a huge cast of spectators, so soon to become actors, saw a sudden burst of light in the sky as a plane was hit, then dropped blazing into the sea. "Everyone expected E Company to be literally destroyed," wrote a 5th Marines corporal, James Johnston. At 0530, the drivers of Lt. Chris Donner's unit went below to warm the engines of their amphibious tractors. The young 1st Marines' forward artillery observer heard a lone, ironic voice singing Rodgers and Hammerstein's "Oh, What a Beautiful Morning." Donner descended to the LST's tank deck, and clambered aboard his vehicle, one among hundreds. They launched at 0630, dazzled by the brilliant sunshine after the darkness of the hold, deafened by the roar of aircraft and naval gunfire. Waves broke over the amtracs as they circled offshore, men sitting atop their craft and waving to neighbours with studied gaiety as they waited for the order to land. Sailors peering down from the steep side of a battleship called: "Give the bastards hell, Marines!" "Good luck!" Then the landing craft and tractors turned for the shore in serried ranks, their wakes whitening the water so that from the air it appeared that a host of sea slugs was approaching Okinawa.

"There was no chatter now," wrote Donner. "Each man's face was tight, teeth set. Even above the roar of the amph's motors we began to hear the crackle of small arms . . . We hit with a jolt that tumbled us in a heap, ground up onto a coral shelf, then onto sand . . . I led the rush out." There was no firing in their immediate area, but one squad heard voices from a cavern, and used an interpreter to shout word to come out and surrender. When no response came, Browning-automatic gunners sprayed the mouth. Inside, Marines found the prostrate forms of several civilians: two men, a woman and a three-year-old boy. Only the child was alive, covered with his mother's blood. "They brought him back to us," wrote Chris Donner, "and Monahan washed the blood off the boy, who had ceased to cry. My team carried him on their shoulders all the rest of the afternoon . . . So this was Easter Sunday warfare. It sickened me."

Corporal James Johnston ran up the beach nursing slender expectations for his own future: "I thought I might get to a pillbox and dump some grenades before they got me." The invaders were disbelieving in the face of their own survival. They encountered only a shell-torn shoreline, a handful of dazed or dead peasants, negligible resistance. "I didn't recognise anything I saw," said Lt. Marius Bressoud of the 3/7th Marines. "There were no pinned-down troops, no bodies." The Americans fanned out north and south, seizing two airfields, advancing in hours across miles of ground for which they had expected to fight for days. Admiral Richmond Turner, commanding the amphibious force, signalled Nimitz: "I may be crazy but it looks like the Japanese have quit the war, at least in this sector." Nimitz snorted back: "Delete all after 'crazy.' "

Yet through the first week of the invaders' residence ashore, Okinawa appeared a deceptively innocent, strikingly beautiful tourist destination. For every American save those who had fought on Saipan, this was a first glimpse of the enemy's land and its people, unlike other battlefields they had experienced. There was no jungle, instead subtropical vegetation. Pines were the commonest trees—Nimitz asked for saplings to be shipped to Guam. There were large, bright, almost tasteless wild raspberries. Every inch of cultivable soil was tilled, hills laboriously terraced. Staff officers amused themselves by shooting pigeons. Units advanced in almost carnival mood, some men riding looted bicycles. One company captured two horses. A Marine broke an ankle falling off one, which in view of subsequent events probably saved his life. Soldiers made Japanese flags out of parachute flare silk, shooting holes in them to sell to sailors for $50 apiece.

Small boys emerged from peasant huts to beg matches, imitating the action of striking them. Marine general O. P. Smith was moved by the sight of an elderly Okinawan woman at the seaside, tearing a piece of paper into shreds then allowing the fragments to flutter away into the water. This was a local superstition: the paper represented a prayer, the force of which was supposed to double each time a fragment turned in the air before its immersion. *New Yorker* correspondent John Lardner was fascinated by the tombs which studded every hillside, the relative tranquillity punctuated by desultory encounters with the enemy: "The roads were narrow and dusty, the villages poor and dingy, but the green island between them was a fine thing to see. Some ridges were so thickly terraced for planting that it was checkered with rice paddies and green squares of sugarcane. Potatoes, beans, garlic, onions, radishes, grew everywhere. The civilians, who were now feeling easier, were walking along the roads and saluting us." Lardner met a truck in which five Americans were sitting with a young Okinawan civilian wounded that morning. A good-natured Marine stuck a cigarette between the teenager's lips. After one puff, the Japanese shuddered and pulled back. Another man said: "What do you want to treat a Jap so good for?"

"Why not?" demanded the cigarette donor.

"Well, why don't they send some of them back to tell those other Japs how good we treat them? Then maybe they would treat us good."

Tenth Army's commander shared Admiral Turner's surprise at the initial Japanese lack of resistance. Marines moving north overcame sporadic opposition without much difficulty. General Buckner was fearful that anticlimax might deprive him of the battle he was keenly expectant to fight. He had been at Kiska in the Aleutians "when the army troops had landed and to their embarrassment had found no Japanese," wrote O. P. Smith scornfully. "He did not want to be involved in another Kiska." Spruance and Turner had wanted Holland Smith of the Marines to command Okinawa. They were overruled by Nimitz, because Smith had made himself violently unpopular among soldiers by sacking an army divisional commander on Saipan.

The substitute choice for command, however, inspired less than universal confidence. Simon Bolivar Buckner was fifty-eight, son of a Civil War Confederate general, "ruddy, heavy-set, but with considerable spring in his step, snow-white hair and piercing blue eyes. His fetish was physical conditioning." During the preparations for Okinawa, the general's enthusiasm for PT had cost his staff sprained ankles, some broken arms and collarbones. He had spent the First World War training fliers, and thereafter filled mostly staff appointments. Smith wrote: "Buckner had surprisingly little troops' duty. His methods and judgements were somewhat inflexible." This grudging view was shared by other officers on Okinawa, whose scepticism would deepen in the months that followed.

Nimitz was right, of course, to have dismissed local commanders' initial bubble of euphoria. After a week of cautious advances, army units in the south of the island were suddenly checked in their tracks by artillery and machine-gun fire. They had reached the first of the immensely powerful concentric lines with which the Japanese had fortified the southernmost six miles of Okinawa. Gen. Mitsuru Ushijima, commanding 32nd Army, charged with defence of the island, allowed himself to be persuaded that he could not stop the Americans on the beaches. Instead, he adopted the plan of his operations officer, Col. Hiromichi Yahara, for "sleeping tactics." One force was concentrated on the northern Mobutu Peninsula, where it offered stubborn resistance from 8 to 20 April. The principal Japanese positions lay in the south, around the capital, Naha, where Ushijima's men had created a chain of fortresses, the so-called Shuri Line. Including local militiamen, 97,000 Japanese were deployed there, crowded into one of the narrowest perimeters of the war.

Through more than two months that followed, U.S. soldiers and Marines assaulted Ushijima's bunkers and trenches, paying with flesh for every yard they gained. The struggle proved more intense than any which U.S. forces had hitherto experienced in the Pacific. As usual, the Japanese had chosen their positions well. They possessed observation points on high ground, hidden machine guns, mines, and defences almost impregnable to frontal attack. Above all, they had guns and plenty of ammunition. The Japanese army, often short of fire support, on Okinawa possessed this in abundance. "The enemy tactic which impressed us most deeply was the intensity and effectiveness of artillery," wrote Marine captain Levi Burcham, "and the fact that this fire covered not only our front line area but also (an experience new to many) well back into rear areas, quartermaster dumps and the like."

The U.S. XXIV Corps once received 14,000 incoming Japanese shells in twenty-four hours. The invaders' advantage of numbers counted for almost nothing, where the enemy could concentrate his forces to hold a front nowhere more than three miles wide, the breadth of the island. Buckner perceived no alternative to launching repeated frontal attacks, which resulted in repeated bloody failures. As heavy rain set in, tens of thousands of men competed for possession of a few score yards of mud. Shellfire churned human body parts, debris and excrement into a ghastly compound from which the stench drifted far to the rear. These were scenes more familiar to veterans of the First World War than those of the Second. After the first weeks, press accounts of the horrors of Okinawa inspired anger and bitter criticism back home in the United States. It seemed incomprehensible that with Germany collapsing, U.S. power triumphant almost everywhere in the world, young Americans should be suffering such an ordeal. How could it be that all the might of U.S. armies, navies and air forces was being set at naught in such a fashion?

The parents of a man killed on Hector Hill wrote a savage letter, branding his officers as murderers for abandoning their son. There was speculation in his unit about what some soldier must have written home to cause the dead man's people to harbour such bitterness. Another letter, from the father of a wounded man, excoriated the army for having put his son into combat without adequate training. Lt. Jeptha Carell of the 3/7th Marines came to believe that married men with children should not be allowed to serve in the front line: "The loss of the father is not only a reason for the family to grieve, it is an economic disaster." When one of his platoon was killed by an American rocket that fell short, Carell wrote to the man's widow, who responded with a pathetic letter saying that she now had five children to care for. The widow ended: "I hope you're satisfied!" James Johnston wrote: "Oh! to see the folks—and snow and city lights and girls and old friends and new ones—and the blessed hills of home. Oh! to eat Mom's wonderful cooking and to drink that cool clear water—and a glass of milk!"

En route to Okinawa, army lieutenant Don Siebert found himself sharing a C-47 "Gooney Bird" with a party of nurses. The girls kidded the young replacements somewhat unkindly, saying that they would see them again on a casevac flight in a couple of days. "Of course this was very, very comforting," wrote Siebert, "but we were too gung-ho to heed the warning, and exacted their assurances that they would give us special care." He himself was troubled, like most newcomers to war, about his own fitness for command: "Would the men accept my leadership? Would I have a problem getting to them?" He read field manuals assiduously all the way to the front, where he joined the 382nd Infantry on line outside Shuri Castle. To Siebert's disappointment, he was assigned to become assistant regimental adjutant and gas officer. He provoked amazement by requesting instead a posting with a line battalion, and was rewarded with a platoon of Fox Company.

The newcomer trudged through heavy rain to take over his woefully under-strength little command, just sixteen strong: "They were strange faces—dirty, drawn, tired, yet the men appeared to have high morale." He was plunged into combat, to see his platoon sergeant immediately evacuated after being wounded by mortar fragments. When another man was killed, Siebert felt ashamed that he had not yet discovered the soldier's name. A young lieutenant, Magrath, clambered out on a rock to take a look at his first battlefield. "Get your ass down!" shouted a sergeant, too late. A bullet hit Magrath in the throat. As he was carried away, he kept asking earnestly whether he would still be able to play his trumpet in a dance band.

In Siebert's first encounter with the Japanese, he was shocked to see an enemy soldier keep running at him, despite being hit repeatedly by carbine bullets. Siebert discarded his carbine in favour of an M1 rifle. "One of the weaknesses of the American army in combat," he wrote, "was night operations. We did little fighting at night, almost no movement . . . The Japs, on the other hand, used the darkness. They fought, moved and resupplied in it." Darkness caused every American soldier, huddled under a poncho to mask the glow of a cigarette, to become acutely sensitive to the risk of surprise. One night in the positions of the infantry company accompanied by gunner Chris Donner, a man panicked when he heard an unexpected noise. He began firing, and killed five of his fellow Marines before somebody shot him down. The company commander, wrote Donner, was thereafter "embittered over this needless loss. The entire outfit moved heavily."

Wandering animals and civilians prompted alerts. White goats were mistaken for infiltrators. Don Siebert's men were dug in at the edge of a big field one night, when they heard rustling and movement. Flares revealed nothing, but there was certainly something out there. The lieutenant told his men to shoot, prompting moans and the squalling of a baby. Siebert was still fearful of Japanese soldiers trying to lure the Americans from their foxholes: "Much against my instincts, I ordered the platoon to open fire; we must have killed the youngster, because there were no more cries. This truly depressed me. However, I believed that it was necessary to protect the lives of my men." And so perhaps it was.

"With afternoon came the order to advance," wrote Chris Donner. "A short round from another artillery shoot so jolted Captain Sweet that he had to be removed . . . As the units, each no more than twenty-five strong, converged on the brushy knoll to our front there was no firing of any kind. Then, walking erect, and only a few yards from the bushes, they were suddenly met by blazing light machine-gun fire, and mortars began raining upon them. There was no cover. They fell, squirmed, and were hit again. A handful managed to get back, including a lieutenant who trembled and shook with terrific sobs, murmuring over and over, 'It was awful, God, it was awful. They all died.' I felt awful myself."

The local mosquitoes were smaller than those of some other Pacific islands, but just as aggressive, and accompanied by a new pest, fleas. Insect life swarmed in clouds around every corpse. Men had plenty of water—too much, with the incessant rain. They supplemented rations with vegetables taken from peasant gardens. Most found that canned rations and stress combined to promote constipation, which they assuaged with a home-brewed laxative made of iron-ration chocolate and canned milk heated on C-2 composite explosive. The principal factor in their lives and deaths, however, was daily attrition from snipers, machine guns, artillery: "When the bullet hit Gosman's head, it sounded as if someone had hit a ripe watermelon with a baseball bat." Each day there were fewer men to sustain the lumbering advances from ridge to ridge. They had phrases for those who survived in body, but were lost in spirit: "the thousand-yard look"; "the bulkhead stare"; "going Asiatic." James Johnston wrote: "I thought of the old verse 'I knew a lad who went to sea / and left the land behind him. / I knew him well—the lad was me / and now I cannot find him.' " A cocky, aggressive replacement named Anderson joined them, and on the first day contemptuously shrugged off Johnston's warnings to stop wandering into caves. Johnston said resignedly: "I'm just trying to keep you alive." After a brief taste of combat on Okinawa, tough young Anderson reported sick, and was never seen again.

Johnston departed too, after being hit by mortar fragments in the Awahaca Pocket. At the field hospital, a voice suddenly called out: "Anyone here from Nebraska?" The Marine responded, and was amazed to find himself talking to a kid he knew from home named Kenny Yant, now a medical corpsman. Yant held Johnston's hand while a surgeon extracted the shrapnel from his body. A little nurse said: "Don't sweat it, Marine. The doc's about got it." Johnston wrote: "Her touch felt like an angel's. She was close enough that I could smell her. She smelt like Camay soap." Discharged from hospital, he was told that he was eligible to go home, but his battalion would like to have him back. He went home.

Rashly exposing himself on Tera Ridge, Lt. John Armiger suddenly cried out that he could see through his binoculars a Japanese sniper taking aim with a telescopic sight. Everyone ducked save Armiger himself, who was fractionally slow to move. A second later, he was fatally hit in the abdomen. On 26 April, a mortar bomb landed beside Lt. Gage Rodman, a company commander in the 17th Infantry: "I knew I was shot, but the only blood I could see was on my leg. Then I caught sight of what seemed like several yards of pink tubing on the front of my trousers . . . One of my assistant squad leaders walked over to me and breaking out his first aid dressing, he made a temporary covering for my exposed intestines . . . At the 102nd Portable Surgical Hospital, I was operated on for the removal of the majority of the shell fragments and the manufacture of a colostomy to replace my severed bowel function." For months Rodman's life was despaired of, though he persisted in attempting to reassure his parents: "You see, I am out of any possible danger now. I am in a rear-area hospital. I might as well tell you I will be out of action for some months to come. I hope you won't worry, because it is all convalescence from here on out." Only on 3 July was the young officer fit for evacuation to the U.S., where he began to suffer brain abscesses, and thereafter remained semi-paralysed.

If the invaders were appalled by their predicament, that of the defenders was vastly worse. Japanese soldiers were dying at ten times the rate of Americans. Captain Kouichi Ito's battalion of the 32nd Regiment used a thousand mortar bombs in twenty hours on 27 April, when it faced its first American attack. Having spent months preparing deeply dug positions, they found themselves instead deployed where they had only hastily scraped foxholes. These offered pitiful protection against U.S. artillery fire, far heavier than anything Ushijima's batteries could put down. Then they met their first American tanks. Like the rest of the Japanese army, the 32nd Regiment was pitifully equipped to deal with them, possessing just two anti-tank guns. These were destroyed within hours by shelling. Thereafter, Ito's companies were forced to improvise, in the only fashion the Japanese army knew. Men were given a mine or shell, and ordered to detonate this against a tank as it approached. Ito tried to say personal farewells, solemnly shaking hands with each soldier designated for the task. Sgt. Kaoru Imai, an NCO whom the captain much liked, ran out after an American tank, clutching a mine, then suffered the humiliation of finding himself unable to catch it up. The turret traversed, the gun fired. Imai was gone.

The pace of attrition was dispiriting. Most of Ito's men had known each other for years. Now, each hour they vanished by scores. "We took three hundred casualties in the first two days," said Ito. His second-in-command, Lieutenant Kashiki, made the dangerous circuit of their perimeter the first night, telling the men how well they had done. Yet all knew how desperate was their predicament. Ito reflected that his father had underestimated their enemy. One of his company commanders said ruefully down a telephone line to the command bunker: "You can't treat these Americans lightly."

The invaders achieved notable successes when defenders were rash enough to leave their positions and counter-attack. Again and again, Japanese efforts to regain ground or surprise the Americans were crushed by firepower. After early bloody failures, however, Ushijima became less obliging about exposing his units. He held them back in their deeply dug defences, leaving it to the Americans to pay the price for movement. Marines and soldiers alike found themselves trapped in an experience as hellish as any of the war. Word of the death of their president, Franklin Roosevelt, on 12 April seemed as remote as a dispatch from the moon. "The news came as a shock," wrote an infantry officer. "The word was passed down to the men, but each had his own problems at the moment, the most important being to keep his hide in one piece." Only the few square yards of ground around them, the men in the next foxhole, possessed meaning. A new list of place-names entered the gazetteer of Pacific horrors: Sugarloaf Hill, Wana Draw, Awacha Gulch, Shuri Castle.

When Lt. Marius Bressoud's Marine company was ordered to undertake a new assault on Wana Ridge, he experienced "an immediate sense of melancholy, as I realised this was my day to die. I had been very zealous about brushing my teeth every morning. I had no toothpaste, of course, but I faithfully hung onto the toothbrush, using it with plain water. Out of habit, I took it out that morning and then said to myself: 'Why should I bother? I will be dead by nightfall.' But I had a second thought: 'Why not brush my teeth? I have time. I will do it, just in case I live.' " Bressoud indeed survived, but his unit's attack failed. "It was not possible to assault entrenched Japanese troops carefully. What were needed were a few nuts who didn't care whether they lived or died, and I Company's level of commitment that day stopped short of madness." One of Bressoud's young Marines was left lying wounded on the hillside, crying, "Mother, mother." The platoon's corpsman gazed forward in bitter frustration. Bressoud told him not to try any heroics, that there was no purpose in having two men rather than one dead or wounded. Finally, however, the corpsman said: "I can't stand it. I'm going to go help him." He scrambled forward. Like the wounded man, he was never seen again.

"Small-unit combat was a continuous stream of decisions that can be agonizing and immobilizing," wrote Lt. Jeptha Carell of the 3/7th Marines. He started his own first action with a mistake. Advancing to attack, his platoon sergeant was shot in the stomach beside him, and a nearby corpsman fell dead. Carell forgot his command responsibility, and knelt trying to save his NCO: "Somehow I had never consciously thought about losing him, and had not adequately prepared myself. I worked over him frantically . . . I was mistaken to take so much time with Jones instead of moving on with the platoon. It reduced the speed and force of our assault on the ridge, and made the attack more difficult for the rest of the company."

Tiny consolations meant much to men who lived as did those of Tenth Army on Okinawa. "Dear Mom and Dad," wrote twenty-year-old gunner Joseph Kohn to his family in New Jersey on 14 May, "every once in a while you come across a fellow who is really a swell Joe. A fellow who is in tanks just happened to start talking and before I knew it he invited me down. Somehow or other he had flour and baking powder, and before you knew it he was making pancakes for me and the rest of the fellows."

Comradeship, love between men, is the only force that makes such circumstances endurable. Marine lieutenant Richard Kennard wrote to his parents on 13 May: "As the weeks go by I have grown to be very fond of my enlisted friend Jack Adamson, raised on a farm in north Wisconsin. He is a perfect Christian and in my eyes the most ideal American boy I have ever known. I have lived very close to him and so know just what I am saying. Jack is the cleanest, most meticulous lad I have ever seen. He is completely unselfish, and always thinks about his buddies in the gun section first. He has worked ever since he could walk. He doesn't smoke, drink or swear. You know a good Christian will always have many friends and yet be little appreciated because there are so few people today who understand what it is like." Kennard had a girlfriend back home named Marilyn, a successful model. If he himself was killed, Kennard asked his parents to see that Jack Adamson got whatever cash he had: "Marilyn won't need it." The claims of intimacy with a man beside whom he shared mortal peril seemed more pressing than those of a girl half a world away.

BUCKNER's headlong assaults on the Shuri Line rekindled familiar interservice animosities. Marines thought soldiers lacked skill, drive, grit. "The Marines and the army don't like each other," wrote corpsman Bill Jenkins. ". . . We thought they were a bunch of scaredycats." Marines relieving the army's 27th Division mocked the depth of their foxholes. A soldier said sourly: "You won't be laughing when 'whistling willy' comes in." Sure enough, within a few hours the Marines were digging even harder for themselves. "We were permitted, if not encouraged, to believe that Army progress was slow because their troops weren't as courageous, capable and well trained as we were," wrote Marine lieutenant Marius Bressoud. "It was only when we ourselves came up against the Shuri bastion that we developed a proper respect for our fellow footsoldiers."

Marine senior officers, however, continued to believe that Buckner's generalship was unimaginative, almost sure to continue to fail, and absolutely sure to cost a lot of lives. They favoured a new amphibious landing in the Japanese rear, for which a reserve division still afloat was available. On 18 April, O. P. Smith told Vice-Admiral Turner that he thought Buckner much too optimistic about the ability of artillery to batter a breakthrough. The admiral agreed, but declared that it was impossible to intervene. "God bless you," Turner said to Smith, his customary farewell. God did nothing to bless Tenth Army, or its tactics, through the weeks which followed. Smith recorded his contempt for Buckner's lack of combat experience. The general, he said, spurned Marine experience of the value of creeping shellfire up to enemy positions, rather than bracketing them. Smith criticised army practice of holding positions as much as eight hundred yards from the nearest Japanese. Marines considered one to two hundred yards more appropriate.

Smith described a visit with Tenth Army's commander to the 27th Division, a formation no one thought much of: "The division was beaten down and did not know whether or not it wanted to fight . . . As General Buckner went round he asked different individuals what they wanted to do most. He was hoping to get the answer that they wanted to go into combat, but they were more interested in going home on furlough." Smith was disgusted to notice that 27th Division had not got around to burying its own dead. Yet the Marines were forced to concede that their own formations could make no faster or cheaper progress than the soldiers.

Fighting in the midst of civilians is always repugnant, never more so than on Okinawa. "On the ground," Chris Donner recorded one day, "lay the body of a young Okinawan, a girl who had been fifteen or sixteen, and probably very pretty. She was nude, lying on her back with arms outstretched and knees drawn up, but spread apart. The poor girl had been shot through the left breast and evidently violently raped." It seemed unlikely that this was the work of Japanese soldiers. Not long after, several men of the infantry unit which Donner was accompanying fell to fire from unseen enemies on a clifftop. Suddenly, the Americans saw a Japanese woman clutching a baby. Convinced that she was spotting for enemy soldiers, some shouted: "Shoot the bitch, shoot the Jap woman!" There was a burst of fire. The woman fell, then struggled to her feet and staggered towards her baby. After more shots, she went down again and lay still. Donner wrote: "None of the men would own up to having fired . . . the ridge was a stinking mess, compounded of half-empty ration tins, dead Japs and human faeces, all covered with hot flies . . . One corporal was dragged back and given a transfusion. His foot was gone at the ankle. When they could bring up a stretcher and start off with the man, he began to smoke a cigarette someone had given him. Then with his face drawn with pain he waved to us and shouted, 'Got mine, fellows. Gonna have liberty now. Good luck to you.' " Marine Eugene Sledge was struck by the sight of a Japanese machine-gunner still sitting at his post, lacking the top of his head. Overnight rain had collected in the open skull. As their unit sat nearby waiting to be relieved, one of Sledge's buddies idly flicked fragments of coral into this receptacle, prompting a splash each time one landed right.

In a rear-area hospital, O. P. Smith inspected combat fatigue cases, of which Okinawa generated thousands. He watched a doctor treating a

Marine in whose foxhole a mortar round had landed. "No man could have portrayed fear as this man did. He kept gurgling 'Mortar, mortar, mortar.' The doctor asked him what he was going to do now. He replied: 'Dig deeper. Dig deeper.' The doctor told him to go ahead and dig. The man got down on his knees and went through frantic motions of digging in the corner of the room." Another man, who had been recommended for a Silver Star, was overcome by guilt about killing so many Japanese. There were others occupying beds, however, for whom the Marine general evinced less sympathy. "I am afraid . . . there are many cases of so-called combat fatigue where the man should not have gotten back to the hospitals." What would Smith have said to a man like medic Bill Jenkins, whose platoon went through double its original strength before the navy man went to his sergeant, removed his pistol belt and said: "You can take this war and shove it, I quit"? The NCO gave Jenkins a mug of coffee and without protest tagged him as suffering from a "psychoneurosis anxiety state." He was evacuated to Saipan.

After their first two days in action, Japanese captain Kouichi Ito's battalion received only ration bread to sustain them. On 2 May they were ordered to participate in a major counter-offensive against two hills held by the American XXIV Corps. At terrible cost, and almost without artillery support, they gained one summit, having driven a mile behind the American front. "We had done our part—but we wondered where everybody else was," said Ito, echoing the sentiments of many soldiers in many battles. Their neighbouring unit failed to capture the second hill. The consequence was that through the days that followed Ito's battalion suffered devastating losses as it strove to hold a salient on the Tanabaru Escarpment, dominated on three sides by the Americans and their artillery concentrations.

On 6 May, Ito was belatedly ordered to pull back. He consoled his men by quoting the German general Mackensen, in a desperate position during the First World War: "Don't think of this as a retreat, but as an advance in a different direction." They had no means of carrying out thirty badly wounded men. Ito moved among these, distributing grenades which should enable them to take some American companions into the next world. One man he knew well, Lance-Corporal Kurokawa, begged him again and again: "Take me away with you. Take me with you. Please. Please." Yet Kurokawa too was left to face death with his grenade. So many close comrades were gone—Ohyama, Mori, Otaki and a host of others whose names Ito forgot. Many more fell during their bloody breakout to a new line a mile back.

The ruins of Naha, Okinawa's capital, fell to the Americans on 27 May. Ushijima retreated to his final positions further south-west, on the Oruku

Peninsula. Here, Ito and his men joined their commander, along with some thousands of other surviving defenders. By the first days of June, the captain found himself left with 135 men, out of the five-hundred-strong battalion he had led into battle: "We were exhausted, morally and physically. We faced the traditional predicament of Japanese warriors of old, with our backs to the wall." They were proud of the losses they had inflicted on the Americans, but understood that the defences were broken. Yard by yard, Buckner's persevering Marines and soldiers had ground down the Japanese 32nd Army. Ito and a few companions were among several hundred men who, rejecting surrender or suicide, took refuge in Okinawa's multitude of caves, scavenging by night for food, with help from local civilians.

The last days of the battle were rendered especially horrible by the presence of so many Japanese women and children among the defenders, some still eager to live, others determined to die. After Lt. Marius Bressoud's Marines blew open a cave mouth, a crowd of civilians emerged, whom he dispatched to the rear. Three remained, badly wounded: a child, its mother and grandmother. Platoon Sgt. Joe Taylor said: "We can't just leave these people, and we can't spare escorts." Bressoud knew the NCO meant that the Okinawans should be put out of their misery, like injured animals. He asked if there was a volunteer to do the job. Nobody spoke. " 'OK,' I said, 'I'll do it myself.' All three were lying motionless on their backs. Some very thoughtful person in the platoon had covered their heads with clean white cloths so that I did not have to look at their faces. I fired one round through each head." Yet the mother and grandmother continued to writhe. Bressoud, a devout Catholic, fired again and again. "By this time the cloths and the heads were a mess. It had not been a neat, gangland-style execution after all. I was overcome with emotion I cannot possibly describe . . . thoroughly ashamed, not because I had killed them, but because I did it in so emotional and unprofessional a manner."

Resistance petered out in the last weeks of June. Yet if Buckner's land campaign represented a shocking experience for American soldiers and Marines, it was matched, perhaps even outdone, by the struggle waged at sea. The battle off Okinawa cost more lives than any other fought by the U.S. Navy in the Pacific war.

2. At Sea

USHIJIMA'S 32nd Army represented the static defence of Okinawa. The hub of Japanese strategy, however, was an air assault upon the invasion fleet on a scale hitherto unseen in the Pacific theatre. The Americans were almost entirely dependent on carriers for fighter cover—the airfields captured ashore remained for weeks within range of Japanese artillery, and could handle few planes. Marc Mitscher's task groups could sustain combat air patrols of not more than 60 to 80 fighters. Against these, the Japanese launched a succession of strikes of which the first, on 6 April, numbered 700 planes, 355 of them kamikazes.

From the destroyer *Howorth*, Yeoman James Orvill Raines wrote one of many passionate letters to his wife, Ray Ellen, back home in Dallas. "We are back up at Okinawa now, we came back very fast (can't tell why yet). Anyway its colder than a well-digger's seat in Montana but everything is OK. No sleep last night due to Bogies but things are squared away now. Bye darling. More later. Poppie." Raines, twenty-six years old, had been a somewhat rootless child of the Depression who settled into a career as a journalist just before the war came. On 6 April, a kamikaze ploughed into *Howorth*'s gun director, killing sixteen men and blowing Raines, badly burned, over the side. He died in the water, in another man's arms. "Your husband," *Howorth*'s captain wrote later to Ray Ellen, "was very popular among officers and men on board this ship. There certainly was no finer bluejacket to be found anywhere." It is to be hoped that Mrs. Raines never knew these were the same phrases offered to the families of every one of *Howorth*'s dead. Yet how could a captain personalise such missives, when they had to be dispatched wholesale?

About four hundred Japanese aircraft broke through the CAP on 6 April. Six ships, including two destroyers, were sunk. Eighteen more were damaged, almost all by kamikazes. This was only the first round of a struggle which persisted throughout the ground campaign for Okinawa, and indeed after its ending. Radio warnings of imminent enemy attack announced "skunks" by sea, "bogies" by air. Thus, perhaps: "Bogey raid four, estimated fifty, bearing 185, distance 30 course 110, speed 300, estimated high, 1114, apparently circling fleet, out."

American defences inflicted fearsome losses. Balloons held aloft a forest of cables over the anchorage, to impede the enemy's approach. Each attack was met by a barrage of fire. Ships' five-inch batteries, firing shells detonated by radio-guided proximity fuses, were joined by massed 40mms and 20mms, filling the sky with black smoke balls, littering decks with mountains of spent cases. Often, the gunners engaged at point-blank range. By scores, Japanese planes collapsed into the sea. But some always escaped, to crash onto their targets with appalling effect. Fighter direction had become a sophisticated art, yet it was also an imperfect one. Cmdr. Bill Widhelm, operations officer of a carrier task group, described how radar detected one Japanese bomber a hundred miles out, at 22,000 feet, and tracked it to forty-three miles. The plane then vanished from every screen in the fleet, was briefly picked up again at sixteen miles, and thereafter only when "about fifteen feet off the stern of the ship."

Tens of thousands of American seamen who badly wanted to live were stunned by the onset of hundreds of Japanese pilots who seemed happy to die. "I don't believe I'll ever forget the noise a plane made as it came racing in," wrote an officer on the carrier *Bennington*, "something like when a plane flat hats a field or a house. But instead of trailing away in the distance, it ends with a sudden startling 'splat!' " An officer watched one Japanese pilot fall without a parachute: "He seemed to float down, arms and legs extended like a sky-diver, his flight jacket puffed out by the air, falling at such a slow rate that we wondered if he might be able to survive." The destroyer *Luce* found itself with three Japanese aircrew prisoners, of whom one proved to be an ex-Berkeley student who spoke fluent English. An officer told a Japanese still eager to commit suicide: "You're out of the war now, you know," but the man seemed obsessed with the loss of his family honour. Another prisoner was Korean, a most reluctant kamikaze conscript, who had successfully averted his intended fate. *Luce*'s crew were wryly amused to find themselves spoon-feeding enemies on whom they had lavished so much verbal hatred. When the prisoners were collected by Marines, however, they received much rougher treatment.

An awed sailor gazed on a destroyer grievously mauled by air attack: "Bombs and shells and even a suicide plane had plowed into her. Her entire superstructure was a mangled mess of melted steel except for the bridge and radio shack. She was crying and bleeding like a dog set upon by a pack of wolves. She needed blood . . . her men were burned, shot, cut, torn and shocked. To me, sitting there so apart from everything but my imagination, she took on human nature. She was a good ship. She was hurt badly and was ashamed but yet proud that she had stood up under all the beating they had given her."

As kamikazes circled *Luce*, her crew saw "meatwagons" closing in—rescue ships anticipating the worst. Cook Freeman Phillips froze at his 20mm gun position. Virgil Degner, his "oppo," holding an ammunition canister, started to say something: "His lips were moving—I had the earphones on—and I didn't know what he was trying to say . . . Then the explosion came . . . a piece of metal flew by and decapitated him. Just like that, his head fell off at my feet. I looked down . . . and I believe his mouth was still trying to tell me something. His body was still up, holding onto that magazine for what seemed like thirty minutes, but I know it was just a few moments. Then the body began to shake, and it just fell over. Soon it just floated away as the water came up."

With so many U.S. fighters airborne, radar operators were often unable to distinguish enemy planes slipping in towards the fleet from every point of the compass. "They scatter like quail," said U.S. fighter pilot Ted Winters of *Lexington*, "and come in from wherever they are staying in the clouds." Anti-aircraft gunnery, especially from transports, was wildly undisciplined, and resulted in frequent "friendly fire" mishaps. When a plane struck a ship, its detonation was often followed by a gusher of flaming gasoline, exploding munitions, carnage among sailors protected by nothing more than helmets, goggles and anti-flash hoods. Hands working below suffered some of the most terrifying experiences. A few minutes after a series of devastating detonations overhead, on 6 April, William Henwood in the engine room of the minesweeper *Emmons* heard the stop bell: "Someone yelled down the hatch and told us to secure and get the hell out. We secured the fires, stopped the fuel oil pump and left. When I first came out of the hatch I was shocked and scared. I saw men swimming in the water and I thought we were going down." The ship had been hit by five kamikazes.

A second big attack on 12 April, by 185 enemy aircraft, resulted in the destruction of almost all the Japanese planes for the loss of two ships sunk and a further fourteen damaged, including two battleships. A flock of kamikazes picked a victim, then launched a coordinated assault of the kind which struck the destroyer *Abele*. Her crew shot down two of twenty attackers, but suffered a suicide strike and a jet-propelled bomb hit, which caused the ship to break in two and sink. After *Douglas H. Fox* was also hit, Cmdr. Ray Pitts wrote: "The first instinct of a destroyer skipper who has been blitzed on radar picket station is to . . . feel that something is fundamentally wrong with the picture. He looks down into the smouldering ruins of his new ship, sees the dead lying in mute rows along the passageways, and wonders if perhaps he has failed either the ship or the dead."

On 16 April, during another mass onslaught, the destroyer *Laffey* was pinpointed by thirty enemy aircraft. Four kamikazes struck her and two planes dropped bombs. The ship survived, but suffered ninety-four casualties. Later that day the carrier *Intrepid* was hit. Between big attacks, smaller-scale raids were mounted, which cost the Americans extravagant quantities of ammunition, and kept weary crews hour after hour at quarters, adding sunburn to the troubles of those on upper decks. Denied hot food, they chewed candy, nursed their bladders—no man could leave his post at Quarters—prayed that today it might be another ship's turn and not their own. James Phillips said: "I was so tired I thought death would be a relief, it would be over. I had the thought, 'Well look, man, just don't shoot at me no more and you can have this whole thing.' " At nightfall it became routine for destroyers to ask permission to sail at flank speed into the wind with all doors and scuttles open for a few minutes, to blow swarms of accursed flies out of the messdecks.

An assault on 4 May resulted in five ships sunk and eleven damaged, all save one by suicide planes. Between the eleventh and the fourteenth, three flagships were damaged—the carriers *Bunker Hill* and *Enterprise*, together with the battleship *New Mexico*. "The fighting off Okinawa became routine," wrote an American carrier commander, "but it was probably the most dangerous brand of routine to be found in the history of WWII." "Jocko" Clark's flag lieutenant sometimes removed bad news from the overnight "Ultra Board" on the bridge until his admiral had eaten breakfast. Suicidal courage was not the exclusive prerogative of the Japanese. On 10 May, two Corsairs intercepted a twin-engined enemy "Nick" at 35,000 feet. One was unable to get within range, and the other's guns froze. Rather than lose his quarry, the American pilot deliberately drove into the Nick's rudder and stabiliser, causing it to crash. The Corsair made an emergency landing without its propeller. The pilot survived to receive a Navy Cross.

When the kamikaze offensive began in October 1944, most of the Japanese pilots were trained and experienced aircrew. Six months later, "special attack unit" commanders had perceived the folly of sacrificing such men. Most suicide pilots were now tyros, trained only to fly a course to a target. More experienced fliers either attempted conventional bombing missions, or provided fighter cover for the kamikazes. Lt. Toshio Hijikata, eldest son of a post office official, had joined the navy from university as a volunteer in 1943. Mocked by elite career officers as a mere hired gun, he rejoined by asking defiantly which of them could fly better than himself. Thanks to a long spell as an instructor in Korea, Hijikata joined 303 Squadron on Kyushu in April 1945 with the benefit of some four hundred hours on Zeroes already in his logbook, a preparation which did as much as luck to keep him alive through the months which followed.

The unit's principal task was to fly high cover for the Okinawa kamikazes. They took off from Kagoshima, rendezvoused with attack planes from nearby Kanoya, and settled down to conserve fuel as best they could on the 350-mile run south. At best, they could achieve only ten minutes' endurance over the battle area. Careless fuel-users found themselves ditching in the sea on the way home. Hijikata had few illusions about his own prospects. "I expected to die. I knew we were going to lose the war—so did everybody. Nobody said it aloud, everybody thought it." He loved flying his Zero, but was acutely conscious that it was outclassed by the American Hellcats. Hijikata was credited with shooting down one enemy fighter, but on most missions he and his comrades could hope only to buy time and airspace for the kamikazes to do their business. Often, his eyes misted with tears as he gazed down at the doomed men flying below him. A significant number were his own former flight students.

Some kamikazes at Kanoya, waiting to sortie, passed their last days on earth helping local peasants with the harvest. Once, a mother and daughter arrived from Tokyo to visit the girl's fiancé. Base officers disingenuously told the women that her young man had already left for deployment to a forward air base near Okinawa. She was obliged to content herself with touching the bamboo bed on which the young pilot had slept. The girl was not informed that he would not be returning from his only operational flight. Petty Officer Hachiro Miyashita, an aircraft maintenance specialist, spent the spring and summer of 1945 at the base of 601 Naval Air Squadron, a kamikaze unit. Pilots' parting instructions decreed blandly: "Once you take off from here, you will not be coming back; you must leave your effects in an orderly state, so that you will not make trouble for others, or invite mockery. You must arrange matters so that after your deaths, people will say: 'As you would expect from a member of the suicide force, he left everything in perfect order.' " So precious were planes, however, that pilots were instructed to return to base if they could not identify a worthwhile target. A significant number turned back with engine trouble, real or imagined. That the pilots were to die was not in doubt, but some received a rain check.

Hachiro Miyashita and his comrades found kamikaze take-offs unfailingly emotional. Ground crews paraded beside the runway, waving caps as the pilots taxied forward with open cockpits, the white scarves that signified their sacrifice fluttering in the slipstream, hands outstretched in farewell. After the engines faded, those left behind drifted uneasily away, sometimes chatting tersely about the departed pilots, already in the past tense: "He was a good chap" . . . "What a naughty boy so-and-so was." The ground crews found it hard to work closely with pilots through a few weeks of training, then launch them to death. A snapshot which Miyashita himself took, of a young airman standing on the wing of his plane as the ground crew fuelled it for the last time, shows a face tense and drawn, as well it might be.

"The whole thing was very moving," said Miyashita. "Once, just as the pilots boarded their aircraft to start up, one shouted in dismay: 'My watch isn't working!' For a flier, a watch is as indispensable as a compass. The man shouted to the group gathered to watch their take-off: 'Who'll lend me a watch?' There was a moment of embarrassed hesitation. Watches were precious. The loan would not be repaid. Then the base commander broke the tension, shouting, 'Take mine!' ' He ran to hand up this parting sacrifice to the young man's cockpit.

Vice-Admiral Ugaki, now commanding all navy "special attack" forces, inspected a kamikaze unit on 27 February. He recorded in his diary with grotesque banality: "I was perspiring in the spring warmth, while warblers sang in the bushes and larks twittered. Whatever is happening to the war, nature comes and goes as always." The admiral often professed to be moved to tears by the kamikazes. Yet he was unembarrassed by dispatching them to die, because he had committed himself to follow them at an appropriate moment. His diary entries leapt from strategic fantasy to humdrum personal detail, in a fashion which invites the derision of posterity. "11 April . . . in the light of so many reported crashes on enemy carriers, there can't be many undamaged ones still operating." Ugaki spent hours cantering across the countryside on horses lent to him by the army, or wandering the fields with a shotgun in search of game. On 13 April he was so irked by his own poor marksmanship that he wrote crossly: "Maybe it is time for me to give up shooting."

Ugaki, like Onishi and others responsible for the kamikazes, had convinced himself that this manner of making war represented an acceptable norm. "By the spring of 1945, there seemed nothing unusual about the idea of suicide missions," said fighter pilot Kunio Iwashita, who flew over Okinawa. "It was a desperate situation. We were losing the war, and pilots were constantly being killed in combat. We felt that a man might just as well sacrifice his life deliberately as lose it in an air battle." Yet Iwashita's view was far from universal. It would be mistaken to suppose that all young Japanese were eager to follow this path to death, or applauded it. Most of those who flew suicide missions to Okinawa had been drafted, accepting the assignment with varying degrees of enthusiasm.

One night a young pilot wandered into the barrack room of Lance-Corporal Iwao Ajiro, with whom he had shared army basic training. "You're a lucky guy, working in signals," said the young man gloomily. "I'm supposed to fly tomorrow." Ajiro sought to console him with a shrug and the familiar catchphrase of the Japanese soldier: "We'll meet again soon enough at Yasukuni." As it happened, Ajiro noted later, "That boy survived. But he did not expect to, and he did not want to die." Toshio Hijikata and his squadron held their CO, Kigokama Okajima, in deep respect, partly because he refused to nominate his own fliers for kamikaze duty. "The job of fighter pilots is to fight," Okajima growled. Senior officers said harsh things to the squadron commander about letting down the navy and the country, but his view prevailed, and his pilots were grateful. Their own duties continued to offer a likelihood of death, but not its certainty.

Most Japanese formations approached Okinawa as high as they could fly, maybe 20,000 feet, but American combat air patrols were always above them. As the sky grew black with the puffballs of massed anti-aircraft fire from the fleet, the suicide bombers dived steeply. Once Hijikata saw a dogfight developing below, and was looking for an opportunity to join it when, without warning, enemy bullets raked his wing. Seized by a moment of naked fear, he pushed the plane into a banking descent and drove towards the sea with a Hellcat on his tail. He was almost in the water when the American broke away. Atsuo Nishikane and Hamashige Yamaguchi, two of the squadron's best fliers, had chased him off. "In the air, they saved my neck again and again," said Hijikata. "We were real soulmates. Like most of the best pilots, on the ground those two were quiet men, but in the sky they were sensational." He nursed his damaged plane carefully home to Kyushu.

Between 6 April and 22 June, the Japanese mounted ten big suicide attacks by day and night, involving 1,465 aircraft, together with conventional air attacks by a further 4,800. About four-fifths of these flew from Kyushu, one-fifth from Formosa. George Kenney, MacArthur's air chief, rejected repeated requests from the navy for increased effort against the Formosan bases, because SWPA's intelligence officers refused to accept that these were being used against Okinawa. The kamikazes sank 27 ships and damaged 164, while bombers sank 1 and damaged 63. A fifth of all kamikazes were estimated to have hit a ship—almost ten times the success rate of conventional attacks. If suicide operations reflected Japanese desperation, it could not be claimed that they were ineffectual. For the sacrifice of a few hundred half-trained pilots, vastly more damage was inflicted upon the U.S. Navy than the Japanese surface fleet had accomplished since Pearl Harbor. Only the overwhelming strength of Spruance's forces, together with the diminishing skills of Japanese aircrew, enabled the Americans to withstand losses on such a scale. Many of those who attacked the American fleet were barely capable of keeping their planes in the air until they found a target. Once an American fighter pilot made an interception, so poor was the enemy's airmanship that it was not unusual for a single Hellcat to shoot down four, five, six Japanese aircraft. Added to that, now that so many kamikaze planes were crewed by pressed men, their spirit and determination visibly diminished. The British naval staff analysis of the campaign said: "What in the Philippines had been a crusade was at Okinawa deprived of all humanity and the virtue went out of it."

The cardinal Japanese misjudgement was target selection. Although the kamikazes achieved notable successes—for instance, sinking two ships loaded with ammunition for the shore battle—many contented themselves with falling upon radar picket destroyers covering the island. These were much easier to reach, since their function demanded lonely station-keeping, far forward of the carrier task forces or transports. Destroyer losses cost seamen's lives, but the ships were almost infinitely replaceable.

For all the trauma of those weeks of incessant alerts, infernos on stricken vessels, at no time did it seem plausible that the kamikazes could reverse the dogged American advance to victory.

INSHORE, the Japanese navy's only contribution to the campaign was made by scores of suicide boats, kindred of Yoshihiro Minamoto's, launched against American ships in the anchorage. A handful inflicted damage, pinpricks by comparison with the aerial onslaught. Just once, in the first week of the campaign, did the Imperial Navy's surface forces attempt to join the battle. On the evening of 6 April off Kyushu, the U.S. submarine *Threadfin* reported a sighting of two large warships and eight destroyers, beyond torpedo range and heading south. By this stage of the war, Magic intercepts were diminishing. Close to home, whenever possible the Japanese communicated by landline rather than radio. Yet it was not hard to guess where this force was probably heading. At 0815 on 7 April, a reconnaissance aircraft from *Essex* spotted the Japanese squadron again, this time heading west across the East China Sea. It was composed of the great battleship *Yamato*, undistinguished veteran of Leyte Gulf, with an accompanying cruiser. It seemed overwhelmingly likely that the enemy intended to turn south in time to approach Okinawa at first light next day.

Through the next four hours, the force was tracked. At 1017, as expected, it turned south. At first, Spruance proposed to hold back his carrier aircraft to maintain their kamikaze watch, and dispatch American battleships to deal with *Yamato*—a strange, possibly romantic notion, never explained. Carrier commander Marc Mitscher successfully argued, however, that the Japanese squadron should be targeted by his strike aircraft, even at the cost of weakening the CAP over the fleet. Soon after 1000, the first of 280 planes took off from the flight decks of Mitscher's Task Force 58: *San Jacinto*, *Bennington*, *Hornet*, *Belleau Wood*, *Essex*, *Bataan*, *Bunker Hill*, *Cabot* and *Hancock*. There were 132 fighters, 50 bombers, 98 torpedo-carriers, launched in successive waves. Fifty-three planes from *Hancock* lost their way, and did not attack. Nonetheless, the Americans were able to send more planes to address the *Yamato* group than the Japanese had deployed against Pearl Harbor. "We looked like a giant crop of blackbirds hunting for Farmer Ito's granary," said Lt. Thaddeus Coleman of *Essex*. The sky was murky—flying conditions were so poor that on Kyushu, kamikaze operations had been cancelled for the day. At 1220, after a difficult flight through rain squalls, the American air fleet found the *Yamato* group. "Sugar Baker Two Charlies," the air group commander called to

Bennington's Helldivers as he surveyed the pattern of fast-moving ships below, "you take the big boy."

Below them lay the largest fighting vessel in the Japanese navy and the world, sister ship of *Musashi*, sunk at Leyte Gulf. "We took a chance and launched where we would be if we were the *Yamato*," wrote Mitscher's chief of staff, Commodore Arleigh Burke. "The *Yamato* thought the same thing—she was there." The battleship displaced 72,000 tons and was protected by armour up to two feet thick. She was served by a crew of more than 3,000 men, boasted a main armament of nine 18.1-inch guns, and possessed as much relevance to the last year of the Second World War as Nelson's *Victory*. Now flying the flag of Vice-Admiral Seiichi Ito, fifty-four-year-old commander of 2nd Fleet, and accompanied by the cruiser *Yahagi*, the huge ship had been dispatched to Okinawa on the most ambitious kamikaze mission of all. The ship was not intended to return, even in the implausible event that it survived the attentions of the enemy. Her orders demanded that she should beach herself after doing her worst to the American fleet, landing surviving crew to join the defenders ashore. Her sailors had been instructed to sharpen bayonets, in anticipation of an infantry role. The squadron was denied air cover, on the grounds that every plane was needed to support kamikaze operations.

The men aboard *Yamato* shared none of their commanders' fantasies. Though Ito and his senior officers accepted their fate in the spirit of samurai, they were privately disdainful of the waste of ships and lives. In an unusual moment of mercy before the ship sailed, fifty newly embarked cadets, fresh from the naval academy, were sent ashore along with the sick. Although those leaving *Yamato* expressed formal regrets, few of their shipmates were fooled. They perceived the sense of reprieve among those who boarded launches for the pier. Some sailors, especially older ones, dispatched their possessions home. Almost all wrote a parting letter. In *Yamato*'s gunroom, at sea on the night of 6 April, an ironic voice demanded: "Which country showed the world what aircraft could do, by sinking the *Prince of Wales*?" There was a vogue for Tolstoy among the battleship's officers, and Ensign Sakei Katono was reading *War and Peace*. Ensign Mitsuru Yoshida, assistant radar officer, sat deep in a biography of Spinoza, haunted by thoughts of all the other books he would never live to read—he was a former law student at Tokyo University. Yoshida, twenty-two, had a friend aboard serving as an interpreter, monitoring American voice transmissions. Kunio Nakatani was a *nisei*—Japanese-American—from Sacramento, caught by the war at a Japanese university. Two of his brothers were serving with the U.S. Army in Europe, and in consequence Nakatani was considerably bullied by shipmates. The young man showed

Yoshida a letter from his mother in the U.S., which had reached him via Switzerland: "How are you? We are fine. Please put your best effort into your duties. And let's both pray for peace." Nakatani now sobbed as he recoiled from the irony of facing death at the hands of fellow Americans.

Through their last days afloat, the crew continued to exercise energetically, especially in damage control. On the night of 6 April, throughout the ship there was heavy drinking and some dancing, a carouse of the damned. In several messes there was folksinging, emotional renderings of "*Kimigayo*," the national anthem. The captain, Rear-Admiral Kosaku Ariga, visited the gunroom bearing a large flask of *sake* for his young ensigns. There were ritual choruses of "*Banzai!*" Yet for all the fatalism on *Yamato*, there was scant enthusiasm. Amid the chronic stench of humanity in closed compartments, some men wondered aloud why, if this was indeed so noble a voyage, Combined Fleet commander Admiral Toyoda had not sailed with them. They debated whether American submarines or planes would send them to the bottom: "We shall be as vulnerable as a man walking alone on a dark night carrying only a lantern." Rice balls were served for breakfast on the morning of 7 April, with the promise of bean soup and dumplings, their favourite battle rations, at supper.

Twenty officers and ratings, stiff with tension, clustered on the bridge. Admiral Ito sat in his high chair with arms folded, a posture he retained through the hours that followed. When they heard that an American sighting of the squadron had been radioed in plain language, rather than encoded, the little command group was irked by the casualness with which the enemy was treating them. At noon, as sailors ate rations at their stations, Ito said with a broad smile: "We got through the morning all right, didn't we?" Forty-one minutes later, under intermittent rain and a sky empty of protective Japanese aircraft, the opening wave of Mitscher's armada struck.

The first American bomb destroyed *Yamato*'s air-search radar, leaving the ship's guns dependent on visual direction. "Using tracer to correct fire," wrote Ensign Yoshida bitterly, "is like trying to catch butterflies in one's bare hands." *Yamato*'s gunnery had never been impressive—at Leyte Gulf the ship failed to score a hit. Now, while every weapon was in action, the relentless concussions of the main armament and clatter of light AA accomplished little. Again and again, bombers pounded the battleship and her escorts as they steered on southwards, while fighters strafed their upper decks. The curtain of Japanese fire scarred many American aircraft milling overhead, but downed pathetically few. On the ship, however, the carnage was appalling. Inspecting the radar compartment after an explosion beneath the bridge, Yoshida found only unrecognisable wrecked equipment and human body parts.

Torpedoes began to slam into *Yamato*'s hull, causing massive damage below. Soon a stream of men were emerging onto the upper deck. Those above were reluctant to slam hatches on the "black gang" still trapped in the engine rooms, but the order was given to flood some compartments anyway. Turrets were traversed by hand when power failed. Exposed light AA-gun positions were strewn with dead and wounded. Yoshida remembered reading a training manual which stated that "a poor ratio of hits is due to human error and inadequate training." An officer had scrawled beside those words: "This is nonsense. Lt. Usubuchi." The upper decks were deluged with water from near misses, and blood from shattered bodies. Half *Yamato*'s bridge crew was dead. Yoshida found most of the survivors, some crudely bandaged with towelling, lying prone at their posts as a third wave of American attackers struck.

Belowdecks, the wardroom crowded with wounded suffered a direct hit from a bomb which wiped out its occupants. The upper works were reduced to twisted wreckage. Wide-eyed men stumbled in the midst of the steel shambles, helpless to aid the maimed and dying. Yoshida slapped the face of a seventeen-year-old rating, to stop his convulsive shaking. Far belowdecks, storeroom clerks gorged themselves on *sake*. What else could they do, and what was the liquor to be saved for? Ito, the admiral, remained in his chair on the bridge even as a fresh explosion hurled flying bodies against him. At the helm was Chief Quartermaster Koyama, an elderly prodigy. Koyama had served as a sailor at Japan's great victory of Tsushima, against the Russians more than forty years earlier. Now, in the last minutes of his life, he witnessed a historic Japanese defeat. Ito's chief of staff, Rear-Admiral Nobii Morishita, a famously brilliant staff officer and poker player, said sardonically of the American assault: "Beautifully done, isn't it?"

The torpedo-carrying Avengers pressed their attacks with great courage. They customarily attacked at three hundred feet, but that afternoon many crews flew much lower, braving the ships' fire to release torpedoes well inside the usual fifteen hundred yards. One of the pilots, Lt. John Davis of *Bunker Hill*, said afterwards: "On the way in I was working for the navy, and on the way out I was working for myself and the crew." Later waves of American attackers were poorly directed and coordinated, because radio communication became confused. Pilots simply chose their own targets, with the Avengers concentrating torpedoes on the biggest. *Yamato* pumped thousands of gallons of seawater into a hull bulge to correct a list. The ship maintained way, and continued to fire her main armament, but was drastically slowed. Four destroyers and the cruiser *Yahagi* were already wrecked or sunk, while those American pilots with fuel to spare machine-gunned survivors in the water. At 1410, a bomb jammed

Yamato's rudder and all power failed. The huge ship swung impotent, listing steeply, her port side awash.

Yoshida noticed a man-sized strip of human flesh hanging from a range finder. Another procession of American planes swung in to attack. On *Yamato*'s bridge Ariga kept repeating monotonously: "Don't lose heart. Don't lose heart." Ito said abruptly, gratuitously: "Halt the operation." His chief of staff saluted. Ito returned the compliment, then shook hands with several officers before leaving the bridge for his quarters, never to be seen again. His adjutant began to follow, only to be restrained by others who said: "Don't be a fool. You don't have to go." The captain ordered all hands on deck, then lashed himself to the chart table. Two navigating officers did likewise. The survivors on the bridge cried "*Banzai!*" thrice. Then Yoshida and several others left the bridge for the last time. Hundreds of men began to seek safety from the foundering ruin of their great ship, still subjected to strafing. No vessel of the Japanese navy carried rafts or lifebelts, for such accessories might suggest that it was desirable to survive defeat.

Dazed, shocked, blackened figures thronged *Yamato*'s deck, where a half-naked officer stood gazing up at their American tormentors. Hysterical, waving a sword, he cried "*Banzai!*" again and again. Another officer was amazed and irked to see some sailors sitting on the foredeck, eating hardtack or smoking, passively awaiting their fate. The ship tilted more steeply still, causing men in scores to fall or jump into the sea, while gun mountings and great fragments of twisted metal broke loose and tumbled overboard. Yoshida wrote: "At the instant *Yamato*, rolling over, turns belly up and plunges beneath the waves, she emits one great flash of light and sends a gigantic pillar of flame high into the dark sky . . . Armour plate, equipment, turrets, guns—fragments of the ship fly in all directions. Soon, thick dark brown smoke, bubbling up from the ocean depths, engulfs everything."

"The prettiest sight I've ever seen," said American Avenger gunner Jack Sausa. "A red column of fire shot up through the clouds, and when it faded *Yamato* was gone." Fires are thought to have triggered a huge magazine explosion as the battleship turned turtle. The smoke pall was visible on Kyushu, a hundred miles distant. It was 1423, less than two hours after the first American attack. Groaning, choking men struggled through the oil coating the sea, "like thrashing around in honey." Some used their last strength to drown themselves. A few sang. As smoke cleared and the sky brightened, an officer cried: "Hooray! We've arrived in the next world!"

The last American attackers departed at 1443, leaving just two Mariner reconnaissance floatplanes circling the battle scene. One of these, defying the nearby enemy, landed to rescue a downed American pilot. The surviving Japanese destroyers were much slower to pick up their countrymen struggling in the water. They awaited formal orders from the mainland to break off the Okinawa operation, which were received only at 1750. Some 269 of *Yamato*'s men were then recovered, while 3,063 perished, along with 1,187 of the escort crews. After the war, Yoshida wrote to the mother of Nakatani, his dead *nisei* friend from Sacramento. She answered: "Nothing gives me greater joy than to know that Kunio fought to the very end . . . and that he attained a death of which, as a Japanese, he need not be ashamed." Mothers need to believe such things to make their losses endurable, yet this was the most futile of all kamikaze operations. The only consolation for the Japanese was that during the American planes' absence from the fleet, a suicide plane hit and badly damaged *Hancock*, killing seventy-two men and injuring eighty-two. Yet by the time the carrier's aircraft returned at 1830, having missed the *Yamato* battle, thanks to effective damage control the ship was able to receive them. The destruction of Ito's squadron, still 250 miles north-west of Okinawa, cost Mitscher's squadrons just ten planes and twelve men killed. Back on the *Yorktown*, Air Group 9 sang: "*Yamato* been a beautiful BB, but BB, you should see yourself now!" It had been a turkey shoot. Mitscher was irritated that four Japanese destroyers escaped.

THE DESTRUCTION of *Yamato* was a mere sideshow, alongside the continuing battle of attrition between kamikazes and American ships. A major attack by 115 aircraft on 27 April disappointed the Japanese. Only ten ships were damaged. The attackers did better on 3 and 4 May, sinking three vessels and killing 450 sailors. At 1005 on 11 May, the first of two Zeroes ploughed into the flight deck of Mitscher's flagship, *Bunker Hill*, starting devastating fires which raged through the ship. Thirty planes on deck carried 12,000 gallons of fuel, all of which burned or exploded. In a succession of skilful manoeuvres, Captain George Seitz saved *Bunker Hill* from absolute destruction by swinging her broadside to the wind, to prevent smoke and flame from engulfing the hull. A steep turn caused tons of fuel to spill harmlessly overboard, but fires burned for hours, asphyxiating scores of men belowdeck, including many firefighters. In the engine and boiler rooms, miraculously undamaged, crews laboured to maintain power in temperatures of 130 degrees. The *Bunker Hill* attacks cost 396 men killed and 264 injured. One of them might have been the post-war movie star Paul Newman. He was ordered to the ship as radioman/gunner in an Avenger with a draft of replacements shortly before the attack, but by a fluke of war was held back because his pilot had an ear infection. The rest of his detail died. As with *Franklin*, hit on 19 March with the loss of

798 lives, on *Bunker Hill* brilliant damage control kept the hulk afloat, but removed Mitscher's carrier from the war.

Just three days later, when another wave of twenty-six kamikazes descended, nineteen were shot down by fighters, six by gunfire. Yet one got through, exploding beneath the forward elevator of the admiral's new flagship, *Enterprise*, and inflicting damage which required her to withdraw from operations. The Americans were fortunate that this was their last fast carrier loss. The overall cost of kamikaze operations to the U.S. fleet off Okinawa was appalling: 120 ships hit, of which twenty-nine were sunk.

THE CAMPAIGN was the first of the Pacific war to which the Royal Navy made a modest contribution. Hitherto, the British Eastern Fleet had merely conducted tip-and-run raids against Japanese installations in the Dutch East Indies and Malaya. Now four British carriers, along with two battleships, five cruisers and escorts, began to operate against Japanese airfields on Formosa, and suffered their share of assaults from kamikazes. "Task Force 57," as Vice-Admiral Bernard Rawlings's force was known, represented an attempt to satisfy Winston Churchill's passionate desire for Britain to play a visible part in the defeat of Japan. Its beginnings were inauspicious. Admiral King was bitterly hostile to any British presence in the Pacific, on both nationalistic and logistical grounds. It required the president's personal intervention to force the U.S. Navy to accede to the prime minister's wishes.

Thereafter, in the first months of 1945 it proved embarrassingly hard to muster a British fleet for Pacific service. The Royal Navy, like its parent nation, was overstretched and war-weary. Australia's shameless dock labour unions delayed the deployment of both warships and the fleet train of supply ships. When Rawlings's ships finally joined Spruance, they were hampered by design unfitness for tropical conditions, which inflicted chronic hardship on crews. British Seafire and Firefly aircraft were too delicate for heavy labour, and British carriers embarked far fewer planes than their American counterparts. Ships like *Illustrious* had been fighting since 1939, and were troubled by old wounds—in mid-April, the carrier was obliged to sail home. Rawlings's fleet struggled to keep up with its vastly more powerful allies. In an early series of air strikes, the British lost forty-one aircraft in 378 sorties, a casualty rate which would have been deemed disastrous even by Bomber Command. Sir Bruce Fraser wrote later in his dispatch: "There can be little doubt that the Americans are much quicker than we are at learning the lessons of war and applying them to their ships and their tactics . . . As a result the British fleet is seldom spectacular, never really modern . . ."

A British war correspondent, David Divine, joined the battleship *King George V* after weeks aboard *Lexington*, which refuelled and resupplied at sea in winds of up to Force 6, in a fashion reflecting the superb professionalism of the 1945 U.S. Navy. Now, Divine watched in dismay as "*KGV* went up astern of one rusty old tanker, which appeared to be manned by two Geordie mates and twenty consumptive Chinamen, and it took us, I think, an hour and a half to pick up a single buoyed pipe-line, fiddling around under our bows." Replenishment operations at sea remained an embarrassment for the British. In a placid sea, an American carrier refuelled in two hours. A British one required all day. A proud service found itself struggling to play a bit part in a vast American drama. Vice-Admiral Rawlings wrote later of the "admiration and . . . it must be admitted . . . envy" with which he followed the sinking of *Yamato*. Flying mishaps inflicted an alarming rate of attrition—in their first twelve strike days, nineteen British planes were lost to flak, twenty-eight in accidents.

The Royal Navy discovered that its most significant assets in Pacific combat were its carriers' armoured flight decks. The extra weight reduced their complement of aircraft, but rendered them astonishingly resistant to kamikazes, in contrast to their fir-decked American counterparts. When a Zero dived vertically onto the carrier *Indefatigable* on 1 April, its aircraft were able to resume landing within an hour. Though HMS *Formidable* suffered damage and fifty casualties when it was hit on 4 May, the ship was soon operational again. On 9 May, *Victorious* was hit twice and *Formidable* a second time, by kamikazes which eluded patrolling British fighters. Here too, the Royal Navy found that inexperience cost dear. Fraser's Seafires and Hellcats shot down a steady stream of intruding Japanese, but lacked the mass which the Americans possessed, together with the refined fighter-direction skills. There was a further twist to British tribulations when the Canadian government announced that only those of its citizens who chose to do so need continue to serve against the Japanese once the war against Germany was over. Despite offers of increased pay, 605 ratings of Rawlings's Canadian-crewed cruiser *Uganda* insisted upon exercising their right to go home. Only with difficulty was the ship persuaded to stay on station until a relief arrived.

The British Pacific Fleet's difficulties mounted with every week of operations. Crew morale suffered from the heat, discomfort and overcrowding: "Except for those engaged in flying operations, it was proving to be a dull war." At the end of April, Admiral King renewed his efforts to remove the Royal Navy from operations against Japan by dispatching Fraser's ships to support the Australian landings on Borneo. This proposal was defeated only by direct British appeals to MacArthur and Kinkaid. At the end of May, to the acute embarrassment of Fraser and the British government, battle damage, crew exhaustion and mechanical failures obliged Rawlings's squadron to withdraw to Sydney for extended repairs. When TF57 departed, it had completed just eleven air-strike days, dropping 546 tons of bombs and firing 632 rockets. It claimed 57 enemy aircraft destroyed, for the loss of 203: 32 to suicide attacks; 30 in a hangar fire; 33 to enemy flak or fighters; 61 in deck landing accidents; and 47 to "other causes." It was a sorry story, indeed one of the most inglorious episodes of the Royal Navy's wartime history. The misfortunes of the fleet reflected the fact that Britain, after almost six years of war, was simply too poor and too exhausted to sustain such a force alongside the United States armada. A British squadron returned to Halsey's command only in the last days of July.

OKINAWA was declared secure on 22 June, eighty-two days after the landings of Buckner's assault force. The U.S. Navy had lost 4,907 men killed, the army 4,675, the Marines 2,928. Another 36,613 men had been wounded ashore, over 8,000 at sea. A further 36,000 soldiers and Marines became non-battle casualties, many of them combat-fatigue cases. Buckner was unable to celebrate the victory he had yearned for. A Japanese shell killed him, unmourned, in the last days. His Japanese counterpart, Gen. Misomu Ushijima, also perished. He and his chief of staff committed ritual suicide in their headquarters cave on 22 June. Nine of his staff officers shot themselves. Dispute persists about how many Okinawan civilians died, because it is uncertain how many were evacuated before the battle began. Estimates range from 30,000 to 100,000, together with around 70,000 of the island's defenders. About 1,900 kamikazes died in their assaults on the U.S. fleet off the island. A total of 7,401 Japanese surrendered, almost half of these local Okinawan conscripts.

Some Japanese officers, including Kouichi Ito, retained a lifelong conviction that Ushijima had been mistaken to allow the Americans an unopposed landing on Okinawa. Yet, given the overwhelming power of the amphibious force, it is hard to believe that any Japanese deployment could have prevented American assault units from getting ashore, or indeed from conquering the island. The defenders could aspire only to what they accomplished—the extraction of a bitter price for American victory. The only tactical option which Buckner never explored, and which might have enabled his forces to prevail more quickly, was that of launching attacks in darkness. The difficulty, however, is that night operations demand exceptionally high motivation and tactical skills, to prevent those carrying them out from simply disappearing, "going to ground," rather than pressing home an assault. It is doubtful that Tenth Army possessed such qualities.

left: A Japanese pilot prepares for his final mission.

center: A suicide plane narrowly misses the U.S. carrier *Sangamon* off Okinawa.

bottom: The USS *Franklin* afire.

OPPOSITE TOP: Marines in one of the innumerable bloody assaults. OPPOSITE BOTTOM: Civilians await their fate. ABOVE: A Marine helps a woman and her baby to safety—most often, such people died.

Toshio Hijikata.

Yoshihiro Minamoto.

Haruki Iki.

Renichi Sugano on a locomotive of the notorious Burma Railway.

Harunori Ohkoshi as a teenage volunteer on his way to Iwo Jima, amid a grave but proud family group

Kisao Ebisawa, the frustrated Okinawa suicidalist.

Toshiharu Konada, who hoped to pilot a *kaiten* human torpedo against the allied invasion fleet.

Yoshiko Hashimoto *(second row, right)* with her family, who paid a terrible price for the 9 March 1945 USAAF firebombing of Tokyo. With their parents are Chieko *(second row, left)*, Hisae *(front row, centre)* and Etsuko *(front row, right)*.

LEFT: Hachiro Miyashita, who dispatched many suicide missions, and *(below)* one of his own photographs of a sombre young pilot watching the fuelling for his plane's last flight.

USAAF B-29s release incendiaries over Japan in May 1945, and *(below)* their formidable commander, Major-General Curtis LeMay.

Chinese

Bai Jingfan, her husband and other guerrillas.

Li Guilin.

Zhuan Fengxiang and her husband.

Liu Danhua.

Weng Shan, proud in his American uniform.

"Tiezi"—Li Dongguan.

ABOVE: Australians search enemy corpses for documents in northern Borneo, June 1945. BELOW: Mountbatten, astride a captured Japanese gun, addresses British troops in Burma.

Three of Slim's Soldiers

John Randle.

Brian Aldiss *(far right)*.

Derek Horsford.

Key Figures in the Final Act

The Big Three at Potsdam.

Henry Stimson.

Leslie Groves and Robert Oppenheimer.

Hirohito.

Anami.

Marquis Kido.

For Japan, the distinction between the carnage wrought by the Tokyo firebomb attacks *(above)* and the atomic bomb on Hiroshima *(below)* was less decisive than it has seemed to posterity.

Distraught Japanese hear the emperor's broadcast on 15 August 1945.

The surrender ceremony in Tokyo Bay aboard the battleship *Missouri*.

American sailors celebrate victory on board the USS *Bougainville*.

At every level, from high command to fighting soldiers, sailors and Marines, Americans emerged from the battle shocked by the ferocity of the resistance they had encountered, the determination of Japanese combatants to die rather than accept defeat. 'People out here attach more importance to the Kamikaze method of attack as an illustration of the Japanese state of mind than as a weapon of destruction," *New York Times* correspondent William L. Laurence wrote from the Pacific. "Considered carefully, the fact that literally thousands of men, many young and in their prime, will go out alone on missions of certain death . . . is not one calculated to breed optimism." Some historians, armed with knowledge of subsequent events, argue that the capture of Okinawa was unnecessary. It did not bring Japan's surrender a day closer. Yet to those directing the operation at the time, it was perceived as an indispensable preliminary to invasion of the Japanese home islands. Okinawa exercised an important influence on the development of events thereafter, through its impact upon the civilian, military and naval leadership of the United States. To capture an outpost, American forces had been obliged to fight the most bitter campaign of the Pacific war. The prospect of invading Kyushu and Honshu in the face of Japanese forces many times greater than those on Okinawa, and presumably imbued with the same fighting spirit, filled those responsible with dismay. At the end of June 1945, staff planners assumed that Operation Olympic, the invasion of Kyushu, would take place four months thence. To the U.S. chiefs of staff, however, any alternative which averted such necessity would be deemed welcome.

So dramatic was the succession of events which crowded into the last months of the war that it is hard to grasp the notion that, in June, the prospect of the atomic bombs did not loom foremost in the consciousness of the U.S. chiefs of staff. At that stage, their hopes of achieving victory without Olympic rested chiefly upon blockade, incendiary air bombardment and Russian entry into the Japanese war. All of these represented more immediate realities and more substantial prospects than the putative fulfilment of the Manhattan Project. The course of the Second World War had so often astonished its participants that no prudent men, even those at the summits of Allied power, could feel assured of how its last acts would play out.

SEVENTEEN

Mao's War

1. Yan'an

U.S. SOLDIERS AND MARINES fighting for their lives in the Ryukyus and Philippines, Slim's men in Burma, Australians in the south-west Pacific, would have found it grotesque had they known how the leaders of their great Asian co-belligerent spent the spring of 1945. Both rival parties for dominance of China held national congresses. True, desultory skirmishing with the Japanese persisted while the Nationalists were meeting in Chongqing, the Communists in Yan'an. The Americans wrung their hands in despair and disgust as the Japanese continued to expand their perimeter southwestwards across the Nationalists' Yunnan Province, resisted with conviction only by the Stilwell-trained Chinese divisions. Neither Chiang nor Mao was any longer interested in contributing to Japan's defeat. That could be left to the Americans in the Pacific. What mattered to them now was to gird their loins, gather their political and military forces, for the civil war that must follow the expulsion of the Japanese from China. The Communist Congress lasted fifty days, from 23 April to 11 June, its ideological writhings coinciding with the agony of Okinawa. Its chief achievement was to confirm the absolute dominance of Mao Zedong. His "thoughts" were thenceforward paramount in every aspect of Chinese Communist creed and deed.

Mao had almost a million men under arms, or what passed for arms among the guerrillas—they lacked artillery, air support and heavy weapons. The question of what these forces did during the Japanese occupation baffled most Americans at the time, and has remained a focus of controversy since. For decades after their domestic victory in 1949, the Communist rulers of China asserted that their followers, unsupported by the Americans, had alone waged effective war against the Japanese. Such Western propagandists as Edgar Snow made extravagant claims for the military successes of the Communists against the occupiers. They contrasted the energy and aggression of Mao's people with Nationalist passivity and sloth. Here is a characteristic Snow flourish: "Though their enemies denounced the Communists' beliefs and attributed to them every shameful excess they could imagine, no one could deny they had wrought a miracle in arms . . . Rarely in the history of modern war or politics has there been any political adventure to match this in imagination or epic grandeur. The job was done by men who worked with history as if it were a tool, and with peasants as if they were raw material."

American officers of the 1944 "Dixie Mission" to Yan'an were taken to watch showpiece operations against the Japanese, about which they reported back to Chongqing as enthusiastically as they were intended to do. Most of Mao's forces, however, spent the war struggling to feed themselves and survive, skirmishing only spasmodically with the Japanese. Today, the myth of Communist dominance of the struggle against the occupiers is discredited even in China. If Chiang Kai-shek's armies were less than effective on the battlefield, Mao Zedong's guerrillas lacked either the will or the combat power to do more than irritate the Japanese. By 1944, 70 percent of Japan's forces in China were committed against the Nationalists. A staff officer at Japan's army headquarters in Nanjing, Maj. Shigeru Funaki, said: "The Communists operated in regions that were strategically unimportant to us. Their troops were much more motivated than the Nationalists, but we sought only to contain them. Our attention was overwhelmingly concentrated on confronting Chiang's forces further south."

"The Communists were not strong enough to offer a major challenge to the Japanese occupation," says a modern Chinese historian, Yang Jinghua. "In the anti-Japanese war, the Kuomintang did most of the fighting, and killed far more of the enemy—I say this, as a Communist Party member for thirty years. Statistics tell the story. Some 1,200 KMT generals died fighting the Japanese, against just ten Communist ones." Zuo Yong, who later became a significant figure in Mao's China, served with the Communist New 4th Army from 1941 to 1945, latterly as a brigade chief of staff. Today, he says: "We had to adopt the strategy and tactics of the weak, as Mao urged in his books. We were staging raids, not serious offensives. We were guerrillas, sometimes living months at a time without fighting a battle. The enemy was too strong for us to do anything else." Zuo is generous in acknowledging U.S. aid to China, even though Washington denied arms to the Communists: "We felt really grateful to the Americans for all their help. One of their planes came down in our area, after being damaged bombing Japan. The pilot was wounded. We helped him to get back to his own people." Another historian, Wang Hongbin, says: "Guerrillas could not realistically engage large bodies of Japanese regular troops. The main achievement of the Communist armies in the war was to win the support of peasants and the respect of the Chinese people." This seems just.

By early 1945, the Communists claimed a combined strength of around 900,000 men for their 8th Route Army in the north and New 4th Army in central China, supported by another two million local militia members. As everywhere in the Second World War, guerrillas flourished chiefly in regions little valued by the occupiers. And like most irregular forces, those led by Mao were more concerned with proselytising for their cause and sustaining human existence in a starving countryside than with engaging the enemy. Li Fenggui, for instance, served eight months with his regiment of 8th Route Army in Shandong Province before acquiring a weapon of any kind. Most men went into action with perhaps ten rounds of ammunition apiece. Li's battalion possessed two light and two heavy machine guns; it acquired a single 60mm mortar only in 1944, artillery never. Most of its weapons were locally made single-shot rifles. Few Communist officers possessed watches, which made the synchronisation of operations difficult.

"For us," said Li, "1945 was not much different from 1940. Everyone was very hungry, everyone was very poor." They led nomadic lives, of stringent austerity. A battalion of seven hundred men billeted itself in a village for a few days, fed by local people. When supplies were exhausted, the column moved on, each man if he was fortunate carrying three days' bread and rice in a food bag. Their circumstances in 1945 had improved in only two respects: most Japanese troops had moved south from Shandong to confront the KMT; and far fewer Chinese were collaborating with the enemy. The ruthlessly pragmatic national ethic recognised that survival required bending with the wind. It had become plain even to peasants that the prevailing weather was no longer Japanese.

"Most nice people, clever people, chose to be Communists," claimed Xu Yongqiang, who in 1944–45 was an interpreter with the Nationalist army in Burma. "They were real Communists, not selfish politicians." He meant that many Chinese idealists and intellectuals gravitated naturally to the left in response to the Nationalists' moral bankruptcy and the hyperinflation which ruined so many people in those years. "The professional middle classes found themselves bankrupted. The wife of the head of our university had to find work as a domestic servant. People were selling their clothes to buy food. It was the middle class who paid for the war." Many Communists all over China languished in Japanese prisons, if they had been fortunate enough to escape execution.

Liu Danhua was a literature student in Harbin, Manchuria, when the Japanese took over. He was disgusted by everything about their behaviour, not least the fact that Japanese fellow students were so much better fed: "They had all the meat and fish. Everywhere we went, everything we did, was under Japanese control. The lives of ordinary people were wretched. I was young and angry. We tried to join the Communists, but for a long time we couldn't find them—they were underground." In 1940, Liu organised a student movement at Harbin University, which became known as the Left Reading Group. They made their pathetic protests by reading banned books, and urging peasants to defy Japanese orders about what crops to plant. They denounced collaborators. Liu taught his group revolutionary songs. He knew little Communist ideology, "but I could see the corruption and tyranny of the Kuomintang and the landlords. I was sure socialism must be the way forward for China."

It was too dangerous to assemble in the university, so they met at the local tax office, where they incited tax collectors to defiance. In 1941, at last they made contact with the Communists, who began to use Liu as a courier. He was soon arrested, however, and interrogated by the usual Japanese methods—beatings, water torture, suspension by his ankles. When these refinements palled on their captors, prisoners were merely left to stand in the snow. After a trial, Liu was sentenced to fifteen years' imprisonment, and served the first of them manacled.

Thereafter, however, his circumstances improved. He shared a cell with seven others, guarded by Chinese who proved not unsympathetic to the prisoners. He was allowed to receive a monthly visit from his wife, Yuan, who brought food wrapped in newspapers. These provided fragments of information about the outside world. He exercised constantly and took cold baths, because he was determined to be fit if he regained freedom. Some of his cellmates were Nationalists, "but there was no tension with us Communists. We were all against the Japanese." He had no paper or pen, but composed poems in his head. Their only books were science texts and the Bible. "I read it, simply to keep my brain occupied. I can't say I enjoyed it—it has always been abused by national rulers to serve their own purposes—but there are good things there."

From 1944, Liu and his fellow prisoners knew that the Japanese were losing the war. Ironically, given Stalin's indifference to China's Communists, Liu felt passionately committed to the Soviets: "At that time, I thought the Russians were wonderful. I was sure imperialism and capitalism were doomed to collapse." In his cell, he knew more about Stalin than about Mao. During the last months of the war, like every prisoner of the Japanese, he expected to be killed before liberation came. The tension between fear and hope became almost unbearable.

THE WAR POLICIES of Chiang and Mao had this much in common: each sought to strengthen his own power base, rather than to assist in the defeat of the Japanese. By a notable irony Mao, whose efforts to gain

American support failed, profited vastly more from the conflict than Chiang, who received billions in aid, together with the wholehearted endorsement of the greatest power on earth. Mao used the war years to build popular support among the peasantry of a kind which the Nationalists never achieved. Communist forces developed a motivation, comradeship and sense of shared purpose quite unknown in Chiang Kai-shek's army.

Li Fenggui, in 1945 a twenty-four-year-old company commander, was typical. He grew up in a village of nine hundred people near Shanghai, dominated by three "rich" landlords and a few "rich" peasants. The natural condition of others, including his own family, was destitution. After a bloody Japanese visit in 1941, Li and a few other villagers formed a little resistance group. Their first act of defiance was both primitive and ruthless. They lay in wait in the fields for a well-known Chinese collaborator who rode past daily on a bicycle. They rushed out, pulled him off his machine, wielded their machetes, and dragged the half-dead figure into the paddy. There, they finished him off and hid the body. Next day, another Chinese agent of the Japanese arrived to question the village headman about the disappearance of his colleague. Such happenings were not uncommon, however. No more was heard about the killing from the authorities.

But local Communists learned of it and approved. One day a stranger came to the village and told Li and his friends: "If you want to fight the Japanese properly, you must become a Communist." Li said: "But I don't know what a Communist is." The stranger said: "A Communist is a friend to poor people. When China is ruled by Communists there will be no more landlords, no more famines, everyone will have enough to eat, proper houses to live in and electricity." Li recalled later: "I had no idea what electricity was, because I had never seen it. But I accepted that it must be a good thing." The visitor helped Li and three others to write applications to join 8th Route Army, one of whose units was encamped a few miles away. Li's parents applauded. His mother made him a pair of cloth shoes. His father, poorest of the poor, nonetheless found money to buy cloth and stitch him a blanket. Thus equipped, he and the others set off one morning, accompanied for the first mile or so of their adventurous journey by a throng of admiring villagers. They were local heroes.

The years that followed were unremittingly harsh, yet Li found them rewarding: "We had such good relationships in the battalion, especially with our commanders. We were like family to each other." He enjoyed the communal concerts, led by the divisional entertainment troupe. Together they sang the famous "Guerrilla Song": "Marksmen all are we, when we shoot we kill!" In the summer of 1944, during the Ichigo offensive, Li's division found itself attacked by an overwhelming force of Japanese, obliged to disperse and flee: "We told the local peasants to hide everything, poison the wells, and come with us. About five hundred joined our retreat. There were just thirty-seven soldiers in our group, three of them wounded. At last we came to the Yellow River. We had to get across it to be safe. The women put small children on their heads. Some peasants helped carry our wounded. The river was deep. Some of those women were not very tall. The water closed over their heads. Children drowned. Hardly anyone could swim. When we finally reached the other side, maybe three hundred of the five hundred who had started the crossing were still with us. We all cried and embraced each other, guerrillas and villagers together. We were supposed to be soldiers, but we were always peasants as well—one family."

In a subsequent battle, Li was badly wounded—hit in the chest and leg. His unit had no medical supplies. They could only wash away the blood with salt water. When the rest of the battalion pulled out, he was left behind in the hut of a peasant named Li Qirong. For a week the wounded man lay undisturbed. Then one morning a Japanese collaborator appeared at the door of the house. "You seem to have visitors," said the man suspiciously. He looked in, saw Li on the bed, and said: "He looks as if he's from 8th Route Army." Li Qirong said angrily: "That's my own son, who was wounded last week when your Japanese friends shot up a lot of people." Not satisfied, the collaborator questioned the village headman. Somehow, Li Qirong persuaded him to support the story. After the collaborator had gone, the guerrilla burst into tears: "My mother first gave me life," he said, "but those people gave it to me a second time." He recovered, and eventually rejoined his unit.

By 1945, Li and his comrades knew little more about Communist ideology than they had done three years earlier. Survival remained their overwhelming preoccupation. Li had risen to become a captain, though he was denied the formal rank because he could not read. Orders were issued verbally, as so few men were literate, but Li's absence of education created problems in recording ammunition states, handling messages and taking roll calls. "Our general was the only really well-educated man in the division," he said.

The sexual climate in the Communist ranks was puritanical. Zuo Yong, twenty-year-old son of a rich peasant, was a student in Shanghai in 1941 when the Japanese burnt down his school: "I decided I would rather fight than find another school." He joined the Communists not for ideological reasons, but simply because their forces chanced to be closer at hand than those of the KMT. After a spell at an "anti-Japanese military school" in Hainan he was posted to New 4th Army as a platoon commander. A year or so later he was billeted in the village house of a family whose father was away at the front, serving as an officer with the Kuomintang. The man's wife was a teacher, with two teenage sons and two daughters of eighteen and nineteen. Zuo persuaded the woman to let her daughters become nurses in a Communist clinic, because there was no longer a chance that they could study. Soon afterwards, the woman said she wanted to meet Zuo's mother, to discuss a serious issue. "I'm afraid that's difficult," said Zuo. "Our village is a long way off." The woman said: "Well, in that case, I'd better talk to you. I think you would make a good husband for one of my daughters." Zuo explained that he could fulfil none of the three alternative criteria for being allowed to marry in the Red Army: he was under twenty-eight, he had not completed ten years' service, and he was not a regimental commander.

Ordinary soldiers were officially denied physical contact with girls. Even the few married women in the ranks were forbidden to touch their husbands in public. Senior officers, however, were provided with arranged wives of eighteen or nineteen. Zuo said: "I remember one girl who was told she was to marry a regimental commander. She asked about him, and was told that he was brave, hard-working, kind. After their first meeting, a comrade demanded: 'Do you like him?' She said: 'How can I tell? I've only seen him once.' " The marriage went ahead anyway. After a while, the girl ran away. Her husband remained enthusiastic, however, and eventually persuaded her to return. "A lot of couples whose marriages were arranged made a go of it together," said Zuo, "but there were divorces. Some of our soldiers were pretty simple fellows from the countryside, not very nice. They took for granted the right to beat hell out of their women."

FOR MOST of the war, Allied intelligence in China was shockingly poor. Stilwell and his successor Wedemeyer knew little about what the Nationalist armies were, or were not, achieving on the ground against the Japanese, and even less about the Communists. Until late 1944, the Communists' base in Yan'an remained a distant lunar world, shrouded in mist. It was known that Mao Zedong and his followers controlled an area the size of France, inhabited by some ninety million Chinese people, in which they had established a radical social and economic regime. Westerners who visited Yan'an asserted that living conditions were better than those prevailing in Nationalist areas. Such reports were compromised, however, by the fact that most of their authors were ideological fellow travellers. Were Mao's people serious Communists, or was he merely a rival warlord to Chiang? This issue mystified American and British officials in Chongqing. John Keswick, a scion of Hong Kong's Jardine Matheson trading house, was a British political adviser. He described the Yan'an regime contemptuously as "nothing more than a provincial government by a group whose policy sprang from agrarian revolt . . . It is unlikely that they would interfere with private property."

Lt.-Gen. Adrian Carton de Wiart was Churchill's personal emissary to Chiang, an appointment which reflected the prime minister's weakness for battlefield heroes, heedless of their other limitations. De Wiart was absurdly brave, veteran of campaigns innumerable, wounded eight times. He neglected to mention his Victoria Cross in his autobiography, presumably on the grounds that a self-respecting soldier should scorn such trifles. He lacked an eye, a hand (after being hit in France in 1915, he bit off his own mangled fingers when a doctor declined to remove them) and any hint of intellect. De Wiart despised all Communists on principle, denounced Mao as "a fanatic," and added: "I cannot believe he means business." He told the British cabinet that there was no conceivable alternative to Chiang as ruler of China.

A British diplomat delivered a shrewder and more nuanced verdict: "The Communists do not, any more than the Kuomintang, think of 'democracy' as a system which gives a chance to opposition parties. What is really meant by the 'democracy' of the Communists is that they are strongly supported by the poorer peasantry." British agents proved wiser than some Americans, dismissing any possibility of a deal between Chiang and Mao. By contrast Patrick Hurley, who became U.S. ambassador in October 1944, for months pursued the chimera of reconciliation. His first actions on arrival were to have a Cadillac appropriate to his status flown to Chongqing, and the ambassadorial residence redecorated. Then he set out to broker a deal between the Kuomintang and the Communists. In Hurley's first weeks, this foolish man confided to his own staff that he could perceive little to choose between Mao and Chiang.

The Nationalists, unsurprisingly, were implacably hostile to any Anglo-American dealings with Mao, and for most of the war the Americans indulged them. But late in 1944, as Washington's disillusionment with Chiang hardened, some contacts developed. John Service, a U.S. diplomat who shared with John Paton Davies a growing respect for the Yan'an regime, met the Communist leaders in August. After years of contending with Chiang's self-importance, pomposity and duplicity, Service was captivated by the charm, humour and apparent frankness of the Communists in general, and Mao Zedong in particular. Mao told him that he had thought of abandoning the name "Communist" for his party, to assuage capitalist fears about its nature: "If people knew us they would not be frightened." He said that China would need American investment after the war: "We must cooperate and we must have American help. This is why it is so important to us Communists to know what you Americans are thinking and planning. We cannot risk crossing you—cannot risk any conflict with you." Mao pleaded for American amphibious landings on the coast of northern China, to open a direct supply route to Yan'an. So eager were the Communists for aid that Zhou Enlai, while acting as Mao's emissary in Chongqing, told Service they were willing to place their troops under American command if the U.S. would arm them. Service, impressed and even entranced, formally recommended to Stilwell that weapons should be sent to the Communists. The general was not unsympathetic.

The idea got nowhere. More than sixty years later it is easy to convict of naïveté those Americans—some in Chongqing, some in Washington—who frustrated Chinese Communist advances. They persisted in backing Chiang Kai-shek when it was plain that his regime was incorrigibly corrupt. Yet the advocates of Mao also showed themselves imperceptive. American visitors, arriving from Chongqing with the rotten taste of Nationalism still fresh in their mouths, were absurdly easily seduced by the Communist leaders. Davies, who flew to Yan'an in October 1944, was enchanted by the "direct, friendly manner" in which Mao strode up to each visitor in turn and shook hands. His physical presence impressed them: the strong chin and prominent mole; long, thick black hair; wide lips. Davies noted Mao's slow gestures, big, soft, heavy frame, mastery of dialectic argument, "the incandescence of personality which develops not in the twinkling of an eye but of easy perception. There is an immense, smooth calm and sureness to him."

The American reported to Washington: "I got the impression that here we were dealing with pragmatists—men who knew their limitations as well as their strengths. And they were confident—confident and patient. They have waited a long time to get where they are now. They are willing to wait much longer." Likewise Raymond Ludden and the five military members of the U.S. Yan'an Observers' Group—the "Dixie Mission"—who travelled on foot and by mule to visit guerrillas. "8th Route Army has a legendary fame in North China as friend and champion of the people," Ludden enthused in February 1945. After years of cynicism and frustration in the Nationalist camp, such men as Service and Davies found the Communists intensely romantic. They swallowed claims for the decency and moderation of Mao's leadership, when shrewder observers recognised that the Communist leader, like Chiang, was engaged in the ruthless pursuit of power. Soft words offered to American emissaries were meaningless.

Mao's personal vices are starkly depicted by modern writers. Jung Chang and Jon Halliday, in an unremittingly dark portrait, highlight his maltreatment of his first two wives, and of a host of unfortunate young women whom he exploited. Many Western as well as Chinese scholars argue contrarily, however, that whatever Mao became after he achieved power, in the wartime years his excesses had not yet manifested themselves. What seems indisputable is that Mao had no interest in liberal socialism. American visitors to Yan'an were foolish to be deluded by the warmth of Communist greetings. They saw, or thought they saw, a group of austere, dedicated patriots committed to fighting the Japanese and creating a better life for China's starving millions. This was fanciful. It is no longer denied in China that Mao's regime in Yan'an engaged in large-scale opium trafficking, and almost certainly also made tactical truces with the Japanese. "Mao and the Communists engaged in the opium trade," says Yang Jinghua, a historian of Manchuria. "How else could they pay their troops? Nothing else that would grow in Yan'an was marketable. In such a situation, you do what you must."

Evidence about Communist parleys with the Japanese is circumstantial, but persuasive. It suited both parties to trade opium, a major industry for the occupying regime. Japan's China Affairs Board, established by Prince Konoe, controlled a $300-million annual traffic, deliberately revived by the Japanese army to weaken the Chinese and raise cash. This was the body whose agents negotiated with Mao's people for supplies. Several of the largest Japanese corporations administered distribution—Mitsubishi in Manchuria, Mitsui in the south. There was intense rivalry over markets, though all the interested parties sought to conceal their roles. By 1944–45 it also suited Communists and Japanese alike to avoid headlong military confrontation. "China was so fragmented at that time, that it remains hard to say with certainty what did or did not happen," shrugs Yang.

Mao's suppression of dissent, however, is undisputed. A young intellectual named Wang Shiwei had languished under house arrest since 1942 for denouncing in an essay the "dark side of Yan'an," the "three classes of clothing and five grades of food," of which the best went to senior cadres while "the sick can't get a bowl of noodles and the young have only two bowls of congee a day." While the rest of the politburo walked everywhere, Mao rode in a Chevrolet van, prominently labelled "Ambulance: Gift of the New York Chinese Laundrymen's National Salvation Association." Young girls are alleged by Chang and Halliday to have suffered chronic sexual predation from party bosses. Dissidents were ruthlessly purged. Wang Shiwei was eventually beheaded. Spies and counter-revolutionaries were identified by torture and confessions. Among denounced intellectuals, suicides were not unknown.

Western visitors were charmed by the apparent casualness of Yan'an, the charm and fluency of Zhou Enlai, the manner in which Mao dropped by people's quarters for cards or gossip, danced energetically though with absolute absence of rhythm at Saturday-night hops. Foreigners joined the cadres to drink *baicha*, "white tea"—hot water. They witnessed a brilliantly staged pantomime. The choice for China was not between a corrupt, brutal, incompetent dictatorship and libertarian socialism. It lay between two absolutist systems, of which that of the Communists was incomparably more subtle and effective, possessed of wide appeal for peasants and intellectuals.

Those Americans in Chongqing and Washington who opposed an alliance with Yan'an made the right call for the wrong reasons. They disdained Mao because they were fearful of undermining Chiang Kai-shek. The proper grounds for refusing aid to the Communists were that war matériel would not have been employed to assist the defeat of Japan. The Soviets took the same view. Moscow's emissaries in Yan'an reported most unfavourably to Stalin on the discipline, battlefield performance and alleged successes of Mao's troops. The Communists had indeed created a remarkable political edifice. The problem from an Allied viewpoint was that their achievement had everything to do with the future of post-war China, almost nothing to do with defeating Japan.

Yet in the wartime years, millions of Chinese peasants passionately believed that Mao held out the promise of a better life. To this day, many of those who served with the Communist guerrilla forces in World War II remember the experience with romantic enthusiasm. For all his shortcomings, Mao was a profoundly inspirational leader. Those modern biographers who claim that his achievement and long maintenance of power in China were founded exclusively upon terror seem drastically to understate the popular support which he mobilised. "The Communists were so much better organised than the KMT," said Wei Daoran, son of a famous Nationalist general, Wei Lihuang, who as a teenager accompanied his father on wartime campaigns. "They had an infrastructure that stretched right through the countryside. When Communist troops passed through a region, they left behind much better memories than the KMT. They offered the peasants some education. If you were talented, the party offered opportunities for advancement. They treated women as equals."

Many women found a fulfilment in the ranks of Mao's Communists which had been wholly unattainable in pre-war China. Bai Jingfan was the daughter of a prosperous merchant from Henan Province who dealt in grain and oil. When the Japanese stormed their village in 1934, the family fled. Bai herself, sixteen at the time, set off alone in determined search of the Communists, whom she perceived as the only convincing opponents of occupation. Initially, she took an eight-day bus journey to Xian. From there, she travelled to Yan'an, where she enrolled in the Party's Women's

University. On graduation she became a propaganda officer. The hardships of her new life counted for nothing beside the exhilaration of working for the cause. She married a rising star of the Communist military hierarchy, and followed him to fight with a guerrilla regiment in Hebei Province.

By May 1944 she had grown accustomed to a wholly nomadic existence, playing cat-and-mouse with Japanese forces. One night, camped in a village, they were awakened at midnight by scouts. An enemy search-and-destroy column was approaching. "It was pitch dark and blowing a gale. Our commander said: 'We've got to get out—fast.' " Hastily seizing weapons and equipment, they set off towards another village, nine miles distant. They had marched barely a mile when the night erupted into gunfire. Somebody said: "The lead platoon has run into the Japanese." Bai's companions said: "We'll have to make a run for it." She had a special problem of her own, however. She was heavily pregnant. After struggling across country for two miles, she felt she could not run another step. In the midst of the fields, she told the others: "Leave me here—I'll find a place to hide." They argued fiercely for a few moments, then took her at her word. After a cold and frighteningly lonely night, early next morning she was able to struggle on to the village rendezvous where she joined her company. The Japanese were still close behind, however. The guerrillas had to keep going. In a few hasty exchanges with the villagers, they found a refuge for Bai, in the hut of a widow with no reason to love the enemy, for they had killed her husband.

For two weeks, they lived peacefully enough. Then, one morning, a boy dashed in shouting: "Japanese come! Japanese come!" At first they were disbelieving. Then they saw enemy soldiers approaching. Once again, Bai had to stumble into flight with her unborn burden. She lasted six miles, as far as another village, before again collapsing exhausted. She threw herself on the mercy of the peasants. They showed her into a deep, narrow hole. In stifling heat and total darkness, she lay secreted when the enemy column arrived. The Japanese announced that they knew people from 8th Route Army were in the village, and proposed to find them. After a search, which came close to Bai's hole but did not discover it, they interrogated a ten-year-old boy and an old man. Both denied all knowledge of any fugitives. After raping the old man's niece in front of the entire village, the Japanese marched on. Bai said: "I felt so guilty, completely powerless to interfere with anything the Japanese did." She was safe, and rejoined her regiment. Soon afterwards, she gave birth to a son. She cherished the profound gratitude, common to all fugitives, of owing her life to strangers who suffered much and risked more.

2. With the Soviets

One of many errors made by Western observers in China was to assume that Communists in Moscow must be sympathetic to Communists in Yan'an, and vice versa. In the winter of 1944–45, when Chinese Nationalist troops were everywhere retreating before the Japanese, the British Joint Intelligence Committee speculated: "If Chinese unable put up even show of determined resistance in defence of such important towns, considerable danger gov might not survive. With breakdown of centralised govt and dispersal Chinese troops, other than those trained and led by Americans, organised Chinese opposition would come only from Communists . . . who might get more support than in past from Russians who might see some advantage in maintaining some Chinese Government in opposition to Japanese."

In reality, however, Stalin had long before reached brutally pragmatic conclusions about China. He believed that Chiang was the only man capable of ruling the country; that Mao was too weak to overthrow him; and that Soviet interests therefore demanded a working relationship with the Nationalists. For years before the war, Chiang received cash and military aid from Moscow. Mao's people in Yan'an were far more isolated politically than Western visitors knew. Though Stalin had funded China's Communists back in the 1920s, not until the war ended did the Soviet leader lift a finger to assist their cause against Chiang. Conversely, in the dark days of 1941–42, when Stalin's emissaries in Yan'an urged Mao to exert all possible military pressure on the Japanese, to diminish the risk that they would join Hitler's onslaught on Russia, the Chinese leader ignored their imprecations.

Yet the Soviets needed information from China, and above all from Manchuria, where Russian and Japanese forces confronted each other across their shared border, and had fought a brief war in 1939. Despite their supposed neutrality towards Japan, the Russians welcomed into the far east of the Soviet Union several thousand Chinese Communist guerrillas who sought refuge from hunger and Japanese harassment. In remote forest areas, under the auspices of Moscow's Far East Intelligence Group, training camps and bases were established. Chinese guerrillas were sent back into their own country to spy and make trouble, in the same fashion as the British SOE and American OSS promoted resistance elsewhere in the world.

The activities of these groups form a remarkable story, largely unknown in the West. Chiang Kai-shek lost much face among Manchurians when he declined to commit Nationalist forces to resist the 1931 Japanese takeover. The local guerrilla bands which formed thereafter were Communist in name, however little ideology they possessed. Stalin's Chinese recruits were drawn from unimaginably wretched backgrounds. Li Dongguan was the child of a peasant in Heilongjiang Province, who started poor and grew relentlessly poorer. The child tended cattle for the local landlord, and quickly became radicalised by the Japanese occupation. One day when a group of boys were making a fishtrap by the river, two Japanese soldiers came by with a dog. One of the children was foolish enough to throw a stone at it. The Japanese unslung their rifles and shot dead not only the stone thrower, but three other children. "I was so shocked. After that, I cared only about fighting the Japanese."

Not long after, a Communist guerrilla group stayed in his village for a few days. He befriended its bugler, a boy about his own age. They played together, as children do, and Li—nicknamed "Tiezi" by his family—helped tend the guerrillas' horses. He told the bugler that he wanted to join the band. "You'll have to talk to Liu, the commissar," said the young warrior. Liu was dismissive: "Look at you—thirteen years old. Life as a guerrilla is no picnic. One day you're crossing mountains in the snow, the next there's nothing to eat. You'd never keep up. Anyway, your family need you at home." "My mother's dead and I needn't tell anybody else," said the boy. Liu shrugged, patted him on the head and said: "We can talk about this again in a couple of years."

Next day, however, when the guerrilla column marched out, behind them in the snow trudged Li. He said nothing to his family, carried only a little rice and a few trifles in a bag. That night, when the guerrillas camped, Li slipped in among them, and slept beside his friend the bugler. It was two days before Liu, the commissar, noticed him. Then he burst out furiously: "What the hell are you doing here? We're going into action tomorrow. Look at your hands—you've got frostbite already. The cold will kill you in a week. Go home where you belong!" But Li did not go home. Through the days that followed, he shadowed his young friend the bugler, helping with camp chores, fetching water, peeling vegetables, feeding the horses. After a month of this, Liu shrugged and said: "OK, you're earning your keep. You can stay with us." Li's family assumed that he was dead. It was fifteen years before his few surviving relations saw him again.

In the times that followed, besides the usual privations of guerrilla life, Li took part in several skirmishes with the occupiers. Once, when his band saw two Japanese vehicles pass by on a road, they knew that they were likely to come back the same way, and laid an ambush. Sure enough, late in the afternoon the trucks reappeared. The guerrillas poured fire into them. When the action was over, they found that they had killed twenty Japanese. Only one made good his escape. There was a bonus: one truck had been carrying a garrison payroll. The guerrillas found themselves laden with cash as well as the weapons of the dead. In China, it was hard to distinguish between banditry and politically motivated resistance, and few tried to do so. Such little battles were rare. The guerrillas' lives were characterised by monotony, privation, and long marches to escape Japanese punitive columns. A combination of all three eventually drove Li's group across the northern border, into Russia.

Li Min's father was head of the anti-Japanese group in his village in Heilongjiang Province. During her brief period of schooling, her teacher proselytised enthusiastically about the virtues of the October Revolution in Russia. He taught them Lenin's song: "With Lenin's birth, a star rose in the sky, beloved of all workers, feared by every capitalist." Min's education ceased, along with the life of her village, after a punitive raid by Japanese troops in 1936. She found herself a young nomad in the forests with a guerrilla band. Her father and brother joined other groups—with which both were killed before she could see them again. In the early years of the Japanese occupation, such groups survived without too much difficulty, receiving help from sympathetic peasants. At its peak, Min's band was seven hundred strong. However, as the Japanese tightened their grip, the plight of their opponents grew harsher. Peasants were rounded up into "protected villages," which they needed passes to leave. Others were deported for slave labour. Large numbers of Japanese immigrants arrived, taking over confiscated Chinese land. Japanese military sweeps of guerrilla areas became progressively more vigorous and ruthless.

It was a fantastically primitive existence, which only the youngest and hardiest could endure. Most of Min's group were aged between seventeen and twenty—"a man of thirty, like our commander, seemed to us incredibly old." They planted their own maize and rice in remote stretches of wilderness, hunted deer, wild boar and bears not only for food but for skins in which to clothe themselves. Like most of the wartime French *maquis*, their chief concern was not with fighting the enemy—for which they possessed scant means—but with survival. They snared rabbits for food and skins with which to sew caps and cloaks. They lived in huts dug deep into the earth, so that only the roofs showed above ground level. They huddled around their fires to fight the winter cold. But fires meant smoke, and smoke brought strafing Japanese aircraft, which killed scores of their people. Of those who survived, many more perished of hunger. Finally, in 1941, they embarked on a twenty-day march which led them across the border into Russia.

Jiang De grew up with Communist guerrillas in Manchuria. Every autumn they came to his village seeking grain and recruits. His uncle, whom Jiang much admired, joined them. Jiang became a small-time spy, collecting fragments of information about Japanese movements, assisted by the fact that he had another uncle working in a local police station. "Nobody took any notice of what a kid like me was doing." One day in July 1943, six guerrillas were in Jiang's house when two Japanese police appeared without warning at the front door. The guerrillas bolted through the back. There was a brief scuffle, in which one policeman was killed while the other fled. A few hours later, three trucks laden with Japanese soldiers and Chinese militia drove up to the village and rapidly deployed around it. They rounded up all fifteen members of the family except Jiang, who escaped into fields with the guerrillas. In captivity, the family paid dearly for their rashness in lingering at home after the policeman's killing. All were tortured in varying degrees, with forced infusions of chilli water, electric shocks and beatings. Jiang's father died under the experience.

After the Japanese had departed with their prisoners, the young man and the guerrillas raided the farm of a local landlord. They seized ten horses and all the grain the beasts could carry, then set off towards the forests. After marching all night, at dawn they realised that they were being pursued. For four hours they lay in hiding with their animals, listening to Japanese voices as troops searched the area. One of the horses began to whinny. They cut its throat. At last it seemed safe to move on. Early next morning, they reached the camp of the seventy-strong guerrilla band, with whom Jiang now threw in his lot. Winter came on. "It was a very difficult time," he said. They were soon desperate for food. They ate some of the horses, and the remainder soon perished of hunger. Eventually, a decision was taken: some men would hold out in the forest until spring. The rest, however, would make for the Russian border. After three weeks' hard marching, and a crossing of the frozen Amur River, they reached Soviet border posts. Jiang delivered a letter which the guerrilla commander had given him, asking that he should be trained and sent back into China.

Zhou Shuling was an illiterate fourteen-year-old when one day in 1934 her Manchurian hamlet was visited by Japanese troops who murdered her grandfather by stuffing chilli plants down his throat until he choked. Her brother, aunt and two uncles were killed by simpler methods. She ran away to join a local Communist guerrilla group of the North-East Anti-Japanese Union: "I refused to become a Japanese slave." There were eleven guerrilla groups in northern Manchuria at this time, some of them no more than bandits. She served with the 3rd Regiment, initially employed as a spy to scout Japanese positions and report where it might be possible to steal weapons or food. On one of these expeditions she met a Japanese patrol. A soldier casually lashed out with his bayonet, gashing her face. Another Japanese intervened, saying: "Oh, leave her alone. She's harmless." He said to Shuling: "Run for it, while you've got the chance." After that encounter, fearful of rejoining her group when the Japanese were on the move and she had no papers, she took refuge for a week with a woman whom she persuaded to give her shelter in return for helping to look after her four children. Then Shuling threw herself on the mercy of a women's religious group. After a week with them, she was able to escape back to her band.

It was a hard life, moving constantly to escape roving Japanese columns, living in caves and woods, once surviving a week without food. In 1938, when she was sixteen, she was told that she was to marry the commander of another group, an old man of twenty-nine named Li Mingshu. "What did I think of him?" She shrugged. "It didn't matter whether I liked or disliked him. That was the way things were done." She lived for several months in the wilderness with Li's 32nd Battalion, until Japanese pressure became irresistible. After the Communist groups in their area had been desperately mauled, and with the loss of hundreds of men, the survivors slipped over the border into Russia, where most of them remained until 1945.

The Russians treated their Chinese guests as well as their own threadbare means allowed: "They respected us, because we had been fighting for the same thing as them," said Li Min. They were issued Russian uniforms, armed and intensively trained for intelligence missions and guerrilla war. Min underwent courses in radio work and parachuting. Clothes to wear, roofs over their heads and a bare minimum of food to eat might seem little enough, but were more than they had known in the forests of northeast China. Min supervised the guerrillas' little library, and acted as assistant to their group's resident intellectual, Chen Lei. He produced a string of pamphlets and reports, and conducted briefings for the group on the state of the war, based on newspaper reading and radio listening. In 1943, Min married Chen Lei. She was twenty-one, he was twenty-five. "It was not an arranged marriage—we simply loved each other. There was somebody else who liked me a lot, but Lei was the one I really cared about."

Marriage in such circumstances was a strange business. There was only the simplest of ceremonies before a few friends, with no spare food or alcohol with which to celebrate. In winter months, the couple were allowed to cohabit in a hut they found for themselves in a derelict Soviet army camp. In summer, however, party rules decreed that men and women should occupy separate quarters, whether married or not. The Chinese were strictly quarantined from all Soviet citizens except their own instructors. They were forbidden to visit the nearest town, Yasta, some forty miles from the guerrilla camps. Yet the union of Lei and Min, unlike so many wartime marriages, lasted through sixty-three years that followed. "I never regret my experience in Russia. I was very lucky. In some ways, it was a good time."

After months of training by Soviet instructors, Li Dongguan joined one of the reconnaissance groups which operated inside China from Russian bases. Over the next seven years he carried out seventy cross-border missions, scouting on foot up to thirty miles inside Japanese-controlled territory, liaising with local guerrillas and reporting on Japanese deployments. In winter the guerrillas usually stayed in their Soviet camps. Though there were occasional ski patrols, deep snow made movement difficult. In summer they worked in four-man teams. Dongguan's favoured companion was a young Korean named Li Yunlong, "a peasant like me, who had shared the same sort of life." They were dropped by jeep on the Russian side of the border, then travelled for three to five days in Japanese territory, clad usually in peasant clothing, occasionally in Japanese uniform, reporting back by radio. They slept mostly in the huts of sympathetic peasants. Unlike most Russian soldiers, they never carried vodka in their rations: "We saved our drinking for when we got back." Only once did they clash head-on with a Japanese patrol, which cost Dongguan a bullet in the shoulder. Fortunately, they had only just crossed the river border. Within hours his companions were able to get him back into Russia.

The young Chinese liked the Russians: "We were all fellow Communists." Once he had mastered the language, he became friendly with Russian officers who used to say: "You like it here. Why not take out citizenship and marry a nice Russian girl?" Dongguan was irked by this: "I am not a Russian—I'm Chinese." "Don't be so small-minded and nationalistic," they taunted him. "I'm not nationalistic!" the young Chinese said angrily. "I'm internationalistic." "Come on," insisted the Russians. "You'd have a much better life here than in China—even when we've dealt with the Japanese there'll be a civil war to come." Dongguan brushed them aside. He met a young Chinese Communist doctor named Zhang Yujie and married her three months later. He enjoyed his life in the Russian camps. Their remoteness held no terrors for a Chinese peasant, and he loved the opportunities to hunt and fish: "There was plenty of game in the forests. We lived pretty well." By 1945 he was twenty-eight years old, one of the most experienced of the guerrillas.

Jiang De joined a course of thirty students, most of them under twenty, who were taught the arts of reconnaissance and wireless operation—which, in the case of Jiang and several others, included some basic literacy skills. "I enjoyed it—I learned so many things I didn't know." Their material needs were served by Russian batmen and cooks, a privilege the teenager had never known. They liked their Russian "headmaster." Jiang said: "I changed a lot—for a start, I learned to read and write. I became a different person."

"The Russians were kind to us," said Zhou Shuling. "I saw how very hard life was in Russia—worse than in China—but they shared what they had. Sometimes, a Russian might only have one potato to eat. But he would share that potato." She herself was trained as a nurse, and during those years of exile bore her husband four children in their tiny room in the bleakness of the Russian north-east. Her husband's career became much more exotic. He was trained as a parachutist, and carried out several intelligence missions in Manchuria. He told her nothing of his abrupt comings and goings. Once, she was amazed to see a Japanese soldier walking up the path to her home. Then she recognised her husband in the hated uniform.

More than a few of the Chinese agents whom the Soviets sent back into Manchuria were captured by the Japanese, who were as confused as the Allies by the tangle of Communist loyalties between Mao and Stalin. In December 1944, Japanese intelligence in Manchuria reported to Tokyo that they had caught two Chinese Communist agents in Dalian, who had been in contact with the local Soviet consul. These men confessed under interrogation to membership of a thirty-strong network of agents in Manchuria, in wireless contact with the Communists in Yan'an. Their group, the prisoners asserted, "at present were mostly inactive awaiting a revolt in Manchuria or a Soviet-Japanese war." It is today impossible to guess whether the captured agents were in reality reporting to Yan'an or to the Soviets.

In addition to the reconnaissance groups, the Russians formed guerrilla refugees into a regular unit, the 88th Independent Brigade. Four of its battalions were Chinese. The fifth was Korean, commanded by Kim Il Sung, who later became ruler of North Korea. Their ranks were stiffened by some Soviet officers of Chinese and Korean origins. In the canteen at their base forty miles from Khabarovsk, they celebrated the German surrender with Russians who offered toasts to victory and to Stalin. The Chinese immediately called for another toast: victory over Japan. The Red Army men enthusiastically joined in. From that day on, the former guerrillas anticipated Soviet entry into the eastern war. When at last it came, the Chinese were bitterly disappointed when the Russians deployed only a handful of the Chinese trainees, committing the others to internal security duties in Manchuria and Korea. Stalin's Chinese clients were deemed a political asset more than a military one.

. . .

JOHN PATON DAVIES and his kind forever afterwards believed that, in the winter of 1944–45, the United States lost a historic opportunity to achieve an understanding with China's future, in the person of Mao, which it sacrificed by clinging to the past, in the person of Chiang. This was naïve. There is no more reason to suppose that Mao would have honoured promises to American capitalists, made under the duress of war, than did Chiang. Both were playing a game with the Americans, Chiang with greater apparent success, Mao with much shrewder understanding of his own people. Edgar Snow, the U.S. journalist who knew Mao for many years and who became one of his most effective Western propagandists, recorded a conversation with him in the 1930s: "Both of us felt a growing conviction that the Communist-Nationalist war in China would in the long term prove more important than the Japanese war . . . Mao correctly predicted the Japanese attack on Western colonies in Asia, Russian intervention in a general war to defeat the Japanese—and end colonialism in Asia. He told me to expect the Japanese to win all the great battles, seize the main cities and communications, and in the process destroy the KMT's best forces . . . at the end of a war which he thought might last ten years, the 'forces of the Chinese revolution' would . . . emerge as the leading power in East Asia."

This seems both a plausible illustration of Mao Zedong's shrewdness and a convincing view of his agenda. In 1945, the U.S. remained implacably unwilling to send military aid to Yan'an. For this, much abuse has been heaped upon Hurley and his kind by liberal contemporaries and historians. Yet the Americans were surely right. It would have availed the Allied war effort nothing to ship arms to the Communists. These would have been used against the Japanese only in showcase operations to impress foreign spectators. By now, the minds of U.S. policy-makers as well as Chinese principals had become fixed upon shaping post-war realities, rather than promoting Japan's defeat on the Asian mainland.

In January 1945, Wedemeyer chaired a meeting with the British at which he asserted emphatically: "Under no circumstances is any material help to be given or negotiations entered into with any provincial authorities or military leaders who are not, repetition not, directly controlled by and owe allegiance to central authorities." A British hand pencilled on the War Office copy of this minute: "Yennan?" Wedemeyer urged everyone present to "come clean" about any "undeclared operations." The British in Chongqing agreed with their American colleagues about very little, but they endorsed Hurley and Wedemeyer's view that it was pointless to arm Mao's people. The British military attaché signalled to London on 27 December 1944: "Seeing that the Communists have not been equipped with modern weapons nor organised and trained to operate with them, I consider that they would be of negligible value for at least a year, even if given all the facilities enjoyed by the central gov forces since 1928. They have never carried out regular ops against the Japs, but have contented themselves with occupying territory from which the Kuomintang tps have withdrawn."

In March 1945 Hurley abandoned his attempt to forge a coalition between Mao and Chiang, and became implacably hostile to Yan'an. The ambassador conducted a dramatic purge of all those whom he deemed Communist sympathisers, including Service and Ludden. He had become convinced that the United States must support Chiang, and Chiang alone. A British visitor met Hurley in 1945. He afterwards asserted that the U.S. ambassador "despised the Chinese [and] asked whether I did not agree that they were hopeless people who must have a strong man on top to keep them in order." As so often when others waver, one man passionately committed to a course of action—Hurley—got his way. America withheld support from Mao, whose guerrillas remained largely passive until August 1945.

John Paton Davies admitted later that he had been mistaken to suppose that Mao Zedong was amenable to democracy. However, the American diplomat was impenitent in his judgement about the virtues of what he and his colleagues saw, liked and admired about Mao's camp in 1944–45: "Yan'an provided the great mass of the population, which had been without hope, with an affirmative, personal way out of the swamps of despair. The way out was through rustic nationalism, based on organized rustic resistance to the Japanese invaders, and a novel feeling of having some say in the shaping of one's individual destiny."

It was unquestionably true that Mao's people in Yan'an were building a base of popular support—however deluded were the Chinese people about Mao's ability to improve their lives—quite lacking for Chiang Kai-shek's regime. Christopher Thorne has written perceptively about the enthusiasm of generations of American foreign policy-makers for identifying a nation's "great man," and fixing upon him—sometimes to the point of obsession—as friend or foe. Americans, Thorne argues, are far less comfortable assessing movements and ideologies than categorising individuals. American policy in China represented a spectacular example of this proclivity. Chiang had become unequivocally the chosen "great man" of the United States. Though Washington grew deeply disillusioned about the Nationalists' will or ability to assist the Allied cause against the

Japanese, and acknowledged the chronic corruption and incompetence of Chiang's government, they stuck with him.

Even if the U.S. had decided to ship military aid to the Communists in 1945, the logistical difficulties were so great that the Japanese would not have been much inconvenienced. No more than the Nationalists were the Communists capable of inflicting defeat upon a regular Japanese army. American support for the Communists might have spared the Chinese people from their later civil war, by hastening the fall of Chiang: it was plain to all but the most blind and bigoted foreigners in China in 1945 that if its people were granted political choice, Chiang must fall. But aid to Mao could not have altered the course of the Second World War in Asia.

Exposure of the delusion that the U.S. could determine the future of China cost Americans only money, but was paid for in blood by the Chinese people. By the spring of 1945, Wedemeyer in Chongqing was making hasty plans for American troop landings at Chinese ports and in Beijing, to pre-empt their seizure by the Communists when hostilities ended. The U.S. general was grudgingly obliged to recognise how formidable Communist forces and organisation had become. By summer, Mao's people in Yan'an displayed a notable smugness The mere fact of their survival against all expectations until the Japanese stood on the brink of defeat enabled them to stand poised to launch the only struggle which mattered to them: for the body and soul of China.

EIGHTEEN

Eclipse of Empires

ALTHOUGH JAPAN and Nazi Germany never significantly collaborated, the collapse of Hitler's regime plainly hastened the defeat of Japan, because it enabled the Allies to transfer significant, though not unlimited, resources to completing the destruction of Hirohito's shrinking empire. In the last weeks of the European war, Japanese emissaries in Berlin pestered leading Nazis in the hope of salvaging something for themselves from the wreckage of Hitler's arsenal. After considerable difficulties, naval representative Vice-Admiral Katsuo Abe secured an interview with Admiral Karl Dönitz on 15 April 1945, and another with Keitel and Ribbentrop on the seventeenth. He begged that the surviving German fleet, and especially its U-boats, should be sent to Japan. The Germans curtly informed Abe that only three of their submarines had sufficient range to make the voyage. Hitler refused to grant the admiral an audience. Ribbentrop explained to the Japanese that the Führer was "extremely busy." Though a handful of U-boats sought refuge in Japan's East Indies ports, embroiled in their own catastrophe the Germans cared unsurprisingly little about providing assistance to an ally close behind them on the brink of the abyss.

A British WRNS signaller, Peggy Wightman, wrote home from Mountbatten's headquarters in Ceylon on 19 April, amid reports that the German war was hastening towards its conclusion: "The news is terrific isn't it? I wonder what you are all feeling like. It is all so remote out here that I think we will all be feeling very funny when the day comes for your rejoicings." Captain Ronnie McAllister, with his Gurkha battalion in Burma, said: "The end of the war in Europe was all very nice, but it didn't mean a lot to us. Our horizon stretched way ahead. We thought we'd have to go into Siam."

On 8 May, a foolish young officer of the Border Regiment ran out in front of his company waving his hat and crying exultantly: "Men! The war in Europe is over!" He was crestfallen by the response: "There was a long silence, while we digested this, and looked through the heat haze to the village where Jap might be waiting . . . then someone laughed, and it ran down the extended line in a great torrent of mirth, punctuated by cries of 'Git the boogers oot here!" and 'Ev ye told Tojo, like?' " Yet Nimitz's Pacific Fleet Strategic Intelligence Section noted with jocular satisfaction on 21 May: "If, as reports have it, the German announcement of the death of Nazism's chief protagonist was accompanied by the massive strains of Wagner's requiem, 'Twilight of the Gods,' it is to the less decorous if more modern jangle of 'Don't Fence Me In' that Nippon, now a Lone Ranger astride a white horse, jogs dolefully towards the last round-up."

At midsummer 1945, major Allied ground operations against the Japanese were in recess. The armies of Slim in Burma, Krueger and Eichelberger in the Philippines, Stilwell—who, to widespread astonishment, was appointed Buckner's successor—on Okinawa, Blamey's Australians in Borneo and the south-west Pacific were engaged in mopping up. It was symbolic of the Japanese condition that some of their starving soldiers resorted to cannibalism. There were cases in New Guinea and Burma of downed Allied aircrew being eaten. Portions of beheaded U.S. carrier flier Marve Mershon were served to senior Japanese officers on Chichi Jima in February 1945, not because they needed the food, but to promote their own virility. Such gestures were not uncommon.

When driven by hunger to eat their own dead, Japanese soldiers favoured flesh cut from the thighs. An account from Biak Island described "many corpses lying round . . . with portions removed with a knife." A Japanese prisoner from the 108th Airfield Construction Unit described seeing three fresh civilian corpses lying in a pool of blood approximately fifteen feet from a jungle path, each with bayonet wounds in the chest, "and flesh was removed from thighs . . . There were many occasions when PW encountered Jap troops offering meat in exchange for potatoes." Even if some such reports were exaggerated, cannibalism was not infrequent among desperate soldiers in far-flung places.

Scattered enemy forces continued doggedly to reject surrender, and Allied soldiers were obliged to risk their lives to deal with them. On the night of 9 June, for instance, four Royal Navy motor launches took part in a characteristic little adventure up a river in southern Burma. Information was received from local people that Japanese were hiding nearby. Accompanied by a police inspector, Lt. Simon Mitchell led his boats up the Pebin until they reached a village named Payabyo. Police inquiries revealed that the Japanese had gone, but the British found a man whose sampan they had used for their escape. He took them to the place where he had deposited the fugitives. The British used loudhailers to summon the Japanese to give themselves up. Rewarded only by silence, the launches formed a line ahead and cruised upstream, pouring 15,000 rounds of automatic fire into the area behind the riverbank. Mitchell and his police companion then landed to make a cautious reconnaissance. To their surprise, and no doubt initial alarm, a Japanese officer and forty men emerged—and surrendered. A year earlier, such docility would have been unthinkable.

"From May onwards, prisoners in a terrible state came in daily," recorded a British gunner unit in Burma, "many of them armed with nothing more dangerous than bamboo spears, and trembling with a mixture of malaria and humiliation." Almost every Japanese soldier, sailor or airman who lived through the war, especially those posted to designated suicide units, afterwards felt obliged to offer elaborate excuses for his own survival. Most such explanations must be deemed fanciful. The truth, surely, was that a substantial number of young men found that the attraction of preserving their own lives overcame the pressures imposed upon them by the demented culture of *bushido*.

But if some proved ready to quit, others did not. To the end, most Japanese who lost their ships at sea deliberately evaded Allied rescuers. On the deck of HMS *Saumarez*, destroyer captain Martin Power was directing rescue operations after sinking a Japanese convoy off the Nicobars, when he suddenly heard a "clang" against the ship. Peering over the side, he saw a bald, heavily built Japanese clinging to a scrambling net with one hand, while hammering the nose of a shell against the hull with the other. Power drew his pistol, leaned over and whacked the man's head. "I could not think of anything else to do—I spoke no Japanese. Blood streaming down his face, he looked up at me, the pistol six inches from his eyes, the shell in his hand . . . I do not know how long I hung in this ridiculous position, eyeball to eyeball with a fanatical enemy, but it seemed too long at the time. At last he dropped the shell into the sea, brought up his feet, pushed off from the ship's side like an Olympic swimmer, turned on his face and swam away."

The main business of the Allies, following the conquest of Okinawa, was the maintenance of the blockade of Japan and the air bombardment by LeMay's B-29s, now joined by carrier aircraft of Third Fleet, together with preparations for Mountbatten's Operation Zipper, an amphibious landing by British and Indian forces on the coast of Malaya, to be staged in defiance of American disdain; finally, of course, there was Operation Olympic, the invasion of Kyushu, Japan's southern island. This was scheduled for November. Despite rumours that Nimitz or even Marshall himself might direct the operation, MacArthur was appointed. His subordinate commanders immersed themselves in the huge task of planning the assault, together with assessing likely Japanese responses. This would be the largest opposed landing in history, with fourteen divisions afloat and twenty-eight carriers deployed in support. Weighty volumes of documentation were prepared in anticipation. "Mass air attacks mixed with frequent small sorties will probably begin as soon as landing is imminent," stated a characteristic forecast from MacArthur's staff dated 25 April, entitled "Estimate of the enemy situation with respect to an operation against southern Kyushu in November 1945," "and continue with great violence until the enemy is convinced his efforts to prevent our landing and consolidation are unlikely to succeed . . . The enemy fleet . . . will probably launch a final desperate suicide attack during the approach or soon after landing. Intense submarine attack by both large and midget subs and 1 man suicide torpedoes may be expected."

MacArthur's behaviour was markedly unimproved by his new responsibilities. Throughout the Okinawa campaign he delivered a stream of criticisms of its conduct, oblivious of the fact that he himself had done no better in the Philippines. His relations with Nimitz worsened: there were persistent "turf wars" and arguments about resources. As late as 8 August, Navy Secretary James Forrestal urged that MacArthur should be replaced as Olympic commander, in the interests of inter-service relations and operational effectiveness. But the general's untiring publicity machine served him better than did his battlefield judgement. His prestige, the American public's belief that he was the embodiment of national retribution against Japan, rendered him unsackable. Forrestal, King and Nimitz were obliged to put up and shut up. If Olympic took place, however, it would be directed by an officer whose military competence and even mental stability seemed increasingly questionable.

One of the most difficult issues for the Allied high command was that of transferring formations from Europe to the Far East. Many British soldiers and civilians who had begun to keep diaries of the Second World War in September 1939 made their last entries in May 1945, perceiving the conflict as ended once the Germans were beaten. Almost every European veteran felt that he had done his part, and expected to go home. Some 5.2 million Americans were serving overseas, only 1.2 million of them in the Pacific. There was dismay in British and U.S. formations under Eisenhower's command when some were told that they would be required to invade Malaya or Japan.

Many men had amassed sufficient points to qualify for demobilisation, drastically weakening units' combat power. Intensive training of replacements was needed before any of Eisenhower's formations would be fit for their destined role in Operation Coronet, the post-Olympic assault on Honshu. For British soldiers in Burma, "repat"—repatriation—had become an obsession. Slim noted that a man in a foxhole, asked what he was, replied not "A Lancashire Fusilier," but "I'm four and two," or "three and ten," indicating his length of overseas service. The British Army reduced compulsory foreign service from four years to three years and eight months in January 1945, then again in June to three and four. The consequence was that thereafter many units found themselves abruptly stripped of experienced men, who were sent home. Slim saw no purpose in trying to hold back the time-expired: "It would have been not only unfair to land such men on Malayan beaches, but unwise."

Yet there were always some eager warriors, especially in special forces and airborne units. Maj.-Gen. James Gavin and other fiery spirits in the U.S. 82nd Airborne expressed disappointment that, after reaching the Elbe, they were offered no chance to fight the Japanese. Elements of British "private armies"—the Long Range Desert Group, Special Boat Service and suchlike—volunteered for the Asian theatre. A brigadier who signed himself "Crasher" Nicholls, commanding the "Special Allied Airborne Recce Force," which was being disbanded in Germany, wrote to SEAC on 1 June 1945, appealing for employment: "I am trying very hard to get myself included in something going to the Far East as I regard War [*sic*] as my job, and as long as there is a War on I want to be in it." By the summer of 1945, however, there were relatively few "Crasher" Nichollses. The higher commanders of the U.S. and British armies were alike dismayed by the prospect of needing to motivate soldiers for further battles when some comrades were already going home, and most were out of harm's way.

THE DUTCH, French and British owners of the old Eastern empires were increasingly preoccupied with regaining their lost territories—and conscious that they could expect scant help from the Americans to achieve this. "We must naturally be prepared for criticism from some quarters whatever we do," the British embassy in Washington observed to the Foreign Office on 13 May. "If we prosecute Eastern War with might and main, we shall be told by some people that we are really fighting for our colonial possessions the better to exploit them and that American blood is being shed to no better purpose than to help ourselves and Dutch and French to perpetuate our degenerate colonial Empires; while if we are judged not to have gone all out, that is because we are letting America fight her own war with little aid, after having let her pull our chestnuts out of the European fire." The U.S. Navy, said the embassy with a sigh, was prone to think both these things simultaneously.

Not only Japan's Asian possessions, but those of the European powers, were perceived to be "in play." Tensions between Britain and the U.S. grew, rather than diminished, as the war entered its final stage. MacArthur made plain that he had no desire for British participation in Olympic. A

Foreign Office official minuted bitterly: 'The Americans are virtually conducting political warfare against us in the Far East and are seeking not only to belittle the efforts which we have hitherto made in that theatre of war, but also to keep us in a humiliating and subsidiary role in the future." Harry Hopkins, Roosevelt's most intimate counsellor in Washington, did not dissent from such a view: "To hear some people talk . . . you would think the British were our potential enemies."

If the Americans were unenthusiastic about the resumption of British hegemony over Burma and Malaya, they were implacably hostile to French retention of Indochina. In 1945 the Japanese achieved a victory there which did nothing to improve their own strategic fortunes, but significantly influenced the future of South-East Asia. They had entered northern Indochina in 1940, to halt the flow of supplies to Nationalist China from the Vietnamese port of Haiphong. In 1941 they introduced 35,000 troops to secure for themselves the colony's rich resources of rice, rubber and tin. The Vichy French administration was permitted to continue in office; the French garrison kept its arms under Tokyo's orders; the hapless Vietnamese people were allowed to starve so that Japanese people might eat.

Early in 1945, however, de Gaulle's government in Paris demanded that the governor, Vice-Admiral Jean Catoux, should adopt a far more aggressive policy. As the local nationalist Vietminh under Ho Chi Minh spread their influence ever more widely, de Gaulle decided that France would only regain possession of Indochina by being seen to contribute to its liberation. The outcome was a disaster. On 9 March the Japanese staged a pre-emptive coup against the Saigon administration, seizing or massacring ill-equipped French troops who sought to resist. By 13 March, the Japanese claimed to have captured 8,500 POWs and killed a further thousand Frenchmen. Saigon Opera House became the Japanese interrogation and torture centre. With wildly confused loyalties, some French colonials found themselves held captive in prisons manned by French guards. Straggling columns of French fugitive soldiers sought to cut a path across country from Tonkin to the Chinese border, beset by both Japanese and Vietminh.

The British were eager to assist these survivors, on both humanitarian and political grounds. If Indochina fell into local nationalist hands, this would represent a disastrous precedent for Burma and Malaya. Yet the Americans, with bases and aircraft in neighbouring China, declined to lift a finger. This provoked one of the most bitter Anglo-American rows of the Japan war. Esler Dening, chief political adviser to Mountbatten, once observed acidly: "I often think that we might on important occasions remind ourselves that we are not yet the 49th of the United States." In

Paris, the enraged de Gaulle complained to U.S. ambassador Jefferson Caffery about the refusal of the U.S. air force in China to fly support missions to his people in Vietnam. He said that he found American policy incomprehensible: "What are you driving at? Do you want us to become, for example, one of the federated states under the Russian aegis?" In Washington, a State Department official minuted contemptuously: "I personally think that the French are making a great fuss over the Indo-China resistance for political reasons only in an effort to smoke out our policy."

Churchill cabled Washington on 19 March: "It will look very bad in history if we were to let the French force in Indochina be cut to pieces by the Japanese through shortage of ammunition, if there is anything we can do to save them." Marshall, however, delegated operational decisions to Wedemeyer in Chongqing, who pleaded logistical difficulties to justify American passivity. Such arguments seemed unconvincing. On 29 March, for instance, two C-47s of Tenth Air Force were dispatched from China to Tonkin to evacuate OSS personnel and six downed American airmen. Frenchmen at the strip where they landed were enraged when the planes arrived empty, without even cigarettes for the destitute colonists. An officer of the British Force 136 signalled: "American name is mud, repeat mud, with French and British alike in this whole episode."

The anti-colonialist policy of the Roosevelt administration in Washington was executed with utmost fervour by OSS teams operating in support of the Vietminh nationalists. American special forces' definition of Vietnamese liberation addressed French rather than Japanese occupation. Sebastian Patti of OSS explicitly told the Vietminh that they enjoyed the wholehearted support of the United States. Another OSS man described Ho Chi Minh as "an awfully sweet guy . . . If I had to pick out one quality about that little old man sitting on his hill in the jungle, it was his gentleness." Washington refused to allow troops of de Gaulle's Corps Leger to be deployed in Asia. French agents parachuted into Tonkin Province by British and Australian aircraft were killed by the Vietminh. After dreadful sufferings as they struggled through the jungles and mountains of northern Vietnam, some 5,000 French fugitives eventually reached China. They were greeted without enthusiasm by U.S. ambassador Patrick Hurley. Urging that they should quickly be removed elsewhere, he described them as "undisciplined, unequipped and destitute refugees and almost useless."

Relations worsened steadily between Wedemeyer in Chongqing and Mountbatten's headquarters at Kandy. On 30 May, the American general asked Washington to suspend lend-lease aid to British clandestine organisations in South-East Asia. He was chagrined to learn that this was impracticable, since in the China-Burma-India theatre U.S. forces were getting "considerable assistance from [the] British through reverse lend-lease." The "turf" dispute about Indochina was settled at Potsdam in July, when the combined chiefs of staff agreed to assign southern Indochina to SEAC, the north to China, at the Japanese surrender. Esler Dening wrote from Mountbatten's headquarters, however: "The division of French Indochina by the parallel of 16 degrees north . . . is going to cause a lot of trouble . . . The division is purely arbitrary and divides people of the same race, while raising new and unnecessary problems to divide French civil administration between here and [Chongqing]."

The consequence, of course, was that when the French returned, the Vietminh had gained a momentum which was to prove irreversible. The West had the worst of all possible worlds. The British showed poor judgement in supposing that the French *status quo ante* might be restored. The Americans allowed Ho Chi Minh to exploit U.S. support for his own political purposes, rather than in pursuit of the struggle against Japan. The cynicism of Wedemeyer and the OSS in denying even humanitarian aid to French troops after 9 March—when they were, after all, fighting the Japanese—invited dismay. The U.S. subsequently forfeited Indochinese goodwill by withdrawing its support from the Vietminh. Here was an ugly subplot to the war which did credit to no one.

A directive from the Political Warfare Executive in London to Mountbatten's command highlighted the political and cultural complexities besetting the theatre: "Keep off Russo-Japanese, Russo-Chinese and Sino-Japanese relations except for official statements. Do not comment on [Chongqing-Yan'an] relations . . . Continue to show that if Germany had prolonged her resistance the devastation would have been yet more terrible. Show that a worse fate awaits Japan if her militarists force her to fight on . . . Continue to avoid the alleged Japanese peace feelers." At Britain's Military Administration School in Wimbledon, and at the Malaya Planning Unit in London's Hyde Park Gate, intensive planning had been taking place for years, in anticipation of the restoration of imperial rule in the east. Many of those involved, however, especially younger officers and civil servants, perceived that they were crafting a hollow crown.

BRITAIN'S Royal Navy was embarrassed by its difficulties in sustaining a small fleet alongside the great American armada off Okinawa. In the spring of 1945, however, it conducted a series of little actions which helped to revive its battered self-esteem. First, on 15–16 May, a destroyer flotilla fought what proved to be the last significant battle between surface ships in the Second World War. Signals intelligence revealed that the 13,380-ton heavy cruiser *Haguro*, with the escorting destroyer *Kamikaze*, was sailing to the Andaman Islands in the Indian Ocean to deliver supplies and evacuate troops. After evading British submarines, *Haguro* was a hundred miles south-west of Phuket when spotted by a Fleet Air Arm Avenger shortly after noon on 15 May. *Saumarez*'s Captain Martin Power, leading five destroyers of "Force 61," headed to attack the Japanese at twenty-seven knots. Given the overwhelmingly superior firepower of *Haguro*'s eight-inch guns, Power hoped to delay an engagement until nightfall, then close with torpedoes. Lest he be in any doubt as to his duty, he received a terse signal from his admiral: "You should sink enemy ships before returning."

The British were relieved when dusk fell without a sighting. Thereafter, despite heavy rain which limited visibility, they were confident of defeating the Japanese when they found them. The destroyers steamed in line abreast, four miles apart, probing for electronic contact. At 2245, at an amazing range of 68,000 yards, *Venus*'s radar picked up the Japanese. An hour after midnight, the five British ships closed in a crescent on the enemy cruiser. *Haguro*, perceiving her danger, began to twist and turn, finally fleeing from the British at her full thirty-three knots. *Venus* missed a perfect chance to attack at almost point-blank range when her torpedo officer misjudged his settings. The British lit the sky with star shell, and began exchanging gunfire with *Haguro*. Splashes from Japanese near misses drenched the British bridge crews. Power said laconically: "If you're only getting wet, there's nothing to worry about." A few seconds later, however, a direct hit wrecked one of *Saumarez*'s boilers. The ship rapidly lost way. Power had one brief chance: he swung the destroyer violently to port and fired eight torpedoes at 2,000 yards. A minute later, *Verulam* dispatched her own salvo.

Three of these sixteen torpedoes achieved hits, throwing up waterspouts beside *Haguro*'s hull "like a Prince of Wales's feathers, more than twice as high as her bridge." *Saumarez* was now hit again, however. Scalding steam burst through the boiler room, killing several men in the most horrible fashion. A terrified bridge lookout abandoned his post and fled below, which caused him later to be court-martialled, dismissed the service and sentenced to six months' imprisonment for cowardice in the face of the enemy. The captain's secretary, supposing from the ship's violent manoeuvres that the helmsman was disabled, engaged the emergency steering aft the funnel. In a spirit which might have won Japanese admiration, an excited petty officer urged the secretary to ram the enemy. Power quickly resumed control, however, and watched *Venus* put another "fish" into the stricken cruiser, whose decks were now awash.

Errant torpedoes swerved in all directions, narrowly missing British ships. The engineer officer of *Saumarez* ordered every other man out of the boiler room before manhandling an unexploded Japanese eight-inch shell up to the deck, aided by a petty officer. He then had his little joke, reporting the lethal projectile's presence to the bridge before adding: "But don't worry, I've thrown it over the side." The flotilla crowded the Japanese cruiser, "snarling round the carcass like a lot of starving wolves round a dying bull." At 0206, *Venus* reported *Haguro* sunk. The British used searchlights to conduct a perfunctory scan of her resting place without finding any survivors, then hastened away to open the distance between themselves and Japanese airfields before dawn. The slightly damaged *Kamikaze* later recovered some of the cruiser's crew.

British submarines operated with increasing energy against Japanese shipping off Malaya and the Dutch East Indies, but the most spectacular exploit was performed by midgets. It was a fantastically dangerous business, conning tiny underwater vessels into enemy harbours. Italians pioneered such techniques, the Japanese used them unsuccessfully, the British refined them. In 1944, Royal Navy "X-Craft" seriously damaged the battleship *Tirpitz* in a Norwegian fjord. When the first "XE-Craft" reached Brisbane in April, the British were crestfallen to discover that the Americans had no interest in promoting their operations. It might be politically necessary for the U.S. Navy to endure a token British presence in the Pacific, but King and his subordinates had no intention of providing opportunities for piratical British adventures—or, as the Royal Navy believed, for the publicity that might accompany successes.

Only in July did the little XE-Craft flotilla get its chance, after a spell of training in which two divers died of oxygen poisoning. Towed by conventional submarines with passage crews, five midgets were dispatched to cut telegraph cables off Hong Kong and Saigon—and, most spectacularly, to attack the heavy cruisers *Myoko* and *Takao* at Singapore. Early on the morning of 31 July, having slipped the tows from their parent ships, Lts. Ian Fraser and John Smart steered two three-man boats up the Johore Strait. That afternoon, Fraser took *XE-3* under *Takao*'s hull. His crewman, Jim Magennis, then emerged from a hatch in frogman kit, to dump the boat's two big mines under the Japanese cruiser.

It was a hair-raising business. First, one charge refused to unlock from *XE-3*'s hull. Then, when Magennis re-entered the boat, for several minutes it appeared that a falling tide had trapped the submarine beneath *Takao*'s bottom. *XE-1*, delayed by encounters with Japanese patrol craft, laid its own mines under the same cruiser. The two little boats made good their escape. That night the charges exploded, severely damaging the cruiser and winning Victoria Crosses for Fraser and Magennis. Strategically, in those last weeks of war their feat was irrelevant. But such small triumphs delighted the Royal Navy, so eager to be seen to contribute to the defeat of Japan.

ONCE OKINAWA was secured and American ground-based aircraft deployed there, the U.S. Navy was at last free to launch an air offensive against the Japanese home islands, which began on 10 July 1945. The first raids were exploratory, probing resistance as American planes struck at strips in the Tokyo plain. Thereafter they attacked with increasing confidence, against ineffectual Japanese defences. The most devastating missions were launched on 14–15 July, against the sea links between Honshu and Hokkaido islands. Of twelve rail ferries, eight were sunk outright and the remainder badly damaged. Shipments to Honshu of coal, lifeblood of Japanese industry, were more than halved overnight. The Japanese had no means of replacing the ferries.

Between air strikes American battleships, joined by the Royal Navy's *King George V*, bombarded coastal industrial installations. Flat-trajectory naval gunfire was much less effective than incendiary attack by B-29s, but drove home to the Japanese that they could now be struck with impunity from the sea as well as the air. Hundreds of planes were destroyed on the ground by carrier strikes, though many more remained camouflaged and dispersed miles from any airfield, awaiting MacArthur's invasion. Inshore shipping was ravaged at will. American aircraft mounted an average of two sorties a day apiece, for a cumulative daily total of more than 2,000. Weather was the chief impediment to Halsey's operations, with thick fogs and heavy seas often frustrating ships' refuelling as well as flying. Isolated kamikaze attacks on the fleet were intercepted and broken up, while the Americans maintained standing fighter patrols—"the big blue blanket"—over mainland airfields, to frustrate enemy take-offs. When the Japanese mounted night counter-attacks, Halsey withdrew his ships further offshore, not from fear that they might be sunk, but because his pilots needed their sleep.

Beyond destruction of the Hokkaido ferries, a critical contribution to the paralysis of Japanese industry, substantive damage inflicted by the carrier planes—"the little ones," as civilians called them—was limited. But the spectacle of Halsey's airborne host overhead, often flying so low that civilians could see pilots' faces, made a deep impression on morale. Hunger and despair were eroding the spirit of the Japanese people, however strong the residual commitment of their soldiers. At Osaka University, students routinely ate locusts boiled in soy sauce and *sake*. Lunch might consist of twenty or thirty insects, half a potato and a salted plum.

Yoshiko Hashimoto, who had survived the March Tokyo air raid in which her parents died and her sister Etsuko was terribly burned, said of this time: "In the last months, the food situation became worse and worse. The black market became an open, public institution." Yoshiko had to feed two sisters, of whom one was desperately injured. She struggled to get medicines for Etsuko, until such things could no longer be bought for any money. All the girl's burns eventually healed except those on her hands, which never received the treatment that might have restored them. To the end of her life, in company Etsuko concealed her hands behind her back.

Col. Saburo Hayashi acknowledged the growing unpopularity of the military, still privileged people among the civilian population: "There was disorderly behaviour by officers and men occupying billets in towns and villages; the military were especially selfish in their attitude to food. Their actions, which provoked intense public hostility, can be attributed to the poor quality of manpower now reaching the armed forces because of the scale of national mobilisation." So desperate was Japan's lack of fuel that millions of civilians, including many children, were committed to digging out pine roots, from which oil might be extracted. Some 37,000 local distillation units produced 70,000 barrels, yielding just 3,000 barrels of aviation spirit.

Each night when Petty Officer Kisao Ebisawa finished duty at Yokosuka naval base, he walked home to a doctor's house in town, where he shared a billet with his wife, Fumiyo. After years at sea, he was grateful for a shore posting which spared him from the fate of his brother, lost aboard a transport in the Pacific. At Yokosuka, naval rations provided the Ebisawas with enough to eat, but even at the base shortages were endemic. In the absence of fuel, sailors provided traction when trucks were used to move equipment.

The Ebisawas' landlord was the matchmaker who had introduced the couple. Fumiyo was a teacher, now a heavily pregnant one, who possessed much of the legendary toughness of Yokosuka people. "I always felt that if anything should happen to me, she would be able to look after herself and the baby," said Ebisawa. They talked between themselves about the future, after Japan's inevitable defeat. Before Ebisawa was called up he had worked for Mitsukoshi, the famous Tokyo department store. He reckoned the firm would take him back, but did not expect to live to apply.

Zero engineer Jiro Horikoshi went to Nagoya station to bid farewell to his wife as he dispatched her to the safety of the countryside. On the platform, contemplating his country's predicament, he burst into tears: "Those of us who knew the awesome industrial strength of the U.S. never really believed that Japan would win this war. We were convinced that our government must intend some diplomatic initiative which would save the situation before it became catastrophic. But now, bereft of any convincing government initiative to enable us to escape, we are being driven to our doom."

Hirohito's people could see for themselves that their defenders had lost control of Japan's airspace. Bombers from the Philippines attacked targets around Formosa and off Korea. LeMay's Superfortresses, in formations up to a thousand strong, broadcast fire by day and night. The Americans dominated sea and sky. Japan's home air bases descended into a routine of alarms and damage control. At Hyakuri, for instance, Petty Officer Hachiro Miyashita gave up trying to reach a slit trench when he glimpsed American fighters—they approached so low that shelter was unattainable. He simply threw himself on the ground as shrapnel rattled down like hail after each bomb explosion. The crews enlisted the aid of soldiers from a neighbouring recruit camp to push aircraft deep into woodland, where they were concealed until immediately before take-off.

USAAF captain Jack Lee DeTour's group commander was obsessed with a desire to sink an aircraft carrier before the end of the war, and was killed making the attempt off Kyushu. DeTour's unit spent the spring flying B-25s out of the Philippines against ships, railyards and fuel-alcohol plants on Formosa. They attacked from heights between 5,000 and 10,000 feet, using a mix of bombs, rockets and machine-gun fire. Shipping strikes were by far the most dangerous, requiring lower-altitude attacks, with a five-second delay on bomb fuses to enable planes to jink clear after attacking. DeTour, a garage owner's son from a small town in Nebraska, was twenty-two, and had been in the war a long time. Frustrated in his ambition to become a fighter pilot, he flew nine hundred hours before entering combat in New Guinea. He spent the summer of 1945 attacking Japanese convoys from a strip on Okinawa. The American pilots fell upon one cluster of enemy shipping, two squadrons strong, off the Korean coast. DeTour was dismayed to see one of his former flight students going down, hit by flak. The bombers hit a destroyer and a merchantman. He was awed by the sight of the stricken ships' disappearance: "It seemed unbelievable that something that big went down so fast."

Admiral "Jocko" Clark of Halsey's Task Force 38 was disgusted to discover that one of his Helldiver commanders, finding a target fogged in, had jettisoned bombs in the sea rather than drop them randomly on Japan: "When I took him to task he said he did not want to kill innocent civilians . . . But any damage to the enemy in war contributed to destroying his willingness to fight. I told this strike leader that he should have dropped his bombs on Mount Fuji, rather than waste them."

If American losses were relatively small, the price of being shot down and captured was always high, not infrequently fatal. On 25 July, Ensign Herb Law flew from the carrier *Belleau Wood* to attack Yokkaichi-shi airfield on Honshu. "We had the usual fun strafing and rocket-firing . . . I was saving my bomb for a juicy target. Just as we were pulling out at low altitude bullets began hitting my plane. My first thought was that it was AA. Much to my surprise, there was a Jap plane directly behind me . . . Where the hell he came from I'll never know. My engine cut out completely, and he got in some more gunnery practice while I looked for a place to land." Law was too low to parachute, and crashed in a field, where he sat on a wing examining a wound in his leg. He enjoyed his first glimpse of the enemy when a Japanese woman approached, and emptied a pistol towards him without effect. Ten minutes later he was encircled by a fiercely hostile crowd, who stripped him naked. He was eventually taken to Osaka: "I had no food or water for three days. I was beaten with clubs, fists, leather straps every day and night. I had lighted cigarettes put to my lips. It is surprising what a man can take and still live."

Halsey deliberately excluded British aircraft from Third Fleet's last strikes against the Japanese navy, claiming to have fallen in with his chief of staff's views: "At Mick Carney's insistence I assigned the British an alternative target. Mick's argument was that although this division of force violated the principle of concentration, it was imperative that we forestall a possible post-war claim by the British that [they] had delivered even a part of the final blow that demolished the Japanese fleet."

Two FUNDAMENTAL propositions still underpinned Japanese strategic reasoning: first, that the Americans must invade their home islands in order to claim victory; second, that in such an eventuality, they could be repelled. All the elements used to such effect on Okinawa would be deployed manifold on Kyushu: fixed defences, kamikaze aircraft, suicide boats, "*oka*" rocket-propelled suicide bombs, suicide anti-tank units. The Japanese army's newly issued *Field Manual for the Decisive Battle in the Homeland* called for absolute ruthlessness in slaughtering any Japanese, old or young, male or female, who impeded the defence or was used as a shield by the invaders. There would be no retreats. Casualties were to be abandoned. Those whose weapons and ammunition were spent should fight with bare hands. Here was a commitment to create not merely an army of suicidalists, but an entire nation.

At Yokosuka naval base, Kisao Ebisawa was instructing a new unit of "*fukuryu*"—"dragon divers"—destined for suicide missions against American landing craft. Many of the 4,000 pupils were teenagers, some as young as fourteen or fifteen. Their only asset was a sacrificial commitment, matching that of the Hitler Youth in Europe. Ebisawa and his fellow petty officers, recognising that the war was lost, recoiled from the enterprise to which these children were committed. "Whoever dreamed it up knew nothing about diving," said the sailor. "First, anyone who had seen the Americans in the Pacific knew that they bombed and shelled everything in sight before making a landing. Shock-waves would kill any diver in the water for miles. *Fukuryu* were supposed to attack in groups, each one carrying a pole charge. It needed only one charge to detonate, for the whole group to go up in smoke. It would have made more sense to pack all those kids off to the mountains to wait for the Americans with grenades." Some instructors were rash enough to make representations to their superiors along these lines, causing them to be posted out of the unit. Thereafter, Ebisawa and his colleagues kept their mouths shut, though they were painfully conscious of the chasm between the enthusiasm of their young students and the cynicism of their commanders.

At his airfield outside Singapore, Lt. Masaichi Kikuchi was deeply unwilling to become a human sacrifice, but *gyokusai*, duty to fight to the last, was deeply instilled in his generation. "It was all a matter of upbringing and education. This was what we had been taught was required of us." Month after month Kikuchi and his unit supervised working parties of Allied prisoners, digging a maze of tunnels, trenches and bunkers for the great defensive battle against a British landing which their commanders were sure would come. Officers made black jokes to each other: "These holes are going to be our graves. We'd better dig them good."

Toshiharu Konada and his fellow midshipmen on the heavy cruiser *Ashigara* volunteered for submarine service when it became plain that Japan's remaining big ships were going nowhere useful. Konada, by then a lieutenant, spent a fortnight at the submarine school at Otake before he and thirteen others in his draft were abruptly informed that they were being transferred to man new weapons named *kaiten*—"heaven-shakers." They had no notion what *kaiten* were, until they reached a training base on the island of Ohtsu. There, at last, they were admitted to the secret. Their craft were human torpedoes, piloted by frogmen sitting astride them. Their commanders claimed that these would transform Japan's fortunes, destroying the enemy's ships as they approached the home islands.

Konada's group were thrilled. "This was a role which made us really happy and excited," he said. Class photographs of himself and his beaming young comrades support this claim. They were all twenty-one-year-olds: "We felt that *kaiten* offered us an opportunity to make a personal difference to the course of the war, to save our country, even." Some 1,375 pilots entered training, but only 150 completed the course before the war's end, because of a shortage of torpedoes. A further fifteen died in training, for *kaiten* were immensely dangerous to their operators. Some pilots suffered respiratory failures, others steered their craft into rocks or were lost in rough seas.

Konada found the atmosphere on his course "very tense and serious; but it was also a very exciting experience." When his detail graduated in December 1944, he himself was retained at Ohtsu for four months to help train the next intake. He found this frustrating, "because I wanted to get on with the job." It became more so as he heard the fate of comrades of his own course, already dispatched against the enemy. There was his roommate Kentaro Yoshimoto, "a very jolly fellow, though not very bright. We used to talk for hours about everything—except the war or death." Yoshimoto and his torpedo were launched on a mission in the Carolines on 20 December, which ended in an anticlimactic technical failure. He set forth on a second operation on 12 January 1945, and was never heard of again.

Likewise Seizo Ishikawa, who had served with Konada in the gunroom of *Ashigara*, "a bold character of passionate loyalties, with a very sharp tongue." Ishikawa's torpedo was launched from the submarine *I-58* off Guam on 12 January. Pilots at the home bases never learned the fates of these men and scores of others, though American records show that they achieved little. By the summer of 1945, to Konada's embarrassment, he found himself the only survivor of the fourteen men in his training detail designated to wear the suicides' white headband. However, his turn seemed sure to come soon enough. In May he was dispatched to command a unit of eight *kaiten* on the island of Hachijo, in the Pacific 140 miles south of Tokyo. The Americans were expected to land on Hachijo before they assaulted the mainland. The *kaiten* crews practiced launches in all manner of tactical circumstances, and worked incessantly on maintaining their frail craft. Konada said proudly: "It was the most rewarding time of my life."

All through the summer of 1945, Japan poured men onto Kyushu, to confront the expected American landings. In January, there had been only one garrison division on the island. Thereafter, the build-up was relentless. American historians Edward Drea and Richard Frank have made important contributions to the study of this period, by highlighting the scale of Japanese reinforcement in the first seven months of the year—almost all revealed to the Americans through signal decrypts. By the end of July, thirteen field divisions were deployed on Kyushu, 450,000 Japanese servicemen, all digging hard. At least 10,000 aircraft would be available to support the defence.

The critical question, of course, was whether these forces represented anything like as grave a threat to an American landing as their raw numbers might suggest. Most of the available planes were trainers or obsolete types, though as kamikazes even these could be deadly. The *kaiten* and *fukuryu* units could be dismissed, likewise Japan's surviving surface ships. Ground formations were as short of firepower and training as all Japanese forces at this stage, although experience in the Philippines and on Okinawa had shown that even raw Japanese units could achieve remarkable results, if their men were committed to death and entrenched in fixed positions. Yet by November 1945, after months of LeMay's planned bombardment of Japanese transport links, food for the military as well as civilian population would be desperately short. As we shall see, the Soviets rolled up Japan's armies in Manchuria with relative ease.

Japanese combat effectiveness in the face of Olympic will never be susceptible of proof. It can only be said that it seems mistaken to judge the fitness of Hirohito's armies to mount "Ketsu"—the operation to defend Kyushu—merely in terms of troop and aircraft numbers. It is possible to speculate that the defences would have crumbled relatively quickly. But no responsible American commander could make such an assumption *at the time*. The only one who did so, MacArthur, merely emphasised his own hubris when he dismissed overwhelming evidence of the enemy's build-up on Kyushu in a signal to Marshall on 9 August: "Throughout the southwest Pacific Area campaigns," said the supreme commander, "as we have neared an operation intelligence has invariably pointed to greatly increased enemy forces. Without exception, this build-up has been found to be erroneous."

This observation represented the reverse of the truth, of course. Again and again in the Pacific, MacArthur had chosen wilfully to underestimate enemy strength, to follow his own hunches rather than to heed signals intelligence. Now, fantastically, he suggested that the enemy was deliberately generating exaggerated information about its own strength, to deceive U.S. intelligence. Richard Frank has written: "It is almost impossible not to believe that MacArthur's resort to falsehood was motivated in large measure by his personal interest in commanding the greatest amphibious assault in history."

Until the last day of the war, MacArthur and his staff continued to plan for Olympic. Yet nobody, with the possible exception of the general, wanted to launch the operation. A British infantryman, gazing at bloated corpses on a Burman battlefield, vented the anger and frustration common to almost every Allied soldier in those days, about the enemy's rejection of reason: "Ye stupid sods! Ye stupid Japanni sods! Look at the fookin' state of ye! Ye wadn't listen—an' yer all fookin' dead! Tojo's way! Ye dumb bastards! Ye coulda bin suppin' chah an' screwin' geeshas in yer fookin' lal paper " 'ooses—an' look at ye! Ah doan't knaw." However the statistics of the Japanese build-up on Kyushu were interpreted, they promised heavy American casualties—of an order of magnitude of at least 100,000.

In an "eyes only" signal to King on 25 May, Nimitz wrote: "Unless [Olympic] is considered so important that we are willing to accept less than best preparation and more than minimum casualties, I believe that the long-range interests of the U.S. will be better served if we continue to isolate Japan and to destroy Japanese forces and resources by naval and air attack." The Pacific C-in-C's resistance to an invasion did not diminish in the months that followed. With the ending of the war in Europe, millions of Allied soldiers had been liberated from the risk of death, and were beginning to go home. In such circumstances, it seemed deeply repugnant that a hapless minority of Americans should again be exposed to mortal peril. Japan's military leaders remained committed to a "decisive battle" for the homeland. The United States, however, was most unwilling to accommodate them.

An age before, in 1942, on Joseph Grew's return from service as U.S. ambassador in Japan, he was dismayed by the American people's abysmal ignorance of their enemy. He delivered lectures around the country, in an attempt to increase understanding of the magnitude of the task which the U.S. faced in overcoming this formidable foe. Grew described his shock on hearing an intelligent American assert blithely: "Of course there must be ups and downs in this war . . . but it's now a question of time before Hitler will go down to defeat—and then we'll mop up the Japs." The events of August 1945 would display, in the most awesome and terrible fashion, the culmination of the process once so insouciantly described as "mopping up the Japs."

NINETEEN

The Bombs

1. Fantasy in Tokyo

IN THE FINAL PHASE of the Second World War, Allied generals and admirals played a minor role in the decisions which precipitated Japan's surrender. These will remain a focus of controversy until the end of time, first, because of the use of atomic bombs; second, because the mountain of historical evidence, detailing the principal actors' words and deeds, stands so high. Much of it invites inconclusive or even contradictory interpretation. Leading figures changed their minds, some more than once. Several wrote disingenuously afterwards, to justify their own actions. The Japanese aspect of the story is rendered opaque by a familiar chasm between what the nation's leaders said, and what each afterwards claimed or is conjectured privately to have thought.

From the winter of 1944 onwards, a significant party in Tokyo was seeking a route by which to end the war, and to overcome the army's resolve to fight to the last. Even the most dovish, however, wanted terms that were not remotely negotiable, including the preservation of Japanese hegemony in Korea and Manchuria, freedom from Allied military occupation, and the right for Japan to conduct any war crimes trials of its citizens. As late as May 1945, the emperor clung to a belief that a victory was attainable on Okinawa, which would strengthen Japan's negotiating position—in other words, that military resistance was still serviceable. On 9 June, he urged the Japanese people to "smash the inordinate ambitions of the enemy nations."

The "peace party" thought and spoke as if Japan could expect to be treated as an honourable member of the international community. There was no acknowledgement of the fact that, in Western eyes, the behaviour of the Japanese since Pearl Harbor, indeed since 1931, had placed their nation beyond the pale. Japan's leaders wasted months asserting diplomatic positions founded upon the demands of their own self-esteem, together with supposed political justice. In reality, their only chance of modified terms derived from Allied fears that a host of men would have to die if an invasion of the homeland proved necessary. As blockade and bombardment, together with the prospects of atomic bombs and Russian entry into the Pacific theatre, progressively diminished the perceived American need to risk invasion, Japan held no cards at all.

Nothing more vividly reflected Tokyo's misreading of its own predicament than its attempts to enlist the good offices of the Soviet Union as an intermediary. Russian abstention from belligerency until August 1945 was among the odder aspects of the global conflict. In April 1941 it served the interests of both Russia and Japan to conclude a five-year Neutrality Pact. Japan's ambitions lay south and eastwards. It needed to secure itself from a threat in the rear. Likewise, even before Russia became committed to its death struggle with Germany, Moscow wanted no complications in Asia. When Hitler's Operation Barbarossa was launched in June 1941, Stalin was thankful to be assured by Richard Sorge, his legendary agent in Tokyo, that Japan would not attack Russia, and thus that the Red Army could safely throw everything into the western war.

Yet if peace on the Russo-Manchurian border suited the two neighbours for three years, by 1944 it no longer suited the United States. A million Japanese soldiers in China might sooner or later be committed against the Americans. An invasion of Manchuria by the Red Army offered the most obvious means of deflecting such a redeployment. Stalin's masses could reprise what they were so spectacularly doing in Europe—saving the lives of Western Allied soldiers by expending those of Russians. As late as 6 August 1945, MacArthur told an off-the-record press briefing in Manila of his eagerness for the Soviets to invade Manchuria: "Every Russian killed is one less American who has to be."

Churchill and Roosevelt were thrilled by Stalin's September 1944 promise to launch sixty Soviet divisions against Japan within three months of Germany's collapse. "When we are vexed with other matters," the prime minister wrote to FDR, "we must remember the supreme value of this [commitment] in shortening the whole struggle." MacArthur was firmly of the view that "we must not invade Japan proper unless the Russian army is previously committed to action in Manchuria." Marshall concurred. American field commanders wanted all the help they could get to diminish the numbers of enemy they might have to confront in the Japanese home islands. From Luzon, Maj.-Gen. Joseph Swing of 11th Airborne Division wrote home in May, dismissing reported British fears about the perils of admitting the Soviets to the Asian war: "Everybody wants the Roosh as soon as he will come and the more the merrier. As to what Uncle Joe Stalin will get in the East . . . he'll demand and probably get anything he wants."

Washington recognised that the Russians would not fight unless they received tangible rewards for doing so. To destroy the Nazis, the Soviet

Union had already contributed twenty-five times the human sacrifice made by all the Western Allies together. After months of equivocation, at Yalta Stalin presented his invoice for an eastern commitment. Moscow wanted from Japan the Kurile Islands and southern Sakhalin; from China, the lease of Port Arthur, access to Dalian as a free port, control of the southern Manchurian railway, and recognition of Russian suzerainty over Outer Mongolia. On the fifth day of the conference, 8 February 1945, Roosevelt agreed to accept Moscow's terms. The U.S. president acted with colonialist insouciance, making important Chinese territorial concessions without consulting the Chinese government. But these arrangements were nominally subject to Chiang Kai-shek's endorsement, and in return Moscow pledged to recognise the Nationalists as China's sole legitimate rulers. Both the Soviet and American delegations went home from Yalta well pleased with their bargain, indifferent to the fact that it would violate the Russo-Japanese Neutrality Pact.

Yet in offering incentives, Roosevelt ignored the fact that Stalin never did—or forbore from doing—anything unless it fitted his own agenda. In 1945, far from the Russians requiring encouragement to invade Manchuria, it would have been almost impossible to dissuade them from doing so. As soon as Germany was beaten, Stalin was bent upon employing his armies to collect Asian booty. Ironies were thus densely woven into the events of the five months following Yalta. On 22 February, the Japanese ambassador in Moscow, Naotake Sato, a former foreign minister, called on Vyacheslav Molotov, Stalin's foreign minister, on his return from the Crimean conference. Sato was assured that bilateral Russo–Japanese relations, the future of the two countries' neutrality pact, had nothing to do with the Americans and the British. This bland deceit was gratefully received in Tokyo. Japan sought Russian goodwill to salvage its tottering empire at exactly the moment Stalin secretly committed himself to loot it.

As the Russians planned and armed for an August descent on Manchuria, however, American enthusiasm for their participation began to falter. Even if U.S. military leaders were eager to see the Red Army committed, politicians and diplomats were much more equivocal. European experience suggested that whatever Stalin's armies conquered, they kept. It seemed rash to indulge further Russian expansionism in Asia. By April 1945, some important Americans would have been happy to break the bargain made with Stalin in February, if they could justify doing so. The Russians, conscious of this, thenceforward possessed the strongest possible interest in ensuring that the Japanese kept fighting. If Tokyo made peace with Washington before Stalin had shifted his armies eastwards and was ready to declare war, the Americans might renege on the rewards promised at Yalta.

Japanese politicians, with extraordinary naïveté, acted in the belief that wooing neutral Russia would serve them better than addressing belligerent America. In reality, there was more willingness among some Western politicians than in Moscow to consider concessions in return for an early end of bloodshed. Winston Churchill was the first and most important Allied leader to propose qualifying the doctrine of unconditional surrender in respect of Japan. Before the combined chiefs of staff in Cairo on 9 February 1945, he argued that "some mitigation would be worthwhile, if it led to the saving of a year or a year and a half of a war in which so much blood and treasure would be poured out." Roosevelt dismissed the prime minister out of hand. British influence on this issue, as indeed upon everything to do with the Pacific war, ranged between marginal and non-existent. The decisions about how to address the Japanese, whether by force or parley, rested unequivocally in Washington.

A strong party in the State Department, headed by former Tokyo ambassador Joseph Grew, now undersecretary of state, favoured a public commitment to allow Japan to retain its national polity, the *kokutai*, of which the most notable feature was the status of the emperor. Grew and his associates believed that the *kokutai* mattered vastly more to the Japanese than it should to anyone else: if assurances on this point would avert a bloodbath in the home islands, they should be given. Secretary of War Henry Stimson and Navy Secretary James Forrestal agreed, as did some media opinion formers. The British embassy in Washington reported to London on 13 May: "There are notes . . . not merely in the ex-isolationist press but eg the *Washington Post*, of the possibility of some modification of unconditional surrender in [Japan's] case and optimistic speculation of likelihood of her early surrender when she perceives the hopelessness of her case, and woven into popular desire for Russian participation in the Pacific War there runs a thin but just perceptible thread, the thought that an American settlement of that area would best be made if USSR were kept out of it."

Yet the White House and its most influential advisers believed that American public opinion would recoil from concessions to the perpetrators of Pearl Harbor, among whom the emperor was symbolically foremost; and that generosity was anyway unnecessary. Japan's predicament was worsening rapidly. The principal uncertainty focused upon whether it would be necessary to invade the home islands. Among U.S. chiefs of staff, Admiral Ernest King, for the navy, and Gen. "Hap" Arnold of the USAAF opposed a ground invasion. While their desire to avoid another bloody campaign was no doubt sincere, both men also had partisan agendas, well understood in Washington. King wanted the world to see that Japan had been defeated by the U.S. Navy and its blockade. Arnold sought recognition of strategic bombing's decisive contribution, in pursuit of his crusade to make the Army Air Forces an independent service. King and Arnold could invoke important opinion in support of their case. Early in April, the U.S. Joint Intelligence Committee predicted that "the increasing effects of air-sea blockade, the progressive cumulative devastation wrought by strategic bombing, and the collapse of Germany" would soon oblige the Japanese to acknowledge that they could not continue the war.

Yet as Germany foundered, King and Arnold allowed themselves to be persuaded that planning must continue for Olympic. Marshall, although he had never been enthusiastic, "went firm." However unwelcome, the invasion option must be kept open. Given the lead time indispensable to a huge amphibious operation, a commitment was needed forthwith. Experience, especially at Iwo Jima and Okinawa, showed that the enemy exploited every day of grace to strengthen his defences, and thus to raise the cost of delaying invasion. The chiefs of staff were also concerned that the American people's patience with the war was ebbing, and thus that it was essential to hasten a closure in the east. On 25 April the joint chiefs of staff adopted JCS 924/15, endorsing Olympic. Their memorandum, which should be regarded as prudent recognition of a contingency, rather than as an ironclad commitment, was forwarded to the president—the very new president—of the United States.

Harry Truman has come to be regarded as one of America's outstanding national leaders of the twentieth century. In the spring of 1945, however, this decent, simple, impulsive man was all but overwhelmed by the burden of office thrust upon him by Roosevelt's death on 12 April. "I felt like the moon, the stars and all the planets had fallen upon me," he told reporters on the afternoon that he was sworn in. "Boys, if you ever pray, pray for me now." One journalist said: "Good luck, Mr. President." Truman said: "I wish you didn't have to call me that." By one of Roosevelt's most hubristic omissions, given the desperate state of his own health, he had made no attempt to ensure that his vice-president was briefed to address the vast issues which now fell to his lot. Until 12 April, Truman was not even a recipient of Magic intelligence bulletins. Those who observed him closely during his first months at the White House believed that much he said and did was motivated by insecurity, a desire to appear authoritative and decisive, though within himself he felt equipped to be neither. Such self-awareness deserves the sympathy of posterity.

On 10 May, responding to perceived Russian breaches of faith in Europe, Truman directed that lend-lease supplies to the Soviet Union should be terminated. Grew and Averell Harriman, U.S. ambassador in Moscow, wanted him to go further, and repudiate the Asian provisions of Yalta. Stimson dissuaded the president from these courses, observing that "the concessions . . . to Russia on Far Eastern matters . . . are . . . within the military power of Russia to obtain regardless of U.S. military action short of war." But Truman's conduct in the months that followed was dominated by a determination to prove his own fitness for office, above all by making no unnecessary concessions to the bullying of the Soviet Union, and by conducting the last phase of the war against Japan with a conviction worthy of his great predecessor, and of his great nation. He now discovered that science promised an extraordinary tool to further these ends.

On 24 April Truman received from Stimson a letter requesting a meeting to discuss "a highly secret matter." Next day, the secretary of war and Maj.-Gen. Leslie Groves, senior officer responsible for the Manhattan Project, revealed to the new president its secrets, about which he had previously received only intimations. "Within four months," wrote Stimson, "we shall in all probability have completed the most terrible weapon ever known in human history, one bomb of which could destroy a whole city." Groves was bent on dropping two, to prove to the Japanese that the first nuclear explosion represented no unique phenomenon.

The Manhattan Project represented the most stupendous scientific effort in history. In three years, at a cost of $2 billion, the U.S.—with some perfunctorily acknowledged British aid—had advanced close to fulfilling a programme which much of the scientific world had thought unattainable, certainly within a time frame relevant to this conflict. At Truman's meeting with Stimson and Groves, he was not warned that he must make a great decision, confront a historic dilemma. He was merely informed of the new weapon's impending maturity. There was no hint of looming controversy. Rather, there was an absolute assumption that if the Japanese continued to fight, atomic bombs would be used against them, as had been every other available destructive tool to advance the conflict's ending.

Technological determinism is an outstanding feature of great wars. At a moment when armadas of Allied bombers had been destroying the cities of Germany and Japan for three years, killing civilians in hundreds of thousands, the notion of withholding a vastly more impressive means of fulfilling the same purpose scarcely occurred to those directing the Allied war effort. They were irritated, indeed exasperated, by intimations of personal scruple from scientists concerned with the weapon's construction. As long as Hitler survived, the Manhattan team had striven unstintingly to build a bomb, haunted by fear that the Nazis might get there first. Once Germany was defeated, however, some scientists' motivation faltered. Their doubts and apprehensions grew about the purposes to which their efforts might be turned.

A group in Chicago formed a "committee of social and political implications" which became known as the Franck Committee. Its members argued in a report submitted to Washington: "The military advantages and the saving of American lives achieved by the sudden use of atomic bombs against Japan may be outweighed by the ensuing loss of confidence and by a wave of horror and revulsion sweeping over the rest of the world and perhaps even dividing public opinion at home." In May 1945, some Manhattan team members made determined efforts to caution America's political leaders. Several wrote letters to the president. Leo Szilard, one of the foremost Chicago scientists, paid a personal visit to the White House. Truman's secretary diverted him to Spartanburg, South Carolina, home of James Byrnes, the president's personal representative on the bomb committee.

Byrnes enjoyed one of the more unusual careers in American history. Sixty-six in 1945, a self-made man of the humblest origins, he had served as congressman, senator and Supreme Court justice. Critics dismissed him as a mere Democratic Party hack and White House crony, but he wielded extraordinary power as director of the Office of War Mobilization, and was widely described as FDR's "assistant president." Embittered by Roosevelt's refusal to offer him the vice-presidency, in the spring of 1945 he had opted to retire into private life when abruptly recalled by Truman, who intended him for secretary of state. At Spartanburg on 22 May, Byrnes was irked to be confronted by the unsolicited Hungarian emotionalism of Szilard: "His general demeanour and his desire to participate in policy-making made an unfavourable impression on me." The scientist, in his turn, was dismayed by Byrnes's unreceptiveness: "When I spoke of my concern that Russia might become an atomic power soon, he said that General Groves . . . told him there was no uranium in Russia." Groves hated Szilard, and indeed had claimed to suspect him of being a German agent.

As the scientist made his case against precipitate use of the bomb, Byrnes interrupted impatiently that Congress would have plenty to say if $2 billion proved to have been expended on the Manhattan Project for no practical purpose. "Byrnes thought the Russians might be more manageable if impressed by military might," recalled Szilard. Nothing could demonstrate this more effectively than the atomic bomb. The Hungarian was disgusted when Byrnes urged him to consider that the bomb might even get Stalin's legions out of his own country. "Flabbergasted" by his host's insensitivity, Szilard walked unhappily back to Spartanburg station. It would have been little consolation to him to know that attempts by the great Danish physicist Niels Bohr to convey the same fears to Roosevelt and Churchill had met with a response even less temperate than that of

Byrnes. The prime minister suggested that Bohr should be confined, to prevent him from venting his dangerous misgivings.

The scientists' scruples counted for little alongside the consensual perception of America's leadership that here was a weapon which could decisively strengthen their hands in confronting the Soviets as well as defeating the Japanese. The builders of the bomb were fatally hampered in their attempts to promote a debate about its use by the fact that security made it impossible, indeed treasonable, even to discuss its existence outside their own circle. Most focused concern not upon the bomb's use, but upon whether a warning should first be given to Japan, and whether the peace of the post-war world might best be secured by sharing America's atomic secrets with the Soviets.

If the scientists had better understood the disastrous strategic predicament of the Japanese in 1945, more would have opposed Hiroshima. As it was, however, the men who knew most about the new weapon were quarantined from awareness of the context in which it would be employed. Meanwhile, the politicians responsible for determining the bomb's use had an inadequate sense of its meaning for civilisation. Byrnes told Truman: "It might well put us in a position to dictate our own terms at the end of the war." Overwhelmingly the most important representative of the Manhattan Project in Washington was not a scientist, but General Groves. Triumphalist about the monumental undertaking of which he was chief administrator, he rejected any notion that his country might fail to exploit its fulfilment.

Groves is one of the least-known significant military figures of the Second World War. It is hard to overstate his importance in sustaining momentum towards the detonation of the bombs over Hiroshima and Nagasaki. A major-general whose rank would have entitled him only to a divisional command in the field, he had been promoted by fate to extraordinary authority. An army chaplain's son, as deputy chief of construction for the army he had played a major role in building the Pentagon. In September 1942 he was a forty-six-year-old colonel eagerly awaiting overseas posting—"I wanted to command troops"—when he was instead ordered to supervise the Manhattan Project. "If you do the job right, it will win the war," he was told.

It seems likely that his superiors said this to reconcile the engineer to a thankless domestic posting, rather than because they believed it at the time. Groves's assignment was unique for a soldier, requiring him to oversee thousands of civilian scientists of the highest gifts and often most wayward personalities, led by Dr. Robert Oppenheimer. Beyond these guiding brains, Groves was responsible for a workforce that eventually grew to 125,000, embracing engineers, administrators and construction personnel, centred upon the development laboratory at Los Alamos, New Mexico, and operating other facilities all over the United States. Most of these people had no notion, of course, about the objective of their labours. The paunchy, bustling general reported only to the secretary of war and the army chief of staff. To Groves's own amazement, as the bomb approached completion he was deputed by Marshall also to assume responsibility for its operational use.

Groves was bereft of tact, sensitivity, cultural awareness, and human sympathy for either the Japanese or the bevy of Nobel laureates whom he commanded. He harassed and goaded the scientists as if they were army engineers building a bridge. Yet his effectiveness demands the respect of history. His deputy, Col. Kenneth Nichols, described him as "the biggest sonofabitch I've ever met in my life, but also one of the most capable. He had an ego second to none . . . tireless energy, great self-confidence and ruthlessness. I hated his guts and so did everyone else, [but] if I was to have to do my part all over again, I would select Groves as boss." At the end of April 1945, the general was exultant. The sun shone brilliantly upon his purposes. A bomb should be ready for testing inside three months, its siblings for use rapidly thereafter. Groves's commitment was critical to the eventual decision to destroy Hiroshima. When other men faltered or their attention was distracted, he never flagged. A week after the White House meeting with Stimson and the general, Truman ordered the formation of the so-called Interim Committee, to advise him on the progress and appropriate use of the bomb. Groves had already established a Target Committee, which selected eighteen Japanese cities as possible objectives, and endorsed the general's view that when the time came, two atomic weapons should be dropped.

When Truman learned of Germany's unconditional surrender on 8 May, therefore, he knew of the extraordinary means the United States was soon likely to possess to impose its will on its enemies and drastically to alter the balance of power between itself and the Soviet Union. Stimson told a colleague: "We really held all the cards . . . a straight royal flush, and we mustn't be a fool about the way we play it . . . Now the thing is not to get into unnecessary quarrels by talking too much . . . Let our actions speak for themselves." At a press conference on 8 May following the end of the war in Europe, Truman restated America's determination to receive the unconditional surrender of Japan's armed forces. He said nothing explicit, however, about the future of the emperor, and emphasised that America did not intend "the extermination or enslavement of the Japanese people."

Next day, Japan defiantly informed the world that the German surrender increased its determination to fight on. The Japanese minister in Berne, alarmed by observing the revulsion towards all things German which followed exposure of their concentration camps, urged Tokyo to avoid giving the world any impression that Japan would follow Nazi policies "at the bitter end." Yet there were still plenty of fantasists. As late as 29 May, Japan's naval attaché in Stockholm expressed his belief that in negotiations the Western Allies would allow Japan to retain Manchuria "to provide a barrier against Russia." He thought Britain would be content to settle for restoration of its Asian colonies. He himself favoured fighting on, because he thought Western dismay about Russian excesses left the Anglo-Americans open to compromise. These messages were read in Washington, via Magic.

While Japan was suffering terrible pain from LeMay's B-29 offensive, it was plain that several months must elapse before the U.S. could launch its next big land campaign, which the Japanese correctly assumed would be an invasion of Kyushu. Japan's peacemakers supposed, therefore, that they still had time to talk. Since early spring there had been some diminution of expectations among civilian politicians. Facing imminent defeat on Okinawa, they aspired only to preserving the *kokutai*, together with Manchukuo's "independence" and Korea's status as a Japanese colony.

If these ambitions were fanciful enough, the fantasies of the military were even more extravagant. As an incentive to the Soviets to maintain their neutrality, the navy proposed exchanging some Japanese cruisers for Russian oil and aircraft. Gen. Korechika Anami was a man of few brains and little imagination, but as war minister he possessed overwhelmingly the most influential voice in the Japanese cabinet. Anami opposed all concessions on the Asian mainland: "Japan is not losing the war, since we have not lost any homeland territory. I object to conducting negotiations on the assumption that we are defeated." More realistic voices urged that Japan should concentrate upon a single limited objective: preserving the imperial system and the homeland's territorial integrity.

Among many leading Japanese, there was a sharp distinction between an outcome of the war which they would privately accept, and that which they would acknowledge in the presence of colleagues and subordinates. Prime Minister Kantaro Suzuki, for instance, favoured peace. In public, however, he continued to exhort the nation to resist to the end, in the spirit of the kamikazes. The politicians feared for their lives if they were identified as defeatists by the military fanatics, and recent Japanese history suggested that their apprehension was well-founded. Admiral Suzuki himself, seventy-seven and deaf, carried the scars of four bullet wounds received in 1936, during an attempt by army ultra-nationalists to overthrow the then government.

The consequence of the peace party's timidity was a stunning incoherence of view, which persisted through to August 1945. Japanese equivocation was bound to incur the impatience, if not incomprehension, of literal-minded Americans, to whom words meant neither more nor less than they expressed. Japan's critical error was to address the quest for peace at the usual snail's pace of all its high policy making. Tokyo was oblivious that, 8,000 miles away, General Groves's titanic enterprise was hastening towards its climax at a far more urgent tempo.

JAPANESE LEADERS feared, indeed anticipated, a Russian invasion of Manchuria. They were nonetheless shocked when, six weeks after Molotov told Ambassador Sato that nothing had happened at Yalta which should alarm his country, Moscow announced the abrogation of the 1941 neutrality pact. In Japanese eyes, Soviet behaviour represented perfidy. Yet on 29 May Molotov received Sato amicably, and assured him that the Soviet statement was a mere technicality, that Russia "has had her fill of war in Europe," and must now address huge domestic problems. Sato, usually bleakly realistic about Soviet pronouncements, was rash enough to swallow this one. U.S. intelligence annotated the Magic decrypt of the ambassador's report to Tokyo: "[The] meeting leaves a mental picture of a spaniel in the presence of a mastiff who also knows where the bone is buried." If it seems extraordinary that the architects of Pearl Harbor could be surprised by another nation's duplicity, that the Japanese could suppose themselves to possess any negotiating hand of interest to Stalin, their behaviour was of a piece with the huge collective self-delusion which characterised Tokyo's conduct in 1945.

In Moscow on 28 May, in response to a question from Harry Hopkins, Stalin said that the Soviet Union would be ready to invade Manchuria on 8 August, though weather would thereafter influence exact timing. Hopkins reported to Truman that Stalin favoured insistence upon Japan's capitulation, "however, he feels that if we stick to unconditional surrender the Japs will not give up and we will have to destroy them as we did Germany." The same week, Japan's foreign minister, Shigenori Togo, appointed Koki Hirota, a former prime minister, foreign minister and ambassador, as his secret envoy to the Soviets, with instructions to pursue their friendship as well as neutrality.

Hirota's first move was to visit Jacob Malik, the Russian ambassador in Tokyo. He expressed admiration for the Red Army's achievement in Europe, a richly comic compliment from an emissary of Germany's recent ally. Malik reported to Moscow that Hirota's overtures, though intended to be deniable, reflected a desperate anxiety by the Japanese government to end the war. He judged success implausible, however, since Tokyo persisted in its determination to cling to Manchuria and Korea. Nor were such fantasies confined to politicians. Jiro Horikoshi, the Zero design engineer, often discussed with friends the prospect of soliciting Soviet aid: "Japan has made special efforts to maintain neutrality with the Russians," he wrote in his diary in May, "and we hoped we could rely on her fairness and friendship in mediating with the Allies."

Meanwhile in Washington on 31 May at a meeting of the Interim Committee Stimson emphasised the magnitude of its agenda: to manage deployment of a weapon that would bring about "a revolutionary change in the relations of man to the universe." James Byrnes flatly rejected a proposal made by Oppenheimer, director of the atomic programme, that its secrets should be shared with the Russians. He also dismissed a suggestion that Soviet representatives should be invited to attend the bomb's testing. Beyond security considerations, America would appear ridiculous in the event of failure. For the same reason he opposed, without dissent from the committee, a formal warning to the Japanese. Oppenheimer himself said that he found it impossible to imagine a demonstration of the bomb—for instance, in the skies off Japan—which would be likely to impress the enemy. Next day, 1 June, the decision was formally recorded: "Mr. Byrnes recommended, and the Committee agreed that the Secretary of War should be advised that, while recognizing that the final selection of the target was essentially a military decision, the present view of the Committee was that the bomb should be used against Japan as soon as possible, that it be used on a war plant surrounded by workers' homes, and that it be used without prior warning."

When Stimson reported these conclusions to Truman on 6 June, the secretary of war made two disingenuous and indeed contradictory observations. He had firmly rejected Groves's proposal to drop the first bomb on the ancient capital Kyoto, hub of Japan's culture. He was unmoved by the general's pragmatic argument that Kyoto was "large enough in area for us to gain complete knowledge of the effects of the bomb. Hiroshima was not nearly so satisfactory in this respect." Tokyo and several other cities had already been discarded as objectives, on the grounds that they were mostly rubble already. Stimson told Truman that, against air force wishes, he had held out for a precision rather than an area target, because he did not want the atomic bombing to be compared with Hitler's mass murders. He also expressed fears that LeMay "might have Japan so thoroughly bombed out that the new weapon would not have a fair background to show its strength." Truman laughed, and said that he understood. Here was a vivid illustration of the inability of two intelligent men to confront the implications of what they were about to do. They had been told the potential explosive power of the atomic bomb, yet no more than the scientists did they know its consequential effects, of which radiation sickness was the most significant. In their minds, as in that of Winston Churchill, the new weapon represented simply a massive multiple of the destructive capability of LeMay's B-29s.

Stimson's role puzzles posterity. He was the most august veteran in the administration, seventy-eight years old. His political career began in 1905, when he was appointed a U.S. attorney for New York by Theodore Roosevelt. A gentleman at all points, known as "the colonel" from his military service in World War I, he had served as secretary of state under Hoover from 1929 to 1933, and presided over the War Department from 1940 to 1945. Stimson disliked many things about total war, above all aerial bombardment of cities. Robert Oppenheimer noted his strictures: "He didn't say that air strikes shouldn't be carried on, but he thought there was something wrong with a country where no one questioned that." In the months preceding Hiroshima, though Stimson was increasingly tired and ill, no American political leader devoted more thought and attention to the bomb. Oddly, given his distaste for incendiary attack, he never expressed principled opposition to atomic devastation. Indeed, he welcomed Oppenheimer's weapon as a means of shortening the war. He strove, however, to serve the Japanese with notice to quit before this horror fell upon them.

The secretary of war's fastidious reservations were quite insufficient to deflect the process now in train. From June onwards, only absolute Japanese submission could have saved Hiroshima and Nagasaki. Thereafter, no explicit political decision was made to drop the bomb; rather, a dramatic intervention from Truman would have been needed to stop it. To comprehend the president's behaviour, the limitations of the man occupying the office, his July Potsdam diary is helpful. This reveals Truman's ingenuous private responses to the personalities and events amidst which he found himself. His narrative possesses an awesome banality. To say this represents not condescension, for Truman's later achievement is undisputed, but mere recognition of his predicament. He was a self-consciously small man much influenced by advisers, notably Byrnes and the former ambassador to Moscow Joseph Davies, because he was morbidly sensitive to his own inexperience.

The president adopted in the case of "Little Boy" precisely the same mechanism employed throughout the war by the democracies to implement strategic decisions. He, the politician, approved the concept, then left its execution in the hands of the military—which meant Groves. The dispatch of *Enola Gay* and *Bock's Car*, in common with all bomber operations, required a sequence of orders, aircrew training, logistical preparation, which was now rolling. In recent years, immense scholarly attention has focused upon the decrypted Japanese diplomatic communications, notably with Moscow, which became available to the Americans between June and August 1945. Yet the salient aspect of these is readily summarised: the Japanese government wanted to end the war, but privately as well as publicly rejected unconditional surrender. Japan's most notable pragmatist, Ambassador Sato in Moscow, vividly articulated in cables to Tokyo his conviction that nothing the Japanese government was minded to propose would prove acceptable to the Allies.

If Sato held this opinion, why should Americans intercepting his messages have been any more impressed? In 1945, the distant chirrups of Morse between Tokyo and Moscow were nowhere near explicit or humble enough to halt the earth-shaking juggernaut being steered towards Japan by Leslie Groves. After the war, Truman falsely claimed that he gave the order to attack Hiroshima at the beginning of August 1945, perhaps because he feared that it would seem shocking to posterity to acknowledge that there was no such moment of deliberate presidential judgement before Col. Paul Tibbets took off. Having acquiesced in the process months earlier, thereafter the president merely remained informed of progress, and did not halt the *Enola Gay*. Tolstoy argues—in the context of Napoleon's 1812 invasion of Russia—that great events possess an impetus of their own, independent of the will of national leaders and commanders. Had he lived through 1945, he would have judged the countdown to the dropping of the bombs a vivid demonstration of his thesis.

The Japanese continued to delude themselves that they had time to talk, time to probe and haggle with each other and with the Allies. They believed that their ability to extract a huge blood price from their enemy before succumbing represented a formidable bargaining chip. Instead, of course, this helped to undo them. It seems irrelevant to debate the merits of rival guesstimates for Olympic's U.S. casualties—63,000, 193,000, a million. What was not in doubt was that invading Japan would involve a large loss of American lives, which nobody wished to accept. Blockade and firebombing had already created conditions in which invasion would probably be unnecessary. New means now promised a summary termination of Japan's defiance, and perhaps also pre-emption of the Soviet onslaught.

Why should the United States have endured prevarication from the sponsors of Pearl Harbor and the Bataan death march, or further duplicity and self-aggrandisement from the bloodstained Soviets? The public face of Japan remained implacable. Given the strains to which U.S.-Soviet relations were now subject, knowledge that the Japanese were seeking terms through Moscow rather than offering submission to Washington could only stimulate American impatience and cynicism. The dropping of the bombs did not represent, as Truman and others later claimed, a direct alternative to a costly U.S. invasion of Japan. The people disastrously influenced by the prospect of Olympic were not Americans, but the Japanese, whom it persuaded to continue the war. Much historic attention has focused upon whether the U.S. should have warned Tokyo that it planned to drop atomic bombs. In truth, Japan's military leadership would have been much more readily confounded by a public American intimation that it did not intend to invade the home islands, unrealistic though such a notion is.

2. Reality at Hiroshima

THE JAPANESE dickered through June, unaware that American attention was now fixed upon two critical events, scheduled for undetermined dates in August: the Soviet invasion of Manchuria and the dropping of atomic bombs. The hawks in Washington, foremost among whom were James Byrnes and Truman himself, were eager that the second should pre-empt the first; that, if possible, the U.S. should be seen to have terminated the Japanese war without Soviet participation. A paper prepared by the War Department's Operations and Plans Division on 12 July asserted the advantages of an early Japanese surrender "both because of the enormous reduction in the cost of the war [by achieving victory without an invasion] and because it would give us a better chance to settle the affairs of the Pacific before too many of our allies are committed there and have made substantial contributions to the defeat of Japan." Yet until the Manhattan Project attained fulfilment, planning continued for the launch of Olympic on or soon after 1 November. The atomic bomb was anticipated, but it must never be forgotten that its putative power did not become proven fact until the test on 16 July at Alamogordo in New Mexico.

In the weeks before the Potsdam summit conference, Stimson and others devoted intensive effort to drafting a proclamation, which they expected to be signed by all the Big Three Allied leaders, offering Japan a last opportunity to surrender before facing unparalleled devastation. The "warning party" in Washington attached much importance to including in such a document an assurance about the preservation of the imperial dynasty. Many hands tinkered with the drafting, seeking a precision of language which would deny Japan's militarists any escape clause. Yet some prominent State Department officials, notably including Assistant Secretary of State Dean Acheson, opposed sparing the emperor. They believed that Hirohito must pay the price for having occupied the throne of a nation which launched a hideous war. By the time the American delegation sailed for Potsdam, rival drafts of the proclamation reposed in several briefcases. The instincts of Truman and Byrnes were much closer to those of Acheson than to those of the would-be compromisers. To eager applause, the president had told Congress on 16 April that "America will never become a party to any plan for partial victory." This remained his position thereafter.

WITHIN the Allied nations, in July 1945 many people who knew nothing of the atomic bomb or the imminent Soviet invasion of Manchuria believed that the eastern war was anyway approaching its end. The British embassy in Washington reported to London on the fifteenth: "The belief that Japan herself is anxious to capitulate on terms less than unconditional surrender has been further nourished by stories of unrest and dissatisfaction inside Japan; reports over the Tokyo radio that the dean of Japanese journalists had openly criticised his government for 'dismissing the loss of strategic islands with superficial optimism.' " A week later, the embassy noted: "Generally it is believed that the Pacific War is rushing towards an early climax." Eichelberger of Eighth Army wrote from the Philippines on 24 July: "A great many people feel . . . that Japan is about to fold up." He added next day: "so many believe that the Japs will quit if Russia comes in." Yet such optimism underestimated the obduracy which still prevailed among Japan's leaders.

In Tokyo, the emperor made his first direct personal intervention at a meeting of the "Big Six," the leaders of Japan's government and armed forces, in the Imperial Palace on 22 June, following defeat on Okinawa. While all those present signified their commitment to continue the war—a mantra as indispensable to every Japanese principal as obeisance to the throne—Hirohito authorised an attempt to pursue negotiations through Moscow. In the days that followed, the Japanese were dismayed to find that Ambassador Malik was "too busy" to meet Hirota again. Now, for the first time, an astonished Ambassador Sato in Moscow was informed that ministers in Tokyo were pursuing at least a modest portion of the policy which for months he had urged in vain. When Malik did receive Hirota on 29 June, however, the Russian found the Japanese talking in fantasies: he advanced proposals for preserving Manchukuo's "independence," for abandonment of some Japanese fishing rights in exchange for Russian oil, together with a general willingness to discuss outstanding issues. This was persiflage, as absurd to Malik as it seems to posterity.

However sincere was Hirohito's desire to initiate a negotiation, so dilatory were the Japanese diplomatic efforts which followed that a month was thrown away—a fatal month for Hiroshima and Nagasaki. The prevarication which characterised the conduct of Japan's leaders in the summer of 1945 represented an appalling betrayal of hundreds of thousands of its soldiers, sailors and airmen who had died in recent campaigns designed to buy time for their country. Such time was squandered. Colonel Tibbets's take-off was now barely five weeks away, Stalin's assault little more. At a meeting of the Soviet Stavka and politburo in Moscow on 26–27 June, the formal decision had been promulgated to launch Russian armies into Manchuria and seize the offshore islands promised at Yalta. Some generals and party leaders urged also occupying the Japanese home island of Hokkaido. Others, including Molotov and Marshal Zhukov, argued that such action would be militarily hazardous, and would enable the Americans to claim a breach of the Yalta terms. Stalin preserved his silence, leaving the issue open to wait upon events.

When Hirota sought a further meeting with Malik in Tokyo on 14 July, in the absence of encouragement from Moscow the ambassador again refused to see him. The next step in this black farce was the nomination of Prince Konoe, yet another former prime minister, to serve as the emperor's personal envoy to the Soviets. Grotesque equivocations accompanied the appointment. To avoid a confrontation with the war party, Konoe was given no formal instructions. Ambassador Sato was urged by the foreign minister: "Please be careful not to give the impression that our plan is to make use of the Russians in ending the war." The exasperated ambassador cabled back, demanding to know how much influence Japanese promises—for instance—of non-annexation or non-occupation of overseas territories were likely to have, when most of these had been lost anyway. He declared that he could never hope to convince such supreme realists as the Soviets "with pretty little phrases devoid of all connection with reality."

But these were all that Tokyo's riven factions could agree to offer. Hirohito's 12 July message to Molotov, conveyed by Sato, declared simply: "His Majesty The Emperor, mindful of the fact that the present war daily brings greater evil and sacrifice upon the peoples of all the belligerent powers, desires from his heart that it may be quickly terminated. But so long as England and the United States insist upon unconditional surrender the Japanese Empire has no alternative but to fight on with all its strength for the honour and existence of the Motherland . . ." The message concluded with a bald assertion that Prince Konoe would shortly arrive in Moscow to seek to "restore peace," bearing a letter confirming the lofty sentiments expressed in the emperor's cable.

. . .

All these exchanges became known to the Americans through Magic intercepts. On 16 July, Stimson noted in his diary: "I received . . . important papers [regarding] Japanese maneuverings for peace." John J. McCloy, his deputy, likewise wrote exultantly: "News came in of the Japanese efforts to get the Russians to get them out of the war. Hirohito himself was called upon to send a message . . . to Stalin. Things are moving—what a long way we have come since that Sunday morning we heard the news of Pearl Harbor!" Forrestal noted: "The first real evidence of a Japanese desire to get out of the war came today . . . Togo said . . . that the unconditional surrender terms of the Allies was about the only thing in the way of termination of the war."

A few miles from the cold, shattered heart of Berlin, in Potsdam's Cecilienhof Palace, Stalin was playing host to the last great Allied summit conference of the war. Each participant perceived the occasion as a critical challenge, none more so than Harry Truman. He was a novice, taking a place at a table crowded with legends, Stalin and Churchill foremost among them. The president, having sailed from Newport News, Virginia, on 7 July, was now installed in a three-storey yellow stucco house at 2 Kaiserstrasse, formerly owned by a German film-maker whose daughters had been raped on the premises barely ten weeks earlier, during its pillage by the Red Army. The building was, of course, densely microphoned by the Soviets, and the NKVD provided domestic staff. It was there that Truman received a memorandum from Stimson, emphasising how urgent had become an American warning to Tokyo.

The principal business to be transacted at Potsdam related to Europe, specifically the future of Germany and Poland. The issues of the Far East war and Soviet participation were also much on the minds of the principals, but a host of great matters competed for the attention of Truman and Byrnes. It would be unjust to perceive their approach to Asian matters as perfunctory. Throughout the conference, however, these had to be addressed in the context of much else. Byrnes, with Joseph Davies, overwhelmingly the most important influences upon the president, took the news of Tokyo's overtures to Moscow much less seriously than did Stimson, McCloy and Forrestal. The secretary of state wrote later that he thought little of this Japanese attempt to "avoid the emperor's removal and also save some of their conquered territory."

Some historians have perceived in Byrnes's attitude a petty nationalism unworthy of the issues at stake. It may be true that he was an unsophisticated man, smaller than his great office, as Truman later decided him to be. Yet if Byrnes's judgements in the summer of 1945 were strongly influenced by domestic political considerations, they do not seem unreasonable. The U.S. was Japan's principal enemy. Throughout the war, the Soviet Union had shown itself obsessively fearful that the Western Allies might make a separate peace with Germany. Britain and the U.S. deferred to Soviet paranoia—rejecting, for instance, every approach from German anti-Nazis until the last days when Hitler's armies in Italy surrendered. Now, Tokyo had chosen to approach Moscow. At a time when Soviet savagery and expansionism in Europe were shocking the world, why should not the U.S. spurn such contortions? Those who criticise America's alleged failure to reach out to the enemy in the last weeks of July 1945, to save the Japanese from themselves, seem to neglect a simple point. If Tokyo wanted to end the war, the only credible means of doing so was by an approach to Washington, through some neutral agency less hopelessly compromised than the Soviet Union.

We know *why* this did not happen: because the Japanese expected to gain more favourable terms from the Russians; and because the war party in Tokyo would have vetoed direct negotiation with the United States. The loss of face would have been unendurable. The State Department's Asian experts thoroughly understood the cultural and political forces which caused the Japanese to behave as they did. When, however, America stood on the brink of absolute victory over a nation which had brought untold grief and misery upon Asia, why should not the enemy bear the burden of acknowledging his condition, and indeed his guilt?

Hitler set a standard of evil among those whom the Allies fought in the Second World War. Some historians, not all of them Japanese, argue that Japan's leaders represented a significantly lesser baseness; and certainly not one which deserved the atomic bomb. Few of those Asians who experienced Japanese conquest, however, and knew of the millions of deaths which it encompassed, believed that Japan possessed any superior claim on Allied forbearance to that of Germany. Post-war critics of U.S. conduct in the weeks before Hiroshima seem to demand from America's leaders moral and political generosity so far in advance of that displayed by their Japanese counterparts as to be fantastic, in the sixth year of a global war. Their essential thesis is that America should have spared its enemies from the human consequences of their own rulers' blind folly; that those in Washington should have displayed a concern for the Japanese people much more enlightened than that of the Tokyo government.

Why, however, should the U.S. either have welcomed a Soviet propaganda triumph in Asia, or humoured the self-esteem of a barbarous enemy? Truman's "firmness" towards Japan certainly reflected a desire to impress his authority upon the Soviets, as well as upon the American people. Yet it is hard to believe that Roosevelt, architect of the doctrine of unconditional surrender, would have behaved much differently, had he survived. In the war against Germany, Stalin took much in return for paying most of the blood cost of victory. He profited from overrunning eastern Europe while the British and Americans dallied west of the Rhine. In the Japanese war, however, the U.S. was unequivocally the victor. It was irksome to see the Soviets on the brink of garnering rich rewards for attending curtain calls after missing all but the last minutes of the play. The principal and overwhelming reason for dropping the bomb was to compel the Japanese to end the war; but it seems entirely reasonable that the U.S. also wished to frustrate Soviet expansionism.

James Byrnes wrote in his memoirs: "Had the Japanese government surrendered unconditionally, it would not have been necessary to drop the atomic bomb." Tsuyoshi Hasegawa, author of one of the more significant recent studies of this period, comments: "Perhaps this statement can be read in reverse: 'If we insisted on unconditional surrender, we could justify the dropping of the atomic bomb.' " Hasegawa's words again prompt the question: why should the U.S. *not* have insisted upon unconditional surrender?

At Truman's first bilateral meeting with Stalin at the "little White House," 2 Kaiserstrasse, on 17 July, the Soviet leader announced that his armies would be ready to invade Manchuria in mid-August. The president wrote to his wife, Bess, next day: "I was scared I didn't know whether things were going according to Hoyle or not. Anyway a start has been made and I've gotten what I came for—Stalin goes to war August 15 with no strings on it. I'll say that we'll end the war a year sooner now, and think of the kids who won't be killed." How can this letter be squared with Churchill's memorandum to Eden at Potsdam: "It is quite clear that the United States does not at the present time desire Russian participation in the war against Japan"? Truman, like many of his advisers, regretted the deal for Soviet intervention in the Far East. Yet at Potsdam he was obliged to make the best of the fact that Yalta could not be undone. The significant phrase in his letter is surely "*with no strings on it.*" Moscow had made no new demands that would further compromise Chinese or American interests. Stalin was not insisting upon a Soviet occupation zone in Japan, as he had intimated to Harry Hopkins that he would.

Yet the U.S. president's words and deeds at Potsdam suggest a lingering confusion of mind about Soviet entry into the Japanese war. The issue is further muddled by false claims Truman made later, notably in his memoirs, about the circumstances surrounding the atomic decisions. All politicians seek to amend their own records. Roosevelt told many untruths, and Churchill's war memoirs are shamelessly self-serving. Truman's writings convey a sense that, at the very least, he was not afterwards wholly comfortable about some of the things he did and did not do in July and August 1945. He injured a strong case by supporting it with notable misstatements of historical fact.

The day before the president wrote the letter to his wife, he had received first news of the successful atomic test in New Mexico of an implosion device similar to "Fat Man," which would be used against Nagasaki. The scientists, under enormous pressure to produce an outcome in time for Potsdam, had achieved "the greatest physics experiment in history." "Little Boy," the gun-type bomb that would be dropped on Hiroshima, needed no test. Truman could henceforward assume, therefore, that the U.S. would soon be able to employ such weapons against Japan. The enemy's early surrender seemed overwhelmingly likely, but what combination of forces would precipitate this outcome was as uncertain as ever. Tsuyoshi Hasegawa writes: "It is clear that [Truman] saw Stalin not as an ally committed to the common cause of defeating Japan, but as a competitor in the race to see who could force Japan to surrender." This assertion is important, because it has become one of the pillars upon which modern critics support their case against Hiroshima. The U.S. president deceived his own people and the world, they say, by claiming that he was employing the atomic bomb to force Japan's surrender. In reality, this was the first military act of the Cold War, designed to overawe America's future enemy, the Soviet Union.

Such a proposition attaches to Truman's behaviour an unmerited malignity. The world in July 1945 seemed a deeply dangerous place not only to the president and to Byrnes, but also to cleverer and better-informed people such as Averell Harriman. Hitler had been destroyed, but the evil of Nazi tyranny was now supplanted in eastern Europe by an almost equally repugnant Communist one. Harriman asserted that the West was threatened with "a barbarian invasion." The Russian conquest of eastern Europe provided Stalin with opportunities for imperial dominance, formally acknowledged at Yalta by an ailing Roosevelt, which the Russians had abused ever since. In Poland, the most conspicuous example, Soviet forces were systematically murdering every citizen who professed support for his country's right to independence and democracy. There were no means short of war whereby Stalin's new dominions could be wrested from him. Churchill's Fulton speech still lay seven months ahead, but on 12 May 1945 he had already used its most momentous phrase: "An iron curtain is drawing down on the Russian front." Moscow's global ambitions were abundantly apparent.

Thoughtful and informed Americans were apprehensive about what new aggrandisement Stalin might attempt in the east. No U.S. invasion of Japan was feasible before November, yet the Soviets would invade

Manchuria in August. When Moscow's armies plunged into China, how likely was it that Stalin would respect his promises to forswear Mao Zedong's Communists, and acknowledge the government of Chiang Kai-shek? There was concern that the Russians might exploit their planned drive into Korea to seize the whole peninsula instead of stopping half-way, at the 38th parallel, as agreed at Yalta. When Stalin's forces staged their amphibious landings in the Kuriles, which had been promised to them, what if they went on to occupy some Japanese home islands? A strong Japanese Communist movement existed, the source of much unease in Tokyo, which might provide the nucleus for a Soviet puppet government. Lest it should seem that such speculation reflected mere paranoia in Washington, it is a matter of fact that when Stalin's armies attacked in August, the Soviet leader held open the option of seizing Hokkaido, and almost certainly would have done so had Japanese resistance persisted.

Truman found himself president at a moment when it was alleged, not least by Winston Churchill, that American naïveté and weakness had licensed Soviet expansionism, and when fear of Communist takeover pervaded many nations. Atomic bombs should allow America to end the war with Japan before Stalin's armies wreaked havoc in Asia. It seems mistaken of some historians to perceive this view as reflecting a crude competitive nationalism on the part of the U.S. government. Truman's and Byrnes's attitude was certainly ruthless, but it lacked neither realism nor statesmanship. They understood, as some people in the West did not yet understand, the depth of evil which Stalin's Soviet Union represented. They may be accused of treating Japan with a summary abruptness which its residual military power did not make necessary. But it was the misfortune of the Japanese in July 1945 that their own prevarication coincided with other imperatives oppressing America's leadership.

To Truman, Byrnes, Acheson and many others, swift victory over the declared present enemy of the democracies would also send an important signal to their undeclared prospective foe. It seems correct to acknowledge that a race to claim victory over Japan took place between America and the Soviet Union in the summer of 1945. The motives of the U.S. government, however, seem deserving of more respect than critics accord them. It also seems mistaken to convey even an implicit impression that the *principal* objective of the Hiroshima bomb was to impress the Soviet Union. This was certainly a highly desirable secondary purpose of Colonel Tibbets's mission. But it remains almost impossible to doubt that the atomic weapons would have been used to hasten Japan's surrender whether or not the Soviets were on the brink of intervention.

If this argument is important in assessing Truman's Hiroshima decision, however, it does not address the question of what manner of warning might first have been given. As far as is known, none of the Americans or British present at Potsdam voiced moral scruples about using the bomb. But the Western Allied leadership exhaustively debated the merits of first presenting an ultimatum to the Japanese, along the lines proposed by Stimson and McCloy. Winston Churchill, in his last days as prime minister after losing the July 1945 British general election, renewed his urging that the unconditional surrender doctrine should be modified.

Truman was not overawed by the greatest Englishman. "We had a most pleasant conversation," he wrote of their first meeting, in a characteristic passage of his Potsdam diary. "He is a most charming and a very clever person—meaning clever in the English, not the Kentucky sense. He gave me a lot of hooey about how great my country is and how he loved Roosevelt and how he intended to love me, etc., etc. I gave him as cordial a reception as I could—being naturally (I hope) a polite and agreeable person. I am sure we can get along if he doesn't try to give me too much soft soap. You know, soft soap is made of ash hopper rye and it burns to beat hell when it gets into the eyes."

Truman rejected Churchill's emollient proposal as swiftly as Roosevelt had done in Cairo. When the prime minister made reference to giving the Japanese "some show of saving their military honour," the president responded tartly that, since Pearl Harbor, they had little of this commodity left. He remained unimpressed when Churchill persisted "that at any rate they had something for which they were ready to face certain death in very large numbers." Churchill told Truman that Stalin had disclosed to him the Japanese peace feelers to Moscow. The Soviet leader, who shortly afterwards repeated the same story to the U.S. president, plainly hoped to exploit this disclosure as earnest that he would conduct no secret bilateral negotiation with Tokyo.

Yet, just as Truman's mention to Stalin at Potsdam that the U.S. "now possessed a new weapon of unusual destructive force" came as no surprise to the Russian leader, so he also probably knew or guessed that the Americans were reading Japanese cipher traffic. Soviet agents had penetrated Western intelligence as thoroughly as they had done the Manhattan Project. A notable feature of Potsdam was the fashion in which the Big Three revealed to each other supposed secrets which were already known to the recipients. Stalin asked Truman how the Americans would like Russia to respond to Japanese overtures. Keep talking, said the president.

And indeed, even while the Allied warlords conferred in Germany, Japanese exchanges with the Russians continued. As agreed between Truman and Stalin, on 18 July Moscow sought clarification of Tokyo's position. Two days later, Ambassador Sato sent a signal to his government, passionately urging that Japan should offer its surrender, subject only to preservation of the *kokutai*. Foreign Minister Togo dismissed this proposal: "The whole country as one man will pit itself against the enemy in accordance with the Imperial Will so long as the enemy demands unconditional surrender," he informed Sato—and, of course, through Magic the Americans—on 21 July. Four days later, Togo told Sato to inform Moscow that if Russia remained indifferent to Japanese requests for mediation, "we will have no choice but to consider another course of action." This plainly signalled a threat to approach the other Allies. Nothing in these messages was likely to persuade Washington that Tokyo had embraced reality. Magic decrypts of messages from neutral diplomats in Japan to their home capitals showed their assessments matching everything the Americans knew from the Moscow-Tokyo exchanges: the Japanese were determined to fight to the end. Their government explicitly rejected the urgings of such rationalists as Sato to accept unconditional surrender.

In Potsdam, debate continued about the wording of Stimson's proposed ultimatum or proclamation to Japan. The Joint Strategic Survey Committee disliked the notion of promising, as the secretary of war wished, that the emperor's position would be protected. Its members, good republicans, preferred to say that "Subject to suitable guarantees against further acts of aggression, the Japanese people will be free to choose their own form of government." The War Department's Operations Division, Stimson's drafters, remained determined to offer a commitment to sustain the emperor, and substituted: "The Japanese people will be free to choose whether they shall retain their Emperor as a constitutional monarchy." The joint chiefs of staff told the president that they favoured the JSSC version, which best fitted the American vision of national rights to self-determination.

On 21 July, General Groves's full report from Alamogordo, brimming with exhilaration, was received in Potsdam: "For the first time in history there was a nuclear explosion. And what an explosion! . . . The test was successful beyond the most optimistic expectations of anyone . . . We are all fully conscious that our real goal is still before us. The battle test is what counts in the war within Japan." When Stimson read Groves's dispatch aloud to Truman and Byrnes at the Little White House, the president looked "immensely pepped up." The news, he told the secretary of war, gave him "an entirely new confidence." McCloy noted in his diary: "The Big Bomb stiffened Truman and Churchill . . . They went to the next meeting like little boys with a big red apple secreted on their persons." Stimson was enraged to learn that Groves had reinstated Kyoto as primary target for the first bomb. He hastened to signal Washington, vetoing the general's choice, though the rationale explained to Truman was scarcely enlightened. Sparing Kyoto, Stimson suggested bizarrely, should ensure "a sympathetic Japan to the United States in case there should be any aggression by Russia in Manchuria."

The War Department, in its turn, signalled to Potsdam that it should be possible to use the first atomic bomb soon after 1 August, depending on weather, and almost certainly before the tenth. On the morning of 23 July, Truman told Stimson that he accepted the latest draft of his "warning message" to the Japanese. He proposed to issue this as soon as possible. On the morning of 25 July Gen. Carl Spaatz, commanding the U.S. Army's Strategic Air Force in the Pacific, received a written order for dropping the two bombs on Japan, approved in Potsdam by Stimson and Marshall. It is uncertain whether Truman saw the document, but its issue was anyway a formality. The directive stipulated: "The 509 Composite Group, Twentieth Air Force, will deliver its first special bomb as soon as weather will permit visual bombing after about 3 August 1945 on one of the targets: Hiroshima, Kokura, Niigata and Nagasaki . . . Additional bombs will be delivered on the above targets as soon as made ready by the project staff."

There was, in other words, no provision for a political pause between the first bomb and the second, to enable the Japanese to consider their position. This was a morally unattractive aspect of the process. Hiroshima was named primary objective nominally because it was a strategic port, but chiefly because it was untouched by LeMay's fire-raisers, and thus would provide a convincing nuclear test site. In Europe, the RAF's Bomber Command had sometimes sought undamaged cities for the same reason—to measure the effectiveness of new techniques of destruction. There is little doubt that Hiroshima would already have been devastated by the Twentieth Air Force had it not been deleted from American fire-raising lists after its appointment as birthplace, or rather death place, of the nuclear age.

The question of whether Soviet operations in Manchuria were still desirable continued to loom large in Truman's mind. Once more he invited the opinions of Stimson and Marshall. The chief of staff responded that a Russian invasion was now superfluous. The mere fact of Moscow's massive deployment on the Manchurian border had deterred the Japanese from moving their Guandong Army. Since, however, the Soviets could take Manchuria whenever they chose, Marshall could see no merit in a formal American policy change. It seemed better to admit the Russians to the Japanese empire in accordance with conditions agreed with the U.S., rather than watch them flood into China on their own terms. Stimson agreed. It is significant to notice that, even at this late stage, Marshall was sceptical about whether atomic bombs would precipitate Japan's surrender. Months earlier, America's foremost soldier had declared that the decision about whether and how to use them must be made by the nation's political rather than military leadership. In July, he continued to focus his own attention upon what Soviet and American armies might do, rather than upon the mission of Colonel Tibbets.

On 24 July, Truman approved the final text of what became known as the Potsdam Declaration. Some suggestions made by Churchill were incorporated. The prime minister had also agreed, with a readiness close to insouciance, that the Americans should thereafter drop atomic bombs without further consultation with Britain. In this, he recognised political reality; yet also, perhaps, he revealed the limits of his understanding about the manner in which this vast event would change the world. A final British attempt to incorporate a modification of unconditional surrender was rejected, as was a new plea by Stimson for more specific assurances about the preservation of the imperial dynasty.

Between Truman's departure from Washington and the issue of the declaration, the success of the atomic bomb test caused the document to assume a changed significance. Stalin, as well as some Americans, assumed that all three Allied leaders in Potsdam would sign a common document, which would also become the Soviet Union's declaration of war on Japan. Yet now that a direct causal link was intended between the document, its rejection, and unilateral American detonation of the bomb, the U.S. delegation had no desire to share its declaration with the Soviet Union.

On 25 July, Truman recorded in his diary: "This weapon is to be used against Japan between now and August 10th. I have told the Sec. Of War, Mr. Stimson, to use it so that military objectives and soldiers and sailors are the target and not women and children. Even if the Japs are savages, ruthless and fanatic, we as the leader of the world for the common welfare cannot drop this terrible bomb on the old capital [Kyoto] or the new [Tokyo]." It is impossible to interpret this passage as anything but a self-conscious attempt by Truman to create a record which would serve his reputation in the eyes of history. After receiving Groves's report, no intelligent person could doubt that a cataclysm of unprecedented horror was to be unleashed upon a Japanese centre of population.

The Potsdam Declaration, signed by the American, British and—in absentia—Chinese leaders, was issued on the evening of 26 July:

> Following are our terms. We will not deviate from them. There are no alternatives. We shall brook no delay.
>
> - There must be eliminated for all time the authority and influence of those who have deceived and misled the people of Japan into embarking on world conquest . . .

- Until such a new order is established . . . points in Japanese territory shall be occupied.
- Japanese sovereignty shall be limited to the islands of Honshu, Hokkaido, Kyushu, Shikoku and such minor islands as determined.
- The Japanese military forces, after being completely disarmed, shall be permitted to return to their homes with the opportunity to lead peaceful and productive lives.
- We do not intend that the Japanese shall be enslaved as a race or destroyed as nation, but stern justice shall be meted out to all war criminals . . . Freedom of speech, of religion, and of thought, as well as respect for the fundamental human rights shall be established.
- Japan shall be permitted to retain such industries as will sustain her economy . . .
- The occupying forces of the Allies shall be withdrawn from Japan as soon as these objectives have been accomplished and there has been established in accordance with the freely expressed will of the Japanese people a peacefully inclined and responsible government.
- We call upon the government of Japan to proclaim now the unconditional surrender of all Japanese armed forces . . . The alternative for Japan is prompt and utter destruction.

The Potsdam Declaration was not dispatched to the Japanese government as a diplomatic communication, but merely broadcast to the world through the media. The Soviets were stunned to find themselves excluded from the signatories, and indeed shown a copy only after the declaration's release. They had come to the conference with their own draft, demanding Japan's unconditional surrender, but using the words "The United States, China, Great Britain and the Soviet Union consider it their duty to take joint, decisive measures immediately to bring the war to an end." This was never presented or discussed.

The Americans were within their rights to confine endorsement of the ultimatum to co-belligerents against Japan, and thus exclude the neutral Soviets. But Stalin could thereafter be in no doubt of America's determination to address Japan in its own way, with minimal reference to Moscow. For once, the Russian leader might have been excused paranoia, in fearing that the U.S. hoped to renege on Yalta, and deny him his promised Asian prizes. From Potsdam he had already telephoned Moscow to demand a ten-day acceleration of the Red Army's timetable for invading Manchuria. He lambasted Beria, his spymaster, for ignorance of the successful American bomb test, which he readily inferred from Truman's hints.

On 29 July at Potsdam, Molotov asked that the U.S. should make a formal request for the Soviet Union to enter the Far Eastern war. The

Americans refused. Truman later claimed that he did not want to give the Russians scope to claim that their intervention decided the outcome of the conflict. Byrnes, in his memoirs, was much more frank. He asserted that, given recent Soviet behaviour and violations of the Yalta Agreement in Europe, he did not want the Soviets in the Asian war, and believed that the atomic bomb would compel Tokyo's surrender without them. Truman responded to Molotov's request with a personal letter to Stalin on 31 July, suggesting that the four Allies' 1943 Moscow Declaration fully justified the Soviet Union in joining the war without any further preliminaries. Such a view scarcely suggested much regard for diplomatic niceties, but there the matter rested. The Soviets left Potsdam enraged by what they perceived as American duplicity.

The party most deluded by the declaration was Japan. When the absence of Stalin's signature was noted in Tokyo, it was supposed that he had chosen to exclude the Soviet Union from the ranks of Japan's enemies; and thus that it remained a plausible intermediary. The Japanese were further heartened by the eclipse of Churchill, following the British election defeat which removed him from the premiership. They supposed this to open prospects of faltering and dissension in the Allied ranks. Some in Tokyo were encouraged by the language of the Potsdam Declaration. Through Moscow, they sought clarification of its vague generalities. At a cabinet meeting on the afternoon of 27 July, Foreign Minister Togo urged making no immediate public response, partly because it would be almost impossible to achieve an agreed position among ministers. The declaration's terms were reported in the Japanese press, omitting only the Allied promise that Japanese soldiers would be allowed to return peacefully home. Newspapers were less restrained than politicians in their reactions: "Laughable Surrender Conditions to Japan," said the heading of an editorial in *Yomiuri Hochi*. Another title, *Asahi Shimbun*, reported: "The government intends to ignore it." *Mokusatsu*, silence in the face of unacceptable words or deeds, is among the principal behavioural tools of Japanese society.

Next day, however, several officeholders headed by Anami, the war minister, declared that silence would not suffice. They insisted that Suzuki should denounce the declaration. The prime minister made a short statement to a press conference, dismissing the American document as "a rehash of the Cairo Declaration. The government does not think that it has serious value. We can only ignore it. We shall do our utmost to see the war through to the bitter end."

Some historians have questioned whether Suzuki indeed used these words in this context. Yet if there is doubt about the exact language, it is undisputed that the Japanese government agreed to make no positive response to the Declaration. The U.S. Associated Press reported on 27 July: "The semi-official Japanese Domei news agency stated today that Allied ultimatum to surrender or meet destruction would be ignored." The emperor himself seems to have made no attempt to question Suzuki's posture. Hirohito has so often been credited with a role as Japan's principal peacemaker that it is important to emphasise his rejection of the Potsdam terms. If the emperor had intervened decisively at this point, rather than a fortnight later, all that followed might have been averted. As it was, this hesitant, inadequate divinity continued to straddle the fence, wanting peace yet still recoiling from acknowledgement of his nation's defeat, and history took its course.

From Moscow, Ambassador Sato continued to bombard Tokyo with imprecations to face reality. "There is no alternative but immediate unconditional surrender if we are to try to make America and England moderate and to prevent [Russia's] participation in the war," he cabled on 30 July. Foreign Minister Togo replied on 2 August, urging patience: "It is difficult to decide on concrete peace terms all at one stroke." He reported, however, that the emperor was closely following developments in Moscow, while Suzuki and the army's leaders explored the question of whether the Potsdam Declaration offered scope for negotiation. American naval intelligence analysts of the Magic decrypts on the declaration reported: "There is a disposition (or determination) of finding in its terms a sufficiently effective emollient for tortured pride which still rebels at the words 'unconditional surrender'."

It is unknown whether Truman read these decrypts or this analysis on his way back from Potsdam. The final conference session took place on 1 August. Stalin left Berlin that day, and the U.S. president early the following morning. Truman had already approved the text of a public statement to be issued in his name when the bomb was dropped. In his eyes, all that now mattered was that the Japanese government refused to respond positively to the Potsdam Declaration. Indeed, the earlier Magic intercepts between Sato and Togo had made Tokyo's rejection certain, since the foreign minister explicitly ruled out unconditional surrender. For weeks past, use of the bomb had been almost inevitable. It now became absolutely so.

Many people of later generations and all nationalities have viewed the dropping of atomic weapons on Japan as events which, in their unique horror, towered over the war as a dark mountain bestrides the plain. In one sense this perception is correct, because the initiation of the nuclear age provided mankind with unprecedented power to destroy itself. Until the bombs had exploded, however, full understanding of their significance was confined to a few score scientists. To grasp the context in which the commitment to bomb Hiroshima was made, it seems necessary to acknowledge the cacophony amidst which all those involved, the political and military leaders of the U.S., were obliged to do their business. These were men in their fifties and sixties, weary after years of perpetual crisis such as world war imposes, bombarded daily with huge dilemmas.

Europe was in ruins and chaos, the Western Allies striving to contend with Stalin's ruthlessness and greed, Britain's bankruptcy, the starvation of millions. Each day brought to the desks of Truman, Stimson, Marshall and their staffs projections relating to the invasion of the Japanese homeland. The U.S. found itself obliged to arbitrate upon the future of half the world, while being implored to save as much as possible of the other half from the Soviets, even as war with Japan continued and mankind recoiled in horror from newsreel films of Hitler's death camps. What could be done about Poland, about millions of displaced persons? About escaping Nazi war criminals and civil war in Greece? Could power in China be shared? Might the rise of the Communists in Italy and France be checked? Japan's beleaguered Pacific garrisons continued to resist even though the Allies initiated no major operations against Hirohito's armies overseas after June 1945. The British were preparing to land in Malaya. Almost every day, LeMay's Superfortresses set forth from Guam and Saipan to incinerate more Japanese cities. Carrier aircraft strafed and bombed the home islands. Casualty lists broadcast grief to homes all over the U.S. and Britain. Apprehension overhung the fate of many thousands of Allied prisoners in Japanese hands.

In judging the behaviour of those responsible for ordering the atomic attacks, it seems necessary to acknowledge all this. The bomb was only the foremost of many huge issues with which these mortal men, movingly conscious of their own limitations, strove to grapple. In the course of directing a struggle for national survival, all had been obliged to make decisions which had cost lives, millions of lives, of both Allied servicemen and enemy soldiers and civilians. Most would have said wryly that this was what they were paid for. The direction of war is never a task for the squeamish. The U.S. had already participated in bombing campaigns which killed around three-quarters of a million German and Japanese civilians, and to which public opinion had raised little objection. It is much easier to justify the decision to drop the atomic bombs than the continued fire-raising offensive of the Twentieth Air Force. "The preoccupation of the historians' debate with the necessity of using the bomb," Lawrence Freedman and Saki Dockrill have written wisely, "has meant that it has been judged strategically against the prospective invasion [of Japan], rather than the actual air bombardment under way at the time and with which it was unavoidably linked in the minds of policy-makers."

Poison gas was the only significant weapon available to the wartime

Allies which was not employed against the Axis. Roosevelt opposed this for moral, or rather propagandistic, reasons; the British chiefly on the pragmatic grounds that the Germans might retaliate against their homeland. As discussed above, the Americans began the war with moral scruples about bombing civilians, but by 1945 had abandoned them. It is a delusion of those who know nothing of battle, to suppose that death inflicted by atomic weapons is uniquely terrible. In truth, conventional shells and bombs dismember human bodies in the most repulsive fashion. The absolutism of atomic destruction merits humanity's horror, and indeed terror, more than the nature of the end which it inflicts upon individuals.

Most of those involved in the atomic decision recognised war, the homicidal clash of belligerents, as the root evil from which mankind should spare itself. After living for years with the bloody consequences of global conflict, they were less sensitive than modern civilians to specific refinements of killing. Many people whose deaths are described in this book would have found nothing uniquely pitiable about the manner in which Hiroshima's and Nagasaki's inhabitants perished, even if they might have been appalled by the scale.

From the inception of the Manhattan Project, it was assumed by all but a few scientists that if the device was successful, it would be used. Some people today, especially Asians, believe that the Allies found it acceptable to kill 100,000 Japanese in this way, as it would not have been acceptable to do the same to Germans, white people. Such speculation is not susceptible to proof. But given Allied perceptions that if Hitler and his immediate following could be removed, Germany would quickly surrender, it is overwhelmingly likely that if an atomic bomb had been available a year earlier, it would have been dropped on Berlin. It would have seemed ridiculous to draw a moral distinction between massed attacks on German centres of population by the RAF and USAAF with conventional weapons, and the use of a single more ambitious device to terminate Europe's agony.

Curtis LeMay regarded the Hiroshima and Nagasaki raids merely as an addition—a redundant and unwelcome addition—to a campaign which his B-29s had already won. LeMay had not the slightest moral qualms about the atomic attacks, but was chagrined that they diminished the credit given to his conventional bomber force for destroying Japan. In late June, he predicted that the Twentieth Air Force would render the enemy incapable of continuing the war after 1 October 1945. "In order to do this," said Arnold, "he had to take care of some 30 to 60 large and small cities." LeMay had accounted for fifty-eight when events rendered it unnecessary to test his prophecy to fulfilment. In the minds of those conducting the war against Japan, the mission of the *Enola Gay* represented only a huge technological leap forward in the campaign already waged for months by the fire-raisers.

One further military point should be made. From August 1945 onwards Truman and other contemporary apologists for the bomb advanced the simple argument, readily understood by the wartime generation of Americans, that it rendered redundant an invasion of Japan. It is now widely acknowledged that Olympic would almost certainly have been unnecessary. Japan was tottering and would soon have starved. Richard Frank, author of an outstanding modern study of the fall of the Japanese empire, goes further. He finds it unthinkable that the United States would have accepted the blood-cost of invading Kyushu, in light of radio intelligence about Japanese strength.

Like any "counter-factual," it is hard to accept this proposition as an absolute. The prospect of the Kyushu landings was wholly unwelcome to America's military and political leadership. Yet in the summer of 1945 Marshall, for one, was committed to keeping open an invasion option—possibly of northern Honshu—partly because he questioned whether the bomb's impact would be conclusive. The U.S. chief of staff recognised the wisdom of Churchill's view that "all things are always on the move simultaneously . . . One has to do the best one can, but he is an unwise man who thinks there is any *certain* way of winning this war . . . The only plan is to persevere." So much that is today apparent was then opaque. So many forces were in play, the impacts of which were unclear.

At the beginning of August 1945, most of MacArthur's officers believed that they *would* have to invade Japan, and even some of those in Washington privy to the atomic secret and to impending Russian intervention thought they *might* have to do so. It was impossible to be sure what an enemy nation which had displayed a resolute commitment to mass suicide might do, when confronted with the last ditch. A 27 July U.S. naval intelligence analysis of Japan's behaviour, written with full access to Magic decrypts, was circulated to all Washington's top policy-makers: "Her unwillingness to surrender stems primarily from the failure of her otherwise capable and all-powerful Army leaders to perceive that the defenses they are so assiduously fashioning actually are utterly inadequate . . . Until the Japanese leaders realize that an invasion cannot be repelled, there is little likelihood that they will accept any peace terms satisfactory to the Allies." Invasion was not a direct alternative to the bomb, but on 1 August 1945, who could be sure what might have to be done if the bomb was not dropped?

So much for military context. What of the political decision? The most obvious question is that of whether Japan might have behaved differently if the Potsdam Declaration had explicitly warned of atomic bombs. The answer, almost certainly, is no. If America's leaders found difficulty in comprehending the unprecedented force they were about to unleash, the Japanese were unlikely to show themselves more imaginative. More than that, the war party in Tokyo, which had crippled Japan's feeble diplomatic gropings, was committed to acceptance of national annihilation rather than surrender. If LeMay's achievement in killing 200,000 Japanese civilians and levelling most of the country's major cities had not convinced the likes of General Anami that surrender was inevitable, there is no reason to suppose that a mere threat of atomic bombardment would have done so.

The principal beneficiary of a warning, even if unheeded, would have been Harry Truman. His decision to insist upon unconditional surrender can be justified for reasons offered above. Japan had done nothing in China and South-East Asia throughout its occupation, or in the prison camps of its empire, to make any plausible moral claim upon terms less rigorous than those imposed upon Germany. Japan would certainly have used atomic weapons if it possessed them. The nation had gambled upon launching a ruthless war of conquest. The gamble had failed, and it was time to pay. It would have well served Truman's historic reputation, however, to have been seen to offer Japan an opportunity to escape nuclear retribution before this was administered. The Potsdam Declaration was a statement of honourable Allied objectives. It was a sham ultimatum, however, because it failed plausibly to describe the nature of the vague sanction which it threatened in the event of non-compliance. The words "prompt and utter destruction" meant much to American drafters, nothing at all to Japanese readers.

Why was no explicit warning given? Because the dropping of the bomb was designed to deliver a colossal shock, not only to the Japanese people but also to the leaders of the Soviet Union. Marshall said to Field Marshal Sir Henry Wilson, head of the British Military Mission in Washington: "It's no good warning them. If you warn them there's no surprise. And the only way to produce shock is surprise." This was precisely the same justification offered by the Japanese military to the emperor in 1941 for declining to give the U.S. notice of its intention to go to war before attacking Pearl Harbor. Japan bears overwhelming responsibility for what happened at Hiroshima and Nagasaki, because her leaders refused to acknowledge that their game was up. However, the haste with which the U.S. dropped the bomb as soon as it was technically viable reflected aforementioned technological determinism, together with political fears focused upon the Russians, as much as military imperatives related to Japan. It is possible to support Truman's decision not to stop the dropping of the bomb, while regretting his failure to offer warning of its imminence.

. . .

LATE ON 6 August 1945, a Top Secret signal flashed from the Twentieth Air Force to Washington, where the time difference caused it to be read just before midnight the previous day: "Subject: Bombs Away Report 509 SBM 13 Flown 6 August 1945 . . . 1 a/c bombed Hiroshima visually thru 1/10 cloud with good results. Time was 052315Z. No flak or E/A opposition." This was followed almost immediately by a second signal: "Altitude: 30,200 feet . . . Enemy air opposition: Nil . . . Bombing Results: Excellent."

"Little Boy," "an elongated trash can with fins" in the words of one of *Enola Gay*'s crew, scrawled with rude messages for Hirohito, exploded 1,900 feet above Hiroshima's Shima Hospital, 550 feet from its aiming point. Tibbets, a supremely professional bomber pilot, described this simply as "the most perfect AP I've seen in this whole damn war." The 8,900-pound device created temperatures at ground zero which reached 5,400 degrees and generated the explosive power of 12,500 tons of TNT. All but 6,000 of the city's 76,000 buildings were destroyed by fire or blast. The Japanese afterwards claimed that around 20,000 military personnel and 110,000 civilians died immediately. Though no statistics are conclusive, this estimate is almost certainly exaggerated. Another guesstimate, around 70,000, seems more credible.

The detonation of "Little Boy," the mushroom cloud which changed the world, created injuries never before seen on mortal creatures, and recorded with disbelief by survivors: the cavalry horse standing pink, stripped of its hide; people with clothing patterns imprinted upon their flesh; the line of schoolgirls with ribbons of skin dangling from their faces; doomed survivors, hideously burned, without hope of effective medical relief; the host of charred and shrivelled corpses. Hiroshima and its people had been almost obliterated, and even many of those who clung to life would not long do so. As late as June 1946, an official press release from the Manhattan Project asserted defiantly: "Official investigation of the results of atom bomb bursts over the Japanese cities . . . revealed that no harmful amounts of persistent radio-activity were present after the explosions." Yet even at that date, thousands more stricken citizens of Hiroshima were still to perish.

Truman received the news aboard *Augusta*, four days out from England on his passage home from Potsdam, as he was lunching with members of the cruiser's crew: "Big bomb dropped on Hiroshima August 5 at 7:15 p.m. Washington time. First reports indicate complete success which was even more conspicuous than earlier test." The beaming president jumped up and told *Augusta*'s skipper: "Captain, this is the greatest thing in history." At Truman's behest, the officer carried the signal to Byrnes, eating at another table, who said, "Fine! Fine!" Truman then addressed crewmen in the mess: "We have just dropped a new bomb on Japan which has more power than 20,000 tons of TNT. It has been an overwhelming success!" The president's delight was apparently unburdened by pain or doubt. He simply exulted in a national triumph. Here was a vivid demonstration of the limits of his own understanding of what had been done. Sailors crowded around the president, asking the question on the lips of millions of Allied soldiers, sailors and airmen across the world: "Does this mean we can go home now?"

In the U.S., first reaction to Hiroshima was overwhelmingly enthusiastic. The British embassy in Washington reported: "The lurid fantasies of the comic strips seemed suddenly to have come true. Headlines sagged under the weight of the drama and the superlatives they had to carry." There was much unseemly flippancy, for American skins had been thickened by forty-four months of war. The Washington Press Club produced a sixty-cent "atomic cocktail." A newspaper cartoonist depicted Truman presiding over an angelic gathering of his advisers, each sprouting wings as they contemplated a bowl of split atoms on the table. The caption read: "The Cabinet meets to discuss sending an ambassador to Mars." At Los Alamos, scientist Otto Frisch recoiled from the exuberance of colleagues who telephoned the La Fonda Hotel in Santa Fe to book tables for a celebration.

Among some ordinary people news of the bomb prompted not triumphalism, but the darkest reflections. A letter to the *New York Times* described Hiroshima as "a stain on our national life. When the exhilaration of this wonderful discovery has passed, we will think with shame of the first use to which it was put." British housewife Nella Last recorded in her diary how she and her Lancashire neighbour received the news: "Old Joe called upstairs, brandishing the *Daily Mail*: 'By Goy, lass, but it looks as if some of your daft fancies and fears are reet. Look at this.' I've rarely seen Jim so excited—or upset. He said: 'Read it—why, this will change all t'world. Ee, I wish I was thutty years younger and could see it aw.' " Mrs. Last, however, reacted very differently: "I felt sick—I wished I was thirty years older, and out of it all . . . This atomic bomb business is so dreadful."

Senator Edwin Johnson of Colorado declared that the bombs proved that universal military training was stupid. President Roosevelt's widow, Eleanor, said it showed the importance of goodwill visits such as Soviet trades unionists were then making to the United States. Leaders of the oil and coal industries issued statements reassuring stockholders that for the foreseeable future the new discovery would have little effect on existing fuels. Some left-wingers demanded that atomic patent rights and means of production should remain controlled by Congress, and not be allowed to fall into the hands of large oil or munitions combines. To the embarrassment even of many capitalists, the prospect of an end of hostilities caused the New York Stock Exchange to fall sharply. A correspondent of the London *Sunday Times* wrote: "It is always unedifying when moneyed interests are revealed as benefiting or believing themselves to benefit more from war than from peace."

Some senior U.S. soldiers in the Philippines were disgruntled to find themselves facing financial loss of a different kind. One of their number had returned from a liaison mission to the Marianas shortly before, reporting that Twentieth Air Force officers had created a $10,000 pool, to bet that the war would end before October. Since MacArthur's people knew that Olympic was not scheduled until November, some hastened to accept the air force wager. "From what we knew and the way it looked to us, that was an easy bet to win. We started taking up the $10,000, but we didn't get very far with it," Krueger's G3, Clyde Eddleman, wrote ruefully. ". . . The next thing we knew Hiroshima disappeared."

A British corporal of Fourteenth Army in Burma, George MacDonald Fraser, noted: "It is now widely held that the dropping of atomic bombs was unnecessary because the Japanese were ready to give in . . . I wish those who hold that view had been present to explain the position to the little bastard who came howling out of a thicket near the Sittang, full of spite and fury, in that first week of August. He was half-starved and near naked, and his only weapon was a bamboo stave, but he was in no mood to surrender."

Nowhere was relief at the dropping of the bomb more intense and heartfelt than in prison camps throughout the Japanese empire. Yet even among those for whom Hiroshima promised deliverance, a few displayed more complex emotions. Lt. Stephen Abbott's closest friend, Paul, a devout Christian, entered their bleak barrack room in Japan and said: "Stephen—a ghastly thing has happened." He described the destruction of Hiroshima, as reported on the radio, then knelt in prayer. Eighteen months later, Abbott wrote a letter for publication in *The Times*, citing his own status as a former POW, and arguing that a demonstration of the bomb would have sufficed: "The way it has been used has not only provided a significant chapter for future Japanese history books but has also convinced the people of Japan that the white man's claim to the ethical and spiritual leadership of the world is without substance."

PRESIDENT TRUMAN'S statement to the world, approved before he left Potsdam, declared that the fate of Hiroshima represented a just retribution for Pearl Harbor: "It was to spare the Japanese people from utter destruction that the ultimatum of 26 July was issued at Potsdam . . . If they do not now accept our terms, they may expect a rain of ruin from the air, the like of which has never been seen on this earth." This time there could be no doubt in the minds of Japan's leaders about exactly what the president's words portended. More atomic bombs would follow "Little Boy." Other cities would share the fate of Hiroshima.

Yet the extraordinary aspect of Japanese behaviour in the wake of the 6 August bombing was that the event seemed to do almost nothing to galvanise Japanese policy-making, to end the prevarication which was already responsible for so much death. The emperor and prime minister learned of the attack only after a lapse of some hours. First reports spoke of "the complete destruction of Hiroshima and unspeakable damage inflicted by one bomb with unusually high effectiveness." At least one senior officer immediately guessed that this was an atomic device, as was soon confirmed by intercepted American radio broadcasts. Other army commanders remained sceptical, however, and saw nothing in the news to soften their implacable opposition to surrender. General Anami, the war minister, privately acknowledged that this was a nuclear attack, and dispatched an investigating team to Hiroshima. He proposed, however, that the government should take no action before hearing its report, which would not be available for two days. Hiroshima at first rendered some ministers more committed, rather than less, to resisting unconditional surrender.

Foreign Minister Togo dispatched a message to Ambassador Sato in Moscow, seeking urgent clarification of the Soviet attitude. Togo went to the Imperial Palace on the morning of 8 August. Hirohito told him that, in the new circumstances, "My wish is to make such arrangements as to end the war as soon as possible." Togo was asked to convey this message to Prime Minister Suzuki. Even now, however, the emperor was vague about means. He certainly did not urge immediate acceptance of the Potsdam terms. The Japanese government failed to adopt the course which could almost certainly have saved Nagasaki from destruction: a swift communication to the Americans declaring readiness to quit. Once again, we know *why* this did not happen: because the decision-making process was so slow, the war party so resolute. But again, also, the question should be asked: how many days of stubborn enemy silence should the U.S., never the most patient society on earth, have been expected passively to endure?

In Moscow, on 7 August Russia's media reported nothing about events in Hiroshima. All that day Stalin remained incommunicado. It is assumed that the Soviet leader was stunned by the news, and fearful that Japan would immediately surrender. But Ambassador Sato's urgent request to meet Molotov showed that this was not so. Japan was still in the war. It was not, after all, too late for the Soviet Union to achieve its objectives. Sato was granted an appointment with Molotov for the evening of 8 August. Stalin meanwhile conducted meetings with a Chinese delegation led by T.V. Soong, Chiang's prime minister and brother-in-law, which was still stubbornly resisting endorsement of some of the terms agreed by Roosevelt at Yalta. Japan's leaders went to bed in Tokyo on the night of 8 August expecting to hear news from Moscow next morning about Sato's meeting with Molotov. This they did, but in a form drastically divergent from their expectations.

When Sato entered the foreign minister's office, Molotov brushed aside his greetings, invited him to sit, and read aloud the terms of his nation's declaration of war. Since Japan had rejected the Potsdam Declaration, said the Russian, "the Allies approached the Soviet Union with a proposal to join in the war against Japanese aggression and thereby shorten the length of the war, reduce the number of victims, and assist in the prompt re-establishment of general peace." Russia accepted the Allied proposals, to save the Japanese people "from the same destruction as Germany had suffered." Less than an hour later, Molotov informed the British and American ambassadors that, in fulfilment of its obligations, his country had declared war on Japan. Harriman expressed the gratitude and pleasure of the U.S., for he could do nothing else. A few hours later, shortly after Truman in Washington heard news of the Soviet action, *Bock's Car* took off from Tinian for Nagasaki.

The second mission was launched without any further Washington directive, and simply because its weapon was ready. Twentieth Air Force's mandate left the timings of both atomic attacks in the hands of local commanders, to be determined by operational convenience. The generals advanced the second strike by two days in the face of warnings of bad weather after 10 August, and "a general feeling among those in the theater that the sooner this bomb was dropped the better it would be for the war effort." Washington's only contribution was passive. The president and his advisers discerned in Japanese silence no cause to order the 509th Bomb Group to halt its operations. At 1102 on 9 August Japanese time, having found Kokura, its primary target, under cloud, Maj. Charles Sweeny dropped "Fat Man" on Nagasaki, his secondary objective, generating the explosive power of 22,000 tons of TNT, killing at least 30,000 people. Since midnight, Soviet armies had been sweeping into Manchuria.

TWENTY

Manchuria: The Bear's Claws

IN THE EARLY hours of 9 August 1945, Japanese outposts on the Manchurian border were bewildered to find themselves first under heavy shellfire, then attacked by infantry, swiftly identified as Russian. In some sectors the picture was confused by torrential rain. "It was the worst thunderstorm I've ever seen," said Soviet sapper Ivan Kazintsev. "The lightning caused us to lose our night vision, our sense of direction—and lit us up for the enemy on Camel Hill. We managed to capture it by dawn, though." Kazintsev's general, A. P. Beloborodov of 1st Red Banner Army, wrote: "Lightning kept flashing unexpectedly. Dazzling streaks split the darkening sky, thunder growing ever louder. Should we delay the attack? No . . . The rain would hinder the enemy as much as ourselves." Beloborodov was right about that. Japanese Imperial General Headquarters issued an emergency order, reporting that the Soviet Union had declared war and started entering Manchurian territory, but adding absurdly: "The scale of these attacks is not large." In reality, the first elements of a 1.5-million-strong Soviet host were in motion: infantry, tank formations, trotting columns of horsed cavalry and mounted infantry, supported by river flotillas, air fleets, guns in tens of thousands. Assault operations extended across land and water fronts of 2,730 miles, from the Mongolian desert in the west to the densely forested coast of the Sea of Japan. This was the last great military operation of the Second World War.

The initial Japanese response accorded with every wider delusion about their nation's predicament. Even those in Tokyo who had accepted that Stalin was "waiting for the ripe persimmon to fall," who were warned of great Soviet troop movements eastwards, believed the Russians would not be ready to attack in Manchuria until that autumn, or even the spring of 1946. This was yet another gross miscalculation of the time available to Japan to find a way out of the war. Among Japanese civilians, the reaction of aeronautical engineer Jiro Horikoshi was typical. He was still reeling from news of Hiroshima when "a still more shocking report came in to us, announcing the bolt from the blue that Russia has declared war." In the early months of 1945, many refugees from the Japanese home islands had moved to Manchuria with all their possessions, supposing that the colony represented a safe haven. Japan's Guandong Army was nowhere near operational readiness. Its best units had been sent to Okinawa or Kyushu. Few demolition charges were laid. Some senior commanders were absent from their posts.

In Nanjing, Japanese staff officer Maj Shigeru Funaki and his colleagues at China Army headquarters said to each other: "At last!" They had always anticipated such an assault, "yet we felt very bitter towards the Russians for doing it now. It was so unfair! We had been obliged to send so many men to other Pacific fronts. It was as if they were burglars breaking into an empty house." In Manchuria, no steps had been taken to evacuate hundreds of thousands of Japanese civilians even from border regions, on the grounds that such precautions would promote defeatism. The Guandong Army's commanders found themselves in the same predicament as the British in Malaya and the Americans in the Philippines in December 1941: struggling to defend wide fronts with weak forces and negligible air support. It was now the turn of Japan's most cherished colony to suffer the fate which had befallen the West's imperial possessions in Asia almost four years earlier.

Russia's official war history declares: "The Soviet Union's aims . . . were . . . the provision of security for its own far eastern borders, which had been subjected to threat again and again by Japan; the fulfilment of obligation to its allies; . . . to hasten the end of the Second World War, which continued to bring incalculable suffering to the people; the desire to provide assistance to the workers of east Asia in their liberation struggle; and the restoration of the USSR's historic rights in territory which Japan had earlier seized from Russia." In truth, of course, Stalin's simple purpose was territorial gain, for which he was prepared to pay heavily. Before launching their assault in Manchuria, the Soviets made medical provision for 540,000 casualties, including 160,000 dead. Here was a forecast almost certainly founded upon an assessment of Japanese paper strength, of much the same kind as the Americans made about a landing on Kyushu.

Since 1941, Stalin had maintained larger forces on the Manchurian border than the Western Allies knew. In the summer of 1945 he reinforced strongly, to create mass sufficient to bury the Japanese. Three thousand locomotives laboured along the thin steel thread of the Trans-Siberian rail link. Men, tanks, guns fresh from the Red Army's triumphs in eastern Europe were loaded onto trains at Königsberg and Insterberg, Prague and Brno, for a journey that took a month to accomplish. Moscow strove to disguise the significance of the huge migration. Soldiers were ordered to remove their Leningrad and Stalingrad medals, to repaint guns emblazoned with such slogans as "On to Berlin!" No one doubted their new objective, however. As the troop trains crawled across Russia, at stations sympathetic locals called to their passengers, craning from windows: "Ah, boys, they are taking you off to fight the Japanese—the *yaposhki*." A veteran muttered wryly: "So this is military secrecy!" Men of Maj. Vladimir Spindler's rifle regiment gave away their bulky European loot to Russian civilians whom they met as they moved east. Spindler gazed pityingly on starving urchins crowding the rail tracks. Some asked wistfully: "Uncles, is our daddy among you by any chance? He fought against the Germans too."

"Everyone slept a lot, catching up on all the sleep we'd lost," said soldier Oleg Smirnov. They discussed the eastern campaign. Most soldiers grudgingly acknowledged that "the samurais," as Russians called the Japanese, had to be dealt with. "We reckoned it would take a month to sort them out," said Smirnov, "which proved about right. Myself, I couldn't help thinking what a pity it would be to die in a little war after surviving a big one." Lt. Stanislav Chervyakov and the men of his *katyusha* rocket unit travelled by train from Prague to Moscow, exhilarated by a delusion that they were going home. They had fought through four long years at Stalingrad and on the Don, in Romania, Austria and finally Czechoslovakia. The first intimation that their rulers had other plans came as they approached the capital. Their train, instead of proceeding to Moscow's central station, took the ring line. Chervyakov was less dismayed than most of his comrades. A career soldier, "I was twenty-two, and I didn't give a damn who I fought."

By contrast, Sgt. Anatoly Fillipov, radio operator with an intelligence unit, was weary of war. He was twenty-eight, and had been the first to bring news to his commander of the June 1941 German invasion, for which he was roundly cursed and told to "cut out the bullshit." In 1943 he was wounded and taken prisoner on a secret mission into neutral Turkey, and badly beaten by his Turkish captors before escaping. Fillipov was in Moscow in May 1945 when told that he was being posted to the Far East. He enlisted the good offices of his brother, a staff college student, to delay his departure until after Victory Day, Stalin's equivalent of VE-Day, twenty-four hours later: "Please, Lyosha, could you ask your commander to get permission for me to stay? I so much want to see the Parade!" Fillipov got this wish, but his wider ambitions went unfulfilled. He was a sailor at heart, raised aboard a Volga river steamer on which his father was an engineer. All he wanted now was a chance to join the merchant fleet and travel the world. He cherished a special dream of seeing Rio de Janeiro. Instead, he went to Manchuria.

Oleg Smirnov was deeply saddened by his unit's journey east. In East Prussia on VE-Day, he had emptied his pistol into the air, holstered it with finality, and declared: "Those were the last shots I shall ever fire." Now he was called upon to fight again. Crossing Lithuania, his train was attacked by anti-Communist partisans, who had to be driven off. Despite the bands and welcomes from local people at every Russian station halt, "we came to realise the price we had paid for victory. Day after day while the train crawled slowly through European Russia we saw around us only burnt-out ruins, chimneys amid charred wastelands, fields scarred by trenches and craters . . . Even beyond the Volga where the villages stood intact, one saw no fit men—only women, old men and cripples. I remember looking out at women dragging ploughs and homeless kids at the stations." A railway guard at Chita scrounged a cigarette from Smirnov and said: "What a host is moving east! The samurais are in for a bad time, and those rats must know it. Look at the Japanese consul here—he sits every day by the river with his fishing rod, counting trains. He can count as many as he likes, but his lot are for it!"

After travelling 6,000 miles from Europe by rail, some units, including Vladimir Spindler's, marched the last two hundred to the Manchurian border across the treeless Mongolian desert in blazing heat. A large influx of young recruits joined them, many weak from malnutrition. These were given hasty training, and as much food as could be spared. "Frankly, most of us hated having to do this," said anti-aircraft gunner Georgy Sergeev, a veteran of the European campaign. "I was due to turn twenty in September. I kept thinking, would I now live to be twenty?" After all that they had survived in the west, now they were back under the sun and stars, living on field rations. Once again, in Sergeev's words, "there was that perpetual uncertainty, not knowing what would happen tomorrow, or whether there would even be a tomorrow."

"I'd taken part in plenty of offensives, but I'd never seen a build-up like this one," said one soldier. "Trains arrived one after another, off-loaded men who formed ranks and marched away across the steppe. The diesels of hundreds of brand-new tanks roared, as they were started up by crews of veterans, *frontoviks*, who had fought in Europe. There were tractors towing heavy artillery, *katyushas*, cavalry, dust-covered trucks, and ever more infantry. Even the sky was crowded there were always bombers, *sturmoviks*, transports overhead." Machine-gunner Anatoly Shilov was bemused to find himself at a wayside station where he was presented with 5 mechanics, 130 raw recruits, and crates containing 260 Studebaker,

Chevrolet and Dodge trucks which he was ordered to assemble, then deliver to a formation sixty miles away. He managed this notable feat by coupling the vehicles in pairs, the front wheels of the rearmost lashed high onto the body of the one in front.

As the infantry marched, "the earth smelt not of sagebrush, but of petrol," wrote a soldier. "Dust hung in a dense cloud over the column, it lay on our faces, rasped between our teeth. It was hot as hell, a hundred degrees or more. Sweat dripped into our eyes, our throats were parched—we could fill only one waterbottle a day." Dust storms whipped the steppe. Captured German mess tins with covers became much prized, because only these excluded sand from everything eaten. Most men lost their appetites for food or cigarettes, caring only about thirst. When they reached a lake, the water proved saline. Those who drank retched in disgust. They marched day and night, with four-hour halts which offered little respite, because the bare earth was too hot for a man to lie upon without discomfort. "It took us a week to reach the Manchurian border. By the finish we were stumbling, falling asleep as we moved. The tramp of marching feet was always audible, even above the roar of tank and vehicle engines, the clatter of tracks."

By early August, 136,000 railway cars had transferred eastwards a million men, 100,000 trucks, 410 million rounds of small-arms ammunition, 3.2 million shells. Even firewood had to be collected from forests and shipped four hundred miles, to enable units deployed in treeless regions to cook their rations. Thirty-five thousand tons of fuel were needed on the Trans-Baikal Front alone, requiring as much haulage capacity as ammunition. As part of Stalin's bargain with the Western Allies, he insisted that the U.S. should help to feed and arm the Soviet soldiers whose participation in the eastern war was expected to save so many American lives. This aspect of their forthcoming campaign did not escape the Red Army: "Guys rubbished the Americans for wanting to get other people to do their fighting," said Oleg Smirnov. Moscow called on the U.S. for 860,410 tons of dry goods, 206,000 tons of liquids—mostly fuel—and 500 Sherman tanks. Most of these commodities and weapons were indeed shipped to Russia's Pacific ports.

As troops approached the frontier, elaborate camouflage and deception schemes were adopted to mask their deployments. Senior generals travelled under false names: the commander-in-chief and victor of the East Prussian campaign, Marshal Alexander Vasilevsky, became "Colonel-General Vasil'ev." Vasilevsky, only forty-nine in 1945, was originally educated for the priesthood. He started his military career as a Tsarist officer, joined the Red Army in 1918 and was commanding a regiment a year later.

Big, handsome, silver-haired, a surprisingly benign figure for a Soviet commander, he served as the Stavka's representative at Stalingrad and Kursk. He was Zhukov's closest colleague, yet never achieved the celebrity of some other marshals—nor incurred the consequent resentment of Stalin.

The Soviet plan called for massive envelopments of the Japanese defences by offensives on three axes, followed by the capture of Sakhalin and the Kurile Islands, and then if possible northern Hokkaido. The Trans-Baikal Front, commanded by Malinovsky, was to attack western Manchuria; Meretskov's 1st Far Eastern Front was to drive into eastern Manchuria, heading for Mukden—modern Shenyang—Harbin and Jilin. In the north, Purkaev's 2nd Far Eastern Front would launch supporting attacks, while a mechanised group headed directly for Beijing. This was to be a blitzkrieg, relying on speed to pre-empt Japanese responses. The Guandong Army—which Moscow estimated at a million men, instead of the actual 713,724, organised in twenty-four divisions—would be denied any respite to form new defensive lines. The so-called Manchukuo Army, raised from local Chinese collaborators, numbered 170,000 but possessed neither will nor means to give much combat support to the Japanese.

The Russians, with 3,704 tanks and 1,852 self-propelled guns, enjoyed a paper superiority of two to one in men, five to one in tanks and artillery, two to one in aircraft. In quality, however, the disparity was much greater. More than a third of the Soviet troops were veterans, as were their commanders. Japanese divisions were woefully understrength. The Guandong Army had been progressively stripped of its best units to reinforce other fronts. Its heavy weapons were entirely outclassed by those of the Red Army. Some Japanese bayonets were forged from the springs of scrapped motor vehicles. Many mortars were homemade. There was sufficient ammunition to issue riflemen only a hundred rounds apiece, without reserves. The Japanese themselves estimated that their formations in China and Manchuria possessed one-third their pre-war combat power.

Soviet soldiers grumbled when, on approaching the border, they were ordered to dig in. "We're supposed to be attacking, aren't we?" they said. They were warned that the Japanese might use biological weapons, and were inoculated against cholera and typhoid. Veterans were dismayed when they saw the poor quality of reinforcements sent to swell their ranks. "These were 'war babies,' " wrote Oleg Smirnov, "weak boys reared on the meagre food available behind the fronts." Men fed to fight under Zhukov and Konev in Europe were amazed to see the condition of those who had served in eastern garrison units, subsisting on starvation rations: "They were simply skin and bones, dressed in shabby uniforms, shod in foot-bandages such as we had never seen." There was a deep psychological divide between "westerners" and "easterners" in the ranks of Vasilevsky's armies.

The marshal's original orders from the Stavka called for his forces to attack on the morning of 11 August, Far East time. Following news of Hiroshima, however, on the afternoon of the seventh he was abruptly directed to advance his timetable by two days. In the hours before the assault, senior officers were briefed on what little was known about the atomic bomb. Implausibly, they were urged to seek any available intelligence about the new weapon which they could extract from Japanese prisoners.

It was evident to Moscow that Japan's surrender had become imminent. It thus became vital to secure Russia's promised prizes, lest the victorious Americans have second thoughts about acquiescence. Soviet reasoning was indistinguishable from that of the British in Burma. It was perceived that only physical occupation of territory could ensure subsequent jurisdiction over it. On 8 August, like thousands of others, Lt. Alexander Fadin and his fellow officers of 20th Guards Tank Brigade were summoned to the unit commander's tent. Hitherto, though every man knew the purpose of the huge mobilisation, it had never been openly avowed. Now, the colonel said: "The time has come to erase the black stain of history from our homeland . . ." Political officers believed that the most plausible motivation which they could offer Soviet soldiers was to invite them to reverse Russia's 1905 defeat by Japan.

To achieve surprise, the Soviets denied themselves air reconnaissance of Japanese positions behind the Manchurian frontier. Their maps were poor, and few displayed contours. The Soviet 15th Army in the north crossed the Amur River with the aid of a makeshift flotilla of commercial steamships, barges and pontoons. In some places the Japanese sought to impede landings by setting fire to floating timber and barges. Soviet gunboats with such names as *Proletariat* and *Red Star* duelled with shore batteries. There was fierce street fighting in Fuchin, until Soviet tanks landed to reinforce the first wave of infantry. One armoured brigade's lead elements were sixty-two miles deep in Manchuria before its rear units got ashore. In nine days, the Amur River Flotilla transported 91,000 men, 150 tanks, 3,000 horses, 413 guns and 28,000 tons of stores. The operation was chaotic, but against weak opposition it worked.

In the north-west, as Sgt. Anatoly Fillipov's vehicles approached the border at Atpor with their unit of the Trans-Baikal Front, a Soviet frontier guard waved enthusiastically: "Say hello to the Manchurians for me!" The central plain, where all the region's important industries and commerce were concentrated, could be reached only by traversing great expanses of

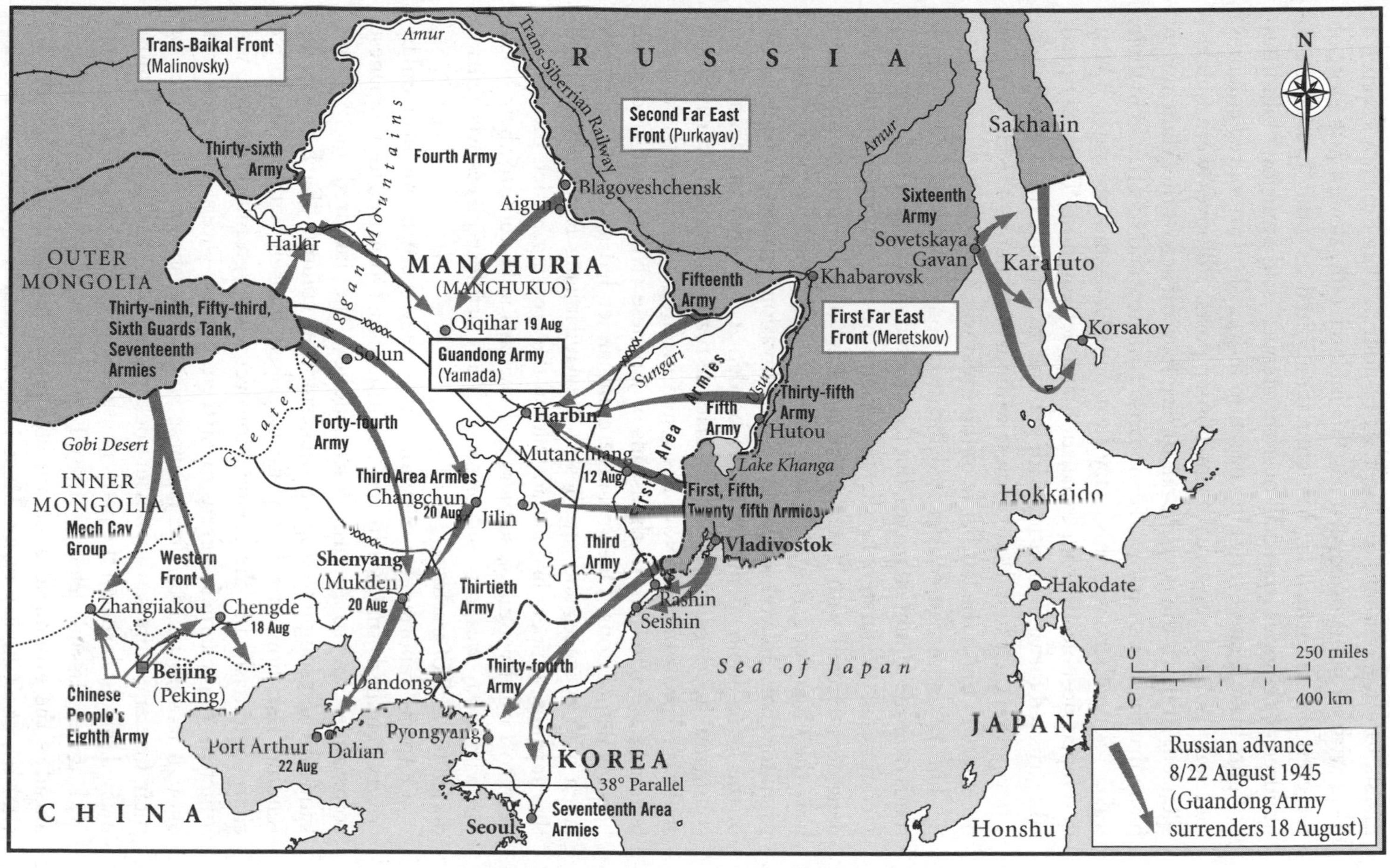

The Russian invasion of China, August 1945

marsh, forest, mountains or desert. At H-hour in Oleg Smirnov's sector, a T-34 with its lights on rattled past his infantry unit, slowed just short of the crest beyond which lay Manchuria, and fired its gun. "Immediately, hundreds of engines roared all over the steppe," said Smirnov, "hundreds of lights blazed, and everything began to move." The armoured columns met only isolated resistance from border posts. Pillboxes were quickly silenced. At dawn the tanks began to race forward across the Manchurian plain, dry riverbeds their roads, motorised infantry and fuel trucks in their wake. "Soon there was this crazy heat and dust—and no water." Men developed nosebleeds from exhaustion and dehydration. They glimpsed lakes, rushed forward shouting with joy, only to perceive them as mirages. They passed their first dead Japanese without sentiment. "We knew it was necessary to finish the last battle of this great war."

The Japanese had constructed fortified zones to protect recognised roads over the mountain passes, but they lacked men and materials to hold a continuous perimeter. In the first hours of the Soviet invasion, the defenders reacted with dazed bewilderment. It is hard to comprehend how the Guandong Army allowed itself to suffer such tactical surprise, when for years Tokyo had feared a Soviet invasion. Japanese officers knew of the huge deployment across the border. As so often in Japan's high command, however, evasion of unpalatable reality prevailed over rational analysis of probabilities. Now, hasty staff meetings were held. A struggle began to evacuate tens of thousands of Japanese civilians and undertake belated demolitions. One Japanese commander led a convoy of trucks laden with evacuees and supplies to the Mudanjiang River, only to find that Japanese sappers had already blown the crossing, which proved too deep to ford. Eventually, soldiers and civilians alike took to their heels, throwing away weapons and baggage. Many artillery pieces were abandoned for lack of tractors.

Outposts reported by telephone that they were being overrun by "overwhelmingly superior forces." A pitiful signal from one local Japanese commander on 10 August described how the hundred men of his kamikaze unit sought to stop a Soviet armoured column: "Each man of the Raiding Battalion's 1st Company equipped himself with an explosive charge and dashed at the enemy. However, although minor damage was inflicted, the charges—seven to sixteen pounds—were not powerful enough to stop tanks." The Japanese were astonished and dismayed by their first encounters with Soviet rocket launchers, the *katyushas* whose massed salvoes carpeted the paths of attacks.

Engineer assault groups of 1st Far Eastern Front were parachuted ahead of the ground advance, to seize intact tunnels and bridges on the vital eastern China railway. Most Japanese guards were stealthily dispatched with knives and clubs, but a few pillboxes offered resistance. After the tunnels were secured, Maj. Dmitry Krutskikh met a cart taking his casualties to the rear. He looked at one boy, no more than eighteen, obviously badly wounded, unlikely to live. Krutskikh asked: "Does it hurt?" The soldier said: "It does indeed, comrade officer, but I'll fight again!" Krutskikh wrote long afterwards: "Sixty years have passed, but still I remember that soldier's voice and eyes. Those firefights were pretty rough." The advancing Russians heard news of the atom bomb attack on Nagasaki. "To be frank," said Major Krutskikh, "we had too much on our minds to pay much attention. And, of course, none of us could imagine the scale of destruction."

On the morning of 9 August, the Guandong Army's commander, Otozo Yamada, called on the palace of Emperor Pu Yi at Changchun. Yamada, a slight, moustachioed cavalry veteran of the 1905 Russo-Japanese war, was habitually solemn and taciturn. Now, crisis rendered him voluble. His assertions of confidence in victory were somewhat discredited by the sudden wail of air-raid sirens, followed by the concussions of falling Russian bombs. Emperor and general retreated to continue their conversation in a shelter.

Pu Yi, a hypochondriac prey to superstition and prone to tears, was consumed with terror that either the Japanese or Chinese would now kill him. A tall, gangling, immature creature of thirty-nine, for years he had indulged his sexual enthusiasms with a bevy of consorts and concubines, his petulant sadism by beating domestics. Under the Japanese, he enjoyed a much-diminished portion of the trappings of majesty. At his court, only ten eunuchs remained of the 100,000 who had served the Ming emperors, or of the hundreds whose quarters he liked to snipe at with an airgun in his earlier life as child-emperor. As nominal ruler of Manchukuo, Pu Yi signed official documents, death warrants and industrial plans without discrimination, earning the loathing of the Chinese people for his collaboration. His pages were recruited from Changchun orphanages, where they languished after their parents were killed by the Japanese. He was saluted as a head of state, yet in reality was merely Japan's most prominent prisoner.

Now, the prospect of becoming a dead one threw him into ecstasies of terror. He began to carry a pistol day and night. On 10 August, a Japanese officer arrived at the palace to announce that the army was withdrawing south. The emperor must prepare to leave immediately for Tunghua. Pu Yi's pleas secured a two-day postponement, but the Japanese said bleakly: "If your majesty does not go, you will be the first to be murdered by the Soviets." When the emperor demanded food, he was told that all his cooks had fled. On the night of 11 August, carrying in the baggage his dynasty's sacred Shinto objects, the wretched little imperial party set off on a slow, faltering private train.

THE CHIEF PROBLEMS facing the Russians were those of terrain. Gunners dragged artillery pieces by brute force through marshes, while infantrymen discarded their rifles to help build tracks for the passage of heavy equipment. Troops of 1st Far Eastern Front ferried across the Ussuri River found themselves wading through chest-high swamps on the Manchurian shore. Engineers struggled to cut wire and clear minefields under torrential rain. Forest approaches were no more hospitable. "Between the trees, thick undergrowth created a carpet of thorns, each as long as a man's finger and sharp as a sewing needle," wrote A. P. Beloborodov. "These created hazards that could cripple an unwary man in minutes, gashing flesh and piercing the soles of boots . . . Streams and creeks were so swampy that even tanks as powerful and manoeuvrable as T-34s became bogged." The Khalkin-Gol River at the southeast border of Manchuria was not more than sixty yards wide and four feet deep, but its racing current overturned trucks and gun tractors. The Russians solved the problem in characteristic fashion, by deploying across the flow a line of Mongol cavalry on their shaggy ponies, riders locked knee to knee. Infantry then waded across upstream of them, gripping the beasts' manes to keep their footing.

Everywhere, the Soviets forced passages. Again and again they confounded enemy strongpoints built to cover roads by cutting across open country. Japanese suicide troops—*smertniks*, as the Russians called them—launched raids by day and night against sappers clearing minefields and in the attackers' rear areas. But these could do nothing to halt the relentless advance. A Soviet account described a rare set-piece action, near Zixincun:

> The road widened somewhat, but nevertheless only two tanks could advance abreast, almost locked together. We glimpsed wooden peasant huts ahead, and heard explosions as Japanese anti-tank guns opened up from the high ground. The column halted to return fire. Some tank crews found ways to bypass the road across country, and broke through to the strongpoint. Fighting became general. Tank engines raced amid a tangle of trenches, pillboxes, dugouts and gun positions . . . Japanese shells often struck home, while huts and grass caught fire. For more than an hour, our forces experienced perhaps their bloodiest battle since the campaign began. Finally the enemy faltered. [We could see] hundreds of retreating Japanese dotting the hills and marshy stream beds. The tanks raced after them.

A Japanese account described suicide teams leaping out from the roadside to attack the foremost Russian armour, while anti-tank guns attempted to knock out the rearmost and block the road. "Yet even when tanks were hit, the damage was slight, for our shells were not armour-piercing," recorded a despairing officer. "The enemy calmly carried out repairs in full view of our lines, his arrogance mocking our impotence . . . We noticed that some tank crews included women." At 0900 on 14 August, a Japanese divisional commander received a report from a position in the Central Sector, delivered by a horseman in the absence of radio or phone links: "Because of the difficulty of holding our positions, the regiment will launch a counterattack behind its colours. This may be our last report."

During the first days, Japanese aircraft offered sporadic resistance. Soviet pilot Boris Ratner's wing began the campaign full of apprehension, given the historic reputation of the enemy's air force, but quickly found its confidence soaring. One Russian flier was lost on his first ground-attack sortie, none thereafter. Pilots struck repeatedly at Japanese troop and vehicle columns. Anti-aircraft fire occasionally holed Russian planes, but brought down scarcely any. A handful of Japanese reconnaissance aircraft were destroyed wherever they appeared. The Russians were surprised to discover that most enemy airfields contained only dummy planes. They began to perceive how feeble were the defences of Manchuria.

The Japanese high command quickly wrote off its own frontier outposts, and set about creating shorter defensive lines well to the rear. This policy was realistic enough, but became hopelessly compromised when Guandong Army headquarters attempted simultaneously to reorganise its formations. Many officers were left uncertain to whom they were reporting, never mind what they were supposed to hold. They lacked time and mobility to redeploy effectively. Some units were still trying to move to new positions when the war ended. "Many Japanese lacked the will to fight hard in Manchuria—they knew the war was lost," said Chinese historian Wang Hongbin. "A million defenders sounds a lot, but these troops had never been obliged to fight a modern enemy such as the Russians were, fortified with all the experience of their campaigns in Europe, and with very strong air support. The Russian war machine was incomparably more advanced, and the Japanese could enlist no local assistance."

RUSSIAN TANK columns advanced ninety-three miles the first day across the desert facing the western Trans-Baikal Front. Some units became lost, disorientated by the great dust clouds they threw up. "Units advanced from hill to hill under the blazing sun, their men rejoicing at each breath of breeze," wrote Col.-Gen. Liudnikov Doroga. "The hills seemed endless, and made distances deceptive . . . Daytime temperature reached ninety-five degrees, and medical officers became alarmed by the threat of heat stroke. Men knew that snatching at a waterbottle only intensified thirst. They endured. Vehicles did not. Engines overheated and radiators boiled. At last, the Grand Hinggang loomed . . . The mountains were bathed in silence. We had got there before the Japanese, and must scale them at once."

Lt. Alexander Fadin of 20th Guards Brigade said: "We were completely exhausted by the heat and the struggle to overcome so many natural obstacles. When the order to halt came and we climbed out of the tanks, men could hardly stand up." Each division reported thirty to forty heat-stroke cases a day. Flimsy canteens cracked, leaving their owners dependent on more fortunate comrades to assuage thirst. "When we found a well, we had to draw water from thirty or forty feet down," said Stanislav Chervyakov. "It was ice-cold, and after drinking some men suffered agonies from twisted guts. Several died. We learned that it was essential for officers to get to wells first and carefully supervise men's drinking. It was an incredibly wild country. We scarcely saw any Japanese. We had been told to expect attacks from their guerrillas, but there were none. We were shocked by the poverty of the Chinese. Their mud huts were such a contrast to what we had grown used to in Europe. Whatever our ranks, they called us all '*Kapitana*'!" The 59th Cavalry Division faced special difficulties, needing water for its ponies and lacking means to carry much. Its commander detailed a special squadron to ride ahead, identifying and securing wells on the line of advance.

Sgt. Georgy Petryakov's principal anxiety was not to get himself killed. He had survived four years of war, spent partly on the German front and partly on garrison duty in the east. Now he had applied for Communist Party membership, that passport to all good things in Soviet life. He wanted to be around to enjoy them. "I could never have believed such a climate possible—thirty degrees below freezing in January, a hundred degrees in August." He hated everything he saw of the parched countryside of Manchuria, including the inhabitants whom they had come to liberate: "What hypocrites the Chinese were! Grinning, bowing, fawning on us," he said in disgust. Yet he was still more repelled by the contempt with which Japanese, even as prisoners, treated Chinese civilians.

Before dawn on 11 August, 39th Army began to force a path up the steep ascent of Grand Hinggang. The Japanese deemed it impassable, and thus had done nothing to fortify the crests. Even small forces covering the approaches would have immensely complicated the invaders' task. As it was, however, the Russians fought only the mountains. T-34 tanks took the lead—American Shermans were less rugged, and used more fuel. In places, tracks were barely ten feet wide, traversed by streams and gullies, each one of which had to be bridged. Some units found their advances blocked by rock walls. Then heavy rain fell, and the wheeled vehicles thrashed helplessly. "At first, we were so thrilled by the rain," said Oleg Smirnov, "and afterwards, how we learned to curse it!" Soldiers have better cause than other men to hate foul weather, for they can seek no refuge from it. Flooded mountain streams pushed great boulders downhill. Soldiers compared the lightning to the flickering of a *katyusha* barrage. Men laboured to push and pull stranded trucks through the mire—they later asserted that they got their vehicles up Grand Hinggang by "fart power." Sometimes a truck slipped off a precipice and sailed into space, to shatter far below. Even in daylight, the low cloudbase forced vehicles to use lights.

On the mountain ascent, engines revved in frenzy as tracks slipped on wet rocks, tanks skidded into deep mud. "Even experienced drivers shook their heads as they gazed up the hills," said Alexander Fadin. His own tank made three attempts on the highest pass, before negotiating it by linking three T-34s with steel cables. Lt. Stanislav Chervyakov, who had been so careless about his assignment to Manchuria when the campaign began, found himself a much less happy soldier amid the defiles of Grand Hinggang. He and his men had to off-load crates of *katyusha* rockets, then haul their big, heavy Studebaker trucks up the mountain on ropes, by main force: "It was hopeless terrain for us, and there was nothing for the *katyushas* to do."

The descent on the far side of Grand Hinggang proved more hazardous than the climb, with tanks careering uncontrollably down steep, slippery defiles. There were constant breakdowns, and still no respite from the rain. At last, the tank crews heard firing ahead. It was their reconnaissance unit, engaged with the Japanese in the town of Lupei. The brigade hastened forward, to find the defences already crushed. They drove curiously past the Japanese positions, noting pole charges lying beside the enemy's dead. A disappointed voice said on the radio net: "We're too late again." That evening of the twelfth, some tanks ran out of fuel. "How's the milk situation?" the battalion commander enquired by radio, in primitive code. Fadin responded that most of his company had only enough diesel for a further twenty or thirty miles. They were ordered to give all but a few litres to their brigade's first battalion, which would keep moving. Next morning, their own tanks were resupplied by transport aircraft which landed in a neighbouring field and off-loaded drums. Soviet aircraft humped to the spearheads 2,000 tons of fuel and seventy-eight of ammunition.

If a tank broke down, it was taken in tow by another. On the plain, the armoured column found that the Japanese had blown dams, flooding huge areas. The only passable line of advance lay down a high, narrow railway embankment from Tunliao to Chzhaniu. With their crews feeling acutely vulnerable, a procession of tanks began to bump along the line. Vibration caused breakdowns and track breakages. Cripples were rammed aside into the waterlogged paddies. A lone Japanese kamikaze aircraft destroyed a T-34 and several soft-skinned vehicles. At last, however, the Russians found themselves back on solid ground, and racing forward.

Some Japanese cavalry put up a fight, but many defenders chose to surrender—1,320 prisoners were taken on the evening of 14 August. Russian veterans of the European war cried "*Hande hoch!*" to enemies who appeared willing to quit, for they knew no words of Japanese. The commander of the Manchukuo 10th Military District arrived in the Russian lines to surrender, at the head of a column of a thousand Chinese horsemen. Though isolated strongpoints held out, most were bypassed. Sixth Guards Tank Army advanced 217 miles in four days, its chief impediments a shortage of fuel for vehicles, water for men. On 19 August, Soviet aircraft landed at Shenyang (Mukden) and Changchun to seize the cities' airfields. Two days later they met their brethren of the armoured columns, arriving overland.

The men of 1st Far Eastern Front found themselves advancing through a maze of wreckage left behind by Soviet bombardment and air attacks: dead men and horses, papers and photographs fluttering loose on the wind, burnt-out vehicles and debris trampled into the mud. The stench was indescribable—a blend of death and excrement, burnt rubber and bloated animals. Victor Kosopalov's regiment was briefly checked by a bee swarm. Gunfire had wrecked the creatures' hives: "They went mad and stung everyone until they were tranquillised with smoke candles."

LI DONGGUAN and his Soviet-sponsored reconnaissance team were working behind the enemy lines as so often before, in the city of Dongan, pinpointing Japanese positions and reporting by radio to their base. Within days they were overrun by the Russians, and the remaining Japanese threw down their arms. Li, in Russian uniform, suddenly found himself confronted by Japanese with their hands held high, bowing in abject submission. "They deserved everything they got," he said laconically. "Nobody had asked them to occupy our country."

Jiang De was among a contingent of Soviet-trained guerrillas who were suddenly mustered at their forest base in eastern Russia on 8 August, to be told: "You're off." They were taken to an airfield, where sixty Chinese in fifteen four-man teams were loaded aboard three transport aircraft, with strict orders that none were to discuss their destinations with others. Then they took off for Manchuria. For Jiang's group, there was an alarming problem. By a characteristic piece of Soviet carelessness, while most of their comrades had received parachute training, they had not. Appalled by the prospect of making their first jump onto a battlefield, they sought to console themselves with the thought that they would play a prominent role in the liberation of their country.

Two hours later, they hurtled into the darkness over Manchuria. Jiang and two of his comrades were lucky enough to survive intact. At first light they contacted local peasants who told them that their fourth comrade had been less fortunate—his corpse lay in the fields. Jiang made radio contact with his Russian base. He was told that it was vital to find the body of their companion, to recover his maps and papers. The peasants led them to the place where he had landed. Sun Chengyu had been a good friend of Jiang. Now, "his corpse looked a shocking mess." The static line of his parachute had snapped when he jumped, and the canopy never opened.

The three survivors, two in Japanese uniform and one in civilian clothes to meet alternative eventualities, set about their business—reporting troop movements and inciting local people to make trouble for the enemy. At lunchtime on 11 August, only a few hours after their landing, peasants reported that a platoon of Japanese had arrived in their village, and were demanding food. "Give it to them," said Jiang. "Try and get them together in one place. Then, when you've got them all eating, find somewhere to hide." The Japanese were wholly unsuspecting when the three Chinese burst into the hut where they sat, and opened a murderous fire with sub-machine guns. When the first magazines were spent, only four or five wounded Japanese still moved. The Chinese reloaded, finished off the cripples, then left the peasants to carry off the corpses in carts to be thrown into the nearby river.

"We felt really pleased with ourselves," said Jiang. "The Japanese had killed so many of our people that it felt wonderful to even the score." They summoned all the villagers they could find, announced who they were, proclaimed that the Japanese were finished, and invited local people to help them to gather information. The young Chinese agents threw away the Japanese uniforms in which they had jumped, replacing them with Russian tunics. Their mission enjoyed one more moment of excitement: on 14 August they spotted a column of Japanese withdrawing from the nearby town of Mudanjiang, and reported this by radio to their base. When a devastating Russian air strike hit the road soon after, they liked to believe that their signal had prompted it. After the attack the agents went down to the road, gathered all the Japanese weapons they could find among the bodies and wreckage, and distributed them to peasants. Next morning, they met a column of advancing Russian infantry "who gave us a great welcome." The three Chinese were dispatched by jeep back to their headquarters in Russia.

In some places there was heavy fighting. "This was no country stroll," said tank officer Alexander Fadin. "The samurais resisted desperately, especially during the first week. All those stories about Japanese suicide soldiers proved to be true." Radio operator Victor Kosopalov's unit approached a pass between two ridges, and suddenly came under fire from the high ground. Everybody dashed for cover, and from behind a rock Kosopalov watched curiously as bullets severed scrub branches over his head and struck sparks off stones. Eventually an officer gave him the coordinates of the Japanese position, which he passed in plain language to divisional headquarters. After a long pause, artillery fire deluged the Japanese. When at last the Russian infantry rose and advanced warily onto the high ground, they met no further resistance. On the summit they found a few Japanese corpses. Kosopalov was struck by the sight of an abandoned field kitchen, still steaming and full of boiled rice. They marched on.

Early on 13 August, Japanese general Yoichi Hitomi of the 135th Division approached the city of Hualin by rail with his staff and reinforcements, only to see the bridge across the Mudanjiang River blow up in their faces. Russian tanks began to shell the stranded train while some men jumped in the river and attempted to swim to safety. Hitomi and his men eventually found a way into Hualin on foot. He took command and for several days repulsed repeated Russian attacks.

Sgt. Anatoly Fillipov's first intimation of resistance from the Japanese garrison at Hailar came when his battalion glimpsed a flock of sheep in the fields, as it advanced towards the town on the evening of 11 August: "Suddenly the sheep were shooting at us: ta-ta-ta-ta! Japanese soldiers had worked their way in among them. They killed six of our men, which caused a bit of a panic." The Russians called down artillery fire on the Hailar defences, which included a deep anti-tank ditch and lines of trenches anchored to pillboxes. Sappers crawled forward to lay charges on the Japanese emplacements. As these exploded, infantry ran up and fired point-blank into the embrasures.

Yet still the attackers could not break through. "Japanese mortar and machine-gun fire was so heavy that we hardly dared raise our heads," said gunner forward observer Dashi Irencheev, whose corporal was killed beside him. "On the evening of 15 August, at about 1700 a battalion of samurais—kamikazes—rushed at us shouting '*Banzai!*' brandishing their swords, tunics unbuttoned and sleeves rolled up. Our gunners wasted no time, and killed half. Then our infantry counterattacked, and overran them. Not one retreated or surrendered. Some wounded samurais killed themselves. The field was littered with bodies." Soon after, a Japanese mortar bomb landed beside Irencheev, so close that he was concussed and deafened. He was eventually dug out by comrades with blood running from his ears. The Japanese in Hailar held out against artillery fire and infantry assault until 18 August, when 3,827 survivors surrendered.

The Russians learned the hard way the importance of protecting their rear echelons. A medical company of 3rd Rifle Division was bivouacked on the night of 14 August when a kamikaze force stormed its positions. The weary Russians were asleep. Japanese were already dragging doctors and nurses out of a vehicle when the alarm was given. After a brief firefight the enemy retreated, taking with them three nurses. Their mutilated bodies, hacked to pieces, were found nearby. This episode, declared an angry Soviet report, was due to "criminal carelessness" by the officers responsible for ensuring their unit's security. A platoon of sub-machine gunners was detailed to provide protection for the medical team.

A key reality of the Manchurian campaign was that the defenders possessed no means of shifting forces in the face of total Russian air superiority and their own lack of vehicles. They were also critically short of anti-tank guns. Yet where the Russians were obliged to attack painstakingly constructed defensive positions, the Japanese resisted stubbornly and inflicted substantial losses. In the east, at the heavily fortified road junction of Mudanjiang, two Japanese divisions fought for two days against 1st Far Eastern Front. A Japanese soldier described the action there on 15 August:

> As soon as our anti-tank guns had been silenced, about thirty enemy tanks appeared in front of 278th Regiment's main positions. They opened fire, inflicting heavy casualties, picking off the defenders one by one and destroying our heavy weapons . . . At about 1600 hours the regiment's telephone link with divisional headquarters was cut. Four enemy tanks were destroyed and five damaged. Soon afterwards, fifteen more tanks appeared in front of the division command post. A squad of five men from the Transport Unit, each armed with a 15-kilogram charge, launched a suicide attack on the leading elements, each man destroying one tank. On seeing this, the rest of the enemy armour hastily made off towards Sudaoling, and their accompanying infantry were also routed.

The respite persuaded the Japanese divisional staff to abandon plans for a final "*banzai*" charge. They maintained a conventional defence for a time, hampered by the fact that their phone lines were cut and radios almost non-existent. On 16 August, a certain Major Ueda of the 278th Regiment arrived at headquarters before dawn to report that the rest of the division had withdrawn. His commanding officer, Colonel Hajma Yamanaka, said simply: "I shall die here. I shall not withdraw in the absence of an explicit order." A few hours later, an overwhelming Russian tank and infantry force attacked their positions. At noon, Colonel Yamanaka respectfully bowed to the east, burned the regimental colour, rallied his survivors and led a counter-attack. When this failed, he and Major Ueda committed *hara-kiri*. Japanese accounts asserted that the capture of Mudanjiang cost them 4,000 dead, while the Soviets claimed 40,000. The truth is probably somewhere in between. The Red Army reckoned that this one battle accounted for half its total losses in Manchuria, including scores of tanks.

The city was cleared only on the evening of 16 August. Many Japanese never learned that they had been ordered to withdraw, and fought to the death. Over-ambitious Soviet spearheads, racing ahead, suffered severely from local counterattacks, but by 20 August they had reached Harbin. Organised resistance in North Korea, overrun by 1st Far Eastern Front, ended on 16 August. Some Japanese units, however, continued fighting for a further ten days. The Russians were grudgingly impressed by the fashion in which enemy strongpoints refused quarter, and had to be reduced by piecemeal bombardment and infantry attack. In the words of David Glantz, foremost Western historian of the campaign: "The defending troops in the Japanese fortified regions put up a tenacious, brave yet meaningless defense . . . Garrisons fought to the point of exhaustion or extermination."

BOTH WITHIN and without Manchuria, the Chinese received news of Stalin's onslaught with mixed feelings. In the first days, local people greeted the Russian armies enthusiastically. Victor Kosopalov's unit was delighted to be met in each village by peasants proffering buckets of springwater: "It was so hot and we were so thirsty—this was the most welcome delicacy they could have given us." Russian soldiers contemplating a flooded torrent were amazed when Chinese on the far bank leapt into the river and swam across to meet their liberators, carrying ropes to facilitate a crossing. Thousands of others went to work alongside Soviet sappers, repairing dams blown by the Japanese. Peasants gave warnings of ambushes. "When we entered the city of Vanemiao," said Oleg Smirnov, "the Chinese welcomed us with cries of '*Shango!*' and '*Vansui!*'—'10,000 years of life to you.' They were waving red flags and almost jumping onto our tank tracks." In reality, local people were most likely crying "*Zhongguo wansui!*"—"Long live China!"—but Smirnov and his comrades were not to know that.

On the Pacific coast, Russian naval infantry launched amphibious assaults to take the towns of Unggi and Najin on 11 and 12 August, and at Chongjin four days later. Even after the defenders were forced out, many continued fighting in the surrounding hills. Units of the Soviet 2nd Far East Front still faced heavy counter-attacks on 15–16 August. Russian warships found themselves duelling with an armoured train ashore. Fighting for Chongjin ended only late on 16 August, when troops of the Russian 25th Army arrived overland to meet the naval infantry.

The emperor Pu Yi's train approached Meheguo on 12 August. The Guandong Army's commander, Yamada, boarded the imperial carriage to report that Japanese forces were everywhere victorious. His assurances were immediately belied by the spectacle of crowds of screaming Japanese fugitives of all ages and both sexes, brawling soldiers and police, at Jelin station. Next day, the emperor arrived at Dalizikou, a coal-mining community set among beautiful mountains. Here, through two days of terror, Pu Yi and his bedraggled little party waited on events, and his fate.

It was plain that Japan was defeated, but it seemed much less obvious what would follow. "Most of us knew that Stalin was doing this for his own reasons," said Chinese Nationalist captain Luo Dingwen. "We had no reason to love or trust the Russians." Xu Guiming was a Chinese clerk at the Japanese Propaganda Bureau in the town of Aihni, on the Manchurian side of the Amur River, now in the Soviet 2nd Far Eastern Front's sector. He lived a few hundred yards from the office building, in a courtyard occupied by three families. There was his own, and that of Zeng, another clerk in the Propaganda Bureau. The third family was that of their landlord, a rich Muslim named Mr. Chen who owned ten cows and was customarily so deep in an opium-induced stupor that events of war and peace passed him by. On the evening of 9 August, a telephone rang in the courtyard. It was the Propaganda Bureau. All its employees were to report to the office immediately, to receive vital news.

Xu reached the squat three-storey building to find Japanese scurrying hither and thither with piles of documents, which they were hurling onto a huge bonfire. Inside, the staff assembled. The director announced that he had received information that Russian forces had crossed the border into Manchuria. Everyone must leave the town by next afternoon. The Japanese staff bowed their heads in abject misery. Xu felt no emotion, for nothing about his employers commanded his sympathy. They all queued to receive three months' salary apiece, then returned home as their workplace was put to the torch.

In the courtyard, Xu found his neighbour Zeng exploiting his ownership of four ponies to flee with his wife, children and what little they could carry. Xu discussed the situation with his own family, which included a brother and assorted children. They decided to seek shelter nearby. By the time they had taken themselves into the fields, darkness had fallen. Exhausted, they huddled together into a slumber which lasted well past dawn. Daylight revealed that while about half Aihni's 20,000 population had fled further afield, many inhabitants like themselves had chosen to remain, watching events which soon unfolded. A procession of Soviet gunboats appeared, steaming steadily downriver. They opened fire, raking the shoreline and pouring shells into the nearby railway station. To and fro the guns ranged, killing an old woman and a cow not far from Xu. Then, as Russian marines began to storm ashore, the head of the local labour union advanced to meet them. "Welcome to the north-east," said this rather brave Chinese. He told the Russians that all the Japanese had gone, and that there were no weapons in the town. Some 4,000 Japanese troops held out nearby, however, surrendering only on 20 August.

THE DAYS and weeks that followed the Russian occupation were a brutal shock to the "liberated" people of Aihni. They witnessed their share of the orgy of rape and destruction which overtook Manchuria. On 13 August, Xu Guiming saw two Russian soldiers accost in the street a local girl named Zhang—half-Russian, half-Chinese, like many people of the region. "We reckon you owe us one," they said, throwing her to the ground. One man held her down while the other bestrode her, and a ghastly little drama took place. Zhang fought fiercely, throwing aside her rapist. This caused the other man to unsling his gun and shoot her. His careless bullets also killed his comrade, however. The occupants of a passing Russian vehicle, seeing what happened, themselves unleashed a burst of fire which killed the murderer. Three corpses were left unheeded in the street.

Xu did not himself witness another local incident which became notorious. A Russian burst into the home of a local policeman, Mr. Su, who was sitting with a man friend and his twenty-year-old wife, newly delivered of a baby. The Russian brusquely ordered the men out, and raped the girl. When he emerged, the outraged Chinese seized and bound him, then thrust him down their well. This incident rendered the avenging Chinese briefly famous, and a local hero. However, when the Communists soon afterwards took control of Aihni, Su was arrested for killing the Russian, "our ally," and summarily shot. His raped wife was denounced as a counter-revolutionary, an outcast, and forbidden ever again to marry or receive the protection of a man.

Xu said bitterly: "This was not justice. Everyone was sickened by the things that happened. The Russians were supposed to be our liberators, our brothers, but we quickly learned to regard them as enemies. They masqueraded as revolutionaries, but in truth they were no more than wolves." Xu himself was fortunate to escape retribution for his time working for the Japanese. "I was too unimportant a person," he shrugged. Like millions of Manchurian Chinese, he now found himself witnessing a drama on which the curtain would ring down in accordance with Moscow's timetable, not that of Tokyo or Washington.

CHAPTER TWENTY-ONE

The Last Act

1. "God's Gifts"

The Operations and Plans Division of the War Department in Washington wrote on 7 August: "Undoubtedly the biggest question in [Japanese] minds is how many atomic bombs have we and where are we going to drop the next one . . . We had a rumor that Suzuki had been made Premier to make peace. If this was true, either there were strings to his appointment or else conditions have changed. Japanese propaganda since the [Potsdam] proclamation has obviously been guided by those 'self-willed militarists' against whom [it] was aimed." This was not far from the mark.

It remains cause for astonishment that, even in the wake of the atomic bombs and the Soviet invasion of Manchuria, the political stalemate in Japan at first appeared unbroken. The military party, dominated by the war minister, Anami, and other service chiefs, argued that nothing had changed: resistance to the death was preferable to accepting the Potsdam Declaration; Japan could still successfully oppose an invasion of the homeland. Admiral Toyoda, the naval chief, fancifully suggested that world opinion would prevent the U.S. from perpetrating another "inhuman atrocity" with atomic bombs. Some civilian politicians were now willing to accept Potsdam, but with familiar conditions: there should be no occupation of Japan, and the Japanese must try their own alleged war criminals. Most ministers, however, cared about only a single issue: retention of the position of the emperor, though there were endless nuances about how this demand should be articulated. There is no doubt that some genuinely feared the spectre of "red revolution" in Japan, of a dramatic and terrible explosion of popular wrath in the wake of defeat, if the stabilising influence of the emperor was removed.

Throughout 9 August, at meetings of the cabinet and Supreme War Council and at the Imperial Palace, these matters were debated. Within the government and service departments, the terms of dispute quickly became known, and provoked frenzied intrigue. Junior officers at the War Ministry, in particular, were appalled by the notion of surrender, and pressed their superiors to have no part of such a betrayal. Vice-Admiral Onishi, begetter of the kamikaze campaign and now deputy chief of naval staff, begged Anami not to yield to the peacemakers. News of the second atomic bomb on Nagasaki appears to have made astonishingly little impact on the leadership one way or another, save that it fulfilled the American purpose of emphasising that "Little Boy" was not a unique phenomenon. Anami speculated wildly that the Americans might possess as many as a hundred atomic weapons.

That evening of the ninth, the "Big Six" members of the Supreme War Council found themselves called to an "imperial conference" in the palace. There, they were told, Hirohito would announce a "sacred decision." The summons reflected fevered efforts by the peace party, in conversations that afternoon between Prince Konoe, Mamoru Shigemitsu and the lord privy seal, Marquis Kido. At first, Kido was aghast at the notion of involving the throne in a matter of such delicacy. "You are advocating a direct decision from the emperor," he told the politicians. "Have you ever thought what embarrassment such a course might cause His Majesty?" The peacemakers, however, knew that only the emperor's personal support might make it possible to overcome military resistance to surrender. They pressed their point. After a forty-minute private conversation between emperor and lord privy seal, the substance of which was never disclosed, Kido returned to report Hirohito's assent to an "imperial conference." The service chiefs agreed to attend, and to hear the "sacred decision," knowing full well what this would be. Most privately recognised that Japan was beaten. Yet still they ducked and weaved, to escape overt complicity in an outcome which their peers and subordinates would deem a betrayal. Slim of Fourteenth Army was surely right when he observed that while Japan's commanders were physically brave men, many were also moral cowards.

The imperial conference began ten minutes before midnight on 9 August. The text of the Potsdam Declaration was read aloud. Foreign Minister Togo tabled a one-condition draft, proposing Potsdam's acceptance provided that no change was demanded "in the status of the emperor under the national laws." War Minister Anami continued to preach defiance, supported by his military colleagues. Soon after 2 a.m. on 10 August, however, Prime Minister Suzuki rose, bowed to the emperor, ignored a protest from Anami and invited the emperor's decision. Hirohito, still seated at the table, leaned forward and said: "I will express my opinion. It is the same as that of the foreign minister." It was necessary to "bear the unbearable." Hirohito spoke harshly of the chasm between the military's past promises and performance. Suzuki said: "We have heard your august Thought." Hirohito then left the room. Everyone present, including the military proponents of continued belligerence, signed a document approving the imperial decision.

Yet the war party was successful in introducing into the Togo draft a significant amendment. This accepted Potsdam "on the understanding that the Allied Declaration would not comprise any demand which would prejudice the prerogatives of His Majesty as a Sovereign Ruler." It was almost inevitable that a phrase open to far-reaching interpretations would be rejected by the United States. Even at this late and terrible hour, in Tokyo resistance to capitulation persisted. As Japan's conditional acceptance of Potsdam was transmitted to the world, within the service ministries desperate intrigue continued. Junior officers were plotting a coup. The civilian politicians feared for their lives.

On 10 August, Japanese military headquarters in Shanghai signalled China Army HQ in Nanjing in some bewilderment. Local Chinese were celebrating Allied victory, its staff reported, cheering in the streets and letting off fireworks. Nationalist radio was reporting that Japan had accepted the Potsdam terms. What were Japanese forces supposed to do? In private, Nanjing staff officers readily recognised that the war was lost, and had started to address the logistical problems of getting a million soldiers and 750,000 civilians back to Japan. No one, however, was ready openly to concede this. Nanjing answered Shanghai: "Ignore it all. Japan has accepted nothing. We fight on."

That same morning of the tenth, when Truman heard news of the Japanese pronouncement, he summoned Byrnes, Stimson and Forrestal to the White House, where they were joined by Leahy, the president's chief of staff. It is an indication of Stimson's curious absence of expectation that any historic climax was imminent that he was due to leave on vacation that day, until he learned of the Japanese message. All those at the White House save Byrnes favoured immediate acceptance. No quibble, they thought, was worth delaying peace. But the secretary of state, still the most powerful influence on the president, said that he was troubled by the Japanese condition. "Unconditional surrender" had always been the demand, indeed a national slogan, of the United States. He argued that to modify this now, when the U.S. was using atomic bombs and Russia had entered the Japanese war, would seem incomprehensible to the American people. Byrnes was perfectly amenable to preserving Hirohito's role. He was merely determined that the world should perceive the throne's survival as the fruit of American magnanimity, not Japanese intransigence.

Truman approved a note drafted by the State Department at Byrnes's behest, which was sent to London, Moscow and Chongqing on the afternoon of 10 August. This stipulated that "from the moment of surrender the authority of the emperor and the Japanese government to rule the state shall be subject to the Supreme Commander of the Allied Powers," and that "the ultimate form of government of Japan shall be . . . established by the freely expressed will of the Japanese people." The British responded immediately, making their only significant intervention. They argued that it was wrong to insist, as the Americans proposed, that the emperor should personally sign the surrender terms. Probably mistakenly, Byrnes accepted this. He ignored Chiang Kai-shek's dissent.

On the tenth also, Truman told the cabinet he had given orders that no further atomic bombs should be dropped on Japan without his explicit authority. It is reasonable to speculate that, in the days since 6 August, a sense of the enormity of the consequences of Hiroshima had darkened the mood of celebration with which the president greeted the first news. He was not alone in this. "Along with a thrill of power and the instinctive pleasure at the thought of Japan cringing in abject surrender, America's deep-rooted humanitarianism has begun to assert itself," the British Embassy in Washington suggested to the Foreign Office in London on 11 August, "and this secondary revulsion has been very marked in private conversation, although it has not yet appeared in the press . . . There is a good deal of heart-searching about the morality of using such a weapon, especially against an enemy already known to be on his last legs."

Truman, however, was determined to maintain pressure on Japan. He rejected the urgings of Stimson and Forrestal to halt conventional bombing. Between 10 and 14 August, LeMay's Superfortresses maintained their attacks on Japan's cities, killing 15,000 people. Technical preparations continued for the release of further atomic bombs, should these prove necessary. A third weapon would be ready for delivery on 19 August. If Tokyo remained obdurate, U.S. assistant chief of staff Gen. John Hull debated with Colonel Seeman of the Manhattan Project the relative merits of dropping more bombs as they became available, or holding back to "pour them all on in a reasonably short time," in tactical support of an invasion. Gen. Carl Spaatz, USAAF strategic bombing supremo, opposed continuing firebomb attacks. This was not, however, for humanitarian reasons: he simply preferred to conserve American lives and effort until the nineteenth, then drop a third atomic weapon on Tokyo.

In Moscow, Stalin perceived that peace was very near, and hastened to complete his treaty with the Chinese Nationalists. By its terms, Moscow recognised Chiang Kai-shek as his country's sole legitimate ruler. However, the Soviet leader sought to introduce a clause whereby Chiang would introduce "national unity and democratisation." The Nationalist delegation rejected this out of hand. Stalin asked: "Don't you want to democratise China? If you continue to attack Communists, are we expected to support [the] Chinese government? We have no wish to interfere, but [it would be] hard for us to support [you] morally when you fight Communists." The Nationalists remained implacable. Stalin shrugged: "Very well. You see how many concessions we make. China's Communists will curse us." But agreement on other issues remained elusive. Only at 3 a.m. on 15 August was the "Treaty of Friendship and Alliance" between the USSR and China finally signed.

That night of the tenth in Moscow, Foreign Minister Molotov told Harriman, the U.S. ambassador, that in the absence of Japanese unconditional surrender, the Soviet thrust into Manchuria would continue. As ever, Tokyo's stubbornness suited Soviet convenience. More dismaying, the Soviets now abruptly asserted that they expected a share in the occupation of Japan, including the appointment of their own supreme commander to serve jointly with MacArthur. Harriman responded furiously, saying that this was an outrageous demand, when Russia had only been in the Japanese war for two days. The Soviets eventually backed off, and accepted MacArthur's appointment as SCAP—Supreme Commander Allied Powers.

On 11 August the Byrnes note was dispatched to the Japanese government. It reached Tokyo in the early hours of the twelfth, provoking bitter disappointment among the peace party. Togo, the foreign minister, was at first disposed to abandon his commitment to bow to Washington. Only with the utmost reluctance did Suzuki and Togo finally agree to accept Byrnes's terms. The most surprising reactions came from some of the military. Deputy Chief of Staff Torashiro Kawabe declared that it was now too late to draw back from surrender, or to question the emperor's decision. He wrote in his diary: "Alas, we are defeated. The imperial state we have believed in has been ruined." Kawabe's superior, Gen. Yoshijiro Umezu, was nicknamed "the ivory mask." He recognised that the war was lost. Toyoda, the naval chief, was similarly resigned. In contradiction to such private realism, however, in the presence of others all three persisted in holding out for conditions. Fearful of their own junior officers, they satisfied their "honour" by submitting a note to the emperor asserting that acceptance of the Byrnes note amounted to acceding to "slave status" for Japan. Hirohito sharply rebuked them, asserting that his own mind was made up. The nation must rely upon American good faith.

The army's general staff drafted its own defiant response for the Supreme War Council to send to the Americans, asserting Japan's determination to continue the war. Fantastically, it also emphasised Japan's refusal to declare war on the Soviet Union, apparently in the hope that Russian mediation still offered a prospect of better terms. This document was never dispatched, of course, but staff officers continued to plot a coup to forestall surrender. Kawabe was told of their intentions, and equivocated. Anami listened to an outline of the coup plan, neither approved nor disapproved, but made suggestions for refining its execution. He agreed to the mobilisation of some units which could secure the Imperial Palace and arrest civilian ministers. Anami's personal position had become further complicated the previous day, when Tokyo papers published in his name an exhortation to Japan's soldiers to fight on, "even if we have to eat grass, chew dirt and sleep in the fields." This display of bellicosity was in reality issued by junior officers without Anami's knowledge. He refused to renounce the statement, however, because it reflected his personal convictions.

Signals were received from a succession of officers in the field, urging that the nation should fight on. Old Gen. Yasuji Okamura, directing Japan's armies in China, cabled: "I am firmly convinced that it is time to exert all our efforts to fight to the end, determined that the whole army should die an honourable death without being distracted by the enemy's peace offensive." Field Marshal Terauchi spoke for his command: "Under no circumstances can the Southern Army accept the enemy's reply." Even by the standards of the Japanese military, in those days the conduct of its leaders was extraordinary. They seemed to care nothing for the welfare of Japan's people, everything for their perverted concept of personal honour and that of the institution to which they belonged. They knew that continued military resistance was futile. Yet they deluded themselves that they not only could, but must, pretend otherwise. Anami told Kido that the army was utterly opposed to accepting the Byrnes note. Among the civilian politicians, some continued to claim that they could endorse no terms which rendered the emperor subordinate to the supreme Allied commander.

Hirohito himself, however, declared that he was satisfied by Washington's assertion that the Japanese people could choose their own form of government. There is significant evidence that he was more affected than his senior officers by the atomic bombings—he quizzed Kido closely about their effects. At 3 p.m. on 12 August, the emperor summoned the men of his family, thirteen princes, to an unprecedented meeting at the palace, at which he explained the situation. All agreed to accept his judgement, including his youngest brother, Prince Mikasa, who had betrayed an earlier peace move to the military. Suzuki, after further vacillation, rallied with Togo to support acceptance of Byrnes's note. Yonai, the navy minister, with considerable courage summoned Admirals Toyoda and Onishi, and sternly reprimanded them for questioning the emperor's will. Yonai confided to a colleague: "The atomic bombs and the Soviet entry into the war are, in a sense, God's gifts." They offered substantive reasons to end the war.

All through 13 August, meetings of the military and civilian factions continued. Hirohito, having embarked hesitantly on the path to surrender, progressively increased the energy of his interventions to secure this. He appears to have exercised private pressure on all the military chiefs to forestall a coup. At 3 p.m., after further sessions of the Supreme War Council and cabinet, Togo reported to the emperor that the war and peace parties were deadlocked. Anami begged the prime minister to delay two days before reconvening the imperial conference—he obviously wanted time to rally the military against surrender. Suzuki refused. A naval doctor attending the ailing prime minister said: "You know that Anami will kill himself?" Suzuki said: "Yes, I know, and I am sorry."

The drama of those days, the constant proximity of disaster, almost defies belief. Only a chance encounter with a Tokyo journalist enabled the peacemakers to prevent the military plotters from broadcasting on national radio an announcement that Japan would fight on. Anami spent hours listening to pleadings from the colonels and majors planning their coup. He still refused to join them, presumably because a wooden-headed interpretation of honour prevented him from taking up arms against the emperor, while precluding him from frustrating the conspirators.

Two days had passed, in which Japan remained silent while the world waited. "The days of negotiation with a prostrate and despised enemy strained public patience," the British embassy in Washington reported to London: "Although the responsible press united in support of the [Byrnes] reply to the Japanese surrender offer . . . the general public were and still are much less tolerant of discredited deities . . . The man in the street seemed keener to hear about Admiral Halsey riding on Hirohito's white horse, as he had boasted he would, than to listen to explanations about the problems of administering Japan." More Japanese died under air bombardment. The Russians swept on across Manchuria.

On the morning of 14 August, at the Imperial Palace Kido was woken by an aide who showed him a leaflet, one of hundreds of thousands showered on Tokyo during the night by B-29s. This gave the text of the emperor's letter of 10 August accepting Potsdam, and the Byrnes response. Neither document had hitherto been seen by the Japanese public. Kido told Hirohito that he feared the propaganda bombardment might precipitate action by the coup plotters. He proposed to force the pace: there should be an unprecedented meeting of all twenty-three members of the cabinet and Supreme War Council, at which the emperor would announce his decision to accept the Byrnes note. Soon after ten, the leaders of Japan began to arrive, taking their places in silence on rows of chairs in the cramped basement shelter, awaiting Hirohito. At 10:50, the meeting began. The military representatives expressed their familiar objections to surrender. The prime minister did not trouble to invite the peace party to rehearse its arguments. He simply invited the emperor's decision.

Hirohito said he was convinced that Japan could not continue the war. He believed the Allies would retain the *kokutai*. He asked everyone present to respect his decision to accept the Byrnes note, and urged the military and naval leaders to persuade their subordinates to do so. He announced his intention to broadcast personally to the Japanese people, to help them accept the shock. He instructed the government to prepare an Imperial Rescript ending the war. Most of his listeners wept. Suzuki rose, thanked the emperor and apologised for the cabinet's failure to reach agreement, which had made imperial intervention necessary. Some postwar scholars have sought to argue that the Byrnes note enabled Japan to quit the war on contracted terms rather than by unconditional surrender, and thus that American stubbornness on the point—prompting the atomic bombs—was spurious. To dismiss this claim, it is necessary only to notice that the leaders of Japan were in no doubt that they submitted at America's mercy and pleasure, which is why so many resisted.

That night of 14 August, junior officers from the Army Ministry, led by Maj. Kenji Hatanaka and Lt. Col. Jiro Shiizaki, staged their coup. It was a feeble adventure, which could nonetheless have had disastrous consequences. First, the two officers and their supporters rushed into Anami's office on the war minister's return from the imperial conference. When he said that he could not support them, adding that "those who disobey will do so over my dead body," the conspirators burst into tears. Army chief Umezu gathered his staff around his own person, making it almost impossible for the rebels to pass orders to outlying units. His vice-chief secured the signatures of every leading military figure, including Anami, on a document committing them to accept the emperor's sacred decision. Senior soldiers began burning documents, a process that continued apace through the weeks which followed, in all Japan's key ministries and headquarters.

Around 4 p.m., Hatanaka and Shiizaki slipped into the compound of the Imperial Palace. They successfully convinced Col. Toyojiro Haga, commanding the 2nd Imperial Guard Regiment protecting Hirohito, that he should join their plot, on the understanding that it enjoyed the army's support. At 11 p.m. the Imperial Rescript, signed by every member of the cabinet, was dispatched to Berne and Stockholm, for onward transmission to the four Allied governments. In his office, Hirohito read the text aloud to a phonograph. Two duplicate records were then secreted in a safe in the empress's office, for broadcast next day. Even as the recording was being made, Hatanaka and Shiizaki drove to the headquarters of the Imperial Guard Division close to the palace, to incite its commander to join their plot. When he refused, Hatanaka drew a pistol and shot him dead. He then forged an order for all seven Imperial Guard regiments to rally to the emperor's "protection." This bluff was at first successful. Troops deployed to cut Hirohito's communications with the outside world.

Hatanaka and Shiizaki themselves hastened back to the palace, and began searching for the records of the imperial broadcast. They interrogated the radio technicians and court chamberlains, but were unable to find either the disks or Marquis Kido. Had they done so, much harm might have ensued. Any delay in the imperial broadcast would have cost lives. The mutiny might have spread. Kido and the emperor himself are thought to have hidden themselves during the hours in which angry and frustrated rebels roamed the palace corridors. Around 1:30 a.m. another plotter, Anami's brother-in-law Masashiko Takeshita, called at the war minister's house to plead once more with him to join the coup. A farcical scene ensued. Anami invited him in and said: "I am going to commit *seppuku*. What do you think?" Takeshita said he had always assumed that this would be Anami's chosen course. He certainly would not attempt to dissuade him. Abandoning his responsibilities to the other coup plotters, Takeshita sat down to drink *sake* with the doomed man. In the distance, they could hear the concussions of bomb explosions. In response to Spaatz's urging that the Twentieth Air Force should lay on "as big a finale as possible," 821 B-29s were attacking Japan that night.

Soon after 3 a.m., troops of Eastern Army arrived at the palace, informed the Imperial Guard soldiers that their orders had been faked, and quickly restored order. Realising that the coup had failed, one plotter, Col. Masataka Ida, drove to Anami's house to report the news. The war minister invited Ida, also, to join him for a farewell drink. There were more tears and embraces. At 5:30 a.m., Anami donned a white shirt given to him by Hirohito, seated himself on the floor facing the Imperial Palace, thrust a short sword into his left abdomen, and made the proper cross and upward cuts. He then severed his own carotid artery. As blood sprayed across the testament before him, Takeshita asked: "Do you want me to help?" Anami said: "No need. Leave me alone." When his brother-in-law found the general still breathing a few minutes later, he took the sword and finished him off. The only mitigation for Anami's contemptible conduct of his own life and death is that he never betrayed the doings of the peace party to the fanatics. Later that morning, Hatanaka and Shiizaki shot themselves.

Given the mind-set of Japan's armed forces, what was remarkable was not that a coup was attempted, but that only a tiny handful of officers chose to participate. For all their anger, and a significant number of suicides in the days to come, the overwhelming majority of soldiers acceded to the emperor's will. If this indicated the strength of Hirohito's influence, it also seems unlikely that it could have been effectual save in the new circumstances created by Soviet entry into the war and the atomic bombs. So powerful was the culture of self-immolation fostered by Japanese militarism over a generation that the instincts of many officers demanded continuing the war, however futile such a course.

Even had Japan chosen to reject the Byrnes note, it is most unlikely that an American invasion of the home islands would have been necessary. The Soviets were within days of reaching the Pacific coast and establishing themselves in the Kuriles. LeMay's B-29s were preparing to launch a systematic assault on Japan's transport network, against negligible opposition, which would quickly have reduced much of the population to starvation. Historians have expended much ink upon measuring the comparative influence of the atomic bombs against that of Soviet intervention in persuading Japan to surrender. This seems a sterile exercise, since it is plain that both played their parts. "For Japan's civilian politicians," asserts Japanese historian Kazutoshi Hando, "the dropping of the atomic bombs was the last straw. For the Japanese army, it was the Russian invasion of Manchuria."

Considering the plight of civilians and captives, dying in thousands daily under Japanese occupation, together with the casualties that would have been incurred had the Soviets been provoked into maintaining their advance across mainland China, almost any scenario suggests that far more people of many nationalities would have died in the course of even a few further weeks of war than were killed by the atomic bombs. Stalin would almost certainly have seized Hokkaido, with his usual indifference to losses. Robert Newman suggests that 250,000 deaths would have occurred in every further month the war continued. Even if this is excessive, it addresses a plausible range of numbers. Starvation and LeMay's fire-raisers would have killed hundreds of thousands more Japanese by the late autumn of 1945. Such an assertion does not immediately render the detonations of the atomic bombs acceptable acts. It merely emphasises the fact that the destruction of Hiroshima and Nagasaki by no means represented the worst outcome of the war for the Japanese people, far less for the world.

Those who seek to argue that Japan was ready to surrender before Hiroshima are peddlers of fantasies. The Tokyo leadership was indeed eager for peace, but on terms rightly unacceptable to the Allied powers. Even after Nagasaki, the peace party prevailed only by the narrowest of margins. While evidence remains fragmentary and inconclusive, Richard Frank is surely right to argue that a critical, if unacknowledged, element in Japanese thinking was awareness that they had lost the chance of a "decisive battle for the homeland." The hopes of the military were pinned upon exploiting an opportunity to defeat a U.S. amphibious assault. Now Japan faced devastation, starvation and probable Soviet invasion, without the need for America to expose its soldiers to the desperate defenders of Kyushu.

It is sometimes suggested that the U.S. would have lost nothing by making explicit its willingness to permit the Japanese people to keep their emperor. However, in the context of Japan's conduct in Asia since 1931, the tens of millions of deaths for which Japanese aggression was responsible, it is hard to perceive any good reason for Truman to have modified his demand for the enemy's unconditional surrender. Byrnes's judgements withstand the tests of history. If there was a strand of triumphalism in American conduct, why should there not have been? The U.S. and its allies had been obliged to expend immense blood and treasure to frustrate the ambitions of a brutal fascistic aggressor. At any time, by acknowledging defeat Japan could have secured peace, escaped the atomic bombs. The fact that its leaders did not do so reflected their own irrational choice, rather than American obduracy. Why should the sensibilities of such men as Anami, Toyoda, Umezu and their subordinates have been indulged, when at last their bloody pretensions were brought to naught?

The emperor himself will never cut a sympathetic figure in Western eyes. Hirohito presided over a society which had brought misery upon many nations. If he was not a prime mover, throughout the war his preoccupation with the preservation of the imperial house caused him to treat Japan's militarists as honourable men and legitimate arbiters of power, to applaud their successes and acquiesce in their excesses. Yet there was a redemptive quality about his conduct in those last days. Albeit belatedly, he displayed a courage and conviction which saved hundreds of thousands of lives. To a man of such instinctive diffidence, his role was entirely unwelcome, but he fulfilled it in a fashion which commands some respect. It is sometimes argued that the Allies were mistaken not to remove Hirohito from his throne in August 1945; that failure to do so allowed the Japanese people to deny the iniquity of the crimes committed in his name, as many do to this day. Nonetheless, whatever his faults in years past, through Hirohito's actions in August 1945 the imperial house worked a passage to its own salvation.

At 7:21 on the morning of the fifteenth, Japan's radio network began to broadcast repeated calls for every listener to tune in at noon, to receive a personal message from the emperor. Following the National Anthem, Hirohito's squeaky tones, speaking in old Japanese almost incomprehensible to many of his subjects, delivered his reading of the Rescript:

> After pondering deeply the general trends of the world and actual conditions obtaining in Our Empire today, We have decided to effect a settlement of the present situation by resorting to an extraordinary measure. We have ordered Our Government to communicate to the Governments of the United States, Great Britain, China, and the Soviet Union that Our Empire accepts the provisions of their Joint Declaration.

He then delivered an exposition of his nation's past conduct which has become familiar to posterity, together with a circumlocution tortured even by Japanese standards, that the war situation had evolved "not necessarily to Japan's advantage." He lamented America's employment of "a new most cruel bomb." He appealed to the armed forces to accept his decision, concluding: "Cultivate the ways of rectitude; foster nobility of spirit; and work with resolution so as ye may enhance the innate glory of the Imperial State and keep pace with the progress of the world." Hirohito's archaic phrases represented a self-serving caricature of Japan's recent history, yet they sufficed for their immediate purpose.

That afternoon, the Suzuki cabinet resigned. The elderly Prince Higashikuni reluctantly accepted the premiership. At 7 p.m. on 14 August Washington time, before a dense throng of politicians and journalists, Harry Truman read the announcement of Japan's unconditional acceptance of the Potsdam Declaration. He then sent a message to the Pentagon and the Navy Department, for onward transmission to American field commanders, ordering the cessation of all offensive operations against Japan. Early in 1943, an editorial in *Collier's* magazine borrowed its headline from Cato's Roman curse upon Carthage: "*Delenda est Japonia.*" Now the American curse seemed fulfilled. Japan was extinguished.

2. Despair and Deliverance

A FEW WEEKS before the Japanese capitulation, Gen. George Kenney's chief air planner warned: "Considering the suicidal tactics and peculiar psychology of the Japs in comparison with the Hun . . . stress the possibility of continued air action regardless of surrender." The Allies anticipated that many Japanese would reject the emperor's call to lay down their arms; that American and British soldiers, sailors and airmen would have to continue to die, suppressing guerrilla resistance or even fighting conventional battles against the four million Japanese troops in the home islands, and three million more scattered across their overseas empire.

In late August 1945 there were indeed difficulties in reconciling some units to defeat, and dramatic suicides by individuals. When Vice-Admiral Matome Ugaki learned of the emperor's broadcast, he ordered planes prepared, drank a farewell *sake* with staff at 5th Air Fleet, then drove to Oita airfield on north-east Kyushu carrying a sword presented to him by Yamamoto, whom he had served as chief of staff. Eleven Suisei dive-bombers stood ready. "Are you with me?" he demanded of the pilots. "Yes, sir!" they cried. Ugaki shook hands with them. A warrant officer whom he dispossessed of his cockpit seat insisted upon squeezing in beside him. During their subsequent flight, Ugaki made a voice transmission: "Despite the courage of every unit under my command over the past six months, we have failed to destroy the arrogant enemy and protect our divine empire, a failure which must be considered my own." He left behind his diaries, together with a farewell note: "I shall vanish into the sky along with my vision." His final flight accomplished nothing save his own extinction, aged fifty-five. All the planes save three, which sensibly turned back with "engine failure," were shot down by American fighters. Ugaki made his death as contemptible as his life, by taking with him so many hapless young men.

In the days that followed, some thousands of Japanese chose immolation rather than acknowledge defeat. Among these were Gen. Shizuichi Tanaka, the Oxford-educated commander of Eastern Army who had suppressed the coup against the palace; Prince Konoe; Vice-Admiral Onishi, prime sponsor of the kamikazes; Marshal Sugiyama and his wife; ten young men who killed themselves on Tokyo's Atago Hill, followed by two of their wives; eleven transport officers who chose to die in front of the Imperial Palace; and fourteen students who killed themselves on the Yoyogi parade ground. Hysteria seized some army officers. Tears fell in torrents across the nation. On a Philippine island, Lt. Hiroo Onoda and his little band of destitute Japanese soldiers found a message left by the Americans: "The war ended on August 15. Come down from the mountains!" Neither he nor the others believed it: "There was no doubt in my mind this was an enemy trick." Onoda remained in hiding for twenty-eight years.

What is remarkable, however, is not how many Japanese rejected surrender, but how many embraced it gratefully, whatever protestations they made to the contrary. This outcome once more highlights the gulf between the private acknowledgement of reality and the public embrace of fantasy which had been the bane of the Japanese nation, and of Asia. Lt. Masaichi Kikuchi and other officers of the Singapore garrison heard rumours of the impending surrender from local Chinese a week before the news became official. Whatever paroxysms of grief these inspired among his career professional comrades, for Kikuchi they represented "a reprieve from a death sentence. For so long, we had all been asking ourselves: when would it be our turn to face the enemy? And to lose our lives?"

On the morning of the fifteenth, in Burma Lt. Hayashi Inoue was preparing to lead a local raid against British troops when he learned that the war was over. "I was overwhelmed with relief," he said. "It was so obvious we were beaten. Each day for months, it had seemed unlikely that one would survive to see the next." High in the hills of Luzon, Gen. Tomoyuki Yamashita still presided at his headquarters. When the surrender was announced, an officer urged the chief of staff to sit with his commander through the night, to prevent him from killing himself. Yamashita reassured them: "Don't worry, I won't go to heaven alone—it would help no one. My duty is to get our soldiers home. Relax and go to bed." A few days later, he assembled the staff of his headquarters, shook hands with each one, gave a final salute, then walked through the trees to give himself up to the Americans. He penned a last poem:

My soldiers have been gathered from the mountains
like wild flowers.
Now it is my turn to go,
and I do so gladly.

Likewise Lt.-Gen. Masaki Honda, who had fought Slim in Burma. At his headquarters in a village named Nangala he told his staff: "We must accept the emperor's announcement. This is the end of the war. I ask you to continue to obey orders and to refrain from any violent action." One of his officers, Maj. Mitsuo Abe, burst out passionately: "The Allies will destroy our heritage and wipe out the Japanese race. The Americans will occupy our country forever. You are our commander. You should commit *seppuku*—and if you dare not, I will show you how!" Honda, who was seated on the floor in Japanese fashion, calmly invited Abe to sit beside him. "You are a staff officer and thus supposed to be intelligent. Can't you understand the emperor's mind? We must bear our misfortunes with courage. Neither the old nor the young must kill themselves; that is not the way to save the nation. We must live on, and build the foundations of the new Japan."

"The men all cried about the surrender," said twenty-four-year-old Yoshiko Hashimoto, who had lost half her family in the March firebombing of Tokyo. "I too cried—but with relief." Ryoichi Sekine, a Tokyo sixteen-year-old, experienced a sense of shame which his father did not share. Mr. Sekine senior said pragmatically: "Now we're going to live in a new world in which the Americans will call the shots." Yoichi Watanuki remembered hearing the triumphal blast of martial music which accompanied Tokyo Radio's announcement of Japan's attack on Pearl Harbor, as an eight-year-old child on 8 December 1941. At school assembly later that morning, the headmaster made three hundred children each in turn mount his rostrum and declaim: "China, America and Britain are the enemies of Japan."

Almost four years later, in the rural village to which the school had been evacuated, on 16 August 1945 Yoichi found himself summoned to assembly along with every other child, even though it was the holiday season. The same headmaster mustered his charges in the playground, then delivered a stern harangue. He said that the shame of defeat fell upon Japan's people, who had failed its warriors. He ordered the children to kneel. Yoichi winced at the pain of the gravel beneath his bare knees. The children had to bow towards Tokyo and recite in chorus: "We apologise to the Emperor because we of the Home Front are responsible for the loss of the war." Yoichi felt angry and resentful. He was sure that he and his kind had done their utmost. Had the headmaster forgotten all those hours they spent digging out pine roots from which pitiful quantities of oil were extracted for aviation fuel? He went home and said to his mother: "Surely we have lost the war because our soldiers were not good enough. They told us a Divine Wind would come, and it didn't. They lied to us, didn't they?"

Lt. Cmdr. Haruki Iki flew a little communications plane to navy headquarters the night before the surrender, for a conference about his wing's invasion suicide mission. On landing, he met two staff officers whom he knew well from navy academy days. They greeted him and said: "Forget about the meeting. An important announcement's due which could change everything. Let's go and have a drink." They got their drinks, then spent the hours which followed in shelters, evading the attentions of American bombers. Then they listened to the emperor's broadcast. Like so many others, Iki dissolved into helpless tears. He flew alone back to his base, to find that most of his aircrew had decamped towards their homes. Iki, furious, dispatched demands for their return, with which most sheepishly complied. He put the disconsolate fliers to work smartening up their planes: "I thought the Americans would be taking them for reparations." Then a terse order arrived from headquarters: all aircraft were to be destroyed. So indeed they were.

Another pilot, Toshio Hijikata, was in a naval hospital, having lost weight and developed chronic fever during the summer months. The doctors diagnosed lung trouble precipitated by combat flying. Other men in his ward seemed vastly relieved to hear the war was over, but Hijikata threw himself out of bed and hitched a ride on a vehicle back to his squadron's base at Kagoshima. "I was sure there would be one last great air battle," he said, "and I wanted to be in it." He was crestfallen to discover that his unit had accepted the surrender.

Maj. Shoji Takahashi, a general staff intelligence officer, had spent a week in Hiroshima as a member of the army's investigating team after the atomic explosion. Takahashi became ill, suffering from what he afterwards assumed was radiation sickness. He learned of Japan's surrender at the airfield on their return to Tokyo. "All the way back to general staff headquarters," he said later, "I was trying to decide how I would kill myself, because I assumed that we would all be expected to do this." It came as a surprise to discover that most officers were content to survive. Amid the profound sense of humiliation which engulfed the army, Takahashi refused an order that he should join the Japanese delegation flying to Manila to receive detailed instructions from the Americans: "I could not bear the idea of being one of those who abased ourselves before MacArthur."

At 1000 on 15 August, twelve kamikaze aircraft were as usual prepared for take-off at Hyakuri air base north of Tokyo. One proved unserviceable, but the remainder left as scheduled to attack the American fleet. Ground crews began to prepare the next wave of thirty for launch soon after noon. The imperial broadcast intervened. Interference was so bad that the crews working under Petty Officer Hachiro Miyashita could not understand a word the emperor said. They assumed that he was simply inciting them to greater effort, and returned to work. Suddenly, a man bicycled up to their dispersal and said: "Didn't you hear? The war's over." The most bewildered men on the airfield were the pilots, who had expected to be dead within two hours. "I watched them walk away to their quarters," said Miyashita. "Their shoulders were hunched, they looked sunk in misery. They were so keyed up for what they were going to do." The ground crews were expected in the mess hall, but even after flying was cancelled, Miyashita and his companions had no appetites. It was only some hours later that a new thought burst upon his consciousness: "I've made it! I've survived the war!" he exulted. That night, when for the first time he saw lights showing in buildings which had been blacked out for years, he began to perceive the merits of peace.

On 17 August there was an attempted mutiny at Atsugi air base, following which a Zero took off and flew to Hyakuri. Its pilot set about single-handedly inciting airmen to resume the struggle. "Don't give up!" he begged them. His appeal met little support. Next day the base commander assembled all officers and NCOs, and delivered a stern harangue about the importance of accepting the surrender terms: "The price for any act of defiance will fall upon the Japanese people," he said sternly. "It is the duty of each of you to keep the men of your commands under strict discipline."

The ground crews emptied aircraft fuel tanks and removed bombs. Next day, they also unbolted propellers to disable the planes.

Lt. Masashiko Ando landed a floatplane at his squadron's base on the Dutch East Indies island of Surabaya, and strolled nonchalantly into the mess. He found other pilots plunged in silent gloom. "What's up?" he demanded. Somebody said: "The war's over." Ando asked flippantly: "Who's won?" The notion that his own nation might acknowledge defeat was beyond his comprehension. "We young officers were like boxers in a ring," he said later. "We had thought only of our own fight. We knew nothing about what was happening to the rest of the war. Now, we simply wondered what would happen to us."

Balwant Singh Bahia, an Indian Army engineer, was sitting with two sergeants in a signal lorry at Tharrawaddy on the main road north of Rangoon, when an NCO called: "Oh, war finish! War finish! They have dropped atom bomb on Japan." I said: "What's that one?" He said: "I come back one minute," and swiftly returned with two small celebratory bottles of beer. Japanese survivors hiding on Okinawa saw the sky illuminated by a brilliant, thunderous firework display of naval tracer, and guessed its significance. Most emerged in the days that followed, to hear recordings of the imperial broadcast played to them by their American captors.

John Sandle's regiment in Burma indulged a brief *feu de joie* on VJ-Day, but "the euphoria of the occasion soon evaporated, to be replaced by a feeling of melancholy at the utter futility of war in which our battalion had lost hundreds of men just to finish up where we had started four years earlier." He was one of only two officers in his unit to have survived the entire campaign. They set Japanese prisoners to work rolling a cricket pitch for their mess.

At Aomi barracks in Japan, senior prisoner Stephen Abbott paraded the inmates in uniform and said: "Today is the greatest day in the history of our time. We must remember, however, that to obtain it millions of all nationalities have died. It is a day, not only for rejoicing, but also for sober thought. You are no longer prisoners of war, but you are soldiers of your countries and upon you rests a great responsibility for good behaviour and dignified example. Remember above all things that you are citizens of the free democracies of the United States and Great Britain. Be true to the ideals which during six hard years we have battled to maintain." After dismissing the parade, Abbott and his fellow POWs waited three weeks for liberation. In the interim, at several other locations in Japan guards murdered captives. Sixteen U.S. B-29 aircrew at Fukuoka were hacked to death with swords.

"What reaction? Absolutely nil," British gunner Fred Thompson wrote at his prison camp on Java. "Perhaps it's because we have been told nothing by the Japs . . . except today 'no work' . . . maybe the reaction will set in later, when we realise what it means—the end of this existence of misery, hunger, humiliation. I thank God that I have survived and my friends here with me." Next day, 17 August, exhilaration at last broke through: "Last night, 339 hearts in this camp missed a beat."

Rod Wells, in Singapore's Changi jail, recoiled in disgust from the fashion in which Japanese began to salute British and Australian inmates, offering them water and cigarettes. A British medical team landed by parachute—big, strapping men whose rude health inspired in the POWs a perverse sense of shame at their own debility. When they saw the pistol on a paratrooper's belt, so institutionalised were the hapless prisoners that they said in alarm: "The Japs won't like that." The British officer responded: "Cheer up. You can tell them what you like, hit them over the head with a hammer, anything. Don't mess around—just give them orders. Treat them like scum, that's all they are." Not all the liberating forces behaved sensitively to prisoners. A repatriation officer who arrived at Lt. Cmdr. George Cooper's camp on Batavia admonished the inmates to realise that they were infinitely better off than concentration camp prisoners he had seen at Belsen and Buchenwald. Several of his hearers walked away in disgust.

Six American paratroopers landed a plane at a prison camp outside Mukden, where senior British and American officers had been held since 1942. "It seemed like talking to men from Mars," wrote Brig. Sam Pearson to his wife. "They had flown from central China with orders to locate us . . . the 1st plane has arrived this morning and been seized by the Nips because the Russians coming in from the north have ordered all movement to stop . . . Those six chaps were very brave men as they nearly met their end at the hands of the local Nips. They were stripped naked and stood up against the wall. How they got out of that fix I don't know, but I agree with the anthem 'God Bless America.' "

When the first parachute food drop landed at the camp on Japan's Shikoku Island where RAF Squadron Leader David Grant was held, "I felt a lump the size of a cricket ball crawling up to my throat. I turned to hide myself. I said to the man next to me: 'Will you let me pass, please. I think I am going to cry.' 'That's OK, old boy,' he said in a broken voice, 'half the bloody camp is crying already.' " At Alf Evans's camp, the Japanese commandant "Charlie Chan" got up on a box and said " 'the wicked Americanos had dropped two terrible deathray bombs and the Japanese people of two towns had been killed and burnt and the Japanese had surrendered.' This was it, this bloody war was over at last. Some of us had made it . . . We all went mad, singing and jumping about, praying to God and thinking of those of our comrades who had died in the three and a half years of suffering." When the Americans arrived, hysterical prisoners fell on them, kissing and hugging their deliverers.

Three American doctor POWs took the extraordinary risk of leaving their camp at Kobe, then travelling across Japan to check in at the Imperial Hotel in downtown Tokyo. Bewildered hotel staff eventually acceded to their importuning. In the restaurant they were served breaded veal cutlets, rice, a vegetable salad and tea off real china on clean linen. When a Kempeitai officer arrived and began fiercely questioning them about their presence, Lt. Murray Glusman jabbed a finger at him and said: "Listen, you goddamned son of a bitch. We won the war. And if you don't treat us with the respect that is our due as officers of the United States Navy, I'll see to it that your ass is strung up from the highest lamp post in Tokyo!"

British POW Andrew Cunningham's brother Stuart, an officer of the Fleet Air Arm, flew into Singapore a few days after the surrender, immaculate in tropical whites. Andrew, a skeleton, looked at him and said: "My God, Stuart, you look fat." Like most prisoners, he was overwhelmed by the experience of freedom: "We came out into a world that seemed wonderful, where people asked 'What would you like for supper?' " Cunningham even found compassion to spare for his former jailers: "I loathed the Japanese, yet at the end I felt desperately sorry for them. We had sacrificed everything, but we'd won. They had sacrificed everything—and lost."

IN THE STREETS of Chongqing, Chinese and Americans embraced each other in the streets. "*Mei kuo ting hao, mei kuo ting hao!*" they cried, "America is wonderful!" Firecrackers exploded, people shouted and cheered sporadically at first, "but growing to a volcano of sound and happiness within an hour." Some shouted in English: "Thank you, thank you!" Captain Luo Dingwen was among many Chinese who cried, "because this meant that for the first time since 1937, I could go home." Captain Yan Qizhi's first thought was: "Who else is alive?" It was weeks before somebody from his Nationalist regiment passed by his village and told his family that he had survived. Eventually he received a letter containing news that they were among the fortunate. Only one of his relations had been killed, an uncle murdered by the Japanese at the school where he taught. Wu Yinyan's Beijing school class was not dismissed to join the celebrating crowds thronging the streets, "and even if we had been, I doubt that we should have chosen to go. After years of subjection, the news was too sudden to be immediately believable. I could not imagine that the war had really ended." For days, fears persisted in occupied regions of China that violent retribution would fall upon those who celebrated the Japanese downfall.

At Unit 731, the Japanese biological warfare research centre in Manchuria, there was a rush to destroy evidence. Lethal injections were given to all surviving Chinese human guinea pigs and site labourers. No Japanese was ever held to account or tried for the monstrous crimes committed there. Though the Americans quickly became privy to the hideous nature of Unit 731's operations, they concluded that it was more profitable to secrete its files and shield its commanders and scientists, for the possible military advantage of the United States.

Within days of the surrender, local Communists arrived at the gates of the Japanese air base outside Beijing where Lance Corporal Iwao Ajiro was stationed, demanding his unit's weapons. "We had to tell them, 'Sorry, we haven't been fighting you. We've surrendered to Chiang Kai-shek, so the guns belong to him.' " The Communists persisted with personal advances to Ajiro, who was a signaller. "They said: 'Come and work for us—we need your skills, we'll give you a good life and find you a wife.' I said: 'You're crazy! I'm young. I want to go home and see my mum.' "

ON THE SOVIET fronts alone, the war continued almost unabated. Stalin had no desire for peace until his armies physically possessed the prizes which they had been promised. MacArthur, absurdly, professed to believe that, as SCAP, Soviet troops were subject to his authority. He sent a signal via Moscow ordering them to "discontinue further offensive action against Japanese forces." The Russians curtly responded that such a matter would be decided solely at the discretion of "the Supreme Commander of the forces of the Soviet Union." In several places in Manchuria, Japanese emissaries seeking to surrender to Vasilevsky's forces were shot out of hand. In others Japanese fought on, neither knowing nor caring that their country had surrendered. On and on swept the Russians, east and southwards.

There was characteristic confusion at Girin airfield on the afternoon of 19 August. Russian troops landed in transport aircraft and deployed. In response to a summons from their commander, Major Belyaev, a Japanese delegation appeared wearing white armbands, unarmed save for swords. There was a parley. The Soviet officer wrote sourly later: "The samurais were playing for time. Eventually one of their officers took from his pocket a white handkerchief, and waved it. Japanese machine guns immediately opened fire on us." The Russians dived for cover, but four men were wounded, and Belyaev's face was cut open by fragments. He shouted at the Japanese officers to stop the shooting, but nothing happened. After a short, sharp firefight the Russians captured four officers and forty men, killing many others. "To be honest, we were so angry that we weren't keen on taking prisoners," said Belyaev. "We'd agreed a ceasefire, and there they were, shooting at us!" The incident was more likely the product of contradictory sentiments in the Japanese ranks than of a "samurai" ruse, but the Russians were disinclined to generosity. In subsequent skirmishes in the nearby town they found some Japanese troops struggling to escape in civilian clothes, others still offering resistance. By the morning of the twenty-first, however, most of the Japanese had surrendered. Belyaev's company was guarding 12,000 prisoners. He observed wryly that these seemed too fearful of falling into Chinese hands to attempt escape.

Souhei Nakamura, son of a teacher of Japanese music who had lived in Manchuria since 1941, was inducted into the Japanese army only a week before the Russians attacked. On 12 August, every man of the five hundred at his depot, all either raw recruits or elderly reservists, was issued with a weapon and a stocking full of rice to tie on his pack, then crammed onto a train south, towards the front. During their march to the station, a Japanese bank manager astonished them by rushing into the street with armfuls of paper money. He broadcast banknotes among the soldiers as they passed, rather than leave them for the Russians.

After days of faltering progress, the recruits disembarked at a halt where they were supposed to join a regiment. They found the place already abandoned by the retreating army, the rail bridge ahead cut by Russian bombing. They had no officers, and milled about uncertainly for hours before glimpsing two figures walking down the track carrying white flags. At first these looked like children. As they came closer, however, the Japanese perceived that they were Russian soldiers, who told them the war was over. Without much concern, indeed with relief, the young recruits surrendered their weapons. Some emotional older men drove their swords into the earth and bent them until they broke, rather than present them to the Soviets. Then they lingered, expecting a train to take them to Korea, and thence home to Japan. "I was nineteen," said Nakamura. "The whole thing of defeat didn't mean much to me. I just felt grateful that because there were five hundred of us all together there, it seemed unlikely the Russians would shoot us."

There was no train to Korea; instead a long, gruelling march under Russian guard. Exhausted soldiers began to throw away packs, personal effects, even boots. It was a time of rains, and they were often trudging through thick mud. They passed a village of Japanese immigrants, where they saw an elderly grandmother beseeching impassive local Chinese to relieve her of a baby which she clutched. A gaggle of Japanese orphans killed a bullock, and distributed slabs of its raw meat to the thankful men. Nakamura noticed that no young women were visible, and guessed that they had been carried off by the Russians. After a few hours, the prisoners were herded on down the road. "I always wondered afterwards what happened to those kids, and all those immigrants." The likely answer was that they starved.

Russian brutality towards their prisoners was cultural rather than personal. Few Red Army men harboured much animus towards the Japanese, only puzzlement about people beyond their experience in appearance and character. "We felt nothing like the hatred we held towards the Germans," said Sgt. Anatoly Fillipov. In Manchuria's "liberated" towns and cities, the victors revelled in rickshaw rides and brothels. Lieutenant Chervyakov acquired a kimono for his mother, as did Boris Ratner on Sakhalin. The pilot was bewildered to see a column of Japanese prisoners struggling past, the men encumbered with packs, their officers even in captivity using soldiers to lug their baggage. As Ratner watched, one Japanese fell down and died. A Japanese prisoner who spoke a little Russian said bitterly to Anatoly Fillipov: "Well, you've got your prize, but it is an unlawful one. Stalin deceived us. He always promised that he would not attack us." Thousands of Japanese soldiers and civilians in Manchuria killed themselves.

For Manchurian women, rejoicing at the defeat of the Japanese soon gave way to horror at the conduct of the Russians, as they found themselves facing wholesale rape: "We didn't like them at all," said Liu Yunxiu, who was twenty-one and living in Changchun. "They stole food, they raped women in the streets. Every woman tried to make herself look as ugly as she could, to escape their attentions. My parents hid me for weeks, in which I was never allowed out of the house." Some Soviet soldiers afterwards claimed that their army's excesses were chiefly committed by veterans of Rokossovsky's front, notorious for its conduct in Europe. "They did not behave very well," said Sgt. Anatoly Fillipov. "They were always showing off, saying 'We're Rokossovsky's boys!' " Souhei Nakamura's thirty-one-year-old aunt, a married woman, offered herself to the conquerors in the absurd hope, she claimed, of sparing some virgin from rape. Her reward was syphilis, which she sought to conceal from her husband when he eventually returned from Soviet captivity, and thus infected him. Communist guerrilla Zuo Yong was among those appalled by the behaviour of the Red Army: "The Russians were our allies—we were all in the same boat. We thought of their soldiers as our brothers. The problem, however, as we discovered, was they had no respect for our people. Their behaviour in Manchuria was appalling." Jiang De, another guerrilla, shrugged: "The Russians simply behaved in the same way they did everywhere else."

EVEN AS SOVIET armies completed the occupation of Manchuria after the Japanese surrender, amphibious units were assaulting the Pacific islands promised to Stalin at Yalta. Eight thousand men were dispatched across five hundred miles of sea to the Kuriles, a chain of some fifty islands situated north-east of Japan. The northern Kuriles were defended by 25,000 imperial troops, of which 8,480 were deployed on the northernmost, Shannshir, eighteen miles in length by six wide. Their morale was not high. This was, by common consent, one of the most godforsaken postings in the Japanese empire.

On the night of 14 August, Shannshir's senior officer, Maj.-Gen. Fusaka Tsutsumi, was alerted by 5th Area Army to listen with his most senior staff to the emperor's broadcast next day. Having done so, Tsutsumi awaited the arrival of an American occupation force, whom he had no intention of fighting. Instead, however, at 0422 on 18 August, without warning or parley a Russian division assaulted Shannshir—and met resistance. For all the Red Army's experience of continental warfare, it knew pitifully little about the difficulties of opposed landings from the sea. From the outset, the Shannshir operation was a shambles, perfunctorily planned and chaotically executed. The landing force was drawn from garrison troops without combat experience.

At 0530 Japanese shore batteries began to hit Soviet ships as they approached. Some assault craft were sunk, others set on fire. Those who abandoned foundering boats found themselves swept away by the currents. The invaders' communications collapsed, as radios were lost or immersed when their operators struggled ashore. Sailors laboured under Japanese fire to improvise rafts to land guns and tanks—the Russians possessed none of the Western Allies' inventory of specialised amphibious equipment. A counter-attack by twenty Japanese tanks gained some ground. What was almost certainly the last kamikaze air attack of the war hit a destroyer escort. Early on the morning of the nineteenth, the Soviet commander on Shannshir received orders to hasten the island's capture. Soon afterwards, a Japanese delegation arrived at Russian headquarters to arrange a surrender. Yet next morning, some coastal batteries still fired on Soviet ships in the Second Kuril Strait, and were heavily bombed for their pains. Tsutsumi's men finally quit on the night of 21 August, having lost 614 dead.

. . .

Sakhalin represented a less serious challenge, for its nearest point lay only six miles off the Asian coast, and its northern part was Soviet territory. But the island was vastly bigger—560 miles long and between 19 and 62 miles wide. Japan had held the southern half since 1905, a source of bitter Russian resentment, now to be assuaged. Sakhalin's terrain was inhospitable—swamp-ridden, mountainous, densely forested. For reasons of prestige, the Japanese had lavished precious resources on fortifying the place. The consequence was that when Soviet troops began an assault on 11 August, their advance made little headway. Only after bitter fighting did they capture the key Honda strongpoint, whose defenders fought to the last man. The weather was poor for air support, and many tanks became bogged. Russian infantry were obliged to struggle through on foot, to outflank Japanese positions. Early on 16 August, however, after the imperial broadcast the Japanese obligingly launched "human wave" counter-attacks, which enabled the Russians to inflict much slaughter. Next day, yard by yard, Soviet troops forced passages through the forests, battering the defenders with air attacks and artillery. On the evening of 17 August, the local Japanese commander in the frontier defensive zone surrendered.

Elsewhere on Sakhalin, however, garrisons continued to resist. When the Soviets' Northern Pacific Flotilla landed a storming force at the port of Maoka on 20 August, they mowed down civilians at the shoreside. Japanese troops opened fire. Thick fog hampered gunfire observation. Defenders had to be painstakingly cleared from the quays and then the city centre. "Japanese propaganda had successfully imbued the city's inhabitants with fears of 'Russian brutality,' " declared a Soviet account disingenuously. "The result was that much of the population fled into the forests, and some people were evacuated to Hokkaido. Women were especially influenced by propaganda, which convinced them that the arriving Russian troops would shoot them and strangle their children." The Soviets claimed to have killed three hundred Japanese in Maoka and taken a further six hundred prisoners. The rest of the garrison fled inland. Sakhalin was finally secured on 26 August, four days behind the Soviet schedule.

Stalin harboured more far-reaching designs on Japanese territory. Before the Manchurian assault was launched, Soviet troops were earmarked to land on the Japanese home island of Hokkaido, and to occupy its northern half as soon as north Korea was secure. On the evening of 18 August, Vasilevsky signalled the Stavka in Moscow, asking permission to proceed with a Hokkaido attack scheduled to last from 19 August to

1 September. For forty-eight hours Moscow was silent, brooding. On 20 August Vasilevsky signalled again, asking for orders. Continue preparations, said Stalin: the assault force should be ready to attack by midnight on 23 August.

Meanwhile the Americans also dallied with possible landings in the Kuriles and at the mainland port of Dalian, to secure bases—in breach of the Yalta agreement—before the Soviets could reach them. Both sides, however, finally backed off. Washington recognised that any attempt to pre-empt the Soviets from occupying their agreed territories would precipitate a crisis. Likewise Truman cabled Moscow, summarily rejecting Stalin's proposal that the Russians should receive the surrender of Japanese forces on north Hokkaido. At midday on the twenty-second the Stavka dispatched new orders to Far East Command, cancelling the Hokkaido landings. The Americans confined themselves to hastening U.S. Marines to key points on and near the coast of mainland China, to hold these until Chiang Kai-shek's forces could assume control. A huge American commitment of men and transport aircraft alone enabled the Nationalists to reestablish themselves in the east during the autumn of 1945.

THE LAST BATTLE of the Second World War was fought at a place few Westerners have ever heard of. Hutou means "tiger's head." In 1945 there were still some tigers in the Wanda Mountains, where the town stands beside the great Ussuri River, eastern frontier of Manchuria. On the Russian shore, forests stretch for miles across flat country. On the Manchurian side, however, steep bluffs rise from the swamps and railway yard at the waterside. Here, beginning in 1933, the Guandong Army created the most elaborate defensive system in Asia: its commanders were rash enough to call it their "Maginot Line." Hutou was centred upon five forts built on neighbouring hills which rise up to four hundred feet above the riverbank. The concrete roofs and walls were nine feet thick, with generators, storerooms and living quarters sunk deep underground, linked by tunnels. The whole system was almost five miles wide and four deep, supported by some of the heaviest artillery in Asia, including 240mm Krupp guns and a 410mm howitzer. The Chinese assert that the 30,000 slave labourers who built the fortress were killed when their work was complete, and indeed many bodies were exhumed after 1945.

To the Japanese, Hutou was an unpopular posting, remote from any pleasures or amenities. For those who occupied its echoing caverns, it was also chronically unhealthy—moisture dripped off the concrete walls, rusted weapons, spoilt food. In winter the bunkers were icy cold, in summer stiflingly hot. Anyone familiar with the 1916 casemates of Verdun would readily have recognised 1945 Hutou. Through the years of war, veteran units had been removed from the fortress garrison and replaced by less impressive human material. Despite evidence of Soviet patrolling and the discovery of pontoons drifting on the Ussuri, Hutou's commander was absent at a briefing on the night of the initial attack, and was never able to return to his post. The defence was therefore directed by the local artillery commander, Captain Masao Oki.

The initial Soviet barrage cut road links and spread terror among the few hundred hapless civilians living behind the fortress. On 9 August, the Chinese inhabitants of Hutou township, a wattle-and-wooden settlement, were awakened in the early-morning darkness by the roar of aircraft overhead, the whistle of falling bombs and thud of shells. Some fell on the Japanese defences, others among the houses, killing five Chinese. Jiang Fushun and his family huddled terrified beside a brick bed, the most substantial object in their flimsy hut. After two hours the shelling stopped, and hundreds of villagers ran out into the street. They saw the horizon rippling with gun flashes from the Russian shore of the Ussuri River, and at once understood that the Soviets were coming. Japanese soldiers ran into the town. Though some buildings were already blazing after being hit by bombs and shells, they merely claimed that an air-raid practice was taking place. All civilians must move immediately into the nearby woods. There was no time to gather food or possessions. Jiang's father cried: "Go-go-go! I'll stay and look after the house." The family fled, along with hundreds of others.

The defenders exploited a lull in Russian artillery fire to move all the garrison's family members and nearby immigrant Japanese farmers into the tunnel system. As well as six hundred regular troops, there were then sheltering underground a thousand civilians, some with militia training and weapons. An hour later, shelling resumed, and at 0800 Soviet infantry started crossing the Ussuri. The Japanese responded with mortar fire. This inflicted some casualties, but within three hours the attackers had secured a bridgehead. Amazingly, Hutou's biggest artillery pieces did not fire. They were short of gunners, and Captain Oki was preoccupied with directing the infantry defence. All that day and the next, Soviet troops continued to shuttle across the river. The local Japanese army commander, Lt.-Gen. Noritsune Shimuzu, telephoned Hutou on the evening of the ninth to deliver a wordy injunction to Oki to hold fast: "In view of the current war situation and the circumstances of the garrison, you are all requested to fight to the last breath and meet your fate, when it comes, as courageously as flowers, so that you may become pillars of our nation." After this heady torrent of mixed metaphors, all contact was lost between the defenders and the outside world.

By nightfall on 10 August the surrounding area was securely in the hands of the invaders. When darkness came the Russians began attacks on the bunker system. All failed. It became plain that, against such strong defences, subtler tactics would be necessary. Through the days that followed, artillery was used to keep Japanese heads down, while infantry and engineer groups inched forward among the trenches. Soon they had isolated the individual forts, and destroyed Japanese artillery observation posts. The condition of the defenders became grim. "After the first [Russian] salvo, we knew the battle could have only one outcome," wrote one of the few Japanese survivors, gunner Gamii Zhefu. "In the tunnels beneath the fort, it was incredibly hot. We were desperate for water. The women were terrified. Then one soldier produced a canteen and gave everyone a sip, which did wonders for our morale. We were also very hungry, however, and started looking for food. We found some cans, ate—and started feeling thirsty again. Soon, for all of us, water became an obsession. It overcame even our fears about the battle and the threat of death. We were reduced to animal needs and desires."

On 13 August, adopting a technique familiar in the Pacific island battles, Russians poured petrol down ventilation inlets and ignited it. Hundreds of defenders and their families perished in the conflagrations that followed. Yet the Japanese continued to surprise Russian troops with sallies, sometimes dislodging the attackers from newly occupied positions. One Japanese rush was led by a twenty-two-year-old probationary officer brandishing a sword, who fell to a Russian grenade. Hutou's gunners, unable to use their huge weapons, destroyed them with demolition charges and formed suicide squads. A Japanese artillery piece was destroyed by a round from its neighbour, firing at point-blank range. The central heights of the fortress changed hands nine times.

The wretched defenders of Hutou knew nothing of the emperor's broadcast on 15 August, nor of their country's surrender. They rejected all Russian calls to lay down their arms. On the seventeenth, a five-man party of local Chinese and captured Japanese carrying a white flag was dispatched from the Soviet lines to tell the garrison that the war was over. The officer who received them dismissed such a notion with contempt. He drew his sword and beheaded the elderly Chinese bearing the Soviet proposals. "We have nothing to say to the Red Army," he declared, before retiring into his bunker. The Soviet barrage resumed. Conditions underground became unendurable. Many of those in the tunnels and casemates suffered carbon monoxide poisoning. "There were plenty of bodies down there," wrote Gamii Zhefu. "I heard a wounded man crying repeatedly 'Water, water,' but no one took any notice of him. I was momentarily excited by seeing a trickle of fluid running across the floor, until I realised that it was leaking from a corpse. I drank it. Another man said: 'That stuff will kill you.' I didn't care. I was dying of thirst anyway."

For hundreds of peasants sheltering in the woods, in the first days there was nothing to eat save a few berries and wild plants. They drank water from the river, and listened to the appalling cacophony of battle on the Hutou hills. A few Japanese immigrants huddled among them, but most had sought the shelter of the fortress. On the fourth day, while fighting still raged, Red soldiers appeared and herded the civilians down to the riverbank, which was now secure. The Russians smashed open a big Japanese food store, and invited the Chinese to help themselves. They were able to make rice soup to sustain them through another ten days of uncertainty and gunfire on the hills above.

On 19 August, a large party of Japanese from the fortress attempted a break for freedom. They were cut down by Russian machine guns. By the twenty-second, almost all the underground bunkers had become untenable. Soviet troops probing cautiously down the steps met a ghastly stench of humanity, cordite and death. In one bunker, the bodies of men, women and eighty children aged between one and twelve were heaped together. In a cavern beneath Strongpoint "Sharp" lay another pile of women's corpses. There was also the detritus of the dead—cooking pots, wire-rimmed spectacles, gramophones, a few bicycles, pin-up pictures of surprisingly smartly dressed "comfort women." The Soviets declared the Hutou Fortified Region secure. Yet for four days more, one isolated Japanese company continued its resistance. Only on 26 August was this remnant snuffed out. Thus, today, a huge Soviet war memorial on the site declares Hutou to be the scene of the final battle of the Second World War. Almost 2,000 Japanese men, women and children perished in and around the fortress, days after the rest of the world celebrated peace.

Russians told the Chinese fugitives in the woods behind Hutou that it was now safe to come out. In a curious introduction to their new lives, these bewildered peasants were shown a propaganda film about the Russian Revolution. A commissar addressed them through an interpreter: "Red soldiers have made great sacrifices in this battle to bring you liberty, and now it is yours." The Japanese were all dead, he said. The villagers could go home. Home? They drifted uneasily back to their huts, to find only ruins and blackened earth. In the ashes of Jiang Fushun's family home lay the body of his father, a bullet through his head, the price of his rashness in staying behind. Every Chinese who ventured into the village during the battle had met the same fate. Those who had relatives elsewhere began long treks in search of sanctuary, but Jiang's family had no one to go to. They lingered among the ruins, scrabbling to build themselves a shelter, scavenging for food. The task was made no easier by the fact that Russian soldiers began to remove everything edible or of value. The Chinese were appalled to see the liberators drive off the horses on which their tiny farms depended. Women were raped in the usual fashion.

Soviet soldiers warned peasants not to approach the forts, which were still littered with mines and munitions. After a few days, however, Jiang and a few others wandered up to the blackened casemates, gazing in revulsion at the unburied corpses of Japanese soldiers and their women. When the Russians finally departed, taking with them even the tracks of the local railway, the thousand or so desolate people left in Hutou found themselves existing in a limbo. The village headman was dead. For more than two years thereafter, no one attempted to exercise authority over them, nor to provide aid of any kind. When the Communists eventually assumed control of their lives, "things became a little better."

Only forty-six Japanese are known to have escaped from the fortress with their lives. "The defence was extraordinarily brave," says Chinese historian Wang Hongbin, "which usually demands respect. But it was also completely futile. It is hard to admire blind loyalty to the emperor at that stage. They all died for nothing."

Lt. Stanislav Chervyakov's rocket battery entered Shenyang having scarcely fired a salvo, and without meeting serious resistance. The soldiers were amazed to meet Russian émigrés, who welcomed them warmly. Chervyakov found himself billeted on one such family. In this city where Russian influence had always been strong, some local people spoke a few words of the language. Chinese stood outside little cafés, urging the soldiers: "Come in, have a drink or a meal!" "*Kapitana, shango! shango!*"—"Good! good!" Sgt. Anatoly Fillipov was delighted to be handed a mess tin of *pelmeni*—ravioli—but became less enthusiastic when he discovered that it was made with donkey meat. "Most of the local people welcomed us with open arms," said tank officer Alexander Fadin. "They were threadbare, in rags, but they gave us masses of flowers, fruit and Chinese food. We could eat all we wanted in the Chinese restaurants for free. We really felt like liberators."

Stalin had promised the Allies that he recognised Chiang Kai-shek's Nationalists as the sole legitimate government of China. This did not prevent Soviet forces in Manchuria from seeking to give Mao's people a head start in the civil war that was now imminent. "I shall never forget my first sight of the People's Army," said Russian gunner Georgy Sergeev. "I saw some men coming down from the mountains. They were in rags, many barefoot. They had no weapons, but each carried a stick with a bundle on its end. So this was the heroic 8th Route Army." Crowds of vengeful Chinese gathered around headquarters and POW cages, shouting at the Russians to surrender the prisoners to them. On 23 August, Soviet front HQ ordered the handover of captured Japanese weapons to nearby Chinese Communist units. To satisfy the letter of Stalin's agreement with the Nationalists, Soviet officers were to have no personal dealings with Mao's people, instead merely to withdraw guards from arms dumps. The first Communist unit arrived in darkness, and laboured by torchlight in complete silence, manhandling crates of weapons and ammunition with furious energy. "When I came back to the depots with my men," said a Soviet officer, Major Belyaev, "they were completely empty, literally cleaned out. The Chinese had even swept the floor and taken away the shelving."

THE EMPEROR PU YI heard news of the Japanese surrender at Dalizikou, where the final drama of his pitiful reign was acted out. For the third and final time in his life, on 15 August he signed an "Abdication Rescript," surrounded by unhappy ministers and privy councillors. His Japanese custodian announced that he was to be evacuated to Japan. He should decide who should accompany him. The emperor chose his brother, two brothers-in-law, three nephews, his doctor and valet. His sole remaining concubine asked through sobs what she was supposed to do. The emperor blandly responded that she could not accompany him: "The plane is too small, so you will have to go by train."

"Will the train get to Japan?"

"Of course it will. In three days at most you and the empress will see me again."

"What will happen if the train doesn't come for me? I haven't got a single relation here."

"You'll be all right."

The inglorious imperial plane landed at Shenyang to transfer its passengers to a larger aircraft for the flight to Japan. Yet even as they waited upon this, Soviet transport planes arrived, disgorging scores of Red soldiers brandishing tommy-guns. A few minutes later Pu Yi became a Russian captive. This was a relief, for more than anything he feared falling into the hands of Nationalist or Communist Chinese. The emperor's Soviet guards were fascinated by their prize, and at first a little awed by the responsibility. Lt. Alexander Zhelvakov, a political officer with 6th Guards Tank Army, was warned by his commander that he would answer with his life for the emperor's security, and believed it. The Soviets shared Pu Yi's perception that if he fell into the hands of Chinese, they would tear him asunder.

"I didn't get a wink of sleep during the night of 20 August," Zhelvakov said later, "and the emperor didn't sleep either—didn't even take off his clothes. He was skinny, quite tall, wearing horn-rimmed spectacles, a dark suit and white shirt. He looked rather ordinary, a little pale, depressed, lost. One could see how nervous he was. His brother never left his side. The two of them looked, to be honest, pretty forlorn and unworthy of their rank. There was absolutely no royal grandeur. Pu Yi kept asking: 'Am I going to be killed? Am I going to be shot?' He seemed shy, indeed pretty scared. Once he understood that no one was going to kill him, he gradually calmed down, cheered up, even began to smile."

Zhelvakov escorted the imperial party and their heaps of expensive luggage onto a transport plane to the Soviet city of Chita, where they were removed to incarceration in a procession of limousines. After Pu Yi departed, one of Zhelvakov's soldiers, a doughty Communist, said sourly: "Comrade Lieutenant, we should have put a bullet in him." The emperor cherished brief hopes of being permitted to go into exile in Britain or the United States. Instead, he spent the next five years in Soviet confinement, for the first of these employed as a compliant witness at successive show trials of Japanese. Returned to Mao's mercy in 1950, Pu Yi ended his days as a gardener in Beijing's Botanical Gardens, dying in 1967.

Soviet transport aircraft flew many Chinese guerrillas back from Russia into Manchuria. On the landing strip at Bei An, Li Min and her party were amazed to see Japanese soldiers, albeit disarmed, talking to their Russian conquerors. The Chinese were even more astonished by the arrogance of some of their vanquished foes. One Japanese officer told them defiantly: "Give us ten years and we'll be back!" An affronted guerrilla, Chen Ming, unholstered his pistol and shot the man dead. The Russians sternly ordered Chen to control himself.

Guerrilla Zhou Shuling returned to Manchuria from Russia in some style, in a car with her husband. His intelligence work finished, he boasted a chestful of Russian medals. Zhou said: "I was so excited, to see my own country again." But that country was ruined by war, and now by Soviet pillage. Soon the Russians began to dismantle and remove wholesale Manchuria's industrial plant. They asserted that this was Japanese property, and therefore represented legitimate reparations for the Soviet Union. Li Fenggui marched into Manchuria with Mao's New 4th Army in October 1945, to find that "the Russians had stripped the peasants of everything—including the women's virtue." When Zhou reached her old village, she met desolation. The sole memorials of her family's residence were four water tanks which had once belonged on the roofs of their houses, and now stood derelict on the blackened earth. Two of her four young children died amid the terrible cold and hunger of their first winter back in China. Her husband became a town chief of police, with herself as a precinct chief.

Zhuan Fengxian knew that the woman who returned to Manchuria from Russia, in the uniform of the Soviet army, was not the illiterate girl "frightened even of spiders" who had gone away to join the guerrillas five years earlier. She had achieved a fulfilment through her wartime experience quite unattainable by a woman, especially a peasant woman, in mid-twentieth-century Chinese society. She and her group flew home in Soviet transport aircraft, and wandered in bewildered horror through the Japanese prison in Shenyang where so many political prisoners had died. "We looked at the gallows, and even the device they had for crushing bodies so that no traces remained. What sort of people could they have been?!" In the chaos of the civil war that now began to overtake China, she had no time to go in search of her family. It was only long afterwards that she discovered that disease had killed her parents, hopelessly weakened by hunger, during the occupation. "They were sick—and they had no money to do anything about it." Her father was fifty, her mother forty. She was reunited with her sisters only in 1949.

"An image of Manchuria after the surrender remains imprinted in my memory," said Red Army radio operator Victor Kosopalov: "A lonely Japanese infantry soldier is limping along the road with a rifle upon his shoulder. One of our tank gunners jumps down from a T-34 beside the road, and gestures to the Japanese to surrender his weapon. The Japanese resists, shaking his head, but the tank man wrests the rifle from him. The Japanese shrinks back, expecting retribution. The tank man gestures him to move on. He limps away . . ."

In Manchuria and the island operations, the Soviets claimed to have killed, wounded or captured 674,000 Japanese troops at a cost to the Red Army of 12,031 dead, 24,425 sick and wounded. Stalin's Far Eastern conquests thus incurred about the same human cost as the American seizure of Okinawa, though characteristically the Russians were far less troubled by their losses. First Far Eastern Front bore the heaviest casualties—6,324 dead; 2nd Far Eastern lost 2,449 killed; Trans-Baikal 2,228; the Soviet Pacific Fleet lost 998 naval infantry. Japan identified 21,000 of its own men killed, but the true figure is probably closer to 80,000.

MacArthur, in his new role as supreme commander Allied powers, ordered all subordinate commanders to postpone reoccupation of Japanese-held territory until after the formal surrender was signed. Seven million Japanese troops remained under arms, in the home islands and across

Hirohito's empire. A British official wrote: "They do not consider that they have been defeated and say so quite openly. They have simply laid down arms on the Emperor's orders. We are thus in a position that, in a few days' time, we shall be setting out to disarm an undefeated army." It was also plainly a matter of urgency to prevent a vacuum of authority across a huge area where local nationalists were poised to challenge the Allies for control. At SEAC, Mountbatten told his staff he was "at a loss to understand why General MacArthur should wish to impose such a dangerous delay." MacArthur said loftily to his British liaison officer: "Tell Lord Louis to keep his pants on or he will get us all into trouble." Mountbatten responded: "Tell him I will keep my pants on if he will take Hirohito's off." SEAC's commander defied MacArthur's orders and rushed help to Allied prisoners in Malaya and the Dutch East Indies. Without prompt succour, these men would have continued to die, as the U.S. general might have paused to consider. It was widely believed that MacArthur's policy was promoted by vanity, a determination to tolerate no distractions from his own great final performance.

The Japanese surrender brought the beginnings of a new round of misery to Indochina. The vanquished occupiers exerted themselves to aid Ho Chi Minh's nationalist Vietminh and inflict further humiliations on the French. In Hanoi, 5,000 French prisoners remained confined for weeks in the citadel, even as the Vietminh hastened to occupy the city. While the Hôtel Metropole continued to serve six-course meals, and shops were stocked with silks, the bodies of Vietnamese who had died of starvation lay in the streets. Even after the surrender, the Japanese dealt brutally with French officers whom they captured. While awaiting Chinese and British occupation forces, they transferred large quantities of money and arms to the Vietminh. Some Japanese deserters joined Ho Chi Minh's ranks. The first British troops found themselves obliged to participate in a bitter struggle for power, indeed an open war, until French units arrived to relieve them. In Saigon, the Americans abruptly withdrew from participation in the Vietnam Control Commission, removing the designated U.S. Army signals team from the Allied occupying force. Brig.-Gen. Timberman, commanding U.S. troops in South-East Asia, asserted that reoccupation of Indochina "had nothing to do with the French."

In the Dutch East Indies, local nationalists swiftly seized control from the Japanese. A bitter and bloody struggle began, which cost thousands of lives in the months that followed, to resist the restoration of Dutch hegemony. "The Japanese," concluded a French observer who had been in Batavia since 1941, "though defeated in a general sense, have 'won the war' in this corner of Asia." They had rendered it impossible for the former European colonial powers convincingly to reassert their authority where they had left off more than three years earlier.

Thousands of British and Indian Soldiers had been preparing for the amphibious assault on Malaya, Operation Zipper. For them, as for American soldiers slated to land in Japan, it was an overwhelming relief that they could now land unopposed. Cecil Daniels's battalion of the Buffs had lost ten officers and 205 men in Burma. Looking back on his personal contribution to the war, the infantryman wrote with touching gaucheness: "I felt I had acquitted myself reasonably well, but . . . could and would have done more (in other words, stuck my head out more), if my parents had not already lost one son in the war. I wanted to spare them the grief of the possibility of losing another son if possible."

From a housing estate in Dagenham, Essex, a cook's mother wrote to the captain of the British cruiser *Nigeria*, serving in the Pacific: "Dear Sir, we send our greatest thanks & congratulations to you, all the crew & my son Jimmy Underwood, mess 42B. It really seems almost unbelievable that peace with Japan has now been proclaimed & so many of our loved ones will now be spared. You have all done so well and we at home owe you so much. To say 'thanks' is such a small word to show the appreciation we feel in our inner souls. To be parted from our loved ones . . . has seemed an eternity. No more weeping and sleepless nights & wet pillows. The 'blitz' all finished and now to make ready for a new home to rest our boys. God speed your return, thanks a million to you, I am faithfully, yours sincerely Mrs. Alice Underwood. PS Let us think for a while of those who have 'passed on for this good cause.' They will NEVER be forgotten."

Captain Kouichi Ito of the Japanese 32nd Regiment was one of several hundred Japanese who escaped captivity on Okinawa, hiding in the island's multitude of caves, scavenging for food with some little aid from local people, digging up potatoes in the fields under cover of darkness. On 22 August, a Japanese prisoner under American escort appeared at the mouth of the cave being occupied by Ito and his handful of companions, and told them the war was over. They hesitated, but finally decided to believe him. They had seen the offshore firework display a week earlier, as U.S. ships celebrated the announcement of victory. "It did not seem likely that the Americans were making this up," said Ito. He emerged, and was taken to hear a recording of the emperor's broadcast. Ito had been officially posted missing, along with the rest of the doomed garrison of Okinawa.

When finally he came home to his parents, he found that while his father had remained convinced that he was alive, his mother had for months been praying for his shade at the shrine for the dead. He found himself collapsing into tears, which he was unable either to check or explain to himself. "I marvelled at my own survival, and could not understand it. I kept thinking of the 90 percent of my men who had died." He felt embittered and frustrated by the collapse of his own hopes for a career as a warrior, as well for his country's defeat. Instead of finding glory in military prowess, he settled down to a humdrum life in his father's transport contracting business. When he married, his wife said sternly: "In the army, you have grown accustomed to having lots of people to boss about, and orderlies to do everything for you. I do not intend to become a replacement for them." It was many years before the ghosts of defeat on Okinawa were laid in Ito's mind, his furious emotions calmed.

THERE WAS MUCH American debate about whether the formal surrender should be signed on Japanese soil, or at sea. Truman, the most famous Missourian, made the decision. The battleship bearing his state's name was at sea south of Japan, and the men were opening a new mail delivery. The chief yeoman dashed up to Captain Murray, her commanding officer, and said: "Captain, *Missouri* is going to be the surrender ship—here's a clipping from the Santa Barbara paper." Murray, a forty-seven-year-old Texan who had only commanded the great vessel since May, found that his own wife had sent him the same cutting. The ship had been at sea for eighteen months, and showed it. An appeal for paint was signalled round the task group. Only a slender supply could be found, because paint stores had been such a fire hazard aboard ships in combat. Men began holystoning decks that had been camouflage-tinted, cleaning every visible part of *Missouri*. The Royal Navy's Admiral Sir Bruce Fraser offered a table for the ceremony, which Murray wanted to accept "because it gave the British a chance to say: 'We contributed something.' " In the end, however, this well-meaning condescension was frustrated. A wardroom table was set up on deck, simply because it was bigger.

On the afternoon of 1 September, the huge battleship eased its way cautiously into Tokyo Bay, wary of mines and kamikazes. A party of Japanese naval officers boarded from a destroyer to offer the keys of the city of Yokosuka, near the ship's intended anchorage. Advancing further, the battleship passed more Japanese destroyers, their guns plugged and depressed, and at last stopped engines some six miles off Yokohama. By nightfall, 260 Allied warships filled the bay.

Mustering the great crowd of dignitaries and onlookers next morning, Sunday, 2 September 1945, proved a challenge. There were 225 correspondents and seventy-five photographers, two of these Japanese, together with representatives of every Allied power. Captain Murray took pains to ensure that the respective flag hoists of MacArthur and Nimitz were exactly level. Two Marines hustled an errant Russian photographer into his proper place, while the Americans scrutinised the Japanese cameramen nervously. Soon after 0800, destroyers delivered MacArthur and Nimitz to the ship.

In Tokyo, there was bitter dispute about who should sign the detested peace documents on behalf of the government. "The feeling of Japan's leaders, now that the war was ended so suddenly, was characteristic," wrote Mamoru Shigemitsu. "They abhorred, as an unclean thing, the act of shouldering responsibility for the deed of surrender, and they did their best to avoid it." He himself was finally appointed, as minister plenipotentiary. At dawn Shigemitsu and a small group, most prominent among whom was Umezu, the army chief, assembled at the prime minister's official residence. They bowed formally towards the Imperial Palace, then drove through miles of empty streets and bombed-out desolation to Yokohama. There, an American destroyer awaited them for the hour-long passage to Halsey's flagship.

The Japanese party came alongside *Missouri* at 0855. Silence fell over the throng as the defeated enemy's representatives, in formal dress and top hats, mounted the gangway and approached the serried ranks of Allied brass. Shigemitsu, who had lost a leg to an unsuccessful assassin's bomb a few years earlier, made every step in visible pain, embarrassing the more sensitive Americans. When the Japanese were in their places, MacArthur, Nimitz and Halsey—the last scowling, as usual—emerged from a hatchway and strode to the mess table, covered with a green cloth. MacArthur delivered a short speech, which even his sternest critics have been unable to fault: "The issues, involving divergent ideals and ideologies, have been determined on the battlefields of the world and hence are not for our discussion or debate," he said. "Nor is it for us here to meet, representing as we do a majority of the people of the earth, in a spirit of distrust, malice or hatred. But rather it is for us, both victors and vanquished, to rise to that higher dignity which alone befits the sacred purposes we are about to serve, committing all our people unreservedly to faithful compliance."

His hands trembled as he read. Even MacArthur seemed a little overwhelmed by the magnitude of the occasion. The Japanese were deeply impressed by the generosity of the sentiments expressed by the supreme commander. For the first time, they felt a gleam of hope for the future. Then they all signed. At 9:25, the silence was broken by a distant drone, then a great roar overhead, as four hundred B-29s and 1,500 carrier planes staged the greatest fly-past in history. The Japanese bowed, retreated, and descended the gangway. MacArthur walked to a microphone, and delivered another slow, majestic speech. "Today the guns are silent," he began. "A great tragedy has ended. A great victory has been won." After rehearsing memories of the long journey from Bataan to Tokyo Bay, he concluded with an appeal entirely worthy of the moment, for mankind to pursue a new spirit of peace: "These proceedings are now closed," he said. Nothing so became MacArthur's tenure of combat command as the manner in which he ended it. The general departed ashore, to begin at the age of sixty-five the most impressive phase of his life, as architect of Japan's resurrection and redemption—also, indeed, of his own.

Aboard *Missouri*, Captain Murray found that no one had thought of locking up the American copy of the surrender document, and hastily did so himself. He frustrated an attempt by the ship's cooks to abstract the table used for the surrender ceremony. Huge and bloody domestic struggles were commencing for the future of Asia, but the war against Japan was ended.

TWENTY-TWO

Legacies

THE MOST CREDIBLE statistics suggest that 185,647 Japanese were killed in China between 1937 and 1941. The Imperial Army lost a further 1,140,429 dead between Pearl Harbor and August 1945, while the navy lost 414,879. At least 97,031 civilian dead were listed in Tokyo and a further 86,336 in other cities, but many more bombing casualties were unrecorded. Over 100,000 died in Hiroshima and Nagasaki. Some 150,000 civilians are alleged to have perished on Okinawa, 10,000 on Saipan, though these latter figures are thought by modern Western scholars to have been exaggerated, perhaps as much as tenfold. Anything up to 250,000 Japanese soldiers and civilians died in Manchuria during the icy winter of 1945, after the war ended, along with many more who served as slave labourers for the Soviets in Siberia through the succeeding decade. Japan's total war dead are estimated at 2.69 million, against 6 million Germans.

Chinese historians today seek to increase figures for their nation's wartime death toll from 15 to 25 or even 50 million. Some 5 million inhabitants of South-East Asia are thought to have perished under Japanese occupation, most of these in Indochina and the Dutch East Indies. None of these numbers are reliable, but they offer an indication of scale. It can confidently be asserted that Japan's human losses were vastly surpassed by those of the nations which it attacked and occupied between 1931 and 1945. The U.S. Army, meanwhile, lost some 55,145 killed in the Pacific conflict, including 3,650 in South-East Asia, compared with around 143,000 in Europe and North Africa. The U.S. Navy lost 29,263 dead in the east, the Marines 19,163. About 30,000 British servicemen perished in the war against the Japanese, many of them as prisoners, by comparison with 235,000 who died fighting the Germans.

The outcome of the Pacific conflict persuaded some Americans that they could win wars at relatively small human cost, by the application of their country's boundless technological ingenuity and industrial resources. The lesson appeared to be that, if the U.S. possessed bases from which its warships and aircraft could strike at the land of an enemy, victories could be gained by the expenditure of mere treasure, and relatively little blood. Only in the course of succeeding decades did it become plain that Japan was a foe uniquely vulnerable to American naval and air power projection. Some modern U.S. historians assert that the pursuit of decisive victory is central to the American way of war. If true, this renders their country chronically vulnerable to disappointment. The 1950–53 Korean conflict proved only the first of many demonstrations that the comprehensive triumph achieved by the U.S. in the Second World War was a freak of history, representing no norm. Modern experience suggests that never again will overwhelming military, naval and air power suffice to fulfil American purposes abroad as effectively as it did in the Pacific war. Limited wars offer notable opportunities to belligerents of limited means. Only total war enabled a liberal democracy to exploit weapons of mass destruction. Even granted such circumstances, posterity has shown itself profoundly equivocal about America's 1945 bombardment of Japan.

In the light of the events of August 1945, it can be suggested that Japan would have surrendered not one day later had U.S. ground forces never advanced beyond their capture of the Marianas in the summer of 1944. It is superficially arguable, therefore, that Iwo Jima, Okinawa and MacArthur's Philippines campaign contributed no more than did Slim's victory in Burma to the final outcome. The Japanese retained large armies with which to defend their home islands. They were induced to quit by fuel starvation, the collapse of industry caused by blockade and in lesser degree aerial bombardment, together with the Soviet invasion of Manchuria and the atomic bombs.

Yet this represents the knowledge of hindsight, which makes possible a judgement wholly unattainable by Allied warlords in 1944–45. It would have been politically as well as militarily unthinkable for large American and British forces to stand idle in the Pacific and South-East Asia, waiting upon the impact of hypothetical scientific, strategic and economic developments. The loss of the Philippines and Burma played at least a marginal part in persuading Hirohito and those around him that their nation was doomed. Consider the implications if Slim's army had *not* crossed the Chindwin, if MacArthur had *not* established himself in the Philippines. Had large Allied armies merely lingered passive after the fall of the Marianas, waiting for blockade and bombardment to force Japan's capitulation, the military leadership in Tokyo would certainly have interpreted this as infirmity of will. The material and moral cost to the United States of LeMay's campaign outweighed its substantive achievement. Yet it would be foolish to doubt that even the most fanatical Japanese were deeply shaken by the destruction of their cities, the loss of between one-quarter and one-third of their national wealth to the B-29s.

At the very least, the 1945 air and land campaigns emphasised the Allies' implacable resolution. Even the war party in Tokyo could not convincingly argue that American commitment, indeed ruthlessness, was inferior to that of samurai, when they beheld Japan's ruined cities, the slaughter of its people in hundreds of thousands, the dogged erosion of its armies. Japan's leaders started the war supposing that their nation's spirit could compensate for its relative material weakness. By August 1945, this proposition was decisively discredited.

Of the atomic bombs, a modern American historian has written: "If the bombing of Hiroshima and Nagasaki was the apogee of the nation-state—for what other political entity could possibly have financed and manned such an undertaking as the Manhattan Project . . . then that moment was also the birth of the universal vulnerability of the nation-state." Not only does the use of the atomic bombs seem to have been justified in the circumstances prevailing in August 1945, but I am among those convinced that the demonstration of nuclear horror, and the global revulsion which it provoked, has contributed decisively towards preserving the world since. If the effects of nuclear attack had not been demonstrated at Hiroshima and Nagasaki, it is overwhelmingly likely that in the Cold War era, an American or Russian leader would have convinced himself that the use of atomic weapons could be justified. Korea in 1950 offers an obvious example, when some U.S. generals, above all MacArthur, favoured exploiting against China the advantages supposedly conferred by America's nuclear arsenal. Such a point is irrelevant to the debate about whether the original decision in 1945 was valid, but is surely worthy of consideration more than six decades later.

For all the absurdity of Britain's hopes of restoring its eastern hegemony in 1945, many of Slim's soldiers of Fourteenth Army retained sentimental memories of the Japanese war as the last gathering of the British Empire in arms. "Dear Sir," wrote Garba Yola, a Nigerian of 82nd West African Division, to his former commander Maj.-Gen. Sir Hugh Stockwell in 1946. "Of course it is a very long time ago since I come back home to my native land, and I hope that these few lines will meet you in an excellent condition. I arrived home safely and found all my people all right, nothing strange to be reported in respect of my present health, only that I always remember you in any circumstances of the day. I have seen the letter you sent me, and I am very glad to see that it comes from you. Give my special compliments to my 'mother' your wife. I enclose herewith my portrait, so that she may know me. Warm compliments from my wife, and my friend Jauro. My father and mother ask me to remember them to you. I would like to hear from you as regards your conditions, and your present place of abode, yours obediently." Slim's 1945 reconquest was among the most successful British campaigns of the war, reflecting the highest credit on its commander and his soldiers. But it represented a last convulsion of empire, rather than a convincing contribution to the defeat of Japan.

In 1947 the British left India. They quit Burma a year later, and Malaya in 1957. The Dutch were forced to abandon their East Indian possessions in 1949, after four years of bloody guerrilla war. The French suffered futile agonies in Indochina before bowing to the inevitable when they lost the battle of Dien Bien Phu to Ho Chi Minh's Vietminh nationalists in 1954. Ironically, the European colonial nations found themselves in much more comfortable economic circumstances after shedding their cherished Asian possessions. These had become drains upon their straitened resources, rather than the assets their owners had supposed. The U.S. granted independence to the Philippines in 1946. That year, Manuel Roxas was elected national president. He had been prominent among Filipino politicians who collaborated with the Japanese occupation regime, and indeed declared war on the U.S. in September 1944. The electoral success of Roxas served to highlight the equivocal attitude of the Filipino people to the Second World War and to the United States.

Far from the Soviets fulfilling fears that they would prolong their presence in Manchuria for imperialistic reasons, Chiang Kai-shek was obliged to beg Stalin's occupying forces to serve overtime, to give the Nationalists time to send their own troops to take possession. The Soviets withdrew between January and May 1946, having systematically pillaged the region of every scrap of industrial plant. They justified this by asserting that their booty was not Chinese property but Japanese-owned, and thus represented legitimate war reparations. Hundreds of thousands of Japanese captives such as Souhei Nakamura found themselves labouring for the Russians in Siberia, enduring cold and starvation. They never knew how many of their number died, because as soon as a man became sick he was removed by the guards, never to be seen again.

Just once in his years behind the wire was young Nakamura allowed to send home a card via the Red Cross in Switzerland, announcing that he was "well and happy," like so many wretched British and American prisoners of the Japanese a few years earlier. The wheel had turned full circle. "It seemed so unjust," said Nakamura. "The world was at peace, and yet there were we, living as prisoners in terrible conditions." They constantly begged of their captors: "When can we go home?" and always received the same reply: "In forty-five days." When the time was up, they asked again, and received the same stony answer: "In forty-five days." Some men became sufficiently impressed by ideological indoctrination to profess Communism on their return to Japan. Nakamura himself was repatriated in July 1948.

Chiang Kai-shek's occupation of Manchuria proved a strategic error. His forces there found themselves cut off as the Chinese civil war developed. Vast quantities of American military aid provided to his armies counted for nothing beside the corruption and incompetence of his regime. In 1949 Mao Zedong became master of China, excluding only the island of Formosa, which became Chiang's pocket nation-state, modern Taiwan. Thus was confounded the Americans' great fantasy of the wartime era, their vision for China, as was the matching British one, of redeeming their Asian empire. The Japanese slogan "Asia for Asians" achieved fulfilment in a fashion undreamt of by those who coined it.

And so to MacArthur. Few today suppose that he ranks among the great commanders of history. Yet so prodigious were his theatrical powers, so remarkable was the achievement of his wartime publicity machine, that he remains the most famous figure of the Pacific war. More than forty years after the general accepted the Japanese surrender, Ronald Spector wrote of him: "Despite his undoubted qualities of leadership, he was unsuited by temperament, character, and judgment for the positions of high command which he occupied throughout the war." MacArthur's megalomania, disloyalty to his own national leadership, pettiness, contempt for intelligence, poor selection of staff and subordinates, refusal to acknowledge error and determination to shape national strategy to conform with his personal ambitions suggest that this verdict errs on the side of generosity. Nonetheless, it is essential also to recognise the charisma, intellect and self-conscious aspiration to nobility which enabled MacArthur at times to scale heights no ordinary commander could achieve, as he did at the Japanese surrender. As post-war ruler of Japan, he displayed a wisdom and magnanimity conspicuously absent from his tenure as supreme commander in the south-west Pacific. It should also be acknowledged that between December 1941 and August 1945, deservedly or no, he became for the American people the embodiment of their national purpose in the east. Nations at war need symbols, and no less so do fighting soldiers: "We thought he was above God," one veteran said to me of MacArthur. Another asserted: "He was the greatest military commander America has ever produced." Even though this is quite untrue, it is noteworthy that some of his old soldiers believe it.

It was MacArthur's good fortune that, after presiding over the initial disaster in the Philippines, he served in a theatre where American material dominance became so overwhelming that his misjudgements and follies were redeemable. The U.S. Navy achieved the decisive victories, but MacArthur was able to reap much of the glory. That dramatic profile in its oversized cap and glinting sunglasses dominated every image of war against Japan. Nimitz, a supremely professional naval officer, neither sought nor received a due share of fame for his stellar performance in the Pacific. The U.S. Navy's achievement was as brilliant, as decisive, as that of the Royal Navy in frustrating Napoleon's tyranny almost a century and a half earlier.

British and American prisioners in Aomi barracks, Japan, had to wait three weeks after the surrender for the first sight of their deliverers. Then one day nine U.S. fighters flew overhead in perfect formation, spotted the huge "PW" letters laid out by the inmates, and dipped low enough for the pilots to wave. It was the prisoners' first glimpse of a friendly outside world for 1,302 days. Stephen Abbott went inside and wept. Before the prisoners departed, he visited the local factory, in the quarry of which he and his comrades had laboured and often died. In the boardroom of the Denki Kagaku Kogyo company, its president said to Abbott: "Our country is in ruins, but you understand Japanese people. We will never lose our pride. Return here in five years and we will be tidy; allow us ten and I know you will find a prospering nation." Soon afterwards, the British and American prisoners quit "those few square yards of Japanese soil we loathed with all our hearts—but on which a volume of human tragedy and learning had been recorded." Even as the prisoners departed, the first elements of MacArthur's army landed in Japan, a force mighty enough to ensure against any belated displays of recalcitrance by the defeated enemy. Officers and men alike gazed in awe at the ruined land before them: "I marvel continually, from what I see, how Japan did so much with so little," wrote Lt.-Gen. Oscar Griswold. U.S. military occupation continued until 1952.

In 1945–46, some Japanese were prosecuted for war crimes. To impose retribution on all those guilty of barbarous acts would have required tens of thousands of executions, for which the Allies lacked stomach. Very few Japanese were called to account for their deeds in China and South-East Asia. The U.S., dominant partner in the alliance, focused its vengeance upon those who had committed atrocities against white men and U.S. colonial subjects. The most prominent figure to be charged was Tojo, who was hanged. Gen. Tomoyuki Yamashita was indicted for his role as Japan's commander in the Philippines when so many atrocities were committed against its people.

The proceedings began on 29 October 1945, and at first the general declined to go into the witness box. When persuaded to do so, he presented an impressive image of dignity and fluency. Convicted and sentenced to hang, he removed his belt and presented it to an American colonel as a souvenir, observing jovially: "You're the only man here fat enough to wear this." Pinioned before being marched to the gallows, he complained of the tightness of the handcuffs, but then strode courageously to meet death. Gen. Masaharu Homma was shot by firing squad in April 1946, convicted of responsibility for the Bataan death march. Homma said: "I am being executed for the Bataan incident. What I want to know is: who was responsible for the deaths of tens of thousands of innocent civilians at Hiroshima and Nagasaki? MacArthur or Truman?" He went gaily to execution, raising a beer glass to the chaplain and interpreter, saying in perfect English: "Come on gentlemen, please. Bottoms up!"

Many people, American as well as Japanese, were dismayed by the fashion in which Yamashita and Homma were done to death. Their trials bore an ugly stamp of kangaroo court proceedings, at which evidence of the generals' opposition to inhumane treatment of civilians and POWs was swept aside. It was widely believed that the sentences represented MacArthur's personal vengeance upon Japanese commanders who had humiliated him in the field. There is, however, a strong contrary argument. Yamashita and Homma were sympathetic and personally honourable figures. Yet they held the responsible commands when unlawful and indeed unspeakable acts were committed against a host of innocents. How could their subordinates be punished for carrying out such deeds, if commanders went free? Japanese atrocities might not have been directly ordered by Yamashita or Homma, but they reflected a culture of massacre in which the entire Japanese military was complicit, and which it worked assiduously for decades to promote.

Even if the generals' executions were symbolic rather than legally proper, they were almost certainly necessary. The American decision to leave Hirohito on his throne caused many Japanese afterwards to suppose that their nation could not have behaved so very badly, if their emperor's reign was permitted to continue. Had Japan's most senior commanders also been judged unaccountable for the ghastly deeds of the nation's soldiers, their survival would have appeared a betrayal of millions dead by Japanese hands. It is plainly true that the 1945–46 war crimes trials, in Europe as well as Asia, represented victors' justice. No attempt was made to impose even token punishment upon Allied personnel who committed unlawful deeds. But it seemed preferable then, as it still does today, to subject to trial some of those responsible for crimes against humanity, rather than to hold none responsible because so many were guilty.

In the wake of Japan's surrender, Hirohito's soldiers, sailors and airmen were shocked to find themselves objects of obloquy among their own people. Public animosity embraced the humblest as well as the loftiest warriors. After years of suffering, all the pent-up frustration and misery of the Japanese people was made manifest in the wake of defeat. Servicemen who had mindlessly accepted the code of *bushido*, and sometimes suffered terribly to fulfil its demands, now faced the contempt of their own nation. Amazingly, the U.S. army of occupation found itself protecting the survivors of the Imperial Japanese Army from the fury of its own people. This was an experience unknown among German veterans who had served in Hitler's legions. Japan's early post-war years were characterised by a collapse of hierarchies, a ruthless pursuit of self-interest reflected in looting, crime and wholesale prostitution, unknown at any other period of the nation's history. Decadence, even depravity, flourished, as the defeated people astonished their conquerors by the fashion in which they abased themselves before all things American. Self-loathing seemed for a time to overtake Japan.

Perhaps this was a necessary part of a cleansing process after the years of military dominance and national self-delusion. From 1950 onwards, stimulated ironically enough by the Korean War, there followed an economic resurrection which awed the world.

YET THE NEW JAPAN proved distressingly reluctant to confront the historic guilt of the old. Its spirit of denial contrasted starkly with the penitence of post-war Germany. Though successive Japanese prime ministers expressed formal regret for Japan's wartime actions, the country refused to pay reparations to victims, or to acknowledge its record in school history texts. I embarked upon this book with a determination to view Japanese wartime conduct objectively, thrusting aside nationalistic sentiments which have clouded the perspective of many British and American writers since 1945. Japanese veterans whom I met proved warmly sympathetic. It is essential for every historian to keep in view the wartime excesses of Allied forces, which seldom incurred censure, far less judicial sanction. Yet it proved hard to sustain lofty aspirations to detachment, in the face of the evidence of systemic Japanese barbarism, displayed against their fellow Asians on a vastly wider scale than against Americans and Europeans. The knights of *bushido*, like those of medieval Europe, made mockery of their lofty ideal of honour by behaving so basely towards the great multitudes whom they deemed undeserving of the protection of their code. In modern times, only Hitler's SS has matched militarist Japan in rationalising and institutionalising atrocity. Stalin's Soviet Union never sought to dignify its great killings as the acts of gentlemen, as did Hirohito's nation.

It is easy to perceive *why* so many Japanese behaved as they did, conditioned as they were. Yet it remains almost impossible to empathise with those who did such things, especially when Japan still rejects its historic legacy. Many Japanese today adopt the view that it is time to bury all old grievances—those of Japan's former enemies about the treatment of prisoners and subject peoples, along with those of their own nation about fire-bombing, Hiroshima and Nagasaki. "In war, both sides do terrible things," former Lieutenant Hayashi Inoue argued in 2005. "If you win, then that justifies any action you have taken. If you lose, you become the guilty party. Surely after sixty years, the time has come to stop criticising Japan for things done so long ago." Maj. Shigeru Funaki, a former staff officer at Japanese army HQ in Nanjing, says sternly: "A lot of the stuff about what Japan is supposed to have done in China is simply invented. At the end of the war, I had to negotiate constantly with Nationalist army officers. None of them said a word about, for instance, a massacre in Nanjing. OK, some people died there, because there was a battle and people die in battles. But this idea that 150,000 or 200,000 were killed—who is supposed to have counted them?" Japanese media tycoon Tsuneo Watanabe has sponsored a major project to review more realistically Japan's record in World War II. Most of his fellow countrymen, however, decisively reject both the concept of self-analysis and his bleak conclusions.

Germany has paid almost $6 billion to 1.5 million victims of the Hitler era. Austria has paid $400 million to 132,000 people. By contrast, modern Japan goes to extraordinary lengths to escape any admission of responsibility, far less of liability for compensation, towards its wartime victims. By an absurd, indeed grotesque, irony, in 1999 the British government chose to make ex-gratia payments to British former captives of the Japanese, having despaired of the perpetrators of their sufferings doing so. Repeated attempts at litigation before Japanese judges, notably by Chinese plaintiffs including former "comfort women," have so far been unsuccessful. Three cases have only recently been rejected by the Supreme Court. Perhaps the most striking example is that of slave labourers, of whom 38,935 Chinese were shipped to Japan, and 6,830 died. They were employed by thirty-five companies, of which twenty-two continue to trade, including Mitsubishi and Matsui Mining. In a recent lawsuit by former Chinese slaves against Mitsubishi, defence lawyers sought to question whether Japan had invaded China. Mitsubishi explicitly denies that it employed forced labour. A ruling in favour of the plaintiffs, said Mitsubishi's counsel, would "impose an unjust burden on future generations of our nation, possibly for centuries to come."

The wartime Japanese minister of commerce and mines was the grandfather of Shinzo Abe, Japan's recent prime minister. Soon after assuming office in 2007, Mr. Abe publicly asserted that many Chinese and Korean comfort women volunteered for their role. Both the Japanese government and the companies targeted for litigation argue that any possible liability towards Japan's wartime victims has lapsed with the passage of time and the September 1951 San Francisco Peace Treaty signed by Japan and forty-eight Allied nations—though China was a conspicuous absentee, and the USSR declined to append its signature. Tokyo also asserts, less than subtly, that it is grotesque for a country with as deplorable a record of respect for human rights as China to seek redress for any past Japanese shortcomings in this field.

Both the policy of denial and the alternative doctrine of moral equivalence are unconvincing, when Japanese brutality was institutionalised for many years before the Allies commenced their own excesses, if excesses they were. Even LeMay's campaign was designed to hasten the end of the war. Many Japanese actions, by contrast, including the torture and beheading of prisoners, reflected a gratuitous pride in the infliction of suffering. Wartime Japan was responsible for almost as many deaths in Asia as was Nazi Germany in Europe. Yet only a few modern Japanese acknowledge as much, and incur the disdain or outright hostility of their fellow countrymen for doing so. The nation is guilty of a collective rejection of historical fact. The treatment of subject peoples and prisoners described in this book is wholly unaccepted by most modern Japanese, even where supported by overwhelming evidence. This sustains a chasm between their culture and ours, which cannot be justified or dismissed by mere reference to differences of attitude between East and West.

Much Western criticism has focused upon the custom of modern Japanese prime ministers paying formal annual visits to the Yasukuni Shrine to honour the nation's war dead, including its war criminals. This, I believe, is mistaken. The leaders of all societies which participated in great conflicts are expected to pay homage to those who fell in them, whatever the demerits of their causes. There is no reason why Japan should be excepted. It seems to me that dismay, indeed repugnance, should instead concentrate upon the refusal of the Japanese people, including their political, educational and corporate leaders, honestly to acknowledge their history. They still seek to excuse, and even to ennoble, the actions of their parents and grandparents, so many of whom forsook humanity in favour of a perversion of honour and an aggressive nationalism which should properly be recalled with shame. As long as such denial persists, it will remain impossible for the world to believe that Japan has come to terms with the horrors which it inflicted upon Asia almost two-thirds of a century ago.

"What comes next, then? What am I going to do?" And immediately he knew the answer: "Nothing. I'm just going to live. Oh, it's marvellous!"

Tolstoy's Pierre Bezukhov after the Franco-Russian campaign of 1812

A BRIEF CHRONOLOGY OF THE JAPANESE WAR

1931 18 September: Japan begins occupation of Manchuria
1933 25 March: Japan leaves League of Nations
1934 21 October: In China, Mao Zedong begins "Long March" to Shensi Province
1936 25 November: Japan signs Anti-Comintern Pact with Germany
1937 7 July: "Marco Polo bridge incident" sparks Japanese invasion of China
13 December: Japanese seizure of Nanjing precipitates massacre of Chinese
1939 May–August: Soviet and Japanese forces clash at Nomonhan on the Manchuria-Mongolia border: Japan decisively worsted
23 August: Nazi-Soviet Pact signed
1 September: Germany invades Poland
3 September: France, Britain, India, Australia and New Zealand declare war on Germany
1940 January: U.S. abrogates 1911 Treaty of Commerce with Japan
22 June: France signs armistice with Germany; Japan insists on closure of Haiphong–Yunnan rail link through French Indochina, supplying Chiang Kai-shek. Eight hundred French troops killed resisting Japanese forces advancing into Indochina.
26 June: U.S.A. imposes embargo on iron and steel scrap shipments to Japan
16 September: U.S. Selective Service Act becomes law, imposing the draft
27 September: Japan signs Tripartite Pact with Germany and Italy
5 November: Roosevelt wins third presidential term
1941 10 January: Siam invades French Indochina
31 January: Siam and French Indochina accept Japanese "mediation"; Japan occupies northern Indochina
22 June: Hitler invades the Soviet Union
26 July: U.S. imposes oil embargo on Japan and freezes Japanese assets
27 July: Japanese occupy Saigon and enter Cambodia
18 October: General Tojo replaces Prince Konoe as Japanese prime minister
7 December: Japanese aircraft bomb U.S. Pacific bases at Pearl Harbor, Hawaii; Wake Island; Midway; Philippines
8 December: Japanese invade Malaya and Siam. Bangkok government surrenders

8 December: The United States declares war on Japan. Japan enters into a state of war with the United States and Britain.
9 December: Nationalist China declares war on Japan, Germany and Italy
10 December: Japanese sink British warships *Prince of Wales* and *Repulse* off Malaya, begin landing on Luzon, Philippines
14 December: Japanese advance into Burma
16 December: Japanese land in Borneo
20 December: Japanese attack Dutch East Indies
22 December: Japanese land at Lingayen, Philippines
24 December: Japanese seize Wake Island
25 December: Hong Kong falls

1942 25 January: Siam declares war on Britain and the United States
2 February: Maj.-Gen. Joseph Stilwell appointed C-in-C to Chiang Kai-shek and C-in-C U.S. forces in the China theatre
3 February: Japan invades Dutch East Indies; Japanese bombers attack Port Moresby, New Guinea
8 February: President Quezon, on besieged Corregidor, asks Roosevelt for immediate Philippines independence, so that the islands can declare themselves neutral and call upon both Japanese and Americans to leave. FDR refuses.
15 February: British garrison of Singapore surrenders to the Japanese; Japanese bomb Darwin, in northern Australia
23 February: Japanese submarine bombards oil refinery at Santa Barbara, California
27 February: Japanese victorious in Battle of the Java Sea
8 March: New Japanese landings on New Guinea
11 March: MacArthur escapes from the Philippines
17 March: MacArthur appointed Allied commander in the south-west Pacific
6 April: Japanese forces land on the Admiralty Islands and on Bougainville in the Solomons, and bomb two towns in eastern India
9 April: U.S. troops on the Bataan Peninsula surrender
18 April: Sixteen B-25 Mitchell bombers, launched from the carrier *Hornet* and led by Gen. James Doolittle, bomb Tokyo; captured U.S. aircrew beheaded by the Japanese
1 May: Japanese take Mandalay
6 May: U.S. forces on Corregidor, Philippines, surrender to the Japanese
7 May: Battle of the Coral Sea costs Japanese and Americans a carrier sunk and another badly damaged on each side, but forces the Japanese for the first time to abandon an amphibious assault against Port Moresby, New Guinea
15 May: In China, Japanese execute one hundred Chinese families in reprisal for the Doolittle Raid
23 May: Stilwell reaches India, after 150-mile march out of Burma with Chinese units; British forces complete withdrawal from Burma
4 June: Japanese attack Midway Island, north-east of Hawaii
6 June: Japanese occupy Kiska in the Aleutians; decisive U.S. naval victory at Midway, with four Japanese carriers sunk and 275 planes destroyed, for American loss of one carrier and 132 planes

7 August: Americans land on Guadalcanal
9 August: Japanese navy sinks four U.S. cruisers off Savo Island, in the Solomons
11 August: Australians driven out of Deniki on the Kokoda Trail in New Guinea
12 August: Japanese land at Buna, New Guinea
27 August: U.S. carrier *Saratoga* badly damaged by submarine attack, leaving *Wasp* only operational U.S. carrier in the Pacific
1 September: Battle of Stalingrad begins
2 September: In North Africa, Rommel withdraws after the decisive failure of his assault on the British defending Egypt at Alam Halfa
8 September: New Guinea: Australian forces driven back in the Owen Stanley Mountains
18 September: New Guinea: Japanese forces obliged to make some withdrawals, Australians poised to start advance on the Kokoda Trail
11–12 October: Solomons: Japanese navy worsted in Battle of Cap Esperance
17 October: Burma: Indian forces begin an advance in the Arakan
23 October: U.S. forces land in North Africa; Battle of El Alamein begins
26 October: Japanese navy victorious in Battle of Santa Cruz, which costs U.S. *Hornet* fatally damaged and *Enterprise* crippled, but Japanese suffer heavy aircraft losses

1943 2 February: Germans capitulate at Stalingrad
13 February: First British "Chindit" operation launched into Burma
2 March: Battle of the Bismarck Sea
20 June: U.S. campaign in New Georgia begins
5 July: Battle of Kursk begins
1 August: Japanese declare Burma independent
3 September: Allies land in Italy
7 October: Mountbatten becomes Allied supreme commander in South-East Asia
14 October: Japanese declare Philippines independent
20 November: U.S. Marines land on Tarawa Atoll
2 December: First chain reaction achieved at Chicago University by the Manhattan Project team

1944 31 January: U.S. forces land in the Marshalls
2 March: Second Chindit operation mounted into Burma
15 March: Japanese Imphal-Kohima offensive begins
22 April: U.S. forces land at Hollandia, New Guinea
April–December: Japanese "Ichigo" offensive in China
17 May: Stilwell's Chinese and U.S. force takes Myitkyina airfield
31 May: Japanese begin withdrawal from Kohima
4 June: Allied forces enter Rome
6 June: D-Day landings in Normandy
15 June: U.S. forces land on Saipan
19 June: Battle of the Philippine Sea begins
18 July: Tojo resigns as Japan's prime minister; Japanese begin retreat from Imphal
20 July: German officers attempt unsuccessfully to assassinate Hitler
15 September: Marines land on Peleliu
20 October: U.S. Army lands on Leyte

24–25 October: Naval Battle of Leyte Gulf
30 October: Lt.-Gen. Albert Wedemeyer replaces Stilwell as senior U.S. military representative in China
6 November: Roosevelt wins fourth presidential term
December: Slim's Fourteenth Army crosses Chindwin into Burma

1945 9 January: U.S. Army lands on Luzon
11 January: British forces begin to cross the Irrawaddy
19 February: Marines land on Iwo Jima
2 March: British advance to Meiktila
9 March: Japanese seize control of Indochina
20 March: British capture Mandalay
1 April: U.S. Army and Marines land on Okinawa
5 April: Koiso resigns as Japan's prime minister, succeeded by Suzuki
12 April: Death of Roosevelt; Truman becomes president
30 April: Hitler commits suicide
3 May: Slim's Fourteenth Army enters Rangoon
8 May: VE-Day in Europe: Germany surrenders unconditionally
16 July: World's first atomic device tested at Alamogordo
17 July: Allied summit meeting in Potsdam
26 July: Churchill resigns as British prime minister following election defeat
6 August: First atomic bomb dropped on Hiroshima
8 August: USSR declares war on Japan, invades Manchuria
9 August: Second atomic bomb dropped on Nagasaki
15 August: VJ-Day: Japan announces its surrender
26 August: Soviet forces declare Hutou fortress secure, completing their campaign in Manchuria
2 September: Japan's surrender signed in Tokyo Bay

ACKNOWLEDGEMENTS

A book of this kind, three years in the making, has been dependent upon help and goodwill from a host of people. First, I should thank my publishers in London and New York, Richard Johnson and Ash Green, together with my splendid editor, Robert Lacey of HarperCollins. My British and American agents, Michael Sissons and Peter Matson, are always wonderfully supportive.

It is often suggested that academic historians are prey to jealousies. By contrast, I am constantly amazed by the generosity of scholars. Dr. Williamson Murray and Dr. Allan Millett offered many pointers at the outset of this project. Both were kind enough to read and comment upon a draft of my manuscript. Without the advice and personal commitment of Dr. Tim Nenninger, it would be impossible for a researcher to make swift headway in the vastnesses of the U.S. National Archive. Tim's help was indispensable in pointing me towards relevant and relatively unexplored material. The U.S. Army's Military History Institute at Carlisle, Penn., is a peerless source of documents and personal narratives, which its staff identified for me. Special thanks are due to Dr. Richard Sommers, together with Dr. Conrad Crane, MHI's director, himself a notable historian. Con commented upon my chapter about Curtis LeMay's air campaign. Dear Dr. Tami Biddle, of the neighbouring U.S. Army War College, gave me copies of many USAAF documents which she had unearthed in the course of her own researches.

The U.S. Marine Corps' historical centre at Quantico, Virginia, is full of good things, and I am grateful especially to Mike Miller for his assistance during my time there. The U.S. Navy's Historical Center at the Navy Yard in Washington, D.C., is another treasure house. Jack Green answered my questions, in person and by e-mail, with endless patience. Thereafter, he corrected scores of technical solecisms in my text, for which I am especially grateful. The library and oral history archive provided a mass of published and unpublished material. Dr. Ronald Spector offered some reflections over lunch in Washington. James Controvitch provided a comprehensive formation and unit bibliography. Col. David Glantz read and commented upon the draft of my chapters on the Soviet invasion of Manchuria, about which he is the foremost Western expert. Richard Frank, who in recent years has established himself as a brilliant historian of the Pacific, drew my attention to his unpublished monograph on Leyte Gulf. He also read my manuscript in advance of its U.S. publication, saving me from some egregious errors. The above, of course, bear no responsibility for my errors or judgements, some of which they will dissent from.

In Britain, Professor Sir Michael Howard, OM, CH, MC, and Don Berry were kind enough to read and discuss this manuscript, as they did that of my earlier book *Armageddon*. The staff at the Imperial War Museum were as splendid as ever, and the museum's collection of personal memoirs gets better every year. The Liddell Hart Archive at King's College, London, and the London Library both provided indispensable assistance.

In Japan, Chako Bellamy located survivors of the wartime era for interview, and accompanied me to interpret at meetings with them. Gu Renquan, the enchanting "Maomao," wife of the distinguished former BBC correspondent and biographer of Mao Zedong, Philip Short, did the same for me in China. Her company was among the foremost pleasures of my travels there. In Russia Dr. Luba Vinogradovna, researcher and interpreter for *Armageddon*, translated a mass of documents and personal reminiscences, as well as conducting interviews with several Red Army veterans of the Manchurian campaign. I have acknowledged individual contributions from eyewitnesses in the source notes, but I would like to offer collective thanks to all those in four countries, many of them very elderly, who answered my questions for many hours, thus contributing much to making this book possible.

My secretary, Rachel Lawrence, is never less than wonderful. My wife, Penny, sometimes thinks it might be best to emigrate when I am writing a book. In truth, however, she knows that I could do none of it without her.

NOTES AND SOURCES

As with *Armageddon*, I have not concluded this book with a formal bibliography, because the published literature is so vast. A catalogue of relevant titles becomes merely an author's peacock display. I have confined myself instead to listing in the source notes works from which I have quoted directly, or cited specific points of information. I have omitted references for quotations which have been familiar for decades in the public domain.

Quotations derived from author interviews are attributed as, for instance, "Al Horsford." Those downloaded from the Veterans' Oral History Archive of the U.S. Library of Congress are attributed as, for instance, "LC Jenkins interview." Principal documentary sources are abbreviated as follows:

British National Archive—BNA
Liddell Hart Archive, King's College London—LHA
Imperial War Museum, London—IWM
U.S. National Archive—USNA
U.S. Navy Historical Center—NHC
U.S. Army Military History Institute, Carlisle—USAMHI
U.S. Marine Corps Historical Center, Quantico, Va.—MCHC
Australian War Memorial—AWM.

Every effort has been made to trace copyright holders, but where this has proved impossible, I offer apologies.

INTRODUCTION

xvii "There are no big battalions" Lord Tedder, *Air Power and War*, London 1948, p. 41.

xix "I agree wholeheartedly" Richard Frank, *Downfall*, Penguin 2001, p. 359; and Robert Newman, *Truman and the Hiroshima Myth*, University of Michigan Press 1995, passim.

CHAPTER ONE · DILEMMAS AND DECISIONS

4 "which may not be until the final" John Paton Davies, *Dragon by the Tail*, Robson Books 1974, p. 274.

5 "Both [nations'] programmes were fuelled" *RUSI Journal*, August 2005.

5 "Japan did not invade independent countries" John Dower, *War Without Mercy*, Faber 1986, p. 5. Dower's works have become indispensable sources for any writer about wartime Japan.
6 "We honestly believed that America" Col. Tsuji Masanobu, *Singapore: The Japanese Version*, Constable 1962, p. 21.
7 "The shame of our disaster" BNA CAB79/79.
7 "It is all very well to say" Brendan Bracken BNA CAB66/29 11.6.43.
7 "The Japanese have proved" *Daily Mail*, 21.1.44.
8 "Never do that again" AI Horsford.
8 "We are of the opinion" LHA Lethbridge Papers Box 1/3.
10 "Americans ought to like" NHC Library.
10 "The cumulative cost" Alvin P. Stauffer, *The Quartermaster Corps Operations in the War Against Japan*, Department of the Army, Washington D.C. 1955.
11 "The people are what" AI DeTour.
11 "Only shipmates were important" Emory Jernigan, *Tin Can Man*, Vandamere Press 1993, p. 167. Jernigan's memoir offers an outstanding record of lower-deck destroyer service in the Pacific.
11 "Eugene Hardy" LC Hardy interview.
11 "Men live conscious" Keith Vaughan, *Journal*, 7 March 1944, Alan Ross 1966.
11 "Relax, we have always won" W. J. Holmes, *Double-Edged Secrets*, Naval Institute Press 1979, p. 125.
12 "All the officers at home" USAMHI Eichelberger Papers 22.7.44.
12 "that terrible, recurrent" Anthony Powell, *The Valley of Bones*, Heinemann 1964, p. 116.
12 "My dear Myrtle" USNA RG496 Box 457 Entry 74.
12 "Here it is a Burma moon" IWM 99/77/1, letters of 25.10.44 and 17.5.44.
12 "Nearly every Jap fights" LHA Gracey Papers 6/1–13.
13 "Dear Mother and Dad" MCHC Kennard Papers.
13 "In 1944 there seemed absolutely" AI Luo Dingwen.
13 "We got the order to retreat" AI Ying Yunping.
14 "They didn't want this baby" AIs Chen Jinyu, Tan Yadong.
15 "In some districts" *North China Herald*, 28.2.40.
15 "Everywhere in Asia" Theodore White and Annalee Jacoby, *Thunder Out of China*, William Sloan, New York 1946, p. xiii.
16 "We understood that" AI Konada.
17 "We realised that Japan" AI Ando.
17 "In Japan, one felt very conscious" AI Funaki.
17 "In October 1944 Lt. Masaichi Kikuchi" AI Kikuchi.
17 "I imagined the Americans" Meirion and Susie Harries, *Soldiers of the Sun*, Heinemann 1991, p. 314.
18 "We have just started" IWM Thompson Papers 87/58/1, letter of 4.11.44.
20 "If brought out, public opinion" *Eisenhower Diaries*, ed. Robert Ferrell, Norton 1981, p. 49.
21 "From everything I saw of him" *The Alanbrooke Diaries*, ed. Alex Danchev and Daniel Todman, Weidenfeld & Nicolson 2001, p. 476.
22 "joy or sorrow" Charles Lockwood and Hans Adamson, *Battles of the Philippine Sea*, New York 1967, p. 7.
22 "At the risk of being naïve" USAMHI Harmon Papers Box 1a/2c, memo from Streett to Handy 31.10.42.

22 "The violence of inter-service rivalry" Air Marshal Sir John Slessor, *The Central Blue*, Cassell 1956, p. 494.
23 "If it were not for his hatred" USAMHI Eichelberger letters, op. cit.
23 "It is generally believed" *New York Times*, 13.4.44.
23 "ruthless, vain, unscrupulous" Churchill College, Cambridge: Journal of Lt.-Gen. Gerald Wilkinson.
24 "The humiliation of forcing me" Quoted Clayton James, *The Years of MacArthur*, Houghton Mifflin 1975, Vol. II, p. 527.
25 "Pearl was mostly brass and hookers" LC Hardy interview.
25 "There were dinner parties" MCHC Smith Papers.
27 "No matter how a war starts" *U.S. Infantry Journal*, April 1945.
28 "conceived of war as something" *On to Westward*, New York 1945, p. 234.
28 "warned me that it was well" MCHC Smith Papers.
29 "I am a doctor" Cato D. Glover, *Command Performance with Guts*, New York 1969, p. 46.
29 "the one great leader" Admiral J. J. Clark, with G. Clark, *Carrier Admiral*, Reynolds McKay, New York 1967, p. 242.

CHAPTER TWO · JAPAN: DEFYING GRAVITY

33 "Even at that stage" AI Kikuchi.
33 "I found that I jumped" AI Miyashita.
34 "It's only to be expected" *Fading Victory: The Diary of Admiral Matome Ugaki, 1941–45*, Pittsburgh 1991, p. 437.
35 "Money-making is the one aim" Quoted Christopher Thorne, *The Issue of War*, Oxford 1985, p. 124.
36 "Whereas racism in the West" John Dower, *Japan in War and Peace*, p. 204. I am indebted to Dower's works for much information in this passage.
37 "didn't really feel that I was in a foreign country" AI Sugano.
38 "To our distress it became evident" Masatake Okumiya and Jiro Horikoshi, *Zero!: The Story of the Japanese Navy Air Force*, Cassell 1957, p. 187.
38 "We would like to obtain" Dower, op. cit., pp. 55–87.
39 "Führer Hitler was an enlisted man" John Toland, *The Rising Sun*, Cassell 1971, p. 474.
43 "Arrests for 'peace preservation' " Dower, *War Without Mercy*, passim.
43 "I contemplated the hardships" Ugaki diary, op. cit., 2.12.44, p. 527.
44 "It would be nice to say" AI Hashimoto.
47 "His father made occasional visits" AI Watanuki.
47 "Why do we need this?" AI Iki.
47 "Before World War II, Japan's experience" AI Nakamura.
47 "We were far too influenced" AI Funaki.
48 "people understood that we were poorly prepared" AI Funaki
48 "Only in 1944 did the war situation" AI Takahashi.
48 "Intelligence became a backwater" AI Hando.
49 "the most formidable fighting insect" Quoted Ronald Lewin, *Slim: The Standard Bearer*, Leo Cooper 1976, p. 381.
49 "first-class soldiers" Gordon Graham, *The Trees Are Young on Garrison Hill*, Kohima Educational Trust, p. 49.
50 "I thought of joining the army" AI Nakamura.
50 "Personality ceased to exist" AI Kikuchi.

50 "The first year as a recruit" AI Inoue.
50 "You are soldiers" AI Ajiro.
51 "I saw innumerable ways of killing people" Laurens van der Post, *The Night of the New Moon*, Hogarth Press 1970, p. x.
51 "After dealing with a score or two" AI Ebisawa.
51 "When a destroyer's cutter" Mitsuru Yoshida, *Requiem for Battleship Yamato*, Constable 1999, p. 144.
52 "Right was what a soldier" Robert Harvey, *The Undefeated*, London 1994, pp. 220–21.
52 "If we were told to defend this position" AI Inoue.
53 "It is the Ishiwara-Tsuji clique" Quoted Harries, op. cit., p. 292.
54 "A lot of our men in that conflict" AI Funaki.
54 "A Japanese POW named Shiniki Saiki" USNA RG337 Box 59 X Corps POW interrogation reports.
54 "The understandable reluctance" J. Broadbent of 1/17th Australians USNA RG337 Box 59.
55 "a Formal Examination of Myself" LHA POW reports 10I610–15.
55 "the Japanese possessed" LHA POW reports 10IR579.
55 "His own reaction" LHA POW reports 10IR648–52.
55 "An aircrew lieutenant captured" LHA I01R599–602.
57 "We felt that it was a mistake" AI Ito.
57 "The whole thing's so silly" Harries, op. cit., p. 171 and passim.
57 "What a sorry spectacle" Arthur Swinson, *Four Samurai*, Hutchinson 1968, passim.

CHAPTER THREE · THE BRITISH IN BURMA

60 "I have noted a regrettable" Quoted Christopher Thorne, *Allies of a Kind*, Hamish Hamilton 1978, p. 452.
60 "The majority of American officers" BNA FO371 F2983/1/61.
60 "The Americans . . . have rather behaved" *Chief of Staff: The Diaries of Sir Henry Pownall*, ed. Brian Bond, Leo Cooper 1974, Vol. II, 14.12.43, p. 125.
60 "Our anti-Americanism" John Hill, *China Dragons*, Blandford 1991, pp. 94–95.
60 "A sheaf of contemporary" BNA WO203/4524.
61 "It would be a brave man" BNA WP(44)326, CAB66/51.
61 "We tried to say" AI Wen Shan, loc. cit.
61 "Some British people even hit them" AI Wu Guoqing.
63 "I began to wonder" Field Marshal Lord Alanbrooke, *War Diaries, 1939–45*, ed. Alex Danchev and Daniel Todman, London 2001, 17.3.44.
63 "The American method" BNA CAB120/707 to Ismay.
63 "The hard fact is" Pownall diaries, op. cit., 29.9.44.
63 "If our operations formed merely" BNA COS 13.3.44 CAB79/84.
64 "I did not hold two articles" Slim, op. cit., p. 249.
64 "It is indeed a disgrace" BNA CAB120/707 7.5.44.
65 "A remarkable and complex character" Pownall diaries, op. cit., p. 201.
65 "I only quote this story" Alanbrooke diaries, op. cit., p. 452.
65 "Mountbatten is in the seventh heaven" Pownall diaries, op. cit., p. 187.
66 "Enjoy yourself" Christopher Somerville, *Our War*, Weidenfeld & Nicolson 1998, p. 273.

66 "If . . . we are relegated" Pownall diaries, op. cit., p. 191.
67 "Imphal . . . yes" Swinson, op. cit., p. 125.
67 "The whole time" Lt. Col. J. Balfour-Oates, *The Jungle Army*, Kimber 1962, p. 176.
68 "Uncle Bill will fight a battle *there*" Slim, op. cit., p. 374.
69 "His appearance was plain enough" George MacDonald Fraser, *Quartered Safe Out Here* HarperCollins 1992, p. 36.
69 "We make the best plans" John Masters, *The Road Past Mandalay*, Michael Joseph 1971, p. 44.
69 "The scenery was superb" Raymond Cooper, op. cit., pp. 53, 59.
70 "Despair became rife" BNA WO203/6320.
71 "The air was thick" Captain Gerald Hanley, *Spectator*, 29.9.44.
71 "The Jap retreat" TL letters of 6.9.44 and 22.9.44, Lethbridge Papers LHA.
72 "Sometimes it is impossible" BNA WO203/279.
73 "There's not much time" Pownall diaries, op. cit., p. 184, 29.8.44.
73 "that the minimum of effort" BNA CAB99/29 15.9.44.
73 "In the UK . . . I found everywhere" Michael Anglo, *Service Newspapers of the Second World War*, London 1977, p. 117.
73 "I was a pale white thing" Brian Aldiss, *The Twinkling of an Eye*, Little, Brown 1998, p. 151.
74 "When our lorry was labouring" ibid., p. 153.
74 "Gurkhas were wonderful chaps" AI Horsford.
74 "The fact that he sung in Welsh" Slim, op. cit., p. 468.
75 "Today I shall win the Victoria Cross" AI Ronnie McAllister.
75 "One can't help feeling very humble" LHA Lethbridge Papers, op. cit.
75 "beard glistening" Gordon Graham, op. cit., p. 74.
75 "Reports of dissension" Pownall diaries, op. cit., p. 148.
75 "An army psychiatrist's report" LHA Stockwell Papers 5/7/4.
76 "I remember dinner parties" AI McAllister.
76 "Sir, that thing is not coming" Randle, op. cit., p. 97.
76 "We thought nothing of the British Army" AI Horsford.
77 "They appeared mildly surprised" BNA WO232/35.
77 "With the Japanese, you could never see" AI John Cameron-Hayes.
77 "A Borderer in Raymond Cooper's company" Cooper, op. cit., p. 102.
77 "He smelt pretty much" IWM Daniels MS 95/33/1.
78 "The screams of the patients" John Leyin, *Tell Them of Us*, Lejins Publishing 2000, p. 159.
78 "The war in Burma was fought" Randle, op. cit., p. 58.
78 "the Japanese still considers himself" BNA WO203/632.
78 "All experience . . . has demonstrated" LHA Messervy Papers.
79 "The Jap selects the most unlikely" LHA Gracey Papers, op. cit.
79 "It seemed a terribly old-fashioned" Fraser, op. cit., p. 26.
79 "but NOT to such an extent as" LHA Gracey Papers, op. cit.
80 "A six-month breakdown of" LHA *Medical History of 20th Indian Division*, Gracey Papers.
80 "One orderly was deputed" John Hamilton, *War Bush*, Michael Russell 2001, p. 332.
80 "John Leyin's crew sang" Leyin, op. cit., p. 178.
80 "Back in harbour we faced" T. Grounds, *Some Letters from Burma: The Story of the 25th Dragoons at War*, privately published, p. 41.

81 "Has he got a chance?" AI Horsford.
81 "A saddler with an Indian Army" AI J. C-H.
81 "Perhaps the reason why the old soldier" Cooper, op. cit., p. 151.
82 "The thought went through my head" Daniels MS, op. cit.
82 "infidelity of soldiers' wives" BNA WO203/4536.
82 "Waiting in the dark" Cooper, op. cit., p. 124.
82 "Anxiety about domestic affairs" BNA WO203/4537.
82 "does not like India or Burma" ibid.
83 "I get reports that certain officers" LHA Stockwell Papers Box 4/2.
83 "Stockwell deplored the poor quality" ibid.
83 "a small outbreak of desertion" BNA WO203/4524.
84 "they would go out on patrol" AI Horsford, loc. cit.
84 "On his own, in the dark" Hamilton, op. cit., p. 226.
84 "Bamboo ladders were built" ibid., p. 213.
84 "Without a murmur of complaint" ibid., p. 175.
85 "I gave Alex" Lt. Col. J. H. Williams, *Elephant Bill*, Hart-Davis 1950, passim.
86 "We had entered an enchanted zone" Aldiss, op. cit., p. 158.
86 "lukewarm, assisting whichever superior forces" LHA Gracey Papers Box 2/24 11.9.44.
86 "with his left leg shattered" Randle, op. cit., p. 72.
87 "The war took a long time" Hill, op. cit., pp. 43, 40.
88 "I didn't worry about it" AI Joe Welch.
88 "Even the miners among us" Hill, op. cit., p. 36.
89 "I'm not carrying a haversack" IWM Daniels MS, op. cit.
89 "We seem condemned to wallow" Churchill Papers 20/176 telegram to Smuts.
90 "Not if they go by train" Philip Mason, *A Matter of Honour*, Cape 1974, p. 502.
90 "Oh, the Indians were very kind" Quoted Somerville, op. cit., p. 258.
90 "Most rankers expected little" Aldiss, op. cit., p. 180.
92 "My daddy always taught me" AI Linamen.
93 "For an instant" Anthony Montague Browne, *Long Sunset*, Cassell 1995, p. 24.
93 "It looked doom-laden" ibid., p. 27.
93 "That night, the sky was red" ibid.
93 "We had superiority in every arm" ibid., pp. 28–29.
94 "When one considers what the Americans" IWM 81/7/1 Romney Papers.
94 "This army is like Cinderella" LHA Lethbridge Papers, op. cit., 27.12.44.

CHAPTER FOUR · TITANS AT SEA

95 "Between 1941 and 1945" Navy Department Bureau of Construction, see J. Furer, *Administrative History of USN in WWII*.
96 "The fighter direction staff" Ronald Spector, *At War at Sea*, Penguin 2001, p. 301.
96 "The inescapable conclusion" Joel R. Davidson, *The Unsinkable Fleet*, Naval Institute Press 1996, p. 97.
98 "day in and day out life at sea" *Flight Quarters*, Veterans Association of the Belleau Wood 1946, p. 75.
98 "You never know where you're going" LC Irwin interview.

98 "Dear Mom and Dad" MCHC Kohn Papers, Joseph Kohn 21.2.45.
99 "you stand back under cover" James Fahey, *Pacific War Diary, 1942–45*, Houghton Mifflin 1963, p. 182.
99 "there weren't many fuck-ups" AI Bradlee.
99 "It was an exhausting life" Ben Bradlee, *A Good Life*, New York 1995, p. 67.
99 "too old for the duty they had" NHC Joe Kenton, *Long Ago and Far Away*, unpublished MS 2000, p. 17.
99 "for lack of anything better to do" LC Irwin interview.
99 "Everyone had a new respect" Jernigan, op. cit., p. 43.
100 "it felt like being taken apart" ibid., p. 45.
100 "I had such a wonderful time" Bradlee, op. cit., p. 76.
100 "time and distance" Jernigan, op. cit., p. 92.
100 "You want to be free again" Fahey, op. cit., p. 182.
100 "On the destroyer *Schroeder*" George W. B. Hall, *Men of the Schroeder*, Reunion Group 1995, p. 66.
101 "Carlos, a lack of formal education" Hall, op. cit., p. 137.
101 "a warping sound" Jernigan, op. cit., p. 121.
101 "Each ship is like a city" ibid., p. 33.
101 "You'd be playing checkers" ibid., p. 126.
102 "He . . . sounded just like a Georgia redneck" Richard W. Streb, *Life and Death Aboard the U.S.S. Essex*, Dorrance 1999, p. 121.
102 "emotionally unstable, evil-tempered" ibid., p. 123.
102 "The old man is getting nastier" Kenton, op. cit., p. 47.
103 "We hadn't spent years learning" AI Bradlee.
103 "the most important thing" NHC Oral Histories Box 5, Burke File.
104 "Every time we bring out" USNA RG38 Box 4 Captain L. J. Dow report.
104 "James Hutchinson of the battleship *Colorado*" NHC, James Hutchinson, *The Love of a Sailor for His Ship*, privately published 1992, p. 66.
104 "Suckers!" Samuel Eliot Morison, *U.S. Naval Operations in World War II*, Vol. XII, p. 79.
105 "Of all the announcements" *Attack Transport: The Story of the U.S.S. Doyen*, University of Minnesota Press 1946, p. 119.
105 "A carrier officer, Ensign Dick Saunders" *Flight Quarters*, op. cit., p. 96.
106 "He ordered the vacant admiral's cabin" NHC RG38 Box 4 Riley file.
106 "There are men out there" ibid., Widhelm file.
107 "The boys in a squadron" ibid., Lamade and Mini files.
107 "The very exacting nature" NHC, Administrative History of the USN in WWII: *Aviation Personnel*, p. 279.
107 "We learned to listen" Gerald W. Thomas, *Torpedo Squadron Four*, Rio Grande Historical Collections 1991, p. 118.
107 "Sherwin Goodman, an Avenger gunner" LC Goodman interview.
108 "Most of our kills were" USNA RG38 Box 4 Winters file.
108 "From pull-out, I looked back" ibid., Lamade file.
109 "What the boys want to do" USNA RG38 Box 4 Caldwell file.
109 "lose their daring" *Aviation Personnel*, op. cit., p. 281.
109 "Combat fatigue is a word we use" USNA RG38 Box 4 Lamade file.
110 "The weather was pretty good" ibid., Bakutis file.
110 "When Lt. Robert Nelson crashed" Charles Patrick Weiland, *Above and Beyond*, Pacifica Press 1997, p. 175.
111 "We were amazed to see the Americans" AI Iwashita.

111 "which sure was a wonderful show" NHC Oral History Files.
111 "Before returning them, we would strip them" Bradlee, op. cit., p. 65.

CHAPTER FIVE · AMERICA'S RETURN TO THE PHILIPPINES

112 "During planning for Third Fleet's" NHC Carney file Box 6.
113 "revealed the concern of a man" Clayton James, op. cit., Vol. II, p. 509.
113 "The two rival roads were . . . converging" Morison, op. cit., Vol. XII, p. 18.
113 "an aloof cocker spaniel" MCHC O. P. Smith Papers.
114 "You will take no prisoners, you will kill every yellow" LC Jenkins interview.
114 "a guy I thought a lot of" ibid.
115 "The boy was not badly hurt" MCHC Smith narrative, p. 117.
116 "The thousands of rounds" ibid., pp. 119, 51.
116 "Bill Atkinson watched" Tom Evans, *Hold Your Head High, Marine*, privately published 2006, p. 35.
116 "Oh my God, I guess" ibid.
117 "I am carrying this guy" ibid., p. 125.
117 "Our troops should understand" USNA RG337 Box 58/206.
117 "Why did you do it?" Evans, op. cit., p. 86.
118 "It is hard to put your finger" MCHC Smith MS, op. cit., p. 93.
120 "For Isaac Waltons" NHC Library.
121 "If I was MacArthur" AI Takahashi.
121 "He could have filled his headquarters" ibid.
122 "This is our final parting" Pu Yi, *From Emperor to Citizen*, Foreign Languages Press, Beijing 1989, p. 234.
124 "The objective is relatively undefended" Quoted Craven and Cate, *The U.S. Army Air Forces in WWII*, Chicago 1953, Vol. V, p. 344.
125 "The navy and air force will attempt" USAMHI Japanese monographs 8489 roll no. 6.
125 "Leyte, like most of the other islands" USAMHI, *Recon Scout*, unpublished MS in McLaughlin Papers Box 5.
125 "As he approached, his face" Robert Shaplen in *The New Yorker Book of War Pieces*, Bloomsbury 1989, pp. 409–14.
127 "The smaller building erupted" USAMHI Newman Papers Box 2.
127 "Regard publicity set-up as excellent" USNA RG496 Box 849 Entry 184.
128 "The simple truth about war" Fraser, op. cit., p. 82.
128 "long before noon" Edmund Love, *The Hourglass*, Infantry Journal Press 1950, p. 216.
129 "You were wet" LC Norman interview.
129 "Forget it," said the colonel" AI Takahashi.
130 "Filipino labour . . . performed manual labour" Craven and Cate, op. cit., Vol. V, p. 373.
130 "Empty casings jingled down" USAMHI George Morrissey diary, Newman Papers Box 6.
130 "It is foolish to land" USNA RG337 Box 58, "Lessons of Leyte."
130 "it is essential that all units" ibid.

CHAPTER SIX · "FLOWERS OF DEATH": LEYTE GULF

132 "Whether the plan is adequate" Ugaki diaries, op. cit., p. 442, 13.8.44.
134 "to engage the full might" ibid., p. 460.

135 "gigantic castles of steel" Winston S. Churchill, *The World Crisis*, Odhams 1923, Vol. I, p. 83.
135 "Why can't our people" Masanori Ito with Roger Pineau, *The End of the Imperial Japanese Navy*, Weidenfeld & Nicolson 1962, p. 125.
136 "It's competitive all the way" NHC Oral History interviews Box 20.
138 "Let's get this over with" A. J. Galantin, *Take Her Deep!*, Algonquin 1997, p. 173.
138 "It was a beautiful day" LC Goodman interview.
138 "Our captain was a" AI Ebisawa.
140 "a Jap sailor yelled" NHC Oral History Narratives Box 32 Tropp file.
140 "absolutely beautiful" USNA RG38 Box 4.
140 "Who can read the heart" Ugaki diaries, op. cit., 6.11.44.
141 "The dive-bombers are not hitting" USNA Lamade report, op. cit., 23.2.45.
141 "Too many targets were attacked" Gerald Thomas, op. cit., p. 71.
141 "Lucky I wouldn't let you go" AI Takahashi.
142 "General situation: enemy aircraft" USNA RG200 Box 59.
144 "Lt. Tokichi Ishii, forty-four-year-old" LHA POW Report 10IR648–52.
146 "we rode the mast" NHC, Howard Sauer, *Battleship Gunner*, unpublished MS 1994.
146 "The Japanese Vice-Admiral Ugaki" Ugaki diaries, op. cit., p. 574.
147 "Never give a sucker" NHC Oral History Narratives Box 24 Oldendorf file.
147 "more like a petty officer" LHA POW Reports 106R638.
147 "All forces will resume the attack" Ito, op. cit., p. 133.
148 "If a man has a nervous wife" William Halsey and Joseph Bryan Halsey, *Admiral Halsey's Story*, McGraw-Hill 1947, p. xi.
148 "he was always sure" Quoted Wilmott, p. 248.
149 "It was not my job to protect" Halsey and Halsey, op. cit., p. 219.
149 "With the conviction that Center Force" NHC Box 6 Carney file, p. 11.

I am indebted in this chapter for some significant reflections offered by Richard Frank in a presentation at the Nimitz Museum of the Pacific War, Fredericksburg, Texas: "Halsey's Great Decision at Leyte Gulf." Frank argues that Kinkaid was substantially more culpable than most historians suggest, and Halsey less so, for the surprise inflicted on Taffy 3. While revising *Retribution* for publication, I was also able to consult the most recent book on Leyte Gulf, *Sea of Thunder* by Evan Thomas (Simon & Schuster 2006), though it did not cause me significantly to change my own conclusions.

150 "the morning sun" Jernigan, op. cit., p. 126.
151 "Halsey's job" John T. Mason, *The Pacific War Remembered*, Naval Institute Press, p. 274.
151 "Our captain announced" NHC Oral Histories.
152 "We went up on the flightdeck" NHC Oral Histories Box 34 RF Whitehead file.
153 "about the same as driving" NHC Oral Histories Box 17 William Kirkland file.
154 "I told the crew" NHC Oral History Collection Box 12 Hathaway file.
154 "Buck, what we need is a bugler" ibid.
155 "As we cleared each other" NHC Oral History Interviews Box 13.
155 "We were weaving back and forth" NHC Box 12 Hagen file.
156 "It takes a lot to go in there" NHC Oral Histories Box 34 RF Whitehead file.

156 "This process lasted" ibid., Box 33 Vieweg file.
157 "At the end of two hours" ibid., Box 34.
157 "Japan was showing signs not only" Ito, op. cit., p. 111.
157 "my mind was extremely fatigued" ibid., p. 166.
157 "the very poor decision" USNA RG200 Box 59, report of 29.10.44.
158 "The second explosion" ibid.
158 "severely burned beyond recognition" NHC Oral Histories Burrell file.
159 "Attention all hands" *Flight Quarters*, op. cit., p. 51.
160 "There wasn't any of this" USNA RG38 Box 4.
160 "mission was to be defeated" Ito, op. cit., p. 142.
161 "We had frantic screams" USNA RG38 Box 4 Dow, op. cit.
161 "It wasn't five minutes" ibid.
163 "Prosecute damage control" NHC Library.
164 "Fifty hours in the water" NHC Box 12 Hagen file.
164 "I guess I missed the best battle" Clark, op. cit., p. 235.
164 "Several Japanese fighter pilots" Rikihei Inoguchi and Tadashi Nakajima with Roger Pineau, *The Divine Wind*, Hutchinson 1959, passim.
165 "In the Philippines, every day" AI Iki.
165 "Everything was urgent" S. Sakai, *Samurai*, Four Square 1974, p. 213.
165 "When a commander is uncertain" Ito, op. cit., p. 161.
166 "Japan is in grave danger" ibid., pp. 37–38.
167 "People in the streets" *Divine Wind*, op. cit., p. 77.
168 "He was afire in the engine" *Flight Quarters*, op. cit., p. 58.
168 "You could of drove a Mack" C. Raymond Calhoun, *Tin Can Sailor*, Naval Institute Press 1993, p. 155.
168 "This type of attack is quite different" NHC Box 26 Purdy file.
169 "If adequate fighter cover not maintained" USNA RG200 Box 59.
169 "I was standing in the open" Hutchinson, op. cit., p. 61.
169 "You just don't know which one's" LC Erwin interview.
170 "The first thing I saw that day" Jernigan, op. cit., p. 176.
170 "rushed over to help get a man" Gerald Thomas, op. cit., p. 92.
170 "I seen these fellows with short sleeves" ibid.
170 "Seven of our bomber pilots" USNA RG38 Box 4 Winters report, op. cit.
171 "The Japanese had perfected" Morison, op. cit., Vol. XII, p. 367.
171 "Logically, suicide attack" Royal Navy Staff History, *War with Japan*, Ministry of Defence 1995, Vol. VI, p. 196.
171 "I could imagine myself in the heat" Bradlee, op. cit., p. 90.
172 "Let no man belittle" Mamoru Shigemitsu, *Japan and Her Destiny*, Hutchinson 1958, p. 340.
172 "We ran afoul of Japanese" NHC Box 6 Carney file, p. 14.
173 "I was somewhat puzzled" NHC Box 15 Inglis report, p. 19.
173 "We came to believe" Jernigan, op. cit., p. 92.

CHAPTER SEVEN · ASHORE: BATTLE FOR THE MOUNTAINS

174 "the Navy succeeded" Japanese monograph 8489 roll 6 USAMHI.
175 "There are only thirty-four men in our company" Diary of Eichi Ogita of 362th Independent Battalion, Japanese Interrogation Reports, LHA.
175 "By 7 November" Japanese Translated Monographs, op. cit.

176 "Men threw away their packs" Orlando Davidson et al., *The Deadeyes: Story of the 96th Division*, Infantry Journal Press 1947, p. 49.

176 "We had just begun to dig in" Morrissey diaries, op. cit., 28.10.44.

176 "I only knew him as a G Company screw-up" Eric Diller, *Memoirs of a Combat Infantryman*, privately published 1959, p. 51.

176 "I saw an undernourished" ibid., p. 70.

176 "Beyond grief inflicted" USNA RG337 Box 59/238.

177 "The task of supply and evacuation" M. Hamlin Cannon, *The U.S. Army in WWII—Leyte: The Return to the Philippines*, Dept of the Army 1954, p. 112.

177 "Floods raced" Jan Valtan, *Children of Yesterday*, Readers Press 1946, p. 187.

177 "I saw the creek bed" Morrissey diaries, op. cit.

177 "The end of the Leyte-Samar" USNA RG200 Box 2 SWPA communiqués.

178 "I'm surprised it isn't going faster" Quoted *Yank*, 19.1.45.

178 "The new john radioed back" USAMHI, Charles Henne, *Battle History of the 3/148th Infantry*, unpublished MS, p. 126.

179 "I don't want this business" USAMHI Bruce Papers Box 9, 12.12.44.

180 "No loud talking or laughing" USAMHI Morrissey diary, op. cit.

181 "The men looked ten or fifteen" USAMHI unpublished MS memoir, p. 134, Aubrey Newman Papers Box 6.

181 "This meant a long war" USAMHI Hostetter MS p. 89, Newman Papers Box 6.

182 "To the Japanese officer" USAMHI WD, *Handbook*, pp. 97, 99.

182 "The Japanese . . . displayed" Cannon, op. cit., pp. 245–52; Sixth Army Operations Report Leyte, pp. 204–12, Report of Col. William Verbeck of 21st Infantry.

182 "The Americans, meanwhile" Estimate by Col. Junkichi Okabayashi, chief of staff of 1st Division, quoted Eighth Army staff study of Japanese 35th Army on Leyte, pp. 5–6.

182 "The difficulties of terrain and weather" USNA RG337 Box 59.

183 "It's your turn in the morning" USAMHI Newman Papers Box 2.

184 "One enemy soldier, about thirty-five yards" Edmund G. Love, op. cit., p. 260.

184 "giving them the appearance" MCHC O. P. Smith Papers.

184 "If they don't quit this shooting" LC Norman interview.

184 "We thought we'd cleaned out" ibid.

185 "It was pleasant to have houseboys" Craven and Cate, op. cit., Vol. V, pp. 388–89.

185 "for the first time" Diller, op. cit., pp. 148–49.

185 "The tactics we have been using" LHA diary of Lt. Suteo Inoue, Japanese interrogation reports.

185 "Soldiers have become very weak" ibid.

185 "As we crouched there" USAMHI, *Recon Scout*, op. cit.

186 "You've got soldiers with no brains" USAMHI Arnold oral history interview.

186 "One of the small number of Japanese" LHA Japanese interrogation reports 10IR644–7.

187 "Another tropical typhoon" USNA RG200 Box 2 SWPA communiqués.

188 "a blazing inferno" Cannon, op. cit., quoting *77th Division Operations Report Leyte*, p. 16.

189 "MacArthur's communiqués are" USAMHI Rodman Papers Box 5.
191 "Perhaps the best way to describe" USAMHI, *Recon Scout*, op. cit.
191 "This theater has been a victim" USAMHI Eichelberger letters, op. cit.

CHAPTER EIGHT · CHINA: DRAGON BY THE TAIL

192 "a huge and seductive" John Paton Davies, *Dragon by the Tail*, Robson Books 1975, p. 429.
193 "In Manchuria in those days" AI Nakamura.
194 "We were victims of those gangsters" AI Wen Shan.
194 "The Japanese forced my father" AI Jiang Zhen.
194 "Every morning we watched corpses" AI Xu Yongqiang.
194 "of lacquerware and porcelain" White and Jacoby, op. cit., p. 19.
198 "my parents felt" AI Liu Yunxiu.
199 "Even when the Japanese" AI Xu Guiming.
200 "China's principal ruler" Biographical details are taken from Jonathan Fenby, *Generalissimo*, Free Press 2003.
200 "The two peoples are nearer" LC Dulles Papers Box 2, Press conference 24.8.44.
201 "Unit 731, the biological warfare" Daniel Barenblatt, *A Plague upon Humanity*, Souvenir Press 2001, passim.
202 "Nowadays the media" AI Ajiro.
202 "More than a million Japanese soldiers" AI Hando.
203 "I have told the president" BNA PREM4 30/11.
204 "a junk heap of old boxes" John King Fairbank, *China*, Harper & Row 1982, p. 243.
204 "She can become at will" Auden and Isherwood, *Journey to a War*, Faber 1938, pp. 66–67.
204 "perfect dears" Peter Clarke, *The Cripps Version*, Allen Lane 2002, p. 156.
205 "Most recruits came simply as prisoners" AI Xu Yongqiang.
205 "If only more people" AI Ying Yunping.
206 "It is difficult" BNA WO203/291 21.1.45.
206 "the campaigns the Japanese" Farmer, *Shanghai Harvest*, Museum Press 1945, p. 103.
206 "One Japanese division" AI Funaki.
207 "The Chinese were poor soldiers" AI Inoue.
207 "One man slowly put four fingers" Farmer, op. cit., p. 143.
207 "The Japanese had so much more" AI Yan Qizhi.
208 "There's nothing to forgive" AI Ying.
208 "a cricket in a tiny straw cage" Davies, op. cit., p. 101.
208 "Ying Yunping, a thirty-year-old" AI Ying Yunping.
209 "We usually relied on what food" AI Luo Dingwen.
209 "Senior officers were suspicious" USAMHI Haydon Boatner Papers Box I "A statement for the record on Barbara Tuchman's *Sand in the Wind*," pp. 5, 9.
209 "To the Japanese soldier" Davies, op. cit., p. 204, 1938 report to the State Department.
210 "At such a moment [our commander]" I. Feng, *Give Me Back My River and Hills*, Macmillan 1945, p. 127.
210 "Additionally, as Christopher Thorne has argued" Thorne, *Allies*, op. cit., p. 567.
211 "The report asserted that a section" USNA RG337 Box 54 Folder 101.

212 "It has been the lowest common denominator" BNA WO203/142.

213 "It was dawn when we fell" White and Jacoby, op. cit., p. 187.

213 "the Japanese army could still march" Fenby, op. cit., p. 289.

214 "Chinese soldiers showed" AI Wen Shan.

214 "I was very lucky" AI Jiang Zhen.

214 "They said what they liked" AI Wu Guoqing.

214 "It might be said that" S. Woodburn Kirby, *The War Against Japan*, HMSO 1964, Vol. IV, p. 194.

215 "All of us must remember" Quoted Davies, p. 269.

216 "I saw a machine gunner" USAMHI Boatner Papers, op. cit.

216 "He was much more than" Letter to John Hart 9.11.59, quoted Lewin, *Slim: The Standard Bearer*, p. 141.

217 "silken clad girls" Edgar Snow, *Journey to the Beginning*, Gollancz 1959, p. 163.

218 "the one abiding sentiment" ibid., p. 164.

218 "incapable—surely to an abnormal degree?" Emily Hahn, *Chiang Kai-shek*, Doubleday 1955, p. 248.

218 "hanging up my shovel" Quoted Davies, op. cit., p. 337.

220 "Al stated that" Jan. 1944 conversation noted by JS, quoted ibid., p. 300.

221 "General Wedemeyer told me with conviction" BNA FO371/41746.

221 "Chiang did some big things" AI Hongbin.

222 "Time is on the side of" Quoted Davies, op. cit., p. 273.

CHAPTER NINE · MACARTHUR ON LUZON

224 " 'Sit down,' said the general" USAMHI Eddleman Papers.

224 "We grew to know his mood" Sgt. Vincent Powers quoted Clayton James, op. cit., p. 584.

224 "treason and sabotage" ibid., p. 588.

225 "At this late stage, after all one had survived" Somerville, op. cit., p. 264.

227 "This is terrible country to fight in" USAMHI Austin MS, op. cit., 3.2.45.

228 "General MacArthur visited" USAMHI Griswold Papers Box 1.

228 "I don't see how I have gotten" USAMHI Eichelberger Papers, op. cit., letter of 23.1.45.

228 "I must insist that you take" Quoted Robert Ross Smith, *Triumph in the Philippines*, Department of the Army, Washington, D.C., 1964, p. 236.

229 "Groaning and writhing on the ground" A.V.H. Hartendorp, *The Japanese Occupation of the Philippines*, Manila 1957, Vol. II, p. 525.

229 "Mrs. Foley kept asking about" Evelyn M. Monahan and Rosemary Neidel-Greenlee, *All This Hell*, Kentucky University Press 2000, p. 160.

229 "They seemed to be using their last strength" Douglas MacArthur, *Reminiscences*, Heinemann 1965, p. 247.

229 "We met more resistance around Nichols Field" USAMHI Eichelberger Papers, "Dearest Miss Em," 23.2.45, op. cit.

230 "On 28 December 1944 the Japanese *kempeitai*" Richard Connaughton, John Pimlott and Duncan Anderson, *The Battle for Manila*, Bloomsbury 1995, p. 72. This entire passage draws heavily on their work.

231 "Throngs of Filipinos" USAMHI Henne unpublished MS, op. cit., p. 41.

231 "The fighting became a shoot-out" ibid., p. 42.

231 "Not many men were ever privileged" ibid., p. 46.

231 "Our forces are rapidly clearing" USNA RG200 Box 2.

232 "MacArthur has visions" USAMHI Griswold Papers, op. cit.
232 "Leaving the near bank" USAMHI Henne MS, op. cit., p. 107.
232 "The sky was a" USAMHI Maj.-Gen. R.S. Beightler: Report on the Activities of the 37th Infantry Division.
232 "Even then the Japanese" USNA RG337 Box 71/491.
233 "I'll never forget the bewildered look" USAMHI Palmer Papers.
233 "Didn't you command HQ Company" USAMHI Eddleman Papers, op. cit.
233 "Such . . . are lonely, personal times" USAMHI Henne MS, op. cit., p. 80.
234 "I hope they don't get VD" ibid., p. 95.
234 "It was . . . so common in combat" ibid., p. 73.
234 "Private Dahlum of the 3/148th" ibid., p. 66.
234 "Suspecting that every closed door" ibid., p. 68.
235 "They grabbed my two sisters" Evidence given at 1946 Yamashita trial, quoted Connaughton et al., op. cit., p. 243.
235 "I had seen the head of an aunt" ibid., pp. 204–5.
236 "When Filipinos are to be killed" *Report on the Sack of Manila*, U.S. Congressional Committee on Military Affairs 1945, pp. 14–15.
236 "Oscar Griswold of XIV Corps" USAMHI Griswold Papers, op. cit.
236 "Don't do that" Luis Esteban, *My War*, unpublished MS, quoted Connaughton et al., op. cit., p. 150.
237 "will not be able to understand" USNA RG338/11061/41 MacArthur 2.9.44.
237 "From then on, to put it crudely" USAMHI Beightler MS, op. cit.
237 "American lives were undoubtedly far more valuable" Ross Smith, op. cit., p. 301.
237 "Those who had survived Japanese hate" *A Question of Identities: Selected Essays*, Manila 1973, p. 77.
237 "C-in-C refused my request" USAMHI Griswold Papers, op. cit.
238 "The assault upon Intramuros was unique" ibid.
238 "It was not a pleasant moment" *Reminiscences*, op. cit., p. 247.
238 "organised drunk" USAMHI Henne MS, op. cit.
239 "I believe the BC [Big Chief] would fight against" USAMHI Eichelberger letters, op. cit.
240 "Of the forty-nine men who are left" Suteo diary, op. cit.
240 "After daybreak, removed arm" LHA interrogation reports, captured diary of SH 19.5.45.
240 "Practically every day" LHA interrogation reports.
241 "They all talked big" Hiroo Onoda, *No Surrender*, Deutsch 1975, p. 57.
241 "all resigned to death" ibid., p. 69.
241 "We tore off the wings" Quoted Harvey, op. cit., pp. 221–22.
242 "absurd orders" USNA RG337 Box 59/238.
242 "It is still something of a mystery" Morison, op. cit., Vol XII, p. 216.
243 "There are unmistakable" Quoted Clayton James, op. cit., p. 717.
243 "It was a long, slow and costly operation" USAMHI Gill Papers Box 1, oral history transcript tape 8.
243 "We sometimes reported" USAMHI Henne MS, op. cit., p. 161.
244 "I looked around to see" USAMHI Lamagna Papers.
244 "They laughed and kept on" USAMHI, Col. Charles A. Henne, *Reduction of the Shobu Group*, unpublished MS 1989, p. 9.
244 "The price that the . . . trail cost" USAMHI Gill Papers Box 1, op. cit.
244 "It seemed the right thing to do" USAMHI Henne MS, op. cit., p. 104.

244 "Col. Bruce Palmer" USAMHI Palmer Papers.
244 "With the torrents of rain" USAMHI Henne MS, op. cit., p. 90.
245 "On those occasions" Stanley L. Falk, *Decision at Leyte*, Norton 1966, p. 21.
246 "South-West Pacific commitment" *Army*, June 1992, p. 61

CHAPTER TEN • BLOODY MINIATURE: IWO JIMA

247 "a waterless island of sulphur springs" USNA RG38 Box 119, Maj. Y. Horie.
247 "We are now getting enemy" MCHC Joseph Raspalair Papers.
248 "You can hardly see sea" AI Ohkoshi.
248 "I . . . thought of the helpless feeling" Patrick Caruso, *Nightmare on Iwo*, Naval Institute Press 2001, p. 17.
249 "clothing and helmet" Johnston, op. cit., p. 73.
250 "I wondered how our plastic surgeons" James Vedder, *Combat Surgeon*, Presidio 1984, p. 37.
250 "This war will be decided" USNA Horie MS, op. cit.
252 "I saw my group leader" MCHC Rodriguez Papers.
252 " 'God, if you save my life I'll go to church every Sunday' " LC Jerry Copland interview.
253 "We had a gross misconception" Caruso, op. cit., p. 73.
253 "we had not seen any of the enemy" MCHC Rodriguez Papers, op. cit.
254 "Low morale, fatigue" MCHC Sayers Papers.
254 "Progress a hundred yards" MCHC Arsenault MS.
254 "Pick some prominent landmark" MCHC Green MS.
255 "At times, it appeared that the only sure way" Caruso, op. cit , p. 109.
255 "not only alive but leaving" MCHC unpublished MS, p. 302.
255 "I got hit in the balls" MCHC Cudworth Papers.
255 "After seeing dead Marines on the island" ibid.
256 "He was a good bit older" AI Ohkoshi.
256 "Once I get back home" Caruso, op. cit., p. 134.
256 "other than feeling sorry for the guys" LC George interview.
257 "Sometimes we were so close" MCHC Watkins MS, p. 182.
257 "In the time that one belly wound" ibid.
257 "You don't need my watch" Caruso, op. cit., p. 31.
257 "He turned out to be my age" Bradlee, op. cit., pp. 78, 80.
258 "It was necessary for officers" MCHC Sayers report, op. cit.
258 "We replacements were despised" MCHC Lane Papers.
258 "My mind traversed the spectrum" Caruso, op. cit., p. 162.
259 "You wanted to know how bad" MCHC Colegrove Papers.
259 "I was never once sore" MCHC Schless Papers, op. cit.
260 "The first guy I ever killed" LC Copeland interview.
262 "It makes me sick" Maj.-Gen. Joseph Swing, *Dear General: WWII Letters, 1944–45*, 11th Airborne Association 1963, letter of 8.3.45.
264 "Captain Kouichi Ito, an army officer" AI Ito.
264 "In ancient times" MCHC Raspilair Papers, op. cit.
264 "There's your uncle" LC Copeland interview.

CHAPTER ELEVEN • BLOCKADE: WAR UNDERWATER

266 "The entire question of Japanese" USNA RG496 Box 809.
267 "Seeing no one on board" USNA RG38 Box 3 ONI.

268 "Ronald Spector has remarked" Spector, *Eagle Against the Sun*, Viking 1984, p. xvi.
270 "It was hard to flush" Artie Akers, unpublished MS, University of Tennessee.
270 "We were essentially a steel bubble" Galantin, op. cit., p. 137.
270 "We had almost disdain for the threat" ibid., p. 96.
271 "for instance, Sam Dealey" Charles Lockwood and Hans Christian Adamson, *Through Hell and Deep Water*, Greenburg 1956.
272 "Use the periscope as little as possible" NHC *Current Doctrine* 1944.
272 "This man seemed to know" Akers MS, op. cit.
273 "It was an impersonal war" Galantin, op. cit., p. 106.
274 "Three hits observed" Theodore Roscoe, *U.S. Submarine Operations in World War II*, Naval Institute Press 1949, p. 441.
275 "Vice-Admiral Charles Lockwood" Charles Lockwood, *Sink 'Em All*, Dutton 1951, p. 124.
275 "Heads ached" Galantin, op. cit., p. 243.
276 "Many will tell you that depth-charging" Walter Jaffee, *Steel Shark in the Pacific*, Glencannon 2001, p. 125.
278 "By the fall of 1944" Galantin, op. cit., p. 203.
279 "It had become an aviator's" ibid., p. 226.

CHAPTER TWELVE · BURNING A NATION: LEMAY

I am indebted for much factual material in this chapter to two sources: Tami Davis Biddle's "Curtis Emerson LeMay and the Ascent of American Strategic Air Power," published in *Realizing the Dream of Flight*, ed. Virginia Dawson and Mark Bowles, NASA, Washington, D.C. 2005; and Ralph Arnold: "Improvised Destruction: Arnold, LeMay and the Firebombing of Japan," published in *War in History*, October 2006, Vol.13.

281 "The best psychological warfare" Gerald Hanley, *Spectator*, 29.9.44.
283 "the use of incendiaries" Chennault, *Way of a Fighter*, Putnam 1948, p. 97.
283 "As we piled out" Carter McGregor, *The Kagu-Tchuchi Bomb Group 40BG*, Wichita Falls Texas, Nortex 1981, p. 49.
284 "had as many bugs" C. E. LeMay and Kantor, *Mission with LeMay*, p. 124.
286 "but they continue with these futile operations" Pownall diaries, op. cit., p. 197.
286 "They are very poor" LC LeMay Papers Box 11.
286 "the B-29 outfits are being filled" ibid., letter to Maj.-Gen. Fred Anderson 18.11.44.
286 "The B-29 project is important to me" ibid.
287 "Sir, it could ignite gas fumes" AI Leon Cobaugh.
287 "I had hoped to find brown-skinned" Brown, *A B-29 Pilot's Memories*.
288 "Leather began to get mouldy" Samuelson diary, B-29 website www.http:B-29.org.
288 "Everyone was on edge the rest of the day" ibid.
288 "3 Dec: The boys are" ibid.
289 "When the clouds broke, Mt. Fujiyama" ibid.
290 "We're all of us poor soldiers" Quoted Kenneth P. Werrell, *Blankets of Fire*, Smithsonian 1996, p. 206.

290 "I had a nice talk with Wray and Cutler" Samuelson diary, op. cit., B-29 website.
291 "I became aware of the sky" Ben Robertson, *The Beginning of the End*, privately published 2004, p. 112.
294 "In our situation, it was pretty much" ibid., p. 102.
294 "Maybe the road ahead" ibid., CL to Norstad 31.1.45.
294 "Morale was terrible . . . Nothing worked" B-29 website.
295 "General LeMay has taken over" Quoted Werrell, op. cit., p. 140.
295 "As early as September 1944" William W. Ralph, op. cit., p. 503.
296 "It is air power that this Country" Lt.-Gen. Barney Giles to Kenney 27.9.44, quoted Ralph, op. cit., p. 505.
296 "To date the Twentieth" USAAF Maxwell AFB Research file 760.317–1.
296 "Whereas the adoption of nonvisual" Conrad C. Crane, *Bombs, Cities and Civilians*, Kansas University Press 1993, p. 76.
297 "A sort of cold fear gripped the crews" 497BG History, p. 19.
297 "There were a lot of unhappy campers" B-29 website.
297 "We might lose over three hundred aircraft" LeMay and Kantor, op. cit., p. 1.
297 "The whole city of Tokyo" B-29 website.
298 "Arnold assured him mendaciously" Ralph, op. cit., p. 519.
298 "blasted large cracks in the myth" *Christian Century*, issue of 21.3.45.
298 "through intensified bombing" *Newsweek*, 2.7.45.
305 "Most of my mail consisted of" Shigemitsu memoirs, op. cit , p. 346.
305 "the most frightful experience" ibid., p. 324.
305 "elements of the population" USNA RG457 Box 24 SRH074–081.
305 "After the war" AI Ando.
305 "An unforgettable mission" B-29 website.
306 "Frequent bombings, particularly night attacks, have made a major impact" RUSSIAN ARKHIV 18. VELIKAYA OTECHESTVENNAYA No.7 (1), Moscow 1997, no. 294, p. 297; from the Review of Military Operations of the USAAF Against Japan Compiled by the Intelligence Department of USSR Main Naval Headquarters (June 1944–March 1945). Source: *TsVMA F.2 Op. 1 D.1019. L.304–9, 313–20.*
306 "It was easy to see that the Nip pilots" Samuelson diary, op. cit., B-29 website.
307 "Mess kits were banged" True personal narrative, loaned to the author.
308 "Personally I have no quarrel" Norstad to LeMay 17.4.45.
308 "Never before or since" MAFB 760-551: USAAF special post-war report on fire-raising.
309 "We were going after military targets" LeMay and Kantor, op. cit., p. 384.
309 "I don't think we thought much" AI True, loc. cit.
310 "It is much easier" IWM Speer Collection Box 5369 SHAEF G2 30.5.45.
313 "this use of psychological warfare" Conrad C. Crane, "Leadership, Technology and the Ethics of Total War: Curtis LeMay and the Firebombing of Japan," in Christopher Kolenda (ed.), *Leadership: The Warrior's Art*, Army War College Foundation Press, Carlisle, Pa. 2001, pp. 205–24.
315 "I imagine if one knew Napoleon" USAMHI Eichelberger Papers, op. cit.
316 "Fear of losing control" Craven and Cate, op. cit., p. 531.
316 "one of the most ruthless" Hoover Institution, Fellers Collection Box 3.
316 "The course and conduct" Crane, *Bombs, Cities and Civilians*, op. cit., p. 173.
317 "Highlight of the entire" Maxwell AFB 760–1 Post-War Narrative.

318 "Nobody involved in the decision" Freedman and Dockrill, "Hiroshima: A Strategy of Shock," *From Pearl Harbor to Hiroshima*, Macmillan 1993, p. 196.
318 "Nothing new about death" Quoted Werrell, op. cit., p. 140.

CHAPTER THIRTEEN · THE ROAD PAST MANDALAY

319 "It might be one of our chaps" Fraser, op. cit., p. 37.
320 "He confused 9 Section" ibid., p. xii.
322 "There was a wonderful" *Northamptonshire Regimental Journal*, Nov. 1952, p. 17.
322 "He is neither pro-Jap" LHA Gracey Papers.
323 "Very few of us" Hill, op. cit., p. 110.
323 "None of them surrendered" ibid.
323 "One of our chaps" IWM 95/33/1 Daniels MS, p. 243.
324 "that it was counterattacked' Woodburn Kirby, Vol. V, op. cit., p. 257.
324 "Despite recent bad behaviour" BNA WO203/1259 23.2.45.
325 "The South Lancs' CO" AI Horsford.
325 "With maddening sluggishness" Woodburn Kirby, Vol. V, op. cit., p. 265.
327 "The tanks took a pasting" AI McAllister.
327 "The Japanese still had the reputation" ibid.
327 "Jap suicide squads dug in" BNA WO203/1259.
327 "Meiktila was a place" AI Inoue.
328 "Here before us" Hill, op. cit., p. 112.
328 "house-to-house" BNA WO203/5315.
328 "We just overran them" AI Horsford.
328 "It's no good, *sahib*!" Sandle, op. cit., pp. 67–68.
328 "We felt it was going to be over" AI J. C-H.
328 "I'm afraid I enjoyed the campaign" AI McAllister.
328 "It was always a disappointment" Slim, op. cit., p. 351.
329 "Among the stream of vehicles" Abe, *On the Staff of Thirty-Third Army*, Fuji Shobo 1953.
330 "Leading troops now only 72 miles" BNA WO203/1259.
330 "Men are the most precious thing" Maj. P. G. Malins of Royal Indian Army Service Corps personal narrative 1981, Gracey Papers LHA.
330 "I turned to see" Fraser, op. cit., p. 83.
330 "If thoo wez a Jap, an' saw this lot coomin' " ibid., p. 93.
330 "The scale of loss on both sides" Michael Hickey, *The Unforgettable Army*, Spellmount 1998.
332 "I began to realise how much" Hill, op. cit., p. 137.
332 "The most incredible thing" Lethbridge Papers LHA.
333 "Dicky [Mountbatten], reinforced by" Quoted Martin Gilbert, *Winston S. Churchill*, Vol. 7, p. 1283.
334 "They looked like beggars" AI Sugano.
334 "Petrol is as precious as blood" AI Inoue.
334 "The old unquestioning confidence" R. Hunt and J. Harrison (eds.), *The District Officer in India, 1930–47*, London 1980, p. 175.
334 "in their leisure time they will talk" BNA WO203/1194.
335 "Exactly what purposes it served" Aldiss, op. cit., p. 180.
335 "I realised that I had longed" ibid., p. 187.

CHAPTER FOURTEEN · AUSTRALIANS: "BLUDGING" AND "MOPPING UP"

336 "They said they were all too tired" G. R. Matthews diaries AWM PR87/79.
337 "deterioration in the morale" Australian Archives Victoria: MP72/1, File 193/1/657.
338 "Many . . . laborers refused to work" Stauffer, *The U.S. Army in WWII*, p. 51.
338 "was directly obstructing the war effort" ibid., p. 115.
338 "apathy amongst large sections" Lacey to Curtin 14.1.43, cited Thorne, *Allies*, p. 304.
338 "The Department may be surprised" ibid., p. 237.
339 "pulling right out of the war" *Sydney Morning Herald*, 8.9.44.
339 "civil war or very near it" Sydney *Daily Telegraph*, 30.10.44.
339 "The Australian government tried" Paul Hasluck, *The Government and the People, 1942–45*, Australian War Memorial, Canberra 1970, p. 630.
339 "The mainspring of Curtin's leadership" ibid., p. 436.
340 "The enemy garrisons which" To Marshall 9.8.44, quoted Clayton James, op. cit., p. 464.
340 "American public opinion" *Melbourne Herald*, 10.1.45.
341 "a rather unpleasant" Tedder letter to wife 10.5.41, Tedder Papers.
342 "not an impressive" Alanbrooke diaries, op. cit., p. 544.
342 "On his head descended" Gavin Long, *The Final Campaigns*, AWM, p. 586.
342 "The best that can be said" D. M. Horner, *Blamey: The Commander-in-Chief*, Allen & Unwin 1998, passim.
342 "We are all just about had" Diary AWM PR89/190.
342 "A feeling of terrible sadness" *War in the Shadows: Bougainville, 1944–45*, AWM 1996, p. 86.
342 "The political and grand strategic" Johnston, op. cit., p. 95.
342 "capable of anything" AWM 3DRL 3825 John Butler letter to wife from New Guinea.
343 "When you get into action" Quoted Johnston, op. cit., p. 81.
343 "75 of us refused to go into action" ibid., p. 236.
343 "I happen to entertain" Commonwealth Debates Vol. 181, p. 1126.
343 "In both Australian and Japanese history" Long, op. cit., p. 386.

CHAPTER FIFTEEN · CAPTIVITY AND SLAVERY

345 "American PWs appeared to be" LHA POW reports microfilm 588.
346 "There was evidence" BNA 16.1.45 WO203/5609.
346 "Their liberators were stunned" BNA WO203/5620.
347 "I dared not look into their eyes" Christopher Bayly and Tim Harper, *Forgotten Armies*, Penguin 2004, pp. 406–7.
347 "In the beginning" AI Idlett.
348 "The Burma railway was a very difficult" AI Renichi Sugano.
348 "men of the arrogant nation" Hino's 1942 book *Batan Hanto Kojoki*, cited Haruko Taya Cook, *Voices from the Front: Japanese War Literature, 1937–45*, unpublished MA thesis, University of California, Berkeley 1984, pp. 59–60, quoted Dower, *Japan in War and Peace*.
348 "There is no doubt that many men just" Romney Papers, op. cit., IWM.

349 "The most junior soldier felt" Stephen Abbott, *And My War Is Done*, Pentland 1991, p. 37.
349 "I saw discipline go down" AI Rosen.
349 "Major D— was about as useful" IWM Young MS 75/124/1.
349 "the white Jap" Hank Nelson, *Australians Under Nippon*, ABC 1985, p. 60.
349 "I know you've been terribly ill" Abbott, op. cit., p. 51.
349 "seems to accept everything" IWM Romney Papers, op. cit.
349 "Flying Officer Erroll Shearn" IWM Shearn Papers 92/36/1.
349 "You are signing away" Coubrough, *Memoirs of a Perpetual Second Lieutenant*, Wilton 1995, p. 90.
350 "During the early months" BNA WO203/3105.
350 "The grandiose picture he draws" IWM Shearn MS IWM 92/36/1.
350 "The Dutch doctors I met" IWM Lyon MS 90/10/1.
350 "There was no love lost" AI Idlett.
350 "There was a weeding-out" AI Paul Reuter.
350 "My life was a nonentity" AI Andrew Cunningham.
351 "wanted to survive" AI Idlett, loc. cit.
351 "I knew some that would not eat rice" ibid.
351 "Australian Snow Peat saw" Nelson, op. cit., p. 42.
351 "I was prepared to eat anything" AI Ashwell.
352 "I've missed the sunshine after rain" LHA Morris Papers, op. cit.
352 "Some men swore" AI Mel Rosen, loc. cit.
352 "Guess my mother thinks" Monahan and Neidel-Greenlee, op. cit., pp. 102, 129.
353 "We were so hungry that" ibid., p. 136.
353 "It was becoming very apparent" Hartendorp, op. cit., p. 311.
353 "My Dear Philip" IWM Sparrow Papers 88/63/1.
354 "Goddammit! That was" Coubrough, op. cit., pp. 92–93.
354 "not a bit like Butlin's" IWM Evans Papers 82/24/1.
355 "In sapper Edward Whincup's" IWM Whincup Papers 91/81/1.
355 "With one exception" Coubrough, op. cit., p. 121.
355 "1/2 pint rice pap" IWM Denis Leigh 1947, thesis on neurological disorders in POWs 77/172/1.
355 "Somehow we keep going" IWM Thompson Papers 87/58/1.
356 "THE BRITISH ALWAYS" Stibbe, op. cit., p. 124.
356 "Some people would steal" AI Reuter.
356 "Sapper Edward Whincup" IWM Whincup Papers 91/81/1.
356 "No one has any sympathy" IWM Romney Papers, op. cit.
356 "We became hardened" P. G. Stibbe, *Return via Rangoon*, Wolsey 1947, p. 162.
356 "You don't know the meaning of frustration" AI Rosen.
356 "that the Japanese, contemptuous of us" Coubrough, op. cit., p. 99.
357 "It was pointless to maintain" ibid., p. 147.
357 "a necessary exercise" IWM 93/8/1 Jackson, "Misadventure," privately published MS.
358 "The ordinary Japanese" Stibbe, op. cit., pp. 55, 196.
358 " 'Mr. M' scythed grass" IWM, David Nicoll, *Young Shanghailander*, 92/14/1.
359 "I cooked it slowly" Nini Hannaford-Rambonnet, *Stand to Attention, Bow, Stand Up*, Batavia Publishing 2005, p. 33.

359 "no one was raped" IWM Lyon MS 90/10/1.
360 "That's what I wanted" IWM Dryburgh Papers 82/19/1.
360 "Not until your hair is grey" Hannaford-Rambonnet, op. cit.
363 "If you wish to live you must" Abbott, op. cit., p. 179.
364 "He was a really kind-hearted Japanese" IWM Lyon MS 90/10/1.
364 "How do you like winning" IWM Shearn MS 92/36/1.
364 "Are you contented" Abbott, op. cit., p. 58.
365 "a terrible tragedy" ibid., p. 66.
365 "I had beriberi" AI Idlett.
366 "I told myself after the war" AI Kikuchi.
367 "At the end of the war" John Glusman, *Conduct Under Fire*, Viking 2005, p. 410.
368 "There was no debate among the doctors" *Baltimore Sun*, 20.5.95.

CHAPTER SIXTEEN · OKINAWA

371 "We bombarded all day long" Hutchinson, op. cit., p. 61.
374 "Everyone expected E Company" Johnston, op. cit., p. 126.
375 "They brought him back to us" MCHC Donner MS.
375 "I thought I might get to a pillbox" James W. Johnston, *The Long Road of War: A Marine's Story of Pacific Combat*, University of Nebraska Press 1998, p. 128.
375 "I didn't recognise anything I saw" MCHC Bressoud MS, "The Way It Really Was. I Think," 1994.
376 "What do you want to treat a Jap" *The New Yorker Book of War Pieces*, Bloomsbury 1989.
376 "He did not want to be involved" MCHC Smith MS, op. cit.
376 "ruddy, heavy-set" ibid.
377 "Buckner had surprisingly little troops' duty" ibid.
377 "The enemy tactic which impressed us" USNA RG127 USMC Operations in WWII—Okinawa.
377 "The U.S. XXIV Corps once received" USNA RG337 Box 70 Tenth Army Report of 28.5.45.
378 "Another letter, from the father of a wounded man" MCHC Siebert Papers.
378 "I hope you're satisfied!" MCHC Carell MS.
378 "Oh! to see the folks" Johnston, op. cit., p. 139.
378 "Of course this was very, very comforting" MCHC Siebert Papers.
379 "One of the weaknesses of the American army" ibid.
379 "embittered over this needless loss" MCHC Donner MS.
379 "Much against my instincts" MCHC Siebert Papers.
379 "With afternoon came the order" MCHC Donner MS.
379 " 'It was awful, God' " ibid.
380 "when the bullet hit Gosman's head" Johnston, op. cit., p. 150.
380 "I thought of the old verse" ibid., p. 122.
380 "Her touch felt like an angel's" ibid., p. 157.
380 "Rashly exposing himself on Tera Ridge" MCHC Carell MS.
381 "You see, I am out of any possible danger" USAMHI Rodman Papers.
381 "We took three hundred casualties in the first two days" AI Ito.
382 "The news came as a shock" USAMHI Henne MS, op. cit.
382 "I can't stand it" MCHC Bressoud MS, op. cit.

382 "Somehow I had never consciously" MCHC Carell Papers.
382 "every once in a while" MCHC Kohn Papers, op. cit.
383 "The Marines and the army" MCHC Jenkins MS.
383 "We were permitted, if not encouraged" MCHC Bressoud MS, op. cit.
384 "On the ground lay the body" MCHC Donner MS, op. cit.
384 "None of the men would own up" ibid.
385 "I am afraid . . . there are many" MCHC Smith Papers, op. cit.
385 "You can take this war and shove it" LC Jenkins interview.
386 "By this time the cloths and the heads" MCHC Bressoud MS, op. cit.
387 "Your husband," *Howorth*'s captain' Yeoman James Orvill Raines, *Good Night Officially: Letters of a Destroyer Sailor*, Westview Press 1994, p. 276 et seq.
387 "Cmdr. Bill Widhelm" USNA RG38 Box 4.
388 "I don't believe I'll ever forget" Cmdr. David Scott, *No Hiding Place off Okinawa*, Naval Institute *Proceedings*, Nov. 1956.
388 "He seemed to float down" MCHC Bressoud MS, op. cit.
388 "*Luce*'s crew were wryly amused" Ron Surels, *DD552: The Story of a Destroyer*, Valley Graphics 1994.
388 "Bombs and shells" Raines, op. cit., p. 162.
388 "His lips were moving" Surels, op. cit., p. 130.
389 "They scatter like quail" USNA RG38 Box 4.
389 "Someone yelled down the hatch" Andrew Wilde (ed.), *The U.S.S. Emmons in WWII*, privately published 1998, p. 21.
389 "The first instinct of a destroyer skipper" Andrew Wilde (ed.), *The U.S.S. Douglas H. Fox in WWII*, privately published 1999, p. 9.
389 "I was so tired" Surels, op. cit., p. 101.
390 "The fighting off Okinawa became routine" Clark, op. cit., p. 227.
390 "I expected to die" AI Hijikata.
392 "By the spring of 1945" AI Iwashita.
392 "You're a lucky guy" AI Ajiro.
393 "What in the Philippines had been" *War with Japan*, op. cit., p. 196.
395 "We took a chance and launched" NHC Box 5 Burke file.
396 "How are you? We are fine" Mitsuru Yoshida, *Requiem for Battleship Yamato*, Constable 1999, p. 10.
397 "a poor ratio of hits is due to human error" ibid., p. 76.
398 "At the instant *Yamato*" ibid., p. 118.
399 "Nothing gives me greater joy" ibid., p. 89.
399 "The destruction of Ito's squadron" Russell Spurr, *A Glorious Way to Die*, Sidgwick & Jackson 1982, passim.
400 "There can be little doubt" Quoted Philip Vian, *Action This Day*, Muller 1960, p. 186.
401 "*KGV* went up astern" Quoted John Winton, *The Forgotten Fleet*, Michael Joseph 1969, p. 114.
401 "Except for those engaged" ibid., p. 140.

CHAPTER SEVENTEEN • MAO'S WAR

404 "Though their enemies denounced" Snow, op. cit., p. 201.
405 "The Communists operated in regions" AI Funaki.
405 "In the anti-Japanese war, the Kuomintang" AI Yang Jinghua.
405 "We had to adopt the strategy" AI Zuo Yong.

405 "Guerrillas could not realistically engage" AI Wang Hongbin.
406 " 'For us,' said Li" AI Li Fenggui.
410 "A lot of couples whose marriages" AI Zuo Yong.
411 "nothing more than a provincial government" BNA FO371/ F6140/34/10.
411 "I cannot believe he means business" ibid.; and Adrian Carton de Wiart, *Happy Odyssey*, Cape 1950, passim.
411 "The Communists do not, any more" BNA FO371/F2375.
412 "the incandescence of personality" Davies, op. cit., p. 345.
412 "I got the impression that here" ibid., p 347.
413 "Mao and the Communists" AI Yang Jinghua.
413 "Western visitors were charmed" Philip Short's *Mao*, John Murray 1999, is probably the best biography for the general reader, while also commanding the respect of scholars. Jung Chang and Jon Halliday's *Mao: The Unknown Story*, Cape 2005, makes fascinating reading as an impassioned polemic, the case for the prosecution. The book, and rival views of Mao, are exhaustively discussed in *The China Journal*, no. 55, Jan. 2006. There are also, of course, many contemporary eyewitness accounts of Mao in wartime Yan'an, some of them cited above.
414 "They had an infrastructure" AI Wei Daoran.
416 "If Chinese unable put up even show" BNA WO203/291 22.12.44.
422 "at present were mostly inactive" USNA RG457 Box 24 SRH 074–081 18.12.44.
422 "In addition to the reconnaissance groups" Vasily Ivanov, *I Fought the Samurais*, Moscow 2006, pp. 310, 312 (Russian-language edition).
423 "Both of us felt" Snow, op. cit., pp. 138, 161.
423 "Under no circumstances is any material help" BNA WO203/291.
424 "Seeing that the Communists have not been equipped" ibid.
424 "despised the Chinese [and] asked" Michael Lindsay, *The Unknown War*, London, Bergstrom & Boyle 1975, cited Thorne, *Allies of a Kind*, op. cit., p. 574.
424 "Yan'an provided the great mass" Davies, op. cit., p. 371.

CHAPTER EIGHTEEN · ECLIPSE OF EMPIRES

426 "extremely busy" USNA RG457 Box 24 SRH074–081.
426 "The news is terrific isn't it?" IWM Wightman Papers 97/34/1.
426 "The end of the war in Europe" AI McAllister.
426 "Men! The war in Europe is over!" Fraser, op. cit., p. 28.
427 "If, as reports have it" USNA RG457 Box 24 SRH074–081.
427 "There were cases" James Bradley, *Flyboys*, Aurum Press 2003, p. 227, gives some vivid examples, but many others are to be found in contemporary files and narratives.
427 "and flesh was removed from thighs" LHA PW interrogation reports 10IR579.
427 "Rewarded only by silence, the launches" BNA WO203/5082.
428 "From May onwards, prisoners" 114 Field Regiment RA, narrative loaned to the author.
428 "I could not think of anything else to do" Winton, op. cit., p. 210.
429 "Mass air attacks" USNA RG496 Box 809.
430 "It would have been not only unfair" Slim, op. cit., p. 522.

430 "I am trying very hard" BNA WO203/55.
430 "We must naturally be prepared" H. G. Nicholas (ed.), *Washington Despatches*, Weidenfeld & Nicolson 1981, p. 559.
431 "The Americans are virtually conducting" BNA FO371/f1955 Sterndale Bennett.
431 "To hear some people talk" Quoted R. G. Sherwood, *Roosevelt and Hopkins*, New York 1948, p. 921.
431 "I often think that we might" BNA WO203/5610.
432 "It will look very bad in history" BNA PREM 3/178-3.
432 "an awfully sweet guy" Quoted Robert Shaplen, *The Lost Revolution*, Deutsch 1966, p. 29.
432 "undisciplined, underequipped and destitute" Unless otherwise cited, all quotations and details given in this passage are taken from Peter Dunn's *The First Vietnam War*, Hurst 1985.
433 "considerable assistance from [the] British" ibid., p. 108.
433 "The division of French Indochina" ibid., p. 112.
433 "Keep off Russo-Japanese" BNA WO203/368 27.7.45.
437 "There was disorderly behaviour" Col. Saburo Hayashi with Alvin D. Coox, *Kogun: The Japanese Army in the Pacific War*, Marine Corps Association 1959, p. 151.
437 "Those of us who knew" Horikoshi diary quoted *Zero!*, op. cit., p. 333.
438 "It seemed unbelievable" AI DeTour.
438 "When I took him to task" Clark, op. cit., p. 209.
439 "We had the usual fun" *Flight Quarters*, op. cit., p. 103.
439 "At Mick Carney's insistence" Halsey and Whittlesey, op. cit., p. 304.
440 "It was all a matter of upbringing" AI Kikuchi.
440 "We felt that *kaiten* offered us" AI Konada.
442 "It is almost impossible not to believe" Frank, op. cit., p. 276.
442 "Ye stupid sods!" Fraser, op. cit., p. 124.

CHAPTER NINETEEN · THE BOMBS

445 "Every Russian killed" James J. Halsema, quoted Clayton James, op. cit., p. 774.
445 "When we are vexed" BNA PREM3/472 17.10.44.
445 "We must not invade Japan proper" U.S. Dept. of Defense, *The Entry of the Soviet Union into the War Against Japan: Military Plans, 1941–45*, Washington, D.C. 1955, pp. 50–51.
445 "Everybody wants the Roosh" Swing, op. cit., 28.5.45.
447 "There are notes" H. G. Nicholas, op. cit., p. 559.
452 "the biggest sonofabitch" Quoted Richard Rhodes, *Ultimate Powers*, Simon & Schuster 1986, p. 393.
452 "We really held all the cards" Stimson diary 14.5.45.
454 "[The] meeting leaves a mental picture" USNA RG457 Box 24.
455 "Japan has made special efforts" Okumiya and Horikoshi, op. cit., p. 335.
456 "To comprehend the president's behaviour" Professor Robert H. Ferrell, *Harry S. Truman and the Bomb*, High Plains Publishing 1996.
458 "both because of the enormous reduction" West Point Archive, George A. Lincoln Papers.
459 "Generally it is believed" Nicholas, op. cit., pp. 593, 595.

459 "A great many people feel" USAMHI, Eichelberger Papers, "Dearest Miss Em," op. cit.
463 "Perhaps this statement" Tsuyoshi Hasegawa, *Racing the Enemy*, Belknap, Harvard 2005, p. 135.
466 "We had a most" Truman diaries, ed. Ferrell, op. cit., 16.7.45.
466 "that at any rate they had something" BNA PREM4 79/2.
473 "The preoccupation" Freedman and Dockrill, op. cit., p. 195.
475 "all things are always" WSC to Portal 7 10.41.
475 "Her unwillingness to surrender" Quoted Frank, op. cit., p. 232.
477 "Subject: Bombs Away" USAF Historical Research gp-509-su July–August 1945.
477 "Official investigation of the results" LC Arnold Papers Box 256.
478 "The lurid fantasies" H. G. Nicholas, op. cit., 11.8.45.
478 "Old Joe called upstairs" 7.8.45, *Nella Last's War*, Sphere 1983.
479 "From what we knew" USAMHI Eddleman Papers.
479 "It is now widely held" Fraser, op. cit., p. xx.
479 "Stephen—a ghastly thing has happened" Abbott, op. cit., p. 95.

CHAPTER TWENTY · MANCHURIA: THE BEAR'S CLAWS

482 "It was the worst" Ivanov, op. cit., p. 381.
482 "This was the last great military operation" This chapter owes much to Col. David M. Glantz's massive two-volume narrative of the campaign, *The Soviet Offensive in Manchuria, 1945*, and *Soviet Operational and Tactical Combat in Manchuria 1945*, Cass 2003, supported by Japanese and Chinese accounts and author interviews, together with interviews with and personal accounts by Soviet veterans.
482 "a still more shocking report" Okumiya and Horikoshi, op. cit., p. 321.
483 "At last!" AI Funaki.
483 "The Soviet Union's aims" VOV 389, P. N. Pospelov, *History of the Great Patriotic War*, Moscow, Voenizdat 1963, Vol. V.
484 "Ah, boys, they are taking you" Ivanov, op. cit., p. 320.
484 "Uncles, is our daddy" ibid.
484 "Everyone slept a lot" ibid., p. 322.
484 "I was twenty-two" AI Chervyakov.
484 "Please, Lyosha, could you ask" AI Fillipov
485 "we came to realise the price" Ivanov, op. cit., p. 320.
485 "What a host is moving east!" ibid., p. 322.
485 "there was that perpetual uncertainty" *Ya Dralsya S Samurayami*, Moscow 2005, p. 383.
485 "I'd taken part in plenty of offensives" ibid., p. 322.
485 "Machine-gunner Anatoly Shilov" Ivanov, op. cit., p. 343.
486 "It took us a week" ibid., p. 324.
486 "Guys rubbished the Americans" ibid., p. 322.
487 "Some Japanese bayonets" USAMHI POW monograph no. 154-b Col. Hiroshi Matsumoto.
487 "They were simply skin and bones" Ivanov, op. cit., p. 325.
488 "In the hours before the assault" ibid., p. 292.
488 "Say hello to the Manchurians" AI Fillipov.
490 "Soon there was this crazy heat" Ivanov, op. cit., p. 327.

491 "Sixty years have passed" ibid., p. 292.
491 "If your majesty does not go" Pu Yi, op. cit., p. 317.
492 "These created hazards" *In the Hills of Manchuria*, *Military Herald* no. 12, 1980, p. 30.
492 "The Russians solved the problem" Ivanov, op. cit., p. 379.
492 "The road widened somewhat" Belobodorov, op. cit., p. 50.
493 "Yet even when tanks were hit" JM154, 293, quoted Glantz, op. cit., Vol. I, p. 173.
493 "Because of the difficulty of holding" Quoted ibid., p. 103.
493 "Soviet pilot Boris Ratner's wing" AI Ratner.
493 "Many Japanese lacked the will" AI Hongbin.
493 "Units advanced from hill to hill" Quoted Glantz, op. cit., Vol. I, p. 178.
494 "We were completely exhausted" Ivanov, op. cit., p. 304.
494 "The 59th Cavalry Division faced special difficulties" ibid., p. 364.
494 "I could never have believed" AI Petryakov.
495 "At first, we were so thrilled" Ivanov, op. cit., p. 331.
495 "We're too late again" ibid., p. 306.
496 "The stench was indescribable" ibid., p. 350.
496 "They went mad and stung" ibid., p. 351.
496 "They deserved everything" AI Li Dongguan.
498 "who gave us a great welcome" AI Jiang De.
498 "This was no country stroll" Ivanov, op. cit., p. 314.
498 "On the summit they found" ibid., p. 351.
498 "Suddenly the sheep were shooting" AI Fillipov.
498 "On the evening of 15 August" Ivanov, op. cit., p. 360.
499 "criminal carelessness" Russian Arkhiv 18, op. cit., no. 338, Political Report from the Chief of Political Department of the 2nd Red Banner Army to the Chief of Political Department of 2nd Far Eastern Front on the Brutal Murder by a Japanese Group of Medical Personnel of 70th Rifle Regiment of 3rd Rifle Division. Source: *TsAMO RF. F.304 Op. 7007 D.160 L.318, 318b, 319.*
499 "As soon as our anti-tank guns" Quoted Glantz, op. cit., Vol. II, p. 121.
500 "I shall die here" JM154 272–23, quoted ibid., p. 124.
500 "The defending troops in the Japanese fortified regions" ibid., p. 255.
500 "It was so hot" ibid., p. 352.
500 "When we entered the city of Vanemiao" Ivanov, op. cit., p. 330.
501 "Most of us knew that Stalin" AI Luo Dingwen.
503 "This was not justice" AI Xu Guiming.

CHAPTER TWENTY-ONE · THE LAST ACT

504 "Undoubtedly the biggest question" West Point Archive, Lincoln Papers.
506 "Ignore it all" AI Maj. Shigeru Funaki.
507 "and this secondary revulsion" Nicholas, op. cit., p. 598.
507 "pour them all on in a reasonably short time" Quoted Hasegawa, op. cit., p. 235.
510 "The days of negotiation" Nicholas, op. cit., p. 603, 18.8.45.
513 "For Japan's civilian politicians" AI Hando.
513 "Robert Newman suggests" Newman, op. cit., passim.
515 "Considering the suicidal tactics" USNA RG207 Box 404, Entry 55.

516 "Despite the courage of every unit" Ugaki diary, op. cit., p. 665.
516 "The war ended on August 15" Onoda, op. cit., p. 75.
517 "a reprieve from" AI Kikuchi.
517 "The Allies will destroy" Mitsuo Abe, *Staff Officer*, Fuji Shobo 1953.
517 "The men all cried" AI Hashimoto, loc cit.
517 "Now we're going to live in a new world" AI Sekine.
518 "Surely, we have lost the war" AI Watanuki.
518 "I thought the Americans" AI Iki.
519 "I was sure there would be" AI Hijikata.
519 "All the way back to general staff headquarters" AI Takahashi.
519 "Didn't you hear?" AI Miyashita.
520 " 'What's up?' " he demanded" AI Ando.
520 "Oh, war finish!" Somerville, op. cit., p. 292.
521 "What reaction? Absolutely nil" IWM Thompson Papers 87/58/1.
521 "The Japs won't like that" Somerville, op. cit., p. 293.
521 "A repatriation officer" George Cooper, *Never Forget, Never Forgive*, Navigator Press 1995, p. 167.
521 "It seemed like talking to men from Mars" IWM Pearson MS 99/3/1.
521 "I felt a lump" *Sunday Pictorial* 7.10.45.
521 "the wicked Americanos had dropped" IWM AR Evans Papers 82/24/1.
522 "Listen, you goddamned son of a bitch" Glusman, op. cit., pp. 437–79.
522 "My God, Stuart, you look fat" AI Cunningham.
522 "*Mei kuo ting hao*" White and Jacoby, op. cit., p. 277.
522 "because this meant" AI Luo Dingwen.
522 "who else is alive?" AI Yan Qizhi.
523 "and even if we had been, I doubt" AI Wu Yinyan.
523 "We had to tell them" AI Najiro.
523 "The samurais were" Belyaev, op. cit., pp. 295–97.
524 "I was nineteen" AI Nakamura.
525 "We felt nothing" AI Fillipov.
525 "The Russians were our allies" AI Zuo Yong.
526 "The Russians simply behaved" AI De.
527 "Japanese propaganda had successfully imbued" "The Northern Pacific Flotilla in the Southern Sakhalin Operation," *VIZh*, no. 2, Feb. 1980, p. 78.
529 "Go-go-go! I'll stay and look after the house" AI Fushun.
529 "In view of the current war situation" Matsumoto monograph, op. cit., p. 191.
530 "After the first [Russian] salvo" *The Last Battle of Hutou*, Beijing 1993, p. 76 (Chinese-language edition).
530 "There were plenty of" ibid., p. 83.
532 "The defence was extraordinarily brave" AI Hongbin.
532 "Most of the local people" Ivanov, op. cit., p. 315.
532 "I saw some men coming down" ibid., p. 384.
533 "When I came back to the depots" ibid., p. 299.
533 "I didn't get a wink of sleep" ibid., p. 336.
534 "Comrade Lieutenant" ibid., p. 337.
534 "Instead, he spent the next five years" Pu Yi, op. cit., p. 324 et seq.
534 "Give us ten years" AI Li Min.
534 "the Russians had stripped the peasants" AI Li Fenggui.
535 "They were sick—and they had no money" AI Fengxian.

535 "An image of Manchuria" Ivanov, op. cit., p. 353.
536 " 'The Japanese,' concluded" BNA FO371 F11097/6390/61.
537 "I felt I had acquitted myself" IWM Daniels MS, op. cit., p. 289.
539 "The feeling of Japan's leaders" Shigemitsu, op. cit., p. 324.

CHAPTER TWENTY-TWO · LEGACIES

543 "If the bombing of Hiroshima" Philip Bobbitt, *The Shield of Achilles*, Penguin 2002, p. 778.
543 " 'Dear Sir,' wrote Garba Yola" LHA Stockwell Papers.
545 "Despite his undoubted qualities" Spector, op. cit., pp. xiv–xv.
546 "Our country is in ruins" Abbott, op. cit., p. 196.
546 "I marvel continually" USAMHI Griswold Papers 18.9.45.

INDEX

A NOTE ABOUT THE AUTHOR

Max Hastings is the author of the critically acclaimed *Warriors*, *Armageddon* and *Overlord*, and thirteen other titles. He has served as a foreign correspondent and as the editor of Britain's *Evening Standard* and *The Daily Telegraph* and has received numerous British Press Awards, including Journalist of the Year in 1982, and Editor of the Year in 1988. He lives outside London.

A NOTE ON THE TYPE

This book was set in Janson, a typeface long thought to have been made by the Dutchman Anton Janson, who was a practicing type-founder in Leipzig during the years 1668–1687. However, it has been conclusively demonstrated that these types are actually the work of Nicholas Kis (1650–1702), a Hungarian, who most probably learned his trade from the master Dutch typefounder Dirk Voskens. The type is an excellent example of the influential and sturdy Dutch types that prevailed in England up to the time William Caslon (1692–1766) developed his own incomparable designs from them.

COMPOSED BY NORTH MARKET STREET GRAPHICS, LANCASTER, PENNSYLVANIA

PRINTED AND BOUND BY BERRYVILLE GRAPHICS, BERRYVILLE, VIRGINIA

BOOK DESIGN BY ROBERT C. OLSSON